EUROPEAN HISTORICAL DICTIONARIES
Edited by Jon Woronoff

1. *Portugal,* by Douglas L. Wheeler. 1993
2. *Turkey,* by Metin Heper. 1994
3. *Poland,* by George Sanford and Adriana Gozdecka-Sanford. 1994
4. *Germany,* by Wayne C. Thompson, Susan L. Thompson, and Juliet S. Thompson. 1994
5. *Greece,* by Thanos M. Veremis and Mark Dragoumis. 1995
6. *Cyprus,* by Stavros Panteli. 1995
7. *Sweden,* by Irene Scobbie. 1995
8. *Finland,* by George Maude. 1995
9. *Croatia,* by Robert Stallaerts and Jeannine Laurens. 1995
10. *Malta,* by Warren G. Berg. 1995
11. *Spain,* by Angel Smith. 1996
12. *Albania,* by Raymond Hutchings. 1996
13. *Slovenia,* by Leopoldina Plut-Pregelj and Carole Rogel. 1996
14. *Luxembourg,* by Harry C. Barteau. 1996
15. *Romania,* by Kurt W. Treptow and Marcel Popa. 1996
16. *Bulgaria,* by Raymond Detrez. 1997
17. *United Kingdom: Volume 1, England and the United Kingdom,* by Kenneth J. Panton and Keith A. Cowlard. 1997
18. *Hungary,* by Steven Béla Várdy. 1997
19. *Latvia,* by Andrejs Plakans. 1997
20. *Ireland,* by Colin Thomas and Avril Thomas. 1997
21. *Lithuania,* by Saulius Sužiedėlis. 1997
22. *Macedonia,* by Valentina Georgieva and Sasa Konechni. 1997
23. *Czech Republic,* by Jiri Hochman. 1997
24. *Iceland,* by Guðmundur Hálfdanarson. 1997
25. *Bosnia and Herzegovina,* by Ante Cuvalo. 1997
26. *Russia,* by Boris Raymond and Paul Duffy. 1998

Historical Dictionary of Hungary

Steven Béla Várdy

European Historical Dictionaries, No. 18

The Scarecrow Press, Inc.
Lanham, Md., & London
1997

SCARECROW PRESS, INC.

Published in the United States of America
by Scarecrow Press, Inc.
4720 Boston Way
Lanham, Maryland 20706

British Library Cataloguing in Publication Information Available

Library of Congress Cataloging-in-Publication Data

Várdy, Steven Béla, 1935-
    Historical dictionary of Hungary / Steven Béla Várdy.
        p.cm. — (European historical dictionaries ; no. 18)
    Includes bibliographical references
    ISBN 0-8108-3254-2 (alk. paper)
        1. Hungary—History—Dictionaries—English. I. Title.
II. Series.
DB904.V37   1997
943.9'003—dc20   96-43058
                                                         CIP

ISBN 0-8108-3254-2 (alk. paper)

This book is dedicated to

the memory of

Professor Ferenc Somogyi

(1906-1995)

a great scholar

and a

marvelous human being

who first inspired me

to follow the path

of Clio's art

CONTENTS

EDITOR'S FOREWORD

Hungary, as this book shows, is more than just the smallish present-day country that bears its name. It is the result of countless historical twists and turns that have shorn it of many nearby areas in which Hungarians still live, some of them parts of earlier Hungarian states or entities. And, given the frequent and substantial emigrations, it is the actual or spiritual homeland of many who have settled in other parts of Europe or on the other side of the world. So, it is certainly a plus that this *Historical Dictionary of Hungary* covers not only today's Hungary but its predecessors, not only Hungarians as narrowly defined but those who fit a broader definition, and also many surrounding peoples and countries, some no longer extant, that have shaped its history.

Given the countless twists and turns, it is most helpful that the book starts out with a broad historical overview that puts things in place. This is followed by a detailed chronology to put things in order. Many of the related persons and events are then presented in the dictionary section. While the focus is essentially historical, there are numerous entries relating to the current, post-communist period. And, while the stress is on the political aspects, there are also many entries on significant persons active in other fields, places of more than just historical interest, and important aspects of the economy, society, and culture. The substantial bibliography includes relevant books and articles on these other aspects as well as the various historical periods. To round things out, there is a list of abbreviations and acronyms, a list of heads of state and, particularly useful for places that have changed owner so often, a glossary of geographical terms.

Steven Béla Várdy knows both the narrower and the broader Hungary very well. He has taught, lectured, and written on them extensively. His many books deal with such historical figures as Attila the Hun and Louis the Great, the periods dominated by the Habsburgs and Ottoman Empires, and Hungarian Americans. Presently professor of European history at Duquesne University, and president and vice president of the premier American and international associations of Hungarian historians, Dr. Várdy has also been a visiting scholar at the Institute of History of the Hungarian Academy of Sciences and the University of Budapest. The *Historical Dictionary of Hungary* draws on this rich experience and marks a major milestone in his career.

Jon Woronoff
Series Editor

AUTHOR'S PREFACE

Hungary is a country whose past is greater than its present. Its name, therefore, stands for different entities at various times in history. Just as the meaning of Yugoslavia has changed since its demolishment to under half its original size, so did the meaning of Hungary, which today is less than 30 percent of its former self. A historian, however, cannot alter the past. He has to deal with it in its original form. Thus, a work of this type, which purports to present the history of a nation and a country through many centuries, has to deal with provinces, towns, and ethnic groups that are no longer part of the country that is called Hungary today.

This poses the problem of the use of geographical names in an area where place names have been altered repeatedly following the redrawing of borders and the creation of new political entities. Since this is a work of history, I have decided to use the historical names, save for the post-World War I period, and except when there are universally accepted English variants (e.g., Vienna for Wien). In line with this policy, therefore, the capital of the Byzantine Empire is always referred to as Constantinople, even though it has been Istanbul for over five centuries. And this approach has also been followed with respect to Historic Hungary, which ceased to exist after the collapse of the Austro-Hungarian Empire in 1918. In most instances, however, two or more versions of these names are given at the beginning of each article. Moreover, a detailed glossary of terms has also been appended that contains most, though not necessarily all, of the variants of these names.

This work is the result of a labor of love. Yet, I could not have completed it without the constant urging and moral support of my wife,

Dr. Ágnes Huszár Várdy, who is a scholar and an author in her own right. I am very grateful for her support and for the fact that she has read the manuscript repeatedly so as to make it as faultless as possible. I am likewise grateful to my fellow historians, Dr. Aladár Komjáthy of Duquesne University and Dr. Thomas Szendrey of Gannon University. They read the manuscript and gave useful advice. This book is undoubtedly better than it would have been without their help.

I have also received the help of many colleagues at the Universities of Budapest, Debrecen, Pécs, and Szeged in Hungary, as well as at the Institute of History of the Hungarian Academy of Sciences. While I cannot list them by name—for there are simply too many—I am very grateful to all of them. I hope that the appearance of this first historical dictionary on Hungary in English will also be of some use to them in their efforts to spread the knowledge about the Hungarian past beyond their country's frontiers.

I would also like to thank my former student and friend, Gregory Brickl., for his technical help in bringing this work to fruition. Without him, I would still be trying to fathom the secrets of the computer.

The maps were prepared by Professor Harold E. Cox of Wilkes University, to whom I am also grateful.

Steven Béla Várdy
Duquesne University

ABBREVIATIONS AND ACRONYMS

AASHH	American Association for the Study of Hungarian History = *Amerikai Magyar Történelmi Társulat* (AMTT)
ACC	Allied Control Commission = *Szövetséges Ellenőrző Bizottság* (SZEB)
AHF	American Hungarian Federation = *Amerikai Magyar Szövetség* (AMSZ)
AHF	*American Hungarian Foundation* = *Amerikai Magyar Alapítvány* (AMA)
AMOSZ	*Amerikai Magyarok Országos Szövetsége* = National Federation of American Hungarians (NFAH)
AMSZ	*Amerikai Magyar Szövetség* = American Hungarian Federation (AHF)
AMTT	*Amerikai Magyar Történelmi Társulat* = American Association for the Study of Hungarian History (AASHH)
ÁVH	*Államvédelmi Hatóság* = Office of State Defense (OSD)
ÁVO	*Államvédelmi Osztály* = Section of State Defense (SSD)
b.	born
c.	circa, century
COCOM	Coordinating Committee for Multilateral Export Controls
CSEMADOK	*Csehszlovákiai Magyar Dolgozók Kultúregyesülete* = Cultural Association of Hungarians in Czechoslovakia
d.	died, dead
DISZ	*Dolgozó Ifjúság Szövetsége* = Federation of Working Youth (FWY)
DOTE	*Debreceni Orvostudományi Egyetem* = Medical University of Debrecen
ELTE	*Eötvös Loránd Tudományegyetem* = Loránd Eötvös University (of Budapest)
FFD	Federation of Free Democrats = *Szabad Demokraták Szövetsége* (SZDSZ)

FIDESZ	*Fiatal Demokraták Szövetsége* = Federation of Young Democrats (FYD)
FYD	Federation of Young Democrats = *Fiatal Demokraták Szövetsége* (FIDESZ)
GDP	Gross Domestic Products
GYOSZ	*Gyáriparosok Országos Szövetsége* = National Association of Industrialists (NAI)
HAC	Hungarian American Coalition = *Magyar Amerikai Koalíció* (MAK)
HC	Hungarian Committee = *Magyar Biztottság* (MB)
HCYF	Hungarian Communist Youth Federation = *Magyar Kommunista Ifjúsági Szövetség* (MKISZ)
HDF	Hungarian Democratic Forum = *Magyar Demokrata Fórum* (MDF)
HFFF	Hungarian Freedom Fighters' Federation = *Magyar Szabadságharcos Szövetség* (MSZSZ)
HFFM	Hungarian Freedom Fighters' Movement = *Hungária SzabadságharcosMozgalom* (HSZM)
HFFWF	Hungarian Freedom Fighters World Federation = *Magyar Szabadságharcos Világszövetség* [MSZVSZ]
HFF(NG)WF	Hungarian Freedom Fighters (National Guardian) World Federation = *MagyarSzabadságharcos(Nemzetőr) Világszövetség* (MSZ[N]VSZ)
HNC	Hungarian National Council = *Magyar Nemzeti Bizottmány* (MNB)
HSP	Hungarian Socialist Party = *Magyar Szocialista Párt* (MSZP)
HSWP	Hungarian Socialist Workers' Party = *Magyar Szocialista Munkáspárt* (MSZMP)
HTLP	Hungarian Truth and Life Party = *Magyar Igazság és Élet Pártja* (MIÉP)
HWF	Hungarian World Federation = *Magyarok Világszövetsége* (MVSZ)
HWM	Hungarian Way Movement = *Magyar Út Mozgalom* (MÚM)
HWP	Hungarian Workers' Party = *Magyar Dolgozók Pártja*

IAHS	International Association of Hungarian Studies = *Nemzetközi Magyar Filológiai Társaság* (NMFT)
JATE	*József Attila Tudományegyetem* = Attila József University (of Szeged)
JPTE	*Janus Pannonius Tudományegyetem* = Janus Pannonius University (of Pécs)
KISZ	*Kommunista Ifjúsági Szövetség* = Communist Youth Federation (CYF)
KLTE	*Kossuth Lajos Tudományegyetem* = Lajos Kossuth University (of Debrecen)
KÖZGÁZ	*Közgazdaságtudományegyetem* = University of Economics
MB	*Magyar Bizottság* = Hungarian Committee (HC)
MADISZ	*Magyar Demokratikus Ifjúsági Szövetség* = Hungarian Democratic Youth Federation (HDYF)
MAOSZ	*Magyar Amerikaiak Országos Szövetsége* = National Federation a Hungarian Americans (NFHA)
MDF	*Magyar Demokrata Fórum* = Hungarian Democratic Forum (HDF)
MIÉP	*Magyar Igazság és Élet Pártja* = Hungarian Truth and Life Party (HTLP)
MINSZ	*Magyar Ifjúság Népi Szövetsége* = Hungarian Young People's Federation (HYPF)
MKISZ	*Magyar Kommunista Ifjúsági Szövetség* = Hungarian Communist Youth Federation (HCYF)
MOVE	*Magyar Országos Véderő Egyesület* = Hungarian National Defense Association (HNDA)
MPs	Members of the Parliament
MSZMP	*Magyar Szocialista Munkáspárt* = Hungarian Socialist Workers Party (HSWP)
MSZSZ	*Magyar Szabadságharcos Szövetség* = Hungarian Freedom Fighters' Federation (HFF)
MSZ(N)VSZ	*Magyar Szabadságharcos(Nemzetőr)Világszövetség* = Hungarian Freedom Fighters (National Guardian) World Federation (HFF[NG]WF)
MSZVSZ	*Magyar Szabadságharcos Világszövetség* = Hungarian Freedom Fighters World Federation (HFFWF)

MTVSZ	*Magyar Történészek Világszövetsége* = World Federation of Hungarian Historians (WFHH)
MÚM	*Magyar Út Mozgalom* = Hungarian Way Movement (HWM)
MVSZ	*Magyarok Világszövetsége* = Hungarian World Federation (HWF]
NATO	North Atlantic Treaty Organization
NDC	National Defense Committee = *Országos Honvédelmi Bizottmány* (OHB)
NÉKOSZ	*Népi Kollégiumok Országos Szövetsége* = National Federation of People's Colleges (NFPC)
NEM	New Economic Mechanism = *Új Gazdasági Mechanizmus* (ÚGM)
NFAH	National Federation of American Hungarians = *Amerikai Magyarok Országos Szövetsége* (AMOSZ)
NLP	National Labor Party = *Nemzeti Munkapárt* (NMP)
NMP	*Nemzeti Munkapárt* = National Labor Party (NLP)
OFB	*OrdoFratrumPraedicatorum* = Dominican Order
OFM	*Ordo Fratrum Minorum* = Franciscan Order
OMGE	*Országos Magyar Gazdasági Egyesület* = National Hungarian Economic Association (NHEA)
OSP	*Ordo Scholarum Piarium* = Piarist Order = Piarista Rend
OTE	*Orvostovábbképző Egyetem* = Graduate Medical University (of Budapest)
POTE	*Pécsi Orvostudományi Egyetem* = Medical Univ. of Pécs
q.v.	*qui vide* = which see
r.	reigned, ruled, tenure in office
SJ	*Societas Jesu* = Jesuit Order = *Jezsuita Rend*
SOTE	*Semmelweis Orvostudományi Egyetem* = Semmelweis Medical University (of Budapest)
SZOTE	*Szent-Györgyi Albert Orvostudományi Egyetem* = Albert Szent-Györgyi Medical University (of Szeged)
SZDSZ	*Szabad Demokraták Szövetsége* = Federation of Free Democrats (FFD)
WFHH	World Federation of Hungarian Historians = *Magyar Történészek Világszövetsége* (MTVSZ)

POLAND

GREAT MORAVIA

KIEVAN RUSSIA

Prague

Cracow

Danube R.

Slovaks Zipsers Kassa

Augsburg

Pozsony Rusyns

HOLY ROMAN EMPIRE

AUSTRIA

Vienna

Nyitra

Esztergom

Székelys

Székesfehérvár

H U N G A R Y

Nagyvárad Kolozsvár

Danube R.

TRANSYLVANIA

Saxons

Pécs Kalocsa

Tisza R.

Nagyszeben Brassó

Laibach

Venice

Zagreb

SLAVONIA

CROATIA

BOSNIA

Belgrade

Vlachs (Romanians)

PAPAL STATES

Zara

Danube R.

BENEVENTO

Spalato

ZETA

SERBIA

Raška

Niš

BULGARIA

Ragusa

•••••••••••• Borders of Great Moravia in the late 9th Century

———————— Borders of Hungary in the mid-13th century

- - - - - - - - Lands south of this line were acquired by Hungary after 1091

MILES
0   50   100

0   150
KILOMETERS

The Austro-Hungarian Empire (Austria-Hungary) in 1914
The border between Austria and Hungary
The border of Bosnia-Herzegovina within the Austro-Hungarian Empire

MILES
0   50   100

0   150
KILOMETERS

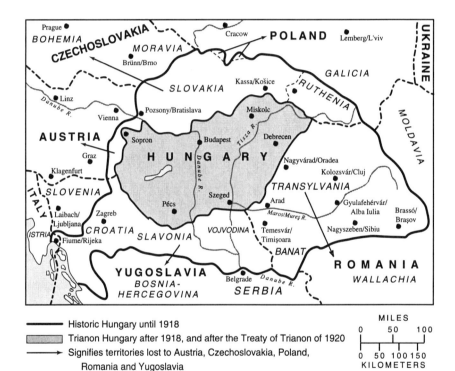

Historic Hungary until 1918

Trianon Hungary after 1918, and after the Treaty of Trianon of 1920

Signifies territories lost to Austria, Czechoslovakia, Poland,
Romania and Yugoslavia

MILES

0   50   100

0 50 100 150
KILOMETERS

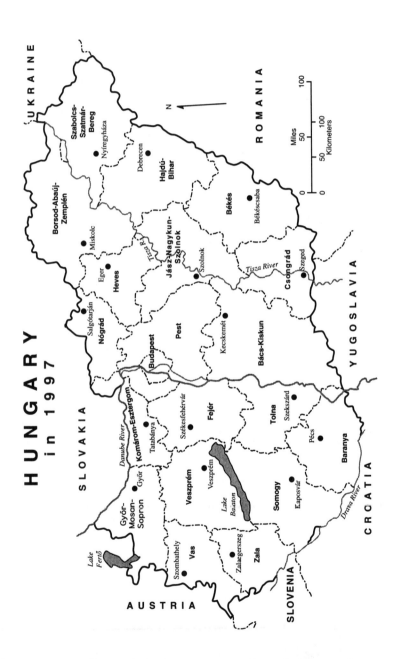

CHRONOLOGY

2000-1500 B.C.	Ancestors of the Hungarians lived among the Finno-Ugric tribes in the northern part of European Russia.
1500-1000 B.C.	The Finnic tribes separated from the Ugric tribes, and while the former moved west, the latter moved southeast to the southern tip of the Ural Mountains.
1000-500 B.C.	A group of Ugric tribes developed into the ancestors of the Magyars, or Hungarians. This took place in an area later to be known as *Magna Hungaria* (Early Hungary), located between the confluence of the Volga and Kama rivers and the Ural Mountains. At this time this group of tribes also picked up the name of "Magyar."
A.D. 9	Romans conquered Pannonia, the western part of future Historic Hungary.
109	Romans conquered Dacia, the eastern part of future Historic Hungary.
271	Romans relinquished Dacia and removed its Romanized population to south of the Danube.
401-10	The Huns conquered the Carpathian Basin and made it the center of their large Eurasian empire.
432-53	Empire of the Huns under Attila. Its center was in future Hungary, and many of its historical traditions became incorporated into the traditions of the Hungarians.
453	Attila's death, followed by a series of civil wars.
463	Many Onogur tribes—among them the ancestors of the future Hungarians—moved westward and settled north of the Caucasus.
465	Attila's Hunnic Empire was fragmented as a result of the fratricidal wars among his sons.

469	Attila's youngest son Irnák ("Csaba" in Hungarian legends) settled with some Huns in Scythia Minor. Hungarian traditions hold that their descendants are the Hungarian-speaking *Székelys* of Transylvania.
527	Byzantine sources mention the Hunnic king "Maugeris," whose name may be connected with the ethnic name of the Hungarians ("Magyars").
567	Establishment of the Avar Empire, centered in the Carpathian Basin, that is, Historic Hungary.
c.600-750	A group of related tribes, the Finno-Ugric Hungarians, left *Magna Hungaria* on the Middle Volga and moved down to *Levedia* on the Lower Don, where they joined the Onogur-Bulgar remnants in the Khazar Empire.
c.630	Establishment of the Khazar Empire centered on the Lower Volga.
c.634	Rise of the Onogur-Bulgar state north of the Sea of Azov, ruled by Khan Kuvrat (Kubrat), which contained Hunnic and proto-Magyar fragments. In the third quarter of the 7th century it was conquered by the Khazars, who thus extended their rule over the Magyar/Hungarian tribes.
c.670-80	The extension of Khazar rule pushed many of the Onogur-Bulgar tribes out of their homeland. One group under Kuvrat's fourth son, Kuber (Kubernek), settled in Pannonia and came to be known as the "Late Avars." Some scholars (e.g., Gyula László) view them simply as an early wave of the Magyars or Hungarians.
c.830	The Hungarian Tribal Federation was formed, which seceded from the weakened Khazar Empire and for a while remained in Levedia north of the Sea of Azov.
c.850	The Hungarian Tribal Federation separated into two groups. The majority moved west to Etelköz, located between the Carpathians and the Black Sea, while a minority moved southeast beyond the Caucasus.
c.870	First reference to the so-called "dual kingship" among the Hungarians, or Magyars. Their supreme ("sacred")

	ruler was called *kende* or *kündü,* but the holder of real power was called *gyilas* or *gyula.*
895	The Hungarians began their conquest of the Carpathian Basin by crossing the Verecke Pass in the Northeastern Carpathians. Consisting of seven Magyar and three Kabar tribes, they were led by Prince Árpád, who occupied the post of *gyula,* and by Prince Kurszán, who was the *kende* or *kündü.*
896	The generally accepted "compromise date" of the Magyar conquest of Hungary. The size of the conquering population was about 500,000, that is, 100,000 families and 20,000 warriors.
899	Beginning of the Magyar raids into Western and Southern Europe.
904	Death of Prince Kurszán, after whose passing the system of dual kingship ended and Prince Árpád took over as the sole ruler.
907	Death of Prince Árpád, who established the Árpádian dynasty, which ruled Hungary until 1301.
955	The Battle of Augsburg (Lechfeld) in Bavaria, where a Hungarian army was defeated by Holy Roman Emperor Otto the Great. This ended their raids into the West.
c.970-97	Reign of Grand Prince Géza, and the beginning of the Christianization of Hungary.
997	Accession of Grand Prince (r.997-1000), later King Stephen (István) (r.1000-38), who Christianized Hungary and later became a canonized saint.
997	Foundation of the Monastery (later Archabbey) of Pannonhalma, which soon became one of the important centers of Hungarian Christianity.
1000	On Christmas day (December 25, 1000) Grand Prince Stephen was crowned Hungary's first Christian king in the city of Esztergom with a royal crown sent to him by Pope Sylvester II.

1001	The foundation of the Archbishopric of Esztergom, followed by the establishment of ten bishoprics. King Stephen also issued his First Law Code in that year.
1031	Death of Prince Emeric (Imre), King St. Stephen's only son. He named his nephew, the Venetian Peter Orseolo, as his heir.
1038	The death of King St. Stephen (August 15), followed by a struggle for the throne and by a pagan reaction against his coerced Christianization of Hungary.
1040s-1060s	Struggle against several Holy Roman Emperors, who tried to incorporate Hungary into the empire. The "Ancient Gesta" *(Ősgeszta),* the source or partial source of many Hungarian chronicles, was composed.
1077-95	Reign of King St. Ladislas (László).
1083	Canonization of King Stephen, Prince Emeric, and Bishop Gerard (Gellért).
1089	The death of King Zvonimir of Croatia, followed by the Hungarian occupation of Slavonia and Croatia (1089-91).
1095-1116	Reign of King Coloman (Kálmán) the Bibliophile, the start of the Crusades (1096), and the consolidation of early feudalism in Hungary.
1102	The final conquest of Croatia and much of Dalmatia and the signing of the *Pacta Conventa.* Croatia became an autonomous part of Hungary, governed by a *bán,* appointed by the king of Hungary.
1131-41	Reign of King Béla II the Blind, who conquered much of Dalmatia, Bosnia, and Rama.
1172-96	Reign of King Béla III, growth of feudalism, growing influence of the Papal court, and the simultaneous development of such royal offices as those of the *nádor* (palatine), *országbíró* (lord chief justice), *bán* (governor of Croatia and other provinces), and *voievod* (governor of Transylvania). Anonymus's *Gesta Hungarorum* was composed during Béla III's rule.

1200	Hungary's population was about two million (i.e., between 1.8 and 2.2 million).
1205-35	Reign of King Andrew II (Endre) and the rise of feudal disunity. Anarchy increased and more power fell into the hands of the regional lords (oligarchs).
1222	King Andrew II was forced to issue the Hungarian Golden Bull *(Bulla Aurea)*, by which he was compelled to share political power with the rising common nobility *(servientes regis)*. The Golden Bull became the foundation stone of Hungarian constitutionalism.
1224	The invited Saxon settlers of Transylvania were given constitutional guarantees for their special privileges. At almost the same time the Teutonic Knights, who violated their obligations to the king, were expelled from Hungary (1225).
1235-70	Reign of Béla IV. He tried to end feudal anarchy, but his plans were derailed by the Mongol invasion.
1241-42	The Mongol invasion of Hungary under the leadership of Khan Batu.
1241 Apr. 11-12	The Battle of Mohi, where the Hungarian Royal Army was destroyed by the Mongols.
1246	King Béla IV defeated and killed Duke Frederick II of Austria, who had imprisoned him during the Mongol conquest and also took Western Hungary. Frederick's death meant the end of the Babenberg dynasty and the start of Hungarian-Czech struggle to gain control over the Babenberg possessions.
1270	Death of King Béla IV, decline of royal power, and beginning of Hungary's fragmentation as a result of the growth of the power of the regional lords.
1272	Election of Rudolph of Habsburg as German king and Holy Roman Emperor.
c.1275	*Gesta Hungarorum* (Deeds of the Hungarians) by Simon de Kéza (Kézai Simon) which emphasized the belief of the Hunnic origins of the Hungarians.

1278	The Battle of Marchfeld, where Emperor Rudolph and King Ladislas IV of Hungary defeatedKing Ottokar of Bohemia-Moravia and thereby established the Habsburgs in Austria and in Vienna.
1301 Jan. 1	Death of King Andrew III (Endre) and the end of the male line of the Árpád dynasty. Hungary became the playground of regional lords (oligarchs), of whom the most powerful was Matthew (Máté) Csák of Trencsén.
1301/08-42	Reign of King Charles Robert (Charles I) of the Neapolitan branch of the French Anjou (Angevin) family, who defeated the oligarchs and saw the penetration of the Western ideals of chivalry and of Italian cultural influences to Hungary.
1329	Vlachs (Romanians) and Rusyns (Ruthens) begin to settle in large numbers in the eastern half of Hungary (Transylvania and Carpatho-Ruthenia).
c.1330	Hungary's population, suffered a drastic decline at the time of the Mongol conquest (1241-42), had again reached two million.
1342-82	Reign of Louis I the Great, which represented the climax of Hungarian empire building.
1351	King Louis's *Decretum,* which proclaimed the uniform rights and privileges of the Hungarian nobility *("unam et eadem nobilitas").*
1358	King Louis acquired the whole of Dalmatia, including the Republic of Ragusa (Dubrovnik), and then organized the Hungarian Admiralty Office *("Admiratus Maritimus Regis Hungariae").*
1367	Foundation of the University of Pécs, Hungary's first university. It was the fourth in Central Europe (Prague 1348, Cracow 1364, Vienna 1365).
1370	The death of Casimir the Great of Poland and the accession of King Louis to the Polish throne (Hungaro-Polish personal union).
1387-1437	Reign of Sigismund of Luxemburg, later Holy Roman Emperor (r.1410-37) and king of Bohemia (r.1419-37),

by virtue of his marriage to Queen Maria (r.1382-95), daughter of King Louis the Great.

1389   Foundation of the University of Óbuda (Old Buda), Hungary's second university. (Some scholars claim that it was founded only in 1395.)

1390s   Growing influx of the early Renaissance spirit into Hungary.

1396   Crusade of Nicopolis against the Turks under the leadership of King Sigismund of Hungary.

1410   King Sigismund was elected Holy Roman Emperor, which resulted in the reorientation of Hungarian foreign policy from a Franco-Italian direction toward Germany (Holy Roman Empire).

1437 June   Outbreak of a major peasant rebellion in eastern Hungary under the leadership of Antal Budai-Nagy (d.1437 December 10/14), which prompted the leading estates of Transylvania to organize themselves into a defensive union at Kápolna.

1437 Sep. 16   Union of Kápolna, the first federation of the three Transylvanian "nations": Hungarians, *Székelys,* and Saxons (Germans). The *Székelys* are Hungarian-speaking alleged descendants of the Huns.

1440   Clash between the constitutional principles of hereditary versus elective monarchy, which ended in the former's victory at the National Diet. This was the first diet that dealt with the "Doctrine of the Holy Crown," which transferred all royal powers from the king to the Crown of St. Stephen and thus made the free election of monarchs possible.

1446   János Hunyadi was elected the regent of Hungary (r.1446-52) and then went ahead to establish Hungary's defenses against the Ottoman Turks.

1456 July 22   Hunyadi inflicted a major defeat on the armies of Mehmet the Conqueror at Belgrade and thereby stopped Ottoman advance for half a century.

1458-90	Reign of King Matthias I, son of János Hunyadi, also known as Matthias Corvinus. Matthias's rule was characterizedby his efforts to break the power of the magnates through political centralization. To strengthen Hungary against Turkish expansion, he gained control over Moravia, Bohemia, Silesia, and portions of Austria, and hoped to become Holy Roman Emperor. Matthias advancedthe cause of Renaissance culture by making Buda into an important center of Renaissance art and learning in East Central Europe.
1467	The foundation of the University of Pozsony (Academia Istropolitana), Hungary's third university.
1470s	The royal book printing and copying shop of Buda moved from the Gothic to the Renaissance style.
1485	King Matthias conquered Vienna and passed the new Palatine Law, which empowered the holder of that office with leading the country during an interregnum. The purpose of this law was to enable Matthias's illegitimate son, János Corvinus, to ascend the throne.
1488	The printing of János Thuróczy's *Chronicon Hungarorum* (Chronicle of the Hungarians), which treats Hungarian history from the very beginnings to August 1477. This work popularized the belief of the direct Hunnic descent of the Hungarians.
1490-1526	Reign of the Jagellonian dynasty, under whom Hungary's power declined drastically.
1514 Apr.-Sep.	The Dózsa Peasant Rebellion that resulted in the perpetual enserfment of the Hungarian peasantry.
1514 Oct.	The Diet of 1514 approved István Werbőczy's *Tripartitum* (printed in Vienna in 1517), which became the primary depository of Hungarian constitutionalism for the next three centuries.
1515	A dynastic pact of mutual succession between the Habsburgs and the Jagellonians at Pozsony and Vienna, sealed by a double marriage.

1526 Aug. 29   Battle of Mohács, where Sultan Süleyman's Ottoman Army of over 100,000 annihilated the Hungarian Royal Army of about 25,000. King Louis II perished, along with 15,000 others, among them many of Hungary's top political and ecclesiastical leaders.

1526 Nov. 11   Crowning of John Zápolya (John I) (1487-1540) as king of Hungary (r.1526-40).

1526 Dec. 16   Ferdinand of Habsburg was proclaimed king of Hungary (r.1526-64) by a rival group of nobles, thus producing two rival kings for the country.

1529   King John became the vassal of Sultan Süleyman, followed by the first unsuccessful Turkish attempt to take Vienna ("First Siege of Vienna").

1536   A new law granted King Ferdinand the right to name a viceroy to administer his section of Hungary. Another law declared Pozsony (Pressburg) the new administrative seat of Royal Hungary.

1538 Feb. 24   The Peace of Várad (Nagyvárad) between Hungary's two kings divided the kingdom on the basis of the status quo. They agreed that in case of King John's death, Hungary would be reunited under King Ferdinand.

1538   Foundation of the Calvinist College of Debrecen, one of several such colleges in Hungary.

1541 Aug. 29   The peaceful occupation of Buda by the Turks through deception. This began the 145 years of Turkish rule in Buda, as well as the threefold division of Hungary.

1542   The establishment of the Viceroyalty Council to administer Royal Hungary under Habsburg rule.

1547   A five-year treaty of peace between Emperor Charles V and Sultan Süleyman, which codified Hungary's trifold division and also obliged the emperor's brother, King Ferdinand, to pay an annual tribute of 30,000 golden florins to the Turkish sultan for the Hungarian territories under his control.

1550	Foundation of a printing press at Kolozsvár (Klausenburg) by Gáspár Heltai and György Hoffgreff, which printed works in Latin, Hungarian, and German.
1550s	Beginning of the construction of a series of frontier fortresses to contain Turkish expansion.
1554	Publication of Tinódi-Lantos's heroic epic, the *Cronica*, about the struggle against the Turks.
1556	King Ferdinand established the Royal War Council *(Consilium Bellicum, Kriegsrat, Haditanács)* in Vienna, which was placed in charge of the defenses of all Habsburg lands.
1556 Sep. 1	King Ferdinand I became Holy Roman Emperor Ferdinand II (r.1556-64).
1564-76	Reign of King Maximilian I (Emperor Maximilian II), known for his Protestant sympathies.
1566	Sultan Süleyman's last Hungarian campaign. He died (September 5-6) during the successful siege of Szigetvár (August 5-September 8) that was defended by Count Nicolaus (Miklós) Zrínyi (c.1508-66). The sultan's death did not deter the Turks from adding more territories to their growing empire.
1568	The Transylvanian Diet at Torda proclaimed the right of religious freedom for the four main Christian denominations: Catholics, Calvinists, Lutherans, and Unitarians.
1571-86	Reign of Stephen (István) Báthory (1533-86) as prince of Transylvania. In 1575 Báthory was also elected king of Poland.
1575	Printing of Gáspár Heltai's Magyar language history of the Hungarians at Kolozsvár, *Chronica az Magyaroknac dolgairól* (Chronicle about the Deeds of the Hungarians).
1576-1608	Reign of King Rudolf I (Emperor Rudolph II) (r.1576-1612), who, while supporting the scientific experimentations of Johann Kepler, had to deal with the Fifteen Years' War.

1584	First printing of the *Corpus Juris Hungarici* (Corpus of Hungarian Laws).
1590	The Protestant clergyman Gáspár Karoli translated and published the first complete edition of the Bible, known as the "Vizsoly Bible."
1591-1606	The Fifteen Years' War between the Habsburg and the Ottoman Empires.
c.1600	The rise of the autonomous "peasant counties" in regions under Turkish occupation.
c.1600-03	The humanist historian István Szamosközy (Zamosius) wrote his histories of Hungary and Transylvania: *Rerum Ungaricarum libri IV* (Four Books on the Deeds of the Hungarians), *Rerum Transylvanicarum Pentades* (The Deeds of Transylvania in Five Books), *Hebdomades* (Seven Books), and *De originibus Hungaricis* (On the Origins of the Hungarians).
c.1600-06	Humanist historian Miklós Istvánffy (1538-1615) wrote his *Historiarum de rebus Ungaricis libri XXXIV* [History of the Deeds of the Hungarians in Thirty-Four Books].
1605-06	Reign of Stephen (István) Bocskai as the prince of Transylvania, who settled many of his *hajdú* fighters (freebooters) and their families in Hajdú, Bihar, and Szatmár counties in East-Central Hungary. He also elevated them to the ranks of the lower nobility.
1606 June 23	The Peace Treaty of Vienna between Prince Bocskai and King Rudolph, wherein Bocskai received guarantees for Transylvania's independence as well as for the freedom of worship for the Protestant peasants of Hungary.
1606 Nov. 11	The Peace of Zsitva-Torok between the Habsburgs and the Ottomans, which restored the status quo and guaranteed armistice for twenty years.
1608	The Hungarian Diet at Pozsony divided itself into the Lower and the Upper House. It also passed a number of significant laws, among them new procedures for the

election of the palatine, obligatory use of Hungarian advisers by the king when dealing with matters relating to Hungary, permission for Hungarian nobles to settle in the German-inhabited cities, and regulation of the migration of serfs. The king was also obliged to finance the upkeep of frontier fortresses and to appoint Hungarian officers to command them.

1608-19   Reign of King Matthias II (Emperor Matthias I), under whom the Thirty Years' War erupted.

1613-29   Reign of Gabriel [Gábor] Bethlen as prince of Transylvania. During Bethlen's reign—which is viewed as the "Golden Age of Transylvania"—that small eastern principality, carved out of the Kingdom of Hungary, became a significant factor in European power-politics.

1616   The future Cardinal Péter Pázmány became the Archbishop of Esztergom and the Primate of Hungary (r.1616-37) and immediately initiated a powerful and successful Counter-Reformation movement.

1618-48   The age of the Thirty Years' War during which the Hungarian princes of Transylvania (Gabriel Bethlen and George Rákóczi I) pursued an anti-Habsburg foreign policy and supported the cause of Protestantism throughout Europe.

1619-37   Reign of King/Emperor Ferdinand II (1578-1637).

1620s   Vlach (Romanian) immigration into eastern and southern Hungary and Croatia. Turkish gypsies immigrated to Hungary and became transmitters of Hungarian heroic lyrics and love songs born amidst conditions of perpetual warfare on the frontier.

1625-45   The election of Nicolaus (Miklós) Esterházy as Hungary's palatine, whose goal was the reunification of Hungary under Habsburg rule.

1626   György Káldi translated and published the first complete edition of the Catholic version of the Bible in Hungarian, *Szent Biblia* [Holy Bible].

1630-48	Reign of George Rákóczi I (1593-1648) as prince of Transylvania, who supported the Protestant cause in the Thirty Years' War.
1630	The Hungarian Diet passed laws regulating the position of the Vlachs [Romanians] who immigrated to Hungary.
1635	Cardinal Péter Pázmány founded the Jesuit University of Nagyszombat (Tyrnau), the predecessor of the present-day University of Budapest (Eötvös Loránd University).
1637-57	Reign of King/Emperor Ferdinand III, who had to deal with ending the Thirty Years' War.
1648	Peace for twenty-two years was concluded between the Habsburgs and the Ottoman Empire.
1648-57/60	Reign of George Rákóczi II as prince of Transylvania. Rákóczi's unfortunate involvement in the Polish War led to his deposition by the Turkish sultan. Thus, after 1657 he was forced to fight for his throne and to share the princely office with other elected or appointed princes.
1651	Count Nicolaus (Miklós) Zrínyi, the great poet and military leader, published a collection of his heroic epics under the title *Adriai tengernek Syrenája* (Mermaid of the Adriatic Sea).
1653	Apáczai-Csere published his *Magyar encyclopédia* (Hungarian Encyclopedia).
1657-1705	Reign of Leopold I (1640-1705), under whom the *kuruc* uprisings took place and the Turks were pushed out of Hungary.
1661-90	Reign of Michael Apafi as prince of Transylvania, whose ineffective rule placed his principality completely under Turkish influence.
1663-64	Habsburg-Ottoman War, initiated by Grand Vizier Ahmed Köprülü's policy of expansion.
1664	The Battle of St. Gotthard (August 1) and the Peace of Vasvár (August 10), ended in the Habsburg-Ottoman

	stalemate. But the Peace of Vasvár was so unfavorable to Hungary that there was a mass indignation throughout the country. It soon led to an anti-Habsburg conspiracy, as well as to the rise of the anti-Habsburg *kuruc* movement.
1666	Start of the "Wesselényi-Conspiracy" against the Habsburg rule in Hungary.
1667	The diet passed additional laws regulating the position of the Vlachs (Romanians) in Hungary.
1670-71	The arrest (1670) and execution (April 30, 1671) of the leaders of the "Wesselényi- Conspiracy."
1672	The formation of the anti-Habsburg *kuruc* armies in Hungary and in Transylvania.
1673	King/Emperor Leopold suspended the Constitution and appointed Johann Ampringen, the Grand Master of the Teutonic Order, as "governor of Hungary" (r.1673-79) to deal with the *kuruc* problems.
1673-76	The forceful Counter-Reformation spearheaded by Primate Szelepcsényi resulted in the arrest of many hundreds of Protestant clergymen. Those who agreed to convert to Catholicism were freed, but the rest were condemned to death, then imprisoned, and finally sold as galley slaves to Venice.
1678-80	Count Imre Thököly was chosen as the leader of the *kuruc* armies, who then began his insurrection against Habsburg rule in Hungary.
1681-1713	Count, later Prince (1687), Pál Esterházy (1635-1713) was elected the palatine of Hungary. Although a pro-Habsburg aristocrat, at times even he spoke up for the protection of the rights of the Hungarian estates against encroachments by Habsburg functionaries.
1682	Sultan Mehmet (Mohammed) IV (r.1648-87) named Count Thököly the "king of Upper Hungary" and also sent him a crown.

1683	The Second Siege of Vienna (July 14-September 12), which ended in Turkish defeat, was the start of the expulsion of the Turks from Hungary.
1686	The reconquest of the old Hungarian capital of Buda (June 21-September 2). The autonomy of Hungary's fiscal administration ended. The first major Serbian immigration to Southern Hungary took place.
1687	General Antonio Caraffa, the commander of the Habsburg Imperial Armies of Upper Hungary, instituted a reign of terror via the so-called "blood tribunal" of Eperjes.
1690	The death of Prince Michael Apafi of Transylvania (April 15), followed by the end of Transylvania's independence. It was integrated into the Habsburg Empire.
1690-1707	Functioning of the so-called *Neoacquisitica Commissio* (New Acquisition Commission), which examined property rights on the reconquered territories and awarded most of the lands to foreigners who had served the Habsburgs well.
1691	A royal charter by King/Emperor Leopold permitted 37,000 Serbian families to settle in Southern Hungary depopulated by the Liberation Wars.
1695-1707	The intensely anti-Hungarian Cardinal Leopold Kollonich (Kollonitsch) (1631-1707) was named archbishop of Esztergom and primate of Hungary. Kollonich had been involved in many of the bloody measures of the Counter-Reformation during the 1670s, and in 1689 he was the primary author of the *Einrichtungswerk des Königreichs Ungarn* [Restructuring Plan for the Kingdom of Hungary], which, if enacted, would have emasculated the nation.
1699 Jan. 26	The Peace Treaty of Karlowitz ended the Liberation Wars (1683-99).
1699-1712	Formation of the "Croatian Military District" in Southern Hungary newly settled by South Slavs.

1703-11	The Rákóczi War of Liberation (second "Kuruc War") against the Habsburgs.
1711 Apr. 30	The Peace Treaty of Szatmár ended the Rákóczi War of Liberation with a compromise.
1711-40	Reign of King Charles III (Emperor Charles VI), the last male member of the Habsburg dynasty.
1717-20	The first partial census after the expulsion of the Turks showed Hungary's population (including Transylvania and the Partium) to be between 3.5 and 4 million. Over half of these were non-Hungarian as a result of the country's depopulation during the Liberation Wars (1683-99) and and simultaneous influx of Vlach (Romanian) and Serbian settlers from the Balkans.
1716-18	Austro-Turkish War ended in the Treaty of Passarowitz (1718), which regained the Banat of Temesvár for Hungary.
1722-23	The Hungarian Diet at Pozsony and the Transylvanian Diet at Gyulafehérvár (Alba Julia) ratified the Pragmatic Sanction issued in 1713, which permitted female members of the Habsburg dynasty to ascend the throne.
1731 Mar. 21	The *Carolina Resolutio* limited the free religious practices of the Protestants and also barred them from administrative offices.
1735	Death of Prince Francis Rákóczi in exile.
1735-42	The great polyhistor, Mátyás Bél, published the first four volumes of his *Notatia Hungariae novae historico-geographica* (Historical-Geographical Description of Modern Hungary).
1739	Publication of Prince Francis Rákóczi's memoirs under the title: *Historie des révolutions de Hongrie* [History of the Revolution in Hungary].
1740-80	Reign of Maria Theresa, the first female head of the House of Habsburg. Her rule was marked by the growth of German and Catholic influence and by the spread of Baroque culture.

1740-48	War of Austrian Succession, which resulted in Maria Theresa retaining her throne, but losing Silesia to Frederick the Great of Prussia.
1745-65	The nominal reign of Francis I, Maria Theresa's husband, as Holy Roman Emperor, which was the result of the fact that German law prevented a female from ascending the Holy Roman Imperial throne. Thus, although she held most of the powers, Empress Maria Theresa was an "empress" only by virtue of the fact that she was married to an emperor.
1745 Dec. 25	The Treaty of Dresden between Austria and Prussia, whereby the Habsburgs relinquished Silesia.
1748 Oct. 23	The Treaty of Aachen (Aix-la-Chapelle) affirmed the great power position of the Habsburgs that had been shaken during the long war.
1754	Introduction of a new tariff system so as to make Hungary—where the nobility was not taxed—pay for the upkeep of the empire.
1758	Maria Theresa first used the title "Apostolic King of Hungary," which went back to the year A.D. 1000, when King St. Stephen (r.997-1038) received a royal crown from Pope Sylvester II.
1760	Founding of the Hungarian Royal Nobles' Guard in Vienna, where each county was represented by two young nobles. The guard soon became the center of a Hungarian national revival movement.
1760s-70s	Continued influx of large number of Vlachs (Romanians) from the Balkans, who were fleeing from the oppressive rule of the Greek Phanaroit princes of Moldavia and Wallachia.
1765	Transylvania was made a Grand Duchy.
1766	Publication of Péter Bod's *Magyar Athenas* (Hungarian Athenas), which contained the life stories of 485 Hungarian authors. Bod also wrote the three-volume *Historia Hungarorum ecclesiastica* (History of the

	Hungarian Church), which remained unpublished until 1888-90.
1767	Maria Theresa's peasant laws regulated the relationship between the lords and their serfs and reducedserf labor *(robot)* to one day per week.
1772	In consequence of the first Polish Partitions, the thirteen Saxon cities of Upper Hungary, that had been pawned by King Sigismund (r.1387-1437), were returned to Hungary.
1777	Maria Theresa's edict on public education *(Ratio Educationis)*established a uniform educational system, introduced a modern curriculum, and made the study of German obligatory.
1779	The port city of Fiume (Rijeka) on the Adriatic Sea was attached to Hungary.
1780-90	Reign of Joseph II, who, next to Frederick the Great of Prussia, was the most noted exponent of Enlightened Despotism.
1780	Launching of the first Hungarian language newspaper, *Magyar Hírmondó* (Hungarian Herald), by Mátyás Rát in Pozsony.
1781 May 13	Joseph II freed the Jews from many of the medieval limitations, but obliged them to assume German family names.
1781 Oct. 26	Joseph II issued his Edict of Toleration, which extended religious freedom to the Protestants and the Orthodox Christians and permitted them to occupy all local and national offices.
1784 May 11	Joseph II's decreeon the obligatory use of German in the empire's administrative and military systems.
1784-87	Hungary's population (including Transylvania), according to a partial census, was 6,443,000, of which 308,000 were nobles. The actual number was probably closer to 8.5 million.
1785 Aug. 22	Joseph II's second decree about the peasantry that ended perpetual serfdom and returned to the peasants the right

	of free movement, although it did not end the peasants' obligations for the use of their plots.
1786	Launching of the second Hungarian language newspaper, the *Magyar Kurír* (Hungarian Courier), in Vienna by Sándor Szacsvay.
1787-91	Austro-Turkish war that ended in *status quo ante bellum.*
1789	Launching of the third Hungarian language newspaper, the *Hadi és Más Nevezetes Történetek* (Military and Other Noteworthy News), in Vienna by Demeter Görög.
1790-92	Reign of Leopold II.
1790-95	Archduke Alexander Leopold (Sándor Lipót) served as the first palatine of the Habsburg family.
1792-1835	Reign of Francis II (Francis I as the Emperor of Austria after 1804), who, during the last two-thirds of his reign, was under the controlling influence of his chancellor, Prince Metternich.
1793-1801	Digging of the "Francis Canal" that connected the rivers Danube and the Tisza.
1794-95	The Martinovics Conspiracy, headed by the ex-monk Ignác Martinovics (1755-95), which resulted in the execution of several good patriots, who were dragged into it by this former Imperial spy.
1796-1847	Archduke Joseph (József) (1776-1847), son of Emperor Leopold II, served as Hungary's second palatine of the Habsburg family. He became the founder of the "Hungarian Habsburgs."
1800	The Reformed (Calvinist) College of Sárospatak introduced Hungarian (Magyar) as the language of instruction.
1801	Founding of the *Georgikon* at Keszthely by Prince György Festetics (1755-1819), which became Hungary's first agricultural academy.

1802-08	Foundation of the Hungarian National Museum, based on Count Ferenc Széchényi's gift of his valuable art collection.
1804	Francis II proclaimed the "Austrian Empire" and assumed the title "Francis I Emperor of Austria."
1805	Hungary's population (including Transylvania) according to a partial census was 7,216,000, of which 345,000 were in the category of nobles.
1805	A new law passed by the Hungarian Diet permitted local authorities to correspond with the Viceroyalty Council in Hungarian (Magyar).
1805	Launching of the political weekly *Hazai Tudósítások* (News from the Homeland), which had a significant role in advancing the cause of the Hungarian (Magyar) language.
1805-12	Publication of *Magyarország históriája* (Hungary's History) by the Romantic Protestant historian, Ésiás Budai (1766-1841).
1806	The second *Ratio Educationis* reemphasized the continued primary use of Latin as the language of instruction in secondary schools.
1808	Publication of the *Magyar századok* [Hungarian Centuries] by the Romantic Catholic historian, Benedek Virág (1754-1830).
1809 May 15	Napoleon issued his "Proclamation to the Hungarian Nation" in which he called upon the Hungarians to rise up against the Habsburgs.
1812-25	A period of autocratic rule, when Francis refused to convene the Hungarian Diet.
1814	By 1814, the Austrian Empire (including Hungary) had mobilized 619,000 soldiers against Napoleon, which equaled the size of Napoleon's Grand Army with which he had invaded Russia.
1814-15	The Congress of Vienna reorganized post-Napoleonic Europe, guided by the principle of legitimacy and by antirevolutionary tendencies. The Congress and the

	period after it was dominated by the repressive spirit of Prince Metternich.
1815	Founding of the *Magyar Tudós Társaság* (Hungarian Scientific Society), the predecessor of the Hungarian Academy of Sciences (1825).
1816	The first gas lights in Pest (later part of Budapest).
1817	Founding of the *Tudományos Gyűjtemény* (Scholarly Compendium) (1817-41), Hungary's first scholarly periodical in the Magyar language.
1820	The first steamship between Buda and Pest.
1821	Launching of the *Aurora* (1822-37), which became the Hungarian Reform Period's most important literary yearbook. In 1837 it was replaced by the *Athenaeum* (1837-43).
1824	Ján Kollár (1793-1852) published the first version of his *Slávy dcera* (Daughter of Slava) and started the Pan-Slavic movement in Hungary.
1825	Publication of István Horvát's (1784-1846) extremely Romantic *Rajzolatok a magyar nemzet legrégibb történeteiből* (Sketches from the Most Ancient History of the Hungarian Nation).
1825-48	The Hungarian Reform Period, which initiated a revival of the nation and ultimately led to the revolution of 1848-49.
1825 Nov. 3	Founding of the Hungarian Academy of Sciences based on Count István Széchenyi's initiative.
1829-44	Publication of György Fejér's (1766-1851) forty-three-volume Latin language documentary collection on Hungarian history, *Codex Diplomaticus Hungariae Ecclesiasticus ac Civilis.*
1830	Act VIII of 1830 permitted the courts to use the Hungarian (Magyar) language side by side with Latin, and directed that all government personnel and lawyers be proficient in both languages.

1830	Count István Széchenyi published his epoch-making *Hitel* (Credit) that placed Hungary upon the path of economic and financial modernization.
1831 Mar. 1	Foundation of the first stock exchange in Pest.
1831 Mar. 16	Start of regular steamship traffic on the Danube.
1832	Kossuth initiated his *Országgyűlési Tudósítások* (Reports from the National Assembly).
1832	The travels of Sándor Bölöni-Farkas (1795-1842) in the United States. His travelogue—*Utazás Észak-Amerikában* (Travels in North America)—was published in 1835.
1834	Opening of the Hungarian language school of the Jewish Congregation of Pest.
1835-48	Reign of the mentally deficient Ferdinand V (Ferdinand I as emperor of Austria).
1835	Foundation of the shipyard at Óbuda.
1836	Act III of 1836 proclaimed that thenceforth all laws will be published both in Latin and in Hungarian.
1837-47	Construction of the Hungarian National Museum.
1837	Kossuth, the leader of the Radicals, was arrested and sentenced to four years of imprisonment.
1837 Aug. 22	Foundation of the Hungarian National Theater.
1839	Baron Miklós Wesselényi (1796-1850), the leader of the Hungarian Reform Movement in Transylvania, was arrested and sentenced to three years of imprisonment for printing the Proceedings of the Transylvanian Diet.
1840	Hungary's population (with Transylvania) reached 8,266,000, of which 395,000 persons, that is, nearly 5% were nobles. The actual population was larger. The populations of Hungary's largest cities were: Pest 64,000, Buda 31,000 (=Budapest 95,000), Debrecen 50,000, Pozsony 35,000, Szabadka 31,000, Zombor 21,000, Székesfehérvár 20,000. For a comparative view, Vienna's population at that time was 333,000.

1841 Jan. 2	Appearance of Kossuth's *Pesti Hírlap* (Pest News) (1841-49), which became the leading herald of the liberal national reform in Hungary.
1841	Public polemics between the two top reform leaders, Széchenyi and Kossuth.
1841	Promulgation of a new, more humane penal code.
1841-49	Construction of the Chain Bridge—Europe's first suspension bridge—between Buda and Pest.
1844	Act II of 1844 made Hungarian (Magyar) the official language of the country.
1846	Opening of the first railway between Pest and Szolnok.
1847-48	The Hungarian Reform Diet at Pozsony passed a series of reforms ending all remnants of feudalism.
1848 Mar. 15	Start of the Hungarian Revolution of 1848-49.
1848 Apr. 7	Formation of the first Independent Hungarian Government under the prime ministership of Count Lajos Batthyány (1806-49). It included such reformers as Count Széchenyi, Lajos Kossuth, Ferenc Deák, and Baron József Eötvös.
1848 Apr. 11	Approval of the "April Laws" by King Ferdinand V and the dissolution of the last feudal diet. The April Laws launched Hungary on the path of democratic modernization.
1848 Spring	Growth of nationalistic agitation among Hungary's national minorities.
1848 May 29	The Transylvanian Diet voted for a reunion with Hungary.
1848 July 5	Convening of the first representative Hungarian Parliament in the city of Pest (Budapest) with 426 representatives from throughout the country.
1848 Sep. 16	In light of the seriousness of the military situation, the Hungarian Parliament appointed a six-member Committee of National Defense *(Országos Honvédelmi Bizottmány)* under the chairmanship of Louis Kossuth.
1848 Sep. 28	Unwilling to approve the growing violence and the approaching Austro-Hungarian confrontation, Count

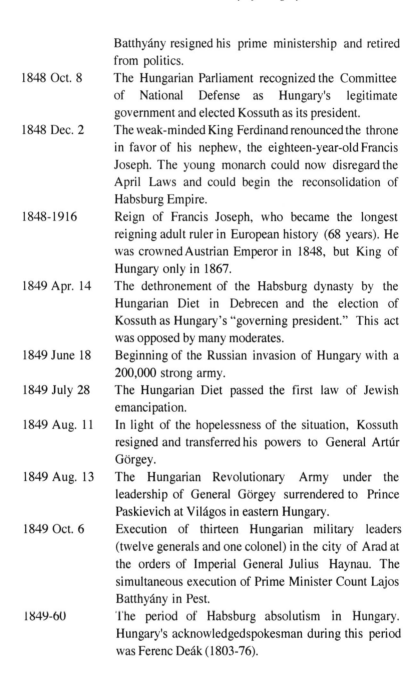

<table>
</table>

Batthyány resigned his prime ministership and retired from politics.

1848 Oct. 8   The Hungarian Parliament recognized the Committee of National Defense as Hungary's legitimate government and elected Kossuth as its president.

1848 Dec. 2   The weak-minded King Ferdinand renounced the throne in favor of his nephew, the eighteen-year-old Francis Joseph. The young monarch could now disregard the April Laws and could begin the reconsolidation of Habsburg Empire.

1848-1916   Reign of Francis Joseph, who became the longest reigning adult ruler in European history (68 years). He was crowned Austrian Emperor in 1848, but King of Hungary only in 1867.

1849 Apr. 14   The dethronement of the Habsburg dynasty by the Hungarian Diet in Debrecen and the election of Kossuth as Hungary's "governing president." This act was opposed by many moderates.

1849 June 18   Beginning of the Russian invasion of Hungary with a 200,000 strong army.

1849 July 28   The Hungarian Diet passed the first law of Jewish emancipation.

1849 Aug. 11   In light of the hopelessness of the situation, Kossuth resigned and transferred his powers to General Artúr Görgey.

1849 Aug. 13   The Hungarian Revolutionary Army under the leadership of General Görgey surrendered to Prince Paskievich at Világos in eastern Hungary.

1849 Oct. 6   Execution of thirteen Hungarian military leaders (twelve generals and one colonel) in the city of Arad at the orders of Imperial General Julius Haynau. The simultaneous execution of Prime Minister Count Lajos Batthyány in Pest.

1849-60   The period of Habsburg absolutism in Hungary. Hungary's acknowledged spokesman during this period was Ferenc Deák (1803-76).

1851-52	Louis Kossuth's six-month tour of the United States, following his liberation from exile in the Ottoman Empire.
1853	Publishing of the first Hungarian emigré newspaper, the *Magyar Száműzöttek Lapja* (Hungarian Exiles' News) in New York.
1853-56	Construction of the tunnel under Castle Hill, which was a continuation of the Chain Bridge built earlier between Buda and Pest.
1855 Nov. 13	Concordat with the Papacy.
1857 May 9	Partial amnesty for those who had participated in the Hungarian War of Liberation against Austria.
1859 Apr.-July	The Austro-Italian-French War that undermined Habsburg power in Italy and forced the Habsburgs to seek accommodation with Hungary.
1860 Apr. 8	Count István Széchenyi committed suicide, after being harassed by authorities following his critical commentary upon the defunct absolutist system.
1860 Oct. 20	Francis Joseph issued the "October Diploma" that restored some of Hungary's autonomy.
1860-67	The Provisional Period or the Age of Provisorium.
1861 Feb. 26	Emperor Francis Joseph issued the "February Patent," which apportioned the representation of all lands (including Hungary) in the Imperial Diet.
1864	The Hungarian Stock Exchange opened in Pest.
1866 Jun.-Aug.	The Austro-Prussian War, ending in Austria's defeat at Königgrätz (Sadowa) on July 3 and the Peace of Prague on August 23. This defeat speeded up the progress toward a compromise with Hungary.
1866 Aug. 1	Horse-drawn tramway service was put into operation in Pest.
1866 Aug. 9	Opening of the Hungarian Zoo, organized by János Xántus (1825-94), who had spent a decade and a half in the United States (1850-64).
1867-71	Count Gyula Andrássy's prime ministership.

1867 May 29	Ratification of the Austro-Hungarian Compromise by the Hungarian Parliament. It transformed the Austrian Empire (1804-67) into Austria-Hungary (1867-1918).
1867 June 8	Francis Joseph was crowned king of Hungary.
1867 Dec. 27	Act XVII of 1867 reasserted the emancipation of the Hungarian Jews, who were first freed by the Revolutionary Government on July 28, 1849.
1868 June 24	Act IX of 1868 guaranteed the autonomy of the Serbian and Romanian Orthodox Churches.
1868 Nov. 17	Francis Joseph signed Act XXX of 1868 (the Hungaro-Croatian Compromise), which gave broad autonomy to Croatia within Hungary.
1868 Dec. 5	Francis Joseph signed Act XXXVII of 1868 (Education Law) that introduced universal and obligatory schooling to Hungary.
1868 Dec. 6	Francis Joseph signed Act XLIV of 1868 (Nationalities Law) that guaranteed extensive rights to all national minorities in Hungary.
1869 Dec. 31	Hungary's population reached 15.5 million (15,512,379).
1871-72	Count Menyhért Lónyay's prime ministership.
1871-79	Count Gyula Andrássy, Sr., served as Austria-Hungary's foreign minister.
1872 Oct. 10	Founding of Hungary's first military college, the "Ludovika Akadémia" at Pest.
1872 Oct. 12	Founding of the Francis Joseph University of Kolozsvár in Transylvania.
1872-74	József Szlávy's prime ministership.
1872 Dec. 31	Unification of the cities of Buda and Pest into Budapest.
1872 Dec.	Launching of the influential *Budapesti Szemle* (Budapest Review) (1872-1944) with the financial support of the Hungarian Academy of Sciences.
1872-76	Construction of the Margaret Bridge *(Margithíd)* between Buda and Pest, across the southern tip of Margaret Island.

1874-75	István Bittó's prime ministership.
1875 Mar. 1	Birth of the Liberal Party (1875-1906) that controlled Hungarian politics for three decades.
1875	Baron Béla Wenckheim's prime ministership.
1875-90	Kálmán Tisza's prime ministership, which turned into the longest tenure in Hungarian history.
1875-84	Construction of the Hungarian National Opera.
1878 July-Sep.	Austria-Hungary's occupation of Bosnia-Herzegovina.
1880 Dec. 31	Hungary's population was 15.7 million (15,739,259).
1880s	Start of a mass economic emigration from Hungary (and Austria-Hungary) to the United States.
1881 Feb. 14	Act III of 1881 established the Gendarmerie.
1881 May 1	Introduction of the telephone system in Budapest.
1883	Protracted nationalistic demonstrations in Croatia against Hungarian control.
1885	Act VII of 1885 reformed the Upper House, limited hereditary membership, and introduced appointed membership for personal merits.
1890-92	Count Gyula Szapáry's prime ministership.
1890 Dec. 31	Hungary's population reached 17.4 million (17,463,791).
1892-95	Sándor Wekerle's first prime ministership.
1894 Dec. 9	Francis Joseph signed the law relating to obligatory civil marriage (Act XXXI of 1894).
1895-99	Baron Dezső Bánffy's prime ministership.
1896	Hungary celebrated the Millennium of the Árpádian conquest of Hungary. Major exhibits and numerous building programs in Budapest (first subway, Andrássy Boulevard, Heroes' Square, People's Garden, House of Parliament, etc.). The date 1896 was selected somewhat arbitrarily, for the Hungarian conquest began earlier and lasted well beyond that year.
1899-1903	Kálmán Széll's prime ministership.
1900	Founding of the influential progressive sociological journal *Huszadik Század* (Twentieth Century) (1900-

	19) connected with the bourgeois liberal movement in Hungary.
1900 Dec. 31	Hungary's population reached 19.2 million (19,254,559).
1902	Founding of the GYOSZ (Federation of Hungarian Industrialists).
1903	Count Károly Khuen-Héderváry's first prime ministership.
1903	Demonstrations by national minorities throughout Hungary.
1903-04	Obstructions by opposition parties in the legislature, leading to physical destructions in the House of Parliament.
1903-05	Count István Tisza's first prime ministership.
1905-06	Baron Géza Fejérváry's prime ministership.
1906-09	Tariff war with Serbia.
1906-10	Sándor Wekerle's second prime ministership.
1907	Climax of the mass emigration from Hungary, when 209,000 Hungarian citizens left for overseas, of whom 193,400 entered the United States. Of the latter, 60,169 were Magyars, while the rest belonged to a host of other nationalities.
1907	Founding of the Christian Democratic Party by Sándor Giesswein (1856-1923).
1907 June-July	Croat obstruction in the Hungarian Parliament.
1908 June	Hungary's first Peasant Congress under the leadership of András Áchim (1871-1911).
1908	Foundation of the influential literary periodical *Nyugat* (West) (1908-41), which was an important champion of Hungary's Westernization.
1910-12	Count Károly Khuen-Héderváry's second prime ministership.
1910 Dec. 31	Hungary's population reached 20.9 million (20,886,487).
1912-13	László Lukács's prime ministership.
1913-17	Count István Tisza's second prime ministership.

1913 Nov. 26	Compromise between the government and the Serbo-Croatian coalition in the Hungarian Parliament.
1914 Spring	Count Mihály Károlyi's tour of the United States.
1914 June 28	Assassination of Archduke Francis Ferdinand, the heir to the Austro-Hungarian throne, at Sarajevo.
1914 July 23	Austria-Hungary's ultimatum to Serbia.
1914 Jul. 28	Declaration of war against Serbia.
1916 Nov. 21	Death of Emperor Francis Joseph.
1916-18	Reign of King Charles IV (Emperor Charles I).
1917 June-Aug.	Count Móric Esterházy's prime ministership.
1917-18	Sándor Wekerle's third prime ministership.
1918 Oct. 23	Establishment of the Hungarian National Council.
1918-19	Count Mihály Károlyi's prime ministership.
1918 Nov. 6	Czech invasion into Northern Hungary (Slovakia).
1918 Nov. 9	Serbian invasion into Lower Hungary (Délvidék).
1918 Nov. 15	Romanian invasion of Transylvania.
1918 Nov. 16	Proclamation of the Hungarian Republic.
1919 Jan.-Mar.	Dénes Berinkey's prime ministership.
1919 Mar. 21	Proclamation of the Hungarian Soviet Republic under Béla Kun.
1919 May 5	Count Gyula Károlyi established his counter-revolutionary government at Arad.
1919 Aug. 1	Resignation of Béla Kun and the fall of the Hungarian Soviet Republic.
1919 Aug. 1-6	Gyula Peidl's prime ministership.
1919 Aug. 9	Admiral Nicholas Horthy, the commander-in-chief of the National Army, established himself as a force separate from the Szeged government.
1919 Aug.-Nov.	István Friedrich's prime ministership.
1920 Mar. 1	Horthy was elected regent of Hungary (1920-44).
1919-1920	Károly Huszár's prime ministership.
1920 Mar.-July	Sándor Simonyi-Semadam's prime ministership.
1920 June 4	Signing of the Treaty of Trianon, which reduced Hungary to about 30 percent of its former size.
1920-21	Count Pál Teleki's first prime ministership.

1920 Aug. 14	Formation of the anti-Hungarian Little Entente by Czechoslovakia and Yugoslavia. Romania joined them in April and June 1921.
1920 Sep. 26	Passage of the *Numerus Clausus* Quota Law, which limited admission to Hungary's universities and law academies to the share of an individual ethnic group or nationality in the country's population.
1920 Dec. 31	Following the Treaty of Trianon (June 4, 1920) and the loss of 70 percent of its territory, Hungary's population was reduced to 8 million (7,990,202).
1921-31	Count István Bethlen's prime ministership.
1921 Oct. 23	King Charles's second and final unsuccessful attempt to regain his Hungarian throne.
1921 Nov. 6	Dethronement of the Habsburg dynasty in Hungary (Act XLI of 1921).
1924 Jan. 8	Hungary is assured Western loans for economic stabilization.
1926 Nov. 11	Reestablishment of the Upper House of the Hungarian Parliament.
1927 Apr. 5	Italian-Hungarian Treaty of friendship, including a promise of help against the Little Entente.
1930 Dec. 31	Trianon Hungary's population reached 8.6 million (8,688,319).
1931 July 14	Hungary's economic crisis erupted.
1931-32	Count Gyula Károlyi's prime ministership.
1932-36	Gyula Gömbös's prime ministership.
1932 Nov. 10-13	Gömbös's visit to Mussolini.
1933 Jan. 17-18	Gömbös's visit to Hitler.
1934 Feb. 4	Resumption of diplomatic relations with the Soviet Union.
1934 Mar. 16	Signing of the Rome Pact by Italy, Hungary, and Austria.
1935 Mar.	Ferenc Szálasi established his fascist Party of National Will *(Nemzeti Akarat Pártja)*.
1936-38	Kálmán Darányi's prime ministership.
1937 Mar. 15	Foundation of the progressive March Front.

1937 Oct. 23	Fusion of several fascist parties into the Hungarian National Socialist Party under Ferenc Szálasi.
1938 Mar. 5	Proclamation of the "Győr Program" of national rearmament.
1938 Mar. 13	*Anschluss* (Union). Nazi Germany occupied Austria and thus became an immediate neighbor of Hungary.
1938 May 29	Implementation of the "First Jewish Law" (Act XV of 1938) that limited Jewish participation in the professions to 20 percent.
1938-39	Béla Imrédy's prime ministership.
1938 Aug.	National celebrations on the nine hundredth anniversary of King St. Stephen's death.
1938 Nov. 2	The First Vienna Award that returned portion of former Northern Hungary (Slovakia) to Hungary.
1939 Mar.	Formation of the Fascist Arrow Cross Party *(Nyilaskeresztes Párt)*.
1939 Mar. 15	Hungary's reoccupation of Carpatho-Ruthenia after the dissolution of Czechoslovakia.
1939 May 5	Passage of the "Second Jewish Law (Act IV of 1939), which defined a Jew as a person who had at least one Jewish parent or two Jewish grandparents.
1939-41	Count Pál Teleki's prime ministership.
1939 Sep. 17	Hungarian government refused to permit the German Army to cross Hungary in their invasion of Poland.
1940 Aug. 30	The Second Vienna Award returned Northern Transylvania to Hungary.
1940 Nov. 20	Hungary joined the Tripartite Pact formed by Germany, Italy, and Japan.
1940 Dec. 12	Hungary signed a "Pact of Eternal Friendship" with Yugoslavia.
1941 Jan. 31	Following the territorial revisions between 1938 and 1941, Hungary's population nearly doubled to 14.6 million (14,683,323).
1941 Apr. 3	Prime Minister Pál Teleki committed suicide as a form of protest for Hungary's joining the German invasion of Yugoslavia.

1941-42	László Bárdossy's prime ministership.
1941 June 26	The bombing of Kassa, allegedly by the Soviets. This was used as a pretext by Prime Minister Bárdossy to declare war against the Soviet Union.
1942-44	Miklós Kállay's prime ministership, in the course of which he tried to get Hungary out of the war through an agreement with the Western powers.
1942-43 Winter	Destruction of Hungary's Second Army in the Soviet Union, near Voronezh.
1943 Aug. 23-28	The Second Conference at Balatonszárszó (Szárszó) by Hungary's Populist intellectuals to find a way out of Hungary's predicament.
1944 Mar. 19	German military occupation of Hungary, to prevent the government from concluding a separate peace.
1944 Mar.-Aug.	Döme Sztójay's prime ministership.
1944 May-July	Collection and deportation of the Hungarian Jews from the provinces.
1944 Aug.-Oct.	Géza Lakatos's prime ministership.
1944 Oct. 11	Signing of an armistice with the Soviets in Moscow.
1944 Oct. 15-16	Regent Horthy proclaimed the armistice and the cessation of all hostilities against the Soviet Army. This was followed by a German-supported coup that overthrew Horthy and installed Szálasi as the head of the government with the titles prime minister and "national leader" *(Nemzetvezető)*.
1944 Dec. 22	Formation of Provisional National Government under the prime ministership of General Béla Dálnoki-Miklós (Béla Miklós), who served until November 7, 1945.
1944 Dec. 25	Start of the Siege of Budapest that lasted until February 13, 1945.
1945 Feb. 24	Mátyás Rákosi became secretary general of the Hungarian Communist Party until Jul. 18, 1956.
1945 Apr. 4	All of Hungary fell to the Soviets and Szálasi's leadership ended. This day came to be celebrated between 1945 and 1990 as "Liberation Day."

1945 Nov. 4	Free elections. The Smallholders' Party won an absolute majority of 57 percent, while the Soviet-supported Communist Party received 17 percent.
1945-46	Zoltán Tildy's prime ministership, at the head of a Coalition government.
1946 Feb. 1	Zoltán Tildy was elected the first president of the Hungarian Republic.
1946-47	Ferenc Nagy's prime ministership.
1946 Aug. 1	End to Hungary's hyperinflation by introducing the *forint* as the new currency.
1947 Feb. 10	Signing of the Peace Treaty of Paris, which made Hungary even smaller than Trianon in 1920.
1947 Apr. 16	Conviction of the leaders of the secret organization "Hungarian Community" *(Magyar Közösség)* for their alleged anti-Soviet conspiratorial activities.
1947 May 30	Prime Minister Ferenc Nagy, while in Switzerland and fearing for his life, resigned his office and decided not to return to Hungary.
1947-48	Lajos Dinnyés's prime ministership.
1947 Aug. 1	Initiation of Hungary's Three-Year Plan.
1947-1949	Communist infiltration and liquidation of all rival political parties.
1848 Feb. 8	Cardinal József Mindszenty was convicted in a political sham trial.
1948 June 13	Formation of a new communist bloc under the name Hungarian Workers' Party
1948-52	István Dobi's prime ministership.
1949 Jan.	In light of the loss of its regained territories, Hungary's territory and population were reduced. In 1949 the size and its population stood at 9.2 million (9,204,799).
1949 Aug. 20	Proclamation of the Hungarian People's Republic under its new socialist constitution.
1949 Sep.	Start of political sham trials against fellow communists and others, and the beginning of the communist reign of terror.

1950 Jan. 1	Initiation of the First Five-Year Plan, which involved unrealistic emphasis on heavy industry and on the forced collectivization of agriculture.
1951 Jun. 17	Start of mass deportations of former "exploiters" from Budapest, in the course of which about 20,000 educated urbanites were resettled to the country's most primitive provinces.
1952-53	Mátyás Rákosi's prime ministership.
1953-55	Imre Nagy's first prime ministership and the beginning of a political thaw.
1955-56	András Hegedűs's prime ministership.
1955 May 14	Hungary joined the Warsaw Pact.
1956 July 18-21	Rákosi was dismissed as the first secretary of the Hungarian Workers' Party. Ernő Gerő was appointed in his place.
1955 Dec. 14	Hungary became a member of the United Nations.
1956 Oct. 23	Start of the anti-communist and anti-Soviet Hungarian Revolution.
1956 Oct. 25	Imre Nagy became prime minister (second time). János Kádár replaced Ernő Gerő as first secretary.
1956 Nov. 1	Formation of the Hungarian Socialist Workers' Party and a Soviet-supported rival government under János Kádár's prime ministership.
1956 Nov. 4	The start of the Soviet invasion of Hungary.
1956 Nov.-Dec.	Exodus of 200,000 refugees from Hungary.
1956-58	Period of violent retributions.
1958-61	Ferenc Münnich's prime ministership.
1958-60	Hungary's Second Three-Year Plan.
1958 June 17	Execution of Imre Nagy and several other prominent leaders of the revolution of 1956.
1958 Dec.	Hungary's population stood at 9,857,016.
1961 Jan. 1	Introduction of the Second Five-Year Plan, to be followed by four others (1965-70, 1971-75, 1976-80, and 1981-85).
1961-65	János Kádár's second prime ministership.

1963 Mar. 22	Proclamation of general amnesty and the initiation of Hungary's liberalization.
1965-67	Gyula Kállai's prime ministership.
1967-75	Jenő Fock's prime ministership.
1968 Aug. 21	Hungary joined (under pressure) the Soviet invasion of Czechoslovakia.
1968 Dec. 4	Initiation of Hungary's New Economic Mechanism, which tried to introduce elements of market economy into the socialist system.
1970 Jan.	Hungary's population stood at 10,314,152.
1970 Aug. 1-15	The first Mother Language Conference, a controversial effort of the Hungarian World Federation to reach out to Hungarians living abroad.
1971 Sep. 28	Cardinal József Mindszenty, who in 1956 found political asylum in the U.S. Embassy in Budapest, was permitted to leave Hungary.
1972 Apr. 19-20	The Constitution was revised and Hungary was proclaimed to be a "socialist republic."
1974 Aug. 9	Visit of President Ford to Hungary as a recognition of the improved Hungarian-U.S. relations.
1975-1987	György Lázár's prime ministership.
1975 Aug. 2	Hungary signed the Helsinki Final Acts concerning European Security and Cooperation.
1976 Dec. 31	The opening of the Hilton Hotel in Budapest.
1977 Sep. 14-16	Signing of the Czechoslovak-Hungarian agreement on the construction of the ill-fated Bős-Nagymaros (Gabčikovo) Power Plant project on the Danube.
1978 Jan. 6	A U.S. delegation headed by Secretary of State Cyrus Vance returned the Holy Crown to Hungary.
1980 Jan. 1	Hungary's population stood at 10,705,000. This was the high point, after which the ongoing population decline began.
1981 Jan. 8-10	Billy Graham's first tour of Hungary. Other tours followed in 1985 and 1989.
1983 Sep. 19-20	Vice President George Bush's official visit to Hungary.
1985 Dec. 15-17	Secretary of State George Shultz's official visit.

1987-88	Károly Grósz's prime ministership.
1987 Sep. 27	Formation of the Hungarian Democratic Forum as a social movement at Lakitelek.
1988 May 24	Kádár was dismissed as the Party's first secretary.
1988 July 20-28	Prime Minister Károly Grósz (also the secretary general of the Hungarian Socialist Workers' Party) made an official visit to the United States.
1988 Oct. 2	Founding of the Federation of Young Democrats.
1988 Nov. 13	Founding of the Federation of Free Democrats.
1988 Dec. 26	Miklós Németh appointed prime minister of Hungary.
1989 June 16	Official state burial for Prime Minister Imre Nagy and his associates, who were executed in 1958.
1989 July 6	Death of János Kádár.
1989 July 11-13	President George Bush's official visit to Hungary.
1989 July 24-25	The Hungarian Democratic Forum was transformed into a political party.
1989 Aug. 19	The first "Pan-European Picnic" in the vicinity of Sopron, which resulted in hundreds of East German tourists crossing over to Austria.
1989 Sep. 10	Hungarian government allowed tens of thousands of East Germans to cross over to Austria and thereby initiated the collapse of the Iron Curtain.
1989 Oct. 6-10	The dissolution of the Hungarian Socialist Workers' Party (1956-89) and the foundation of the Hungarian Socialist Party (ex-communists).
1989 Nov. 9	Opening of the Berlin Wall and the fall of the Iron Curtain.
1989 Dec. 21	Outbreak of the anti-Ceausescu uprising in Romania, which began with Ceausescu's campaign against the Hungarian Calvinist pastor, László Tőkés, in November of that year in Timiśoara (Temesvár), Transylvania, Romania.
1990 Jan. 1	Hungary's population was aging fast and it declined to 10,355,000, representing a loss of 350,000 since 1980.
1990 Jan. 24	Act 1990:IV extended full freedom of worship to all religious denominations.

1990 Jan. 31	Fifty-nine Catholic religious orders were reestablished in Hungary.
1990 Feb. 9	Reestablishment of the diplomatic relations (broken on April 4, 1945) between Hungary and the Vatican.
1990 Mar. 1	The Parliament abolished state monopoly over education and permitted the establishment of denominational schools, as well as religious education in state schools.
1990 Apr. 27-28	The Dalai Lama visited Hungary.
1990 Mar.-Apr.	Elections for the first post-communist Parliament. The results: Hungarian Democratic Forum: 165; Federation of Free Democrats: 91; Smallholders' Party: 44; Hungarian Socialist Party: 33; Christian Democratic People's Party: 21; Federation of Young Democrats: 21; independent candidates: 6; multiparty candidates: 4; Agrarian Federation: 1; for a total of 386.
1990 May 13	Reestablishment of diplomatic relations between Hungary and the Sovereign Order of Malta.
1990 May 23	Assumption of power by the new post-communist government under József Antall's prime ministership.
1990 June 2	Establishment of the Hungarian Christian-Jewish Council for the continuation of a religious dialogue.
1990 July 23	Reestablishment of the Hungarian Scout Association's membership in the International Scout Federation.
1990 Aug. 20	Celebrations of St. Stephen's day as a national holiday, for the first time since World War II.
1990 Sept. 15	The arrival of Ambassador Sándor Keresztes to the Vatican.
1990 Oct. 27	The taxi blockade that almost led to the fall of the Antall government.
1990 Nov. 6	Hungary became a member of the European Council.
1990 Dec. 17	The opening of the Jewish American Foundation School in Budapest.
1991 Feb. 15	Foundation of the Federation of Catholic Journalists.
1991 July 1	Dissolution of the Warsaw Pact.
1991 June 19	The last Soviet army unit left Hungary.

1991 Feb. 15   Treaty of Mutual Cooperation among Hungary, Poland, and Czechoslovakia was signed at Visegrád, Hungary, by József Antall, Lech Wal'esa, and Václav Havel.

1991 May 1-4   The remains of Cardinal József Mindszenty were exhumed at Mariazell, Austria, and reinterred in the Basilica of Esztergom, next to the other primates.

1991 Aug. 16-20   Pope John Paul's first visit to Hungary.

1991 Sep.-Oct.   Prime Minister Antall's visit to the United States.

1992 Mar. 24-31   Meeting of the Protestant World Congress in Budapest.

1992 Aug. 18-22   Third Hungarian World Congress in Budapest.

1992 Aug. 20   Publication of a critical study by István Csurka, which began the split in the ruling Hungarian Democratic Forum between the Conservative-Nationalists and the Populist-Nationalists. It also began Hungary's slide from popularity in the Western press.

1993 Apr. 20-23   President Árpád Göncz's visit to the United States for the opening of the Holocaust Museum.

1992 Sep.   The Protestant Theological College at Sárospatak, founded in 1531 and closed in 1951, was reopened.

1993 Dec. 12   Prime Minister Antall's died and his office was assumed by Péter Boross (to July 15, 1994).

1994 Jan. 1   Hungary's population declined to 10,278,000.

1994 May   The first post-communist Hungarian government, headed by the Hungarian Democratic Forum, was voted out of power. The new ruling coalition was consisted of the Socialist Party and the Federation of Free Democrats. The new Hungarian Parliament was constituted as follows: Socialist Party: 209; Federation of Free Democrats: 69; Hungarian Democratic Forum: 38; Smallholders' Party: 26; Christian Democratic People's Party: 22; Agrarian Alliance: 20; Liberal Civic Alliance and Entrepreneurs' Party: 1.

1994 July 15   The former communist foreign minister of Hungary, Gyula Horn, assumed the prime ministership.

1994 Dec. 5   President Bill Clinton's official visit to Hungary.

1995 Mar.	Introduction of the shock therapy austerity program know after the Minister for Financial Affairs, Lajos Bokros (b.1954), as the "Bokros Package."
1995 June 4-12	Prime Minister Horn's visit to the United States.
1995 Sep.	Introduction of tuition at Hungary's institutions of higher learning.
1995 Oct.-Nov.	Mass demonstrations and strikes against the Horn government's inability to stop the rapid decline of living standards in Hungary.
1995 Dec. 12	Hungary (town of Taszár) became the staging ground for American troops going to Bosnia.
1995 Dec. 31	Sanctions against Serbia had cost Hungary over three billion dollars in trade.
1995 Dec. 31	Hungary's gross foreign debt has risen to over thirty-three billion dollars.
1996 Jan. 13	President Clinton visited U.S. troops in Hungary. He was received by President Árpád Göncz and Prime Minister Gyula Horn.
1996. Jan. 18	Prime Minister Gyula Horn inaugurated Hungary's millecentennial celebrations with a speech in the Hungarian Parliament.
1996. Jan. 27	Hungary's population stood at 10,250,000, i.e. 460,000 below the 1980 level. This was the result of declining birthrate.
1996. Mar. 4	The first post-communist ruling party, the Hungarian Democratic Forum, that had lost the elections in 1994, was split by internal factionalism. The more liberal wing established the Hungarian Democratic People's Party *[MagyarDemokrataNéppárt]*.
1996 Apr. 1	The Slovak Parliament ratified the Hungarian-Slovak Basic Agreement, but without granting collective rights to the country's large Hungarian minority.
1996 May 9	Ferenc Glatz, one of Hungary's most respected historians, was elected president of the Hungarian Academy of Sciences.

1996 Summer   Series of celebrations commemorating the one-thousand-one-hundredth(millecentenary) anniversary of the Árpádian conquest of Hungary.

1996 June 13-18 Fourth Hungarian World Congress in Budapest.

1996 Sep. 7-8   Pope John Paul's second visit to Hungary.

1996 Sep.   The quality of life declined significantly, but Hungary's gross foreign debt also declined to twenty-five billion dollars (net foreign debt to 13.2 billion dollars). This means that the "Bokros Package" is indeed working, and that there may be a hope for an improved quality of life for the average citizen.

1996 Sep.-Oct.   The eruption of the so-called "Tocsik scandal." A legal counselor by the name of M. Tocsik was allegedly paid 804 million Hungarian forints ($5,200,000) for her "legal advice" in the process of the privatization of state and communal property. Many claim that this is only the top of the iceberg of the various potential financial scandals involving billions of forints.

1997 Jan. 1   Hungary's population declined to under 10,200,000.

GLOSSARY OF GEOGRAPHICAL TERMS

ABBREVIATIONS

B	= Bulgarian		OG/v	= Old German, variant
CS	= Czech/Slovak		OH	= Old Hungarian
CH	= Common Hungarian usage		P	= Polish
E	= English		R	= Romanian
G	= German		R/v	= Romanian, variant
GR	= Greek		RU	= Russian
H	= Hungarian		S	= Slovak/Slavic
H/v	= Hungarian, variant		SC	= Serbo-Croatian
I	= Italian		SL	= Slovenian
L	= Latin		T	= Turkish
OG	= Old German		U	= Ukrainian/Rusyn

CITIES, TOWNS, FORTRESSES, SETTLEMENTS

Adrianople (E)	Edirne (T)	Hadrianopolis (L)	Drinápoly (H)
	Adrianoúpolis (GR)	Jedrene (SC)	Odrin (B)
Alba Iulia (R)	Gyulafehérvár (H)	Karlsburg (G)	Carlopolis (L)
Aquincum (L)	Óbuda (H)	Altofen (G)	
Balázsfalva (H)	Blasendorf (G)	Blaj (R)	
Bártfa (H)	Bartfeld (G)	Bardejov (CS)	
Belgrade (E)	Beograd (SC)	Nándorfehérvár (OH)	Belgrád (H)
Beregszász (H)	Lampertshaus (G)	Beregovo (RU)	Berehovo (CS,U)
Beszterce (H)	Bistritz (G)	Bistriťa (R)	
Besztercebánya (H)	Neusohl (G)	Banská Bystrica (CS)	
Bistriťa (R)	Beszterce (H)	Bistritz (G)	Neosolio (L)
Blaj (R)	Balázsfalva (H)	Blasendorf (G)	
Brassó	Kronstadt (G)	Braśov (R)	Brassovia (L)
Bratislava (CS)	Pozsony (H)	Pressburg (G)	Istropolis (L)
Braśov (R)	Brassovia (L)	Brassó (H)	Kronstadt (G)
Breslau (G, E)	Wrocław (P)	Vraclav (CS)	Boroszló (H)
Brno (CS)	Bruna (L)	Brünn (G)	

41

Brünn (G)	Brno (CS)	Bruna (L)	
Bucharest (E)	Bucuresti (R)	Bukarest (H)	Bükreś (T)
Buda(H)	Ofen (G)	Budin (T)	Budim (CS)
Budapest (H, E)	Pest-Buda(OH)	Pesth-Ofen (OG)	Ofenpesth (OG/v)
Cluj (R)	Kolozsvár (H)	Klausenburg (G)	Claudopolis (L)
Cluj-Napoca (R/v)	Cluj (R)	Kolozsvár (H)	Klausenburg (G)
Constantinople (E)	Istanbul (T)	Sztambul (OH)	Constantinopolis (G)
	Czargrad (R)	Czarhorod (U)	Czarigrad (B)
Cracow (E)	Kraków (P)	Krakau (G)	Krakkó (H)
	Cracovia (L)	Krakov (CS, R)	Kroke/Kruke (SC)
Csanád (H)	Tschanad (G)	Cenad (R)	
Danzig (G)	Gdańsk (P)	Gedanium (L)	Danszka (OH)
Debrecen (H)	Debreczen (OH)	Debrecinum (L)	Debreczin (G)
Dévény	Devín (CS)	Theben (G)	
Dubrovnik (SC)	Ragusanum (L)	Ragusa (I, E)	Raguza (H)
Eger (H)	Agria (L)	Erlau (G)	Egri (T)
Eisenstadt (G)	Kismarton (H)		
Eperjes (H)	Preschau (G)	Prešov (CS)	Priashiv (U)
Érsekújvár (H)	Neuhäusel (G)	Nové Zámky (CS)	Novum Castellum (L)
Eszék (H)	Esseg (G)	Osijek (SC)	Mursa (L)
Esztergom (H)	Strigonium (L)	Gran (G)	Ostrihom (CS)
Fiume (I, H)	Rijeka (SC)	Tarsatica (L)	
Forchtenstein (G)	Fraknó (H)		
Fraknó (H)	Forchtenstein (G)		
Gdańsk (P)	Danzig (G)	Gedanium (L)	Danszka (OH)
Güns (G)	Kőszeg (H)		
Güssing (G)	Németújvár (H)		
Győr (H)	Arrabona (L)	Raab (G)	Yanik (T)
Gyulafehérvár (H)	Carlopolis (L)	Karlsburg (G)	Alba Iulia (R)
Hunyadvár (OH)	Vajdahunyad (H)	Eisenmarkt (G)	Hunedoara (R)
Istanbul (T)	Constantinople (E)	Konstantinápoly (H)	Constantinopolis (GR)
Kanizsa (OH, CH)	Nagykanizsa (H)	Gross-Kanischa (G)	Kanije (SC)
Karlowitz (G, E)	Karlovici (SC)	Karlóca (H)	
Kassa (H)	Cassovia (L)	Kaschau (G)	Košice (CS)
Kiev (E)	Kiew (G)	Kijev (H)	Kyiv (U)
Késmárk)H)	Caseoforum (L)	Käsmarkt (G)	Kežmarok (CS)
Kismarton (H)	Eisenstadt (G)		
Kolozsvár (H)	Klausenburg (G)	Claudopolis (L)	Cluj (R)
Komárno (CS)	Komárom (H)	Komorn (G)	

Komárom (H)	Komorn (G)	Komárno (CS)	
Königgrätz (G)	Hradec Králové (CS)		
Königsberg (G)	Kenigsberg (RU)	Kaliningrad (RU)	Królewiec (P)
Košice (CS)	Kassa (H)	Kaschau (G)	Cassovia (L)
Kőszeg (H)	Güns (G)		
Kronstadt (G)	Brassó (H)	Braśov (R)	Brassovia (L)
Laibach (G)	Ljubljana (SL)	Lubiana (I)	Emona (L)
Ljubljana (SL)	Laibach (G)	Emona (L)	Lubiana (I)
Lemberg (G, E)	L'viv (U)	Lvov (RU)	Lwów (P)
Lőcse (H)	Leutschau (G)	Levoča (CS)	Lewocza (P)
Mohács (H)	Mohatsch (G)	Mohacs (E)	Mohać (S)
Munkachevo (U)	Munkács (H)	Munkatsch (G)	Munkačevo (CS)
Munkács (H)	Munkachevo (U)	Munkačevo (CS)	Munkatsch (G)
Nagykanizsa (H)	Kanizsa (OH, CH)	Gross-Kanischa (G)	Kanije (SC)
Nagyszeben (H)	Szeben (CH)	Hermannstadt (G)	Sibiu (R)
Nagyszőlős (H)	Vinogradov (RU)	Vynohradiv (U)	Sevluš (CS)
Nagyszombat (H)	Tirnavia (L)	Tyrnau (G)	Trnava (CS)
Nagyenyed (H)	Enyed (H/v)	Aiud (R)	
Nagyvárad (H)	Várad (OH, CH)	Grosswardein (G)	Oradea (R)
Németújvár (H)	Güssing (G)		
Nicodemia (GR, E)	Izmit (T)		
Nógrád (H)	Novigrad (CS)	Neugrad (G)	
Novi Sad (SC)	Újvidék (H)	Neusatz (G)	Neoplanta (L)
Nyitra (H)	Neutra (G)	Nitra (CS)	
Óbuda	Aquincum (L)	Altofen (G)	
Ödenburg (G)	Sopron (H)	Soproń (CS)	Scarbantia (L)
Ofen (G)	Buda (H)	Budin (T)	Budim (CS)
Oradea (R)	Oradea Mare (R/v)	Nagyvárad (H)	Grosswardein (G)
Orsova (H)	Orschowa (G)	Orśova (R)	
Osijek (SC)	Eszék (H)	Esseg (G)	Mursa (L)
Passarowitz (G, E)	Požarevac (SC)	Pozsarevác (H)	Pasarofça (T)
Pécs (H)	Fünfkirchen (G)	Quinque Ecclesiae (L)	Pečuj (SC)
Pest (H)	Pesth (G)	Contra Aquincum (L)	
Pozsony (H)	Istropolis (L)	Pressburg (G)	Bratislava (CS)
Prague (E)	Praha (CS)	Prag (G)	Prága (H)
Prešov (CS)	Eperjes (H)	Preschau (G)	Priashiv (U)
Pressburg (G)	Pozsony (H)	Bratislava (CS)	Istropolis (L)
Ragusa (I, E)	Ragusanum (L)	Dubrovnik (SC)	Raguza (H)
Rijeka (SC)	Fiume (I, H)	Tarsatica (L)	

Rodostó (H, I)	Tekirdağ (T)	Raedestus (L)	Rhaidestos (GR)
Salonika (E)	Slonicco (I)	Saloniki (G)	Thessaloníki (GR)
	Saloniki (G, R)	Selānik (T)	Solun (B, SC)
Sarajevo (SC, E)	Sarajewo (G)	Bosna-Saray (T)	Szarajevó (H)
Satu Mare (R)	Szatmárnémeti (H)	Szatmár (OH)	Sathmar (G)
Smederevo (SC)	Szendrő (H)	Semendria (G)	Semendire (T)
Satu-Mare (R)	Szatmár (H)	Sathmar (G)	
Segesvár (H)	Stenarum (L)	Schässburg (G)	Sighişoara (R)
Selmecbánya (H)	Schemnitz (G)	Banská Štiavnica (S)	
Sibiu (R)	Nagyszeben (H)	Hermannstadt (G)	Szeben (CH)
Sirmium (L)	Mitrowitz (G)	Sremská Mitrovica (SC)	
Sombor (SC)	Zombor (H)		
Sopron (H)	Scarbantia (L)	Ödenburg (G)	Soproń (CS)
Spalato (I, H)	Spalatum (L)	Split (SC)	
Split (SC)	Spalato (I, H)	Spalatum (L)	Salonae (L)
St. Gotthard (E)	Szentgotthárd (H)	Szent-Gotthárd (OH)	Sankt Gotthard (G)
Subotica (SC)	Szabadka (H)	Zabotka (OH)	Maria-Theresiopel (G)
Szatmárnémeti (H)	Szatmár (OH)	Sathmar (G)	Satu-Mare (R)
Szeben (H)	Hermannstadt (G)	Nagyszeben (H)	Sibiu (R)
Szeged (H)	Segedinum (L)	Szegedin (G)	Segedin (SC)
Székesfehérvár (H)	Fehérvár (CH)	Alba Regia (L)	Stuhlweissenburg (G)
Szendrő (H)	Smederevo (SC)	Semendria (G)	Semendire (T)
Szentgotthárd (H)	St. Gotthard (E)	Sankt Gotthard (G)	Monošter (SC)
Szigetvár (H)	Limusa (L)	Sigetvar (SC)	Sigeth (G, T)
Szombathely (H)	Savaria (L)	Steinamanger (G)	Sambotel (SC)
Temesvár (H)	Temeschwar (G)	Timišvar (SC, T)	Timişoara (R)
Timişoara (R)	Temesvár (H)	Temeschwar (G)	Timišvar (SC, T)
Torda (H)	Salinopolis (L)	Thorenburg (G)	Turda (R)
Trencsén (H)	Laugaritio (L)	Trentschin (G)	Trenčin (CS)
Újvidék (H)	Neoplanta (L)	Neusatz (G)	Novi Sad (SC)
Ungvár (H)	Uzhgorod (RU)	Uzhhorod (U)	Užhorod (CS)
Várad (OH, CH)	Nagyvárad (H)	Grosswardein (G)	Oradea (R)
Varna (E, B)	Odessos (GR)	Várna (H)	
Vasvár (H)	Eisenburg (G)	Castrum Ferrum (L)	
Vienna (E)	Vindobona (L)	Wien (G)	Bécs (H)
Warsaw (E)	Warszawa (P)	Warschau (G)	Varsó (H)
Zagreb (SC)	Agram (G)	Zágráb (H)	Zagabria (L)
Zara (I, E)	Iader (L)	Zadar (SC)	Zára (H)
Zsitva-Torok (OH)	Zsitvatorok (H)		

COUNTRIES, PROVINCES, GEOGRAPHICAL REGIONS

Alföld (CH)	Nagy Alföld (H)	Great Hungarian Plain (E)	
Ardeal (R)	Siebenbürgen (G)	Transylvania (E)	Erdély (H)
Asia Minor (E, L)	Anatolia (E, H)	Anadolu (T)	
Austria (L, E)	Österreich (G)	Ausztria (H)	
Austrian Empire (E)	Kaisertum Österr. (G)	Osztrák Birodalom (H)	
Austria-Hungary (E)	Österreich-Ungarn (G)	Ausztria-Magyarország (H)	
	Habsburg Empire (E)	Austro-Hungarian Empire (E)	
Bácska (H)	Bačka (SC)	Bachka (E)	
Banat (E, SC)	Bánát (H)	Bánság (H/v)	
Bavaria (E)	Bayern (G)	Bajororszag (H)	Bavorsko (CS)
Bohemia (E, L)	Čechy (CS)	Böhmen (G)	Csehország (H)
Bosnia (E)	Bosnien (G)	Bosna (SC, T)	Bosznia (H)
Burgenland	Várvidék (H)	Nyugat Magyarország (H/v)	
Carpatho-Ruthenia (E)	Transcarpathia (E)	Subcarpathia (E)	Kárpátalja (H)
	Carpatho-Ukraine (E)	Podkarpatská Rus (CS)	
Croatia (E)	Hravatska (SC)	Horvátország (H)	
Csallóköz (H)	Schütt (G)	Zhitny Ostrov (S)	
Czech Republic (E)	Česká Republica (CS)	Csehország (H)	
Erdély (H)	Transylvania (E)	Siebenbürgen (G)	Ardeal (R)
Great Hungarian Plain (E)	Nagy Alföld (H)	Alföld (CH)	
Great Moravia (E)	Moravia Magna (E)	Velika Morava (CS)	Nagymorávia (H)
Habsburg Empire (E)	Austrian Empire (E)	Austria-Hungary (E)	Austria (E, L)
Hungary (E)	Magyarország (H)	Ungarn (G)	Hongrie (F)
	Ungheria (I)	Vengria (RU, U)	Wegry (P)
	Ungaria (R)	Madarsko (CS, SC)	Macaristan (T)
Magna Hungaria (L)	Great Hungary (E)	Early Hungary (E)	
Máramaros (H)	Maramureś (R)	Maramarosh (U)	
Moldavia (E)	Moldva (H)	Moldova (R)	Boğdan (T)
Moravia (E)	Mähren (G)	Morava (CS)	Morvaország (H)
Moravia Magna (L)	Great Moravia (E)	Early Moravia (E)	Nagymorávia (H)
Oltenia (E, R)	Little Wallachia (E)	Szörényi Bánság (OH)	
Ottoman Empire (E)	Turkish Empire (E)	Ozmán Birodalom (H)	
Partium (L, E)	Részek (H)		
Sáros (H)	Šariš (CS)	Sharysh (U)	
Satu Mare (R)	Szatmár (H)	Sathmar (G)	Sathmarium (L)
Siebenbürgen (G)	Transylvania (E)	Erdély (H)	Ardeal (R)
Silesia (E)	Schlesien (G)	Slezsko (CS)	Śląsk (P)

Slavonia (E)	Slavonija (SC)	Szlavónia (H)	Tótország (OH)
Slovakia (E)	Slovensko (CS)	Szlovákia (H)	Felvidék (H/v)
	Észak Magyarország (OH)		
Slovenia (E)	Slovenija (SL)	Szlovénia (H)	
Syrmia (E)	Szerémség (H)	Sirmium (L)	Srem (SC)
Szatmár (H)	Sathmar (G)	Sathmarium (L)	Satu Mare (R)
Szepesség (H)	Zipserland (G)	Spiš (CS)	Spisz (P)
Szerémség (H}	Sirmium (L)	Srem (SC)	Syrmia (E)
Transylvania (E)	Siebenbürgen (G)	Erdély (H)	Ardeal (R)
Vajdaság (H)	Délvidék (H/v)	Vojvodina (SC)	Voivodina (E)
Voivodina (E)	Vojvodina (SC)	Vajdaság (H)	Délvidék (H/v)
Volhynia (E)	Lodomeria (L, H)	Volyn' (RU, U)	Woľyń (P)
Wallachia (E)	Havasalföld (H)	Muntenia (R)	Tara Rom. (R)
	Eflāk (T)	Walachei (G)	Vlashko (B)
Zipserland (G)	Szepesség (H)	Spiš (CS)	Spisz (p)

WATERS

Azov Sea (E)	Palus Maeotis (L)	Azovi-tenger (H)	
Balaton (H)	Plattensee (G)	Blatenské jazero (CS)	
Black Sea (E)	Chernoye More (RU)	Karadeniz (T)	Pontus (L)
Danube (E)	Donau (G)	Duna (H)	Dunaj (CS)
	Ister (L, GR)	Danubius (L)	Dunāre (R)
	Dunai (RU, U)	Dunav (B)	Istros (GR)
Drava (SC)	Drau (G)	Dráva (H)	
Lajta (H)	Leitha (G)		
Maros (H)	Marosch (G)	Mureś (R)	
Morava (E, SC, CS)	Morva (H)	Margos (GR)	
Mura (H, SC, SL)	Mur (G)		
Mureś (R)	Maros (H)	Marosch (G)	
Nyitra (H)	Neutra (G)	Nitra (CS)	
Rába (H)	Raab (G)		
Sava (E, SC)	Save (E)	Száva (H)	Sabos (GR)
Szamos (H)	Samosch (G)	Someś (R)	
Temes (H)	Temesch (G)	Timiś (R)	
Tisza (H)	Theiss (G)	Tisa (CS, SC, R)	Tysa (U)
Vág (H)	Waag (G)	Vah (CS)	
Vistula (E)	Wisľa (P)	Weichsel (G)	Visztula (H)

HEADS OF STATE

PERIOD OF "DUAL KINGSHIP (?-907):
Holders of the Office of "Kende"
Levéd (Levedi, Előd)   mid-9th c.
Kurszán (Kusan, Cusan)   c.890-904
Holders of the Office of "Gyula"
Álmos   c.880-895
Árpád   895-907

PERIOD OF THE ÁRPÁD DUKES (907-997):
Árpád's five sons in unknown order and time period: 907-c.945
  Levente (Liüntika), Tarhos (Tarkatzus), Üllő (Jelekh)
  Jutas (Jutocsa, Jutotzas), Zoltán (Zaltas, Zsolt, Solt)
Fajsz (Falitzi, Falics)   c.945-c.955
Taksony   c.955-c.970
Géza (Géjza, Gyécsa)   c.970-997
Vajk (later: King Stephen I)   997-1000/38

PERIOD OF THE ÁRPÁD KINGS (1000-1301):
Stephen I (St. Stephen; István)   997/1000-1038
Peter Orseolo (first time)   1038-1041
Aba Sámuel   1041-1044
Peter Orseolo (second time)   1044-1046
Andrew I (Endre, András)   1046-1060
Béla I   1060-1063
Salamon   1063-1074
Géza I   1074-1077
Ladislas I (St. Ladislas; László)   1077-1095
Coloman (Kálmán the Bibliophile)   1095-1116
Stephen II (István)   1116-1131
Béla II (Béla the Blind)   1131-1141
Géza II   1141-1162

47

Stephen III (István)	1162-1172
Ladislas II (László) (rival king)	1162-1163
Stephen IV [István] (rival king)	1163-1165
Béla III	1172-1196
Emeric (Imre)	1196-1204
Ladislas III (László)	1204-1205
Andrew II (Endre, András)	1205-1235
Béla IV	1235-1270
Stephen V (István)	1270-1272
Ladislas IV (Ladislas the Cuman; Kun László)	1272-1290
Andrew III (Endre, András)	1290-1301

PERIOD OF THE PŘEMYSLIDE, WITTELSBACH, ANJOU, LUXEMBURG, HABSBURG, HUNYADI, JAGELLO, AND ZÁPOLYA KINGS (1301-1526/53):

Vencel (Wenceslas) (Přemyslide)	1301-1305
Otto (Otto the Bavarian) (Wittelsbach)	1305-1307
Charles I (Charles Robert; Károly) (Anjou)	1307-1342
Louis I (Louis the Great; Lajos) (Anjou)	1342-1382
Maria (Mary) (Anjou)	1382-1395
Charles II (Charles the Little) (rival king) (Anjou)	1385-1386
Sigismund (Zsigmond) (Luxemburg)	1387-1437
(Coruler with wife, Maria, 1387-95;	
Holy Roman Emperor, 1410-37)	
Albert (Albert II as Holy Roman Emperor) (Habsburg)	1437-1439
Vladislav I (Úlászló) (Jagello)	1440-1444
(Interregnum, 1444-46)	
(John/János Hunyadi , "Regent," 1446-53)	
and "Captain-General," 1453-56)	
(Michael/Mihály Szilágyi, "Regent," 1458)	
Ladislas V (László) (Habsburg)	1453-1457
Matthias I (Matthias Corvinus; Mátyás) (Hunyadi)	1458-1490
Vladislav II (Úlászló) (Jagello)	1490-1516
Louis II (Lajos) (Jagello)	1516-1526
John I (János) (rival king) (Zápolya, Szapolyai)	1526-1540
John II (John Sigismund) (rival king) (Zápolya)	1540-1553

PERIOD OF THE HABSBURG KINGS (1526-1918):

Ferdinand I (Holy Roman Emperor, 1556-64)	1526-1564
Maximilian I	1564-1576
(Maximilian II as Holy Roman Emperor)	
Rudolph I	1576-1608
(Rudolph II as Holy Roman Emperor, 1576-1612)	
Matthias II	1608-1619
(Matthias I as Holy Roman Emperor, 1612-19)	
Ferdinand II (Holy Roman Emperor)	1619-1637
(Gabriel Bethlen, "Elected King," 1520-21)	
Ferdinand III (Holy Roman Emperor)	1637-1657
Ferdinand IV ("Elected King," but he never ruled)	1647-1654
Leopold I (Holy Roman Emperor)	1657-1705
(Imre Thököly, "King of Upper Hungary,"1682-85)	
Joseph I (Holy Roman Emperor)	1705-1711
(Francis Rákóczi II, "Governing Prince,"1705-11)	
Charles III (Charles VI as Holy Roman Emperor)	1711-1740
MariaTheresa	1740-1780
(Her husband, Francis of Lorraine/Lothringen, Holy Roman Emperor, 1745-65)	
Joseph II (Holy Roman Emperor, 1765-90)	1780-1790
Leopold II (Holy Roman Emperor)	1790-1792
Francis I (Emperor of Austria, 1804-35)	1792-1835
(Francis II as Holy Roman Emperor, 1792-1806)	
Ferdinand V	1835-1848
(Ferdinand I as Emperor of Austria)	
Francis Joseph (Emperor of Austria)	1848-1916
(Louis Kossuth, "Governing President,"1849)	
Charles IV (Charles I as Emperor of Austria)	1916-1918

HEADS OF STATE (1918-1997):

Archduke Joseph August (Regent, Oct. 27-29)	1918
Michael Károlyi (President, Jan. 11-Mar. 21)	1919
Sándor Garbai (President, Mar. 21-Aug. 1)	1919
(President of the Revolutionary Governing Council of the Hungarian Soviet Republic)	

Archduke Joseph August (Regent, Aug. 7-23)	1919
Nicholas Horthy (Miklós) (Regent)	1920-1944
Ferenc Szálasi ("National Leader")	1944-1945
Zoltán Tildy (President of the Republic)	1946-1948
Árpád Szakasits (President of the Republic, 1948-49)	1948-1950
(Chairman of the Presidential Council, 1949-50)	
Sándor Rónai (Chairman of the Presidential Council)	1950-1952
István Dobi (Chairman of the Presidential Council)	1952-1967
Pál Losonczi (Chairman of the Presidential Council)	1967-1987
Károly Németh (Chairman of the Presidential Council)	1987-1988
Bruno F. Straub (Chairman of the Presidential Council)	1988-1989
Mátyás Szűrös (Provisional President of the Republic)	1989-1990
Árpád Göncz (President of the Republic)	1990-

HUNGARIAN PRINCES OF TRANSYLVANIA:

Queen Isabella ("Guardian Regent" for her son John II)	1540-1551
John II (John Sigismund)	1540/56-1571
(Nominally King of Hungary, 1540-53)	
Stephen Báthory (also King of Poland, 1576-86)	1571-1586
(Christopher Báthory, Viceroy, 1576-81)	
(Sigismund Báthory, Viceroy, 1581-86)	
Sigismund Báthory (first time)	1586-1597
Sigismund Báthory (second time)	1598-1599
AndrewBáthory	1599
(Michael the Brave of Wallachia claimed the title	
of prince, but was never elected, 1599-1600)	
Sigismund Báthory (third time)	1601
Sigismund Báthory (fourth time)	1601-1602
Moses Székely	1603
Stephen Bocskai	1604-1606
Sigismund Rákóczi	1607-1608
Gabriel Báthory	1608-1613
Gabriel Bethlen ("Elected King of Hungary," 1620-21)	1613-1629
CatherineBrandenburg(Bethlen'swidow)	1629-1630
Stephen Bethlen	1630
George Rákóczi I	1630-1648

George Rákóczi II	1648-1657/60
Francis Rákóczi I (elected in 1652, but never ruled)	
Francis Rhédey (rival prince)	1657-1658
Ákos Barcsay (rival prince)	1658-1660
John Kemény	1661-1662
Michael Apafi	1662-1690
Imre Thököly ("King of Upper Hungary," 1682-85)	1690
Francis Rákóczi II	1704-1711
(Hungary's "Governing Prince," 1705-11)	

PRIME MINISTERS OF HUNGARY:

Count Lajos Batthyány	1848
BertalanSzemere	1849
Count Gyula (Julius) Andrássy	1867-1871
Count Menyhért (Melichor) Lónyay	1871-1872
József (Josef) Szlávy	1872-1874
István (Stefan) Bittó	1874-1875
Baron Béla Wenckheim	1875
István (Stefan) Tisza	1875-1890
Count Gyula (Julius) Szapáry	1890-1892
Sándor (Alexander) Wekerle (first time)	1892-1895
Baron Dezső (Desider) Bánffy	1895-1899
Kálmán (Koloman) Széll	1899-1903
Count Károly (Karl) Khuen-Héderváry	1903
Count István (Stefan) Tisza	1903-1905
Baron Géza Fejérváry	1905-1906
Sándor (Alexander) Wekerle (second time)	1906-1910
Count Károly (Karl) Khuen-Héderváry (second time)	1910-1912
László (Ladislas) Lukács	1912-1913
Count István (Stefan) Tisza (second time)	1913-1917
Count Móric (Maurice) Esterházy	1917
Sándor (Alexander) Wekerle (third time)	1917-1918
Count Mihály (Michael) Károlyi	1918-1919
Dénes (Denis) Berinkey	1919
Sándor Garbai (also president of Governing Council)	1919
Gyula (Julius) Peidl	1919

István (Stefan) Friedrich	1919
Károly (Karl) Huszár	1919-1920
Sándor (Alexander) Simonyi-Semadam	1920
Count Pál (Paul) Teleki	1920-1921
Count István (Stefan) Bethlen	1921-1931
Count Gyula (Julius) Károlyi	1931-1932
Gyula (Julius) Gömbös	1932-1936
Kálmán Darányi	1936-1938
Bélalmrédy	1938-1939
Count Pál (Paul) Teleki (second time)	1939-1941
László Bárdossy	1941-1942
Miklós (Nicholas) Kállay	1942-1944
Döme Sztójay	1944
Géza Lakatos	1944
Ferenc Szálasi (also "National Leader")	1944-1945
Béla Miklós (overlapping with Szálasi)	1944-1945
Zoltán Tildy	1945-1946
Ferenc Nagy	1946-1947
Lajos Dinnyés	1947-1948
István Dobi	1948-1952
Mátyás Rákosi	1952-1953
Imre Nagy (second time)	1953-1955
András Hegedűs	1955-1956
Imre Nagy (second time)	1956
János Kádár (first time)	1956-1958
Ferenc Münnich	1958-1961
János Kádár (second time)	1961-1965
Gyula Kállai	1965-1967
Fock Jenő	1967-1975
György Lázár	1975-1987
Károly Grósz	1987-1988
Miklós Németh	1988-1990
József Antall	1990-1993
Péter Boross	1993-1994
Gyula Horn	1994-

HISTORICAL INTRODUCTION:
HUNGARY AND THE HUNGARIAN PAST

OVERVIEW

Hungary is situated in the very heart of Central Europe, right in the middle of the Carpathian Basin, which it used to occupy in its entirety until 1918. Its post-1918 neighbors included Austria, Czechoslovakia, Romania, and Yugoslavia. Since the disintegration of Czechoslovakia, Yugoslavia, and the Soviet Union in the early 1990s, however, it is surrounded by seven distinct states: Austria, Slovakia, Ukraine, Romania, Little Yugoslavia (Serbia), Croatia, and Slovenia.

Until the end of World War I, Hungary was three and a half times its present size. It was also part of the Austro-Hungarian Empire, which used to be one of the European great powers. Since Austria-Hungary's and Historic Hungary's dismemberment, however, it has become one of the small-sized European states. With an area of 35,919 square miles (93,030 square kilometers) and a declining population of 10.3 million (on January 1, 1995 it was 10,250,000), it is comparable in size to Indiana and populationwise to Ohio. Within Europe it is in the same category as Czechia (Czech Republic) and only slightly larger and more populous than modern Austria.

In contrast to most of its neighbors, which have large national minorities, Hungary today is basically an ethnically-linguistically homogeneous state, where—according to the 1990 census—the Magyars (Hungarians) constitute 98.5 percent of the population. The remaining 1.5 percent is divided among the ethnic Gypsies (142,683), Germans (37,511), Croats (17,577), Slovaks (12,745), Romanians (8,730), Serbs (2,953), and Slovenians (2,627), as well as some Poles, Greeks, Bulgarians, and Armenians. At the same time, however, there are significant Hungarian minorities in the so-called "Successor States," which—in their original form—had been carved out of Austria-Hungary following World War I. The majority of these Hungarians live in areas that had been part of Historic Hungary for the better part of a millennium, that is, until the shifting of the borders above their heads. These include well over two million Hungarians in Romania (mostly in Transylvania), 700,000 in Slovakia, 500,000 in the states carved out of former Yugoslavia, 200,000 in Ukraine, and 50,000 in Austria, for a total of 3.5 million. To these neighboring Hungarians must be added those hundreds of thousands who have emigrated overseas, the majority of them living in the United States. Today, the latter and their descendants number over 1.5 million.

In wake of the nearly half a century of communist domination, the majority of the Hungarians are not very religious: official statistics on religious affiliation are not even available. Yet, according to a 1992 survey, two-thirds of them are formally Catholic (67.8 percent) and one-fifth formally Calvinist (Reformed) (20.9 percent). The remaining 11.3 percent is divided among Lutherans (Evangelicals) (4.2 percent), several smaller Protestant denominations (2.3 percent), and self-proclaimed nonbelievers (4.8 percent). Conspicuously absent are the Jews, who in 1941 constituted 4.3 percent of Hungary's population. They do not show up in these statistics partially because of the Holocaust, partially because of their emigration to Israel, and partially because the remaining 100,000 are either nonbelievers or simply decline to identify themselves as Jews. Even so, Hungary's Jews still constitute the largest Jewish community in today's East Central Europe.

Hungary has a moderately developed economy with a January 1996 per capita Gross Domestic Product (GDP) of $4,273. This puts her well below Austria ($19,000), on the same level with Czechia ($4,221), but significantly above such other neighbors as Croatia ($2,936), Russia ($2,629), Poland ($2,468), Slovakia ($2,222), Romania ($1,250), Bulgaria ($1,136), Little Yugoslavia ($972), and Ukraine ($676). Comparatively speaking, Hungary has fallen behind in the 20th century. In the early 1900s, when Austria-Hungary was still in existence, Hungary's developmental level approximated that of Italy, Spain, and Finland. By the 1990s, however, it has fallen dramatically behind all three of these states that have three times Hungary's GDP (Italy:

$17,500, Finland: $15,900; Spain: $13,200). This comparatively massive retardation is the result of a number of factors. The two most significant of these are the destruction of Austria-Hungary after World War I and the introduction of a communist economic policy after World War II. The first of these destroyed a well-functioning economic unit, while the second created an economic infrastructure that was both misdirected and also isolated from international economic developments. The economic reforms connected with the so-called New Economic Mechanism (NEM) in 1968 did help the situation somewhat. But being unable to extricate itself from the clutches of a disintegrating socialist system, Hungary's efforts were still doomed to failure. As it turned out, most of the NEM's achievements were really the results of Western loans. The reforms did produce the much-touted "goulash communism" that made Hungary the darling of the West and the envy of the East for a few years in the late 1970s and early 1980s. But they did so at the expense of the future, that is, by mortgaging the well-being of as yet unborn generations. Ultimately, the system collapsed under its own weight, and dragged the whole nation with it.

ORIGINS OF THE HUNGARIANS (MAGYARS) (-A.D. 1000)

The early roots of the Magyars—as the Hungarians call themselves— are lost in the mist of history. All we know for certain is that when they first appeared in written documents in the 6th through the 9th centuries, they were primarily Finno-Ugric in speech and Turkic in their way of life. In other words, they combined the hunting-gathering traditions and language of the peaceful Finnic and Ugric peoples with the belligerent equestrian culture—and some of the linguistic traditions—of the Turkic horse-nomads. This combination makes it rather likely that they were a composite people, who rightfully claim both of these distinct roots. Thus, while the Turkic Huns are probably not their direct ancestors as claimed by romantic Hungarian lore, sufficient Hunnic ethnic and cultural remains went into the making of the Magyars for them to make the traditions of Attila and his Hunnic Empire into a significant component of their own beliefs and traditions.

Scholars tell us that mainline Hungarians are in fact descendants of those Finno-Ugric tribes who in the second millennium B.C. occupied the northern part of today's European Russia, and who subsequently developed into such distinct nationalities as the Finns, Estonians, Hungarians, and a score of other smaller nationalities scattered through the Russian Federation. In the period between 1000 and 500 B.C., a group of Ugric tribes separated from the mass of Finno-Ugrians and settled in today's Bashkiria, in the area between the confluence of the Volga and Kama rivers in the west and the Ural Mountains in the east. It was in this area—later to be known as Magna Hungaria—where they developed into proto-Hungarians and also picked up the national name of Magyar. During the second half of the first millennium A.D. they moved down south to the Pontic Steppes (north of the Black Sea), where they mixed with various Hunnic and other Turkic remains, especially the Onogurs, and incorporated the latter's traditions into their own. They also completely altered their way of life by assuming the equestrian culture of the Turkic horse-nomads. In the course of this ethnic mixing, they—but especially their leading classes—became bilingual, and spoke both Magyar and Turkic. Their contact with the Onogurs was particularly significant, for it is from them that they assumed the name Onogur (= Ten Tribes) by which they came to be known in the West; for example Ungar (German), Ungherese (Italian), Vengr (Russian), Hongrois (French), Hungarian (English). The "H" in the case of the latter two versions is derived from the general belief in their Hunnic ancestry.

While most of the Hungarian tribes remained on the Pontic Steppes until the late 9th century, some of them probably migrated west several centuries earlier. Hungarian traditions know of at least two conquests of the Carpathian Basin, which became their permanent homeland. Some believe that the "First Conquest" refers to the Hunnic invasion of the 5th century, when the Carpathian Basin became the center of Attila's vast Hunnic Empire. Others, however, point to the Avar invasion of the 6th century. More recently, it was the "Late Avar" or Wangar (Onogur, Ungar) invasion of the 670s that was judged to be the most likely First Hungarian Conquest, that was followed 220 years later by the Second Conquest—that is, the Árpádian Conquest of Hungary—whose traditional date has been set at A.D. 896.

Before this final conquest, the bulk of the Hungarians continued to live on the Pontic Steppes, in regions known as Levedia (until c.850) and then Etelköz (c.850-c.890) to the east of the Carpathian Mountains. Initially they were vassals of the Khazar Empire, but by the mid-9th century they freed themselves from Khazar control and united into the Hungarian Tribal Federation under the institution of "dual kingship." Their sacred ruler was known as the *kende,* who in those years was Levéd (Előd). He was followed by Kurszán (d.904), who participated in the conquest of the Carpathian Basin. The actual political power and military leadership, however, was in the hands of the *gyula,* which office was held by Prince Álmos (r. c.845-895), and then by the latter's son, Prince Árpád (r.895-907). Árpád is the one who is credited with having carried out the Hungarian conquest of the Carpathian Basin. He followed this up by establishing the foundations of future Hungary as well as of the Árpád dynasty that was to rule Hungary for the next four centuries until 1301.

The Árpádian Conquest was accompanied by the destruction of a Slavic State known as Magna Moravia ("Great Moravia"), which was really a small state whose name means "Early Moravia." This was followed by the distribution of the conquered lands among the victorious seven Magyar and three Kabar (Turkic) tribes, all of whom mixed with the remnants of the earlier ethnically-linguistically related settlers.

The Carpathian Basin's central section around today's Budapest was occupied by Árpád's Magyar tribe, which gave its name to the whole nation. This was followed by several decades of marauding expeditions against the Western Christian World, as well as in the direction of the Byzantine Empire in the south. Most of these campaigns, however, were the undertakings of individual tribes, who were able to do so because of the absence of strong princely power. These military expeditions continued until 955, when one of the marauding armies suffered a major defeat at the hands of Emperor Otto the Great in the vicinity of Augsburg (Battle of Lechfeld). This defeat helped Prince Taksony (r.955-970) to reassert central control and to start the process of integrating the loose tribal federation into a nation. This process of unification was speeded up by Prince Géza (r.970-997), who permitted both versions of Christianity to penetrate his country. This Christianization was completed by his son, Vajk, later to be known later as King St. Stephen (r.997-1038). After having been crowned as Hungary's first Christian king (December 24, 1000) with a crown presented by Pope Sylvester II (Holy Crown of Hungary), King Stephen made Catholicism the obligatory faith of his country. At the same time he shaped his people into a unified nation, while also laying down the structural foundations of a centralized feudal state.

MEDIEVAL CHRISTIAN KINGDOM (1000-1526)

The next three centuries of Árpádian rule in Hungary saw the expansion of Hungarian power into the Balkans. This was done partially by making Croatia-Slavonia into an autonomous part of the Kingdom of Hungary (1089/1102-1918), and partially by acquiring control over such Balkan provinces as Bosnia, Rama, Dalmatia, as well as the northern part of Serbia and the western part of future Wallachia.

This expansion was accompanied by the influx of Western culture and learning, as well as by the growth of social polarization. The latter process, in turn, led to the birth of the nobility, whose rights and privileges were laid down and codified by the Golden Bull of 1222 ("Hungarian Magna Carta"). The first two centuries of the Christian period also saw the development of a complex administrative system based on the importation of the Carolingian county system to Hungary. This building of the administrative infrastructure was accompanied by the growth of urbanization and the introduction of mining and manufacturing. The primary instruments of this urbanization and industrialization were the German settlers, who were given special privileges in return for their know-how and industriousness.

These positive developments were halted for a while by the Mongol invasion and the resulting destruction of Hungary (1241-1242), as well as by the subsequent disintegration of royal power. The decline of central control at the end of the 13th century was accompanied by the rise of a dozen regional lords (oligarchs) who began to partition the country and created various mini-kingdoms for themselves. Their rise coincided with the end of the Árpád dynasty (1301), and their disruptive power was brought to a halt only by the coming of the House of Anjou from Naples. The Anjou rulers defeated and destroyed the oligarchs, reasserted royal power in Hungary, and established strong dynastic and diplomatic ties with the Piasts of Poland, and the Luxemburgs of Bohemia, and the Holy Roman Empire. They also encouraged the influx of Italian and French culture into the country, founded Hungary's first institution of higher learning (University of Pécs, 1367), and at the same time laid the foundations for Hungary's great power position in Central Europe. Thus, by the 1370s,—while renouncing his claim to the Kingdom of Naples—the power of Louis the Great (r.1342-1382) extended over Poland, much of the northern Balkans, as well as over the new Vlach (Romanian) principalities of Moldavia and Wallachia. True, the Hungarian-Polish union did not survive King Louis's death, but his son-in-law, Sigismund of Luxemburg (r.1387-1437), replaced it with a Hungarian-Czech union, while at the same time also ascended the throne of the Holy Roman Empire in 1410.

Sigismund's rule coincided with the appearance of the Turks on Hungary's southern frontiers, and his death was followed by increasingly violent confrontations with the Ottoman Empire. Hungary's defenses were manned by the country's regent, János Hunyadi (r.1446-1456). Hunyadi halted the Turkish advance at the Battle of Belgrade (July 22, 1456), and his son—Matthias Corvinus (r.1458-1490), who became Hungary's last great native monarch—even added to his kingdom.

King Matthias's goal was to build a European coalition against the expanding Ottoman Empire. For this reason he wished to become Holy Roman Emperor so he could enlist the resources of the German-Italian World. Matthias never made it to the office of the emperor, but he did annex Moravia, Silesia, Lusatia, and even Lower Austria with the Imperial city of Vienna (1485). His death (1490), however, prevented him from completing his goal. Moreover, Matthias's lack of a legitimate heir replaced his effective rule with that of the incompetent Jagellonians, who started Hungary upon the path of rapid national decline.

During King Matthias's reign, Hungary's capital city of Buda was the center of Renaissance culture and learning in East Central Europe. (Hungary by this time had three universities: Pécs 1387, Óbuda 1389 or 1395, and Pozsony 1467.) His death was followed by the disintegration of royal power and by the country's slide to feudal anarchy. This meant the rise of the power of the feudal lords once more, accompanied by their growing exactions from the already overburdened peasantry. These exactions, in turn, culminated in the Dózsa Peasant Revolution of 1514, which was followed by the enserfement of the peasantry (1514). The resulting social and political disorganization also led to the end of Hungary's real independence, which came to a crushing end at the Battle of Mohács against the Ottoman Turks (August 29, 1526).

WITHIN THE HABSBURG DYNASTIC EMPIRE (1526-1867)

Although defeatedby Sultan Süleyman (r.1520-1566), Hungary would still have had a chance to recover, had the country possessed an effective national leader. But there was no such leader. Moreover, the nobility complicated things by electing two rival kings—John Zápolya (r.1526-1540) and Ferdinand of Habsburg (r.1526-1564)—which made it impossible for them to unite into a single camp. In point of fact, instead of uniting against the common enemy, the two kings fought one another and thus made it possible for the Turks to take Buda (1541) and also to trisect Hungary for the next century and a half. The country's western and northern segments evolved into "Royal Hungary" under the rule of the Habsburgs; its eastern half developedinto the Principality of Transylvania, nominally a vassal state of the Ottoman Empire, but in effect ruled by its Hungarian princes; while its south-central section gave birth to "Turkish Hungary," which was fully integrated into the Ottoman administrative and legal system. Moreover, for the next century and a half, Hungary became the battleground between the Habsburg and the Ottoman Empires, inflicting untold misery and destruction upon the country and its people.

The "Liberation Wars" of the late 17th century (1683-1699) freed Hungary from the Turks, but imposed upon it a wrathful Habsburg rule, which for a while was even more destructive than its predecessor. Thus the exploited Hungarians rose in a series of rebellions ("wars of liberation") against the Habsburgs, first under Count Imre Thököly (1678-1690), and then under Prince Francis Rákóczi (1703-1711). The last of these liberation wars endedin the compromise Peace of Szatmár (April 30, 1711), which, with certain limitations, guaranteedHungary's autonomy within the Habsburg Empire.

The 18th century was a period of recuperation for Hungary and its people. At the same time it was also an age when the much-devastated country became even more multinational than before by the implantation of hundreds of thousands of foreign settlers. These included Swabians from Germany, Frenchmen from Alsace-Lorraine, Serbians from the Pashalik of Belgrade, Rusyns and Orthodox Jews from Galicia, and a flood of Vlach (Romanian) shepherds from Wallachia and Moldavia. These newcomers—especially the Vlachs and the Serbians— inundated the country's eastern and southern regions (Transylvania and Voivodina), and sowed the seeds of Hungary's dismemberment after World War I.

In consequence of the continuous influx of foreigners, Hungary's population became so diverse that by the turn of the 18th to the 19th century the Magyars became a minority in their own country. The same period also saw the rebirth of Hungarian national consciousness and the birth of the Hungarian National Revival Movement. The leaders of this movement came from the lower segments of the Hungarian nobility, who remained untouched by the Habsburgization and Germanization policy that had engulfed the titled aristocracy in the 18th century. It was the better educated members of the common nobility who came in touch with the ideas of the French Enlightenment and awoke to their own Magyar identity. This awakening process was accompanied by cultivation of the Magyar language and by the development of modern Hungarian literary and historical studies. This was necessary because during the past centuries, in consequence of the dominance of the Latin, Magyar had been pushed into the background and Magyar language literary and historical studies had only been cultivated sporadically. In the 18th century Latin was partially replaced and complemented by German, which again hindered the development of the Magyar.

The rebirth of Hungarian national consciousness was accompanied by the influx of the ideas of political liberalism, which became important components of the politicized National Revival Movement between 1825 and 1848. This movement produced a number of significant political and social reforms, among them the emancipation of the serfs and the termination of the special privileges of the nobility (1848). Ultimately, it led to the revolution of 1848-1849, which, for a moment at least, created a politically independent Hungary. This independence, however, proved to be both brief and illusory. Hungary was simply not ready for full independence, not only because of its economic and political underdevelopment and the educational-cultural backwardness of its peasant masses, but also because of its inability to cope with the nationalism of its ethnic minorities, who were tearing the country apart even while the Hungarians were in the process of trying to establish their own independence. Defeat would have been inevitable even without Russian intervention. But the Russian invasion of June 18, 1849, speeded up the conditions that led to the Hungarian surrender at Világos (August 13, 1849).

In retrospect it is evident that Lajos Kossuth, the acknowledged leader of the Revolution and the "Governing-President" of Hungary after the dethronement of the Habsburgs (April 14, 1849), simply misjudged the power relationship between the Habsburgs and the Hungarians. Nor was he able to perceive—as did his great rival, Count István Széchenyi— that, in spite of all past difficulties, Hungary's chances were much greater within than without the Habsburg Empire. In addition to the far greater economic opportunities that such a large state could offer, it was precisely Hungary's position within the Habsburg Empire that guaranteed its territorial integrity in that age of intense nationalism. Not even Kossuth's subsequent plan for a Danubian Confederation could have replaced the guarantees offered by the empire. If implemented, Kossuth's plan would have placed the Hungarians into a much worse position vis-à-vis the other nationalities than the solution they achieved through the Austro-Hungarian Compromise of 1867. The compromise ended the period of Habsburg absolutism (1849-1867) and transformed the Austrian Empire into the dualistic state of Austria-Hungary, in which the Hungarians alone among all nationalities were assigned the role of an equal partner with the Austrians.

THE AUSTRO-HUNGARIAN EMPIRE (1867-1918)

The dualistic arrangement created by the Austro Hungarian Compromise satisfied most of the reasonable demands and expectations of the Magyars. In point of fact, their relative political weight in the empire was greater than their numbers would have warranted. Thus, the greatest shortcomings of the compromise were not the unfulfilled goals of the Hungarians, but rather the disregard of the aspirations of the dozen or so other nationalities. In the long run, it was precisely these ignored aspirations that came to undermine this otherwise commendable experimentation in national coexistence.

Notwithstanding its many shortcomings, Austria-Hungary was a state that in many ways was enviable, especially in light of what came after. It offered the protection of a great power to its citizens, and at the same time extended the opportunities of a large economic unit to all of those who wished to take advantage of them. True, the percentage of its enfranchised citizens was relatively small. But there were a significant number of parties and political groupings organized along both ideological and nationality lines. They represented—and sometimes represented too emphatically—the specific interests and aspirations of individual groups and nationalities. In light of the national and ethnic intolerance that came to characterize 20th-century Central Europe, Austria-Hungary was a relatively tolerant political entity. At the same time, it was also flexible with respect to economic opportunities and social mobility. During the half a century of its existence, it was the scene of amazingly speedy economic, industrial, cultural-educational, and public health developments, and of a rapid and rather successful urbanization process. Moreover, during the same period it created such a well-functioning modern infrastructure that some of the components of this system have survived right up to our own days. Thus, even with its frailties and imperfections, Austria-Hungary was much preferable to the politically, economically, and ideologically fragmented Central Europe that followed its dismemberment. The latter was most characterized by national rivalries and ethnic intolerance, which was and is amply displayed by the growing number of economically unviable and politically unstable ministates.

The assassination of Archduke Francis Ferdinand at Sarajevo (June 28, 1914), which dragged the world into a major war, also turned out to be the death warrant of Austria-Hungary. The Dual Monarchy's involvement in that protracted world conflict undermined its stability to such a degree that it was unable to survive a defeat. To this must be added the new emphasis upon the principle of national self-determination, which was first applied—rather unfairly—after World War I. Although a well-intended idea, this principle proved to be a disaster in practice, and its negative effects are still with us today. It set the stage for the dismemberment of large multinational empires (and later even of smaller multinational states), and thus became the brewing ground for the violent ethnic conflicts that have ravaged that part of Europe ever since. The most recent manifestation of this malady is the slaughter that is taking place in Bosnia today. The preservation of Austria-Hungary and other large political entities could well have precluded such violent manifestations of human intolerance.

The disintegration of the Austro-Hungarian Empire was accompanied by Historic Hungary's dismemberment, an act that was basically unavoidable. As feared by Széchenyi, and as foreseen by a number of other thoughtful Hungarian statesmen, post-Turkish Hungary's multinational character made the preservation of its territorial integrity in an age of violent nationalism a virtual impossibility—except within the confines of the Habsburg Empire. This was a truism that pragmatic statesmen knew and accepted, but many sonorous independence-oriented politicians of the Dualist Period simply failed to recognize. Yet what made this dismemberment even worse was the fact that it took place under the worst possible circumstances, that is, in the midst of a defeat and thus without regard to the much-extolled principle of national self-determination. As such, the Treaty of Trianon (June 4, 1920) that codified this mutilation, deprived Hungary of over 70 percent of its territory and well over 60 percent of its population. A country of 125,600 square miles (325,422 sq. km.) was reduced to mere 35,900 square miles (92,963 sq. km.), and its population was cut from 20.9 to 7.6 million. Moreover, because of the lack of fairness on the part of the peacemakers, close to one-third of the Magyar nation (about 3.5 million people) were left on the other side of the new frontiers. Many of these lived right next to the borders and were transferred only for economic, military, and strategic considerations—in direct violation of the very same principles in the name of which Austria-Hungary and Historic Hungary were dismembered. This fact became the most significant determining factor in the history of interwar Hungary.

TRIANON HUNGARY (1918-1945)

The end of World War I was followed in rapid succession by a series of revolutions that saw the disintegration of Historic Hungary and ended in the establishment of a conservative political order under the regency of Admiral Nicholas Horthy (r.1920-44). The first of these revolutions produced the liberal-socialist regime of Count Michael Károlyi (October 1918-March 1919), the second one resulted in the establishment of the Hungarian Soviet Republic under Béla Kun, characterized by the reign of Red Terror (March-August 1919), and the third one brought about a conservative reaction and was marked by a White Terror (August 1919-March 1920). These revolutions and the subsequent counterrevolution ended with the election of Horthy as the regent of Hungary (March 1, 1920), which, in turn, initiated a period of conservative-national social order that resembled the system of the Dualist Period in every respect, except in the latter's grandness and the relative flexibility in social and economic matters. The Horthy Regime turned out to be more rigid than its predecessor, but this rigidity was partially the result of the radically declined opportunities in the much-reduced country. It was also a by-product of the fact that most of the Horthy Regime's efforts were concentrated on the issue of territorial revisionism.

Aside from its drastic economic and social impact, the Treaty of Trianon also produced a so-called "Trianon Syndrome" in Hungary, which became a national malady that permeated all aspects of Hungarian national life for the next quarter of a century. This psychological affliction, combined with the unwillingness of the Western powers to listen to Hungary's just complaints, made it virtually certain that in the course of time the country would slide into the embrace of the Italian-German alliance system. Of all the great powers, only these two states—who themselves were revisionists—were willing to hear out Hungary and support its goals for at least a partial revision of its patently unjust new frontiers.

Given the fact that Hungary's whole infrastructure was destroyed, all its communication and transportation lines severed, and all its industries shorn of their customary raw material deposits and natural markets, the problems that the country faced after its dismemberment were horrendous. To these must be added the burden presented by the hundreds of thousands of refugees from the detached territories. Most of these were upper- and upper-middle class people who were forced to leave their traditional homelands because they did not fit into the plans of the ruling elite of the newly created states. Yet, with the exception of late 1920s and early 1930s that were years of worldwide depression, rump Hungary's economy and society recuperated relatively quickly and remarkably well. The credit for this recuperation must be given to Prime Minister Count István Bethlen (r.1921-1931), whose tenure in office represented a period of rebuilding, consolidation, and the elimination of extremism from Hungarian public life. Few of his successors had the capacity to build upon his achievements, nor dedication to pursue a policy of moderation. Thus, during the 1930s, Hungary came to be caught up in the drift toward the Right, which proceeded in spite of Regent Horthy's dislike of the socially radical ideologies of Fascism and Nazism.

While life in Hungary remained far from easy even after the so-called "Bethlen-consolidation," the new cultural policy, initiated and orchestrated by Hungary's minister for religion and public education, Count Kunó Klebelsberg (r.1922-1931), was unusually successful. Klebelsberg's so-called "neo-nationalism" was based upon the belief in Hungarian intellectual preeminence in the Carpathian Basin and upon the desire to retain and use that preeminence as a magnet for others. The policy that was derived from this ideology was meant to serve the cause of revisionism through intellectual and educational achievements. Thus, neo-nationalism was politically motivated, yet it resulted in the total revamping of Hungary's educational system. It brought about the establishment of hundreds of new primary and secondary schools and in the creation of several new or relocated and radically improved institutions of higher learning. Klebelsberg was also responsible for the establishment of a number of important foreign centers of Hungarian historical research (Vienna, Berlin, Rome, etc.) that were meant to demonstrate the true nature of the Hungarian intellect and thus gain supporters for Hungarian revisionist goals.

Regent Nicholas Horthy himself was a conservative man and a reluctant reformer, but he was neither a tyrant nor an authoritarian. He was more like a benevolent monarch, who scrupulously observed the words and the spirit of the law. He refused to employ unconstitutional methods of governance and always acted against all perpetrators of disorder—be they on the left or the right. He disliked Fascism and Nazism equally, and would have refused to cooperate with Italy and Germany, had France or England—the latter of which he intensely admired—been willing to negotiate about Hungary's legitimate complaints and grievances. Thus, even with the growth of Hitler's shadow over Hungary, Horthy tried to keep his diminished country from becoming a simple satellite to its giant neighbor.

This keeping of the distance became increasingly difficult after the *Anschluss* (March 12-13, 1938), which made Nazi Germany an immediate neighbor of Hungary; and even more difficult after the two Vienna Awards (November 2, 1938; August 30, 1940), when—with German and Italian help—Hungary regained the Magyar-inhabited sections of Southern Slovakia and Northern Transylvania. These fully justifiable territorial revisions were complemented by Hungary's military reconquest of Carpatho-Ruthenia (March 15, 1939) from a dismembered Czechoslovakia, as well as the heavily Magyar-inhabited section of Voivodina (Bácska and Baranya) and the Mura region (April 3, 1941) from disintegrating Yugoslavia. While these were territories that should have been left to Hungary after World War I, the fact that they were regained with German-Italian help made Hungary look bad in the eyes of the West. They also placed that country squarely into the Axis camp and virtually predestined its entrance into the war on the wrong side. That in turn assured that Hungary would again suffer the consequences of a military defeat in the form of territorial losses.

Although pushed into the war by the force of circumstances (June 26, 1941), Hungary proved to be an "unwilling satellite" for Germany and tried to get out almost as soon as it had entered. This desire for a separate peace with the Western powers became especially strong after the destruction of the Second Hungarian Army at the Don River in the winter of 1942-1943. The man in charge of this goal was Prime Minister Miklós Kállay (r.1942-1944), whose efforts eventually triggered Hungary's German occupation (March 18, 1944) as well as the subsequent German-supported elevation of the leader of the Hungarian Arrow Cross Party, Ferenc Szálasi, to power (October 15-16, 1944).

The German occupation was followed by the collection, deportation, and destruction of most of the Hungarian Jews from the provinces, and after Szálasi's rise to power, even the deportation of some urban Jews and various other elements who dared to speak up against the Arrow Cross excesses. Even Regent Horthy found himself under arrest and in German captivity during the last few months of the war.

As the war wound down and Hungary was being overrun by the Soviet Red Army, a group of anti-German politicians formed a Provisional National Government (December 22, 1944) in the city of Debrecen and began the process of extricating the country from this partially self-inflicted catastrophe. Under the prime ministership of General Béla Dálnoki-Miklós (r.1944-1945), they established a political coalition with the inclusion of all so-called progressive political parties, including the recently legalized Communist Party that had the full support of the Soviet occupying forces.

FROM SOVIET OCCUPATION TO REVOLUTION (1945-1956)

Following the end of the war—which for Hungary occurred on April 4, 1945—the Provisional Hungarian Government was overseen by the Allied Control Commission. It was presided over by Marshal Voroshilov of the Soviet occupying forces, who employed various legal and extralegal means to aid the communists under the leadership of Mátyás Rákosi, who had just returned from his Moscow exile. Even so, the first free elections (November 4, 1945) resulted in the complete victory for the Smallholders Party, which gained 57 percent of the votes. The Smallholders' could have governed alone, but Soviet pressure forced them into a coalition government, where the politically most sensitive posts — those in charge of Interior, Police, and Military Intelligence — were all taken over by the Communist Party. This took place in spite of the fact that the communists had garnered only 17 percent of the popular votes. The communists also took control over the "People's Courts" and various "Screening Committees" and used their ill-gained new powers not only to punish real war criminals, but also to get rid of all political rivals. It was under such conditions that the country's reconstruction was undertaken and that Hungary was forced to sign the

Peace Treaty of Paris (February 10, 1947). This treaty reducedHungary to its interwar size and also deprived it of three additional Magyar-inhabited villages that were awarded to Czechoslovakia.

Thus, Hungary's involvement in World War II on the wrong side proved to be very expensive. In addition to being compelled to give up the territories regained a few years earlier, it also deprivedthe country of 800,000 to 900,000 of its citizens who fell victim to the war and close to half of whom were of Jewish origin. But what was perhaps equally devastating was the fact that the Treaty of Paris forced Hungarians to relinquish all their hopes for the establishment of ethnically-linguistically just frontiers, leaving many millions of their fellow nationals under foreign rule for the foreseeable future.

The communists tolerated the coalition government only until 1947. In May of that year they forced Prime Minister Ferenc Nagy (r.1946-1947) to resign, and at the same time they accused other party leaders of various political crimes. They either compelled these politicians to flee to the West, or subjected them to sham trials and various forms of punishments. Simultaneously, they engineered the takeover of the coalition parties by various crypto-communists. A year later the communists were ready for a complete takeover. In June 1948 they merged the Communist Party and the now completely pliable Social Democratic Party into the crypto-communist Hungarian Workers' Party, and then forced all other parties to fade away.

The director and orchestrater of this takeover was Mátyás Rákosi, who between 1945 and 1956 was the general secretary or first secretary of the Hungarian Communist Party (1945-1948) and its successor, the Hungarian Workers' Party (1948-1956). For a brief period, during the height of his power, he also served as the prime minister of Hungary (r.1952-1953). Rákosi's dominance, especially after the 1948 takeover, was most characterizedby a new Red Terror that outdid its predecessor more than a hundred fold. The Secret Police (ÁVÓ, ÁVH) terrorizedthe whole country to the point where Hungarian society began to resemble Soviet society during the Stalinist purges. The communist reign of terror appeared to hit people indiscriminately. During the period between 1949 and 1953 virtually no one could feel safe. After eliminating all rival political parties and their leaders, and after convicting the head of the

Hungarian Catholic Church, Primate Cardinal József Mindszenty (February 8, 1949) of "espionage," the purges penetrated the party itself. Many rival communist leaders—including the once powerful Minister of Interior László Rajk (September 24, 1949) and a series of other communist and crypto-communist politicians—fell victim to Rákosi's wrath. This purge was accompanied and followed by the forced collectivization of agriculture (1948-1956), by the introduction of a totally irrational industrialization drive (1948-1956), by the deportation of tens of thousands of conservative urban elements from Budapest to the provinces (June 1951), by the establishment of concentration camps (e.g., Recsk) for the unexecuted "enemies" of the regime (1950-1953), and by the development of a personality cult that virtually deified Rákosi, making him into the "Father of the Nation."

This communist reign of terror ended only in 1953, and then it did so primarily in consequence of Stalin's death and the resulting thaw in the Soviet Union and in Soviet-American relations. After the workers' unrest in Poland and East Germany, the new Soviet leadership saw it advisable to order an end to Rákosi's terror in Hungary. Rákosi relinquished the prime ministership to the much more humane Imre Nagy (r.1953-1955), but he retained control over the party. Nagy immediately altered the political atmosphere. He ended the reign of terror and undertook a policy of political and social relaxation. This involved releasing most political prisoners, ending of deportations, and dissolving the penal colonies.

This period of relative easing lasted for two years, after which Rákosi made a brief comeback (1955-1956), but without being able to alter the chain of events set in motion by his predecessor. Nagy's release of thousands of inmates from the Recsk concentration camp and from other prisons—many of whom used to be dedicated followers of Marxism and of the Communist Party—rapidly altered the public's perception about Rákosi and his system. Firsthand information about the crimes of his terroristic regime circulated rapidly among the population as well as among the increasingly disenchanted party members. And coming as it did from former comrades-in-arm, this information produced a whole series of disaffected and embittered intellectuals who used to be staunch supporters of the system. They became totally disenchanted with their former ideals and personal idols and demanded that the culprits be called to account. This "revolt of the mind"—as two of the participants labeled it later—soon undermined the belief in the whole communist system.

Some of the regime's most vocal intellectual critics congregated in the so-called Petőfi Circle in Budapest. Rákosi would have preferred to crush the Circle, but in light of Nikita Khrushchev's revelations about the horrors of the Stalinist system at the Twentieth Party Congress of the Soviet Communist Party (February 1956), he was prevented from doing so. This growth of intellectual disaffection and the resulting social unrest rapidly unraveled Rákosi's rule. In July 1956, the erstwhile "Father of the Nation" was unceremoniously stripped of his powers and dismissed from his posts. His replacement by the equally tainted Muscovite Ernő Gerő at the head of the party, however, could not stop the chain of rapidly unfolding events. By the fall of 1956, conditions reached a boiling point. Thus, when on October 23rd of that year a peaceful demonstration in support of the Polish uprising turned violent, the Hungarian Revolution of 1956 suddenly gushed forth.

The eruption of violence led to the fall of Gerő and to the return of Imre Nagy to power (October 25). By this time the brief but universally hailed anti-communist and anti-Soviet Hungarian Revolution (October 23-November 4, 1956) was in full swing. For a while it shook the very foundations of the Soviet Empire. But given the lack of Western help and the start of the ill-timed Suez War against Egypt (October 30, 1956), which had put an end to Soviet hesitation at intervention, the revolution was doomed to failure. Yet, in the long range its impact was so powerful that things never returned to what they were before. In point of fact, most of the developments of post-revolutionary Hungary can be attributed to this brief and glorious uprising.

After a few days of nominal military withdrawal, while the Soviet leaders were assessing the international situation, the Red Army began to move into Hungary (November 4, 1956) and soon put an end to this challenge to Soviet power. The revolution suffered a military defeat, communist control was restored, but the ideals of the revolution never faded. In fact, these undefeated ideals were responsible for laying the foundations of those economic and political reforms that within a decade and a half had transformed Hungary into the envied homeland of the much-touted "goulash communism." The revolution also resulted in the exodus of 200,000 refugees to the West. They were young, capable, and willing to work. They very rapidly came to constitute a powerful Hungarian intelligentsia and a significant Hungarian interest group in many of the Western countries, from Europe to Australia and North America.

FROM REVOLUTION TO THE FALL OF COMMUNISM (1956-1990)

The restoration of communist rule initiated a relatively stable and protracted, although initially very vindictive period in Hungarian history. It was a period that is inseparably linked with the name of János Kádár. Kádár's role during and immediately after the revolution still constitute an enigma in modern Hungarian history. He is known to have been a convinced communist from the time of his early youth, who had worked in the underground for a decade and a half before becoming the leader of Hungary's clandestine Communist Party toward the end of World War II. Yet, upon the repatriation of the emigré communists, Kádár had to take a backseat to Rákosi, Gerő, Farkas, and a number of other Muscovites. Moreover, although he served the reconstituted Communist Party faithfully, in 1951 he too fell victim to Rákosi's purges. In contrast to many others, however, he managed to survive and even to make a comeback during and after the revolution of 1956.

In the course of the first few days of the revolution, Kádár worked in unison with Imre Nagy (r.October 25-November 4), but in late October or early November he broke with the revolutionary government and joined forces with the Soviets. On November 1, 1956, he founded the pro-Soviet Hungarian Socialist Workers' Party, and three days later established the Hungarian Socialist Workers-Peasants' Government, which came to dominate Hungary for the next thirty-three years.

Hungary's postrevolutionary period connected with Kádár's name can be divided into four distinct phases: the period of retributions and consolidation (1956-1963), the period of relaxation and reorientation (1963-1970), the period of "goulash communism" (1970-1985), and the period of disintegration (1985-1989). With the exception of the final year, Kádár was the first secretary of the Hungarian Socialist Workers' Party (r.1956-1988) throughout this period. Moreover, during the early phase of this epoch, he also served twice as the prime minister of Hungary (r.1956-1958, 1961-1965).

Postrevolutionary retributions took the form of mass imprisonments and hundreds of death sentences, culminating in the execution of Imre Nagy and several of his close colleagues in June 1958. Contrary to some highly exaggerated earlier accounts, the number of the executed was closer to 500 than to the many thousands that were circulated by the rumor mills of those years. To these executed revolutionaries must be added another 500 or so, who fell victim to the violence of the revolution itself. Thus, although not as encompassing as originally presumed, the post-revolutionary executions still far outstripped—perhaps twenty times—the Habsburg vengeance that followed the defeat of the revolution of 1848-1849. As such, they constitute an eternal blot upon the name of János Kádár, which not even his subsequent efforts at creating a "communist society with a human face" can ever obliterate.

Postrevolutionary retributions were paralleled by a general political and economic consolidation that placed Hungary once more upon the road toward socialism. Discounting the initial years of retributions, this communist rule cannot be compared to the viciousness of the Rákosi Regime. Apparently, having been shaken thoroughly by the events of 1956, Hungary's communist rulers did not dare or want to go to such extremes. Moreover, convinced of the misdirection of the pre-revolutionary regime, they wanted a new orientation. Thus, they waited only long enough to feel secure before launching the country on its path of political and economic liberalization.

Political liberalization began in 1963 with the proclamation of a general amnesty for the "crimes" of the revolution. This new policy injected a bit of freedom and laxity into the lives of Hungary's citizens and eventually turned the country into "the happiest barracks in the socialist camp." Economic liberalization started a few years later in 1968 with the introduction of the New Economic Mechanism (NEM). The NEM was an ingenious, but ultimately futile effort to mix socialism with capitalism. Yet, it enabled the Hungarians to improve their lives through petty entrepreneurship and various other profit-making ventures, and thus transformed the country into the land of the much-envied "goulash communism."

This comparative freedom and economic success made Kádár into a popular man during the late 1970s and early 1980s, in spite of the fact that these achievements were the results of many factors besides the policies initiated by his regime. Thus, political liberalization was a partial by-product of the growing detente between the United States and the Soviet Union, while economic liberalization was linked to several specific factors within the Soviet bloc itself. From Hungary's point of view, these factors included the presence of a primitive Soviet market with its almost unlimited capacity to absorb shoddy Hungarian-made goods and food products that could not have been sold anywhere in the West; the availability of cheap Soviet oil and natural gas that was sold to Hungary at below world market prices; and the market protection that Hungary derived from its membership in the Council of Mutual Economic Assistance (COMECON or CMEA), which included the Soviet Union and all its East European satellites. To these factors must be added the increased availability of Western loans, which made it possible for Hungary's political leadership to keep alive hopelessly outdated factories and other industrial establishments, and thereby satisfy the craving of the people for economic security combined with a degree of material advancement.

The only area where the Kádár Regime failed to live up to the limited expectations of its subjects was its lack of sufficient attention to the growing problems of the Hungarian minorities in the neighboring states. The fate of these conationals was especially desperate in Romania (mostly in the former Hungarian province of Transylvania), where the oppressive Ceausescu Regime initiated a reign of terror that was to result in the total assimilation and annihilation of the over two million Hungarians who had been left on the other side of the border. Under growing popular pressure, by the 1980s even Kádár was forced to deal with this issue. But this made the already unfriendly relationship between the two countries even worse, without really helping the minorities. Only the 1989 revolution that led to the overthrow of the Ceausescu

Regime in December of that year prevented the situation from deteriorating even further.

"Goulash communism" and the conditions it created made the Hungarians relatively happy. But as it was the result of a situation that fed upon itself, it could not go on indefinitely. The time came—as it did also in the Soviet Union—when the future could simply not afford to support the present. That's when the process of disintegration set in, which ultimately caused the whole Communist World to collapse. In Hungary's case, this took place in the late 1980s. It started with the forced retirement of Kádár (May 22, 1988) and the formation of such opposition groups and political parties as the Hungarian Democratic Forum (September 27, 1987), the Federation of Young Democrats (October 2, 1988), and the Federation of Free Democrats (November 13, 1988). The process of disintegration continued with the transformation of the hitherto dominant Hungarian Socialist Workers' Party into the much more mellow Hungarian Socialist Party (October 6-10, 1989). Kádár lived just long enough (July 6, 1989) to witness the official reburial of Imre Nagy (June 16, 1989), which must have been a psychological torment for the leader of dying Hungarian communism.

The final straw in the regime's disintegration and self-liquidation came in the late summer and fall of 1989 when Prime Minister Miklós Németh (r.1988-1990) and Foreign Minister Gyula Horn (r.1989-1990) decided to open Hungary's western borders and let thousands of East German tourists exit to Austria (August 19 and September 10, 1989). This, in turn, put powerful pressures upon the communist regimes in Czechoslovakia and East Germany, which soon led to the fall of the Iron Curtain, as well as to the breaching of the Berlin Wall (November 9, 1989).

In the fall of 1989, the government of Prime Minister Miklós Németh transformed itself from a communist to a nonpartisan caretaker government and prepared the ground for Hungary's first free multiparty elections. These elections took place in two rounds in March and April 1990, from which the Populist-oriented Hungarian Democratic Forum emerged victorious. It garnered over 40 percent of the seats (165 Members of the Parliament = MPs) in the new post-communist legislature, while its strongest rivals, the Urbanist-oriented Federation of

Free Democrats gained less then 25 percent (91 MPs). The ideological differences between these two parties, however, made it impossible for them to form a grand coalition. Thus, the Democratic Forum allied itself with such other moderately conservative groups as the Smallholders' Party (44 MPs) and the Christian Democratic People's Party (21 MPs), which produced a grand total of 230 MPs (60 percent) against the disunited opposition of 156 MPs. As a shocking aftereffect of this collapse, the heirs of the Hungarian Socialist Workers' Party were represented in the new Hungarian Parliament only by 33 MPs, that is, by a mere 8.55 percent.

THE POST-COMMUNIST PERIOD (1990-1996)

On May 23, 1990, the first post-communist government, under the leadership of Prime Minister József Antall (r.1990-1993), took over the helm of Hungary. This happened at a moment when the country was at the height of its popularity and in many ways was the darling of the Western World. There was a general euphoria in the whole country and everyone expected something new, grand, and uplifting. This euphoria, however, soon evaporated as the new post-communist regime found itself amidst a multitude of insolvable difficulties. The country's two greatest immediate problems were the question of political accountability and the issue of the twenty-one billion dollars' worth of gross foreign debt that had accumulated during the period of "goulash communism." For whatever reasons—not the least of which was the lack of adequate preparation on the part of the intellectuals who suddenly found themselves in responsible governmental positions—neither of these problems was ever solved. Perpetrators of past crimes continued to prosper through the "privatization" of state properties right into their own pockets, while the burden of foreign debt grew further by leaps and bounds—reaching thirty-two billion dollars by the end of 1995. Moreover, many pent-up emotions surfaced almost overnight and undermined normal human relationships in the country. At the same time the nation became polarized economically, socially, as well as ideologically. The growing body of increasingly impoverished intellectuals, white collar workers, and retirees found itself confronted with a small group of venal *nouveaux riches* who openly flaunted their fortunes. The Populist-Urbanist controversy also resurfaced and spilled over into many aspects of Hungarian social and intellectual life. And as the nation's internal problems grew, so did its difficulties abroad. In addition to the growing and emotionally charged conflicts with its immediate neighbors over the treatment of the Hungarian minorities (whom the new regime immediately took under its protection), the country's hard-won popularity abroad also declined very rapidly. Thus, seemingly unable to deal with the nation's multiple predicaments, the Hungarian Democratic Forum suffered a major defeat in the elections of May 1994. In point of fact, this defeat was so thorough that the Democratic Forum was reduced to the rank of one of the minor opposition parties in the Parliament (38 MPs representing a mere 9.84 percent). As opposed to this, the Hungarian Socialist Party (the former communists) gained an absolute majority, controlling 209 (54.15 percent) of the 386 seats in the Hungarian Parliament.

The disillusioned Hungarian voters ejected the Forum-lead government, but their expectations from the new socialist regime under Prime Minister Gyula Horn (July 15, 1994–) also remain unfulfilled. At the end of 1996 Hungary was once more in a state of social malady and national pessimism. While the population enjoyed near-complete political and personal freedom, a sizable portion of the people survived on the brink of despair. According to a report by the International Labor Organization, at the end of 1996 about one-third of Hungary's population lived on the edge or under the official poverty level. Moreover, according to a October 1996 survey by Gallup-Hungary, fifty-five percent of the country's population felt that the Kádár Regime was preferable to the current political and social order. These negative views about post-communist Hungary of the mid–1990s are substantiated and underlined both by the descending life expectancy as well as by the country's rapid population decline.

Naturally, there are still many of those who believe in a future for Hungary. They do so largely on the basis of their knowledge of Hungarian history. It tells them that no matter how bitter the people and how hopeless the future, the nation always stands up and ultimately

always survives. Our survey of the past does seem to agree with them
and appears to substantiate their optimism.

Could anything have been done to prevent this social, political, and
national misfortune that overwhelmed Hungary and its first post-
communist regime? There are those who claim that, given the problems
they have inherited, the hapless regime was doomed to failure. Others,
however, are convinced that had the leadership of the Hungarian
Democratic Forum paid less attention to ideological and personal
squabbles, and more to pragmatic politics, they could have avoided most
of these pitfalls. Some of these critics—among them the prominent
Hungarian-American financier, George Soros—also believe that with the
right approach, at that unique moment in history in 1990, even
Hungary's stifling foreign debts could have been reduced. According to
this view, the leaders of the Democratic Forum were so blinded by their
newfound powers that they were simply unable to perceive their own
shortcomings and thus unwilling to accept reasonable advice.

To end on a positive note, it should be pointed out that as a result
of the strict austerity program introduced in 1995, Hungary's international financial position has improved significantly in 1996. By the fall
of that year, its gross foreign debt has declined to around twenty-eight
billion dollars, its reserves were up to over thirteen billion, and its net
foreign debt tumbled to just slightly over fourteen billion dollars.
Inflation has been checked and is declining, the budget deficit is
decreasing, exports are increasing, foreign direct investments are still
coming in at a steady rate, and the country's international credit rating
has improved significantly. Moreover, Hungary is edging ever closer to
membership in the NATO, as well as in the European Economic
Community. These are all positive signs, which should soon have a
beneficial impact upon the domestic social scene as well. The problem is
that these changes are still beyond the comprehension of the average
Hungarian citizens, who do not as yet feel the positive influence of these
developments. They only see the continuous rapid decline of their living
standards, and consequently view with some nostalgia the simple,
somewhat controlled, but socially secure days of the 1980s.

THE DICTIONARY

- A -

ABA SÁMUEL (c.990-1044). King of Hungary (r.1041-44) and—depending on the sources—either a nephew or a brother-in-law of King St. Stephen. During King Péter's first tenure (1038-41) (q.v.) Aba Sámuel served as the country's palatine *(nádor)* (q.v.). After Péter's deposition the Hungarian magnates elected Aba Sámuel their king. But the deposed Péter soon gained the support of Holy Roman Emperor Henry III (r.1039-56), which resulted in a new German-Hungarian confrontation. During his short reign, Aba Sámuel relied mostly on the support of the commoners of Hungary's tribal-clan society, who were still attached to the traditional ways and religious beliefs. This policy, however, resulted in his alienation from the magnates and from the Church hierarchy. His enemies then combined against him, and with Emperor Henry's help—following Aba Sámuel's excommunication by the Pope—defeated him at the Battle of Ménfő (Győr county) in July 1044. Aba Sámuel fled the battle, but was captured and unceremoniously executed. Later he was buried at the Monastery of Abasár in Heves county.

ABSOLUTISM IN HUNGARY (1849-60). While there were several absolutist periods in Hungarian history, the term "Age of Absolutism" is generally reserved for the decade that followed the defeat of the Hungarian Revolution of 1848-49 (q.v.) and was connected with the name of Austria's minister of interior (r.1849-59), Alexander Bach (q.v.). For this reason that period is also known as the "Bach Period" or the age of the "Bach Regime." It began with the reign of terror initiated by General Julius J. Haynau (q.v.), and was characterized by the suspension of all Hungarian laws of 1848 vintage, and by turning Hungary into a province of the Austrian Empire (q.v.). Although the Patent of 1853 legitimized the end of serfdom that had been abolished by the Hungarian Diet (q.v.) in early 1848, several other features of feudalism were retained. The majority of the Hungarian nobility followed the policy of passive resistance (q.v.) and supported occasional conspiratorial efforts. The system began to unravel in 1859 with Austria's loss in the Austro-Italian-French War of that year, and then came to an end with the October Diploma (q.v.) of 1860 and the February Patent (q.v.) of 1861. It was replaced by the Provisorium (q.v.) in 1861, and then by Austro-Hungarian Dualism (q.v.) in 1867.

ACADEMIA ISTROPOLITANA (1467). The Latin name of the University of Pozsony, Hungary's third institution of higher learning, founded by King Matthias Corvinus (q.v.) in 1467, at the Western Hungarian city of Pozsony (Pressburg, Bratislava) (q.v.). (See also University of Pozsony.)

ACADEMY OF SCIENCES see **HUNGARIAN ACADEMY.**

ÁCHIM, ANDRÁS L. (1871-1911). One of Hungary's first peasant politicians, who, as an editor and a member of the Hungarian Parliament (q.v.), fought vehemently for the rights of small peasants against the interests of the large estates. First elected to the Parliament in 1905, Áchim's aggressiveness resulted in his being ousted from that body in 1906. He was also taken to court for alleged agitation against the existing social order, but was exonerated. In 1908 Áchim founded the "Union of Peasants, Agricultural Workers, and Construction Workers" *(Kisgazdák, Földmunkások és Kubikusok Szakegylete)*, and then had himself reelected to the Parliament in 1910. His persistent agitation for democratic political and agricultural reforms and his continued aggressiveness soon turned the wrath of the ruling social classes against him. Although defended by such heralds of social-political reform as the poet Endre Ady (q.v.), this growing political animosity, combined with certain personal animosities, ultimately ended in Áchim's assassination by the Zsilinszky brothers. It is an irony of history that one of his assassins—Endre Bajcsy-Zsilinszky (q.v.)—later became a herald of social progress and a martyr of political liberalism in Hungary.

ACSÁDY,   IGNÁC   (1845-1906).   Hungary's   pioneer   economic
historian of the so-called Positivist School (q.v.), whose most
influential works were *The History of Hungarian Serfdom (A
magyar jobbágyság története)* (1896), and his two-volume *The
History of the Hungarian Empire (A magyar birodalom története)*
(1904). Although starting out as a journalist and a literary man, and
being largely a self-trained historian, Acsády's turn to economic
historical topics during the 1880s made him into one of the founders
of the Hungarian Economic History School. In addition to the
above-mentioned volumes, his other important works include:
*Hungary's Finances during the Rule of FerdinandI (Magyarország
pénzügyei I. Ferdinánd uralkodása alatt)* (1888), *The Size of
Hungary's Serf Population after the Battle of Mohács (A magyar
jobbágy-népesség száma a mohácsi vész után)* (1889), and *Hungary's
Population in the Age of Pragmatic Sanction (Magyarország
népessége a pragmatica sanctió korában)* (1896).   Acsády also
contributed two large volumes—volumes 5 and 7 on the periods
1526-1508 and 1657-1711—to Hungary's ten-volume "Millennial
History" entitled *History of the HungarianNation (Magyar nemzet
története)* (1895-98), published under the editorship of Sándor
Szilágyi (q.v.).

ACZÉL, GYÖRGY (1917-91). Communist politician and for three
decades the "cultural dictator" of the postrevolutionary Kádár Regime
(q.v.). Coming from a working class family, Aczél developed
himself into a self-styled intellectual, who made it a point to keep in
personal touch with Hungary's literati even the the time when he
was in control of their destiny. Having joined the Communist Party
(q.v.) in 1935, Aczél became an active communist politician on the
county level immediately after World War II (q.v.). In 1949 he was
arrested as a "Titoist spy" and spent five years in prison, where he
became a close friend of János Kádár (q.v.), who had suffered similar
fate at the hands of the Rákosi Regime (q.v.). After the Hungarian
Revolution of 1956 (q.v.), when Kádár assumed the leadership of the
country, Aczél went with him and served in various party and
ministerial positions. He remained a member of the Communist

Party's Central Committee for over three decades(1956-89) and of the Politburo for nearly two decades (1970-88). In 1985 Aczél resigned from all political and governmental posts and became the director of the newly founded Institute of Social Sciences (1985-89), while also serving as an elected member of the Hungarian Parliament (1985-89).

Following the collapse of communism in 1989-90 (q.v.), Aczél left Hungary and settled in Vienna (q.v.), where died at the end of 1991. Although a staunch communist, Aczél had sufficient intellectual sensibilities to appreciate intellectual labor. He prided himself with being able to converse and to correspond with Hungary's top intellectuals on a one to one basis. During the last two decadesof his active life, he published about a dozen books. Most of them contain his political speeches and essays on society and culture, but some of them deal with the life and achievements of Hungary's great literati and artists, such as Attila József (q.v.) and Béla Bartók (q.v.). Aczél's as yet unpublished correspondence will throw considerable light on Hungary's intellectual world in the period between the late 1950s and the late 1980s.

ADALBERT [ST. ADALBERT] (c.955/6-97). Originally called Vojtěch, Adalbert was a member of the ruling Slavnik dynasty of Moravia (q.v.). Having chosen religious life, he became the Bishop of Prague in 983. Adalbert was active in spreading Christianity not only in the Czech lands (q.v.) of Bohemia (q.v.) and Moravia, but also in Hungary (q.v.), Poland (q.v.), and Prussia. In 994-95 Adalbert spent about a year in Hungary, during which time he established close relationships both with Prince Géza (q.v.) and his son Vajk, the future King St. Stephen (q.v.). In 996 Adalbert left for missionary work in Poland and the Baltic region, where he was murdered by the pagan Prussians (the original non-Germanic Prussians) (q.v.). Bishop Adalbert's influence in Hungary was so momentous that later King St. Stephen named the Cathedral of Esztergom (q.v.), then Hungary's capital and permanent ecclesiastical center, after him.

ADRIATIC [ADRIATIC SEA, ADRIA]. This segment of the Mediterranean Sea separates the Balkans (q.v.) from Italy. The northern half of the Adriatic's eastern coast—including Dalmatia (q.v.) and the Republic of Ragusa (Dubrovnik) (q.v.)—had been part of the Kingdom of Hungary (q.v.) for prolonged periods of time between the 11th and 16th centuries. Northern Dalmatia and the city of Fiume (Rijeka) (q.v.) remained part of Historic Hungary (q.v.) up to the collapse of the Austro-Hungarian Empire (q.v.) in 1918.

ADY, ENDRE (1877-1919). The greatest lyricist of 20th-century Hungary (q.v.), whose aesthetically new and socially progressive writings published after 1906 had an unusual impact upon the intellectual and political life of the nation. In his days Ady was perhaps the most powerful voice for the need of a thorough social reform in his native land. At the same time he was also the primary herald of the new literary and aesthetic orientation represented by French symbolism. Although inspired by "decadent" Paris, Ady still drew heavily from Hungarian national and Protestant biblical traditions. Viewed by the contemporary social and political establishment as a rabble-rouser and as a representative of Western moral decay, Ady would not be silenced. He failed to outlive the old regime, but his powerful presence survived. Moreover, his inimitable poetry is still among the most powerful voices of social progress and modernism, and also of the need for national coexistence in the Carpathian Basin (q.v.).

AEHRENTHAL, COUNT ALOYS (1854-1912). The foreign minister of Austria-Hungary (q.v.) between 1906 and 1912. He was responsible for the 1908 annexation of Bosnia-Herzegovina (q.v.) and thus for the precipitation of the so-called Bosnian Annexation Crisis of that year. This crisis aggravated the already strained relationship between Austria-Hungary and Russia (q.v.), worsened the relationship between the Dual Monarchy (q.v.) and Serbia (q.v.), and thus prepared the ground for the assassination of Archduke Francis Ferdinand (q.v.) at Sarajevo (q.v.) in June 1914, which served as the immediate cause of World War I (q.v.).

A.E.I.O.U. The five vowels of the alphabet that have been used by the members of the Habsburg dynasty (q.v.) ever since Emperor Frederick III (r.1440-93) to advertise their belief in their own greatness. Some of the most common Latin and German wordings assigned to these letters include: *Austriae Est Imperare Orbi Universo* (To Austria belongs the domination of the whole world), *Austria Erit In Orbe Ultima* (Austria will survive until the end of the world), *Alles Erdreich Ist Oesterreich Untertahn* (The whole world is ruled by Austria). By the early 1860s, however, when the Habsburgs were being squeezed out of the German Confederation (q.v.), Emperor Francis Joseph (q.v.), upon his return to Vienna, was greeted by the following interpretation: *Auch Eine Illumination Ohne Ursache* (This too is a festivity without any substance).

AGE OF ABSOLUTISM see ABSOLUTISM IN HUNGARY.

AGE OF REFORM see HUNGARIAN REFORM PERIOD.

AGGLUTINATIVE LANGUAGES. Languages that create word forms or new words primarily through the addition (gluing) of suffixes or prefixes to the original root word. Most of these languages are in the Ural-Altaic (q.v.) category, and within that in the Finno-Ugric (q.v.) family of languages, to which Hungarian or Magyar (q.v.) also belongs. An example of such an agglutination is the construction created out of a word, *szent,* that originally came from the Latin *sanctus (saint): meg-SZENT-ség-telen-ít-het-etlen-ség-ed-del,* but written as a single word. This translates approximately into the following: "with your ability to withstand desanctification."

AGRICULTURAL TOWN see OPPIDUM.

AJTONY (d. c.1003). Leader of one of the conquering Hungarian tribes that had settled in eastern Hungary (q.v.) in the vicinity of the Maros and the Kőrös rivers. During the period of political centralization, which coincided with the rule of Prince Géza (r.970-97) (q.v.) and of his son King St. Stephen (r.997/1000-38) (q.v.), Ajtony tried to make his tribal lands into an independent principality. Motivated by political considerations, he converted to Byzantine/Orthodox Christianity (q.v.) and even founded an Orthodox Christian monastery in his capital of Marosvár (later Csanád) named after St. John the Baptist, but he continued to live as before and also opposed the country's centralization. Soon after his accession to the throne, King St. Stephen sent an army against Ajtony under the leadership of Csanád, who defeatedhim and shipped his severed head back to the king. Ajtony's defeat was only one of King St. Stephen's efforts in creating a centralized Christian Hungarian Kingdom.

ALBA IULIA [APULUM] see **GYULAFEHÉRVÁR.**

ALBA REGIA see **SZÉKESFEHÉRVÁR.**

ALBERT I [ALBRECHT I] (1397-1439). Albert I as king of Hungary and Bohemia, Albert II as Holy Roman Emperor, and Albert V as Grand Duke of Austria, was the first Habsburg (q.v.) ruler of Hungary (r.1437-39), who succeeded to the Hungarian throne because of his marriage to Emperor/King Sigismund's (q.v.) daughter, Elizabeth, in 1422. Having no son of his own, Sigismund named Albert as his successor and by 1424 appointed him viceroy of his Czech lands of Bohemia (q.v.), Moravia (q.v.), and Silesia (q.v.). After Sigismund's death in 1437 the Hungarian Estates (q.v.) elected Albert king of Hungary, while in 1438 he was also elected king of Bohemia as well as Holy Roman Emperor. In his capacity as king of Hungary, Albert was very much under the control of the Hungarian aristocracy (q.v.), who basically ran the country during his protracted periods of absences to the distinct displeasure of the lower nobility (q.v.). In light of the increasing Ottoman Turkish (q.v.) advancesin the south—which resulted among others in the loss of the important Hungarian outpost of Szendrő (Smederevo)in 1439—King Albert decidedto lead a campaign against the Turks. His armies, however, barely reachedthe confluence of the Danube (q.v.) and the Tisza (q.v.) rivers in Southern Hungary, when they were decimated by dysentery. Partially because of the spread of this disease, and partially because of the Turkish decision to turn against Bosnia (q.v.), Albert opted to return home. He never made it, for he, too, fell victim to the disease. He was buried in the royal city of Székesfehérvár(q.v.), leaving behind his pregnant wife, who soon bore him a son, later to be know as Ladislas V Posthumus (q.v.).

ALFÖLD see GREAT HUNGARIAN PLAIN.

ALISPÁN see VICE LORD LIEUTENANT.

ALLIED CONTROL COMMISSION (1945-47). A joint body established by the victorious powers after World War II (q.v.) in the defeated states for the purposes of overseeing the implementation of the terms of the armistice and creating conditions necessary for the preparation and the signing of postwar treaties. The Hungarian version of the Allied Control Commission (ACC) functioned between 1945 and 1947, chaired by the Soviet Marshal Clement Y. Voroshilov (1881-1969), who abused his position by actively advancing the cause of the Communist Party of Hungary (q.v.). As such, the ACC was indirectly involved in the preparation of a total communist takeover.

ALLÓDIUM [MAJORSÁG]. That portion of a feudal estate that was retained by the lord for his own use to be tilled through obligatory serf labor. In Hungary, these allódiums initially were worked by peasants who were in a servile status and thus basically slaves (servus) (q.v.) of the landowners. With the gradual introduction of feudalism (q.v.), these slaves were replaced by bonded serfs (q.v.), which system survived until the serf emancipation of 1848 (q.v.).

ÁLMOS (c.819-95). Father of conquering Prince Árpád (q.v.), who, prior to the Árpádian conquest of Hungary (q.v.), was the leader of the Hungarian Tribal Federation (q.v.) both in Levedia (prior to A.D. 850) (q.v.) and in Etelköz (c.850-95) (q.v.). According to Hungarian legends, Prince Álmos was the son of the tribal chief Ögyek (Ügyek) and of his wife Emese. Other sources identify his father as Elöd. Allegedly, he received his name—which means "sleepy" or one connected with sleep—because before his birth his mother dreamt of a son who would one day be the progenitor of a dynasty of great kings. Although Álmos had ruled the Hungarian Tribal Federation (q.v.) before its conquest of the Carpathian Basin (q.v.), like Moses of the Israelites, he was never destined to enter the Promised Land. Hungarian chronicles tell us that in 895, at the age of about 76, he became the victim of a ritual murder on the frontiers of the new country, either to pay for the recent Hungarian losses to the Pechenegs (Patzinaks) (q.v.), or to ensure that the conquest would be a successful one. Some believe that the story about Álmos's killing is simply a figurative borrowing from earlier traditions, such as those of Moses and Romulus. Others, however, feel that this ritual murder did in fact take place, perhaps in line with the traditions of the Khazar Empire (q.v.), according to which the Khazars (q.v.) sacrificed their sacred ruler, the *khagan* (q.v.), if he lived beyond a certain predetermined number of years. This fate could also befall his second in command, the *beg* (q.v.), who was the holder of all executive powers—like the *gyula* (q.v.) among the Hungarians. Such a ritual murder may also take place after a lost battle or in case of a major catastrophe during his tenure.

AMERICAN ASSOCIATION FOR THE STUDY OF HUNGARIAN HISTORY [AASHH]. The AASHH was founded at the December 1970 convention of the American Historical Association for the purposes of unifying those scholars who have interest in the study and teaching of Hungarian history. The founders included Professors Béla K. Király (q.v.), Peter Sugar, Peter Pastor, and Steven Béla Várdy, who were soon joined by Professors George Bárány, István Deák, Joseph Held, and several others. All of those mentioned have served as the Association's presidents, some of them more than once. The AASHH is under the direction of a president, who is aided by the vice president and the secretary-treasurer. It sponsors panels and round table discussions at the annual meetings of several scholarly associations, including the American Historical Association (of which it is an associate organization), the American Association for the Advancement of Slavic Studies, and the Duquesne University History Forum. The AASHH also hands out book prizes every year. In 1990 it became associated with the newly founded World Federation of Hungarian Historians (q.v.).

AMERICAN HUNGARIAN FEDERATION [AHF] [AMERI-KAI MAGYAR SZÖVETSÉG = AMSZ]. Founded in 1906 in Cleveland, Ohio, to represent the interests of Hungarian immigrants, for most of the nine decadesof its existence the AHF was the largest and most influential Hungarian umbrella organization in the United States. In the 1920s it concentrated its activities in propagandizing against the unjust Treaty of Trianon (q.v.) that mutilated Historic Hungary (q.v.) in 1920, while during World War II (q.v.) it tried to point out that Hungary was an unwilling satellite on the side of the Axis and should be judged accordingly. During the 1950s through the 1980s its main effort was directed toward fighting communism and promoting the cause of the liberation of Hungary. Since the fall of communism in 1989-90, it concentrated its efforts to secure American help for the mother country. In the course of its history, the AHF was often challenged by rivals and splinter organizations. The most significant of these challenges came from the National Federation of American Hungarians *(Amerikai Magyarok Országos Szövetsége)* (q.v.), foundedin 1984 after an internal struggle in the AHF. This was followed by the establishment of several other splinter and rival groups, including the National Federation of Hungarian Americans *(Magyarok Amerikai Országos Szövetsége)* (q.v.) in 1989, the Hungarian American Coalition *(Magyar Amerikai Koalíció)* (q.v.) in 1992, and the American Council of the Hungarian World Federation *(Magyarok Világszövetsége Amerikai Tanácsa)* in 1993, but none of them managed to became universally accepted. Recently, these umbrella organizations made several unsuccessful efforts to merge into a single organization, probably under the name of the original American Hungarian Federation.

AMERICAN HUNGARIAN FOUNDATION [AHF] (1954). Founded in December 1954 by August J. Molnár (b.1927) at Elmhurst College (near Chicago, Illinois) under the name American Hungarian Studies Foundation, transferred in 1959 to New Brunswick, New Jersey, in close proximity and some degree of cooperation with Rutgers University, and renamed American Hungarian Foundation in 1974, the AHA is the most important North American depository of Hungarian American archival and library materials relating to the Hungarian American past. In addition to serving as a center for scholarly research, giving small grants, and sponsoring the booklet series *Hungarian Reference Shelf,* since the early 1970s the AHF has also published the *American Hungarian Studies Foundation Bulletin* (1971), the *Hungarian Studies Newsletter* (1973), as well as several major volumes. Since 1964 it has also presented Distinguished Service Awards and Washington Medals to prominent Hungarian Americans— particularly to those who have been successful in business, industry, film, science, and politics—with only an occasional inclusion of scholars in the humanities. In 1989 the AHF established its Hungarian Heritage Center (moving to its new headquarters in 1994), which houses its archives, library, and museum, as well as its research center. The AHF and the Hungarian Heritage Center have an ongoing cooperative working relationship with Rutgers University, or more specifically with its off-and-on Hungarian Studies Program (1959) and its small Hungarian Institute (1992).

ANABAPTISTS. A radical populist movement within 16th-century Reformation. The Anabaptists rejected many of the accepted Christian dogmas, refused to baptize their infants, and underwent a second baptism as adults. They viewed the world as basically evil and turned away from it, waiting for the prophesied new millennium and for Jesus Christ's Second Coming. They believed that in that new brave world of virtue the rich and powerful would be humbled, and the poor and powerless would be uplifted. One of the immediate results of this movement was Thomas Münzer's (c.1480-1525) peasant revolution in 1524 that embroiled most of the southern

German states. Because of their radical social views, the Anabaptists were detested and persecuted by almost all governments and religious denominations. Trying to escape persecution, a number of them left the Holy Roman Empire (q.v.) and settled in Northern Hungary (q.v.) and Transylvania (q.v.). There they worked primarily as potters, producing high-quality earthenware that came to be known as *habána*. Those who survived earlier persecutions were eventually forced to accept Catholicism in the 18th century. Some of their views survived in Hungary (q.v.), which were later incorporated into the beliefs of the Baptists (q.v.) of later years.

ANATOLIA [ASIA MINOR, ANADOLI]. A peninsula of Asia, divided from Southeastern Europe by the Straits of Bosphorus and the Dardanelles, where the Ottoman Turkish Empire (q.v.) developed, and whence it conquered the Balkans (q.v.) and much of Hungary (q.v) between the 14th and the 16th centuries. Today it is the site of the Republic of Turkey.

ANCIENT GESTA [ŐSGESZTA] (c.1050s). The most ancient of the Hungarian chronicles, which was lost in its original form, but portions of which have been incorporated into later chronicles. The *Ancient Gesta* was updated on at least two occasions, once in the 1120s and then in the early 1150s. The oldest existing chronicle, Anonymus's (q.v.) *Gesta Hungarorum (Deeds of the Hungarians)* (q.v.), dating from the late 12th century, used the version of the *Ancient Gesta* that was produced under King Stephen II (q.v.) around 1127. Simon de Kéza (Simon Kézai) (q.v.), on the other hand, in producing his own *Gesta Hungarorum* (c.1283), used the original version of the *Ancient Gesta*.

ANDRÁSSY, COUNT GYULA [JULIUS], SR. (1823-90). One of the chief architects of the Austro-Hungarian Compromise of 1867 (q.v.), Count Andrássy served as post-Compromise Hungary's first prime minister (1867-71) and then as the Dual Monarchy's (q.v.) foreign minister (1871-79). Descendant of an old aristocratic family, and being a product of the Age of Reform (1825-48) (q.v.),

Andrássy became active in politics during the 1840s as a supporter of the great reformer, Count István Széchenyi (q.v.). But after being elected to the Hungarian Diet (q.v.) in 1847, he switched over to the more radical Lajos Kossuth (q.v.). Following the outbreak of the Hungarian Revolution in March 1848 (q.v.), Andrássy was appointed his native Zemplén County's Chief Lord Lieutenant (q.v.) and also the commander of its national guard. He participated in Hungary's (q.v.) Revolution and War of Liberation (q.v.) against the Habsburgs (q.v.), and for a while as one of the adjutants of General Artúr Görgey (q.v.). During the last months of the war, Andrássy was sent on various diplomatic missions to Constantinople, Paris, and London. After Hungary's defeat in August 1849, he fled the country and spent the next nine years in exile, mostly in Paris. During his absence he was condemned and hanged in effigy (1851).

By the end of the 1850s Andrássy became disenchanted with emigré politics and turned into an advocate of a compromise with Austria. Thus, after gaining a pardon in 1859, he returned home and joined Ferenc Deák's (q.v.) circle to work for a compromise. Elected to the Hungarian Parliament (q.v.) in 1861, he became the Speaker of the Lower House in 1865, and had a lion's share in working out the terms of the Compromise of 1867. Between 1867 and 1871 Andrássy headed the first post-Compromise Hungarian Government, in which capacity he concluded an agreement with Croatia (q.v.) in 1868, and promoted several laws to placate Hungary's national and religious minorities (q.v.). He likewise became a staunch defender of dualism (q.v.) against its many critics and opponents. Fearing the decline of Hungary's influence within the Dual Monarchy (q.v.), in 1870 Andrássy frustrated the Czech-initiated efforts to replace dualism with Austro-Hungarian-Czech trialism (q.v.). In 1871 he became Austria-Hungary's foreign minister and in that capacity reoriented the empire's foreign policy toward the Balkans (q.v.). He also sought to placate the French. Yet, at the same time, he established a close alliance with the new German Empire (q.v.) to oppose Russian (q.v.) expansion into the Balkans (q.v.). In 1878 Andrássy had a major role in calling the Congress of Berlin (q.v.) to deprive Russia of its recent gains against the Ottoman Empire (q.v.).

His efforts were repaid by Austria-Hungary's acquisition of Bosnia-Herzegovina (q.v.). While this act brought that hotbed of Balkan revolutionary activities under the empire's control, it was achieved at considerable expense and much loss in human lives. For these reasons Andrássy lost much of his popularity, which led to his resignation in 1879. A day before his retirement, however, he signed the Dual Alliance (q.v.) with Germany, which became the capstone of his foreign policy, motivated largely by his fear of Russia and Pan-Slavism (q.v.). His son, Count Gyula Andrássy, Jr. (q.v.), became the Dual Monarchy's last foreign minister.

ANDRÁSSY, COUNT GYULA [JULIUS], JR. (1860-1929). The son of Count Julius Andrássy, Sr. (q.v.), and a prominent statesman and constitutional scholar of the late-Dualist Period (q.v.). In 1885 Andrássy was elected to the Hungarian Parliament (q.v.) as a member of the Liberal Party (q.v.) that supported the compromise with Austria (q.v.). In 1894-95 he served as Hungary's minister at the Imperial Court (q.v.) in Vienna (q.v.), between 1906 and 1910 he was his country's minister of interior, while in October 1918 he served as the dying empire's last foreign minister. Being a staunch supporter of the Austro-Hungarian Compromise of 1867 (q.v.), Andrássy always followed a policy of cooperation with Vienna. With the decline and collapse of the Liberal Party and the subsequent loss of support for the compromise, in 1905 Andrássy founded and led the ephemeral Constitutional Party *(Alkotmánypárt)* that stood on the principles of 1867. In 1919, following the collapse of Austria-Hungary, Andrássy was one of the founders of the Hungarian Anti-Bolshevik Committee in Vienna. After the collapse of Béla Kun's (q.v.) Hungarian Soviet Republic (August 1, 1919) (q.v.), he returned to Hungary and organized the so-called Legitimist forces (q.v.) that worked for a Habsburg (q.v.) restoration in Hungary. Andrássy was involved in Emperor/King Charles's (q.v.) second failed attempt to return to Hungary in 1921, after which he joined the small Christian National Unity Party *(Keresztény Nemzeti Egyesülés Pártja)* and continued to represent the voice of Legitimism (q.v.) in the Hungarian Parliament right up to his death in 1929.

Count Andrássy's most significant scholarly works include: *About the Compromise of 1867 (Az 1867-es kiegyezésről)* (1896), and a three-volume synthesis,*The Development and Struggles of Hungarian Statehood (A magyar államiság fejlődése, küzdelmei)* (1901-11), a shorter version of which also appeared in English under the title *Development of Hungarian Constitutional Liberty* (1908).

ANDREW, PRINCE [ANDRÁS, ENDRE] (1327-45). Royal prince of Hungary and king of Naples (r.1344-45). Son of Charles I (Charles Robert) (q.v.), the first Anjou king of Hungary, and brother of King Louis I the Great (q.v.). Having been taken to Naples at the age of six, Prince Andrew was to marry his second cousin Johanna (Giovanna), queen of Naples (r.1343-81), and then inherit the Neapolitan throne on the basis of a family pact among the Anjous. His great uncle, King Robert (r.1309-43), however, changed his mind and left his throne to his granddaughter Johanna, who was already Andrew's wife. Never being accepted by the Neapolitans as their own, Prince Andrew was openly humiliated by Johanna and her string of lovers. Andrew's brother, King Louis of Hungary, was eventually able to purchase papal ascent for Andrew's crowning as the king of Naples at the price of 80,000 golden florins, but this act only sealed Andrew's fate. He was strangled with Johanna's knowledge at Aversa. Although this murder horrified contemporary Europe, continued papal protection and King Louis's inability to capture Johanna, in spite of his repeated invasions of Italy, prevented her punishment until after King Louis's death. This amoral Neapolitan courtesan was strangled at the orders of her successor, Charles of Durazzo, who later also claimed the Hungarian throne under the name Charles II (q.v.). Prince Andrew was buried in the so-called Louis Chapel of the Cathedral of Naples, where his grave can still be seen today.

ANDREW I [ANDRÁS, ENDRE] (c.1015-60). King of Hungary (r.1046-60), son of King St. Stephen's cousin Vazul (Vászoly) (q.v.), and father of King Salamon (q.v.). After his father's blinding for political reasons in the 1030s, Andrew and his brothers, Levente and Béla (q.v.), fled abroad. Andrew ended up in the Kievan court (q.v.) of Yaroslav the Wise (r.1015-53), marrying the latter's daughter Anastasia. He returned to Hungary (q.v.) in 1046 at the request of an alliance of Hungarian lords who wished to depose King Peter (q.v.), who had sworn allegiance to Emperor Henry III (r.1039-56). Andrew's rise to the throne was also aided by the outbreak of a pagan uprising under Vata (q.v.), who viewed Peter as a foreign stooge and wished to eradicate all Western influences, including Christianity, from Hungary. Although helped by this uprising, upon his victory against Peter, Andrew turned against Vata and his reactionary supporters. King Andrew spent his initial years as a ruler restoring the prestige of royal power, reestablishing the position of the Catholic Church (q.v.), and trying to normalize his country's relations with the Holy Roman Empire (q.v.). Upon failing to do so, he recalled his brother Béla from exile (c.1048) and named him ruling prince of one-third of Hungary. He also entrusted Prince Béla with organizing the country's defenses and promised him succession to the throne. As a result of these efforts, both of Emperor Henry III's attempts to conquer Hungary failed. In 1051 Prince Béla's troops repulsed the German invasion at the Vértes Hills in Trans-Danubia (q.v.), and in 1052 they sank the Imperial Armada in the vicinity of Pozsony (q.v.). In 1054 and 1055 King Andrew and Prince Béla went on the offensive against the Holy Roman Empire, their armies penetrating deep into Carinthia, Austria (q.v.), and Bavaria. Emperor Henry III's death in 1056 ended the German-Hungarian struggle, and the new peace was sealed by the betrothal of Andrew's son, Salamon, to Henry III's orphaned daughter. In violation of his earlier promises to leave the throne to Béla, in 1058 Andrew had his six-year-old son Salamon crowned king. This led to Béla's flight to Poland (q.v.) and then to an open armed conflict between the two brothers. King Andrew was wounded in this battle and died soon thereafter. He was buried in the Benedictine Abbey of Tihany, founded by him in 1055. His grave and remains were found there in 1891.

ANDREW   II   [ANDRÁS,   ENDRE]   (1176/77-1235). King of
Hungary (r.1205-35), son of King Béla III (q.v.), and the younger
brother of King Emeric (q.v.). After the death of his father in 1196,
his brother entrusted Andrew with the governance of Hungary's
southwestern provinces, where, with the support of a group of
dissident magnates, he soon began to act as an independent ruler.
This led to a military encounter between the two brothers in 1199
and then to an uneasy peace in 1200. Andrew rose in rebellion again
in 1203, which led to his imprisonment, and then to a new
agreement that made him the guardian of Emeric's young son,
Ladislas III (q.v.). Ascending the throne in 1205, Andrew proved to
be much less a forceful king than expected on the basis of his earlier
actions. In fact, he turned into a weak and vacillating ruler who
permitted domestic social and economic conditions to deteriorate.
Andrew devoted much of his reign to pursuing an unsuccessful
policy of expansion into Galicia (q.v.). During his frequent and
prolonged absences, the country's leadership fell into the hands of
his first wife, Gertrude of Merania (1184/86-1213) and those of her
foreign favorites. This led to a conspiracy on the part of a group of
native lords, which, under the guidance of Ban Bánk (q.v.), resulted
in Gertrude's murder in 1213. While punishing the killers
themselves, Andrew permitted most of their co-conspirators to
remain in high office. This turned his oldest son, Béla IV (q.v.),
against him, and ultimately led to a prolonged struggle between
father and son. Having aspirations to secure the Latin throne of
Constantinople (q.v.), and having inherited from his father the
obligation to fight against Islam, in 1217-18 Andrew undertook to
lead a crusade to the Holy Land. Although this crusade proved to be
just as unsuccessful as Andrew's other foreign ventures, he returned
home with the title "King of Jerusalem." Upon his return, King
Andrew found the country in political turmoil and financial chaos.
There was a virtual civil war between the magnates, whom he had
endowed with huge land grants from the royal domains, and the
lesser nobility *(servientes regis = royal servants)* (q.v.), who were
being pressed into the service of these powerful magnates. Given
these conditions, Andrew was forced to call an assembly of the lesser

nobility and satisfy their most essential demands by issuing the Golden Bull *(Bulla Aurea)* in 1222 (q.v.), wherein he guaranteed their rights, and which thus became the foundation stone of Hungarian constitutionalism. The issuance of the Golden Bull and the dismissal of many of his foreign advisers failed to satisfy Andrew's critics, who coalesced around his son Béla, who had held the title of "junior king" (q.v.) ever since 1214. Béla strongly disagreed with his father's policies, and also resented the latter's squandering of royal estates. In 1225 Andrew expelled the Teutonic Knights (q.v.) from southeastern Transylvania (q.v.), whom he had settled there in 1208. The following year he reorganized the country's administrative system, placing his three sons into governing positions in Transylvania, Slavonia (q.v.), and Galicia (q.v.), and then in 1231 he issued a revised version of the Golden Bull. But none of these measures led to improvements in Hungary. In 1234 Andrew married the Italian Beatrix of Este (1212-45). This was his third marriage, which produced a posthumous son, Stephen (István), whose son Andrew III (q.v.), in turn, became the last ruling member of the Árpád dynasty. King Andrew II died in 1235, following his campaign against Frederick Babenberg (q.v.) of Austria, who subsequently was defeated and killed by King Béla IV in 1246. Andrew was buried in the Cistercian Monastery of Egres.

ANDREW III [ANDRÁS, ENDRE] (c.1265-1301). The last king of Hungary (r.1290-1301) of the Árpád dynasty (q.v), and King Andrew II's (q.v.) grandson from his third marriage, and as such, the child of his posthumous son, Prince Stephen. Having been born and brought up abroad, Andrew III was really a foreigner. He ascended the Hungarian throne only with the strong support of the Catholic hierarchy and the lower nobility (q.v.), who preferred him against the Anjou (q.v.) claimants, and stood by him against the powerful regional lords (q.v.). Much of Andrew's short reign was devoted to the struggle against these oligarchs (q.v.). He also had to fight against Charles Martel and Charles Robert (q.v.) of the Italian Anjous, who were supported in their aspirations to the Hungarian throne by the papacy. His simultaneous struggle against the Habsburgs (q.v.) ended in 1296, when he married Albert Habsburg's (r.1298-1308) daughter Agnes, and then supported him in his fight for the throne of the Holy Roman Empire (q.v.). Andrew III died unexpectedly in the middle of a new offensive against the Anjous. He only had a daughter from his first marriage, wherefore the Árpád dynasty, that had ruled Hungary for over four centuries, had come to an end. Andrew III was buried in the Church of St. John of the Franciscans (q.v.) of the city of Buda (q.v.).

ANGEVIN DYNASTY see **ANJOU DYNASTY.**

ANGYAL, DÁVID (1857-1943). One of Hungary's great historians of the so-called Positivist School that dominated Hungarian historical studies (q.v.) in the late 19th and early 20th centuries. Between 1909 and 1929 Angyal was professor of history at the University of Budapest (q.v.), and then director of the Hungarian Historical Institute in Vienna (1929-35). During these three decades he was the mentor of a number of great interwar Hungarian historians, most of whom, however, left Positivism and became proponents of the Wilhelm Dilthey-inspired *Geistesgeschichte (szellemtörténet)* orientation (q.v.) that dominated Hungarian historical thinking from the mid-1920s until the mid-1940s. Angyal's most important historical works include his two-volume *Biography of Imre Thököly of Késmárk (Késmárki Thököly Imre életrajza])* (1988-89), a volume in Hungary's ten-volume "Millennial History" entitled *Hungarian History from the Age of Matthias II to FerdinandIII(Magyarország története II. Mátyástól III. Ferdinándig)* (1897), his *Transylvania's Political Connections with England (Erdély politikai érintkezései Angliával)* (1902), and his essay collection entitled *Historical Studies (Történelmi tanulmányok)* (1937). As a representative of traditional liberal thought of the Age of Dualism (1867-1918) (q.v.), Angyal felt out of place in interwar Hungary (q.v.), marred by psychological scars and political excesses stemming from the country's mutilation after World War I (q.v.).

ANJOU [ANGEVIN] DYNASTY. The French-Italian family that ruled Hungary (q.v.) between 1307 and 1395. Its members included Charles I (Charles Robert) (r.1307-42) (q.v.), Louis I (Louis the Great) (r.1342-82) (q.v.), and Mary (r.1382-95) (q.v.)—the latter of whom reigned jointly after 1387 with her husband Sigismund of Luxemburg (r.1387-1437) (q.v.). The ranks of the Anjou rulers also included the rival king Charles II (r.1385-86) (q.v.)—known in Hungary as "Charles the Little"—who came from the Neapolitan branch of the family and reigned as counter-king for a few months before being killed by Mary's supporters. The Anjou family brought a period of greatness to Hungary after the chaos of the late 13th and early 14th centuries. Charles I ended the country's fragmentation and Louis the Great built an empire that stretched from the Adriatic (q.v.) and Black Sea (q.v.) in the south to the Baltic Sea (q.v.) in the north. The Anjou period also saw a massive influx of Italian and French influences to Hungary, as well as the foundation of Hungary's first two universities: Pécs in 1367 (q.v.) and Óbuda in 1389 or 1395 (q.v.).

ANONYMUS [ANONYMOUS] (c.1190s). Known also as the "Unknown Notary of King Béla" *(Anonymus Belae Regis notarius),* this chronicler is the author of *Gesta Hungarorum (Deeds of the Hungarians)* (q.v.), which is the first extant chronicle of early Hungarian history. He identified himself only as "Master P, the erstwhile notary of the King Béla"—without indicating which of the four Bélas he was referring to. Thus, Anonymus's identity and period have been subjects of scholarly debate for over two centuries. Nowadays there is a general agreement among historians that he had been the notary of King Béla III (r.1172-96) (q.v.), and that he wrote his chronicle soon after the king's death in the late 1190s. It is also believed that Anonymus probably picked up his knowledge about medieval *gestas* (q.v.)—literary compilations of romantic myths and historical tales—during his studies at the University of Paris, after which he joined the Hungarian Royal Court Chancery (q.v.). Being a typical medieval chronicler, Anonymus had the tendency to project the conditions of his own age back into the earlier centuries. For this reason, his *Gesta Hungarorum* has to be used with caution. At the same time, however, his work did preserve important elements of pre-Christian Hungarian national traditions, stretching to before the 9th-century Árpádian conquest of Hungary (q.v.). Scholars believe that one of Anonymus's goals with this work was to support the proprietary claims of Hungary's traditional landed families by grounding their claims in the Hungarian conquest (q.v.). This support was needed against the legal-constitutional claims of the new aristocracy, who—although recent transplantees—were close to Hungary's monarchs and thus in a favorable position to gain control over much of the country.

ANTALL, JÓZSEF (1932-93). Historian, archivist, and the first post-communist prime minister of Hungary (1990-93). In October 1989, Antall was elected president of the Hungarian Democratic Forum *(Magyar Demokrata Fórum)* (q.v.), the political party that dominated Hungary's first post-communist government. In May 1990 he became Hungary's prime minister. Being a typical representative of the moderately conservative Christian Democratic philosophy that has dominated much of European political life in the recent decades (e.g. Italy, Germany), Antall followed a policy of moderation both in socioeconomic reforms as well as with regard to political retributions toward former communists. But having inherited the economic chaos of a failed political system, and having to work with a governmental apparatus whose members were unprepared for the leadership positions into which an accident of history had thrust them, after three and a half years of governance Antall lost most of his early popularity. Before his death in December 1993—when he was replaced by Péter Boross (q.v.)— Antall and his party were being blamed for all the drawbacks of the new system that was especially harsh on the retirees, white collar workers, and on those members of the intelligentsia who had refused to get involved in the party politics of the Hungarian Democratic Forum. Antall's death saved him from the inglorious defeat suffered by his party in the May 1994 elections, which returned the reform communists (q.v.) to power.

ANTI-SEMITISM.   Jews have been part of Hungarian society ever since the Magyar conquest of the Carpathian Basin (q.v.) in the late 9th century. Yet, we know of no manifestations of anti-Semitism until after the spread of Christianity in the 11th and 12th centuries. Beginning with the 13th century, however, Hungary also began to experience elements of Christian anti-Semitism, but that had nothing to do with the racially motivated anti-Semitism of our own age. Modern Hungarian anti-Semitism has its roots partially in the Law of Jewish Emancipation of 1868, which permitted the Jews "to become successful" in Hungarian society, and partially in various late-19th-century racist theories that, under the guidance of loud demagogues, had turned many of the unlettered common folk against the Jews. The first important manifestations of this movement took place in the 1880s, and it included the Blood Libel of Tiszaeszlár (1881), the establishment of an ephemeral National Anti-Semitic Party (1883), and the political and journalistic activities of Győző Istóczy (1842-1915) and Gyula Verhovay (1849-1906). The next phase came after the collapse of the Hungarian Soviet Republic (q.v.) in 1919, and took the form of the so-called White Terror (q.v.). The third phase appeared just before and during World War II (q.v.) and was connected with the spread of Nazism. It included the Jewish Laws of 1938, 1939, 1941 (q.v), as well as the Hungarian Jewish Holocaust in 1944-45 (q.v.). In spite of these periodic flare-ups of political anti-Semitism, since their emancipation in 1868, the Hungarian Jews (q.v.) were much better off than their coreligionists in Poland (q.v.), Russia (q.v.), and Romania (q.v.). This was partially true because—in contrast to the practice in the latter countries, where they were viewed as national minorities—in Hungary they were viewed and treated simply as "Hungarians of the Jewish faith." As such, they were much more readily accepted by their non-Jewish fellow Hungarians, and consequently were able to participate fully in—and contribute significantly to—the economic, social, and cultural life of the nation. The Holocaust had decimated the Hungarian Jews in 1944-45, and for this reason some of the survivors left their homeland permanently. Yet, even today, Hungary has the largest Jewish population in East Central Europe (q.v.).

Moreover, those who remain (c.100,000) view themselves almost exclusively as Hungarians. After the collapse of the communist system in 1989-90 there occurred a revival of anti-Semitism in all of the countries of the former Soviet bloc. Yet, as demonstrated by several recent surveys—including one by the American Jewish Committee in 1991—this revival was least evident in Hungary. According to these surveys, Hungarians today are far less anti-Semitic than are the Romanians (q.v.), Russians (q.v.), Poles (q.v.), Slovaks (q.v.), or any number of other nationalities in the region with the exception of the Czechs (q.v.).

APÁCZAI-CSERE, JÁNOS (1625-59). A prominent social philosopher and educator, and the author of the first real Hungarian encyclopedia. Born into a Székely (q.v.) lower noble family, Apáczai-Csere was educated at the Calvinist colleges of Kolozsvár (q.v.) and Gyulafehérvár (q.v.). In 1648 he left for Holland, where he studied for four years and earned a doctorate in 1652. In 1653 he returned home to become professor of poetics at the College of Gyulafehérvár. Since he favored the ideas of the Puritans, he soon lost his position. In 1656, Prince George Rákóczi II (q.v.) appointed him the director of the College of Kolozsvár, where he remained until his death three years later. Apáczai-Csere published his pioneering *Hungarian Encyclopedia [Magyar Encyclopaedia]* in 1653. It proved to be the first Hungarian—and a pioneering European—attempt to prepare a compendium of all human knowledge within the confines of a single work. Two-thirds of Apáczai-Csere's *Encyclopaedia* is devoted to natural sciences, medicine, and astronomy, while one-third embraces the arts and humanities.

Like his older and better known contemporary, John Amos Comenius (q.v.), Apáczai-Csere was also concerned with the quality and the pedagogical aspects of education. He developed his views concerning new pedagogical methods in his *Little Hungarian Logic (Magyar Logigácska)* (1654) and in his *On the Supreme Need of Schools (De summa scholarum necessitate])* (1656). In these works he proposed the establishment of a multitiered and uniform educational system that would use the vernacular language and reduce religious control to the minimum. Apáczai-Csere also recognized the need for a secular university that would disregard religious ideologies and produce experts in specific fields of human activity. His most significant philosophical works are *About the Human Mind (De mente humana)* (1658) and *Natural Philosophy (Philosophia naturalis)*, the latter of which remained in manuscript form. Apáczai-Csere's death at the age of thirty-four ended the promising career of a great social and educational philosopher. His *Collected Pedagogical Works (Válogatott pedagógiai művei)* were first published in 1899, while his *Hungarian Encyclopaedia* appeared several times, including a facsimile edition in 1976.

APAFI [APAFFY], MIHÁLY (1632-90). The last ruling prince of Transylvania (r.1661-90), who was placed on the throne by the Ottoman Turks (q.v.), and whose death signaled the incorporation of his principality into the Habsburg Empire (q.v.). Having been captured during Prince George Rákóczi II's (q.v.) unfortunate campaign in Poland (q.v.) in 1657, Apafi spent the next four years in the captivity of the Tatar Khan of Crimea (q.v.). During these four years Transylvania (q.v.) witnessed Prince Rákóczi's desperate struggle to retain his throne (1657-60), Ákos Barcsay's (q.v.) appointment as his successor by the Turks (r.1658-60), the election of John Kemény (q.v.) by the Transylvanian estates (r.1661-62), and then the Turkish engineered election of Mihály Apafi in 1661. Apafi proved to be a weak and vacillating ruler, who left most of the governing to his wife, Anna Bornemisza, and to his unscrupulous chancellor, Mihály Teleki (q.v.). As a vassal of the Ottoman Empire (q.v.), he participated in several of the sultan's anti-Habsburg campaigns (1663, 1679, 1683), but at the same time negotiated with Emperor Leopold I (q.v.). For a while Apafi supported Imre Thököly's (q.v) anti-Habsburg campaign (1677-78), but after the Second Siege of Vienna (1683) (q.v.), which proved the decline of the Ottoman Turks, he renewed his negotiations with the Habsburgs. Forced to accept Habsburg vassalage for Transylvania (1688), Apafi lived the remaining two years of his life in the

Fortress of Fogaras in total depression. After his death he was buried in the Saxon church of Almakerek in southeastern Transylvania.

APOSTOLIC KINGSHIP [APOSTOLI KIRÁLYSÁG]. This was one of the titles of the kings of Hungary, which—according to tradition—reached back to King St. Stephen (q.v.), who allegedly received it form Pope Sylvester II (r.999-1003), along with the so-called "Holy Crown of Hungary" (q.v.). After this title lapsed for lack of usage, it was revived and renewed by Maria Theresa (r.1740-80) (q.v.), who had Pope Clement XIII (r.1758-69) reaffirm it in the year 1758. The possession of this title increased the Right of Patronage (q.v.) of the Hungarian kings to a point where they had full control over appointment to high Church offices and they could even interfere in papal elections.

APPEAL PARTY [FELIRATI PÁRT] (1861). One of the parties at the Hungarian Diet (q.v.) of 1861, the other one having been the Resolution Party (q.v.). Both of these parties protested against Emperor Francis Joseph's (q.v.) autocratic rule in Hungary (q.v.), but they disagreed as to how their views should be communicated to the monarch. The Appeal Party wished to do so in the form of an "appeal to the king," while the Resolution Party wished to do so in the form of a sharply worded "resolution." Ultimately, it was the Appeal Party under the leadership of Ferenc Deák (q.v.) that won the day, and thus laid the foundations for the Austro-Hungarian Compromise of 1867 (q.v.).

APPONYI, COUNT ALBERT (1846-1933). A prominent conservative statesman of the Dualist Period (q.v.) and the interwar years (q.v.), who served twice as Hungary's minister for religion, culture and education (1906-10, 1917-18). Although Apponyi began his political career in 1872 as a supporter of Austro-Hungarian dualism (q.v.), by 1903 he had become a loud exponent of various Hungarian independence movements, and thus contributed to the undermining of the health of the Austro-Hungarian Empire (q.v.). He carried his nationalism into the Education Law of 1907 ("Lex Apponyica"), passed under his leadership, which did have some progressive social features, but by its linguistic and ideological demands aggravated the sensitivities of Hungary's national minorities (q.v.). Following the collapse of Austria-Hungary and Historic Hungary (q.v.) after World War I (q.v.), Apponyi reassessed his views and became a strong proponent of Legitimism (q.v.) in Hungary. He spent most of the postwar years abroad, first as the head of the Hungarian delegation to the Peace Conference at Versailles (1919-20), and then as Hungary's representative to the League of Nations (1923-33). Apponyi described the political experiences of his long life in several reminiscences, including his two-volume *Memoirs [Emlékirataim]* (1922-34), and his *Experiences and Reflections [Élmények és emlékek]* (1933).

APRIL LAWS (1848). The reform laws passed by the last Hungarian Feudal Diet (q.v.) in wake of the Hungarian Revolution (q.v.) that began on March 15, 1848. The April Laws were accepted and sanctioned by King Ferdinand V (q.v.) on April 11 of that year. The most important of these laws included: (1) an annual Parliament elected on the basis of a suffrage system that extended the right to vote from the nobility to the non-noble intelligentsia, the artisans, as well as all peasants who owned at least a quarter section of a so-called "peasant plot"; (2) the establishment of an independent Hungarian government responsible to the elected Parliament; (3) the foundation of a Hungarian National Guard for the defense of the country; (4) the abolishment of all censorship for printed works; (5) the unification of all parts of the Hungarian Crown Lands (q.v.)— including Transylvania (q.v.), the Partium (q.v.), and the Military Frontier District (q.v.)—into a single administrative entity; (6) the elimination of all feudal obligations, including the tithe to the Catholic Church; 7) equality before the law for all citizens; and (8) equality of all religious denominations and complete religious equality for all. Following the defeat of the Hungarian Revolution in August 1849, most of the April Laws were rescinded, and not even the Austro-Hungarian Compromise of 1867 (q.v.) restored all of them completely.

AQUINCUM. One of the important Roman settlements on the territory of today's Budapest (q.v.), more specifically in its northwestern section that used to be the separate city of Óbuda (q.v.). Founded in the middle of the 1st century A.D., Aquincum served as the capital of Lower Pannonia. It reached its high point in the 2d and 3rd centuries, when its population was around 10,000. After that it began its decline, along with the Roman Empire itself. Aquincum was destroyed toward the end of the 4th century, largely as a result of the so-called Barbarian Invasions.

ARAD. One of the oldest cities of Historic Hungary (q.v.), which after World War I (q.v.) was awarded to Romania (q.v.). Founded in 1029, soon after Hungary's Christianization (q.v.), it was named after one of King St. Stephen's (q.v.) faithful military vassals. Starting out as a military fortress, Arad became an important Hungarian city for nine centuries. Occupied by the Ottoman Turks (q.v.) in 1551, it remained under their rule until 1685. Following its reconquest by the Christian forces, it was rebuilt, strengthened, and made into a important center of Habsburg (q.v.) power in Hungary. During the Revolution and War of Liberation of 1848-49 (q.v.), Arad was the scene of the final meeting of the Hungarian Government. It was from there that Lajos Kossuth (q.v.) left for his exile in Turkey. On October 6, 1849, Arad was also the scene of the execution of thirteen Hungarian revolutionary leaders (twelve generals and one colonel) by the commander-in-chief of the Habsburg armed forces, Baron Julius Haynau (q.v.). Although the city's population was 70% Hungarian, the Treaty of Trianon (1920) (q.v.) awarded it to Romania, along with such other parts of Historic Hungary as Transylvania (q.v.) and the eastern belt of the Great Hungarian Plain (q.v.). Its current population is 150,000.

ARANY, JÁNOS (1817-82). Hungary's greatest epic poet, who, after many decades of teaching, tutoring, and editing, ended his career as the secretary (1865-70), and then secretary general (1870-79), of the Hungarian Academy of Sciences (q.v.). Like most of his contemporaries, Arany was also the product of 19th-century romantic nationalism. Yet, in contrast to most of his lettered contemporaries, he stood for moderation and compromise. He is known primarily as the author of such epics as the "Toldi Trilogy" about a 14th-century national hero, and of the unfinished "Hunnic Trilogy" about Attila (q.v.), his brother Buda (q.v.), and his youngest son Csaba (q.v.). Arany was also the greatest master of the Hungarian ballad. Although never actively involved in politics, Arany's influence was pervasive over the whole landscape of Hungarian cultural life and historical thinking.

ARCHDUKE [ERZHERZOG, FŐHERCEG].   Since 1453 the title of the members of the House of Habsburg (q.v.). Emperor Frederick III (r.1440-93) endowed the members of his dynasty with this title to distinguish them from all of the other princes of the Holy Roman Empire (q.v.). This title was transferred to Hungary at the time of the ratification of the Pragmatic Sanction (q.v.) in 1723. It was perpetuated even after the dissolution of the Holy Roman Empire (1806) and the almost simultaneous creation of the Austrian Empire (q.v.) in 1804. It was being used also used by the Hungarian branch of the Habsburg dynasty, which developed in the 19th century. Although still being used by some, the title lost its legal significance in 1945.

ARISTOCRACY [ARISZTOKRÁCIA, FŐNEMESSÉG].   The word is derived from a Greek term that means "the rule of the most exalted." In classical times members of the aristocracy consisted of those wealthy and influential families who generally participated in the country's leadership. In medieval times this term came to be applied to the upper layers of society, who possessed both large estates and were appointed to important administrative offices. In the course of time the titles of these offices became hereditary ranks, including prince, duke, marquis, count (earl), viscount, and baron. A good example of this process is the title "count," which originally was a simply the administrator of a "county," but later became a hereditary aristocratic title. The titled aristocracy constitutes a thin upper layer of the nobility. In Hungary, this upper layer consisted of only a few hundred families—among over a hundred thousand noble families—whose members constituted less than one percent of the noble class. Their role is also discussed under the term "higher nobility" (q.v.).

ARMALIST [ARMALISTA]. The class name for members of one of the lower layers of nobility (q.v.) in Hungary, who were ennobled via a royal rescript called *armalis.* They had the right to use coat of arms *(arma),* but were not granted estates, and as such they lived under very modest circumstances. At times they were even obliged to pay taxes, wherefore they were also called '"taxed nobility" *(taksás nemesek)* (q.v.). Since the 16th century, most ennoblements in Hungary took place via an *armalis*—be these done by the Habsburg kings (q.v.) or the princes of Transylvania (q.v.). Thus, by the 18th and 19th centuries, the majority of the Hungarian common nobility (q.v.) were in this category.

ÁRPÁD (845/55-907). Son of Prince Álmos (q.v.), ruling prince *(gyula)* (q.v.) of the conquering Hungarians or Magyars (q.v.), leader of the Magyar tribe (q.v.) that gave its name to the Hungarian tribal federation (q.v.) and to the nation that grew out of it, and founding father of the Árpád dynasty (q.v.) that ruled Hungary (q.v.) for over four centuries (9th c.-1301). During the period of conquest Árpád shared his powers with Kurszán (q.v.), the nominal supreme ruler *(kende, kündü)* (q.v.) of the tribal federation. Kurszán's death in 904 gave Árpád the chance to end the age old practice of "dual kingship" (q.v.) and to unify the powers of the *kende* and the *gyula* into that of a single ruling prince. As the de facto leader of the Hungarians during the conquest, it was Prince Árpád who led them through the Verecke Pass in the Northeastern Carpathians (895) and who completed the conquest of the whole Carpathian Basin (q.v.) in the course of the next few years. Árpád had five sons—Levente, Tarhos, Üllő, Jutas, and Zoltán (q.v.)—of whom only the latter appears to have ruled for any significant time. After his death Árpád was buried according to ancient Hungarian traditions next to the source of a creek in the vicinity of Óbuda (q.v.). Some years later, his Christianized heirs had a chapel built over his grave, which gradually developed into a settlement known for centuries as Fehéregyháza.

ÁRPÁD ACADEMY (1966). A learned association founded in 1966 under the auspices of the Hungarian Association (q.v.) of Cleveland, Ohio, the Árpád Academy recognizes scientific, scholarly, and artistic excellence by inviting Hungarians abroad to "corresponding" and "full membership." The Academy has its annual meetings in Cleveland, in conjunction with the annual Hungarian Congresses, organized for many decades by the Hungarian Association's founding President, John Nádas (q.v.). At that time the newly elected members present summaries of their scholarly research or artistic achievements. Since its foundation, the Árpád Academy had at least a half a dozen presidents, but its secretary general and its moving spirit for the last three decades had been Professor Ferenc Somogyi (1906-95) (q.v.), who held that position from 1966 until his death in 1995. Although membership in the Árpád Academy is based on scholarly, scientific, and artistic qualifications, given its connection with the tradition-oriented Hungarian Association, ideological and political considerations have also played a role in the invitation of new members.

ÁRPÁD DYNASTY. The dynasty that was founded by Prince Árpád (q.v.) in the late 9th century, and which ruled Hungary for over four centuries until 1301. The Anjou dynasty (q.v.) that followed the Árpáds was also related to them in the female line, as was the Habsburg dynasty (q.v.) that ruled Hungary from 1526 until 1918. The greatest rulers of the Árpád dynasty included Kings St. Stephen (q.v.), St. Ladislas (q.v.), Béla III (q.v.), and Béla IV (q.v.). The Árpáds were intermarried with the Rurik dynasty (q.v.) of Kievan Russia (q.v.), the Piast dynasty (q.v.) of Poland (q.v.), the Přemyslide dynasty (q.v.) and the Luxemburg dynasty (q.v.) of Bohemia (q.v.), the Habsburg dynasty (q.v.) of Austria (q.v.) and the Holy Roman Empire (q.v.), the Dukas dynasty of the Byzantine Empire (q.v.), as well as with the rulers of Serbia (q.v.), Bosnia (q.v.), Croatia (q.v.), Venice, Naples, Scotland, and several other states.

ÁRPÁDIAN CONQUEST OF HUNGARY (895-96). The conquest of the Carpathian Basin (q.v.) by the Hungarians or Magyars (q.v.) under the de facto leadership of Prince Árpád (q.v.). This late-9th-century conquest is distinguished from various earlier appearances of the Hungarians in that region. The number and specific time frame of these earlier conquests are debated by scholars, as is the very occurrence of these conquests. More recently the notion of a "Double Conquest" (q.v.) was popularized by Gyula László (q.v.), the first of which refers to the so-called "Late Avars" (q.v.) of the 7th century.

ÁRPÁDS see **ÁRPÁD DYNASTY.**

ARROW CROSS PARTY [NYILASKERESZTES PÁRT]. The most significant of the Hungarian fascist political parties established in 1939 in imitation of the German National Socialist (Nazi) Party. In the course of the 1930s several such competing parties were established in Hungary (q.v.), but by the end of that decade most of them came to be united under the leadership of Ferenc Szálasi (q.v.) of the Arrow Cross Party. The latter was so named because of its emblem—a cross ending in four arrows—which was created in imitation of the German swastika, and which was worn in combination with a green shirt. The ideology of Szálasi's Arrow Cross Party combined elements of national chauvinism with social demagogy. The former emphasized territorial revisionism and the unique destiny of the Hungarians in the Carpathian Basin ["Carpathian-Danubian Great Fatherland"], while the latter combined demands for radical social reform with an irrational anti-Semitism (q.v.) that wished to exclude the Jews (q.v.) from the life of the nation. Both of these ideological trends had a powerful impact on a significant portion of Hungary's lower and lower middle classes, especially the urban poor, the petty bourgeoisie, and various déclassé elements. Relying on these "popular" ideologies and a powerful

demagogy, and enjoying the financial support of Nazi Germany
(q.v.), the Arrow Cross Party did make considerable headway in the
late 1930s. In the elections of 1939 they received 16.2 percent of
the popular votes and seated forty-two parliamentary members, while
after the Second Vienna Award (August 30, 1940) (q.v.)—which
resulted in Northern Transylvania's (q.v.) return to Hungary—they
managed to enlist about 300,000 of the country's bureaucrats.
Although the Arrow Cross Party's popularity declined during World
War II (q.v.), Regent Horthy's (q.v.) fumbling attempt to leave the
war on October 15, 1944, gave Szálasi the chance to assume
political power in Hungary. The Arrow Cross Party's rise to power
resulted in a reign of terror that culminated in the Hungarian Jewish
Holocaust (q.v.) and in the country's wanton destruction. Following
the war, Szálasi and his immediate supporters were brought to trial,
condemned, and executed. The majority of the Arrow Cross Party
members who had stayed at home, however, saved themselves by
immediately joining the ranks of the Communist Party (q.v.) that
also employed social demagogy and was in need of new recruits.

ASBÓTH, ALEXANDER [SÁNDOR] (1811-68). An engineer and
a lieutenant colonel in the Hungarian Revolution of 1848-49 (q.v.),
who, for a while was an adjutant of Lajos Kossuth (q.v.).
Following his flight to Turkey (1849), he emigrated to the United
States (1851), where he worked in various engineering jobs until the
outbreak of the Civil War. In 1861 he joined the Union Army,
fought in Missouri, Arkansas, and Kentucky, was severely wounded
in Florida, and rose to the rank of a major general. Following the
Civil War Asbóth was appointed the U.S. ambassador to Argentina
and Uruguay. He died in Buenos Aires in 1868 in direct
consequences of his war injuries, and he was buried in the local
English cemetery. In 1990 his remains were brought back to the
United States and reinterred at Arlington National Cemetery.

ASIA MINOR see ANATOLIA.

ASSIMILATION. National and linguistic assimilation has been a natural component of human society and human relations for thousands of years. The best examples of this process include the linguistic Arabization of the Egyptians and other North African peoples after the 7th century, the linguistic Slavization and ethnic assimilation of the Turkic Bulgarians (q.v.) in the 9th and 10th centuries, and the English speaking Americanization of all immigrants to the United States since the late 17th century. This natural process of assimilation had not become a disturbing issue until the rise of modern nationalism in the 19th century, when because of unusual efforts at forced assimilation, accompanied by much greater sensitivity to this issue, governmental assimilation policies have poisoned interethnic relations in many parts of the world.

During the age of Austro-Hungarian dualism (1867-1918) (q.v.), the Hungarians have been accused of using various legal and extra-legal means to increase their numbers at the expense of their Slovak (q.v.), Rusyn (q.v.), Romanian (q.v.), German (q.v.), Croat (q.v.), and Serb (q.v.) citizens. Since Historic Hungary's (q.v.) dismemberment (1918-20), however, it is the Hungarians who are complaining about the increased assimilationist pressures upon them in the so-called successor states (Czechoslovakia, Romania, and Yugoslavia, and more recently also Slovakia, Serbia, Croatia, and Ukraine). The most extreme efforts at denationalizing the Hungarians were undertaken in Romania during the rule of the communist dictator Nicolae Ceausescu (r.1965-89). Since the collapse of communism (1989-90), however, these pressures have also increased in the newly independent states of Slovakia (q.v.) and diminished Little Yugoslavia (Serbia and Montenegro) (q.v.).

ASTRIK [ASZTRIK] (d.1044). Also known as Anastas (Anasztáz), Astrik was an aide to Bishop Adalbert of Prague (St. Adalbert) (q.v.), who accompanied the latter to Rome in 993, and then on his Christianizing mission to Poland in 996. After Bishop Adalbert's death at the hands of the pagan Prussians (q.v.), Astrik went to Hungary (q.v.), where he was named the abbot of Pécsvárad and then the archbishop of Kalocsa. According to the early 12th-century *Hartvik Legend* on the life of King St. Stephen (q.v.), in the year A.D. 1000, it was Astrik whom Prince Vajk (i.e., King St. Stephen) dispatched to ask for the Pope's help for Hungary's Christianization (q.v.). And when Pope Sylvester II (r.999-1003) agreed, it was again Astrik who carried the royal crown ("Holy Crown of Hungary") (q.v.) back to Hungary, where it was used to crown Vajk, under the name of Stephen, the first Christian king of Hungary.

ATILLA. A colorful and braided military jacket worn by Hungarian cavalry *(hussar = huszár)* regiments ever since the 16th century. But this word, derived from the name of Attila the Hun (q.v.), was not used to refer to this jacket until the early 19th century, when it was also adopted by the Prussians. The word "Atilla" is often confused with "Attila"—the famous and feared ruler of the Huns (q.v.).

ATTILA (c.400-53). King of the Huns (r.433/34-53) and creator of the great Hunnic Empire (q.v.) that centered on Hungary (q.v.) and stretched from the Rhine and lower Danube (q.v.) in the West to beyond the Caucasus and Ural Mountains in the East. Attila was by far the most powerful ruler of the Age of Barbarian Invasions, who brought scores of Turkic, Germanic, and Slavic tribes under his control, and who compelled the East Roman or Byzantine Empire (q.v.) to pay tribute to him. Although Attila suffered a temporary setback at the Battle of Catalaunum [Chālons-sur-Marne] (q.v.) in 451, he recuperated rapidly and invaded Italy in 452. He may have also conquered the crumbling Western Roman Empire had he not died suddenly in 453.

The French and Italian chronicles—and Anglo-Saxon historical tradition based upon these chronicles—view Attila as a vicious barbarian and attribute to him evil acts that in most instances occurred many years before or after his time. Hungarians (q.v.), however, regard him as a national hero. This view is based on certain medieval Hungarian chronicles that assert that the Hungarians are the descendants of the Huns, and that Attila was the forefather of Prince Árpád (q.v.), who had conquered Hungary in the late 9th century and founded the dynasty that ruled Hungary for over four centuries. Attila is also viewed positively in Germanic traditions as reflected in the late 12th-century "[Song of the Nibelungs" *(Nibelungenlied),* where he is portrayed as a great medieval king, who is endowed with all the virtues of a chivalrous medieval knight. According to the contemporary Priscos (mid-5th c.) —as preserved by the 6th-century Jordanes—Attila was buried in a triple sarcophagus (made of gold, silver, and iron), and all those who participated in his burial were slain to conceal the site of his final resting place. Hungarian tradition adds that this burial site was in the bed of the Tisza River (q.v.) in central Hungary, whose waters were temporarily diverted.

ATTILA'S SWORD. Known also as the "Sacred Sword" or the "Sword of God" *(Isten kardja),* according to Priscos and Jordanes, this long-lost sacred sword promised its owner the domination of the world. It was allegedly found by a shepherd, whose heifer had stepped into it accidentally. He immediately took it to Attila (q.v.), king of the Huns (q.v.), who, upon receiving it, became convinced that destiny intended him to rule the whole world. He thus undertook several major campaigns against the two Roman Empires. There exists at this time in the Viennese Imperial Treasury an ancient sword known as "Attila's sword" (but also known as Charlemagne's sword), which had been in the possession of the Árpádian rulers (q.v.) of Hungary (q.v.) until 1071. In that year the deposed King Salamon (q.v.) presented it to Otto of Bavaria. Tradition holds this sword is the "Sword of God," but scholars tell us that it is in fact a late 9th-century Hungarian sword.

ATTILA'S TREASURE see NAGYSZENTMIKLÓS.

AUGSBURG, BATTLE OF (955). This German-Hungarian encounter, also known as the Battle of Lechfeld, took place in southern Bavaria (q.v.) at the confluence of the Lech and Wertach rivers.

There, the Holy Roman Emperor Otto the Great (r.936-73) defeated two Hungarian armies led by Lehel (q.v.) and Bulcsú (q.v.). Even though Otto's victory involved only two of the western Hungarian tribes, it was sufficiently meaningful to end Hungarian marauding expeditions to Western Europe.

According to unsubstantiated traditions, of the two Hungarian armies only seven persons survived, who were then mutilated. Their ears and noses were cut off and then they were sent home as deterrents to further invasions. Although victorious, the Germans also lost many thousands. Among them was Prince Konrad, Emperor Otto's treacherous son-in-law, who had enticed the Hungarians to attack his father-in-law. According to Hungarian traditions, Konrad was killed personally by Lehel with his battle horn before his execution. Lehel did this to punish Konrad for his treachery, and to force him to became his servant in the other world. (Hungarian traditions held that those killed in battle will serve their killers in afterlife.) A battle-scarred horn, claimed to be the horn of Lehel, is preserved in the town of Jászberény in Hungary.

AULIC NOBILITY. The collective name for those members of the Hungarian aristocracy (q.v.) and upper clergy (q.v.), who followed an unquestionably pro-Habsburg policy during the 18th and 19th centuries. With the rise of nationalism, these aulic nobles were generally viewed as traitors to the national cause.

AURORA. A literary almanac founded and edited by the Romantic author Károly Kisfaludy (q.v.), and published between 1822 and 1837, which served as an important forum for the Hungarian political reform movement that led to the revolution of 1848-49 (q.v.). Literary and political activities have had a close symbiotic relationship in Hungary ever since the start of the Hungarian national revival movement (q.v.) in the 18th century. But in those early decades, this relationship was even closer than today, and the "Aurora Circle" had played a very important role in this revival.

AUSTRIA. This term has a number of overlapping meanings. Originally it referred to the Frankish frontier land conquered by Charlemagne around A.D. 800 and known for a while as *Ostmark (Eastern March)*. Later this term—changed in German to *Österreich (Eastern Empire)*—came to mean those provinces around Vienna (i.e., Upper Austria, Lower Austria, Carinthia, Carniola, Styria, etc.) that became the core of the Habsburg dynastic state (q.v.) after Rudolf I (q.v.) had awarded them (1282) to his own two sons, Albert and Rudolf.

Between the 16th and the early 19th centuries, the term Austria was routinely used to refer to the collection of all of those eastern principalities and kingdoms that were ruled by the members of the Habsburg dynasty (q.v.). This usage was legalized in 1804, when Holy Roman Emperor Francis II (q.v.) declared all of his lands to be part of the new "Austrian Empire" (q.v.) and proclaimed himself "Francis I, Emperor of Austria." The Austro-Hungarian Compromise of 1867 (q.v.) transformed the "Austrian Empire" into "Austria-Hungary" (1867-1918) (q.v.), but for the sake of brevity and simplicity this dualistic state was also often simply referred to as "Austria". Since World War I (q.v.), the term Austria refers only to the small German-speaking republic that is located between Switzerland and Hungary, to the south of Germany (q.v.) and the Czech Republic (q.v.), and to the north of Italy and former Yugoslavia (q.v.). Its area is basically identical with the Habsburg's core provinces of the 15th century.

AUSTRIA-HUNGARY [AUSTRO-HUNGARIAN EMPIRE] (1867-1918). One of the European Great Powers in the late 19th and early 20th century, with a population of 52 million (1910) on a territory of 668,000 square kilometers (257,950 square miles). The state was founded on the basis of the Austro-Hungarian Compromise of 1867 (q.v.), which transformed the Austrian Empire (q.v.) of the Habsburg dynasty (q.v.) into a dualist state, consisting of two near-independent political entities. Both halves of Austria-Hungary had their own parliaments and governments, and they both ran their own internal affairs on the basis of their own constitutions. They were bound together by the person of their common ruler into a "personal union" (q.v.), who was simultaneously the emperor of Austria and the king of Hungary. They also had a common foreign policy, a common Imperial and Royal Army (q.v.), as well as a common budget to support their common affairs. At the same time, they also had two separate small domestic armies and two separate national budgets.

The two halves of Austria-Hungary lived in a monetary and tariff union, and they coordinated their common foreign, financial, and military affairs through two sixty-member delegations, whose members were elected by their respective parliaments. The financial and military terms of the Compromise of 1867 were renegotiated every ten years, and in case of impassé the emperor/king had the right to rule by decrees. Austria-Hungary's weaknesses included the uneven economic development of its component parts, its relatively slow industrialization, its lack of colonies in an age of economic imperialism, the national heterogeneity of its population, and the lack of adequate political representation of this population in an age of growing nationalism.

Austria-Hungary also got involved in a costly arms race that pitted the Triple Alliance (Austria-Hungary, Germany, Italy) (q.v.) against the Triple Entente (Britain, France, Russia) (q.v.). Its most positive feature included its unification of nearly two dozen separate nationalities into a single political and economic unit, which kept them from fighting each other. It also gave them more by way of protection and economic opportunities than was offered later by the small successor states (q.v.) that had been created after Austria-Hungary's dissolution.

AUSTRIAN EMPIRE. The name of the Habsburg Empire (q.v.) between 1804 and 1867. With the imminence of the dissolution of the Holy Roman Empire (q.v.) by Napoleon (r.1799/1804-15), the Habsburg rulers transformed their many dynastic holdings into the Austrian Empire and proclaimed themselves the "Emperors of Austria." The Austrian Empire was reshaped into Austria-Hungary (q.v.) by the Austro-Hungarian Compromise of 1867 (q.v.).

AUSTRO-HUNGARIAN ARMED FORCES. The armed forces of Austria-Hungary (1867-1918) (q.v.) consisted of land forces, naval forces, and during World War I (q.v.) also of a small Air Force. The land forces were made up of three distinct entities: the Common Imperial and Royal Army, the Austrian *Landwehr*, and the Hungarian *Honvéd*. Their manpower supply was based on the obligatory draft law of 1868 (amended in 1912), which made every male between the ages of 19 and 42 subject to draft. Obligatory service included two years of active service and ten years in the reserves. The cavalry demanded three years of active service and seven years in the reserves. The number of annual draftees was apportioned between Austria (q.v.), Hungary (q.v.), and Bosnia-Herzegovina (q.v.) on the basis of population figures. In 1916 these figures for the Common Imperial and Royal Army were 91,482 for Austria, 68,187 for Hungary, and 7,763 for Bosnia-Herzegovina. There were an additional 26,979 draftees for the Austrian *Landwehr* and 25,000 draftees for the Hungarian *Honvéd,* which were separate national armies comparable to the National Guard. The Common Imperial and Royal Army was stationed in sixteen cities throughout the empire, while the *Landwehr* and the *Honvéd* were stationed in fifteen cities, some of them overlapping with the Common Army. Education of the officer corps was conducted in two war academies, three common military academies, one *Landwehr* academy, one *Honvéd* academy, and fifty-seven secondary-level military schools.

At the start of World War I, the standing armies of Austria-Hungary numbered 1,338,000 men, which during the war increased significantly. The Austro-Hungarian Navy was small, geared primarily to the Adriatic (q.v.) and the Eastern Mediterranean. Its roots went back to the Turkish Wars of the late 17th and early 18th century, but its real development took place only in the late 19th and early 20th century, particularly after the Russo-Japanese War of 1904-05. Its official name since 1889 was the "Imperial and Royal Austro-Hungarian Navy," and in 1914—before the start of World War I—it consisted of fifteen battleships, twelve cruisers, several dozen smaller units, and about 20,500 men. The Austro-Hungarian Air Force, established during World War I, was even less significant.

Against 353 British, 280 French, and 218 German airplanes, it only had forty-two units. The number of its trained pilots (ninety-three) was also only about one-third of that of the other three great powers. Only Russia and Italy were behind Austria-Hungary in air power.

AUSTRO-HUNGARIAN COMPROMISE [AUSGLEICH] OF 1867. An agreement between Hungarian and Austrian political leaders for the restructuring of the Austrian Empire (q.v.) into the dualistic state of Austria-Hungary (q.v.). Concluded and approved in May 1867, this agreement ended the Age of Absolutism (q.v.) and Provisorium (q.v.) that followed the defeat of the Hungarian Revolution of 1848-49 (q.v.). It came into being as a result of Austria having been pushed out of Italy (1859) and Germany (1866), and of Austria's growing fear of the creeping Russian imperialism in the Balkans (q.v.). Being at odds with most of the non-German citizens of his empire ever since 1848, having suffered substantial military and territorial losses in the subsequent years, and having become isolated diplomatically in Europe, Emperor Francis Joseph (r.1848-1916) (q.v.) and his Austrian advisers felt that they had no choice but to restore normalcy at home.

Of the various possibilities, they chose to come to terms only with one of their subject nationalities, the Hungarians (q.v), whom they judged to be the most important. The result was the creation of Austria-Hungary (1867-1918), an unusual dualistic state that had two dominant and well over a dozen subject nationalities. The lack of satisfaction of the latter's national aspirations was the most significant flaw of the Austro-Hungarian Compromise, as well as the most threatening shortcoming of the state it had created. The main Hungarian architects of the compromise were Ferenc Deák (q.v.), Count Gyula Andrássy (q.v.) and Baron József Eötvös (q.v.). The Austrian side was represented by Emperor Francis Joseph and by his new prime minister, Count Friedrich von Beust (r.1867-71).

AUSTRO-HUNGARIAN DUALISM. The system under which Austria-Hungary (q.v.) or the Austro-Hungarian Empire functioned between 1867 and 1918. This dualism was the result of the Austro-

Hungarian Compromise of 1867 (q.v.), which transformed the Austrian Empire (q.v.) into Austria-Hungry (q.v.).

AUSTRO-HUNGARIAN EMPIRE see AUSTRIA-HUNGA-RY.

AUSTRO-MARXISM. A dominant ideological orientation in early 20th-century Austria-Hungary (q.v.), which rejected both the necessity of a violent socialist revolution, as well as the obligatory nationalization of private property. The Austro-Marxists wanted to achieve their social goals within the context of parliamentarism, and they believed that the national minority question (q.v.) should be solved by means of cultural autonomy for all national minorities. Its most important exponents included Victor Adler (1852-1918), Otto Bauer (1881-1938), Rudolf Hilferding (1877-1941), and Karl Renner (1870-1950).

AUSTRO-SLAVISM. A Czech-initiated political movement in mid-19th-century Austrian Empire [Austria-Hungary] (q.v.), which hoped to unite all of the small Slavic nationalities (q.v.) of the empire so as to demand for them a controlling partnership in the multinational state of the Habsburgs (q.v.). The most important proponent of this ideology was the Czech historian Francis Palacký (1798-1876).

AUXILIARY SCIENCES OF HISTORY [TÖRTÉNETI SEGÉDTUDOMÁNYOK]. The collection of those specialized fields of study that aid historical research, especially research in the medieval and classical periods. These disciplines include archeology, chronology, epigraphy, genealogy, heraldry, numismatics, and sfragistics (i.e., the study of seals). In a wider sense they also include ethnography, ethnology, folklore, linguistics, and historical geography.

AVARS. A Turkic people, close relatives of the Huns (q.v.), who emerged from Central Asia under the leadership of Khan Baján (c.562-602) in the 560s. After uniting with some Hunnic remnants on the Pontic Steppes (q.v.), they conquered the Carpathian Basin (q.v.)—future Historic Hungary (q.v.)—from the the Germanic Gepids in 567. They created an empire which during its height stretched from the Baltic to the Adriatic Sea (q.v.) and also included the Pontic Steppes north of the Black Sea (q.v.). During the 630s and 640s, the Avars were pushed out of the Black Sea region by the related Onogur-Bulgarian state ruled by Khan Kuvrat, which also had some Hunnic remains and proto-Magyars or early Hungarians.

In the middle of the 7th century, the Avar state underwent an internal turmoil, and in the 670s it was inundated by a new wave of invaders characterized by griffin tendril ornamentation, who are referred to as the "Late Avars" (q.v.) or Wangars, and who then revived the failing Avar Empire. According to recent research, these "Late Avars" or Wangars may in fact have been the proto-Magyars (early Hungarians) led by one of Khan Kuvrat's sons, Kubernek, who had transplanted a segment of the population of the Onogur-Bulgarian state to the Carpathian Basin (q.v.). Some scholars call this the "First Conquest" to distinguish it from the Árpádian Conquest (q.v.) of the late 9th century.

According to traditional views, in the early 9th century, this revived Avar Empire fell victim to the attacks of Charlemagne's Frankish and Khan Krum's Bulgarian Empires. Recent research, however, indicates that the reason for this collapse was primarily the desiccation of the region, which took hold of the lowlands in the period between 720 and 820 and destroyed conditions for normal life. Many of the Avars moved out into the surrounding hilly areas and merged with the Slavs (q.v.). Others—including the proto-Magyars of the "First Conquest"—survived this destruction, but a century later they merged with the Magyars or Hungarians of the Árpádian Conquest of the late 9th century.

AVAR EMPIRE   see AVARS, LATE AVARS.

AVITICITAS   [ŐSISÉG]. A legal tradition that prevented the alienation of the common property of a noble clan. In the 11th century this law applied only to the lands originally occupied by the individual clans. But King Coloman's (q.v.) law of the early 12th century extended this practice also to the lands that had been granted by King St. Stephen (q.v.) a century earlier. This law clearly distinguished between "hereditary estates" and "acquired estates" — the former of which could not be sold or otherwise disposed of. This ancient tradition is closely related to the system of "entailed estates" (q.v.), which developed later.

ÁVH [ÁLLAMVÉDELMI HATÓSÁG, OFFICE OF STATE DEFENSE] see **SECRET POLICE.**

AWAKENING HUNGARIANS [ÉBREDŐ MAGYAROK]. An irredentist and partially anti-Semitic organization founded in November 1918 for the purposes of preventing Historic Hungary's (q.v.) mutilation as a result of Austria-Hungary's (q.v.) defeat in World War I (q.v.). The association's anti-Semitism stemmed largely from the large presence of Jews (q.v.) in the leadership of the communist movement and Hungarian Soviet Republic (q.v.), which was viewed by the Awakening Hungarians as largely responsible for the loss of the war. The members of the Association of Awakening Hungarians were actively involved in various antirevolutionary and anti-Semitic activities. But after the consolidation of Admiral Horthy's (q.v.) conservative regime in the early 1920s, they lost their influence and were pushed into the background. Later, a number of them became associated with the Hungarian Revisionist League (q.v.) and with various insignificant anti-Semitic groups.

AZOV SEA [SEA OF AZOV, PALUS MAEOTIS, MEOTISZ TENGER]. It is a northern bay of the Black Sea (q.v.) that serves as the delta of the Don River. Its importance in Hungarian history is connected with the legend that claims that the two "sister nations"—the Huns and the Hungarians (Magyars)— originated from that region. According to the "Legend of the Wondrous Stag" (q.v.), these two nations are the descendants of the two brothers, Hunor and Magor (q.v.), the sons of the legendary King Nimród. They abducted and married the daughters of the equally legendary King Dúl, and then became the progenitors of the two nations. Attila's (q.v.) youngest son, Irnák—Csaba (q.v.) in Hungarian tradition—also went back with some Hunnic remains to the Azov Sea area following the breakup of his father's empire in the period between 453 and 469.

- B -

BABENBERG DYNASTY. The family that had ruled Austria (q.v.) and a number of related provinces between 976 and 1246. Of Frankish origin, the family took its name from its estate at Bamberg in the late 9th century. In 976 Luitpold Babenberg (d.994) received Ostmark (Austria) as a feudal fief from Emperor Otto II (r.973-83) and thus he became the progenitor of the dynasty that ruled Austria for nearly three centuries. Between 976 and 1156 the Babenbergs held the title Marquis (q.v.), and between 1156 and 1246 Dukes of Austria. The last member of the dynasty was Duke Frederick the Belligerent (r.1230-46), who initiated several campaigns against Hungary (q.v.), without much success. In 1241, at the time of the Mongol invasion (q.v.), he feigned to help King Béla IV (q.v.), but secretly incited the Cumans (q.v.) against the beleaguered Hungarians (q.v.). After Béla's defeat by the Mongols at the Battle of Mohi (April 11-12, 1241) (q.v.), Frederick offered asylum to the king, but then took him captive and forced him to ransom himself by relinquishing his treasures and transferring to him three western Hungarian counties. After the Mongols' withdrawal, King Béla IV got even with Frederick by reconquering the three counties (1242) and then by defeating him in the Battle of the Leitha in 1246. Frederick was killed at this battle and with his death the dynasty of the Babenbergs came to an end. They were replaced on the throne some three decades later by the Habsburgs (q.v.), who held on to Austria until 1918.

BACH, ALEXANDER [SÁNDOR] (1813-93).The first commoner in the Austrian Empire (q.v.) to be named a minister in the Habsburg Imperial Government (q.v.). His name is inseparably linked with the Age of Absolutism (q.v.) that descended upon Hungary (q.v.) after the defeat of the revolution of 1848-49 (q.v.). Appointed minister of interior in 1849, until the spring of 1852,

Bach was under the shadow of Prince Felix Schwarzenberg (q.v.). But following the latter's death, he became the primary executor of Habsburg absolutism to a point, where the whole decade of the 1850s came to be named after him as the "Bach Period." Bach started out as a liberal, and he also introduced some progressive reforms during the 1850s. But because of the repressive postrevolutionary policies that he represented, his name has a very negative connotation in Hungary. He fell from power in 1859 as a result of Austria's defeat in the Austro-Italian-French War of 1859. After the Austro-Hungarian Compromise of 1867 (q.v.), he withdrew from politics completely.

BACHKA [BAČKA] see BÁCSKA.

BÁCSKA [BACHKA, BAČKA]. The southernmost section of the lands between the Danube (q.v.) and the Tisza (q.v.) rivers of former south-central Hungary (q.v.), most of which was awarded to newly created Yugoslavia (q.v.) after World War I (q.v.). Bácska now makes up much of the autonomous region within Serbia (q.v.), known as Voivodina (Vojvodina) (q.v.). Its most important cities are Szabadka (Subotica) and Újvidék (Novi Sad, Neusatz). Following the collapse of Yugoslavia in 1941, Bácska was returned to Hungary for the duration of World War II (q.v.). After the war it went back to Yugoslavia, and following the second disintegration of that state, it remained with Serbia or Little Yugoslavia (q.v.).

BAJCSY-ZSILINSZKY, ENDRE (1886-1944). A politician and a publicist, who started out as the defender of the old order before World War I (q.v.) and as an exponent of "racial purity" during the early 1920s. Then he gradually altered his views and moved in the direction of democratic pluralism. During World War II (q.v.) Bajcsy-Zsilinszky became one of the most important critics of Hungary's (q.v.) pro-German foreign policy and of the whole pro-Nazi orientation. Following the takeover of the Hungarian government by the fascist Hungarian Arrow Cross Party (q.v.) on October 15, 1944, Bajcsy-Zsilinszky was arrested and two months later executed for his so-called antistate activities. The three phases of his political life are best represented by his assassination of the radical peasant leader András Áchim (q.v.) in 1911, by his co-founding of Party for the Defense of the Race *(Fajvédő Párt)* (q.v.) in 1923, and by his above-mentioned daring opposition to the German-Nazi takeover of Hungary during World War II.

BAKÁCS see BAKÓCZ.

BAKÓCZ, TAMÁS [BAKÁCS, THOMAS] (1442-1521). Cardinal-archbishop of Esztergom, primate of Hungary (r.1498-1521), and the head of the Hungarian Catholic Church (q.v.). Bakócz was a typical product of the Hungarian Renaissance (q.v.). Born as the son of a simple peasant artisan, he was enlisted into the ranks of prospective priests in his youth. He studied at the Universities of Cracow and Padua, after which he came to the attention of King Matthias Corvinus (q.v.), who appointed him to his Chancery (q.v.) in 1474. By 1483 Bakócz had become the king's private secretary (1483-90). In the meanwhile he was also appointed the bishop of Győr (r.1486-91). At the time of King Matthias's death in 1490, Bakócz outwardly supported the king's illegitimate son, János Corvinus (q.v.), but secretly sided with the widowed Queen Beatrix (q.v.). Soon he also deserted her in return for the promise of the Chancellorship (1490) from King Ulászló II (r.1490-1516) (Vladislav Jagello of Bohemia) (q.v.). During the early reign of this weak and vacillating king—while secretly negotiating with the Habsburgs (q.v.)—Bakócz acquired so much powers that he was called the Hungary's "second king." In 1491 he became the bishop of Eger (q.v.), in 1498 the archbishop of Esztergom (q.v.) and Hungary's primate (q.v.), and in 1500 a cardinal of the Catholic Church.

In 1512, in anticipation of the papal elections, Bakócz left for Rome, where during the interregnum he became a member of the Catholic Church's governing council. He spread his wealth generously, wherefore he was considered one of the main contenders to the papal throne. During the first round he received eight votes, and was second only to the even wealthier Giovanni Medici, who ultimately won the election and became Pope Leo X (r.1513-21). As a consolation prize, Leo X appointed Bakócz the leader of a new anti-Turkish crusade, which Bakócz announced in Buda (q.v.) on April 16, 1514. But this undertaking fizzled, as the crusading peasant armies, led by György Dózsa (q.v.), refused to fight the Turks (q.v.). Instead, they turned against their own lords, thus precipitating the so-called "Dózsa Peasant Revolution" (q.v.). Following the suppression of this uprising—for which the Hungarian lords blamed Bakócz—the latter lost much of his prestige. He was even censured by the national diet (q.v.). Bakócz then withdrew into semiretirement to Esztergom and died soon thereafter in partial disgrace. A man of humble birth, Bakócz rose to power and accumulated wealth mostly through illegitimate means. Like most Renaissance personalities, he was totally amoral. Yet, at the same time, he was also a powerful patron of the arts.

BALATON. Hungary's and Central Europe's largest lake, located in the center of Trans-Danubia (q.v.), which during the Turkish times (q.v.) served as a frontier region between the Ottoman (q.v.) and the Habsburg Empires (q.v.). Lake Balaton's northern shore is dotted with mountain castles and fortifications in the midst of one of Hungary's best wine-growing regions. In the post-World War II (q.v.) period the lake was developed into an international resort, especially for tourists from Germany, Italy, and, to a lesser degree, from the countries of Eastern and Southeastern Europe.

BALATONSZÁRSZÓ see **SZÁRSZÓ.**

BALKANS [BALKAN PENINSULA]. The peninsula to the south of Historic Hungary (q.v.), between the Black Sea (q.v.) and the Adriatic Sea (q.v.). Its southern protrusion is the Greek Peninsula, which is bounded by the Aegean and Ionian Seas. The Balkans had been an area of interest and expansion for the Hungarians ever since their conquest of the Carpathian Basin (q.v.). During the 11th through the 15th centuries, they usually controlled its northern fringes, where they conquered established states such as Croatia, Bosnia, and portions of Serbia. They also established defensive Banats (q.v.) there against the Byzantine (q.v.) and the Ottoman Empires (q.v.).

BALOGH, ÁDÁM (1665-1711). One of Prince Francis Rákóczi's (q.v.) top generals, and the only one of peasant birth, in the Rákóczi War of Liberation (1703-11) (q.v.). Balogh was captured by the Habsburg Imperial Armies in 1710 and executed in 1711. Because of his close relationship with the common folk of Hungary, he is a frequent subject of Hungarian folk songs and folk ballads.

BAN [BÁN, BANUS, BÁNOK]. Derived from the Avar-Turkic word meaning "rich," this was the title of the governors of medieval Croatia (q.v.), who were appointed by the Hungarian kings after Dalmatian Croatia had become an associated state of the Kingdom of Hungary (1091/1102-1918) (q.v.). In the course of the 12th and 13th centuries, this title was also awarded to the governors of various other South Slavic lands that at one time or another became provinces of Hungary. In consequence of the Ottoman Turkish (q.v.) advances in the 15th and early 16th centuries, most of these southern banats ceased to exist. Thus, after the Battle of Mohács of 1526 (q.v.), only the ban of Croatia-Slavonia functioned. The title of *ban* was also used by the governor of Croatia in the period between the Hungaro-Croatian Compromise of 1868 (q.v.) and the collapse of the Austro-Hungarian Empire (q.v.) in 1918.

BANAT OF TEMESVÁR see TEMESVÁR, BANAT OF.

BANATS [BÁNSÁG, BÁNSÁGOK]. Provinces or associated states governed by *bans* appointed by the kings of Hungary. Medieval Hungarian banats included Dalmatia (q.v.), Croatia (q.v.), Slavonia (q.v.), Bosnia (q.v.), Ozora, Só, Macsó, Barancs, Kucsó, and Szörény (q.v.). Others were formed towards the end of the Turkish occupation (q.v.), the best known among them being the Banat of Temesvár (q.v.) that remained in Turkish hands until the

Treaty of Passarowitz in 1718 (q.v.). By the 19th and 20th centuries, this section of the former Great Hungarian Plain (q.v.)—borderedby the Tisza (q.v.), Danube (q.v.), and the Maros Rivers—was simply referred to as "Bánát." The Treaty of Trianon of 1920 (q.v.) divided this province between Romania (q.v.) and Yugoslavia (q.v.).

BANDÉRIUM   [BANDERIA].   A component of the late medieval Hungarian military organizational system. The term is derivedfrom the Italian "bandiera" (banner with a coat of arms), probably brought to Hungary by the armies of Louis the Great (q.v.) that had invaded the Kingdom of Naples several times in the mid-14th century. It replaced the "vexillum" (flag) used by the Árpádian kings (q.v.). A bandérium was a military formation under a single military leader, usually a powerful baron, who gathered his forces under his own family banner and coat of arms. By the 15th century, this system of individual baronial armies expanded to many members of the wealthy landed nobility (q.v.) who originally were not members of the baronial group (q.v.). Collectively known as the "bannered lords" *(domini banderiati; zászlósurak),* they held considerable political and military power, especially in times of weak monarchs.

BÁNFFY, BARON DEZSŐ (1843-1911). A member of the ruling Liberal Party (q.v.), Speaker of the Parliament (1892-95), and Hungary's prime minister (r.1895-99), Bánffy was known for his irreconcilable opposition to all liberal reforms. These included various antiminority and antiworking class measures, as well as the breaking up of parliamentary opposition (1896). His first two years as prime minister were spent in preparing Hungary (q.v.) and Budapest (q.v.) for the country's Millennium (1896) (q.v.), with the result that during those years Budapest was built into a world-class metropolis. After the millennial celebrations, Bánffy's tyrannical personality brought him into an open conflict with the Hungarian Parliament (q.v.), which ultimately led to his resignation. He returned to politics in 1904 under the flag of the newly founded New Party *(Új Párt),* which, however, did not prove to be a lasting force in Hungarian politics. Bánffy retired again in 1906. Both of his important works reflect his irreconcilable approach to the national minority question: *Hungarian Nationality Policy [Magyar nemzetiségi politika]* (1902), and *About the Croatian Question [A horvát kérdésről]* (1907).

BANGHA, BÉLA (1880-1940). A Jesuit publicist and politician, and one of interwar Hungary's (q.v.) most influential spokesmen of the so-called "Christian National Idea" (q.v.). Bangha was a powerful orator and writer, and used his communication skills to combat all leftist ideas and movements, as well as to propagate his conservative nationalist and partially anti-Semitic views. To further his views, in 1913 he established the periodical *Hungarian Culture [Magyar Kultúra]* (1913-23), in 1918 he founded the Catholic "Central Publishing House" *(Központi Sajtóvállalat),* and in the early 1930s he served as the editor-in-chief of the four-volume *Catholic Encyclopedia (Katolikus Lexikon)* (1931-33). Bangha was also the moving spirit of the "Congregation of Mary" *(Mária Kongregáció)* movement in Hungary, and while in Rome (1923-26), he edited the congregation's periodical, *Actes Ordinata.* He wrote hundreds of articles in dozens of journals and newspapers, and also authored about two dozen books on contemporary social and religious issues. His most important works include: *Personality Sketches from the Life of the Catholic Church (Jellemrajzok a Katolikus Egyház életéből)* (1909), *Organizing Our Spiritual Life and the Congregation of Mary (Hitéleti szervezkedésünk és a Kongregáció)* (1915), *The Rebuilding of Hungary and Christianity (Magyarország újjáépítése és a kereszténység)* (1920), *The Jesuit Order and its Enemies (A Jezsuita rend és ellenségei)* (1928), *Catholicism and the Jews (Katolicizmus és a zsidóság)* (1933), and the German-language work *Light on the Jewish Question (Klärung in der Judenfrage)* (1934). To further his goal abroad, Bangha also visited many of the emigré Hungarian communities in North and South America (1922, 1934), and then described his experiences in two separate books: *My Mission to America (Amerikai missziós körutam)* (1923), and *Under the Southern Cross (Dél keresztje alatt)* (1934).

BÁNK [BÁNK BÁN] (13th c.). Generally known as "Bánk Bán"—the latter being one of his official titles—Bánk is widely known because he was made into the hero of József Katona's (1791-1830) drama of the same name (1814) that deals with the assassination of Queen Gertrude in 1213. Before becoming the Steward of the Queen's Household *(királynéi udvarbíró)* in 1211-12 and Hungary's palatine *(nádor]* (q.v.) in 1212-13, Bánk served as the *ispán (comes)* (q.v.) of half a dozen counties, and also as the *bán* (q.v.) of Croatia-Slavonia (1208-09; 1217-18). In 1213 Bánk was a participant, but not the leader of the conspiracy, that led to the assassination of Queen Gertrude, the first wife of King Andrew II (q.v.) and mother of King Béla IV (q.v.). She was disposed of because of her preference for foreigners to the detriment of the native aristocracy (q.v.). Although escaping capital punishment, Bánk was removed from office and much later suffered the loss of all his estates. Katona's drama attributes Bánk's participation in the conspiracy to the seduction of his wife by the Queen's brother, Otto of Merania (Merano, South Tyrol). This, however, is an unsubstantiated claim that first appeared in late-13th-century Austrian chronicles.

BAPTISTS. This Christian denomination was founded in England in 1609, and is based on some of the views of the 16th-century Anabaptists (q.v.). The Baptist Church was first organized in Hungary (q.v.) in the mid 19th century and given legal recognition in 1905. Although achieving equality with all the other religious denominations in 1947, it too had to suffer the consequences of the communist takeover (q.v.). The Baptists became active again with Billy Graham's visits during the 1980s, and especially after the collapse of communism (q.v.) at the end of that decade. During the critical decade of the 1980s, their most prominent spokesman was the Hungarian-American clergyman-physician, Alexander Haraszti (b.1920), who accompanied Billy Graham to Hungary, as well as to several other Soviet bloc countries.

BARCSAY [BARCSAI], PRINCE ÁKOS (1610-61). Appointed prince of Transylvania (r.1658-60) during the last three years of

Prince George Rákóczi II's (q.v.) contested reign. A scion of a prominent Transylvanian Hungarian family, Barcsay served in various high offices during the reigns of George Rákóczi I and II (q.v.). In 1657, while George Rákóczi II was absent on his Polish campaign, he served as the latter's viceroy in Transylvania (q.v.). After the Turks (q.v.) deposed Rákóczi in the fall of 1657 for his involvement in the Polish War, Grand Vizier Mehmet Köprülü (q.v.) appointed Barcsay in his place. Following Rákóczi's death in 1660, Barcsay resigned in favor of the newly elected János Kemény (q.v.). Yet Kemény still had him assassinated in the summer of 1661.

BÁRDOSSY, LÁSZLÓ (1890-1946). Hungarian politician with rightist political convictions who was Hungary's prime minister (1941-42) at the time of the country's joining World War II (q.v.). Starting his career in 1913, Bárdossy served in various capacities in the Hungarian Ministry of Culture and Education, and in the Ministry of Foreign Affairs. Between 1930 and 1941 he occupied diplomatic posts in London and Bucharest. In 1941, he was named in rapid succession the foreign minister (February 4) and prime minister (April 3) of Hungary. Because of his strong pro-German leanings, Bárdossy had a role in assisting the German attack against Yugoslavia (q.v.) (April 6), and he also bears much responsibility for Hungary's declaration of war against the Soviet Union (June 27), which dragged the country into the war. Bárdossy's name is likewise linked to the Third Jewish Law (q.v.) (August 8) as well as to the so-called "Bloodbath of Újvidék" (January 21-25, 1942), whose perpetrators he permitted to flee to Germany (q.v.). Because of growing disagreements between Regent Horthy (q.v.) and Bárdossy, the latter was forced to resign on March 7, 1942. But he continued to pursue a vocal pro-German orientation right up to the end of the war. Following World War II Bárdossy was tried, condemned, and executed as a war criminal (January 10, 1946).

BARON [BARONES, BÁRÓ]. Originally the title of Western European feudal lords, who were vassals of the king. In Hungary this title was first used in the early 13th century in reference to owners of large estates who had been appointed to the highest offices in the royal administration. Among them were the palatine (q.v.), the lord chief justice (q.v.), the royal treasurer (q.v.), the *voievod (vajda)*(q.v.) of Transylvania (q.v.), and the *bans* (q.v.) of various associated provinces or banats (q.v.). In the 14th and 15th centuries under the Anjou (q.v.) and Luxemburg (q.v.) dynasties, only the most powerful regional lords were counted as barons, who usually formed themselves into "Baronial Leagues" (q.v.). Starting with the 15th century, the title "baron" was beginning to be awarded by the king as a sign of royal recognition, without appointment to any specific royal office. Starting in the 16th century this title became hereditary within certain families. In the 18th century it was also made available to those who were awarded the Order of Maria Theresa or the Order of St. Stephen, established specifically to recognize political fidelity to the Habsburgs (q.v.). During Austro-Hungarian dualism (1867-1918) (q.v.), a number of successful families—among them recently assimilated Jews (q.v.)—were also awarded this title as a sign of royal recognition for their achievements in industry, business, scholarship and the arts.

BARONIAL LEAGUES [BÁRÓI LIGÁK] (14th-15th c.). These were alliances of powerful landowning aristocrats during the age of the Anjous (q.v.), Luxemburgs (q.v.), early Jagellonians (q.v.), and the early Habsburgs (q.v.). The baronial leagues came into being in times of domestic crises. During the weakening of royal powers, such powerful families as the Bebek, Cillei (q.v.), Garai, Horváti, Hunyadi (q.v.), Kanizsai, and the Lackfi clans united into frequently shifting and often rival temporary alliances. With the consolidation of royal power by King Matthias Corvinus (q.v.) after 1458, these baronial leagues all disintegrated.

BAROQUE. Baroque refers to the artistic style and spirituality of the age that followed the Renaissance (q.v.). This trend began in late 16th-century Italy and Spain and lasted in many European countries until the second half of the 18th century. Its social and political foundations included the Catholic Counter-Reformation (q.v.) and monarchical absolutism. Its most recognizable features were mobility, complex spatiality, richness of colors and forms, formalism, and overdecoration to the point of grotesque. These features appeared mostly in architecture and the plastic arts. In Hungary, the Baroque art and spirituality appeared only in the second half of the 17th century and survived to the very end of the 18th century. Its most important visible features manifested themselves in architecture and literature.

BAROSS, GÁBOR (1848-92). One of the noted exponents of Hungary's modernization and industrialization during the Dualist Period (q.v.). In addition to various lesser offices, during the last six years of his life Baross served as his country's minister of transportation (1886-89) and then minister of commerce (1889-92). In these capacities he nationalized and modernized Hungary's railroads, developed the country's sea shipping via the Hungarian port of Fiume (Rijeka) (q.v.), and also modernized its postal and telegraph system. While working for these goals, Baross often came into conflict with Austrian financial interests, earning him much criticism from the western half of the Dual Monarchy (q.v.).

BARTÓK, BÉLA (1881-1945). An internationally acclaimed Hungarian composer, pianist, and music scholar. Ever since 1905 Bartók was involved in the study of folk music, which he collected in contemporary Northern Hungary (q.v.), Transylvania (q.v.), and even in North Africa. In addition to the music of his own people, he was especially interested in Slovak (q.v.) and Romanian (q.v.) folk music. Between 1914 and 1919 he wrote a number of ballets and operas, while after 1920 he devoted much of his energy to worldwide concert tours and to the cultivation of folk music. Bartók left Hungary in 1940 as a form of protest against the country's rightward drift. He died in New York in relative poverty. His remains were returned to Hungary in 1988. Bartók's pioneering work in folk music enriched 20th-century classical music significantly,

while his emigration was an act of major political protest against
the inhumanity of Nazism.

BASTA, GEORGE [GYÖRGY BÁSTA] (1544-1607). A
Habsburg Imperial General of Italian birth, who is known for his
unusual cruelty in Hungary (q.v.) and Transylvania (q.v.) during the
second half of the Fifteen Years' War (1591-1606) (q.v.).
Recognizing the destructiveness of the German mercenaries, in 1599
he proposed that they be replaced by a permanent Hungarian standing
army. Yet his presence in Transylvania is still remembered as the
most vicious and destructive among all rulers. He is also recalled by
the so-called "Basta wagons" *(Básta szekerek)*, carriages that were
drawn by the peasants themselves in the absence of the draft animals
that had been killed off. A military leader of some note, Basta
produced two significant works on military strategy: *The Master of
the General Camp (Il maëstro di campo generale)* (1606), and
Leadership of the Light Cavalry (Governo della cavalleria leggiera)
(1612). His collected papers were published later under the title
*General George Basta's Papers and Correspondence (Básta György
hadvezér levelezése és iratai)* (2 volumes, 1901-13).

BÁTHORY, PRINCE ANDREW [ANDRÁS] (1566-99).
Cardinal of the Catholic Church (q.v.) and, after one of the several
resignations of Sigismund Báthory (q.v.), briefly, the prince of
Transylvania (r.1599). Having grown up in the Polish royal court
of his uncle, King Stephen Báthory (q.v.), Andrew joined the ranks
of the clergy early in life and became the bishop of Varmia while
still a child. He reached the rank of a cardinal at the age of eighteen.
In March 1599 Andrew Báthory replaced his erratic nephew,
Sigismund Báthory, as the prince of Transylvania. But given the
chaotic conditions, his reign proved to be a very brief one. He was
killed by a group of *Székelys* (q.v.), who sided with the invading
Michael the Brave (r.1593-1601) of Wallachia (q.v.).

BÁTHORY, PRINCE CHRISTOPHER [KRISTÓF] (1530-
81). Brother of Stephen Báthory (q.v.) and viceroy of Transylvania

(q.v.) who, during the first half of the latter's rule in Poland (q.v.), was the de facto prince of Transylvania (r.1576-81). According to contemporary accounts, Christopher Báthory's reign was one of the best periods in Transylvania's history. His rule was characterized by wisdom, moderation, and justice. Báthory was able to maneuver between the Habsburgs (q.v.) and the Ottoman Turks (q.v.). Sultan Murad III (r.1574-95) viewed him as an honorable and reliable vassal, and for this reason forbade the pasha of Temesvár (q.v.) to undertake plundering expeditions into his principality.

BÁTHORY, ERZSÉBET [ELIZABETH] (1560-1614). The aunt of Prince Gabriel Báthory (q.v.) of Transylvania (q.v.) and the most notorious member of the Báthory family (q.v.), who is also known as the "Vampire Countess of Hungary." Elizabeth Báthory was a sexual deviate and a sadist, who in the decade before her imprisonment is known to have tortured many scores of young peasant girls to death. Condemned in 1611 by Hungary's highest Palatine Court, Elizabeth Báthory spent the last three years of her life immured in the castle of Csejthe in Lower Hungary (q.v.), which had been the site of many of her foul deeds. The peasants of Csejthe believed that she continued to haunt the region for many decades after her death in the form of a vampire.

BÁTHORY FAMILY. One of Hungary's great historical families, which descended from the Gutkeled Clan. The name Báthory was assumed by one of their better known ancestors, Bereczk (1277-1332), in the late 13th century after his estate of Bátor. Two of his sons, Lukács and János, were the progenitors of the two branches of the family: Lukács of the Ecsedi branch and János of the Somlyói branch. Although forming two distinct families, the members of the two branches continued to intermarry and both of them rose to great political prominence between the late 15th and the late 17th centuries. They produced bishops, cardinals, lord chief justices of Hungary (q.v.), *voievods* and princes of Transylvania (q.v.), and even a king of Poland. The last member of the Báthory family was Zsófia

(Sophie) (1629-80), wife of Prince George Rákóczi II (q.v.) and mother of Prince Ferenc Rákóczi I (q.v.)

BÁTHORY, PRINCE GABRIEL [GÁBOR] (1589-1613). Prince of Transylvania (r.1608-13), who ascended the throne with the help of the *hajdú* (q.v.) mercenaries in the aftermath of the Fifteen Years War (1591-1606) (q.v.). Gabriel replaced his weak and vacillating relative Sigismund Báthory (q.v.), and could have become a successful ruler had his violent personality and openly immoral life not turned the Transylvanian Hungarian aristocracy (q.v.) and the Saxon burghers (q.v.) against him. In the period between 1610 and 1613 he also antagonized both the Ottoman Turks (q.v.) and the Habsburgs (q.v.). In order to save his throne, by 1613 he would have been willing to make concessions to the Ottoman Empire (q.v.), including giving up the fortress city of Várad (Nagyvárad) (q.v.). The proposed concessions, however, so enraged his *hajdú* supporters that they killed him.

BÁTHORY, PRINCE SIGISMUND [ZSIGMOND] (1572-1613). Prince of Transylvania (r.1586-97, 1598-99, 1601, 1601-02), son of Prince Christopher Báthory (q.v.), and nephew of King Stephen Báthory (q.v.) of Poland (q.v.). Sigismund Báthory ascended the throne of Transylvania after the death of his uncle, who had also been the absentee prince of Transylvania (q.v.). Although his principality was a vassal state of the Ottoman Empire (q.v.), Prince Sigismund broke with the Porte (q.v.) in 1594, and then allied himself with Emperor/King Rudolph II (q.v.). For this he was made prince of the Holy Roman Empire (q.v.) and given a Habsburg (q.v.) archduchess in marriage (1595). He then joined the Habsburgs in their protracted struggle against the Ottoman Empire (1591-1606). In 1597 he transferred Transylvania to Emperor Rudolph in exchange for the Principality of Oppeln-Raitbor in the Holy Roman Empire (q.v.). Having second thoughts about this exchange, he reclaimed his Transylvanian throne (1598), only to resign once more in 1599 in favor of his uncle, Cardinal Andrew Báthory (q.v.). Soon after Andrew's death (October 31, 1599),

Sigismund assumed the Transylvanian throne once more (1601-02), only to resign again. After this, he lived in Bohemia (q.v.) under the shadow of the Habsburgs, who in 1605 supported his candidacy to the Transylvanian throne against the claims of Stephen Bocskai (q.v.). But on this occasion Sigismund declined to be drawn into the Transylvanian quagmire. In 1611 the Habsburgs accused him of a political conspiracy, for which he was imprisoned for about a year in the Royal Castle of Prague (q.v.). Sigismund Báthory was a man of unstable personality. His chaotic foreign and domestic policy did considerable harm to Transylvania and its relationship with the surrounding states.

BÁTHORY, PRINCE/KING STEPHEN [ISTVÁN] (1533-86). Prince of Transylvania (r.1571-86) and King of Poland (r.1576-86), where he is known under the name *Stefan Batory*. Báthory studied at the University of Padua in Italy, and then served as a page at the court of King/Emperor Ferdinand I (q.v.). Initially (1540-63) he supported Ferdinand, but then in 1556 he shifted his allegiance to John Sigismund of Transylvania (q.v.). After the latter's death in 1571, Báthory was elected Prince of Transylvania (q.v.). He fought for the internal consolidation of his small principality, which he viewed as the last outpost of once independent Hungarian statehood. Consequently, he opposed its incorporation into the Habsburg Empire (q.v.). In 1576 Stephen Báthory was elected king of Poland, but also retained his position as prince of Transylvania. During the first five years of his kingship he relied on his brother, Christopher Báthory (q.v.) to govern Transylvania in his name. After the latter's death in 1581 he established a governing council that was headed by his nephew, Sigismund Báthory (q.v.). Even while absent, he attended to most Transylvanian affairs personally via the Transylvania Chancery that now functioned in Cracow. Stephen Báthory's unfulfilled dream was to establish a federation of Poland, Transylvania, and Hungary, and thus put an end to both Turkish and Habsburg encroachments upon the dismembered Kingdom of Hungary (q.v.). In Poland he fought for royal centralization, and also put up an effective struggle against Ivan IV the Terrible (r.1533/47-84) of Moscow, preventing the latter from establishing a foothold on the eastern Baltic region. Stephen Báthory is highly respected both by Hungarians and by Poles—the latter of whom regard him as one of their greatest kings.

BATTHYÁNY, COUNT LAJOS [LOUIS] (1806-49). A progressive statesman during the Hungarian Reform Period (1825-48) (q.v.) and Hungary's first prime minister at the time of the revolution of 1848-49 (q.v.) (r.March 17-October 2, 1848). During his extensive travels in Western Europe, Batthyány had become an admirer of Western political and social reforms, and upon having been elected to the Hungarian Diet (q.v.) in 1830, he became a vocal supporter and later one of the leaders of the so-called "opposition" that clamored for basic reforms. He became an early supporter of Lajos Kossuth (q.v.) and in 1847 was elected to the presidency of the Opposition Party (q.v.). Following the outbreak of the revolution and the introduction of the April Laws (q.v.), Batthyány was appointed to head the first Hungarian responsible government. After the revolution became radicalized, followed by a break between Hungary and King Ferdinand V (q.v.), Batthyány resigned his prime ministership and withdrew from politics. Later he returned to work toward a compromise with Austria (q.v.). In spite of these efforts, in January 1849 Prince Alfred Windischgraetz (q.v.) had him arrested for high treason. After many months of incarceration in Buda (q.v.), Pozsony (q.v.), Laibach, and Olmütz, Batthyány was condemned to death. Although even the court recommended clemency, General Haynau (q.v.) had him executed on October 6, 1849, and thereby made him into a martyr of the Hungarian Revolution.

BATU KHAN (d.1255). Grandson of Genghis Khan (1162-1227), founder of the Empire of the Golden Horde (r.1243-56) (q.v.), and the leader of the Mongol armies that conquered and destroyed Hungary (q.v.) in 1241-42. As the son of Genghis Khan's oldest son, Juchi, in 1225 Batu had inherited the western quarter of the Mongol Empire that stretched from the Aral and Caspian Seas to the north and the west. In pursuance of the orders of his uncle, the Great

Khan Ogotay (r.1228-41), in 1237-40 Batu conquered the East Slavic lands of the former Kievan State (q.v.). He followed this up by the temporary conquest of Poland (1240-41) and Hungary (1241-42), and then—after being unable to gain the office of the Great Khan—by the foundation of the Khanate of the Golden Horde and its capital city of Saray on the Lower Volga. While Batu never returned to Hungary, his impact on Hungarian historical developments was immeasurable. His descendants continued to dominate the East Slavs (q.v.) for over two centuries.

BAVARIA [BAYERN]. One of the five original duchies in what later became the Holy Roman Empire (q.v.), Bavaria had been incorporated into Charlemagne's Carolingian Empire already in 788, and then ruled by members of the Carolingian dynasty until 911. The Carolingians were succeeded by various members of the Saxon and the Swabian dynasties, and then in 1070, by the Welf family (1070-1180), which competed for the Imperial crown with the Hohenstaufen dynasty. In 1180 Bavaria was gained by the Wittelsbach family (1180-1918), which ruled it until the end of World War I, when Bavaria became a federal state of the new German republic. Hungarians have been in close—both friendly and antagonistic—contacts with the Bavarians already at the time of the Árpádian conquest (q.v.) of Hungary (q.v.). This relationship was deepened by the frequent intermarriage between the Bavarian and Hungarian ruling families that began with King St. Stephen (r.997/1000-38), who married Gisella (q.v.), the daughter of Prince Henry II (r.955-77). Later the Hungarians and the Bavarians often allied themselves with each other against the emperors, even though Bavaria had always remained part of the Holy Roman Empire. Many of the German immigrants to Hungary also originated in Bavaria, and Bavarian cultural influences were pervasive in Hungary through much of the Middle Ages and the Early Modern Period. Today Bavaria is the largest state (land) in modern Germany (27,217 sq. mi.) with a population of eleven million. Its capital city Munich (München) is a city of 1.3 million and one of the important cultural centers of Central Europe.

BAY, ZOLTÁN (1900-93). One of Hungary's leading physicists, who—after serving as professor of physics at the University of Szeged (1930-35) and then professor of nuclear physics a the Technical University of Budapest (1935-48)—spent over four decades in the United States (1948-93). He was professor of nuclear physics at George Washington University (1948-55), and then section head at the National Bureau of Standards (1955-72). Bay was one of the developers of radar astronomy, which made him into a potential Nobel Laureate. In addition to scores of scholarly articles on his pioneering research, Bay is the author of a number of books, among them *Atomic Physics (Atommagfizika)* (1946), *From the Moon Echo to the New Meter (A holdvisszhangtól az új méterig)* collection of translated western language articles (1985), *Selected Studies (Válogatott tanulmányok)* (1989), and *Life is Stronger (Az élet erősebb)* reminiscences (1990).

BEATRIX OF ARAGON (1457-1508). The second wife of King Matthias Corvinus (q.v.) and the daughter of the Neapolitan King Ferdinand of Aragon. Beatrix became Hungary's queen through her marriage to King Matthias in 1476. During the next fourteen years she had a significant role in the influx of high Renaissance culture (q.v.) to Hungary, and especially in spreading this culture at the royal court of Buda (q.v.). Having remained childless in this marriage, King Matthias selected his illegitimate son, János Corvin (Johannes Corvinus) (q.v.) as his successor. Beatrix, however, wanted the throne for herself. Thus, after Matthias's death in 1490, she supported the claim of the Czech ruler King Vladislav (Úlászló II in Hungary) (q.v.) with the hope of a marriage. A mock marriage did in fact take place with the collusion of Bishop (later Cardinal Archbishop) Tamás Bakócz (q.v.), which helped to consolidate King Vladislav's position, but ended Beatrix's chances in Hungary. She retired to Italy, where she was forced to witness the fall of her family. Queen Beatrix died in Naples in 1508, where she is buried at the Monastery of San Pietro.

BEG see BEY.

BÉKEFI, REMIG (1858-1924). A noted Hungarian historian of the Positivist School (q.v.), who was a pioneer of Hungarian cultural history *(Kulturgeschichte)*. After two decades as professor of cultural history at the University of Budapest (1893-1911), Békefi became the abbot of the Cistercian Monastery of Zirc. Although this made him leave academic life, he continued his historical scholarship and produced a number of additional significant works. Most of his important monographs deal with the history of Hungarian abbeys, churches, castles, and schools. His best known works include the multivolume histories of the Abbeys of Pilis (1891-92), Cikádor' (1894), and Pásztó (1898-1902), and such major syntheses as *The History of the Cistercian Order in Hungary (A cisterci rend története Magyarországban)*(1896), *Religious and Moral Life in Hungary under the Árpáds (Vallásos és erkölcsös élet Magyarországon az Árpádok alatt)* (1896), *The History of Slavery in Hungary (A rabszolgaság története Magyarországon)* (1901), *The History of Education in Hungary from 1000 to 1883 (Az iskolázás története Magyarországon 1000-1883-ig)* (1907), *The Árpáds, as the Organizers of the Christian Church and Culture in Hungary (Az Árpádok, mint a keresztény egyház és művelődés szervezői)* (1908), and *The History of the Chapter Schools in Hungary till 1540 (A káptalani iskolák története Magyarországon 1540-ig)* (1910).

BÉL, MÁTYÁS [MATTHIAS] (1684-1749). One of 18th-century Hungary's greatest historians and polyhistors, and the transplanter of the German *Staatenkunde (State Science)* to Hungary (q.v.). As the purest Hungarian exponent of that school, Bél undertook a complete survey of the Hungarian state—including its historical, political, constitutional, legal, administrative, social, economic, and cultural development. He began to publish the results of his research in several multivolume works, among them the *Sources on Hungarian History (Adparatus ad historiam Hungariae)* (1735-46), and the *Historical-Geographical Description of Modern Hungary (Notatia Hungariae novae historico-geographica)* (1735-42). Although publishing dozens of volumes, most of Bél's scholarship remained in manuscript form. His impact upon contemporary Hungarian historical scholarship and historical thinking, however, was decisive.

BÉLA I (c.1016-63). King of Hungary (r.1060-63), son of Prince Vazul (Vászoly) the Blind (q.v.), and brother and successor of King Andrew I (q.v.). After spending a decade and a half abroad following the blinding of his father in the early 1030s, Béla returned to Hungary in 1048 to help his brother in the latter's struggle against Holy Roman Emperor Henry III (r.1039-56). His successful defeat of the invading German armies in 1051 and 1052 made him very popular, and he was viewed both by King Andrew I and the people in general as the heir to the throne. But the birth of Andrew's son, Salamon (q.v.), who was named heir to the throne in 1058, altered the relationship between the two brothers. The resulting military conflict ended in King Andrew's death and Béla's accession to the throne at the end of 1060. Béla's rise to power was followed by an another pagan rebellion under the leadership of the son of Vata (q.v.), which he subdued. King Béla died in an accident while preparing to defend his throne against Salamon, who was supported by the Emperor Henry.

BÉLA II [BÉLA THE BLIND] (c.1108-41). King of Hungary (r.1131-41) and the nephew of King Coloman (q.v.). Having been blinded by his own uncle at the age of five, along with his rebellious father Prince Álmos (c.1075-1129), Béla II ascended the throne after the death of his cousin, King Stephen II (q.v.). Being unable to rule personally, much of the power fell into the hands of his wife, Queen Ilona (Helena), the daughter of Prince Uroš Nemanja (r.1130-c.1140) of Serbia. In 1131 Béla II and his wife were instrumental in punishing the lords implicated in his own and his father's blinding (sixty-eight of whom were butchered at the Diet of Arad), while in 1132 he defeated Prince Boris (1113-55), his illegitimate cousin and rival for the Hungarian throne. In the mid-1130s Béla II extended Hungary's rule over much of Bosnia (q.v.) and Rama (q.v.), and in 1137 he named his five-year-old son "Prince of Bosnia," while he himself assumed the title "King of Rama." Béla II also incorporated parts of Dalmatia (q.v.), including its capital Spalato (Split) into his kingdom. King Béla II died soon after the death of his energetic wife. He left two daughters and three sons, all three of whom became kings of Hungary. He was buried in the royal capital of Székesfehérvár (q.v.).

BÉLA III (1148-96). King of Hungary (r.1172-96), grandson of Béla II the Blind (q.v.), son of Géza II (q.v.), and brother of Stephen III (q.v.). Based on an 1163 agreement between Byzantine Emperor Manuel I (r.1143-80) and King Stephen III, Prince Béla was sent to the Byzantine court in Constantinople (q.v.) at the age of fifteen. There he was renamed Alexios, betrothed to Manuel's daughter Maria, and named heir to the throne of the Byzantine Empire (q.v.). Upon the birth of Manuel's son in 1169, however, Béla's betrothal and position as the heir ended. After the death of his brother in 1172, he was sent home to assume the Hungarian throne. Béla III was crowned with papal support in early 1173, after which he pursued a steady pro-Roman policy. Although inheriting a tradition of conflict with the Byzantine Empire, he declined to attack the Byzantines until Emperor Manuel's death in 1180. In that year he was unsuccessful in his effort to gain the Byzantine throne, but during 1180-82 he did regain Sirmium (q.v.) and Dalmatia (q.v.) for Hungary (q.v.), while after his 1191 war with Venice he also forced the the Dalmatian cities to accept Hungarian rule. In 1188 Béla III intervened in Kievan affairs and temporarily conqueredGalicia (q.v.) for Hungary. The following year he saw Emperor Frederick Barbarossa's (r.1152-90) crusaders through Hungary, and at the same time permitted his rebellious brother, the imprisoned Prince Géza, to join the crusaders in their quest for the Holy Land. After the death of his first wife, Agnes Anna of Antioch, in 1184, Béla III married Margaret Capet of France, which increased French cultural influences in Hungary. Béla III was responsible for introducing the use of written records in royal administration as well as for the establishment of the first permanent Hungarian Royal or Court Chancery (q.v.). Béla III was also a patron of industry, commerce, and the arts. Hungary's first extant chronicle, the *Gesta Hungarorum* (q.v.) by Anonymus (q.v.), was compiled under his rule. He strengthened central power in Hungary, yet at the same time granted large estates to his favorites. Béla III died in 1196, leaving three sons and three daughters. Two of his sons, Emeric (q.v.) and Andrew II (q.v.), became kings of Hungary. He was buried in the royal capital of Székesfehérvár (q.v.). Five centuries later, in 1898, he was reinterred in the Matthias Cathedral of Budapest (q.v.). Béla III is viewed as one of Hungary's most significant medieval rulers.

BÉLA IV (1206-70). One of the best known kings of Hungary (r.1235-70) who is also known as "the second founder" because of his successful rebuilding of Hungary (q.v.) after the Mongol Conquest of 1241-42 (q.v.). The son of the King Andrew II (q.v.) whose name is linked with the Golden Bull of Hungary (q.v.), and of Gertrude of Merania (Merano or South Tyrol), who had been assassinated by a group of Hungarian lords in 1213, Béla was crowned king already in his father's lifetime in 1214. Following his crowning he held the title of "junior king" (q.v.) and soon came into conflict with his weak and vacillating father. Béla resented his father's lukewarm handling of his mother's assassins, his squandering of royal estates, and the steady decline of royal power because of the terms of the Golden Bull of 1222. His initial clashes with his father led to his flight to Austria (q.v.) in 1223. Father and son soon reconciled, however, after which Béla was appointed the governor of Slavonia (q.v.) and then of Transylvania (q.v.). In those positions he tried to reclaim some of the squandered royal property, but this policy led to a new conflict with his father in 1228. During the late 1220s and early 1230s Béla initiated a policy of conquest toward the Balkans (q.v.). He fought against the Cumans (q.v.) and the Bulgarians (q.v.), and in 1230 founded the military Banat of Szörény (q.v.) in the western part of what later became Wallachia (q.v.). Following King Andrew's death in 1235, he ascended the throne as Béla IV and promptly undertook to punish those implicated in his mother's murder. He also undertook to reclaim royal property handed out by his father. These efforts, however, were soon halted by the impending Mongol invasion, the news of which was first brought to Hungary by the Dominican friar Julianus (q.v.) in 1236.

In 1239 Béla permitted a tribe of Turkic Cumans (q.v.), fleeing from the Mongols, to settle in Hungary under the leadership of Khan Kuthen (q.v.). He was hoping to use them as auxiliaries against the Mongols. The widespread distrust of the Cumans among the Hungarian lords, however, led to Kuthen's assassination in 1242. After Kuthen's death, the Cumans joined the Mongols in their onslaught against the Hungarians and then moved down to the Balkans. The Mongols appeared in 1241 under the leadership of Khan Batu (q.v.), and defeated the Hungarian forces in a series of battles. The most serious was the Battle of Mohi (q.v.) on April 11-12, 1241, where the Hungarian Royal Army of 60,000 was completely annihilated. King Béla first fled to Prince Frederick Babenberg (q.v.) of Austria (q.v.), who took him captive and exacted ransom from him. Then via Zagreb and Spalato, he fled to the Island of Trau in the Adriatic Sea (q.v.). Béla IV was saved only by the news of the death of the Great Khan Ogotay (r.1227-41) in Mongolia, which prompted Khan Batu to speed back to the east to defend his interests in the upcoming elections.

After the withdrawal of the Mongols, King Béla immediately set to work to rebuild the country. He encouraged immigration to repopulate the Hungary, undertook a program of castle building on royal estates, ordered cities to surround themselves with masonry fortifications, encouraged the development of a well-heeled burgher class, and, in direct opposition to his earlier policies, began to grant lands to those lords who were willing to build stone fortresses on their estates. Simultaneously, Béla initiated a policy of marriage alliances with several of the surrounding dynasties and also recalled the Cumans to strengthen his hand in case of a new Mongol invasion. In 1246 he took his revenge against Frederick Babenberg of Austria, who died in the Battle of Leitha (June 15, 1246). He also reconquered those western provinces that he had been forced to relinquish for his freedom in 1241.

In light of the end of the Babenberg dynasty, Béla IV engaged in a lengthy struggle with Ottokar II (r.1253-78) of Bohemia (q.v.) for the Austrian possessions. For a while he gained control over Styria (1250-61), but then in 1261 he was forced to give it up to Ottokar.

The last phase of King Béla IV's life was taken up by the struggle against his rebellious son, Stephen V (q.v.), who had already been crowned "junior king" in 1245. In 1258 Stephen became the governor of Styria, but in 1262 he rose against his father, after which he became the co-ruler of the country's eastern half, including the Trans-Tisza region and Transylvania (q.v.).

Following a second conflict in 1264-65, Béla IV was progressively pushed into the background. In 1267 he and his son issued a joint Royal Patent in which, for the first time, they recognized the country's upper administrative-military class *[servientes regis = royal servants]* (q.v.) as a noble order, who were to be represented in every annual "diet" (q.v.) by two or three of their kind from every county. Such a diet was promptly held at Esztergom (q.v.). King Béla IV spent his final days in company of his daughter, the future St. Margaret (q.v.) of Hungary, in the Dominican Abbey on an island on the Danube (q.v.) (today's St. Margaret's Island in Budapest). He was buried in the Church of the Minorites at Esztergom (q.v.).

BELGRADE [BEOGRAD, NÁNDORFEHÉRVÁR]. Capital of Yugoslavia (1918), and, before that of Serbia, Belgrade was originally a Roman outpost under the name of *Singidunum*. Following the collapse of the Roman colonial empire, it came under the rule of the Huns (q.v.), Avars (q.v.), Bulgars (q.v.), Byzantines (q.v.), Serbians (q.v.), Hungarians (q.v.), Ottoman Turks (q.v.), Habsburgs (q.v.), and Ottoman Turks again, before it became the capital of autonomous (1816-78), later, independent Serbia (1878-1918). Its significance from the Hungarian point of view is that through much of the 12th through the early 16th century it was a Hungarian outpost under the name of *Nándorfehérvár*. It was at Belgrade where in 1456 the great Hungarian general and regent of Hungary, János Hunyadi (q.v.), defeated Sultan Mehmet the Conqueror (r.1451-81) and thus prevented the Turks from moving into Central Europe. This victory is connected with the so-called *angelus* (tolling of bells at noon), which allegedly was proclaimed by Pope Calixtus III (r.1455-58) to commemorate Hunyadi's victory.

BELLA GERANT ALII, TU, FELIX AUSTRIA, NUBE! [LET OTHERS WAGE WAR, YOU LUCKY AUSTRIA, MARRY!] This saying was allegedly coined by Emperor Maximilian I (r.1493-1519) and it defines the basic Habsburg policy, which held that it is always preferable to increase family possessions through appropriate marriages, than through risky wars. The Habsburgs (q.v.) contracted several such marriages in the late 15th and early 16th centuries, which increased their holdings to a point where Emperor Charles V (r.1519-56) was able to declare that "The sun never sets in my empire." The most important and profitable of these marriage alliances included the Burgundian marriage (1477), which gained the rich Low Countries for them, the Spanish marriage (1496), which acquired Spain and the Spanish colonies in the New World, and the Jagellonian marriage (1515), which resulted in the incorporation of Hungary and Bohemia into the Habsburg possessions.

BELOS, BAN (d.1163). Son of Prince Uroš (r.1130-c.40) of Serbia (q.v.) and the brother-in-law of King Béla II the Blind (q.v.), who, by virtue of that position, served as the ban of Croatia (q.v.) and Slavonia (q.v.) from the 1130s through the 1150s. After Béla II's death in 1141, Ban Belos became the guardian of the minor Géza II (q.v.), and for over a decade (1145-57) he also served as the palatine (q.v.) and de facto ruler of Hungary. In 1157 Belos became involved in a rebellion by the king's brother, the future Stephen III (q.v.), after which both of them had to flee for their lives. Ban Belos returned to Hungary after King Géza's death in 1162, but he could never reestablish his former influence and thus faded out of history.

BEM, JÓZEF [JOSEPH, JÓZSEF] (1794-1850). A Polish military officer, who became the most popular general in the Hungarian Revolution of 1848-49 (q.v.), and then ended his life as a Turkish pasha under the name Murad Tevfik. A graduate of the

Polish Infantry School at Cracow, as a young officer Bem participated in the Napoleonic invasion of Russia of 1812. Having been part of an anti-Russian conspiracy in 1822, after which he was imprisoned, Bem willingly joined the Polish Revolution of 1830-31, where he acquired national fame as an able artillery officer. After the defeat of that revolution he fled to Western Europe, where he lectured, wrote, and worked for the resurrection of Poland (q.v.). Bem took advantage of the upheavals of 1848 to join the revolutions in the Austrian Empire (q.v.). He arrived in Hungary (q.v.) in November 1848, and by December of that year Lajos Kossuth (q.v.) had appointed him the commander-in-chief of the Hungarian Armies in Transylvania (q.v.), where Hungary's great national poet, Sándor Petőfi (q.v.), served as his adjutant. General Bem proved to be a successful military strategist and a legendary leader whose troops viewed him as their father and called him "Father Bem" *(Bem Apó).*

Bem's and Hungary's fortunes began to change in June of 1849, when a 200,000 strong Russian Army invaded the country under the command of Prince Ivan Paskievich (1782-1856). Outmanned and overwhelmed by the Russian and Austrian forces, General Bem lost the Battle of Segesvár (July 31)—where Petőfi was killed—and then the Battle of Temesvár (August 9). After Hungary's capitulation at Világos (August 13) (q.v.), General Bem fled to the Ottoman Empire (q.v.) along with thousands of Hungarians. In order to avoid extradition to Austria, he converted pro forma to Islam and then enlisted into the Ottoman Army. He ended his life as the military governor of Syria in Aleppo. General Bem is viewed as a national hero both by the Poles (q.v.) and by the Hungarians.

BENEDICTINES   [BENEDICTINE   ORDER,   ORDO SANCTI   BENEDICTI,   BENCÉSEK].   The   first   Catholic monastic order founded in A.D. 529 by St. Benedict of Nursia (480-543), who also established the first Catholic monastery at Monte Cassino, Italy. The Benedictines had played a significant role in the spreading of Christianity and Christian culture throughout Europe, including Hungary (q.v.), which was Christianized at the turn of the millennium. They settled in Hungary in 996, when they established their first monastery at Pannonhalma (q.v.) under Prince Géza (q.v.). Following their settlement there they became involved in the religious, cultural, and political life of the nation, and while doing so they established dozens of additional monasteries. At the insistence of Emperor Joseph II (q.v.), the Benedictine Order was disbanded in 1786, but reestablished again in 1802. Following their reemergence, the Benedictines limited themselves to educational activities, which they are still pursuing today in a growing number of secondary schools. They have survived even the communist regime (1948-89), which has disbandedmost religious institutions. The center of the Hungarian branch of the Benedictines is still the Arch Abbey of Pannonhalma, headed by an arch abbot with the rank of a bishop.

BENEFICIUM [JAVADALOM]. Name of the estate granted by the ruler to a feudal vassal in return for feudal services, or, in case of the Catholic Church, the rights and privileges enjoyed by a churchman by virtue of his appointment to a specific office, such as a canon, abbot, or bishop. In case of the vassal's violation of feudal obligations, the dying out of the vassal's family, or the termination of an ecclesiastical office, the *beneficium* reverted to the monarch. In Hungary, after the regulation of the *robot* (q.v.) obligations in 1776, the high-yielding fertile lands were also referred to as *beneficium*.

BENYOVSZKY, COUNT MÓRIC ÁGOST [MAURICE AUGUST] (1741-86). One of the best known Hungarian adventurers and soldiers-of-fortune. Born into a well-to-do noble family, Benyovszky was destined for military service by virtue of his birth. His dislike of the Habsburg Imperial Army, however, soon led to his resignation and to his withdrawal to one of his estates, first in Hungary (q.v.) and then in Poland (q.v.). In the latter country he became involved in an anti-Russian nobles' rebellion (1767), which resulted in his capture (1769) and exile (1770) to Kamchatka in Eastern Siberia. Benyovszky did not remain in captivity for long. He escaped within a year with the help of the local Russian governor's daughter, who accompanied him on his journey back home via the Aleutian Islands, Alaska, Japan, Taiwan, and Macao. For a while Benyovszky ended up in French colonial service at Ile de France (today's Mauritius). From there he was sent to the island of Madagascar to conquer it for the French. While engaged in that undertaking he established such a rapport with the natives that—if we can believe his memoirs—in 1776 they elected him their "king." This earned for him the animosity of the French governor of Ile de France, which in turn led to his resignation and to his return to Europe. The French government naturally refused to acknowledge his "kingship," but his past services still earned for him the title of baron (q.v.). Leaving France disenchanted, Benyovszky returned home, where he tried to persuade Queen Maria Theresa (q.v.) and Emperor Joseph II (q.v.) to support his colonizing venture in Madagascar. They refused to do so, but in 1778 they raised him to the rank of a count (q.v.). In 1782 Benyovszky departed for America to offer his services to George Washington. Although his offer was rejected, in 1785 he was able to persuade a number of Baltimore merchants to underwrite his Madagascar venture in return for the promise of hefty financial returns. Benyovszky left for Madagascar in the same year with the 500-ton ship *Intrepid*, and upon his arrival immediately resurrected his former "kingship." But his "reign" proved to be very short. On May 23, 1786, he was attacked and killed by a French expeditionary force. Benyovszky left behind a wife and two children in Baltimore, from where they soon returned to Hungary. According to some sources, one of his sons remained in America and settled in Texas, where some of his descendants may still be living today.

BERCSÉNYI, COUNT MIKLÓS [NICHOLAS] (1665-1725). The top general of the Hungarian *kuruc* (q.v.) armies and Prince Francis Rákóczi's (q.v.) chief aide in the Rákóczi War of Liberation (1703-11) (q.v.). Before becoming an anti-Habsburg rebel, Bercsényi served in several major military and administrative posts, including that of the Habsburg military commissioner (1696-98) for Upper Hungary (q.v.). During the late 1690s he became increasingly disenchantedwith Emperor Leopold I's (q.v.) absolutism and began to plot the overthrow of Habsburg rule in Hungary. He enlisted the support of young Francis Rákóczi, whose mother, Ilona Zrínyi (q.v.), and foster father, Imre Thököly (q.v.), had been involved in an anti-Habsburg struggle from 1678 until the Peace Treaty of Karlowitz in 1699 (q.v.). When the plot was discovered in 1701, Rákóczi was arrested and Bercsényi fled to Poland. After Rákóczi's own escape, he and Bercsényi joined forces and tried to gain the support of Charles XII (r.1697-1718) of Sweden and Louis XIV (r.1643-1715) of France. Although they received nothing but promises, the Rákóczi War of Liberation did in fact break out in the spring of 1703, initiated by the oppressed peasantry of the upper Tisza (q.v.) region. From that moment on, Bercsényi was involved in every phase of the struggle, remaining Prince Rákóczi's right-hand man to the very end. When during Rákóczi's and Bercsényi's absence, Rákóczi's commander-in-chief, Count Sándor Károlyi (q.v.), negotiated the Peace Treaty of Szatmár (April 30, 1711) (q.v.), Bercsényi refused to accept its terms. Like Rákóczi, he stayed abroad. Between 1711 and 1716 he lived in Poland, but with the outbreak of the Austro-Turkish War in 1716 he moved to the Balkans (q.v.). In 1717 Bercsényi organized an unsuccessful military expedition against Habsburg Hungary (q.v.), but after the Treaty of Passarowitz (July 21, 1718) (q.v.), which ended their hopes, he joined Rákóczi in the Ottoman city of Rodostó (today's Tekir Daǧ) on the Aegean Sea. He died and was buried there in 1725, but in 1906 his remains were brought back to Hungary.

BEREGFFY [BEREGFY, BERGER], KÁROLY (1889-1946). Hungary's minister for defense in the last phase of World War II (October 16, 1944-April 4, 1945), during the regime of Ferenc Szálasi (q.v.). Before the Arrow Cross takeover on October 15, 1944, Beregffy was the commander of the Third Hungarian Army with the rank of a colonel-general. He was a dedicatedadmirer of Hitler's Germany (q.v.) and its Nazi ideology (q.v.). After the war he was repatriated from Germany, and along with other members of

Szálasi's government, he was tried and executed as a war criminal (March 12, 1946).

BEREND, IVÁN T. (b.1930). An economic historian, student of Zsigmond Pál Pach (q.v.), who, along with György Ránki (q.v.), was a young star of Marxist historiography in Hungary. During the final decade of the Kádár Regime (q.v.), however, Berend became a "Westernizer"—although somewhat more belatedly than Ránki. After receiving his degree from the University of Budapest (q.v.), Berend taught in various capacities at the University of Economics (q.v.) (1953-90), and served as the president both of the Hungarian Historical Association (q.v.) (1975-82) and of the Hungarian Academy of Sciences (q.v.) (1985-90). During the 1980s Berend was cultural adviser to the top leadership of the Hungarian Socialist Workers' Party (q.v.). After the collapse of communism (q.v.), he left Hungary (q.v.) and became a professor of history at the University of California at Los Angeles. In 1995 he was elected president of the International Association of Historians. Berend authored over a dozen books, virtually all of them on the economic history of modern Hungary (q.v.) and East Central Europe (q.v.), and the majority of them jointly with György Ránki. Several of these books are also available in English: *Hungary: A Century of Economic Development* (1974), *East Central Europe in the Nineteenth and Twentieth Centuries* (1977), *Underdevelopment and Economic Growth: Studies in Hungarian Social and Economic History* (1979), and *The European Periphery and Industrialization, 1780-1914* (1982). Berend's own books include *Capital Intensity and Development Policy* (1985), *European Economy, 1780-1914 (Európa Gazdasága, 1780-1914)* (1987), *Hungarian Economic Reforms* (1988), *Transition to Market Economy at the End of the 20th Century* (1994), and *Central and Eastern Europe 1944-1993: Detour from Periphery to Periphery* (1996).

BERLIN, CONGRESS OF (1878). One of the two most significant meetings of the Great Powers in the 19th century—the other one being the Congress of Vienna of 1814-15 (q.v.). This meeting took place in wake of the Russo-Turkish War of 1877-78 and the resulting Treaty of San Stefano (March 3, 1878), which gave too many advantages to Russia. Pressured by the other Great Powers, Russia was compelled to attend the Congress of Berlin (June 13-July 13, 1878) and to relinquish many of her gains made a few months earlier. Serbia (q.v.), Romania (q.v.), and Montenegro were given full independence. But recently resurrected Greater Bulgaria—which would have been a Russian client state and a bridgehead on the Balkans (q.v.)—was cut into three parts: Bulgaria, Eastern Rumelia, and Macedonia. Of these parts only Bulgaria (q.v.) gained a near independent status, while the other two went back under Ottoman control. The most important by-product of the Berlin Congress was the transformation of the traditional Prussian-Russian friendship into a German-Russian animosity, giving birth to the Dual Alliance (q.v.) between Germany (q.v.) and Austria-Hungary (q.v.) and to the gradual polarization of Europe into two rival armed camps: the Triple Alliance (q.v.) and the Triple Entente (q.v.).

BERZEVICZY, GERGELY (1763-1822). An influential pioneer economist, the first significant exponent of Adam Smith's ideas in Hungary, and the author of several significant works on Hungarian economy. After some years at the Viceroyalty Council (q.v.), during the 1790s Berzeviczy came into contact with the Hungarian Jacobins (q.v.), with whose ideas he sympathized. Having escaped detection and arrest, in 1795 he retired to his family estate at Kakaslomnic and devoted the remaining twenty-seven years of his life to writing major works on economic theory and foreign trade. His first significant relevant volume was *About Hungary's Commerce and Industry (De commercio et industria Hungariae)* (1797), which he wrote in Latin. This was followed by some study and travel in the German lands and then by the publication of his German language *The Furthering of the Nordic Commerce (Die Erweiterung des nordischen Handels)* (1814). His major theoretical work, *Public Economy and Politics (Oeconomia Publico Politica)* (1818) remained unpublished till 1902. Berzeviczy was an influential apostle of the free economic system, and for this reason he was also a champion of the termination of all aspects of feudalism.

BESSENYEI, GYÖRGY [GEORGE] (1747-1811). Writer, philosopher, and one of the leading exponents of the Hungarian National Revival Movement (q.v.). Between 1765 and 1782 Bessenyei lived in the imperial capital of Vienna (q.v.) and up to 1773 he was a member of the Hungarian Royal Nobles' Guard (q.v.), which had been established by Queen Maria Theresa (q.v.) in order to spread Viennese cultural influences and the German language among the Hungarian provincial nobility (q.v.). While in Vienna, Bessenyei became acquainted with the culture and ideas of the French and English Enlightenments and came to recognize the need to renew Hungarian learning and culture, in particular the Hungarian (Magyar) language (q.v.) that had been neglected in the previous centuries because of the dominance of the Latin (q.v.). Bessenyei undertook a major effort to cultivate that language, to expand its vocabulary, to use it in his literary and philosophical works, and to enlist others in the effort to make Magyar the primary language of the Hungarian nation. In 1782 Bessenyei returned to Hungary (q.v.) and lived on his estates in Szabolcs and Bihar Counties. Starting with his epoch-making *Tragedy of Ágis (Ágis tragédiája)*, published in 1772, most of his influential works appeared in the two decades before 1790. Virtually all of them were *belles lettres*, and they all conveyed important social, political, and national messages. Bessenyei was a true 18th-century rationalist, who initially championed Voltaire's enlightened despotism, but then switched over to the more democratic ideas of Rousseau. None of his works written after 1790 under the influence of the French Revolution was permitted to be published by the censor. In fact, some of them are still in manuscript form today.

BETHLEN, PRINCE GABRIEL [GÁBOR] (1580-1629). The most highly regarded prince of Transylvania (r.1613-29) and one of the truly great personalities in Hungarian history, whose reign is generally viewed as the golden age Transylvania. Coming from a

Transylvanian-Hungarian noble family, in the period between 1595 and 1613 Bethlen served at the courts of Princes Sigismund Báthory (q.v.), Moses Székely (q.v.), Stephen Bocskai (q.v.), and Gabriel Báthory (q.v.). Throughout this period he supported an anti-Habsburg and pro-Turkish foreign policy, believing the Ottoman Turks (q.v.) to be more tolerant and more willing to accept Transylvania's separate identity than the Habsburgs (q.v.). Bethlen's ultimate goal was the reestablishment of an independent Hungarian state, and he hoped to use the Transylvanian throne as a stepping-stone toward this end. The outbreak of the Thirty Years' War (1618) gave Bethlen an opportunity to initiate the struggle against the Habsburgs. In 1619 he allied himself with the rebellious Czechs and undertook to besiege the center of Habsburg power, Vienna (q.v.). The Habsburgs were able to force him to give up the siege, but by that time he already had all of Royal Hungary (q.v.) under his control. Moreover, the Hungarian Diet (q.v.) of Besztercebányahad also elected him "King of Hungary." While very flattering to Bethlen, in wake of the Habsburg victory over the Czechs at the Battle of the White Mountains (1620), he decided not to use his new royal title and to sign the compromise Treaty of Nikolsburg (January 6, 1622). Based on this treaty, he relinquished his royal title, returned the Holy Crown of Hungary (q.v.) to Ferdinand II (q.v.), and promised to review all his land grants. In return, however, he was given the Principalities of Oppeln and Ratibor in Silesia (q.v.), and gained seven additional north-eastern Hungarian counties and 50,000 florins per year for his lifetime. Bethlen devoted the 1620s to the development of the lands and principalities under his control. He encouraged commerce and industry, supported education, subsidized the arts, and also established a mercenary standing army to further his political goals. His repeated military efforts against the Habsburgs proved to be less than fully successful. Yet, he still managed to retain Transylvania's independence, assured religious toleration for the Hungarian Protestants (q.v.), and gained a voice in Hungarian politics. Throughout this period he continued to seek broad anti-Habsburg alliances with the Protestant states of Europe. To this end he married Catherine Hohenzollern of Brandenburg

(1604-49), the daughter of Elector George William (r.1619-40), and also joined the Westminster Alliance composed of England, Holland, and Denmark. Bethlen's sudden and unexpected death on November 15, 1629 prevented him from pursuing his plans concerning the reestablishment of the territorial integrity of Hungary. On the Transylvanian throne, he was followed in rapid succession by his wife (r.1629-30), his brother, István Bethlen (r.1630), and then by several members of the Rákóczi (q.v.) family.

BETHLEN, COUNTESS KATA (1700-59). Countess Bethlen was one of the most learned aristocratic ladies of 18th-century Transylvania, whose *Short Autobiography by Herself (Életének maga által való rövid leírása),* written during the last two decades of her life, is a jewel of 18th-century Hungarian literature. She was married twice, first to Count László Haller (1717) and then to Count József Teleki (1722), but both of her husbands died. So did all her children, which prompted her to call herself "Orphaned Kata Bethlen" *(Árva Bethlen Kata),* by which name she came to be known in history. Countess Bethlen found refuge from her many personal tragedies in an almost fanatical devotion to her Calvinist faith. With the help of her court chaplain, the learned Péter Bod (q.v.), she collected a large private library, which aided her in her writings. Her collected works were published two centuries later as *Writings and Letters (Írásai és levelezése)* (1922-23), while her personal reminiscences appeared under the title *Autobiography (Önéletírás)* (1963).

BETHLEN, COUNT STEPHEN [ISTVÁN] (1878-c.1946). The prime minister of Hungary (1921-31), and one of the most significant conservative-nationalist Hungarian statesmen of the 20th century. Coming from an old aristocratic Transylvanian-Hungarian family whose members included princes of Transylvania (q.v.), Bethlen had served for fifteen years in the Hungarian Parliament (1903-18) (q.v.) before the collapse of Austria-Hungary (q.v.). During the postwar revolutions (1918-19), Bethlen left Budapest (q.v.) for Vienna (q.v.), where he became one of the leaders of the

Anti-Bolshevik Committee that represented the interests of the so-called "Szeged Government" (q.v.) that opposed Béla Kun's (q.v.) Hungarian Soviet Republic (q.v.). In 1920 he was a member of the Hungarian Peace Delegation to Versailles, and in 1921 he became the prime minister of Hungary at the head of the National Unity Party *(Nemzeti Egység Pártja)* (q.v.). Bethlen had a role in thwarting King Charles IV's (q.v.) return to the Hungarian throne (October 23, 1921) and also in the official dethronement of the Habsburg dynasty (q.v.) (November 6, 1921). In 1922, while engaged in the restoration of order in the mutilated country, he engineered a fusion with two peasant parties, which resulted in a unified governmental party under the name of United Party *(Egységes Párt)* (q.v.).

During the 1920s Bethlen devoted his efforts to the consolidation of the social and economic conditions in Hungary. He did this by disbanding the various rightist freebooter bands, by securing loans from the League of Nations and other Western sources, and by raising taxes. In 1926 his position was shaken somewhat by the so-called "Frank-forgery case" (French franks were being forged in Hungary with the involvement of several highly placed individuals), but he managed to hold on to power. At the same time he also began to end Hungary's diplomatic isolation within the clutches of the Little Entente (q.v.) by turning progressively to fascist Italy (q.v.), with which he signed a Treaty of Friendship and Arbitration in 1927. The economic crisis stemming from the Great Depression forced Bethlen to resign (August 18, 1931), but he continued to wield considerable power as a close friend and adviser of Regent Horthy (q.v.).

In 1939 Bethlen became a member of the Upper House (q.v.) of the Hungarian Parliament, where he fought valiantly against the various anti-Semitic measures—Jewish Laws (q.v.)—that were being introduced under German pressure. Sensing that Germany (q.v.) was going to lose the war, by 1943 he became the chief spokesman of a pro-British orientation. He hoped to save Hungary's conservative regime through a separate treaty with the Western Allies. Following the German occupation of Hungary (March 19, 1944) (q.v.), Bethlen went into hiding, but still continued to advise

Horthy in his efforts to save the country and the regime even at the expense of a dialogue with Moscow. In December 1944 Bethlen was taken into Soviet custody. As he refused to cooperate with them in the establishment of a communist regime, he was taken to Moscow (April 28, 1945), where he died in captivity sometime between October 1946 and November 1947.

BETHLEN, PRINCE STEPHEN [ISTVÁN] (1580s-1648). Prince of Transylvania for a brief period (September 28-December 1, 1630), following the death of his brother, Prince Gabriel Bethlen (q.v.), and the death of his brother's widow, Princess Catherine [Katalin] Brandenburg(q.v.). Unwilling the face the challenges of the office, Bethlen resigned a mere two months after his election and transferred the princely office to the newly elected George Rákóczi I (q.v.). In 1636 he had second thoughts about his action and tried to take it back, but his efforts proved to be fruitless.

BETWEEN TWO PAGANS [KÉT POGÁNY KÖZT]. A common expression in the 16th and 17th centuries to refer to the fact that Hungary had become a permanent battleground between the Habsburg (q.v.) and the Ottoman Empires (q.v.). Both of these external powers were resented, and many a time various groups of Hungarians allied themselves with one or another of these powers as the "lesser of two evils." This happened, for example, during the late 17th and early 18th centuries, when this division was represented by the struggle between the *kuruc* (q.v.) and the *labanc* (q.v.) factions.

BETYÁRS. Robin Hood like peasant highwaymen in late-18th- and 19th-century Hungary, who "dropped out" of society because of feudal tyranny, personal mistreatments, excessive work obligations on the feudal estates, or illegal financial exactions on the part of the landed nobility (q.v.). Most of the *betyárs* became outlaws only accidentally, largely through a spontaneous reaction to repeated exploitations and personal humiliations. Few of them lived very long after becoming *betyárs,* for they were usually hunted down and executed. But while they lived in illegality, they survived from highway robbery. They robbed the rich and often gave to the poor, who shielded them in return. The most notorious betyárs included Bandi Angyal (1760-1806), Marci Zöld (1790-1816), Jóska Sobri (1810-37), Jancsi Patkó (1825-62), Pista Patkó (1827-62), Imre Bogár (1842-62), and Sándor Rózsa (1813-78)—of whom only the last mentioned died a natural death at the relatively old age of sixty-five. But he did so in prison, and after many years of incarceration.

BEY [BEG]. A Turkish rank below the rank of a pasha (q.v.), which originally was the title of tribal and clan leaders. In the Ottoman Empire (q.v.), *bey* was the title of the sons of pashas, and later the title of provincial administrators who were in charge of *sanjaks* (q.v.) or districts administered by *sanjak beys.* The largest administrative districts or eyālets were under the governance of *beylerbeys.* (q.v.) This term was also the title of the secondary ruler of the Khazar Empire (q.v.), below the Khagan (q.v.). During the 16th and 17th centuries, Turkish Hungary (q.v.) was under the domination of several dozen of these *sanjak beys.*

BEYLERBEY [BEGLERBEG, BEY OF BEYS]. *Beylerbeys* were the highest ranking administrators of the Ottoman Empire, who were in charge of major provinces known as *eyalets* or *vilayets.* The beylerbeys also had the military title of *pasha* (q.v.), wherefore the provinces under their command were also known as *pashaliks* (q.v.). In Hungary (q.v.) the pasha of Buda always had the title of beylerbey, and he was basically in charge of all of Turkish Hungary (q.v.), and to a lesser degree of autonomous Transylvania (q.v.)

BIBÓ, ISTVÁN (1911-79). One of 20th-century Hungary's most compelling progressive social thinkers, whose influence has been growing ever since his death. Although a scholarly social philosopher, Bibó became involved in politics as a result of his arrest by the Arrow Cross Government (q.v.) in 1944. After World War II (q.v.) he was active in the National Peasant Party (q.v.), taught at the University of Szeged (q.v.), was a researcher at the Teleki Institute (q.v.), worked at the Library of the University of

Budapest (q.v.), and, during the revolution of 1956 (q.v.), also served briefly as a "State Minister" in Imre Nagy's (q.v.) government. Following the revolution Bibó was arrested and imprisoned (1957-63), and then worked in the Hungarian Central Statistical Office (1963-71). During the 1930s, Bibó had fallen under the influence of Hungarian Populism (q.v.), but after a while, he came to view the Populists as too parochial and self-limiting. Thus, he increasingly became a spokesman for a necessary compromise between the two main non-Marxist intellectual trends in Hungary: Populism and Urbanism (q.v.). Bibó wrote his most influential theoretical essays in the period between 1945 and 1948. These include *The Crisis of Hungarian Democracy (A magyar demokráciaválsága)* (1945), *The Misery of the Small States of Eastern Europe (A kelet-európai kisállamok nyomorúsága)* (1946), and *The Jewish Question in Hungary after 1944 (Zsidókérdés Magyarországon 1944 után)* (1948). Bibó's works were published posthumously under the title *Collected Works (Összegyűjtött munkái)* (4 vols., 1981-84), and *Selected Studies (Válogatott tanulmányok)* (3 vols, 1986). A selection of his studies also appeared in English under the title *Democracy, Revolution, Self-Determination: Selected Writings* (1991).

BIEDERMEIER. A Central European cultural style of Viennese origin that dominated much of the Habsburg Empire (q.v.) and Hungary (q.v.) during the first three quarters of the 19th century. It represented the taste of the bourgeois middle classes, and its impact was strongest on home decorations, industrial arts, and wearing apparel. Its main characteristics included simplicity, usefulness, and coziness. It remained the preferred cultural style for the urban middle classes and the rural nobility through much of the 19th century.

BÍRÓ, LÁSZLÓ JÓZSEF (1899-1986). A Budapest-born journalist, painter, sculptor, and inventor of the ball point pen. Bíró first showed the prototype of his invention at the Budapest International Fair in 1931, but it took another decade, and a move to Argentina, before he was able to perfect it for mass use. The first successful version of the pen was marketed in 1943 under the name of *Eterpen*. But not until the establishment of the French company, BIC (Bíró Crayon), did Bíró's ball point pen take off and become universally accepted. Bíró related the history of his invention in his *A Silent Revolution [Una revolutión silenciosa]* (1969).

BLACK ARMY [LEGIO NIGRA, FEKETE SEREG] (1467-92]. The powerful standing army of King Matthias Corvinus (q.v.), composed largely of paid soldiers, including many Czech, Polish, German, and South Slavic mercenaries. Its name was probably derived from one of its leaders, "Haugwitz the Black" (Fekete Haugwitz), although popular belief claims that it was connected with the color of its uniforms. The Black Army was composed of infantry and heavy cavalry, but there were also a considerable number of artillery and light cavalry units. The members of the Black Army were trained by professional condottieri according to the most up-to-date military strategy. Their role in the Hungarian armed forces was very similar to that of the Janissaries in the Ottoman armies. King Matthias used the Black Army in many of his wars, including his conquest of Moravia (q.v.), Silesia (q.v.), and much of Austria (q.v.), along with the city of Vienna in 1485 (q.v.). Following King Matthias's death in 1490, the decline of central power resulted also in the disintegration of this magnificent army. Some of is component units, which resorted to banditry, were dispersed in 1492 by one of Matthias's best generals, Pál Kinizsi (d. 1494).

BLACK SEA [PONTUS EUXEINOS, CHERNOYE MORE, KARADENIZ]. An enclosed sea to the east of the Balkan Peninsula (q.v.), which is connected to the Mediterranean Sea via the Bosphorus, the Sea of Marmara, and the Dardanelles. The Empire of Louis the Great (q.v.) in the 14th century extended to the Black Sea in the southeast of Hungary. The Azov Sea (q.v.) is part of it, and it is divided from its main part by the Crimean Peninsula (q.v.). On its northern shores are the Pontic Steppes (q.v.), the home ground of the Hungarians for several centuries before the Árpádian Conquest (q.v.) of the Carpathian Basin (q.v.).

BLOOD OATH [VÉRSZERZŐDÉS]. An agreement in a clan or tribal society to end the ongoing blood feud (vendetta) by uniting under a single leader. According to Anonymus (q.v.), this is what took place among the Hungarian tribes in Etelköz (q.v.), when in the mid- or late-9th century they joined into the Hungarian Tribal Federation (q.v.) and accepted Álmos (q.v.) and his descendants as their leaders in perpetuity. The Hungarian Blood Oath involved the mixing of the blood of all of the tribal leaders into a cup, and then each of them drinking from this mixture so as to make all of them blood brothers to each other.

BOCSKAI, PRINCE STEPHEN [ISTVÁN] (1557-1606). Prince of Transylvania and Hungary (r.1604-06), whose name if connected with the "Bocskai War of Liberation" (1605-06). Born into a Hungarian noble family, Bocskai was reared at the Viennese Imperial Court (q.v.). In 1592 he was appointed the military commander of the Fortress of Várad (Nagyvárad) (q.v.), in which capacity he became one of the chief spokesmen of the anti-Turkish and pro-Habsburg orientation in his immediate homeland, Transylvania (q.v.). The Fifteen Years' War (1591-1606) (q.v.) between the Habsburg (q.v.) and the Ottoman Empires (q.v.) soon dragged Transylvania into that struggle. Bocskai had an important role in aligning Transylvania with the Habsburgs, which he did in the hope of throwing off Turkish vassalage. The promised Habsburg help, however, failed to materialize and consequently Transylvania became an open battlefield leading to its near-total destruction. The most destructive of the occupying forces were those of the Imperial General George Basta (q.v.), whose cruelty led to a series of uprisings in the course of 1603-06. Having dared to protest against Basta's reign of terror, Bocskai was arrested and interred in Prague (1602-04) (q.v.). Following his release in 1604, he returned home and promptly initiated an anti-Habsburg uprising that resulted in his election as prince of Transylvania (February 21, 1605) and the

"Ruling Prince of Hungary" (April 20, 1605). The war that ensued compelled Emperor/King Rudolph (q.v.) to negotiate with Bocskai. The latter reciprocated, partially because of the growing dissent within the ranks of his supporters—rivalry between his nobles (q.v.) and the *hajdús* (q.v.)—and partially because he did not wish to make himself into a vassal of the Ottoman Sultan. In the resulting Peace Treaty of Vienna (September 23, 1606) (q.v.) Rudolph promised to uphold the rights and privileges of the Hungarian-Transylvania nobility, and also to respect the religious freedom of the Protestants (q.v.). Moreover, he made seven eastern Hungarian counties part of Bocskai's Transylvania, and promised that Transylvania would not be reunited with Hungary until after the death of Bocskai and all his male descendants. Bocskai likewise had a role in the signing of the Peace Treaty of Zsitva-Torok (November 11, 1606) between the Habsburg and the Ottoman Empires, which ended the Fifteen Years War. After the conclusion of these treaties, the grateful Bocskai settled all of his *hajdú* supporters into newly founded privileged *hajdú* towns and districts (q.v.), and gave them privileges comparable to those of the *Székely* (q.v.) nobility of Transylvania. Bocskai died December 29, 1606, leaving a testament in which he urged his followers to uphold Transylvania's independence until more favorable conditions would permit its reunification with Hungary (q.v.).

BOD, PÉTER (1712-69). A noted Calvinist churchman, theologian, and historian, whose three-volume Latin language *Hungarian Church History (Historia Hungarorum ecclesiastica)*—published in its entirety only a century after his death (Leiden, 1888-90)—is among the very best synthetic historical works written in 18th-century Hungary. Coming from a Székely (q.v.) lower noble family, Bod studied at the Calvinist College of Nagyenyed, and then at the University of Leiden in Holland. Returning home in 1743, he became the court chaplain of Countess Kata Bethlen (q.v.). In 1749 he moved to Magyarigen in Transylvania, where he became the pastor of the local Reformed Congregation. Bod remained and worked in this small town until his death two decades later. In the meantime, in 1758 he became the notary of the Seniorate (Classis) of Gyulafehérvár (q.v.), and in 1767 he was elected notary of the whole Transylvanian Synod (Diocese).

Bod was a prominent exponent of progressive Hungarian culture and learning in Transylvania and a forerunner of Hungarian Enlightenment (q.v.). His *Magyar Athenas* (1766), which contains the learned biography of 485 Hungarian writers, was the first significant Hungarian biographical lexicon. His works on Protestant theology show a great deal of learning and erudition. Bod consciously used the Magyar language in most of his writings in direct opposition to the existing trend that favored Latin. Thus, outside of the above-mentioned *Hungarian Church History,* he wrote most of his works in vernacular Magyar.

BODNÁR, GÁBOR (1920-1996). Cofounder and for five decades the leader of the Hungarian Scout Federation in Exile (1946-95), which was first centered in Germany (1946-51), and then in Garfield, New Jersey (1951-). For many years Bodnár had edited the Federation's periodicals: *Hungarian Scout (Magyar Cserkész)* and *Leadership News (Vezetők Lapja])* He is also the author of several educational and scouting books, including *Scouting in Hungary* (1986), which also appeared in Hungarian (1980, 1989) and in German (1982). After the collapse of communism, Bodnár established direct contacts with the reborn Hungarian scouting movements (q.v.) in Hungary (q.v.) as well as with those of the Hungarian minorities in Transylvania (Romania) (q.v.), Slovakia (q.v.), and Carpatho-Ruthenia (Ukraine) (q.v.). (See Scouting in Hungary.)

BOGOMILS [BOGUMILS]. A Christian heretical sect of Persian origin that first appeared in 10th-century Bulgaria (q.v.) and was named after a Bulgarian Paulician monk by the name of Bogomil (Philotheus, Amadeus, Gottlieb). During the next two-three centuries it spread to the Northern Balkans (q.v.), and even to Italy (q.v.), Southern France, and parts of the Holy Roman Empire (q.v.), where it appeared under such diverse names as Poblicani, Patareni, Cathari, Albigenses, Texerantes, and Tisserantes. The Bogomils attributed the act of creation both to God and to the Devil. God, being all good, was responsible for the creation of the invisible spiritual world, while the Devil was responsible for the creation of the visible material world that was evil. This view produced a belief that all material things, including the human body, were innately evil, which, in turn, led to the rejection of all material pleasures, including various kinds of food, sex, and procreation. Occasionally, some far-out manifestations of this belief even led to such extreme acts as self-castration. By the 13th century, Bosnia (q.v.) had become the center of Bogomilism. Because of Hungary's (q.v.) interest in and occasional control of that province, and because Bogomilism extended even to such southern Hungarian provinces as Slavonia (q.v.) and Szerémség (q.v.), a number of Hungarian kings —for example Emeric (q.v.), Louis the Great (q.v.), Sigismund (q.v.), and Matthias Corvinus (q.v.)—were obliged to lead military crusades against them. Following the Ottoman Turkish conquest (q.v.) of Bosnia in the 15th century, most of the Bogomils converted to Islam, their descendants being the Bosnian Muslims of today.

BOHEMIA. The western half of Czechia (Czech Republic) (q.v.) and the former Czech Kingdom (q.v.), which emerged as a state in the 10th century but was never able to extricate itself from the confines of the Holy Roman Empire (q.v.). By the end of the 10th century it united with its smaller eastern neighbor, the Margravate of Moravia (q.v.). These two lands together, with the later addition of the Duchy of Silesia (q.v.), made up the core of the medieval Czech Kingdom, throughout its existence as an independent or as an autonomous state. After 1526, Bohemia, Moravia, and Silesia became part of the evolving Habsburg Empire (Austria-Hungary) (q.v.), and—with the exception of most of Silesia—remained so until its dissolution at the end of 1918. The Czech Kingdom (Bohemia, Moravia, Silesia) had played a continuously important role in Hungarian history, partially as a regional rival (10th-15th c.) and partially as an associated state (e.g., 1440-57, 1490-1526, 1527-1918).

BOHEMIAN CROWN LANDS [LANDS OF THE BOHEMIAN CROWN, CZECH KINGDOM]. The main components of the Czech Kingdom or Lands of the Bohemian Crown were the Kingdom of Bohemia (q.v.), the Margravate of Moravia (q.v.), and the Duchy of Silesia (q.v.). The latter, however, was contested by the Poles, Czechs, Hungarians, Austrians, and the Prussians, and was permanently lost to the Czechs (q.v.) in the War of Austrian Succession (q.v.) in the middle of the 18th century.

BONFINI, ANTONIO (1427-1502/03). An Italian Humanist court historian in the service of King Matthias Corvinus (q.v.). After having made a name for himself in Italy (q.v.), Bonfini arrived at Matthias's court at Buda (q.v.) in 1486. There he became the personal companion and reader of Queen Beatrix (q.v.). But King Matthias also entrusted him with writing a complete history of Hungary and the Hungarians, which he did under the title *Deeds of the Hungarians (Rerum Ungaricarum decades)*. For the earlier centuries Bonfini relied heavily on various Hungarian chronicles, which he colored with the imagination of court historians. The most detailed and most valuable section of his work is the one that deals with the reign of Matthias Corvinus, which is also the most original one. Because of Bonfini's brilliant style and language, his work became and remained the ideal for all Hungarian historians for about two centuries.

BORBÁNDI, GYULA (b.1919). An influential emigré intellectual of moderate Populist leanings, who for over three decades was the founding editor-in-chief of the influential *New Horizons (Új Látóhatár)*(Munich, 1958-90), the most highly regarded Hungarian periodical in the West. Borbándi and his periodical always represented quality and moderation, characteristics that were usually scarce among the emotionally charged emigrés. While editing his periodical, Borbándi was employed in the Hungarian Section of Radio Free Europe and was also involved in the work of the Hungarian Institute *(Ungarisches Institut)* of Munich. At the same time he authored a number of highly regarded works on modern

Hungarian history, among them: *Hungarian Populism (Der Ungarische Populismus)* (1976), *The Story of the Hungarian Emigration (A magyar emigráció életrajza)* (1985), and a collection of essays and recollections entitled *Five Hundred Miles [Ötszáz mérföld)* (1989).

BOROSS, PÉTER (b.1928). Hungary's prime minister (December 12, 1993-July 15, 1994), in the country's first post-communist government, who completed József Antall's (q.v.) term in office, after the latter succumbed to cancer. Prior to his prime ministership, Boross was Hungary's minister of interior and one of the leaders of the Hungarian Democratic Forum (q.v.).

BOSNIA. A state in the center of recently dissolved Yugoslavia (1918-91), whose history goes back to the Middle Ages, when it had a close association with Hungary (q.v.). Inhabited by South Slavs (q.v.) ever since the late 6th century, Bosnia took shape in the 10th century, along with the smaller Herzegovina (Hum until the 15th c.) to the south of it. Although as large as Croatia-Slavonia-Dalmatia (q.v.), it was unable to preserve its independence for any protracted period of time. Controlled occasionally, in full or in part, by the Serbs (q.v.), the Croats (q.v.), and the Byzantines (q.v.), in the 12th century (1135) Bosnia came under Hungarian rule, at which time the Hungarian rulers also assumed the title "King of Rama" (a section of Greater Bosnia). Thereafter, Bosnia became a battleground between Hungary and the Byzantine Empire (q.v.).

During the same period, Bosnia witnessed the arrival of the Bogomil heresy (q.v.) from Bulgaria, which soon became an official state religion, and against which several crusades were led at the urging of Rome. The climax of Bosnian history was reached under Ban Kulin (r.1180-1204) and Ban Tvertko (r.1353-91), the latter of whom also assumed the title "King of Bosnia" in 1377. In the 15th century Bosnia was gradually occupied by the Turks (q.v.), ending in its incorporation into the Ottoman Empire (q.v.) in 1463. In 1482, the much smaller Herzegovina was also incorporated into the Ottoman state. The Ottoman conquest was followed by the mass conversion of the Bogomil heretics to the religion of Islam, which placed the Bosnians into a very favorable position within the Ottoman Empire. The Bosnian beys had a major leadership role in the empire. Their descendants are the Bosnian Muslims (q.v.) of today. Bosnia-Herzegovina remained under Turkish rule until the Congress of Berlin (q.v.) in 1878, when it was placed under Austro-Hungarian (q.v.) administration, which annexed it officially in 1908.

The Bosnian capital of Sarajevo was the scene of the assassination of Archduke Francis Ferdinand (q.v.) in 1914, which served as the spark for the eruption of World War I (q.v.). Between 1918-41 and 1945-92 Bosnia was one of the component republics of Yugoslavia (q.v.). During World War II (q.v.) it was part of Croatia. In February 1992 it proclaimed its independence, but ever since that time it has been involved in an ongoing civil war fought mostly between the Bosnian Muslims and the Bosnian Serbs. The war wound down in 1996, but the situation is still unresolved at the beginning of 1997.

BOSNIA-HERZEGOVINA see **BOSNIA.**

BOSNIAN MUSLIMS. One of the three major ethnic groups in Bosnia, the other two being the Serbs (q.v.) and the Croats (q.v.). All three of them are South Slavs (q.v.), and it is really their distinct religious culture (Catholic, Orthodox, and Muslim) that divides them. The Bosnian Muslims are direct descendants of the Bosnian Bogomils (q.v.), a heretical Christian sect, against whom the Hungarian kings led many crusades during the Middle Ages.

BOURGEOIS RADICALISM [POLGÁRI RADIKALIZ-MUS]. A liberal political and ideological trend in early 20th-century Hungary (q.v.), which was particularly popular among the urban intellectuals and petty bourgeoisie. The bourgeois radicals demanded the introduction of universal suffrage, sweeping land reforms, control of banks, limitation of the power of industrial trusts, termination of all nationality discrimination, and the restriction of the influence of established churches in domestic politics. In foreign policy, they were anti-militarists and proponents of international collaboration among nations. Many of their leaders were members of the Galilei Circle (q.v.), composed of radical intellectuals. In 1914 they brought to life the National Bourgeois Radical Party, which championed their cause, but which never became a significant political force. Their most prominent intellectual spokesman was Oscar Jászi (q.v.), the editor of the prominent sociological periodical, *Twentieth Century (Huszadik Század)* (1900-19) and the author of several significant political and sociological works. In 1918-19 the Bourgeois Radicals participated in the revolutionary government headed by Mihály Károlyi (q.v.), but after the consolidation of the conservative Horthy Regime (q.v.), they rapidly lost their influence. Following Jászi's emigration, their most prominent spokesman was Rusztem Vámbéry (q.v.), the editor of the periodical *Our Century (Századunk)* (1926-39).

BOYARS. The socially, politically, and militarily dominant landed nobility in Bulgaria, Russia, and the Vlach (Romanian) principalities of Moldavia (q.v.) and Wallachia (q.v.). Boyar was a generic name also of the feudal nobility in medieval Bulgaria (9th-14th c.). In Kievan Russia (Kiev Rus') (q.v.) the boyar class was born out of the fusion of the tribal aristocracy *(starets)* and the princely retinues *(druzhina),* and came to be represented in the feudal princely council *(duma).* The boyars dominated Moldavian and Wallachian society ever since the 14th century, and continued their dominance of that society even after the creation of united Romania in 1862. They retained their near-feudal powers and social position right up to the end of World War II (q.v.).

BRATISLAVA see **POZSONY.**

BRODARICS, ISTVÁN [STEPHANUS] (1470-1539). A Humanist historian and King Louis II's (q.v.) last chancellor, before the latter's death at the Battle of Mohács (q.v.) in 1526. Following this catastrophe, Brodarics decided to support John Zápolya (q.v.) against Ferdinand I (q.v.) in wake of the double election. For a while he served as King John's emissary in various diplomatic posts, then was appointed the bishop of Pécs (1532) and Vác (1537). Having participated in the Battle of Mohács, Brodarics wrote the only eyewitness account of that encounter: *The True History of the Conflict Between the Hungarians and the Turkish Sultan Süleyman at Mohács (De conflictu Hungarorum cum Solymano Turcarum imperatore ad Mohach historia verissima)* (1527).

BUDA. Hungary's medieval capital in the period between the mid-13th century and 1541. In 1872 it was merged with the city of Pest to form the modern capital of Budapest. (See also Budapest.)

BUDAPEST.   Hungary's capital city of about 2.1 million people (1995) that was formed in 1872 through the merging of the medieval cities of Buda, Pest, and Óbuda (q.v.). Situated just to the south of the Roman fortress city of Aquincum (q.v.), the cities of Buda and Pest, located respectively on the western (right) and eastern (left) bank of the Danube River (q.v.), became a royally sanctioned crossing (ferry) as early as 1148. The construction of the fortress of Buda on top of Castle Hill was begun by King Béla IV (q.v.) in 1247, immediately after the Mongol conquest of Hungary (q.v.). Buda became a royal capital under the Anjou kings (q.v.) in the 14th century, while under the Renaissance king, Matthias Corvinus (q.v.), it evolved into the unquestioned administrative and cultural center of Hungary. At the same time, Pest, built on the site of the Roman fortress Contra Aquincum, evolved into a commercial town with a heavy presence of Ismaelites (q.v.) and other Balkan peoples.

Falling under Turkish occupation between 1541 and 1686, Buda's and Pest's significance declined. This was all the more true as the country's administrative center was shifted northeast to the city of Pozsony (Pressburg, Bratislava) (q.v.) close to the Austrian border. Following the expulsion of the Turks (1699), both Buda and Pest became Royal Free Cites, and then were inundated by German settlers (q.v.). In the late 18th century, under Maria Theresa (q.v.), Buda again became a seat of several governmental offices (e.g., Viceroyalty Council, Royal Treasury, etc.) as well as of the country's only university that was transferred from Nagyszombat (Tyrnau, Trnava) (q.v.) in 1777. During the same time Pest grew into an important commercial center, and the two cities progressively grew together—first via a pontoon bridge built in the early 18th century, and then through the first permanent suspension bridge in Europe (the "Chain Bridge"). The latter had been constructed as an undertaking of Count István Széchenyi (q.v.) in the period between 1841 and 1848.

During the revolution of 1848, the official capital of Hungary was transferred from Pozsony to Pest. Then, with the merging of Buda, Pest, and Óbuda into a single city in 1872, the newly formed city of Budapest became the country's administrative center. But even after this merger, the old fortified city of Buda—which housed the royal palace, many of the governmental offices and ministries, and for a while also the Hungarian Parliament—continued to be the center of power in Hungary. Only after World War II (q.v.) did Buda give way to Pest as the primary center of power. Today, one-fifth of Hungary's population lives in Budapest.

BUKOVINA [BUKOWINA]. A province on the northeastern borders of Historic Hungary (q.v.) between the Carpathians (q.v.) and the upper Dniester River. Having been under Turkish rule for two centuries, in 1774 it was attached to the Habsburg Empire (q.v.). After World War I (q.v.) it became part of Romania (q.v.), while after World War II (q.v.) it was split between Romania and the Soviet Union. Following the collapse of the Soviet Union at the end of 1991, Soviet Bukovina was inherited by independent Ukraine (q.v.) The Romanian part of Bukovina is the homeland of the Bukovinian *Székelys,* who are close relatives of the Hungarian-speaking Transylvanian *Székelys* (q.v.).

BULCSÚ (d.955). One of the commanders of the marauding Hungarian armies in the mid-10th century, who was defeated at the Battle of Augsburg (Lechfeld) (q.v.). Bulcsú was executed at the orders of Emperor Otto the Great in 955, along with his fellow commander, Lehel (Lél) (q.v.). Between 945 and 955, Bulcsú led a number of military expeditions into the Holy Roman Empire (q.v.), Italy (q.v.), France, and the Byzantine Empire (q.v.), where he was allegedly converted to Christianity. In 955 he invaded the German lands at the invitation of the rebellious Bavarian princes, who then deserted him at Augsburg. Bulcsú was the forefather of the so-called Vérbulcsú clan of Hungary (q.v.).

BULGARIA see BULGARS.

BULGARS [BULGARIANS].   Today one of the Slavic-speaking people of the Balkans (q.v.), who were originally Turkic in speech and were probably the remnants of the Huns (q.v.). Having moved to present-day Bulgaria in the late 670s (official date: A.D. 680) from the region of Crimea (q.v.) and the Azov Sea (q.v.), they mixed with the local Slavic population (q.v.) and established a significant state, which for two centuries (9th and 10th) dominated much of the Balkans and the eastern half of the Carpathian Basin (q.v.). Slavic literacy was born in Bulgaria at the time of Czar Boris (r.852-89, 993), when two Greek brothers, Sts. Cyril and Methodius (q.v.), used Bulgarian Slavic to create a Slavic liturgical language (A.D. 863), which is known today as Old Church Slavonic (q.v.). They then spread this literary language throughout the Orthodox Slavic Christian World, along with the teachings of Byzantine Christianity (q.v.).

The Hungarians of the Árpádian conquest (q.v.) came into contact and conflict with the Bulgarians in the late 9th century, and, in the course of the 10th century, were able to eliminate all Bulgarian presence from Historic Hungary (q.v.). In the course of the 12th through the 14th centuries, Bulgaria was often subject to Hungarian incursions, and some of the Hungarian monarchs even assumed the title "King of Bulgaria." The Bulgarians came under Turkish domination in the late 14th century and remained part of the Ottoman Empire (q.v.) until the late 19th (1878) and early 20th centuries (1908). Bulgaria fought two world wars on the side of Germany, as a result of which it lost some territories. Having been a Soviet satellite state for nearly half a century, it is now in the process of democratization.

BULLA AUREA see GOLDEN BULL OF HUNGARY.

BURGENLAND [WESTERN HUNGARY, VÁRVIDÉK, NYUGAT-MAGYARORSZÁG]. The eastern province of Austria (c.1375 sq. miles), which until 1921 had no name and separate existence, and had been part of Historic Hungary (q.v.) for ten centuries (c.900 to 1921). It was carved out of Sopron and Vas Counties after World War I (q.v.) and attached to Austria (q.v.) by the Treaty of Trianon (q.v.). Because of its proximity to Austria, in the course of the centuries, Burgenland's population became increasingly Germanized. The region's most important city used to be Sopron (Ödenburg) (q.v.), but in 1921 that city voted to stay with Hungary (q.v.) in the only plebiscite that was permitted by the victorious Allies for the defeated country. After Burgenland's separation from Hungary, the region's second largest city, Eisenstadt (Kismarton) became its capital. In the fall of 1921 some demobilized Hungarian army units tried to preserve Burgenland for Hungary through guerrilla activities, which activities included even the proclamation of a separate state called the "Banat of Leitha" *(Lajta Bánság)* (q.v.). But the threat of Allied intervention forced Hungary to give up this territory to its former partner, Austria (q.v.).

BURIAN, COUNT STEFAN [ISTVÁN] (1851-1922). Austro-Hungarian diplomat and one of the late foreign ministers of the Dual Monarchy (q.v.) (1915-16 and 1918). After serving in various diplomatic posts in Alexandria, Bucharest, Belgrade, Moscow, Sofia, and Stuttgart (1882-1903), in 1903 Burian was appointed Austria-Hungary's common financial minister, in which capacity he prepared the annexation of Bosnia-Herzegovina (q.v.) (1908). In January 1915, Burian was appointed Austria-Hungary's foreign minister, a position he retained until after Emperor Francis Joseph's (q.v.) death on November 21, 1916. He served once more in the same capacity during the final months of World War I (q.v.) (April-October 1918).

After the war he wrote and published his memoirs under the title: *Three Years from the Time of My Leadership during the War (Drei Jahre. Aus der Zeit meiner Amstführung im Krieg])* (1923).

BYZANTINE CATHOLICISM [GREEK CATHOLICISM]. This branch of Christianity came into being at the Union of Brest in 1596, when a significant majority of the Ukrainian and Belorussian Orthodox Christians (q.v.) united with Rome. On the basis of this agreement, they accepted the supremacy of the Papacy and joined the Catholic Church, but at the same time retained many of their distinct practices, including the use of the Church Slavonic liturgical language and married priesthood. The Union of Brest was followed by several similar unions that affected Historic Hungary (q.v.). These included the Union of Ungvár (Uzhgorod) (1646) that involved most of the Carpatho-Ruthenians (q.v.), and the Union of Transylvania (1700) that brought many of the Transylvanian Vlachs (Romanians) (q.v.) into union with Rome. These ex-Orthodox Christians came to be known in Europe as Greek Catholics. In the United States, however, they changed their name to Byzantine Catholics — largely to avoid being mistaken for Greeks.

BYZANTINE CHRISTIANITY [ORTHODOX, EASTERN CHRISTIANITY]. The branch of Christianity that evolved in the Byzantine Empire (q.v.) and was centered on Constantinople (q.v.). After the fall of the Western Roman Empire (5th c.) and the development of the Papacy as the dominant institution of Christendom (5th-8th c.), Byzantine Christianity became the most important rival of the Rome-centered Catholic Church. Although both versions of Christianity believed in identical dogmas, some of their practices were different. Western Christianity functioned only in Latin (until the Reformation in the 16th century), and Byzantine Christianity used only Greek until the late 9th century, when the Old Church Slavonic (q.v.) was accepted as a liturgical language for the newly converted Slavs (q.v.). One of the main characteristics of Byzantine Christianity was "Caesaropapism"—a doctrine according to which the Byzantine emperors were the possessors of all temporal and spiritual powers, that is, they were the heads of both the state and the church. Later this doctrine was transferred to Moscow, where the Russian czars also functioned under its principles.

Next to the Byzantine emperors, the top leaders of Byzantine Christianity were the nominally coequal patriarchs of Constantinople, Antioch, Jerusalem, and Alexandria. In practice, however—because of his proximity to political power—the patriarch of Constantinople emerged as the first among equals. Later, other patriarchates were also founded in Bulgaria (924), Serbia (1346), and Russia (1589)—the last of these gradually replacing the patriarchate of Constantinople (q.v.) as the most significant church leader in the Byzantine Christian World. This was the result of the Ottoman Turkish conquest of Constantinople (1453) and the subsequent development of the Doctrine of the Third Rome in Moscow (1510), in light of which the Russian czars claimed spiritual and temporal leadership over all of the Orthodox Christian World.

Byzantine Christianity first entered Hungary (q.v.) in the 10th century, but then it was pushed out by Roman Christianity, which became the country's official religion around A.D. 1000. It returned again later, but largely through the immigration of Vlachs (Romanians) (q.v.) and Carpatho-Ruthenians (q.v.) into the eastern and northeastern provinces of Historic Hungary (q.v.). Many of the latter joined Rome in the 17th and 18th centuries and thus became Greek or Byzantine Catholics (q.v.).

BYZANTINE CIVILIZATION see **BYZANTINE EMPIRE, BYZANTINE CHRISTIANITY.**

BYZANTINE EMPIRE. The customary name of the East Roman Empire, which began to deviate from its western part in the early 4th century when Emperor Constantine the Great (r.311-37) transferred the capital to Constantinople (q.v.). It survived the fall of the Western Roman Empire in 476 by nearly a millennium, right up to the conquest of Constantinople by the Ottoman Turks (q.v.) in 1453. The Byzantine Empire became the home base of Byzantine Christianity (q.v.), which ultimately produced two distinct but related subcivilizations: one based on Constantinople and functioning in Greek, and the other based on the South and East Slavs (q.v.) and functioning in Old Church Slavonic (q.v.). The latter also used the Cyrillic alphabet (q.v.) devised by Sts. Cyril and Methodius (q.v.) in the late 9th century (862).

Through most of the 10th through the 13th centuries, the Byzantine Empire controlled much of the Balkans (q.v.). Consequently, as Historic Hungary's (q.v.) immediate neighbor, it influenced and affected Hungarian history significantly. Although the two states were competing for control over the northern Balkan Peninsula and the Dalmatian coastline (q.v.), in the mid-12th century there was still a serious plan for a Byzantine-Hungarian union. Devised by the childless Emperor Manuel (r.1143-80), the unified empire was to be headed by the son of the Hungarian ruler, the future King Béla III (q.v.). Although Byzantine Civilization was the first of the Christian cultures to influence Hungary in the 10th century, the country ultimately converted to Roman Christianity (1000) and thus became part of Western Christian Civilization.

The conquest of Constantinople by the Fourth Crusaders in 1204 resulted in the temporary demise of the Byzantine Empire and in the creation of several small feudal Latin states on its territory. In 1261 the Byzantines reconquered the Constantinople and Emperor Michael VIII (r.1259/61-82) reestablished the Byzantine Empire under the Paleologus dynasty. This later empire, however, was only a shadow of its former self. Yet, it still lasted for two more centuries, until the conquest of Constantinople by the Ottoman Turks (q.v.) in 1453.

BYZANTINE RITE see BYZANTINE CATHOLICISM.

BYZANTINES see BYZANTINE EMPIRE, BYZANTINE CHRISTIANITY.

- C -

CALIPH [KHALĪF, KHALĪFA]. Head of the Islamic World after the death of Prophet Mohammed in 632. Until the mid–11th century the caliphs of Damascus (661–750) and Baghdad (750–1055) were the spiritual and temporal leaders of most of the Islamic World. Following the Seljuk Turkish conquest of Baghdad in 1055, however, they were relegated to the spiritual sphere only. After the Mongol conquest in the mid-13th century, the caliphs established themselves in Egypt (1260–1517). Then in the early 16th century they transferred this title to the conquering Ottoman Sultans (q.v.)), who held it until after the collapse of the Ottoman Empire (q.v.) following World War I (1922). Sultan Süleyman (q.v.), who conquered Hungary (q.v.) in the 16th century, was also the caliph of the Islamic World.

CALVINIST CHURCH see REFORMED CHURCH.

CANON [KANONOK]. A learned priest, above the parish priest, who is usually a member of a Cathedral Chapter (q.v.). Starting with the 12th century, canons in Hungary (q.v.) usually had a significant income, lived on the level of the middle nobility (q.v), and were the best representatives of higher ecclesiastical culture.

CARAFFA, COUNT ANTONIO (1646–93). A Habsburg general of Italian birth whose unusual cruelty and inhumanity during the early phase of the "Liberation Wars" (1683-99) (q.v.) in Hungary (q.v.) made his name despised all over the country. In 1686 Emperor Leopold I (q.v.) appointed Caraffa the commander-in-chief of the Habsburg Imperial Armies of Upper Hungary (q.v.), with the goal of ending the so-called "kuruc" uprising (q.v.) under the leadership of Prince Imre Thököly (q.v.). In 1687 he captured the important fortress of Eger (q.v.) from the Turks, and in the same year he also established the infamous "Eperjes Blood Tribunal"—officially to find out the details of an alleged "conspiracy" against Emperor Leopold, but actually to extort money from the wealthy citizens of the city of Eperjes. Caraffa had a scaffold built in the center of the town right under his own windows, where the accused citizens were forced to undergo the tortures that Caraffa's diseased mind had devised. After many months of terror, the palatine (q.v.) and other pro-Habsburg Hungarian aristocrats were able to have Caraffa recalled. But he was soon appointed to another important military post. In January 1688 he captured the fortress of Munkács defended by Thököly's wife, Countess Ilona Zrínyi (q.v.), while in May of the same year he forced Prince Apafi (q.v.) of Transylvania (q.v.) to declare the transfer of his loyalties from the Turks (q.v.) to the Habsburgs (q.v.). A few days later he also captured the city of Brassó, followed by the torture and execution of many of its prominent citizens. In 1690 Caraffa returned to Vienna (q.v.), prepared a memorandum for the conquest of Transylvania, and then spent the remaining three years of his life fighting the French under the command of Prince Charles of Lorraine (q.v.).

CAROLINA RESOLUTIO [CAROLINA RESOLUTION] (1731). An important edict issued by King Charles III (Emperor Charles VI) (q.v.) on March 21, 1731, that regulated and circumscribed the rights of the Protestants (q.v.) in Hungary. It limited Protestant religious services to private homes and to those places of worship that had already been specified in 1681. This document obliged the Protestants to pay the tithe to Catholic parish priests, to observe Catholic holidays, and, in case of a judicial process, to take the Catholic oath. It placed Protestant marriages under the authority of Catholic episcopal courts, permitted mixed marriages to be performed only by Catholic priests, and obliged the children of mixed marriages to be raised as Catholics. It also forbade apostasy from the Catholic Church under the threat of a heavy penalty, and in a secret clause it likewise instructed that the Protestants should not be employed in the state bureaucracy. The *Carolina Resolutio* also divided the Reformed (Calvinist) (q.v.) and the Evangelical (Lutheran) (q.v.) Churches into four districts or superintendencies, and declared (in an 1734 addendum) that the elected superintendents could only serve with royal approval.

CARPATHIAN BASIN. The largest geographical unit on the middle Danube River (q.v.) between Dévény (Devín) and Orsova, surrounded on three sides by the Carpathian Mountains. From the late 9th century to 1918 it was the site of Historic Hungary (q.v.). Next to the northern and the eastern foothills of the Carpathians, the largest subregions of the Basin include the Great Hungarian Plain (q.v.) and the Transylvanian Plateau, which is divided from the Great Plain by the Bihar Mountains. The political and economic unity of the Carpathian Basin was shattered by Austria–Hungary's (q.v.) dismemberment after World War I (q.v.) and by the creation of a half a dozen small states on its territory. Since its fragmentation, Hungary occupies less than one-third of its former territory and shares the Carpathian Basin with Slovakia (q.v.) (up to 1993, Czechoslovakia) (q.v.), Ukraine (q.v.) (up to 1991, the Soviet Union), Romania (q.v.), Little Yugoslavia (q.v.) or Serbia (q.v.) and Croatia (q.v.) (up to 1991 Yugoslavia) (q.v.), and, to a degree, with Austria (q.v.).

CARPATHIAN MOUNTAINS. The crescent-shaped mountain range that surrounds much of the Carpathian Basin (q.v.). The mountain range stretches in the shape of a horseshoe from the region of today's Bratislava (Pozsony) (q.v.) to the confluence of the Danube (q.v.) and the lower Morava River and to the northwestern edge of the Balkan Mountains in today's Serbia (q.v.). Its component units include the Little Carpathians and the White Carpathians in the northeast, the Beskides in the north, the Eastern Carpathians in the northeast and east, and the Transylvanian Alps or Southern Carpathians in the southeast and the south. The Carpathian Chain is complemented by the Dinaric Alps in the south and by the Alpine foothills (Julian Alps and the Karavanka) in the southwest. The highest elevation of the Carpathian Mountain range is the High Tátra in the center of the Beskides (2,655 meters = 8,711 feet).

CARPATHO-RUSYNS [UHRO-RUSYNS, HUNGARIAN-RUSYNS, CARPATHO-RUTHENIANS, CARPATHO-UKRAINIANS]. A small East Slavic (q.v.) nationality related both to the Russians (q.v.) and the Ukrainians (q.v.), whose ancestors began to move into the northeastern section of Historic Hungary (q.v.) during the late Middle Ages and continued doing so in the modern period, largely for economic reasons. Their separate national consciousness began to evolve only at the turn of the 19th to the 20th century, to a large degree under the influence of those who had emigrated to the United States and became conscious of their distinct identity. Their homeland, Sub-Carpathia *(Kárpátalja)* or Carpatho-Ruthenia (q.v.), was lost to Hungary (q.v.) and attached to newly created Czechoslovakia (q.v.) by the Treaty of Trianon (q.v.) after World War I (q.v.). Hungary regained Sub-Carpathia in 1939, but then lost it again in 1945, when it became part of the Ukrainian Soviet Republic of the Soviet Union (q.v.). During Soviet rule, the Carpatho-Rusyns were forcibly denationalized. But many of them still retained their national consciousness, for since the collapse of the Soviet Union (December 31, 1991) and the birth of an independent Ukraine (q.v.), they reasserted themselves once more. This reborn ethnic consciousness also emphasizes the Carpatho-Rusyns' historical relationship to Hungary and the Hungarians.

CARPATHO-RUTHENIA [KÁRPÁTALJA, CARPATHO-UKRAINE, TRANS-CARPATHIA SUB-CARPATHIA]. A small, mountainous, northeastern section of Historic Hungary (q.v.) of about 5,000 square miles, with a population of 1.1 million. Most of the latter are Carpatho-Rusyns (q.v.), but there are also about 200,000 Hungarians (q.v.) and a lesser number of Russians (q.v.), Slovaks (q.v.), and Romanians (q.v.). After World War I (q.v.) Carpatho-Ruthenia was attached to newly created Czechoslovakia (q.v.), in 1939 it returned to Hungary, in 1945 it was acquired by the Soviet Union (q.v.), and after the dissolution of the latter state (December 31, 1991) it became part of the independent Ukraine (q.v.). Carpatho-Ruthenia's main cities include Ungvár (Uzhhorod, Uzhgorod), Munkács (Munkachevo), Beregszász (Berehovo, Beregovo), Nagyszőlős (Vynohradiv, Vinogradov), and Huszt (Hust).

CATALAUNUM, BATTLE OF (451). The largest and one of the most important military encounters between Attila the Hun [q.v.] and the civilized West, which took place in A.D. 451 on the plains of Catalaunum, between Châlons-sur-Marne and Troyes in central France. The West was represented by the Roman armies of Aëtius Flavius (390–454) and the Visigothic armies of Theodoric II (419– 51). Although this battle is often passed off as a Western victory, it was really a draw, resulting in the withdrawal of both armies, after very heavy losses in human life. Attila's forces remained basically intact, which made it possible for him to invade Italy (q.v.) and conquer a dozen Italian cities in 452 virtually unopposed.

CATHEDRAL CHAPTER [CAPITULUM, KÁPTALAN]. In the medieval Catholic Church, "Chapters" were advisory councils of bishops and archbishops. They consisted of several canons (q.v.) under the leadership of a provost or a dean. There were also lower type chapters that functioned next to important non-episcopal churches. Cathedral Chapters had been established in Hungary (q.v.) already in the 11th century, and until 1874 they also performed notarial functions, that is, the functions of public notaries.

CATHOLIC CHURCH IN HUNGARY. Catholicism was introduced into Hungary in the late 10th century under Prince Géza (q.v.), and then made into the country's official faith by King St. Stephen (q.v.) in the early 11th century. Stephen was responsible for building the administrative infrastructure of the Catholic Church through the foundation of eight bishoprics, two archbishoprics— Esztergom (q.v.) and Kalocsa—as well as through the establishment of well over a dozen monasteries. With Hungary's (q.v.)

Christianization by Rome, the Catholic Church immediately acquired a unique presence in the country. It infiltrated Hungary's administrative and educational structure, and it also acquired large landed estates. The Hungarian Catholic Church remained part of the country's ruling establishment right up to World War II (q.v.).

Ever since King St. Stephen's time, the head of the Hungarian Catholic Church was the archbishop of Esztergom, who usually was also made a member of the College of Cardinals. Moreover, since the 13th century, he likewise held the title of primate of Hungary (q.v.), and between 1715 and 1945 "Prince Primate of Hungary." While the Protestant Reformation (q.v.) of the 16th century weakened the Catholic Church's hold on Hungary's population, the Counter-Reformation (q.v.) turned the situation around. Hungary once more became largely a Catholic country.

Since the mid–17th century, the Hungarian Catholic Church has two branches: the Roman Catholic Church that follows the Latin Rite and the Greek Catholic Church that follows the so-called Byzantine Rite (q.v.). The latter is the product of various religious unions, such as the Union of Ungvár (Uzhgorod) in 1646. This union transferred the religious allegiance of the Carpatho-Rusyns (q.v.) of Sub-Carpathia (q.v.) from the Orthodox Christian Church (q.v.) into the fold of the Roman Catholic Church, but without compelling them to give up their traditions, among them the use of the Slavic liturgical language (q.v.) and married priesthood. A similar union was also concluded by the Orthodox Christian Vlachs (Romanians) (q.v.) of Transylvania (q.v.) in 1700.

Throughout its millennial history, the Hungarian Catholic Church controlled many schools, colleges, and universities, and the predecessor of the current University of Budapest (ELTE) (q.v.) was also founded in 1635 as a Jesuit school of higher learning. After World War II (q.v.) and the communist takeover of Hungary (q.v.), the Catholic Church was disestablished and shorn of its traditional powers and possessions. Since 1990, however, it is the process of regaining some of its former position and property. In 1992 it even established its own university, the Pázmány Péter Catholic University of Budapest.

CENTRAL ASIA [TURANIAN PLAIN]. Original homeland of the Turkic horse nomads (q.v.), who moved into Eastern and Central Europe in a series of invasions, starting with the Huns (q.v.), and continuing with the Avars (q.v.), Bulgars (q.v.), Khazars (q.v.), Pechenegs (q.v.), and the Cumans (q.v.). The Finno-Ugric (q.v.) Magyars (q.v.) or Hungarians, who descended from northeastern Europe, came into contact with these Turkic peoples in the period between the 5th and the 9th centuries. They mixed with them and picked up their lifestyle. Thus, when they appeared on the fringes of Western Civilization, the Magyars were also thought to be one of these Central Asiatic horse nomads and were often referred to by the names of these invaders, among them the Huns and the Turks *(Turkoi)*. In the 13th century, Central Asia became part of the great Mongol Empire, from where—with the help of Turkic auxiliaries—the Mongols (q.v.) launched their invasion of Europe.

CENTRAL EUROPE. Historically, Central Europe included the eastern half of Western Christendom that stretched from the western limits of German linguistic line up to the borders of the Orthodox Christian World (q.v.). During much of the second millennium, its main components were the Holy Roman Empire (q.v.) (including the Czech Kingdom) (q.v.), Poland (q.v), Historic Hungary (q.v.) (including Croatia-Slavonia-Dalmatia and Transylvania) (q.v.), and the Baltic states of Lithuania, Latvia, and Estonia. It excluded the Balkans below Historic Hungary, as well as the Eastern Slavic lands to the east of Poland and Hungary. After World War II (q.v.), Central Europe was cut into two by the Iron Curtain (q.v.), and its eastern half came to be called East Central Europe (q.v.).

CENTRAL EUROPEAN UNIVERSITY [CEU]. Founded in 1991 by the Hungarian-American businessman George Soros (q.v.) to advance the cause of "open society," the CEU is an English language postgraduate school that functions mostly in Budapest and partially in Prague. It emphasizes the social sciences, and its student body comes from all of the former communist states that used to constitute the Soviet Union and its East European empire. The CEU has been accredited by the New York Board of Higher Education but it still has some problems with Hungarian authorities, who seem to frown upon this kind of international institution of higher learning within the ranks of their own traditional universities.

CENTRALISTS. The name of a group of young liberals during the decade before the revolution of 1848-49. The Centralists were fighting for the establishment of a constitutional democratic state that would be based on the principles of centralism at the top (hence their name), and on local autonomy at the bottom.   The most significant personalities of this group were Baron József Eötvös (q.v.), László Szalay (1813–64), Antal Csengery (q.v.), Ágoston Trefort (1817–88), and Baron Zsigmond Kemény (1814–75).

CENTRAL POWERS. The term by which the members of the Triple Alliance (q.v.)—Germany (q.v), Austria-Hungary (q.v.), and Italy (q.v.)—were known between 1882 and 1914. As Italy refused to honor her treaty obligations in 1914, and soon joined the Triple Entente (q.v.), during World War I (q.v.) the term Central Powers was used to refer to Germany, Austria-Hungary, and their allies, the Ottoman Empire (Turkey) (q.v.) and Bulgaria (q.v.).

ČERNOVIĆ, ARSEN [ARZÉN CSERNOVICS] (c.1633– 1706). Serbian patriarch of Ipek [Peć], who established contacts with the Habsburgs (q.v.) during the so-called Liberation Wars (1683–99) (q.v.) and in 1690 received permission from Emperor Leopold I (q.v.) to migrate with about 37,000 to 40,000 Serbian families—c. 200,000 souls—to Southern Hungary (q.v.). This act initiated the mass migration of Serbs (q.v.) to the region of present-day Voivodina (q.v.), which two centuries later (1918) resulted in the amputation of that territory from Historic Hungary (q.v.). Patriarch Černović's arrival to Hungary (q.v.) brought about the transplantation of the center of the Serbian Orthodox Church to the city of Újvidék (Neusatz, Novi Sad) (q.v.), which in the early 19th century became the base of the Serbian national revival movement.

Ultimately, this movement led to the independenceof Serbia (q.v.) (1878) and to the creation of Serbian-led Yugoslavia (q.v.) (1918).

CHANCELLOR [CANCELLARIUS, KANCELLÁR]. The head of the Royal Court Chancery (q.v.) in medieval Hungary (q.v.). First mentioned in the late 12th century under King Béla III (q.v.), the chancellorship was made into a permanent office in the 13th century. During the next several centuries, it was usually filled by high churchmen (bishops or archbishops), who were friends of the ruling monarchs and thus could be entrusted with the royal seal.

CHANCERY see ROYAL CHANCERY.

CHARLES I [CHARLES ROBERT, CAROBERTO] (1288-1342). King of Hungary (r.1301/07–42), who is known primarily as Charles Robert. He came from the Neapolitan branch of the Anjou dynasty (q.v.) and became a claimant to the Hungarian throne immediately after the death of the last member of the Árpád dynasty (q.v.), Andrew III (q.v.), in 1301. After several years of unsuccessful efforts to establish his claim to the throne, in 1307 Charles Robert was finally acknowledgedas the king of Hungary. In 1309 he was crownedin Buda (q.v.), and then in 1310 with St. Stephen's crown (Holy Crown of Hungary) (q.v.) in the medieval capital of Székesfehérvár (q.v.). Upon consolidating his rule on the Hungarian throne, Charles Robert set to work to cut down the power of the regional lords or "oligarchs" (q.v.) who had torn the country apart during the dynastic interregnum. Charles broke the Amadé lords and weakened the power of Máté Csák (q.v.) in the Battle of Rozgony in 1312. In the following years he also subdued several other oligarchs (Borsa Kopasz, István Ákos, Henrik Kőszegi, László Kán, Ugrin Csák, and Miklós Pók), but he was unable to complete the country's reunification until after the death of Máté Csák in 1321. The defeatedoligarchs were replaced by Charles's supporters, coming either from the original Magyar clans (e.g., Lackfi, Debreceni Dózsa, Szécsi, Széchényi) or from the ranks of transplanted foreigners (e.g., Drugeth). His preferencefor the new faces may have prompted Felicián Záchʼs (d.1330) assassination attempt against the king in 1330, which the latter avenged by exterminating the whole Zách family and its relations.

Recognizing the importance of economic developments, Charles Robert supported the growth of cities, manufacturing, and industry. He encouraged the immigration of miners and artisans from Bohemia (q.v.), whom he settled in the new mining towns of Upper Hungary (q.v.). He introduced the Hungarian golden *forint* (Florin] (q.v.) as a stable national currency, began to collect "regale" ("royal share") on such monopolies as salt, gold, and silver mining, and minting, and introduced obligatory fees on the operation of mills, inns, butcher shops, town fares, bridges, and fords, as well as domestic and foreign trade.

King Charles Robertʼs foreign policy was characterized by wars of conquest and dynastic alliances. In 1333 he was able to have his younger son, Andrew (q.v.), accepted as the heir to the Neapolitan throne, while in 1339 he concluded a treaty of mutual succession with his brother-in-law, Casimir the Great (r.1333–70) of Poland. He also played the role of a European peacemaker at the Congress of Visegrád in 1335 (q.v.), where he was able to iron out the differences between King Casimir (r.1335–70) of Poland, King John (r.1310–46) of Bohemia, and several Silesian and German princes. Charles Robert had also played the role of a mediator between Poland (q.v.) and the Order of the Teutonic Knights (q.v.).

CHARLES II [CHARLES THE LITTLE] (1354–86), King of Hungary (r.1385-86). A member of the Neapolitan branch of the Anjou dynasty (q.v.), who, since the age of eleven (1365), had been reared in his cousinʼs Royal Court in Hungary (q.v.). Between 1371 and 1376 Charles governed Southern Hungary with the title prince of Dalmatia-Croatia. Then in 1380, when King Louis the Great (q.v.) transferred to him his own claim to the throne of Naples, Charles led a Hungarian army to Italy (q.v.) to make good this claim. While in Rome, Pope Urban VI (r.1378–89) had him crowned king of Naples (1381), after which he got rid of both of his rivals either by assassination (Johanna, 1382) or by outliving them

(Louis of Anjou, 1384). Charles could have remained king of Naples had he not become embroiled in a conflict with the Pope, who had him excommunicated in 1385. This act coincided with a call to the Hungarian throne by a group of lords who were dissatisfied with the reign of Queen Maria (q.v.) and her widowed mother Elizabeth. Charles entered Hungary and was crowned king at the end of 1385 in the presence of the two queens. His rule, however, lasted less than two months, for in February 1386 he fell victim to a conspiracy led by the Queen Mother in cooperation with the Garai clan (q.v.). King Charles—who was called "Little" because of his small stature —was buried in the Monastery of St. Paul next to the fortress of Visegrád (q.v.), but only in 1390, after his excommunication had been lifted.

CHARLES III [HOLY ROMAN EMPEROR CHARLES VI] (1685-1740). King of Hungary and Holy Roman Emperor (r.1711–40), who, for a period during the War of Spanish Succession (1701–15), was also the King of Spain (r.1706–14). Charles was the brother of Joseph I (q.v.) and the father of Maria Theresa (q.v.), and thus the last male member of the Habsburg dynasty (q.v.). Although the Peace of Rastatt (1714) forced him to relinquish the Spanish throne, he received in return Milan, Mantua, Tuscany, Naples, and Sardinia in Italy (q.v.), as well as southern Netherlands (Belgium) and some territories on the Rhine River. Charles began his rule over Hungary (q.v.) by signing the Peace of Szatmár in 1711 (q.v.), which ended the Rákóczi War of Liberation (1703–11) (q.v.). Thereafter, he relied heavily on the pro-Habsburg Hungarian aristocracy and on the new landed nobility of foreign extraction who had been granted estates in the former Turkish-ruled and depopulated territories of Southern Hungary. During his reign, Charles waged two major wars against the Turks: one in 1716-18, which ended with the Peace of Passarowitz in 1718 (q.v.), and gained for him the Banat of Temesvár (q.v.), Northern Serbia (q.v.) with Belgrade (q.v.), and Little Wallachia (Banat of Szörény) (q.v.); and one in 1736–39, which ended with the Peace of Belgrade in 1739, whereby he had to relinquish Northern Serbia and Little Wallachia.

Under Charles's reign, parts of Southern Hungary were made into Military Frontier Districts (q.v.) with their own separate administrative system. Charles also established a standing army and the Hungarian Viceroyalty Council (q.v.) at Pozsony (q.v.) (1723). After the death of his only son, Charles promulgated the Pragmatic Sanction (q.v.), which, among others, established the right of Habsburg succession in the female line. He devoted much of his time and efforts to have the terms of this document accepted both at home and abroad, which was ratified by the Hungarian Diet in 1723. Charles was also responsible for issuing the so-called "Carolina Resolutio" (q.v.), which circumscribed and curtailed the rights of the Protestants in Hungary. He was followed on the throne by his daughter, Maria Theresa (q.v.), the only female Habsburg ruler. Together with her husband, Francis of Lorraine (Emperor Francis I) (q.v.), she initiated the Habsburg-Lorraine dynasty (q.v.) in Hungary and the Holy Roman Empire (q.v.).

CHARLES IV [AUSTRIAN EMPEROR CHARLES I] (1887 –1922). King of Hungary, Emperor of Austria (r.1916-18), and the last ruling member of the Habsburg-Lorraine dynasty (q.v.). Charles became heir to the Austro-Hungarian throne after the assassination of Archduke Francis Ferdinand (q.v.) at Sarajevo (q.v.) on June 28, 1914, and then ascended the throne after Emperor Francis Joseph's (q.v.) death on November 21, 1916. Aware of the impending defeat of the Central Powers (q.v.), Charles immediately set to work to extricate his empire from the war through a compromise peace. He also tried to influence the German Empire's policy in that direction. At the same time he altered Austria-Hungary's (q.v.) domestic policy by pressing for extended franchise rights to the national minorities (q.v.). On October 16, 1918, he proclaimed the federalization of Austria-Hungary, but the collapse of the Central Powers, followed by a series of revolutions, forced him to relinquish his thrones of Austria (November 11) and Hungary (November 13) and to resettle with his family in Switzerland. In 1921 Charles made two desperate attempts to regain his Hungarian throne, but without success. On the second occasion this effort led to a military encounter with Hungary's elected regent, Admiral Nicholas Horthy (q.v.), at the Battle of Budaörs (October 23, 1921). Charles was defeatedand captured, and then taken by the British to the Island of Madeira, where he died within a few months (April 1, 1922).

CHARLES ROBERT see CHARLES I.

CHERNOVICH see ČERNOVIĆ.

CHRISTIAN DEMOCRATIC PEOPLE'S PARTY [KERESZTÉNYDEMOKRATA NÉPPÁRT] (1989). One of the coalition partners in the first post-communist government headed by József Antall (q.v.) in the period between 1990 and 1994. The roots of this party reach back to the late 19th century, and more specifically to the birth of Christian Socialism (q.v.) in Hungary (q.v.). The followers of this movement established the Catholic People's Party *(Katolikus Néppárt)* (1894-1918) and the Federation of Christian Social Associations *(Keresztényszociális Egyesületek Szövetsége)* (1904-43), followed four decadeslater by the Christian People's Party *(Keresztény Néppárt)* (1943-45), and the Democratic People's Party *(Demokrata Néppárt)* (1945-48). The movement was resurrected at the time of the collapse of communism (q.v.) in 1989, and is currently under the leadership of György Giczy (b.1953).

CHRISTIANIZATION OF HUNGARY. The official date is A.D. 1000, when the future St. Stephen (q.v.) was crowned king of Hungary with the crown—the Holy Crown of Hungary (q.v.)—sent to him by Pope Sylvester II (r.999–1003). This was followed by the official and obligatory Christianization of the whole country. But this process of Christianization had begun at least a half a century earlier, when many Hungarians, including some top leaders, accepted Christianity in its Byzantine form (q.v.). Others were Christianized by Latin priests, including Stephen's father, Prince Géza (q.v.). But until Stephen's decision to make Hungary part of the Western Christian World, these Christianizations were only sporadic and voluntary. After A.D. 1000, the acceptance of Christianity became universal and obligatory. Moreover, the mass infusion of Western Christianity (Catholicism) also brought with it various other elements of Christian Civilization, including literacy in Latin and higher forms of social organization and administration.

CHRISTIAN NATIONAL IDEA [KERESZTÉNY NEMZETI GONDOLAT]. A politico-ideological orientation that was born during the post–World War I (q.v.) revolutions in Hungary (q.v.), as a rival force to liberalism, socialism, and communism, the latter of which culminated in the Hungarian Soviet Republic (q.v.) under the leadership of Béla Kun (q.v.) in 1919. During the interwar years (q.v.), the Christian National Idea became a kind of official ideology of the Horthy Regime (q.v.), although only in its "conservative-national" form. Two other of its variations were frowned upon. These included a right radical version that moved in the direction of fascism (q.v.) and ultimately climaxed in the Arrow Cross Party (q.v.); and a "folk-national" *(nép-nemzeti)* version that was part of mainline Populism (q.v.) during the late 1930s and early 1940s.

The Christian National Idea was ostracized and proscribed during the four decades of Soviet occupation and communist domination of Hungary. It was resurrected again in 1989-90, at the time of the collapse of the communism, when it became an official component of the intellectual foundations of the ruling governmental coalition, led by the Hungarian Democratic Forum *(Magyar Demokrata Fórum)* (q.v.), the political party that governed Hungary between 1990 and 1994. Its two strains during the post-communist period included the "conservative-national" and the "folk-national" forms. The former was represented by Prime Minister Antall (q.v.) and his supporters, while the latter found a spokesman in István Csurka (q.v.) and his Populist colleagues, whose vocal nationalism displayed both xenophobia and elements of a persecution complex. The general disenchantment with the performance of the government led by the Hungarian Democratic Forum, and the even greater disappointment with Csurka's demagogy, undermined the credibility of the Christian National Idea in Hungary. Although still alive, it had suffered a significant, but probably only a temporary, setback in the elections of 1994.

CHRISTIAN SOCIALISM [KERESZTÉNY SZOCIALIZ-MUS]. This political movement was born in the last quarter of the 19th century as a rival to political liberalism and revolutionary socialism (Marxism). It wished to solve society's social problems through the application of Christian charity and by the gradual elimination of the major social and economic differences within that society. Thus, while protecting the principle of private ownership, it stood up against the exploitation of the workers. The movement was given a powerful boost by two papal encyclicals: Pope Leo XIII's *Rerum novarum* (1891) and Pope Pius XI's *Quadragesimo anno* (1931).

In 20th-century Hungary, numerous associations and political parties were born under the aegis of this ideology, some of which also established federations. These include the Catholic People's Party *(Katolikus Néppárt)* (1894) under the leadership of Count Nándor Zichy (1829-1911), and the "Federation of Christian Social Associations" *(Keresztényszociális Egyesületek Szövetsége)* (1904) headed by the Catholic priest and social philosopher, Sándor Giesswein (1856–1923) (q.v.). Since then, numerous political parties had carried the flag of Christian Socialism, both before the rise (1945-48) and since the fall of communism (1989–90). The current Hungarian political party that best represents this ideology is the Christian Democratic People's Party *(Kereszténydemokrata Néppárt)* that entered the Hungarian Parliament (q.v.) in May 1990. But this orientation was, and is, also represented by the Hungarian Democratic Forum *(Magyar Demokrata Fórum)* (q.v.) that had dominated Hungary's first post-communist government (1990–94).

CHRONICLE [CHRONICON, KRÓNIKA]. A type of medieval historical work that narrates historical events in a chronological order. The authors of chronicles generally followed the antique models and very seldom mentioned anything that was in any way unfavorable to their subjects—be these nations, rulers, or events.

Chronicles are related to the medieval *gesta (deeds)*(q.v.), which describe the activities of prominent persons or nations. Although some medieval Hungarian historical works are called chronicles, most of them are in the category of *gesta*.

CHRONICLE OF BUDA [CHRONICON BUDENSE, CHRONICA HUNGARORUM] (1473). The first book printed in Hungary, barely two decadesafter the printing of the Bible by Johannes Gutenberg (c.1398–1468) in 1450–55. The *Chronicon Budense* is a Latin language compilation of several 14th-century Hungarian chronicles (i.e., those of Márk Kálti, Johannes the Minorite, and Johannes Küküllei), followed by a chronological account of the history of the period between the death of Louis the Great (d.1382) (q.v.) and the first fifteen years of the reign of Matthias Corvinus (r.1458–90) (q.v.). It was printed by András Hess (q.v.) in his printing shop in Buda (q.v.) with the financial support of László Karai, the Catholic provost of the capital city. Ten copies are known to exist of this first printed Hungarian chronicle.

CHRONOLOGY. In everyday usage it is the arrangement of dates and events in the order of their occurrence. In the discipline of history, however, chronology also means a subdiscipline that studies the various calendar systems that have been used in the course of history, as well as their relationships to each other. Although nowadays the universally accepted system is the Gregorian Calendar introduced by Pope Gregory XIII (r.1572–85) in 1582, for religious purposes there are still many other systems in use. These include the Hebrew calendar for the Jews, the Islamic calendar for the Moslems, and the Julian calendar for the Orthodox Christians. In the course of the past five to six millennia, there had been systems based both on lunar and solar cycles. The Jews measured time from the moment of biblical creation (3,761 B.C.), the Greeks from the first Olympic games (776 B.C.), and the Romans from the foundation of the city of Rome (754 B.C.). The Christians do so from the presumed year of Jesus Christ's birth, while the Moslems from the *Hijrah [Hegira],*that is, the flight of Prophet Mohammed from Mecca to Medina (622 A.D.). The Hungarians had switched to the Julian calendar immediately after their Christianization in the early 11th century, and then to the Gregorian Calendar in 1582.

CHURCH SLAVONIC [OLD CHURCH SLAVONIC]. The liturgical language of those Slavs (q.v.) who are Orthodox Christians (q.v.) or Byzantine Catholics (q.v.). Church Slavonic is based on the 9th-century Bulgarian Slavic made into a written language by the two Greek brothers, Sts. Cyril (q.v.) and Methodius (q.v.), who were also responsible for creating the Cyrillic alphabet (q.v.). Church Slavonic and the Cyrillic alphabet are still being used today by the Russians (q.v.), Ukrainians (q.v.), Belorussians, Carpatho-Rusyns (q.v.), Serbs (q.v.), Bulgarians (q.v.), and the Macedonian Slavs, as well as other Slavic and non-Slavic groups that follow the Byzantine Rite (q.v.). The Vlachs (Romanians) (q.v.) used it until their Latinization Movement in the 19th century. Although Byzantine Christianity had penetrated Hungary (q.v.) in the 10th century, Church Slavonic was not used until much later, when Orthodox Slavs—Rusyns (q.v.) and Serbs (q.v.)—began to settle in the country's northeastern and south-central regions.

CILLEI FAMILY. Taking their name from the Styrian town and fortress of Cilli (Celje), the Cilleis transplanted themselves to Hungary (q.v.) during the reign of King Louis the Great (r.1342–82) (q.v.). Rising steadily in social prominence, they established marriage alliances with the ruling families of Hungary, Poland (q.v), and Bosnia (q.v.), as well as with such grand Hungarian magnates as the Frangepán (q.v.) and the Garai (q.v.) families. The Cilleis reached the height of their power during the first half of the 15th century. The most prominent members of the family included: King Sigismund's father-in-law, Herman (c.1360–1435), who served as the bán of Croatia-Slavonia (1404–08, 1423–35) and was Hungary's most powerful oligarch during Sigismund's reign; Herman's daughter and Sigismund's wife (after 1437), Borbála (1392–1451), whose daughter Elizabeth married Sigismund's successor, Albert of Habsburg (r.1437–39) (q.v.), and thus became

Hungary's queen; and Borbála's nephew, Ulrich (1406–56), who was Hungary's foremost kingmaker during the chaotic decadesfollowing Sigismund's death, and for a while also the guardian (1452–56) of the minor King Ladislas Posthumus (q.v.). Ulrich Cillei viewed the members of the Hunyadi family (q.v.) as his main rivals and did everything to undercut their power.

CIS-LEITHANIA [LAJTÁNINNEN]. Meaning, "on this side of the Leitha River", this term was generally used to refer to the Austrian half of the Austro-Hungarian Empire (q.v.) after 1867. Viewed from Vienna, the Hungarian half was called Trans-Leithania *(Lajtántúl)* (q.v.). From the Hungarian perspective, the position of these terms was exactly reversed. Nevertheless, international scholarly literature usually follows the Viennese perspective and uses Trans-Leithania with referenceto the western or Austrian half of Austria-Hungary.

CISTERCIANS [CISTERCIAN ORDER, SACER ORDO CISTERCIENSIS, SO. Cist]. A Roman Catholic religious order foundedin 1098 in the French town of Citeaux (Cistercium) by the Benedictine abbot Robert. The Cistercians believed in poverty, simplicity, meditative spirituality, and in the nobility of physical labor. During the 12th through the 15th centuries, they had a significant role in the development of European agriculture. Since the High Renaissance (q.v.), however, they were primarily concerned with education. In architecture they favored the transitional style between the Romanesque (q.v.) and the Gothic (q.v.), which they helped to spread throughout Europe.

The Cistercians appeared in Hungary in the 12th century, having established their first monastery at Cikádor in Tolna County. Soon they foundedseveral other monasteries as well, among them those of Pilis, Pásztó, Szentgotthárd, and Zirc. During the Turkish occupation in the 16th and 17th centuries, the Hungarian branch of the order, along with its schools and monasteries, fell victim to the destructive warfare between the Habsburg (q.v.) and Ottoman Empires (q.v.). The order was reestablished in the 18th century, at which time its monastery at Zirc became its headquarters. Thereafter, the Cistercians devoted themselves almost exclusively to education. With the communist takeover in 1948 their schools were nationalized and the order disbanded. It was reestablished in 1989, at which time its members resumed their teaching activities.

CITIZENSHIP. Citizenship is a person's membership in the community of a state, involving legal rights and obligations. The concept of citizenship in the modern sense of that term evolved in the early 19th century. In Hungary the notion of Hungarian citizenship *(állampolgárság)*was first codified by a comprehensive law in 1879 (Act 1879:L), based largely on the German concept of *Staatsbürgerschaft*. This law remained in force until 1948, although it was modified twice: first by Act 1922:XVII to accommodated those who have lost their citizenship as a result of the Treaty of Trianon (q.v.); and then by Act 1939:XIII to deprive those political emigrés who have assumed the citizenship of other states following their emigration. Act 1948:XL replaced the original law of 1879 and assigned the right of decision concerning citizenship to the communist controlled government. This law was altered by Act 1957:V, which reasserted the principle of descent and also limited the right of dual citizenship. It was altered again by the constitutional changes that accompanied the collapse of communism (Act 1889:XXXI and Act 1990:XL), which further amended the notion of citizenship, dual citizenship, and the ways one could claim or reclaim Hungarian citizenship rights.

CIVIS. Latin for citizen of the Roman Empire and also of the Western European cities during the Middle Ages. In Hungary this term was first used to refer to the inhabitants and caretakers of episcopal fortresses during the 11th and 12th centuries. In the period since the late 17th century the term *civis* was used as a designation for the well-to-do burghers of the large agricultural towns *(mezőváros)* (q.v.) of the Great Hungarian Plain *(Alföld)* (q.v.). The latter were almost exclusively of peasant origin, who had grown rich through agricultural endeavors. The term *civis* was first used in this sense by the citizens of Debrecen (q.v.), which was and is the center of Hungarian Calvinism and is known as the "Calvinist Rome."

CLARK, ADAM [ÁDÁM] (1811-66). A Scottish engineer who, upon the urging of Count István Széchenyi (q.v.), in 1834 settled in Hungary (q.v.), where he became the builder of Europe's first major suspension bridge, the so-called "Chain Bridge" (officially Széchenyi Chain Bridge) over the Danube (q.v.). Constructed in the period between 1842 and 1849, this still existing bridge joins the formerly twin cities of Buda and Pest (modern Budapest) (q.v.). On the Buda side it leads into the tunnel built by Clark between 1852 and 1857, which links the heart of the capital with the region beyond Castle Hill, while on the Pest side it ends in Roosevelt (formerly Francis Joseph) Square. Clark's most heroic deed was his sabotaging of the Austrian General Heinrich Hentzi's attempt to blow up the bridge during the revolution of 1848-49 (q.v.). In the fall of 1944, the Chain Bridge was blown up by the Germans and it was not rebuilt until 1949. In 1855 Adam Clark married into the Áldásy family of Buda, and his descendants are still living in Hungary today.

CLUJ [CLUJ-NAPOCA] see **KOLOZSVÁR.**

COAT OF ARMS [ARMA, CÍMER]. The personal insignia of individuals, families, institutions, countries, provinces, or countries, coats of arms have developed parallel with the rise of the mounted knighthood in the 11th and 12th centuries. They experienced their greatest popularity in the 14th and 15th centuries. Some coats of arms developed naturally, while others were specifically commissioned or granted by late medieval rulers. The main components of a coat of arms are the shield that contains the insignia, the helmet which saddles the shield, and the crest. Most of coats of arms also have external decorations that surround and support the shield, including human, animal, or imaginary figures. Coats of arms of rulers, aristocrats, and top ecclesiastical dignitaries may also have other components, including tents and robes.

In Hungary, the granting of coats of arms was introduced by the members of the Anjou dynasty (q.v.) in the 14th century, about a hundred years later than in Western Europe. Hungary's traditional coat of arms evolved progressively since the 14th century and its makeup and use was first regulated by laws in 1896 and 1898. After the communist interlude of over four decades (1948–90)— which saw the use of communist emblems that had no connections with the Hungarian past—Hungary's traditional coat of arms was restored by Act 1990:XLIV.

COCOM [COORDINATING COMMITTEE FOR MULTI-LATERAL EXPORT CONTROLS]. A coordinating organ of the chief Western countries aimed at overseeing the export of the main capitalist states to the communist states. During the period of superpower bipolarity (1945–91) the COCOM's primary goal was to prevent the influx of cutting-edge high technology to the Soviet bloc (q.v.) and other communist states, including Hungary (q.v.).

COLLECTIVIZATION. Forced collectivization was developed in the Soviet Union (q.v.) and then transplanted to Hungary (q.v.) after World War II (q.v.). Following the communist takeover of power in 1948, a policy of collectivization was introduced, which resulted in the elimination of private plots and the creation of large agricultural collectives or kolkhozes (q.v.). Because of the opposition of the Hungarian peasantry, this forced collectivization produced much human misery and a decline in agricultural production. Following Stalin's death in 1953, forced collectivization ended, and by the fall of 1956 most collectives had been dissolved. After the failed Hungarian revolution of 1956 (q.v.), however, collectivization was resumed and by 1961 it was basically completed. But these collective farms proved to be much less productive than expected, and they also destroyed the traditional work ethic of the Hungarian peasants (q.v.). The lack of profitability of the collective farms became increasingly evident during the 1980s, as a result of which many of them were dissolved in the early 1990s. In the meanwhile, however, the young generations have left the countryside, and those who remained also lost touch with the traditional methods of land cultivation. As a result, Hungarian agrarian society is now in a state of crisis, which may not be resolved until the establishment of large-scale capitalistic agricultural production.

COLLEGIUM   GERMANICO-HUNGARICUM.   Founded in 1552 by Pope Julius III (r.1550–55) as "Collegium Germanicum" for the education of German priests, in 1573 Pope Gregory XIII (r.1572-85) endowed the college and raised it to the rank of a university.   In 1578 Pope Gregory also founded the "Collegium Hungaricum" for the education of Hungarian priests. But as the latter college had few students, it was soon merged with its earlier counterpart under the name of "Collegium Germanico-Hungaricum." Because of its association with the Jesuit Order (q.v.), which was dissolved temporarily in 1773, the Collegium Germanico-Hungaricum also ceased to function for about three decades. Reopened by Pope Pius VII (r.1800–23) in the early 19th century, it resumed its original functions, which it still pursues today. Of the Hungarian secular priests who studied within its walls, nearly fifty became bishops of the Hungarian Catholic Church (q.v.), and seven rose to be prince primates (q.v.) of Hungary (q.v.).

COLLEGIUM   HUNGARICUM.   The name of institutions established in 1927 by Count Kunó Klebelsberg (q.v.) in four European capitals (Berlin, Vienna, Rome, and Paris) for the purpose of serving as centers for Hungarian studies. Located in ornate palaces and possessing their own libraries, study rooms, sleeping quarters, and common areas, these Collegium Hungaricums housed Hungarian scholarship holders, who included university students as well as established scholars. They usually spent a year or two in these foreign capitals furthering their studies and searching the local archives for materials connected with the Hungarian past.   Count Klebelsberg founded these institutions during the 1920s in his capacity as Hungary's minister of culture and education in order to advance the cause of Hungary and Hungarian culture in the world.

With the triumph of communism after World War II (q.v.), these institutions were all dismantled in their original form. The buildings were retained, but they were transformed into propaganda centers for the new regime. The collapse of communism ended this misuse of the Collegium Hungaricum system and initiated a gradual rebuilding process that is still going on today.

COLLEGIUM THERESIANUM see THERESIANUM.

COLOMAN [KÁLMÁN] (c.1070–1116). Known as "Coloman the Bibliophile" *(Könyves Kálmán),* King Coloman (r.1095–1116) was the son of King Géza I (q.v.), and the nephew and successor of King St. Ladislas (q.v.). Originally Coloman was destined to be a priest, and in the early 1090s he was in actuality consecrated the bishop of Várad (Nagyvárad)(q.v.). After the death of his uncle, however, he decided to claim the throne himself. He refused to accept the rule of his younger brother, Álmos (c.1070–1127), although the latter already held the title king of Croatia (r.1091–96). The civil war that followed King Ladislas's death ended in Coloman's victory. Thereupon, Álmos received the *Dukátus* (q.v.), which he held until 1107. Being bitter about having lost out to his brother, during the next two decades Álmos became involved in about half a dozen conspiracies against King Coloman. As a result of the conspiracy of 1115, Coloman had Álmos and his son Béla [future Béla II] (q.v.) blinded. For a while Álmos lived in domestic exile, but then in 1125 he conspired with Coloman's son, the future King Stephen II (q.v.). To escape execution, he fled to the Byzantine Empire (q.v.). Although Coloman was originally not meant to be the king of Hungary, he did turn into a capable ruler. He continued his predecessor's foreign policy of expansion into the Balkans (q.v.), conquering all of Croatia (q.v) and Dalmatia (q.v.) in the course of 1102–03, and establishing the office of the *Bán* (q.v.) for these provinces.

King Coloman undercut the power of the Republic of Venice by allying himself with the Norman rulers of Sicily. He continued the close dynastic alliance with the Grand Dukes of Kiev (q.v.)

begun by his predecessors, and he also pursued friendly relations with the Papacy. He conceded to the popes the right of investiture (1106), and he also introduced priestly celibacy (1112). In contrast to most contemporary rulers, Coloman was a learned man, whose court was an important center of culture, learning, and scholarship. One of the literary result of this scholarship is the so-called *Hartvik Legend of St. Stephen* (q.v.). Another one was the now lost *Ancient Gesta (Ősgeszta)* (q.v.), which was begun in the mid-11th century, and parts of which are preserved in several later chronicles. Coloman also issued two law codes (c.1110 and 1116), in the first of which he abolished witch trials. He asserted that witches did not exist, which placed him centuries ahead of his time. Following his death, King Coloman was buried in Székesfehérvár (q.v.), next to the King St. Stephen (q.v.), who had always been his ideal.

COMENIUS, JOHN AMOS [JAN AMOS KOMENSKÝ] (1592–1670). A prominent Czech educator and social philosopher, who was born in the Moravian town of Uherský Brod (Hungarian Ford), which is the basis of the claim that he may have been of Hungarian ancestry. Comenius is known primarily for his educational methods developed in his *Great Didactic (Didactica Magna)* (1628–32), where he elaborated the foundations of modern pedagogical methods, some of which are still being used today. Several of his textbooks have been in use all over Europe for a century and a half. Being a member, and eventually a bishop, of the pietistic Moravian Brethren, Comenius sought to produce a world view that combined religious tolerance with pragmatism, optimism, and the appreciation of the ideas of humanism. Being driven out of his homeland by the ravages of the Thirty Years' War (q.v.), Comenius wandered through many countries of Europe, including Hungary (q.v.), where he found refuge under the protection of Prince George Rákóczi II (q.v.) of Transylvania (q.v.). It was during his professorship at the Calvinist College of Sárospatak (1650–54) that he wrote his path-breaking work on the philosophy of pansophism, which he published a few years later under the title *The Great Visible World (Oribis sensualium pictus)* (1658).

COMES [ISPÁN] NO. 1. In the period from the 11th through the 15th centuries, the terms *comes* and *ispán* (Lord Lieutenant)— the latter being derived from the Slavic *župan*—were the titles of royal officials in charge of the "royal counties" (q.v.). During the first two centuries after the Hungary's Christianization (11th–12th centuries) many other top royal administrators and temporal lords were also referredto by this title. Starting with the 15th century, however, the centrally appointed administrator of the royal counties assumed the enhanced title of *főispán* (Supremus Comes or Chief Lord Lieutenant) (q.v.).

COMES [GRAF, GRÓF, COUNT] NO. 2. From the late 12th century on the title *comes* came to be associated not only with "royal counties" (q.v.), but also with large hereditary estates. But in the latter case, the title of the estate owners came to be translated as *gróf* (from the German *Graf*) and not as *ispán* (from the Slavic *župan).* Starting with the 15th century, the ranks of these *comeses* or counts *(grófok)* were replenished by those large estate owners who were granted this title specifically by the kings of Hungary. The first example of such a grant of title was the case of János Hunyadi (q.v.) and his descendants, who were made perpetual counts *(comes liberi et perpetui)* of Beszterce. Starting with the late 17th century, the ranks of these hereditary counts were further increased by those who were granted the same title by the Habsburg rulers in their capacity as Holy Roman Emperors. The latter became imperial counts or counts of the Holy Roman Empire (q.v.), as was the case with the member of the Teleki family (q.v.), who were made imperial counts in 1697.

COMES PALATINUS [PALATINUS] see PALATINE.

COMMON NOBILITY [KÖZNEMESSÉG]. The collective name for the largest segment of the Hungarian nobility that had separatedfrom the upper nobility or aristocracy (q.v.) in the 13th century and subsequently came to be represented in the Lower House (q.v.) of the Hungarian Diet (q.v.). In the course of the next seven centuries the common nobility became differentiated into many subgroups, based largely on the economic and social position of these groups. The poorest segment of the common nobility consisted of the *armalists* (q.v.), who received patents of nobility in the course of the 16th through the 19th centuries, but without any property to go with it. Thus, they were often forced to survive on small peasant plots. The top layer of the common nobility consisted of the *propertied nobility (birtokos nemesség)* (q.v.) whose members usually held significant landed estates, and were in charge of local and county administration, but lacked the prestigious titles that would have placed them into the category of the titled nobility or aristocracy. In between these two layers were various groups known as the *sandaled nobility (bocskoros nemesség)* (q.v.), *seven-plum-treed-nobility (hétszilvafás nemesség)* (q.v.), and the *taxed nobility (taksás nemesek)* (q.v.), consisting of former propertied nobility who lost their estates through fragmentation or carelessness. In the 19th century, many of these lower noblemen were merged into a uniform gentry class (q.v.), which became active in local and national politics and also filled most of the administrative posts in Hungary's modern bureaucracy.

COMMUNISM, COLLAPSE OF (1989-90). This act was the culmination of a long process that was connected with the disintegration of the Soviet Union (q.v.) during the leadership of Mikhail Gorbachev (r.1985–91) as well as with the collapse of Hungary's so-called "Goulash Communism" (q.v.). The Kádár Regime (q.v.) came to an end in 1988 with János Kádár's (q.v.) forced resignation (May 20), the simultaneous appointment of Károly Grósz (q.v.) as the general secretary of the Hungarian Socialist Workers' Party (HSWP) (q.v.), followed by the appointment of Miklós Németh (q.v.) as Hungary's prime minister (November 24, 1988). This collapse continued in 1989 with the opening up of Hungary's western borders for the East German refugees (August 19 and September 11), with the foundation of several rival political parties, and finally with the HSWP's self-liquidation (October 6–10). The communists relinquished political powers in May 1990, when Hungary's first post-communist government took over under the leadership of the Hungarian Democratic Forum (q.v.) and Prime Minister József Antall (q.v.). The other members of the coalition were the Smallholders' Party (q.v.) and the Christian Democratic People's Party (q.v.)

COMMUNIST PARTY OF HUNGARY [KOMMUNISTÁK MAGYARORSZÁGI PÁRTJA]. Founded on November 20, 1918 by Béla Kun (q.v.) and his associates, this party was the representative of Lenin's Bolshevism in Hungary (q.v.). It tried to implement communism during the five months of the Hungarian Soviet Republic (q.v.) in 1919, but failed miserably. During the interwar years (q.v.) it functioned only as an illegal underground party, with many of its top leaders in exile in the Soviet Union (q.v.). Toward the end of World War II (q.v.) in September 1944, the party reorganized itself under the name of Hungarian Communist Party *(Magyar Kommunista Párt)* and was involved in the formation of Hungary's first postwar coalition government. The coalition lasted only until 1947, after which the party eliminated its rivals with Soviet help. It also forced through a fusion with the purged Social Democratic Party (q.v.), and in June 1948 assumed the name of Hungarian Workers' Party (HWP) *(Magyar Dolgozók Pártja).* This was the party, which under the leadership of Mátyás Rákosi (q.v.), orchestrated a total communist takeover and introduced a reign of terror in Hungary. Following the Hungarian Revolution of 1956 (q.v.), which was suppressed with Soviet help, the disorganized HWP immediately reorganized itself into the Hungarian Socialist Workers' Party (HSWP)*(Magyar Szocialista Munkáspárt)* (q.v.) under János Kádár's (q.v) leadership. It dominated Hungary for the next three decades, right up to the communist collapse (q.v.) in 1989. In November of that year the HSWP split into two separate parties: the Hungarian Socialist Party (HSP) *(Magyar Szocialista Párt)* and the minuscule Hungarian Socialist Workers' Party *[Magyar Szocialista Munkáspárt].* Both of these parties claim descent from the original HSWP, but only the HSP controls the resources of the old party. The elections of 1990 pushed both of these parties out of power, but the HSP still became one of the important opposition parties in the Parliament. The elections of 1994 again favored the HSP, which once more became the largest political party, and was returned to power in coalition with the liberal Federation of Free Democrats (q.v.).

COMMUNIST REGIME IN HUNGARY (1948-89/90). The four decades of communist rule between 1948 and 1989/90. The first decade was characterized by Mátyás Rákosi's misrule (1948–53, 1955–56), followed by the progressively liberalizing János Kádár (q.v.) (1956–88) and his successors (1988–89/90). These two main periods were divided by the Hungarian Revolution of 1956 (q.v.), while Rákosi's rule was cut into two by the temporary emergence of the much more humane Imre Nagy (q.v.) (r.1953–55).

COMMUNIST-SOCIALIST EMIGRATION (1919-20). This emigration consisted of those politically active persons who became involved in Count Mihály Károlyi's (q.v.) liberal-socialist (1918–19) and Béla Kun's (q.v.) communist revolutions (1919), and who then were forced to flee following the restoration of a conservative regime under the leadership of Admiral Nicholas Horthy (q.v.) (r.1920-44). Many of these emigrants were left-leaning intellectuals, but a good number of them were industrial workers, who became involved in socialist and communist labor movements and political activities. Next to Károlyi and Kun, the best known spokesman of this emigration was the noted social thinker, Oszkár Jászi (q.v.).

COMMUNIST TAKEOVER OF HUNGARY (1947–49). This process began in 1947, with the gradual liquidation of the anti-communist leaders of the rival political parties, including Ferenc Nagy (q.v.), the leader of the Smallholders' Party (q.v.) that had gained an absolute majority (57 percent) in the elections of November 1945. The takeover continued with the forced merging of the Hungarian Communist Party (q.v.) and the Social Democratic Party (q.v.) into the Hungarian Workers' Party (q.v.) and the election of Mátyás Rákosi (q.v.) as the party's general secretary

(June 1948). Finally, this takeover culminated in 1949 with the introduction of the communist reign of terror, which included political mock trials, mass arrests, mass purges, and deportations.

COMMUNIST YOUTH ORGANIZATIONS. Youth organizations have been part of the communist movements around the world almost from the very start. This was also true in Hungary (q.v.), where both the Communist Party (q.v.) and its youth organization, the Federation of Young Communist Workers in Hungary *(Kommunista Ifjúmunkások Magyarországi Szövetsége)*, functioned illegally during the interwar period (1919-44) (q.v.). Toward the end of World War II (q.v.), the revived communist movement established the new Communist Youth Federation *(Kommunista Ifjúsági Szövetség = KISZ)* (October 1944), which a few months later was transformed into the Hungarian Democratic Youth Federation *(Magyar Demokratikus Ifjúsági Szövetség = MADISZ).* After the communist takeover in 1948, the MADISZ and several of its rival youth organizations were forcibly merged into the Hungarian Young People's Federation *[Magyar Ifjúság Népi Szövetsége = MINSZ]*, which in 1950 was transformed into the Federation of Working Youth *[Dolgozó Ifjúság Szövetsége = DISZ]*. The revolution of 1956 (q.v.) resulted in the disintegration of both the Hungarian Workers' Party (q.v.) and the DISZ. They were replaced by the Hungarian Socialist Workers' Party (HSWP) (q.v.) and the Hungarian Communist Youth Federation *(Magyar Kommunista Ifjúsági Szövetség = MKISZ)* — the latter of which was commonly referred to as the KISZ. It was dissolved, along with the HSWP, in the fall of 1989. Membership in the DISZ and the KISZ was virtually obligatory for one who wished to advance in society, and it was also an important precondition for party membership after coming of age.

CONQUERING MAGYARS [HUNGARIANS]. This term usually refers to those seven Magyar (q.v.) and three Kabar (q.v.) tribes that were involved in the late–9th century conquest of the Carpathian Basin (q.v.). It is also known as the Árpádian conquest of Hungary (q.v.), so as to distinguish it from one or several earlier conquests preserved in medieval Hungarian chronicles (q.v.) and incorporated into the modern notion of "Double Conquest" (q.v.).

CONRAD VON HÖTZENDORF, COUNT FRANZ (1852–1925). Austrian field marshal, noted military author, chief-of-staff of the Austro-Hungarian Imperial Armies (q.v.) (1906-11, 1912-17), and one of the most noted generals of World War I (q.v.). As the head of the Austro-Hungarian Armed Forces (q.v.) Conrad von Hötzendorf was an advocate of a preventive war against Serbia (q.v.) and Italy in the period before World War I (q.v.). During the first three years of the war, he planned and executed all of the major Austro-Hungarian military campaigns. Following the death of Emperor Francis Joseph (q.v.) on November 21, 1916—while retaining his command over the armed forces—Conrad von Hötzendorf began to lose his influence. This was the result of his continued support of the military alliance with the German Empire (q.v.). During the final year of the war, he was replaced as chief-of-staff and assigned command of the Austro-Hungarian Armed Forces on the Italian front. After the war he published his five-volume memoirs under the title: *From My Service Years, 1906-1918 (Aus meiner Dienstzeit 1906-1918])* (1921-25).

CONSTANTINE PORPHYROGENITUS (r.913-59). Byzantine emperor, son of Leo the Wise (q.v.), and the author of *On the Administration of the Empire (De administrando imperio)* (c.952), which is one of the main authentic sources on early Hungarian history. Chapters 38 through 40 deal exclusively with the Conquering Magyars (q.v.), whom Constantine identifies as Türks. Hungarian historians have been using this work since 1739.

CONSTANTINOPLE [ISTANBUL, KONSTANTINÁPOLY, SZTAMBUL]. The capital of the Eastern Roman, later of the Byzantine Empire (q.v.), built by Constantine the Great (r.306/11–37) upon the ruins of ancient Byzantium in the early 4th century. It survived as a Christian city until its conquest by the Ottoman Turks (q.v.) in 1453, although in the period between 1204 and 1261 it was under the control of the Latins and Western Christianity. After its conquest by Mehmet the Conqueror (r.1451–81), the city was renamed Istanbul and became the capital of the Ottoman Turkish Empire (q.v.) until its dissolution following World War I (q.v.). In the 10th century, Constantinople was like a magnet that drew invaders, including the Hungarians, to its doors. During the 11th through the 15th century, when they competed for the control over the Balkans (q.v.), Hungarian-Byzantine relations were generally more antagonistic than friendly. Yet, there were a number of marriages between the two ruling houses, and Hungarian leaders and envoys would often visit Constantinople. In the middle of the 12th century, there was even a plan for a Byzantine-Hungarian Union, which was not implemented because a son was born to Emperor Manuel I (r.1143–80). Thus, the candidacy of the future Hungarian king, Béla III (q.v.), to the Byzantine throne was dropped. Constantinople—under the name of Istanbul—also played a significant role in Hungarian history during the period of the Turkish occupation in the 16th and 17th centuries. During those years the fate of Hungary and its people depended to a large degree upon the whims of the Ottoman Porte (q.v.) in Istanbul.

CONSTITUTION see HUNGARIAN   CONSTITUTION.

CONSTITUTIONAL   COURT   [ALKOTMÁNYBÍRÓSÁG].
Established in 1989 by Act I of the Revised Constitution (q.v.) and its obligations defined by Act 1989:XXXII, the Hungarian Constitutional Court began to function on January 1, 1990. Legally it is seated in the city of Esztergom (q.v.), but in practice it functions in Budapest (q.v.). The Constitutional Court consists of fifteen independent jurists (although at this moment it is manned only by nine), who are elected by the Hungarian Parliament for the purpose of examining the constitutionality of legal decrees and regulations. The court has the right to nullify all laws and regulations, as well as to suspend the application of laws judged to be unconstitutional. Its role also includes registering political

parties, passing judgments on conflicts arising out of interparty rivalries and elections, and protecting basic civil and human rights. In these respects, therefore, the role of the Constitutional Court is similar, although not quite as encompassing as that of the U.S. Supreme Court. The decisions of the Constitutional Court are binding on everyone, without the right of appeal.

CORPUS JURIS HUNGARICI [CORPUS OF HUNGARIAN LAWS]. Name of the collection of Hungarian laws reaching back to the first law code of King St. Stephen (q.v.) issued in 1001. The first collection of Hungarian laws was undertaken in the mid–16th century (c.1544) by István Ilosvay, the Catholic provost of Eger. This was followed by several other compilations in the course of the next three centuries. The largest ongoing compilation of Hungarian laws is the so-called "Millennial Edition" begun on the occasion of Hungary's millennium (1896), the first volume of which appeared in 1899. A major bilingual (Latin and English) edition of the same laws was undertaken in the United States during the 1980s. The initial two volumes appeared recently under the title *The Laws of the Medieval Kingdom of Hungary—Decreta Regni Mediaevalis Hungariae, 1000-1301* (1989) and *The Laws of the Medieval Kingdom of Hungary—Decreta Regni Mediaevalis Hungariae, 1301-1457* (1992). Until 1832, all Hungarian laws were written in Latin. Between 1832 and 1844, they became bilingual — with parallel Latin and Hungarian columns. Since 1844, they are promulgated and published only in Hungarian.

CORVINA LIBRARY [BIBLIOTHECA CORVINIANA]. The late-15th-century library of King Matthias Corvinus (q.v.), which allegedly rivaled the best libraries of contemporary Europe. The Corvina Library held several thousand illuminated volumes, and consisted of the works of the best known classical and medieval Christian authors. Named after the famed Renaissance king of the Hunyadi family (q.v.), both the library and the individual volumes are called "Corvina." Most of the Corvina volumes were destroyed during the early phase of the Turkish conquest (q.v.), but about 250 of them are still in existence. Of these, about one-fifth are in Hungary, while the rest are scattered throughout the main libraries of the Western world, including the United States.

CORVIN, JÁNOS [JOHANNES CORVINUS] (1473–1504). King Matthias's Corvinus's (q.v.) illegitimate son and designated successor, who was named the count of Hunyad and the prince of Liptó already in his father's lifetime. After the latter's death, he served as the Bán of Croatia-Slavonia (q.v.) (1495-97, 1498-1504), and also acquired the titles king of Bosnia (q.v.) and prince of Slavonia (q.v.). János Corvin tried to ascend his father's throne in 1490, but without success. Eventually he was forced to come to terms with Hungary's elected king, Vladislav II [Úlászló II] (q.v.) of the Jagellonian dynasty (q.v.). Corvin's efforts to become Hungary's palatine (q.v.) in 1503 were also frustrated. He died the following year and was buried in the Pauline Monastery of Lepoglava in Southern Hungary (Slavonia) (q.v.).

COUNCIL SYSTEM [TANÁCSRENDSZER]. Based on models developed in the Soviet Union (q.v.), the council system consists of several layers of allegedly representative councils *(soviets)*. This system was introduced to Hungary (q.v.) in 1950. Although it had the trappings of self-government, in fact all of the councils were staffed and controlled by the ruling Communist Party (q.v.). After the collapse of communism in 1989-90 (q.v.), the council system was replaced by a system of local autonomy *(önkormányzat)* (q.v.).

COUNT see COMES [GRÓF] NO. 2.

COUNTER-REFORMATION. It was the Catholic Church's effort to contain the Protestant Reformation (q.v.) and to regain territories and peoples lost to the zeal of the new faith. The most important weapons of the Counter-Reformation's were the Holy Office of the Inquisition and the Jesuit Order (q.v.). In addition to the popes, the most ardent advocates of this movement were the Habsburgs (q.v.) in their capacity as the rulers of the Holy Roman Empire (q.v.). In

Hungary (q.v.), Counter-Reformation began at the turn of the 16th
to the 17th century under the leadership of Cardinal Péter Pázmány
(q.v.), archbishop of Esztergom (q.v.) and primate (q.v) of Hungary.
As a result of the Counter-Reformation, Protestantism was pushed
back and Hungary became once more primarily a Catholic country.

COUNTERREVOLUTION   (1919–20). In a limited sense, this
counterrevolution was the triumph of the conservative-nationalist
forces under Admiral Nicholas Horthy's (q.v.) leadership against
communism represented by Béla Kun's (q.v.) Hungarian Soviet
Republic (q.v) in 1919. In a broader sense, it refers to the whole
period of Horthy's Regime (1920–44). Horthy had consolidated his
rule and gotten rid of the right radical fringe groups and "freebooter
armies" in the early 1920s, and then settled Hungary on a course of
moderate conservatism. This "kingdom without a king" had a
multiparty system and a functioning parliament, but in practice it
was closer to what is often called "directed democracy." In the past,
Marxist historians generally referred to Horthy's Regency as
Hungary's "Counterrevolutionary Regime"—which was more of a
political judgment than a critical assessment of the situation.

COUNTY see HUNGARIAN COUNTY SYSTEM.

COUNTY ASSEMBLY see HUNG. COUNTY SYSTEM.

COURT CHANCERY see CHANCERY.

COURT COUNCIL [HOFRAT, UDVARI TANÁCS].   The
Imperial Council of the Habsburgs (q.v.) in Vienna (q.v.), which
during the Middle Ages was very similar to the Hungarian Royal
Council (q.v.). With the rise of the Habsburg dynasty upon the
Hungarian throne in 1525, Ferdinand I (q.v.) tried to transform the
Court Council into a universal body that would have handled the
affairs of all of his lands, including newly acquired Bohemia (q.v.)
and Hungary. This effort, however, proved to be impossible. Thus,
by the 17th century, the Court Council became essentially a judicial

forum for the German-speaking provinces of the Habsburg Empire (q.v.). The Court Council's original intended role was gradually taken over by the so-called Secret Council (q.v.).

CRIMEA see **CRIMEAN PENINSULA.**

CRIMEAN KHANATE. A fragment state of the Golden Horde (q.v.), inhabited by the Crimean Tatars (q.v.), that came into existence in 1449 and then in 1475 became a vassal state of the Ottoman Turkish Empire (q.v.). The Crimean Khanate generally participated in the Ottoman wars of the 16th and 17th centuries, and in conjunction with these wars its armies usually invaded Transylvania (q.v.) and other parts of the dismembered Hungarian Kingdom (q.v.). In 1657 Sultan Mehmet IV (r.1648–87) relied on the Crimean Tatar Khan to defeat Prince George Rákóczi II (q.v.) for disobeying him and getting involved in the Polish War. The Crimean Khanate also launched continuous raids against Muscovite Russia (q.v.), but with the gradual decline of the Ottoman Empire, in 1774 it was detached from the Ottomans, and in 1783 annexed to the Russian Empire (q.v.). The Crimean Khanate remained part of the Russian Empire (q.v.) and the Soviet Union (q.v.) until the very end. In 1992 it went with independent Ukraine (q.v.), to which it had been administratively attached in 1954.

CRIMEAN PENINSULA [CRIMEA]. The peninsula that juts into the northern part of the Black Sea (q.v.) and separates the Azov Sea (q.v.) from its main section. According to the "Legend of the Wondrous Stag" (q.v.), which describes the mythical origins of the Huns and the Hungarians, the national genesis of these two nations took place in Meotis (Maeotis), which is generally identified by scholars with Crimea and with a section of the Pontic Steppes (q.v.) immediately to the north of it. Occupied by the Mongols (q.v.) in the 13th century, it became part of the Khanate of the Golden Horde (q.v.), and then in the 15th century of the Crimean Khanate (q.v.), which in 1475 became a vassal state of the Ottoman Empire (q.v.). In 1783 Crimea was attached to Russia (q.v.), inherited by the

Soviet Union (q.v.), and in 1992 by independent Ukraine (q.v.). In the early 1850s the peninsula was the site of the Crimean War (1853–56), which ended in Russia's defeat and in the diplomatic isolation of the Austrian Empire (q.v.). This diplomatic isolation was one of the factors the forced Emperor Francis Joseph (q.v.) to conclude the Austro-Hungarian Compromise of 1867 (q.v.).

CRIMEAN TATARS [TARTARS]. Turkic-speaking remnants of the inhabitants of great Mongol Empire's (q.v.) westernmost section, the Khanate of the Golden Horde (q.v.), which became fragmented in the 15th century. One of its fragment states was the Crimean Khanate, inhabited by the Crimean Tatars. They were ferocious fighters, who were the most feared units of the Ottoman armies during the 16th and 17th centuries. They launched continuous raids against Muscovite Russia (q.v.), Polish-Lithuanian Commonwealth (q.v.), and Transylvania (q.v.). With the decline of the Ottoman Empire (q.v.), in 1783 Crimea was annexed by Russia and the Crimean Tatars disappeared into oblivion. The rise of modern nationalism and their continued attachment to Islam made them resent their being controlled by the atheistic Soviet Union (q.v.). Thus, during World War II (q.v.), many of them viewed the invading Germans as liberators. For this, Stalin had them deported into Central Asia, where many thousands perished. Some of those who survived did return during the late 1980s and early 1990s, but their desire to regain their possessions and achieve special recognition was thwarted both by the Russians and the Ukrainians.

**CROATIA [CROATIA-SLAVONIA, CROATIA-SLAVONIA
-DALMATIA].** An associated state of the Kingdom of Hungary (q.v.) between 1091/1102 and 1918. Having moved down from present-day Southern Poland (q.v.) at the invitation of Emperor Heraclius (r.610–41) in the early 7th century, the Croatian tribes began to organize themselves into a centralized state in the 9th century. Their first crowned ruler was King Tomislav (r.910–28) whose successors generally called themselves "Kings of the Croatians and the Dalmatians" right up to the end of their

independence in 1091. Throughout this period Croatia was limited to the region to the south of the Sava and the Kulpa Rivers. The northern half of present-day Croatia was known as Slavonia (q.v.) and was part of Hungary (q.v.). The death of King Zvonimir (r.1076-89) precipitated a Hungarian intervention (1091) and the annexation of Croatia. This act was legalized by the Pact Conventa of 1102 (q.v.), an agreement between the Hungarian king and the Croatian lords. The Hungarian ruler Coloman (q.v.) was crowned king of Croatia in 1102, after which that country remained part of Hungary as an associated state for over eight centuries. At various times during the Middle Ages, Croatia was administered by the junior members of the Hungarian royal family, usually with the title "Prince of Dalmatia and Croatia" (12th century) or "Prince of Dalmatia, Croatia, and Slavonia" (13th century). At other times it was governed by a *ban* (governor) (q.v.) appointed by the king, whose function was similar to that of the palatine *(nádor)*(q.v.) in Hungary.

Upon ascending the Hungarian and Croatian thrones in 1526 and 1527, respectively, the Habsburgs assumed the title "King of Dalmatia, Croatia, and Slavonia," but continued to govern the "triune kingdom" with the aid of appointed *bans*. During the period of Turkish conquest (q.v.) in the 16th and 17th centuries, the southeastern part of Croatia, along with central Hungary, became part of the Ottoman Empire (q.v.), while the remaining section was turned into a perpetual battleground between the Habsburgs (q.v.) and the Ottoman Turks. During those critical centuries, many of the prominent Croatian aristocratic families became Magyarized (Hungarianized), including the Zrínyi (q.v.), Frangepán (q.v.), Batthyány (q.v.), and Draskovics families. The members of these families acquired high positions and became powerful proponents of the idea of a unitary Hungarian state. Following the expulsion of the Turks in the late 17th and early 18th centuries, the Habsburgs tried to weaken the ties between Hungary and Croatia, but without much success. In 1790 Croatia was again placed directly under the authority of the Hungarian Viceroyalty Council (q.v.).

The growth of modern nationalism and the switch from Latin to the vernacular languages in the 19th century undermined the relationship between the two countries and led to a growing effort of self-assertion on the part of the Croatian national leaders. This was evident during the revolution of 1848–49 (q.v.), when, under the leadership of Bán Josef Jellachich (1801–59), the Croats supported the Habsburgs against the Hungarians. The lack of appreciation by the Habsburgs, however, brought the Hungarians and the Croats together once more. This made it possible for them to come to terms in the Hungaro-Croatian Compromise of 1868 (q.v.)—which followed the Austro-Hungarian Compromise of 1867 (q.v.). The agreement of 1868 reestablished Croatia's position as an associated state of Hungary. This relationship remained intact until the dissolution of the Austro-Hungarian Empire (q.v.) in 1918, when Croatia became a component of the newly founded state of the "Kingdom of the Serbs, Croats, and Slovenes"—later renamed Yugoslavia (q.v.). During World War II (q.v.)—enlarged with Bosnia —Croatia became a nominally independent puppet state of Nazi Germany (q.v.). After the war it was made part of reassembled Yugoslavia. Then, in 1991, as a result of Yugoslavia's dissolution, Croatia became an independent republic.

CROATIA-SLAVONIA   see   **CROATIA, SLAVONIA.**

CROATIA-SLAVONIA-DALMATIA   see **CROATIA, SLAV -ONIA,   DALMATIA.**

CROATS [CROATIANS].   South Slavic people (q.v.), about 4.4 million strong, who are close ethnic and linguistic relatives of the Serbs (q.v.), but represent a different subcivilization. The Croats settled in the southern part of present-day Croatia (q.v.) in the early 7th century, where by the 10th century they created their own state and were Christianized by Rome. This act of having opted for Catholicism—in contrast to Orthodox Christianity (q.v.)—separated them permanently from their Serb brethren. It created a cultural and religious chasm between them, which they were never able to bridge. This chasm was further increased by the Croats' eight centuries of coexistence with the Magyars (q.v.) in the Catholic Kingdom of Hungary (q.v.), while the Serbs were under Byzantine (10th–14th c.) and Turkish-Islamic (15th–19th c.) influence and control. During the eight centuries of coexistence with the Hungarians, the Croat nobility had played a significant part in the political leadership of Hungary, and many of them ultimately became Hungarians. This friendly coexistence between the two peoples was disturbed by the rise of modern nationalism that led to increased antagonism in the 19th century. It was this antagonism that pushed the Croats to seek unity with the Serbs and other South Slavs after World War I. Their experiences in the new state of Yugoslavia (q.v.), however, turned out to be an unfortunate one, which led to the disintegration of that state twice within a period of seven decades. Being the products of Western Christian Civilization, the Croats are Catholics and use the Latin alphabet, while the Serbs are Orthodox Christians (q.v.) and use the Cyrillic alphabet (q.v.).

CROWN LANDS OF ST. STEPHEN see HISTORIC HUNGARY.

CSABA LEGEND (c.435–69+). The youngest son of Attila the Hun (q.v.) is also known in history as Irnák, whose mother was allegedly the daughter of the Roman Emperor Honorius (r.395–423). According to Hunnic legends found in medieval Hungarian chronicles, Prince Csaba survived the fratricidal struggle that followed his father's death (453). After losing to his older brother Aladár, who was supported by German tribes, Csaba fled to the Eastern Roman (Byzantine) Empire (q.v.), from where he moved with his followers on to Scythia (q.v.) in the East. He left about three thousand of his fighters on the Field of Csigla in Eastern Transylvania (q.v.), who allegedly became the ancestors of a tribe of Hungarians known as the *Székelys (Siculi, Szekler)* (q.v.). The same legend also perpetuated the belief that Prince Csaba promised to return, should his people ever be in danger. This return was to take place on the "Path of War" *(hadak útja)* up in the sky, which is equated in the same legends with the Milky Way.

CSÁK, MÁTÉ [MATTHEW] (c.1260-1321). The most powerful of Hungary's so-called regional lords or "oligarchs" (q.v.) during the chaotic period that saw the dying out of the Árpád dynasty (q.v.) and the emergence of the Anjous (q.v.) to the Hungarian throne (1290s – 1320s). A member of the ancient Hungarian clan of Csák, Máté was born into power. After having served as King Andrew III's (q.v.) Master of the Horse *(magister agazonum)* (1293–96) and Hungary's palatine *(nádor)* (1296–97), he took advantage of the disintegration of central power to establish himself as the virtual ruler of the country's northwestern region, which later came to be known as Lower Hungary (q.v.). Máté Csák ruled his personal realm—named after him as "Matthew's Land" *(Mátyusföld)*—from the fortress of Trencsén on the Vág River. Although he was excommunicated by the Papal Legate Gentilis for opposing Hungary's crowned monarch, King Charles I [Charles Robert] (q.v.), and although he lost the important Battle of Rozgony against the king on June 15, 1312, Máté Csák was still able to preserve much of his regional lordship until his death in 1321. After his death, his lands were reintegrated into Hungary (q.v.), along with the lands of all other defeated regional oligarchs.

CSALLÓKÖZ [SCHÜTT, ŽITNÝ OSTROV]. The largest island on the Danube River (q.v.), located between the cities of Pozsony (Bratislava) (q.v.) and Komárom (Komárno) (q.v.). Fifty-three miles long, and between nine and eighteen miles wide, it is a low-lying island subject to many floods. Precisely for this reason, during Turkish times (q.v.) it became the haven for many tens of thousands of Hungarians who were fleeing from the perpetual warfare on the Habsburg-Turkish frontier. Notwithstanding its purely Hungarian population, in 1918 Csallóköz was attached to newly created Czechoslovakia (q.v.) and renamed Žitný Ostrov. Nowadays, its traditional way of life is being endangered by the construction of the ill-fated Bős-Nagymaros (Gabčikovo) dam project on the Danube.

CSANÁD (early 11th c). A prominent Hungarian clan leader and ardent supporter of King St. Stephen (q.v.) who was responsible for defeating Ajtony (q.v.) in 1002–03, after the latter's rebellion against royal centralization and the introduction of Christianity. After Ajtony's defeat and death, King Stephen granted Csanád the former's province, whose capital, Marosvár, was now renamed in honor of Csanád. In 1030 the town of Csanád became the center of a new bishopric, whose first incumbent was St. Gerard (Gellért) (q.v.), one of Hungary's pioneer Christianizers. Soon after this, the city of Csanád also became the administrative center of the newly formed Csanád County.

CSÁNGÓ [CHANGO]. The tribal name of a group of Hungarians, who live to the east of the Carpathian Mountains (q.v.) in Moldavia (q.v.) and Bukovina (q.v.), that is, in present-day northeastern Romania (q.v.). The original Csángós were descendants of those Hungarians who had failed to cross the Carpathian Mountains at the time of the Árpádian conquest (q.v.) of Hungary (q.v.) in the late 9th century. Their numbers increased in the 10th century through the assimilation of various groups of Cumans (q.v.), and in the 15th and 16th centuries, by the flight of many Hungarians from the vicissitudes of the Hussite Wars (q.v.) and feudal exploitation represented by the introduction of bonded serfdom (q.v.). Moreover, their numbers also increased in the 18th century by those who fled from being pressed into service at the newly formed Military Frontier Districts (q.v.). Most of the Csángós continued to practice hunting, fishing, animal husbandry, and small-scale agriculture right into the 20th century. They remained isolated from the rest of the world in their secluded villages, and thus preserved many of those ancient cultural and linguistic traditions that had already been lost by the Hungarians of Hungary.

CSÁNKI, DEZSŐ (1857-1933). Historian, archivist, and one of the prominent exponents of historical geography in Hungary (q.v.) who was responsible for transplanting the Hungarian National Archives to its present home in 1923. In addition to serving as director of the National Archives, Csánki edited its main journal, *Levéltári Közlemények (Archival Proceedings)*and published many scholarly works in his chosen discipline. His magnum opus is the five-volume *Hungary's Historical Geography in the Age of the Hunyadi Family (Magyarország történelmi földrajza a Hunyadiak korában)* (1890-1913; with a posthumous volume in 1941). His other important works include *Árpád and the Árpádian Kings (Árpád és az Árpádok)* (1903), *Sketches from the Age of King Matthias (Rajzok Mátyás király korából)* (1886-1930), and the posthumous *Documentary Sources of the History of Budapest (Budapest történetének okleveles emlékei)* (1936).

CSÁRDA. A Hungarian village or a *puszta* (prairie) inn, which came to be romanticized in the 19th century in connection with the life of the *betyárs* (peasant highwaymen) (q.v.) who frequentedit. In this way the *csárda* became widely known and used in Western literature. It also gave birth to the name of the well-known Hungarian dance, the *csárdás* (pronounced "chahrdash"), which began as a peasant dance in these village inns of Hungary.

CSELE CREEK [CSELE PATAK]. A small creek in Trans-Danubia that empties into the Danube River (q.v.) to the north of Mohács (q.v.), the site of the fateful battle on August 29, 1526, which resulted in Hungary's (q.v.) defeatand the beginnings of the country's occupation by the Ottoman Turks (q.v.). King Louis II (q.v.) died in the flooded waters of the Csele while fleeing from the victorious Turks.

CSEMADOK [CSEIISZLOVÁKIAI MAGYAR DOLGOZÓK KULTÚREGYESÜLETE, CULTURAL ASSOCIATION OF HUNGARIAN WORKERS IN CZECHOSLOVAK-IA]. Founded in 1949, for four decadesthe CSEMADOK was the only representative organization of the Hungarian minorities (q.v.) in Czechoslovakia (q.v.). Its central office was, and is, in the Slovak capital of Bratislava (former Pozsony) (q.v.). It has about 500 chapters scattered throughout the country, whose goal is to nurture Hungarian culture in Slovakia (q.v.) (up to the end of 1992, Czechoslovakia). Although often accused of collaboration with those in power (especially with the Slovak communists), the elected leaders of the CSEMADOK often spoke up for the rights of the Hungarian minority in Czechoslovakia. Following the collapse of communism in 1989–90 and the rise of several Hungarian political parties in Czechoslovakia (since January 1, 1993 Slovakia), the CSEMADOK's relative influence has declined. In 1993 it has renamed itself the Cultural Association of Hungarian Workers in Slovakia *(Szlovákiai Magyar Dolgozók Kultúregyesülete)* and tries to limit its activities to cultural matters and to issues concerning Hungarian autonomy in Slovakia.

CSENDŐRSÉG see GENDARMERIE.

CSENGERY, ANTAL (1822-80). Statesman, economist, and historian during the period that embraced the revolution of 1848–49 (q.v.) and the Austro-Hungarian Compromise of 1867 (q.v.). As a close friend and associate of Baron József Eötvös (q.v.), during the 1840s Csengery was a member of the so-called Centralist Circle (q.v.). Although involved in the March revolution of 1848, like Eötvös, Csengery also opposed violence and supported the idea of a compromise with Vienna (q.v.). Later, as a close confidant of Ferenc Deák (q.v.), Csengery had a significant role in the preparation of the Austro-Hungarian Compromise. A publicist of great renown, Csengery also wrote historical works and did research on Hungarian mythology. In the latter field he was in constant disagreement with Arnold Ipolyi (q.v.), the founder of Hungarian mythological studies. Csengery's writings were published in his *Collected Works (Összegyűjtött munkái)* (5 vols., 1884), and his *Unpublished papers and notes (Hátrahagyott iratai és feljegyzései)* (1928).

CSEPEL ISLAND [CSEPEL SZIGET]. The second largest island on the Danube (q.v.), immediately to the south of Budapest. It is thirty miles long and two to six miles wide. At the time of the Hungarian conquest (q.v.) in the late 9th century, Csepel became the property of Prince Árpád (q.v.). Having lost its inhabitants during the Turkish occupation (q.v.) in the 16th–17th centuries, the island was repopulated after 1698 by its new owner, Prince Eugene of Savoy (q.v.), who brought in German and Serb settlers. In the 19th and 20th centuries Csepel became the hub of Hungary's steel, machine, and automobile industry, and its northern part was incorporated into Budapest (q.v.).

CSERNOCH, JÁNOS (1852-1927). Cardinal-archbishop of Esztergom (q.v.) and prince primate (q.v.) of Hungary (r.1913-27), Csernoch was one of the early advocates of Christian Socialism (q.v.). He became a member of the National Catholic People's Party *(Országos Katolikus Néppárt)*, in which capacity he tried to further social reforms in line with the interests of the Catholic Church (q.v.). As the head of the Hungarian Catholic Church, he had a significant role in opposing and undoing post–World War I (q.v.) socialist-communist revolutions and in helping to consolidate the conservative regime of Admiral Nicholas Horthy (q.v.). Although one of the chief spokesmen of the so-called "Legitimists" (q.v.) who favored Habsburg (q.v.) restoration in Hungary, when King Charles's (q.v.) attempts to return failed in 1921, Csernoch tried to serve as a bridge between the deposed king and regent Horthy.

CSOÓRI, SÁNDOR (b.1930). Poet, essayist, and cultural politician in post-communist Hungary. Coming from a poor peasant family, Csoóri rose to prominence under the influence of Marxism and the social revolution it represented. In wake of the revolution of 1956 (q.v), however, he became disenchanted with communist ideology and embraced Hungarian patriotism, with special attention to the fate of the persecuted Hungarian minorities (q.v.) in the neighboring states. During the 1980s Csoóri became one of the most visible and vocal critics of the Kádár Regime (q.v.). In 1987 he and a few of his friends called a meeting of the Populist-oriented dissident intellectuals at Lakitelek (q.v.), which resulted in the establishment of the Hungarian Democratic Forum *(Magyar Demokrata Fórum)* (q.v.), initially as a social movement and subsequently as a political party. Although one of the kingmakers of the post-communist coalition government of Prime Minister József Antall (q.v.), Csoóri declined to become an active politician, but turned his attention to cultural activities. Since December 1991 he functions as the president of the Hungarian World Federation (HWF) (q.v.) and devotes much of his attention to the fate of the Hungarian minorities in the neighboring countries. Although Csoóri had stayed out of active party politics, even his indirect involvement politics through the activities of the HWF has partially undermined his former popularity and his role as the "sage of the nation."

CSURKA, ISTVÁN (b.1934). Playwright, publicist, and politician. Although originally he studied to be an actor, Csurka opted to become an author. Imprisoned for his part in the revolution of 1956 (q.v.), he was initially frightened into silence. The growing liberalization of the Kádár Regime (q.v.) during the 1970s, however, made him into an even bolder playwright. His plays were highly popular and they all had hidden messages. By the 1980s Csurka had developed into an acclaimed author and a vocal exponent of Hungarian patriotism. Attempts to silence him only made him more bold and more popular. In 1987 he attended the founding congress of the Hungarian Democratic Forum (HDF) *(Magyar Demokrata Fórum)* (q.v.), where—along with Sándor Csoóri (q.v.)—he too became one of the kingmakers of the party that evolved out of it. In contrast to Csoóri, however, Csurka became an active politician.

   With the installation of the HDF-led coalition government in May 1990, he rose to be one of the most influential members of the new regime. His xenophobia, his hardly concealed anti-Semitism, and his thoughtless pronouncements, however, soon made him a source of embarrassment to the new government. The last straw was his publication of a long essay on August 20, 1992, which detailed his views about the failings of the regime. Although many of his observations were correct, this soon led to an open break with the HDF's Antall-faction and to his eventual ejection from the party. Undaunted, Csurka established the "Hungarian Way Movement" *(Magyar Út Mozgalom)* (q.v.) and the "Hungarian Truth and Life Party" *(Magyar Igazság és Élet Pártja)* (q.v.). Although in 1994 his party failed to gain representation in the Parliament, Csurka is using the above two institutions and his weekly newspaper entitled *Hungarian Forum (Magyar Fórum)* (q.v.) to advance his political agenda. At the moment he is in a duel both with the HDF and with various "leftist, cosmopolitan interest groups." The latter include the two parties of the current ruling coalition (July 1994): the ex-communist Socialist Party (q.v.) and the liberal Federation of Free Democrats (q.v.).

CUMANS [CUMANI, COMANI, KIPCHAK, POLOVTSI, KUN]. A Turkic tribal group that emerged out of Central Asia (q.v.) in the mid–11th century (c.1054). They destroyed the power of the related Pechenegs (q.v.) on the southern Russian steppes and extended their rule from the Ural River to the lower Danube (q.v.). Between the late 11th and the early 13th centuries they repeatedly raided Hungary (q.v.), Kievan Russia (q.v.), and the Byzantine Empire (q.v.). In 1223, however, they were defeated by the Mongols (q.v.) at the Kalka River on the Azov Sea (q.v.). Fleeing from the Mongol invaders, the Cumans pressed against the borders of Hungary. Then, with the start of the major Mongol invasion (q.v.) under Khan Batu (q.v.) in 1237, King Béla IV (q.v) permitted them to settle in Hungary under the condition that they would convert to Christianity. They did convert superficially, but their nomadic way of life displeased the Hungarians, who also presumed them to be the secret allies of the Mongols. Thus, at the time of the Mongol invasion in 1241, the Hungarians attacked the Cumans and killed their leader, Prince Kuthen (q.v.). Thereupon the Cumans began a systematic destruction of the country. Then they moved down to Bulgaria (q.v.). A few years later King Béla IV invited them back and settled them on a section of the Great Hungarian Plain (q.v.) that came to be called *Kunság* (Cumania). Thereafter, the history of the Cumans is intimately intertwined with that of the Hungarians. They gradually intermixed with their hosts, and by the early 16th century they even lost their native language.

CUMAN DISTRICTS AND TOWNS IN HUNGARY [KUN-SÁG, CUMANIA]. A group of disconnected districts in the center of Historic Hungary (q.v.) between the Danube (q.v.) and the Tisza Rivers (q.v.), and on the Middle Tisza, at the confluence of the Zagyva and the Kőrös Rivers. These districts had been settled by the Cumans (q.v.) between the late 11th and the late 13th centuries and then became closely associated with the Jazyg districts inhabited by the Jazyges *(Jászok)* (q.v.). These Cuman and Jazyg regions and towns enjoyed a degree of autonomy that survived in a limited form until 1876. In more recent times the region was divided into two fragmented sub-regions: Greater Cumania *(Nagy-Kunság)* and Lesser Cumania *(Kis-Kunság),* both of which were in close proximity to and in association with Jazygia *(Jászság).* The most important Cuman towns that survived the Turkish occupation (q.v.) include Halas, Szabadszállás, Mezőtúr, Kisújszállás, and Karcag. The most important Jazyg town is Jászberény, which is the site of the famous Horn of Lehel (q.v.).

CUNARD LINE. Founded in 1839, a century later (1934) it merged with the "White Star Line" and changed its name to "Cunard White Star Line." The high point of its history was the period of the four decades before World War I (q.v.) when nearly two million Hungarian citizens, over four million inhabitants of Austria-Hungary (q.v.), and many more millions from various other countries emigrated to the United States. The simple Hungarian economic immigrants of those years Magyarized the name of Cunard Line to "Gunár Lina," which became a major component of their everyday existence. By virtue of its role as the primary carrier of the Hungarian immigrants, the Cunard Line had become an indelible part of the history of Hungarian emigration to America.

**CURIA [KÚRIA, MAGYAR KIRÁLYI KÚRIA, HUNGAR-
IAN ROYAL CURIA].** After the Pragmatic Sanction of 1723
(q.v.), this was the common name of the highest level Hungarian
Royal Court *(Magyar Királyi Kúria)*, as well as of the so-called
Seven-Person Court *(Hétszemélyes Tábla)* (q.v.)—the latter of
which was of medieval origin. Between 1884 and 1949, Curia was
also the name of Hungary's Supreme Court of Appeals. In 1949 it
was replaced by the Supreme Court *(Legfelsőbb Bíróság)*, and then
in 1990 by the Constitutional Court *(Alkotmánybíróság)* (q.v.).
The term *Kúria* was likewise used after 1723 as a generic term to
refer to various types of royal courts.

CYRIL AND METHODIUS (9th c.). Two Greek brothers, known
as the "Apostles of the Slavs," who by virtue of having created the
Cyrillic alphabet (q.v.) and having carried Byzantine Christianity
(q.v.) to Great Moravia (q.v.), are considered to be the founding
fathers of Orthodox Christian Slavic Civilization. Born in
Thessaloniki (Salonika), an area where in those days Slavic was
spoken alongside Greek, the two brothers grew up in a bilingual
situation. Thus, when the time came in A.D. 863 to Christianize
the Moravians, they were the ones who were selected by Emperor
Michael III (r.842–67) and Patriarch Photius (r.858–67, 877–86) to
prepare an alphabet suitable for the Slavic language (q.v.). They
were also asked to translate portions of the New Testament into the
Slavic language and to carry Byzantine Christianity (q.v.) to the
heathen Slavic peoples. Cyril (c.826–69)—whose original name
was Constantine—and Methodius (c.815–85) had already been
involved in such a mission a few years earlier (A.D. 860) in the
Khazar Empire (q.v.) with the intention to convert the Khazars to
Christianity. They failed to do so, for the Khazar leadership opted to
convert to Judaism. But on the way back, while crossing the
Crimean Peninsula (q.v.), they encountered some Magyars
(Hungarians) (q.v.), over two decades before the Árpádian Conquest
(q.v.) of the Carpathian Basin (q.v.). Methodius also encountered
them during the 880s on the lower Danube (q.v.). If we accept the
traditional view that Great Moravia was in today's Western Slovakia

(q.v.) and Eastern Moravia (q.v.), then the Christianizing efforts of Sts. Cyril and Methodius failed—at least in the sense that Orthodox Christianity did not survive in Moravia. But if we follow the new theory which holds that Great Moravia was in today's Northern Serbia (q.v.), then they were successful both in perpetuating Byzantine Christianity there, as well as in laying the foundations of the written language among the Orthodox Slavs.

CYRILLIC ALPHABET. The alphabet devised by Sts. Cyril and Methodius (q.v.) in the early 860s for the purpose of reducing the Slavic language to writing. The Cyrillic alphabet was based on the Greek alphabet and geared to 9th-century Bulgarian Slavic spoken in the Balkans (q.v.). It became the alphabet of all Slavs who accepted Byzantine or Orthodox Christianity (q.v.) from Constantinople (q.v.). With some minor changes, it is still being used today by the Bulgarians (q.v.), Serbians (q.v.), Macedonian Slavs, Russians (q.v.), Ukrainians (q.v.), and Belorussians. It is also being used for writing the Orthodox Slavic liturgical language, the so-called Old Church Slavonic (q.v.), by other Slavs who are Byzantine Catholics (q.v.), such as the Carpatho-Rusyns (q.v.). The Cyrillic alphabet has been used in Hungary since the 10th century by the Orthodox Christians, and since the 17th century by the Byzantine Catholics.

CZAR [TSAR, CÁR]. Derived from the name of Julius Caesar (c.100–44 B.C.), this term has become the title of imperial rulers among various Slavic peoples (q.v.). The first to use it was Czar Simeon of Bulgaria (r.893–927), followed by Czar Stephen Dušan of Serbia (r.1331–55), and then by Czar Ivan IV the Terrible (r.1533/47–84) of Moscow. In the case of the Muscovite grand dukes, this title evolved gradually after the fall of Constantinople (q.v.) to the Ottoman Turks (q.v.) in 1453, although Ivan III (r.1462-1505) and Vasili III (r.1505-33) used it only occasionally. The first Muscovite ruler to be officially crowned czar was the above-mentioned Ivan the Terrible in 1547. In 1721 Peter the Great (r.1682/89–1725) exchanged the title of czar with that of *imperator,* but in common usage the Russian rulers were still referred to as czars right up to the end of the Russian Empire (q.v.) in 1917. Since the 16th century the heir to the Russian throne was referredto as *czarevich* (son of Czar), and then between 1841 and 1917 as *caesarevich*(son of Caesar). The title czar was also used recentlyby the rulers of Bulgaria (1909–46) and Montenegro (1908–18).

In Hungary the title czar *(cár)* was claimed only by one person, the Serbian freebooter Jován Černy (Iván Cserni, Iván Fekete) (d.1527), who had established himself in Southern Hungary in the period after the disastrous Battle of Mohács (August 29, 1526) (q.v.). Jován took advantage of the political chaos following Hungary's defeat by the Ottoman Turks (q.v.) and the subsequent controversy between the two rival kings—John Zápolya (q.v.) and Ferdinand of Habsburg (q.v.)—and established himself as the "czar" of a mini-kingdom in Hungary's south-central region. Based largely on the support of the local Serbian peasants who had fled from the Turkish conquest of the Balkans (q.v.), Jován "reigned" less than a year. He was defeatedand killed by King John Zápolya's forces in July 1527. Traditionally, the Hungarians used the title *cár* (czar) for the rulers of the above Slavic states, and *császár* (also derivedfrom the name of Caesar) for the rulers of the Roman, Byzantine (q.v.), Holy Roman (q.v.), and Ottoman Empires (q.v.). Later the latter term was also extended to the rulers of China and Japan, as well as to such other rulers who called themselves emperors.

CZECHIA [CZECH REPUBLIC]. This state came into being on January 1, 1993, as a result of the dissolution of Czechoslovakia (q.v.). It embraces the western half of former Czechoslovakia, i.e. two provinces of the former Czech Kingdom (q.v.), Bohemia (q.v.) and Moravia (q.v.). Czechia is the most industrialized, urbanized, and Westernizedof all of the states of East Central Europe (q.v.), which is the result of the fact that Bohemia and Moravia had remained part of the German cultural world—the Holy Roman (q.v.) and Habsburg Empires (q.v.)—from the 10th to the early 20th century. Czechia or the Czech Republic—the latter being a frequently used awkward term—embraces 30,449 square miles and has a population of 10.4 million, of whom 94 percent are Czechs (q.v.).

CZECH LANDS see **BOHEMIAN CROWN LANDS.**

CZECH KINGDOM see **BOHEMIAN CROWN LANDS.**

CZECHOSLOVAKIA. A state formed out of Austria-Hungary (q.v.) after World War I (q.v.), consisting of the Czech Kingdom (Bohemia and Moravia) (q.v.) and former Northern Hungary (Slovakia) (q.v.). Czechoslovakia survived only for seven decades, and even then only in two segments (1918–39 and 1945–92). The First Republic consisted of Bohemia (q.v.), Moravia (q.v.), Slovakia (q.v.), and Carpatho-Ruthenia (q.v.), while the Second Republic only of the first three—the last having been attached to the Soviet Union (q.v.) in 1945. At the end of 1992 Czechoslovakia was dissolved, giving birth to Czechia (Czech Republic) (q.v.) and Slovakia (q.v.).

CZECH REPUBLIC see **CZECHIA.**

CZECHS. West Slavic people, close relatives of the Slovaks, who have been part of the German-dominated Holy Roman Empire (10th c.–1806) and Habsburg Empire (q.v.) (1526–1918) for a whole millennium. As a result of this, they became more Westernized and more urbanized than any of the other peoples of East Central Europe (q.v.), save the Germans (q.v.). The Czechs have been Christianized by Rome, wherefore they have been part of Western Civilization ever since the 10th century. They use the Latin alphabet, and during the pre-modern periods they also used the Latin literary language, switching gradually to German in the 18th century. Starting with the late 14th and early 15th centuries, the Czech intellectual and cultural world was influenced by Hussitism (q.v.), which in the course of time merged with Protestantism (q.v.). Having lost much of their nobility after the Battle of the White Mountains in 1620, and having been saddled with an alien noble class after that national catastrophe, the Czech national revival was largely in the hands of intellectuals who rose out of the ranks of the lower classes. For this reason, modern Czech historical and political traditions were always more democratic and pragmatic than those of their immediate neighbors, such as the Poles and the Hungarians, whose national revival movements were controlled by their nobility. Although speaking a Slavic language, in their way of life and attitudes, the Czechs are more similar to the Germans than to most of their Slavic brethren, including the closely related Slovaks (q.v.).

CZERNIN, COUNT OTTOKAR (1872–1932). Austrian diplomat of Czech origin, who was one of Austria-Hungary's last foreign ministers (December 23, 1916–April 14, 1918). Czernin represented Austria-Hungary (q.v.) at the Peace Treaty of Brest-Litovsk in February (Ukraine) and March (Russia) of 1918. After World War I (q.v.) he became a member of the Austrian National Council, but in 1924 he withdrew from politics. Czernin's memoirs appeared under the title *In World War (Im Weltkrieg)* (1919).

- D -

DACO-ROMAN-ROMANIAN CONTINUITY. Theory espoused by Romanian historiography which claims that the Romanians (q.v.) of today—who until 1862 were known simply as Vlachs (q.v.) —are the descendants of the ancient Dacians and of their Roman conquerors. Romanian historians also assert that this ethnic mixing between the conquerors and the conquered took place in present-day Transylvania (q.v.) in the 2nd and 3rd centuries A.D. Historical and linguistic research, however—which is elaborated, among others, in the new edition of *The Cambridge Medieval History*—clearly indicates that the Romanian language developed in close proximity to the Albanians in the Balkan Peninsula (q.v.).

The Valchs did not reach the Carpathians (q.v.) until the 12th century, and did not appear in any significant numbers in Transylvania (q.v.) until the 13th century. That was also the time they populated Wallachia (q.v.) and Moldavia (q.v.), which provinces emerged as near-independent principalities in the 14th century, and then survived under the shadows and partial control of Hungary (q.v.) and Poland (q.v.) until they were incorporated into the Ottoman Empire (q.v.) at the end of the 15th century.

The roots of the theory of Daco-Roman-Romanian continuity reach back to the 18th century, when it evolved under the impact of nascent nationalism that tried to create a "grandiose past" for the Romanians. From a political point of view, the significance of this theory became especially important after the Treaty of Trianon (q.v.) that awardedTransylvania and other nearby Hungarian territories to Romania (q.v.). Thereafter, the Romanians developed this theory into a national ideology, with the goal of proving their alleged "historical rights" to Transylvania. During the Ceausescu Regime (1965–89) it became an officially mandated dogma that no one had the right to question.

DALMATIA. A province of former Yugoslavia (q.v.), now part of
Croatia (q.v.), which consists of a narrow coastal plane between the
Adriatic Sea (q.v.) and the Dinaric Alps, and of well over a hundred
islands next to it. Its most important cities—all of them sea ports
—are Rijeka (Fiume), Zadar (Zara), Split (Spalato), Dubrovnik
(Ragusa), and Kotor (Cattaro). Originally inhabited by the Illyrians,
Dalmatia became part of the Roman Empire as early as 156 B.C.
Roman rule was followed by that of the barbarians and then of the
Byzantines (q.v.). Starting with the 7th century, it was gradually
settled by migrating Slavs (q.v.), who mixed with the Illyrians and
in the course of the next few centuries altered the ethnic-linguistic
character of the whole province. During the 11th through the 15th
centuries, Dalmatia was a bone of contention among the Byzantines
(q.v.), Venetians, and the Hungarians (q.v.). Hungarian domination
became almost complete in the 14th and 15th centuries, only to be
replaced in the 16th and 17th centuries by that of the expanding
Ottoman Turks (q.v.). The 18th century witnessed the reemergence
of Venetian rule (1718–97), which was followed by that of Austria
(q.v.) (1797–1805), France (1809–14), and then Austria again
(1814–1918). In 1918 most of Dalmatia became part of the newly
formed Yugoslavia (q.v.), and since 1991 of independent Croatia
(q.v.). The Dalmatian cities and city states—especially Zara (q.v.)
and Ragusa (q.v.)—had played significant roles in medieval
Hungarian history. Fiume (q.v.), on the other hand, was the only
Hungarian port city in the period between 1776 and 1918.

DÁLNOKI-MIKLÓS, BÉLA (1890–1948). Professional army officer with the rank of a colonel-general, who, during the last phase of
World War II (q.v.), became Hungary's (q.v.) prime minister in the
Provisional National Government that functioned between December
22, 1944, and November 15, 1945. After three decades of active
military and diplomatic service, in 1942 Dálnoki-Miklós was named
aide-de-camp of Regent Horthy (q.v.), in which capacity he became a
vocal proponent of the policy espoused by Prime Minister Kállay
(q.v.) of seeking a separate peace with the Western Powers. After the
Szálasi Coup on October 15, 1944 (q.v.), which placed the fascist

Arrow Cross Party (q.v.) into power, Dálnoki-Miklós deserted to the Soviets (q.v.). They persuaded him to participate in the creation of a rival political authority, the Provisional National Assembly *(Ideiglenes Nemzetgyűlés)* and the Provisional National Government *(Ideiglenes Nemzeti Kormány)*, that began to function over three months before the collapse of the fascist regime. In his capacity as prime minister, Dálnoki-Miklós tried to follow a policy of moderation, but he was unable to counteract the power of the Soviet-supported Communist Party of Hungary (q.v.). He remained active in the Hungarian Parliament (q.v.) for two more years after leaving the office of prime minister, but he could not change the trend of events. Dálnoki-Miklós could have left Hungary at the time of the liquidation of all rival political parties in 1947–1948, but he chose to stay. He died in November 1948, only a few months after the total communization of Hungary.

DANUBE RIVER [ISTER, DANUBIUS, DUNA, DONAU, DUNAJ]. The longest and most important river in Central Europe (q.v.), which has played a constant and significant part in the history of Hungary (q.v.). It crossed Historic Hungary (q.v.) from the northwest (near Dévény) to the southeast (near Orsova), and in the course of the past two millennia had served both as a barrier as well as a connecting link between various parts of the Carpathian Basin (q.v.). Three of Hungary's former capitals—Esztergom (q.v.), Buda (q.v.), and Pozsony (q.v.)—are located on its banks, as is the current capital, Budapest (q.v.). Because of its economic importance to much of Europe, commerce on the Danube has been regulated by international agreements ever since 1616, although it was not made into an "international river" until the Peace Treaty of Paris of 1856 that ended the Crimean War.

DANUBE BASIN. The basin that embraces the Danube River (q.v.) and its tributaries, which includes such subregions as the Alpine lands of Bavaria (q.v.) and Austria (q.v.), the Czech Basin, the Carpathian Basin (q.v.), and the Wallachian Basin of Wallachia (q.v.) and northern Bulgaria (q.v.). The lands and peoples of the Danube

Basin have been bound together by various political, economic, and cultural bonds for the better part of the past two millennia.

DANUBIAN PRINCIPALITIES. The common name of Wallachia (q.v.) and Moldavia (q.v.) in the 19th century, before their unification in 1862 into a single state under the name of Romania (q.v.). After 1862, the Vlach inhabitants of these provinces began to call themselves Romanians. They were driven by the romantic-nationalistic notion that asserted that they are descendants of the Romans and the Dacians.

DANUBIAN TELEVISION [DUNA TELEVÍZIÓ]. A special television station in Budapest established in 1992 for the purpose of broadcasting Hungarian cultural programs to the Hungarian minorities in Transylvania (q.v.), Slovakia (q.v.), Carpatho-Ruthenia (q.v.), Voivodina (q.v.), Croatia (q.v.), Slovenia (q.v.), and Austria (q.v.). Its activities are closely linked to those of the Hungarian World Federation (q.v.)

DARÁNYI, KÁLMÁN (1886-1939). A right-leaning conservative politician, who for two years (1936-38) before World War II (q.v.) served as one of Hungary's lesser known prime ministers. Succeeding to the prime ministership after the death of the flamboyant Gyula Gömbös (q.v.), Darányi continued the latter's foreign policy based on increasing reliance upon Italy (q.v.) and Germany (q.v.). At home, however, he pursued a more conservative social policy than Gömbös, who used to be a proponent of moderate social reform. In 1937 and 1938, while standing up to the extreme right, Darányi signed several laws (such as the extension of the privileges of the regent, limiting voting rights, and limiting the freedom of the press) that singled him out as an exponent of both conservative nationalism and a sympathizer of the rightist trends in politics. Soon after his resignation, Darányi became the president of the Hungarian Parliament (q.v.), a position he retained until his death in November 1939.

DARVAS, JÓZSEF (1912-73). One of those Populist (q.v.) writers, who became a full-fledged communist and then served the communist system faithfully until just a few years before his death. Darvas first achieved prominence in 1937 with the publication of the sociographical portrayal of his native town, *The Largest Hungarian Village (A legnagyobb magyar falu)*. Representing the left wing of Hungarian Populism (q.v.), he worked for a communist takeover of, even though he was a member of the National Peasant Party (q.v.). Between 1947 and 1956, Darvas served in various ministerial positions, but after 1956 he reoriented his activities toward literature and to the presidency of the Hungarian Writers' Federation (1959–73). During the last few years of his life, Darvas began to reassess his past political role and moved closer to his original Populism. In 1968 he initiated a new series of Populist socio-graphical works under the collective title: "The Discovery of Hungary" *(Magyarország felfedezése)*. During the 1960s and 1970s, his political involvement was limited to the vice presidency of the Patriotic People's Front (q.v.) (1960–73) and to a nominal membership in the Presidential Council (q.v.) (1971–73).

DÁVID, FERENC (c.1510–79). The founder of Unitarianism (q.v.) and perhaps the most original thinker of the Hungarian Reformation (q.v.). Having studied in Wittenberg, the center of German Lutheranism (1545–48), Dávid returned home to become an exponent of the spirit of the new faith, mingled with the thoughts of Erasmus of Rotterdam (c.1466–1536). After serving as school master and pastor in various Upper Hungarian (q.v.) and Transylvanian (q.v.) towns, in 1557 he finally moved to his birthplace, the city of Kolozsvár (q.v.), where he became the bishop of the Hungarian Lutherans. During the 1560s he came into contact with some of the Anti-Trinitarian views of Michael Servetus (1509/11–53), was influenced by them, and subsequently became their most radical exponent in Hungary. In fact, he went beyond Servetus, for he denied even the divinity of Jesus Christ and almost reached the position of 18th-century Deists.

Having become Prince John Sigismund's (q.v.) court chaplain in 1564, Dávid initiated a systematic effort to convert the Hungarians to his new faith. At the same time he stood up for the freedom of conscience and had a significant role in the resolution of the Diet of Torda (1568), which asserted the right of all clergymen to teach their own interpretations of the Bible. This is often viewed as Europe's first law of religious freedom. Following John Sigismund's death, the new prince of Transylvania, Stephen Báthory (q.v.), turned against Ferenc Dávid, who thus ended his life in the prison fortress of Déva. While still under the protection of John Sigismund, Dávid spread his views orally and in writing. In the course of 1567–70, for example, he held a number of inconclusive debates with Péter Melius-Juhász (q.v.), who was one of the most powerful exponents of Calvinism (q.v.) in Hungary (q.v.). At the same time Dávid was also expounding his ideas in such writings as *Short Explanations (Rövid magyarázat)* (1567), *A Short Guide. (Rövid útmutatás) (1567), Disputations Derived from the Foundation of the Holy Scriptures (A szentírásnak fundamentumából vett magyarázat)* (1568), and *A Description of the Debates of Várad (A váradi disputátiónak előszámlálása)* (1569).

DEÁK, FERENC [FRANCIS] (1803-76). One of the most highly respected Hungarian statesmen and legal scholars of the 19th century who is known as the "Sage of the Nation" *(haza bölcse)* and is considered to be the "father" of the Austro-Hungarian Compromise of 1867 (q.v.). Coming from the ranks of the non-titled landed nobility (q.v.) of Western Hungary during the Era of Reform (1825–48) (q.v.), Deák became one of the most important voices for moderate social and political changes. As a member of the Diet (q.v.) during the early 1840s, he chaired the committee that produced major legal reforms, including a new and more humane penal code. Following the outbreak of the March Revolution of 1848 (q.v.), Deák became one of the formulators of the so-called "April Laws" (q.v.). Then, after the the establishment of Hungary's first responsible government (April 7, 1848), he was named the country's first minister of justice, in which capacity he eliminated all remaining legal vestiges of feudalism (q.v.). With the radicalization of the revolution and the coming of the Vienna-inspired military attacks by Ban Joseph Jellachich (q.v.) of Croatia (q.v.), however, Prime Minister Lajos Batthyány (q.v.) resigned and Deák also left governmental service. Later, after Kossuth (q.v.) took over the country's leadership, Deák returned briefly to political life. But then, when he realized the impossibility of a compromise between Austria (q.v.) and Hungary (q.v.), he withdrew to his country estate at Kehida, Zala County. Deák emerged from seclusion in 1850, when he politely rejected a call for legal consultation by the Austrian minister of justice, Anton Schmerling (1805-93). With this act Deák initiated what came to be known as the "passive resistance" to Habsburg absolutism (q.v.). In 1854 he moved to Pest (Budapest])(q.v.), where he took up residence in the Hotel English Queen, which soon became the meeting place of all of the moderate politicians, who looked to Deák for guidance and leadership. It was at the Hotel English Queen where he elaborated his basic political approach, which consisted of sticking to the royally sanctioned April Laws, while at the same time pursuing a policy of noncollaboration.

After suffering a series of foreign policy reverses, by the end of the 1850s, Emperor Francis Joseph (q.v.) was ready for a compromise. The Hungarians were divided into the two rival and antagonistic factions. These included the "irreconcilables," who were still looking to the exiled Kossuth for guidance, and the "compromisers," who would have been willing to accept some sort of arrangements with Austria (q.v.) Among the latter it was Deák's "Appeal Party" (q.v.)—versus the so-called "Resolution Party" (q.v.) —that gained the upper hand and went to work to come up with an acceptable arrangement. Deák sketched the main outlines of such an arrangement in his so-called "Easter Article" of April 16, 1865. While reasserting the constitutionality of the April Laws, he expressed his willingness to accept certain compromises, including common affairs in foreign, military, and financial matters. The Austro-Hungarian Compromise (q.v.) was finally concluded on the basis of these ideas. The compromise meant that Hungary had to relinquish some of its sovereignty. But at the same time it ended absolutism, and also made the country into an influential partner within a European great power. It is indicative of Deák's modest personality that, after concluding the Austro-Hungarian Compromise of 1867, he declined to head the new government. He also refused all honors and titles and stayed in the background during his remaining nine years.

DEÁK PARTY [DEÁK PÁRT] (1865-75). A political party founded for the purposes of achieving a political compromise with Austria (q.v.), and named after the main architect of the Austro-Hungarian Compromise of 1867 (q.v.). The roots of the Deák Party reach back to the so-called Petition Party *(Felirati Párt)* of 1861 (q.v.), which—in disagreement with the hard-line Resolution Party *(Határozati Párt(* (q.v.)—tried to move the country in the direction of a reasonable compromise with Austria (q.v.). After achieving the compromise, the Deák Party became Hungary's ruling party for the next eight years. In 1875 it merged with the so-called Left-Center of the Hungarian Parliament (q.v.) under the leadership of Kálmán Tisza (q.v.). Out of this merger was born the Liberal Party *(Szabadelvű Párt)* (q.v.), which governed Hungary (q.v.) until 1905.

DEBRECEN [DEBRECZEN, DEBRECZIN]. Known as the "Calvinist Rome," Debrecen is Hungary's second largest city with a population of 225,000. It is also one of the country's regional cultural centers, with a number of important cultural institutions and with one of Hungary's major universities. A typical example of the so-called "agricultural towns" *(oppidum, mezőváros)* (q.v.) of the Great Hungarian Plain (q.v.), Debrecen evolved from the fusion of several villages and towns, each founded in the 13th century. Being on the frontiers of Royal Hungary (q.v.), Turkish Hungary (q.v.), and Transylvania (q.v.), it grew rapidly, and in the 16th century it became an important center of artisanship, trade, agriculture, and animal husbandry. The wealthy burghers, who came to be known as *civis* (q.v.), acquired large landed estates outside the city limits. It was also in the 16th century when Debrecen became one of the important centers of Hungarian Calvinism (q.v.), its first Reformed

(Calvinist) bishop having been Péter Melius-Juhász (q.v.). Its still existing Reformed College was founded in 1538, and its first printing press in 1561. Although falling under Turkish control in 1554, Debrecen managed to preserve its own identity and its own way of life. It was among the first Hungarian cities to switch from Latin to Hungarian in its cultural and educational institutions. In 1849 it became briefly the temporary capital of Hungary (q.v.), where the dethronement of the Habsburgs (q.v.) was proclaimed. This was also true at the end of World War II (q.v.), when Debrecen once more became the seat of the Provisional National Assembly and of the Provisional National Government.

DEMBINSZKY, HENRIK [HENRYK DEMBINSKI] (1791-1864). A Polish freedom fighter, who in 1848-49 became a Hungarian general and one of the commanders-in-chief of the Hungarian Revolutionary Armies. During the Polish Revolution of 1830-31, Dembinszky served as the military commander of Warsaw. After the defeat of the revolution, he went into exile in Paris. In 1848 he traveled to Hungary (q.v.), where Kossuth (q.v.) appointed him the commander-in-chief (January 29–March 3, 1849). As he turned out to be an ineffective commander, he was relieved and transferred to command the Army of the Northeast (April 19–August 30). Dembinszky became commander-in-chief again (July 30–August 9) just before the Hungarian surrender at Világos (August 13) (q.v.). After the defeat of the revolution, Dembinszky fled to the Ottoman Empire (q.v.), then returned to his Paris exile, where he wrote his reminiscences about the Hungarian Revolution. They appeared posthumously under the title *Dembinszky in Hungary (Dembinszky Magyarországon)* (1874).

DEMSZKY, GÁBOR (b.1952). One of the founders and leaders of the Hungarian Dissident Movement (q.v.) centered on the periodical *Beszélő (Speaker)*, who since the fall of 1990 is the lord mayor of Budapest. During the 1980s Demszky was perhaps the most harassed, and thus best known member of the Urbanist (q.v.) branch of the Hungarian Dissident Movement (q.v.). In 1988 he participated in the founding of the Federation of Free Democrats (FFD) *(Szabad Demokraták Szövetsége)* (q.v.), and for the next two years also served as the FFD's executive secretary. In May 1990 Demszky became a member of the Hungarian Parliament (q.v.), while in November of that year he was elected the lord mayor of the Hungarian capital, a position he also retained after the 1994 elections.

DEPORTATIONS IN HUNGARY. The first mass deportations in Hungary took place in the summer and fall of 1944, when several hundred-thousandHungarian Jews (q.v.) were collected and taken to death camps in Germany (q.v.). This was repeated on a much smaller scale in 1951, when about twenty-thousand of the "former exploiters" were deported from Budapest (q.v.) to the remote countryside. Their homes were confiscated, and then were awardedto various communist party functionaries.

DÉZSMA [DECIMA] see TITHE.

DIET [DIÉTA, ORSZÁGYŰLÉS]. The Hungarian Feudal Parliament (q.v.) before the rise of the modern parliamentary system in 1848. The origin of the diet goes back to the Golden Bull (q.v.) in the 13th century, when the king *(rex)* found himself confronted with the state or nation *(regnum)*. In those days the "nation" consisted of the upper clergy (q.v.) and the nobility *(nobiles)* (q.v.)—the latter including the secular aristocracy *(barones)* (q.v.), and, toward the end of that century, also the common nobility (q.v.) that had evolved out of a class of "royal servants" *(servientes regis)* (q.v.). By 1300 the legislation of laws was a prerogative that was increasingly shared by the king and the diet. After the promulgation of the Golden Bull (q.v.) in 1222, all members of the above-mentioned leading classes could participate personally in the annual diets. In the course of the 14th and 15th centuries, however, it became increasingly common for the lower nobility to participate through their elected representatives. In the 16th century, the de facto polarization of the noble class into the upper and the lower nobility was legalized by the introduction of a bicameral legislature. The upper clergy and the secular aristocracy *(barones)* continued to represent themselves in the Upper House (q.v.), while the rest of the nobility were represented by their elected emissaries in the Lower House (q.v.). This practice was then codified by Act I of 1608. This bicameral system survived the end of feudalism (1848) and the rise of the modern parliamentary system. The extension of voting rights and the inclusion of prominent nonaristocratic persons in the Upper House, however, changed the composition of both houses of the Hungarian Parliament (q.v.).

DIPLOMATICS [DIPLOMATIKA]. One of the Auxiliary Sciences of History (q.v.), which deals with the origins, physical appearance, language, style, authenticity, and legal-constitutional significance of medieval and early modern documents (diplomas). The latter were usually issued by rulers, high administrative and church officials, and occasionally even by powerful individuals for official purposes. In Europe, most of these diplomas were written in Latin, and they were usually sealed by a hanging seal made of gold, silver, or wax. Those with a golden seal contained some of the most important royal or imperial resolutions and they were called "golden bulls"— such as the Golden Bull of Hungary of 1222 (q.v.).

DISPLACED PERSONS [DPs]. Persons of many nationalities, faiths, and political beliefs, who after World War II (q.v.) found themselves in defeated and destroyed Germany (q.v.) or Austria (q.v.), and then either could not or did not wish to return to their homelands. In the course of time about 755,000 of them emigrated to the United States: 120,000 under the War Brides Act of 1946, and 635,000 under the two Displaced Persons Acts of 1948 and 1950. There were about 18,000 Hungarians among their ranks — with perhaps another 9,600 coming under the McCarran-Walter Act of 1952 and the Refugee Relief Act of 1953. The majority of these represented the upper and upper-middle echelons of interwar Hungarian society. Many of them were former army officers, bureaucrats, and other white collar professionals with nontransferable degrees in military science, law, and the humanities. Thus, they could not fit well into American society. But their children—while retaining bilingualism, as well as dual identity and affiliation—became assimilated, and did so very successfully.

DISSIDENT MOVEMENT IN HUNGARY (1977–89). The Hungarian Dissident Movement was basically a movement of writers, poets, historians, and other intellectuals. It was in many ways an unavoidable by-product of the economic and political liberalization introduced by the Kádár Regime (q.v.) in the late 1960s. This liberalization made it possible for Hungarian intellectuals to put forth daring ideas and even to engage in some protest activities. The first real sign of this protest movement was the signing of "Charta 77" put out by Czech intellectuals in Prague (q.v.) in 1977. After the initial 34 signatures, it was ultimately signed by 256 Hungarians, all of whom were placed under publication interdiction by the Kádár Regime. These reprisals, however, failed to stop the movement. It continued and resulted in the publication of the *Bibó Memorial Volume [Bibó emlékkönyv]* (1980), in which scores of Hungarian intellectuals came together to honor István Bibó (q.v.), whose writings best represented the spirit of tolerance and cooperation in East Central Europe (q.v.).

In addition to protesting against the policies of the regime, this work brought together the representatives of the two main ideological orientations of Hungarian intellectual life: the Populists (q.v.) and the Urbanists (q.v.). After this common effort, the two orientations diverged once more, giving birth to two distinct and often rival dissident movements. The Urbanists gathered under the flag of the underground periodical *Speaker (Beszélő)* (1981-). They demanded liberal political reforms, organized showy protest movements, and in general, propagandized against the Kádár Regime with the help of their Western sympathizers. The Populists, on the other hand, devoted their attention primarily to the worsening fate of the Hungarian minorities (q.v.) in the surrounding Successor States (q.v.). They wrote about the problems of these minorities under the oppressive communist-chauvinist regimes in Romania (q.v.),

Slovakia (Czechoslovakia) (q.v.), and Carpatho-Ruthenia (q.v.). They visited these minorities whenever possible and then presented lengthy petitions to Hungarian governmental and party leaders, demanding intervention on their behalf. They were especially upset with the violently chauvinistic Ceausescu Regime (1965–89) in Romania (q.v.).

The rise of Gorbachev in the Soviet Union (q.v.) (1985), the simultaneous introduction of a more liberal suffrage law in Hungary (1985), and the growing disenchantment with the Bős–Nagymaros [Gabčikovo] Hydroelectric Power Plant on the Danube (q.v.) (1985) gave a new impetus to the Hungarian Dissident Movement. These events encouraged the two orientations within the movement to come together in a joint conference, which they did at Monor in 1985, but without any success in ironing out their differences. After 1985, events sped up very rapidly. In 1986 there were joint mass protests on the thirtieth anniversary of the Hungarian Revolution of 1956 (q.v.). In the following year (1987) the first gathering of Populist intellectuals took place at Lakitelek (q.v.), which was attended by the most popular "reform communist" politician, Imre Pozsgay (q.v.), and which also gave birth to the Hungarian Democratic Forum (HDF) (q.v.) as a social protest movement. The same year also witnessed a mass protest prompted by the unwelcome political program of the newly appointed prime minister, Károly Grósz (q.v.). These protest movements were organized primarily by the Urbanist intellectuals around the *Beszélő*, who in 1988 transformed their movement into a liberal political party, the Federation of Free Democrats (FFD) (q.v.). By the time of the elections of 1990, the FFD was one of the two main political parties in Hungary, and after May of that year, it became the main parliamentary opposition party of the first post-communist government (1990-94) headed by the Populist HDF. Four years later (1994), the FFD became a partner in Hungary's current coalition government with the ex-communist Socialist Party (q.v.).

The year 1988 witnessed the second meeting of the Populist intellectuals at Lakitelek, where they decided to turn the HDF into a political party. The leaders of the HDF had a major role in tearing down the communist system in 1989. As a result of this, in May of 1990, the HDF became the ruling political party within the first post-communist government. With this victory, the polarization of the Hungarian Dissident Movement was completed and the difference between its Populist and Urbanist orientation became even more pronounced. Occasionally, this disparity turned into outright animosity, as demonstrated by the activities of István Csurka (q.v.) and his group of "folk-national"*(nép-nemzeti)* activists. Notwithstanding their disagreements, however, both of these orientations of the Hungarian Dissident Movement had a major role in undermining and tearing down the ruling communist system in Hungary.

DISZ see COMMUNIST YOUTH MOVEMENTS IN HUNGARY.

DIVAN [DIVÁN]. The Imperial Council of the Ottoman Empire (q.v.) that was responsible for the affairs of the state. Consisting of the top dozen or so military, administrative, financial, and judicial leaders of the empire, the Divan was initially chaired by the sultan (q.v.), and then from the mid-16th century onward by the grand vizier (q.v.). Through much of the 16th and 17th centuries, the fate of the former Kingdom of Hungary (q.v.) — including Turkish Hungary (q.v.), Transylvania (q.v.), and even Habsburg Hungary (q.v.) — was in the hands of the Divan in Istanbul (q.v.).

DIVIDE ET IMPERA [DIVIDE AND CONQUER]. An expression that has been part of Hungarian consciousness and history-writing ever since the 16th century. It has been used especially by the members of the Habsburg dynasty (q.v.) of Vienna (q.v.) in their role as the rulers of a large multinational empire that also included the Kingdom of Hungary (q.v.). In the 19th century this took the form of playing the national minorities (q.v.) — Croats (q.v.), Romanians (q.v.), Carpatho-Rusyns (q.v.), Serbians (q.v.) , Slovaks (q.v.) — against the rebellious Hungarians (Magyars)] (q.v.) so as to undercut the latter's power position in Hungary and within the Habsburg Empire (q.v.).

DOCTRINAIRES [DOKTRINÉREK]. In general, this term refers to those who are dedicated followers of a particular ideology. In Hungarian history, however, it was applied to a group of young liberal reformers during the 1840s, who were also known as the Centralists (q.v.). Their leader was Baron József Eötvös (q.v.).

DOCTRINE OF THE HOLY CROWN see HOLY CROWN, DOCTRINE OF.

DOBÓ, ISTVÁN (c.1500–72). One of the heroes of Hungary's struggle against Ottoman Turkish occupation (q.v.) in the 16th century. As a member of the upper nobility (q.v.) of Hungary, between 1549 and 1552 Dobó was the commander of the fortress of Eger (q.v.). His most heroic deed was stopping a 60,000-70,000-strong Turkish army under the command of Grand Vizier Ahmed and Ali Pasha of Buda with a garrison of only 2,000, and thus saving Upper Hungary (q.v.) for the Christian World. In recognition of the significance of his deed, King Ferdinand I (q.v.) awarded him the fortresses of Déva and Szamosújvár, and then in 1553 named him the *voievod* of Transylvania (q.v.). In 1556, when Transylvania again broke away from the Habsburgs (q.v.), Dobó lost his possessions there, but King Ferdinand compensated him with the grant of new estates, as well as with the command of the fortress of Léva. In 1566, at the time of Sultan Süleyman's (r.1520–66) last campaign, Dobó rallied his forces to prevent the sultan from advancing to Vienna (q.v.). Yet, in 1567 he was accused of having switched over to John Sigismund (q.v.) of Transylvania, for which Emperor Maximilian (q.v.) had him arrested at the Diet of Pozsony in December 1569 (q.v.). After over two years of imprisonment, Dobó was able to prove his innocence and was permitted to return home, where he died a few months later.

DOHNÁNYI, ERNEST [ERNŐ] (1877-1960). An internationally known composer, pianist, and conductor, who at various times had served as a student, a professor, and the director of the Liszt Music Academy of Budapest (q.v.). Being a supporter of the cultural policies of the neoconservative Horthy Regime (q.v.) in interwar Hungary (q.v.), Dohnányi left the country at the end of World War II (q.v.) and in 1949 settled in the United States. While teaching at Florida State University, he also traveled as a concert pianist. He was known as one of the most gifted performers of his time. Perhaps because of his long stay in Germany (q.v.) during the formative years of his life, Dohnányi never became an advocate of the use of the elements of Hungarian folk music in modern musical compositions, as did his better known contemporaries Béla Bartók (q.v.) and Zoltán Kodály (q.v.). Dohnányi started a musical dynasty, with several of his offspring having become prominent musicians andconductors.

DOMANOVSZKY, SÁNDOR [ALEXANDER] (1877–1955). One of the gifted historians of the first half of the 20th century, who was the most noted exponent of the Hungarian Civilization School *(Kulturgeschichte, müvelődéstörténet)*, and also the most able administrator of the historical profession in Hungary. As a professor at the University of Budapest (1914–48) (q.v.), he also initiated agricultural historical studies. He edited and published several medieval chronicles, wrote a number of works on the economic life of medieval cities, authored a few histories of Hungary, and also edited and coauthored a major four-volume *History of Hungarian Civilization (Magyar müvelődéstörténet)* (1939-42). While writing, teaching, and directing dozens of doctoral dissertations in the area of economic and agricultural history, Domanovszky ran the affairs of the Hungarian Historical Association (1916-46) (q.v.). Moreover, simultaneously he edited for three decades (1913-43) the association's official journal, *Centuries (Századok).*

DOMINICANS [DOMINICAN ORDER, ORDO FRATRUM PRAEDICATORUM = OFB]. In Hungarian *domokosok* or *dominikánusok*, this Catholic religious order was founded by St. Dominic (c.1170-1221) of Castilia in 1215 with the goals of spreading Christianity among the pagans, regaining heretics for the true faith, and cultivating the dogmas of the Catholic Church.   The

Dominicans had a significant role in the inquisition that climaxed in the 16th century. They settled in Hungary in 1221 with the intention of converting the pagan Cumans (q.v.). From Hungary (q.v.) they traveled far and wide in Eastern Europe and Asia, and one of their members, Frater Julianus (q.v.), was the first to bring news of the Mongol invasion (q.v.) of Europe.

DOUBLE CONQUEST. The theory put forth by Gyula László (q.v.) during the 1970s, which holds that the Árpádian conquest (q.v.) of the late 9th century was only the last of perhaps several earlier conquests. According to László, Árpád's invasion had been preceded by at least one other Hungarian conquest of the Carpathian Basin (q.v.), that of the so-called "Late Avars" (q.v.) around A.D. 670. Based on archeological, ethnographic, linguistic, and other evidence —including historical traditions preserved in early Hungarian chronicles—he identified the "Late Avars" as "Early Hungarians." Others pursued this theory even further, asserting the occurrence of several earlier conquests. It is to be noted here that Hungarian chronicle traditions also view the Hunnic invasion of the early 5th century as one of these earlier "Hungarian conquests."

DÓZSA, GYÖRGY (c.1470–1514). The leader of the Hungarian peasant rebellion of 1514. A member of the *Székely* (q.v.) nobility and a man of some achievements in the fight against the Turks (q.v.), Dózsa was selected to be the military commander of the anti-Turkish crusade proclaimed by Cardinal Archbishop Tamás Bakócz (q.v.) after his unsuccessful bid for the papacy. The volunteers were to meet in the vicinity of Pest (q.v.), on the opposite side of the Danube (q.v) to the royal capital of Buda (q.v.), with the goal of organizing into a crusading army. But the gathering peasants were so disenchanted with their lords that the prospective anti-Turkish crusade soon turned into an antifeudal rebellion. Dózsa, who was also disenchanted with the way things were developing in Hungary, went along with the peasants. In his May 18 proclamation issued in the town of Cegléd he openly sided with the peasants and began a series of military operations against the armies of the nobles (q.v.).

On May 26 he defeated one such feudal army, which he followed up by the capture of the cities of Arad (q.v.) and Lippa. He also began the siege of Temesvár (q.v.). But this siege gave time to the nobles to organize new armies and challenge Dózsa's crusaders. On July 15 Dózsa was defeated, wounded and captured by János Zápolya (q.v.), the *voievod* of Transylvania (q.v.), who subsequently became the king of Hungary. Following his capture Dózsa was tortured and executed. Through his actions and his heroic death he achieved immortality by becoming one of the most revered heroes of the peasant masses of Hungary.

DÓZSA   PEASANT   REVOLUTION   [PEASANT   WAR] (1514). The revolution under the leadership of György Dózsa (q.v.), which was originally intended to be a Christian crusade against the Ottoman Turks (q.v.), but which soon turned into an anti-feudal rebellion on the part of the peasants of Hungary. After their defeat, the peasants were permanently bound to the soil and thus became serfs. With minor exceptions, serfdom (q.v.) remained unchanged in Hungary until the revolution of 1848 (q.v.).

DRACULA   [VLAD   THE   IMPALER,   VLAD   III,   TEPES] (c.1431-76). Prince of Wallachia (r.1456-62) and a man of diseased mind, who — as the son of Vlad II, Dracul (Devil or Dragon) (r.1435-46) — came to be called Dracula (Little Devil or Son of the Devil) by his own people. Although fighting against the Turks (q.v.), his cruelty eventually compelled King Matthias Corvinus (q.v.) of Hungary (q.v.), Dracula's overlord, to have him imprisoned (1462-76). Mixed with various vampiristic elements, Vlad's sadistic deeds gave birth to the Dracula legend that was later incorporated by Bram Stoker (1847-1912) into his novel of the same name (*Dracula*, 1897). It was also incorporated into a number of Hollywood movies, in which Count Dracula was most famously played by the Hungarian American actor Béla Lugosi (1883-1956).

DRANG NACH OSTEN [PUSH TO THE EAST]. The German drive to the East had begun under the Frankish emperor Charlemagne (r.771-814), and then continued through the next eleven-hundred years right up to the early part of the 20th century. Although initially simply the natural expansion of the German tribes from their westerly homeland in search of more living space, by the 9th and 10th centuries this expansion took the form of spreading Christianity among the heathen Slavs (Poles, Czechs, Moravians, Slovaks, Slovenes, Croats) and non-Slavs (Magyars, Prussians, Livs, Lithuanians, Latvians, Estonians, Finns) of East Central Europe (q.v.). By the 12th through the 14th centuries, many of the Germans moved into the region as invited settlers, who were sought after by the native rulers for their know-how in the area of urbanization, artisanship, and advancedagricultural methods. Many of the important cities of Poland (q.v.), Bohemia (q.v.), and Hungary (q.v.) were founded by these German settlers, who for a while acquiredrights and privileges that were envied even by the native nobility.

With the rise of modern nationalism, a significant percentage of the German urban dwellers became assimilated into the native population. Some of those who lived in compact German-speaking areas remained Germans (e.g., the Sudeten Germans of Bohemia, the Swabians of Hungary, and the Saxons of Transylvania), but then most of them were expelled in wake of World War II (q.v.). The German *Drang nach Osten* came to a halt at the time of World War I (q.v.), after which they were pushed back repeatedly, loosing significant territories after both world wars.

In Hungarian history this German *Drang nach Osten* had both positive and negative results. On the one hand, it compelled the Hungarians to fight a defensive struggle against German incursions for several centuries. On the other hand, the influx of German know-how enriched Hungarian culture significantly, and it also aided the country's modernization through much of its history.

DRAVA [DRAVE, DRAU] RIVER. The river that for many centuries had formed the borderline between Hungary (q.v.) proper and the triune kingdom of Croatia-Slavonia-Dalmatia (q.v.). It runs parallel to the Sava (q.v.), which is to the south of it. Between the two rivers are the northern part of Croatia (q.v.) and the provinces of Slavonia (q.v.) and Szerémség (q.v.). The Drava empties into the Danube (q.v.) where that river turns to an easterly direction.

DUAL ALLIANCE (1879). A secret military alliance between Germany (q.v.) and Austria-Hungary (q.v.) in wake of the new German-Russian antagonism that followed the Congress of Berlin of 1878. This alliance stated that the two states would extend help to each other if Russia were to attack either one of them. Moreover, if attacked by another state, they would each remain neutral. The Dual Alliance was the first in a series of alliances that ultimately polarized Europe into two armed camps: the Triple Alliance (1879–82) (q.v.) and the Triple Entente (1893–1907) (q.v.). These alliance systems bound all of the European great powers and many of the smaller states into two competing power groups, and thus served as one of the underlying causes of World War I (q.v.). Hungary's position within the Dual Alliance made it impossible for her to stay out of the war. The loss of the war, however, doomed her territorial and national integrity.

DUAL IDENTITY AND AFFILIATION. A common phenomenon in the modern world, where there are increasing number of individuals, who feel spiritual and cultural affinity to more than one nation or state. This holds true for many Hungarians, both at home and abroad. Those at home may possess dual loyalties because of their origins and incomplete assimilation into the Hungarian nation. Those in the neighboring states have dual affiliations, because their nationality and emotional loyalties do not coincide with their citizenship (i.e., the Hungarian minorities in Romania, Slovakia, Serbia, Croatia, Slovenia, and Ukraine). Those abroad profess dual identities, because even after a certain degree of assimilation, they still have strong emotional bonds to the mother country and to their nation at home.

DUALISM. The union of two sovereign states, usually bound together by the person of a single ruler who may have two distinct titles in the two countries. Hungary had been involved in such dualistic "personal unions" at various times with Poland (q.v.), the Czech Kingdom (q.v.), and Habsburg Austria (q.v.). The last of such unions came into being with the Austro-Hungarian Compromise of 1867 (q.v.), which transformed the Austrian Empire (q.v.) into Austria-Hungary (1867–1918). Both halves of the Dual Monarchy (q.v.) were completely separate and independent in their domestic policies, even to the point of having two separate citizenships. At the same time they were bound together by the person of the ruler —who was an emperor in Austria and a king in Hungary—as well as by their common foreign policy, military affairs, and financial affairs as far as these related to these common matters. (See also Austria-Hungary.)

DUALIST PERIOD [AGE OF DUALISM, 1867-1918] see **AUSTRIA-HUNGARY.**

DUAL KINGSHIP see **SACRED DUAL KINGSHIP.**

DUAL MONARCHY see **AUSTRIA-HUNGARY.**

DUBROVNIK see **RAGUSA.**

DUKAL AGE [FEJEDELMEK KORA] (c.896-1000). The period between the Árpádian conquest (q.v.) and the coronation of St. Stephen (q.v.) as the first Christian king of Hungary (q.v.). The first half of this period (c.896–955) was characterized by internal disunity, tribal independence, and incessant marauding expeditions to Western Europe and the Byzantine Empire (q.v.). The second half (955–1000), on the other hand, was exemplified by centralization, Christianization, establishment of princely powers, and the molding of the tribes into a nation. During the first six decades, princely powers had sunk so low that not even their reigns are really known. We only know that some of those who ruled after Árpád (q.v.) probably included his five sons, Levente (q.v.), Tarhos, Üllő, Jutas, Zoltán (q.v.), and Fajsz — the first five of these being Árpád's sons, and the last probably Jutas's son. The princes of the second half of this period included Taksony (r.955–70) (q.v.), Géza (r.970–97) (q.v.), and Vajk (r.997–1000). The latter became King St. Stephen (q.v.), who from A.D. 1000 onward ruled as a Christian king.

DUKÁTUS [HERCEGSÉG]. Ever since the early 11th century, the members of the Hungarian ruling family — outside the ruler who bore the title of king—had the rank of a duke *(dux)*.   During the 10th through the 13th centuries, the heir to the throne—usually the king's son—was placed in charge of about one-third of Hungary (q.v.), which he governed with all the rights and privileges of a king. This system of governance was referred to as the *dukátus*. Starting with the 16th century some prominent members of the Hungarian aristocracy (q.v.) also began to assume the title of duke or prince. Then, in the course of the 17th and 18th centuries, a few of these families acquired the rank of the "Prince of the Holy Roman Empire."   The latter included the Esterházy (q.v.), the Batthyány (q.v.), and the Grassalkovich families, as well as the archbishop of Esztergom (q.v.), who thereafter was also known as the prince primate (q.v.) of Hungary.

DURAY, MIKLÓS (b.1945). During the 1970s and 1980s Duray was the best known Hungarian dissident in Czechoslovakia (q.v.), who after the fall of communism (1989) founded the "Coexistence Political Movement" *(Együttélés Politikai Mozgalom),* which in 1990 became the largest Hungarian political party in Czechoslovakia (since 1993 Slovakia).   Although harassed and persecuted ever since 1973, when he assumed the leadership of the Hungarian dissident movement in Czechoslovakia, after the fall of communism he was rehabilitated. Since 1990 Duray serves as an elected member of the Czechoslovak (1990-92), later Slovak (1993-) Parliament.   His most important works, many of them published illegally, include: *Report from Slovakia (Szlovákiai jelentés)* (1982), *In the Dog House (Kutyaszorító)* (autobiography, 1983), and *Under the Double Yoke (Kettős elnyomásban)* (1988).

- E -

EAST CENTRAL EUROPE [ZWISCHENEUROPA]. A term popularized after World War II (q.v.) in conjunction with the eastern half of former Central Europe (q.v.) that had fallen under Soviet (q.v.) control. The countries normally included in this category were Poland (q.v.), Czechoslovakia, (q.v.), Hungary (q.v.), Romania (q.v.), Yugoslavia (q.v.), Bulgaria (q.v.), Albania, and occasionally East Germany. At times, also included were such countries absorbed by Russia (q.v.) and the Soviet Union (q.v.) as Estonia, Latvia, Lithuania, and perhaps Ukraine (q.v.) and Belorussia—although the latter two were usually excluded, because they have always been part of the Orthodox Christian World (q.v.).

Historically speaking, East Central Europe covered the region between the German and the Russian-speaking worlds that stretched from the Baltic down to the Black Sea (q.v.) and the Adriatic (q.v.). Traditionally, the most significant states in this area used to be Poland (q.v.), Bohemia (q.v.), and Historic Hungary (q.v.). At the end of the Middle Ages, its central section became part of the Habsburg Empire (q.v.), its southern section of the Ottoman Empire (q.v.), and its northern section of the Russian (q.v.) and Prussian (q.v.) states. Occasionally, East Central Europe was also referred to as Eastern Europe (q.v.), although its meaning was ambiguous, for often it also included the European part of the Soviet Union (q.v.).

EASTERN CHRISTIANITY see BYZANTINE CHRISTIANITY, ORTHODOX CHURCH IN HUNGARY.

EASTERN EUROPE. Traditionally, that part of Europe that stretches from the Eastern borders of Poland (q.v.) and Hungary (q.v.) or the Habsburg Empire (q.v.) to the Urals, and is inhabited primarily by Eastern Slavs (q.v.) who are followers of Orthodox or Byzantine Christianity (q.v.). Following World War II (q.v.), when

Europe was cut into two by the Iron Curtain (q.v.), the term Eastern Europe was also applied to such Central (q.v.) or East Central European (q.v.) states as Poland, Czechoslovakia (q.v.), and Hungary. This state of affairs lasted until the collapse of communism in 1989-90, when these "borderlands of Western Civilization" began to refer to themselves once more as Central European states.

EAST ROMAN EMPIRE see BYZANTINE EMPIRE.

EAST SLAVS see SLAVS.

ECCLESIASTICAL SOCIETY [ORDO ECCLESIASTICUS, EGYHÁZI TÁRSADALOM]. This segment of society consisted of religious institutions and their personnel. At the time of Hungary's (q.v.) Christianization, the members of its Ecclesiastical Society consisted mostly of foreigners, including Greeks, Germans, Italians, and Czechs. They were soon joined by the newly Christianized native Hungarians. Yet, throughout the late medieval and early modern periods, foreigners constituted a significant portion of the ecclesiastical personnel, playing especially important roles at the Royal Court and in the newly established religious orders and their monasteries.

Initially, there was little difference between the monastic and the secular clergy, and their hierarchical differences were also minimal. This relatively egalitarian nature of the Hungarian Ecclesiastical Society began to disintegrate in the 13th century, and by the 14th century it became strictly polarized into three distinct classes: the upper, middle, and lower echelons. The upper clergy (q.v.) consisted of the archbishops, bishops, deans of cathedral chapters, heads of major religious orders, and abbots of royal monasteries, whose position came to approximate that of the lay aristocracy (q.v.). The middle clergy consisted of the members of the cathedral chapters, large collegiate chapters, canons, archdeacons, and rectors of large parishes, whose position and income approximated that of the non-titled landed nobility (q.v.). The lower layer was made up of village priests, chaplains, assistant priests of larger churches, seminarians, and theology students, and their position was comparable to that of the lower nobility (q.v.).

The members of the Hungarian Ecclesiastical Society were bound together by their common identity, their dedication to the Catholic Church, and their identical literary culture, which, during the Middle Ages, distinguished them from the largely nonliterate lay nobility. They alone possessed the right to deliver the sacraments to the faithful, they were the intermediaries between men and God, and they were exempt from taxation as well as from lay jurisdiction. They were also distinguished from their lay counterparts by their obligatory celibacy (in Hungary, after 1092), which freed them from family obligations and made them even more dedicated to the church and its religious institutions.

Although theoretically any free man could become a member of the Ecclesiastical Society, in practice, with a few exceptions, the upper layers of that society were reserved for the corresponding members of the lay society. Moreover, after the great Dózsa Peasant Rebellion of 1514 (q.v.), when the Hungarian peasant masses were pushed into bonded serfdom (q.v.), it became legally impossible for peasants to take advantage of the social mobility previously available through the Catholic Church. Thus, until the middle of the 19th century, the upper and middle layers of the church hierarchy were occupied only by the members of the Hungarian nobility.

ECKHARDT, TIBOR (1888–1972). One of interwar Hungary's prominent politicians, the leader of the Independent Smallholders' Party (q.v.) who in 1941 emigrated to the United States—with the tacit approval of Regent Horthy (q.v.)—so as to prepare the ground for a postwar rapprochement between the two countries. Eckhardt gained prominence during the revolutions of 1918–19, when he became associated with the anti-communist "governments" of Arad (q.v.) and Szeged (q.v.). In the 1920s he moved to the right and joined such groups as the Association of Awakening Hungarians (q.v.) and the Hungarian National Independence (Race Protective) Party *(Magyar Nemzeti Függetlenségi [Fajvédő]Párt)*, and in 1928 he became the Executive President of the Hungarian Revisionist League (q.v.). During the 1930s Eckhardt moderated his political stance, joined (1930) and assumed control (1932) over the Smallholders' Party, and then became an advocate of an anti-German and a pro-English orientation in Hungarian politics. In the United States he founded the unsuccessful "Free Hungary Movement" (1941-42) (q.v.). He also became active in the American Hungarian Federation (q.v.) and in the Hungarian National Council (q.v.), where he represented a conservative and even a legitimist (q.v.) orientation.

ECKHART, FERENC (1885-1957). One of Hungary's great legal, constitutional, and economic historians whose theories concerning Hungary's constitutional development created much furor in interwar Hungary (q.v.). This was especially true about his *The History of the Doctrine of the Holy Crown (A Szentkorona-eszme története)* (1941), wherein he claimed that the alleged uniqueness of Hungary's constitutional development was a figment of someone's imagination. He believed that this doctrine was analogous to similar doctrines in Bohemia (q.v.) and, to a lesser degree, in Poland (q.v.) —countries whose economic developments were similar to that of Hungary. For the same reason, he rejected the alleged similarities between Hungarian and English constitutional developments, which was an idea that was very popular in Hungary. During Eckhart's professorship at the School of Law of the University of Budapest (1929-57) (q.v.), he authored about a dozen major works, most of them forward-looking and controversial. He summarized his views about Hungary's constitutional development in his *Hungarian Constitutional and Legal History (Magyar alkotmány- és jogtörténet)* (1946). Eckhart spent the last ten years of his life trying to adjust to Marxism, but without much success.

ECONOMIC EMIGRATION see **EMIGRATION FROM HUNGARY.**

EDICT OF TOLERATION see **TOLERATION, EDICT OF**

EDUCATION IN HUNGARY. Five types of educational institutions developed in Medieval Europe: (1) Monastery schools attached to the headquartersof various monastic orders (5th c.); (2) cathedral and chapter schools, connected with the seats of bishoprics or archbishoprics (8th c.); (3) parish schools at some of the more important rural congregations (9th c.); (4) guild schools in the rising burgher towns, where many artisans were concentrated in trade guilds (12th c.); and (5) universities, many of which evolved from earlier cathedral schools (12th c.). Parish schools were elementary institutions, while monastery, cathedral, and chapter schools were secondary institutions that emphasized the seven liberal arts and functioned almost exclusively in Latin. The seven liberal arts included the more practical *quadrivium* (mathematics, geometry, astronomy, and music) and the more humanistic *trivium* (grammar, logic, and rhetoric). Urban schools, on the other hand, stressed artisanship and practical knowledge, and did so mostly in the vernacularlanguages.

Educational developments were slightly delayed in Hungary (q.v.), but in the course of the 11th through the 14th centuries, these five different types of schools also developed there. The last of them were the artisan schools and the universities, both of which appeared in the 14th century. The former of these were generally known as "German schools"—largely because of the heavy presence of German settlers in Hungary's urban centers, and also because they functioned mostly in German. In addition to the special skills needed by a particular guild, these urban schools taught practical subjects, including mathematics, geography, and business correspondence.

The rise of these urban schools was paralleled by the founding of the early Hungarian universities. The first of these was the University of Pécs (1367) (q.v.), followed by the University of Óbuda (1389) (q.v.), the University of Pozsony *(Academia Istropolitana)* (1467) (q.v), and then the still existing University of Budapest (1635) (q.v.)—the last of which was originally established at Nagyszombat (q.v.). In the meanwhile, momentous changes have taken place that altered the political fortunes of Hungary. The 16th century witnessed the Ottoman Turkish conquest (q.v.) of much of

the country, followed by its trisection into Royal Hungary (q.v.),
Turkish Hungary (q.v.), and Transylvania (q.v.). This was paralleled
by the spread of Protestantism (q.v.) and then by a religious-
ideological struggle between the Catholic and the Protestant
Churches. To aid them in this struggle, the Protestant
denominations established many schools, a few of which (e.g.,
Debrecen, Sárospatak, Marosvásárhely, Brassó, Bártfa) developed
into institutions of higher learning whose primary purpose was the
education of clergymen for the new faith.

Primary education was rare and sporadic until the 18th century,
and more common in Protestant than in the Catholic regions. In
1777, under the impact of the Enlightenment, Empress Maria
Theresa (q.v.) issued the *Ratio Educationis* (q.v.), an education law
that tried to introduce a centralized and uniform educational system,
and also extended state control over religious schools. This law was
amended in 1806 by a new education decree issued by Emperor
Francis I (II) (q.v.). Although introduced with the intent of
modernization, neither of these laws had any real impact on mass
education. During the revolution of 1848-49 (q.v.), the revolutionary
government elaborated a plan for a uniform national educational
system, but it had no time to implement it. This process of
modernization was continued during the Age of Absolutism (q.v.)
and Provisorium (Provisional Period) (q.v.), but with centralizing
and Germanizing tendencies. The introduction of the uniform eight-
grade *Gymnasium* system (10–18 yrs.) and the six-grade *Realschule*
system (10–16 yrs.)—on top of a four-year primary school—with an
increased use of the German language, was also meant to serve these
goals.

The foundations of a uniform Hungarian educational system
were laid down by the Education Law of 1868 (Act XXXVIII), which
established an obligatory six-year elementary education throughout
the country, and at the same time also created a multipath system of
secondary education. Some of these paths led to elite education and
opened the doors to university studies, while others led to general
education and ended in various *culs-de-sac,* without any possibility of
further education. Moreover, a significant majority of primary

educational institutions remained in the hands of the churches and continued the practice of religious indoctrination. This dual system of education survived right up to the end of World War II (q.v.), when a uniform mass educational system was introduced on the Soviet model. This meant an end to religious education, the introduction of eight-year primary and a four-year secondary school system, and a rapid expansion of higher education. Between 1950 and 1990, most of the secondary schools consisted of specialized "technikums" that offered practical education, with only minimal emphasis on traditional culture and learning.

University education also expanded in the second half of the 19th and the early 20th century, mostly through the foundation of new institutions of higher learning. These included the Technical University of Budapest (1782/1857) (q.v.), the University of Kolozsvár (1872; moved to Szeged in 1921) (q.v.), the University of Pozsony (1912; moved to Pécs in 1923) (q.v.), and the University of Debrecen (1914) (q.v.). Following World War II (q.v.), several new universities came into being, partially by separating a number of agricultural, chemical, economic, medical, and theological faculties from the traditional universities (1945–51), and partially by establishing dozens of new institutions of higher learning. Most of these, however, were small institutions that resembled specialized colleges rather than comprehensive universities.

Simultaneously with the rapid expansion of higher education, the research capacity was also expanded, primarily by separating research from teaching, and transferring most research activities from the universities to the newly created research institutes of the totally restructured Hungarian Academy of Sciences (q.v.). This Soviet system of education survived until the end of the communist regime in 1989–90. At the moment, it is being revised, either through a partial return to traditional models or by borrowing Western, especially American, models. The latter is particularly true for higher education, where American-type university structure and degrees are being introduced. These include the Ph.D. as a research doctorate, as well as the increased use of English as a language of instruction.

EGER [ERLAU]. City in northeastern Hungary, the capital of Heves County, with a population of 67,000 (1989), which is one of the important centers of Hungarian wine production. Its historical importance was especially great during Hungary's Turkish occupation (q.v.) in the 16th and 17th centuries, when its fortress was one of the important Christian strongholds until 1596. Its greatest historical moment occurred in 1552, when, under the leadership of István Dobó (q.v.), it stopped a major Turkish military offensive and thus thwarted Ottoman expansion for nearly half a century. Eger was conquered by the Turks in 1596, and retaken by Christian forces in 1687.

ELECTIVE KINGSHIP. A system that developed in 14th-century Hungary (q.v.), Bohemia (q.v.), and Poland (q.v.), whereby—after the dying out of the respective native dynasties (1301, 1305, and 1370), the nobility reserved the right to elect their own kings. While this system functioned already in the 14th century, not until the Diet (q.v) of 1447 was it officially proclaimed in Hungary. The Hungarian nobility preserved this right until the Diet of 1687, when they renounced it in light of the Habsburg (q.v.) success in pushing the Turks (q.v.) out of Hungary.

ELIZABETH, EMPRESS [ERZSÉBET] (1837-98). Wife of Emperor Francis Joseph (q.v.), and as such, the empress of Austria and queen of Hungary. She was the daughter of Prince Maximilian II (1808-88) of Bavaria, who married Emperor Francis Joseph (q.v.) in 1854, by whom she had three daughters and one son. The latter was the unfortunate Archduke Rudolf (q.v.), who committed suicide at Mayerling in 1889. Unhappy in the stiff court circles of Vienna, Elizabeth became enamored with Hungary (q.v.) and the chivalrous Hungarian aristocracy (q.v.), and also learned Hungarian fluently. This attachment was reciprocated by the Hungarian nobility, upon whose insistence Elizabeth was also crowned queen of Hungary. This took place at the time of Francis Joseph's coronation as king of Hungary in conjunction with the Austro-Hungarian Compromise of 1867 (q.v.), which Elizabeth helped to bring about.

ELIZABETH, SAINT [SZENT ERZSÉBET] (1207–31). The daughter of King Andrew II (q.v.), who at the age of fourteen (1221) married Louis, the son of the marquis of Thüringia. They had three children, before her husband died in a crusade led by Emperor Frederick II (r.1212–50) in 1227. As a widow she was compelled to leave the fortress of Wartburg along with her children, eventually ending up in Marburg. Under the influence of her confessor, Conrad of Marburg, she dedicated the remaining years of her short life to charitable activities, including the building of a hospital in honor of St. Francis of Assisi. Already regarded a saint while still alive, she was officially canonized in 1235, in the year of her father's death and her brother's, Béla IV's (q.v.), accession to the throne of Hungary (q.v.). The Teutonic Knights (q.v.) selected Elizabeth as their patroness, and the Franciscan Order (q.v.) became the most ardent propagator of her cult. During the 13th and 14th centuries, a whole circle of legends evolved around Elizabeth, most of which became incorporated into the the the Érdy-Codex of the early 16th century.

EMIGRATION FROM HUNGARY. Hungarians have been migrating to neighboring countries throughout the last five centuries. Major migrations, however, did not taken place until the turn of the 19th and 20th centuries, and then largely to the United States. If we examine these Hungarian emigrations since the 16th century, we find that they were motivated by three distinct considerations: (1) search for adventure, (2) the need to escape political persecutions, and (3) the desire for a better livelihood. The first of these produced only sporadic and limited exoduses and was usually limited to individuals or individual families. The second resulted in numerically more significant political emigrations, usually after failed revolutions, civil wars, or military conquests. The third brought about the mass migration of peasants and workers, usually with the seldom fulfilled intention of repatriation.

While the greatest number of persons emigrated for economic reasons, the majority of the identifiable emigration waves were political in nature. Thus, during the past three centuries, Hungary witnessed about seven major emigration waves, six of which were primarily politically motivated. The six political emigrations included: (1) the "Rákóczi Emigration" following the Rákóczi War of Liberation (1703-11) (q.v.) against the Habsburgs (q.v.), led by Prince Francis Rákóczi II (q.v.); (2) the "Kossuth Emigration" (q.v.), after the Hungarian Revolution of 1848–49 (q.v.), under the leadership of Lajos Kossuth (q.v.); (3) the "Communist-Socialist Emigration" (q.v.) after the revolutions of 1918-19 (q.v.), whose leaders included Count Mihály Károlyi (q.v.) and Béla Kun (q.v.); (4) the great "Intellectual Emigration" (q.v.) of the 1930s, following Hitler's rise to power and the spread of the Nazi ideology in Hungary; (5) the great "Political Emigration of 1944–47" (q.v.), following World War II (q.v.), that forced much of the social-economic-political elite of the interwar Hungary (q.v.) into exile; and (6) the "Political Emigration of 1956" (q.v.), following the Hungarian Revolution of 1956 (q.v.), that landed about 200,000 Hungarian emigrants in Western countries, including Europe, North America, and Australia. The single emigration that was basically of economic nature was the great turn-of-the-century "Economic Emigration" of the pre-World War I (q.v.) years (c.1880-1914) that brought more Hungarians to the United States than all the political immigrations together.

In the course of the 19th and 20th centuries, altogether about 2.3 million Hungarian citizens left Hungary. Of these about one million were Magyars (q.v.) or ethnic Hungarians, 80% of whom (800,000) ended up in the United States. The large majority of them (650,000 to 700,000) arrived before 1914. They constituted the great Economic Emigration, which consisted mostly of peasants, unskilled workers, and some displaced skilled workers who were driven to the United States by their lack of livelihood in their homeland. Only about 118,000 came since World War I—a good third of these (47,000) during the interwar years (q.v.), and nearly two-thirds (71,000) after World War II.

Of all the immigrant waves, those coming after World War I made the greatest impact upon American society. The Hungarian intellectuals, scientists, and artists, who came during the 1930s to escape Nazism, were catalysts in the upsurge of American scientific and intellectual life. The Displaced Persons (DPs), who left Hungary between 1944 and 1947, and arrived in the United States between 1948 and 1952, represented the political and social elites of interwar Hungary. The "Fifty-sixers" of "Freedom Fighters," who came after the failed anti-Soviet Revolution of 1956 (q.v.), were geared to the process of modernization and made significant contributions to the scientific, scholarly, intellectual, and business life in the United States. A trickle Hungarian immigration continued through the next four decades—motivated during the 1960s and 1970s by political and, during the 1980s and 1990s, by economic considerations.

Ever since the appearance of the economic immigrants in the late 19th century, Hungarians in North America were polarized socially, having transferred their class consciousness from Hungary to their lives in the United States. Therefore, the educated among them did not wish to have much to do with those of peasant and working class background. The most highly educated among them, who also possessed transferable skills, easily merged into American society. They kept little or no contacts with Hungarian ethnic communities. The economic immigrants and the literary and administrative intelligentsia with no transferable skills, however, were usually forced to start out as physical laborers.

The most important institutions of the economic immigrants were the churches, fraternals, newspapers, and various cultural associations connected with the first three. The educated political immigrants cut themselves off from these organizations completely and founded their own cultural and political associations and newspapers. They generally met their social inferiors only in the churches, and even there they segregated themselves. The economic immigrants stayed out of American political life for quite a while. Few of them became U.S. citizens until after World War I, and they were also reluctant to leave their own ethnic enclaves to meet Angol-American society. Thus, not until the rise of the first native-born generation was there any meaningful involvement in domestic politics. The immigrant generations continued to be attached to Hungary, but their political activism consisted only of supporting the political goals of the mother country. This was even more true for the political immigrants, whose primary concern was always Hungary. With the passing of time, however, some of them also became active in American political life. Hungarian immigrants to the United States contributed a great deal to American society. The contributions of the turn-of-the-century economic immigrants were limited mostly to brawn power, while the political immigrants enriched American cultural, intellectual, and scientific life. They were involved in the creation of the American film industry (e.g., Adolph Zukor [q.v.] and William Fox). At one time they dominated America's great symphony orchestras (e.g., Fritz Reiner, George Széll, Eugene Ormándy (q.v.), Antal Doráti, and Sir George Solti). They were in the forefront of the creation of American atomic power (Edward Teller [q.v.] and Eugene Wigner [q.v.]), space technology (e.g., Theodore von Kármán [q.v.] and Leo Szilárd [q.v.]), computer revolution (e.g., John von Neumann [q.v.], and Andrew Grove [q.v.]), and more recently, even international finance (George Soros [q.v.] and Andrew Sarlós). As a matter of fact, educated Hungarians did so well in the United States that Laura Fermi, the wife of the great Italian scientist Enrico Fermi, was forced to speculate about "the mystery of the Hungarian talent." She did this in her highly regarded book *Illustrious Immigrants* (1968).

EMERIC [IMRE] (c.1174–1204). King of Hungary (1196–1204), the oldest son of King Béla III (q.v.) and his French wife. In 1182 his father had Emeric crowned king and in 1194 appointed him to rule over Croatia-Dalmatia (q.v.). His short reign was characterized by an unending rivalry with his rebellious brother, Andrew (King Andrew II) (q.v.), a continued expansion toward the Balkans (q.v.) into the lands of the Bogomil heretics (q.v.), and the beginnings of the loss of much royal property through large land grants to the rising aristocracy (q.v.). The struggle between the two brothers often broke into open warfare (e.g., 1197, 1199), although later they reconciled and led joint invasions to the Balkans. In 1201–02 they led successful campaigns against the Serbians (q.v.), after which Emeric assumed the title "King of Serbia." In 1202 they were victorious over the Bulgarians (q.v.). But when the defeated Bulgarians appealed to the Papacy for help, in return for switching over to Latin Christianity, King Emeric prevented the papal envoys from reaching Bulgaria (q.v.). Emeric's relationship with the Papacy was also worsened by the capture of the Dalmatian city of Zara (q.v.) by the Crusaders (November 24, 1202). The squandering of royal property —to be continued by his brother, King Andrew II—undermined the power of the monarchy by cutting down the king's power base and by creating several groups of powerful landed aristocrats. The latter included even the upper clergy, who turned against the king. King Emeric's last days were devoted to assuring the throne for his son, Ladislas III (q.v.), who was still a child. He had Ladislas crowned (August 26, 1204) and then named his brother Andrew as the latter's guardian. Ladislas survived his father's death only by a few months.

EMERIC, SAINT [SZENT IMRE] (c.1007-31). The only son and heir of King St. Stephen (q.v.) who, although married to a Byzantine princess, remained childless. Reared by Bishop St. Gerard (q.v.), who had a major role in Hungary's Christianization (q.v.), Emeric allegedly vowed to live a celibate life. He fell victim to a hunting accident, leaving King Stephen without a direct heir to the throne. Because of his saintly life, Emeric was canonized, along with his father, on November 4, 1083. He was also buried in the royal capital of Székesfehérvár (q.v.). His legend was authored by a Benedictine monk at the Monastery of Pannonhalma (q.v.) somewhere between 1109 and 1112. St. Emeric's fame spread far and wide, even into Italy, where his name became "Amerigo." Allegedly, Amerigo Vespucci's parents named the 16th-century Italian navigator after the Hungarian saint. Thus, indirectly, the name of King St. Stephen's son was appended to the new continent, America, discovered by Columbus and his followers.

ENCYCLOPEDIAS, HUNGARIAN. The first Hungarian encyclopedia was written and published by János Apáczai-Csere (q.v.) in 1653. This was followed by dozens of other attempts in the 18th and the 19th century, mostly on the basis of French and German models.

The first major modern Hungarian Encyclopedia was *Pallas's Great Encyclopedia (Pallas Nagy Lexikona)* (18 vols., 1893–1900), which was followed by the even more comprehensive *Révai's Great Encyclopedia (Révai Nagy Lexikona)* (21 vols., 1910-35), and then by the somewhat smaller *Encyclopedia of the New Age (Új Idők Lexikona)* (24 vols., 1936–42). These three major undertakings were paralleled by a comprehensive biographical encyclopedia entitled *Hungarian Writers (Magyar Írók)* by József Szinnyei (14 vols., 1891–1914), and followed by its still ongoing sequel of at least comparable size by Pál Gulyás and János Viczián, *Hungarian Writers (Magyar Írók)* (1939–).

The first half of the 20th century also witnessed the publication of several smaller multivolume encyclopedias, as well as a number of specialized ones, including the *Hungarian Legal Encyclopedia (Magyar Jogi Lexikon)* (6 vols., 1898–1907), the *Economics Encyclopedia (Közgazdasági Lexikon)* (3 vols., 1898–1901), *Hungarian Literary Encyclopedia (Magyar Irodalmi Lexikon)* (1926), and the *Jewish Encyclopedia (Zsidó Lexikon)* (1929). After World War II (q.v.) came the *New Hungarian Encyclopedia (Új Magyar Lexikon)* (6 vols., 1960–62; 2 supplements, 1972, 1981), which is saturated by Marxism and represents a radical decline both in size and in quality. This was followed by several multivolume specialized encyclopedias, such as the *Hungarian Literary Encyclopedia (Magyar Irodalmi Lexikon)* (3 vols., 1963–65), the *Encyclopedia of Music (Zenei Lexikon)* (3 vols., 1965), the *Hungarian Biographical Encyclopedia (Magyar Életrajzi Lexikon)* (2 vols., 1967–69; 2 supplements, 1981, 1994), the *Encyclopedia of Art (Művészeti Lexikon)* (4 vols., 1981–84), the *New Hungarian Literary Encyclopedia (Új Magyar Irodalmi Lexikon)* (3 vols., 1994), the *Early Hungarian Historical Encyclopedia (Korai Magyar Történeti Lexikon)* (1994), and virtually dozens of other specialized works.

The next major universal encyclopedia, originally planned for forty-two volumes, was undertaken in the early 1970s, but the initial volumes of the significantly reduced project appeared only recently under the title *Great Hungarian Encyclopedia (Magyar Nagylexikon)*

(1993–). This is paralleled by the ongoing publication of the Hungarian version of the *EncyclopaediaBritannica* (1993–).

ENLIGHTENED DESPOTISM. Enlightened despotism put forth by Voltaire (1694-1778) as the ideal form of government believed in the rule of a so-called "philosopher king" who would utilize all his abilities in the service of his nation and state. Next to the better known Frederick the Great of Prussia (r.1740–86), the most worthy of these enlightened despots was Emperor Joseph II (q.v.) of Austria (q.v.), who refused to have himself crowned king of Hungary (q.v.) precisely to be able to carry out his plans for modernization without having to violate the feudal traditions embodied in the ancient Hungarian constitution (q.v.). His modernization efforts, however, ran counter to the interests of the nobility (q.v.), who sabotaged it and linked this sabotage effort to the rising Hungarian National Revival Movement (q.v.). By calling Joseph's efforts anti-Hungarian, the nobles could defend their class privileges under the guise of standing up for Hungarian national rights. Many of Joseph's reforms failed precisely because—instead of using persuasion and consensus-building—he tried to implement them via imperial decrees, that is, through despotic means.

ENLIGHTENMENT. Enlightenment was an ideological and philosophical trend that began in late-17th-century England (Hobbes, Locke, Newton), reached its climax in 18th-century France (Montesquieu, Rousseau, Voltaire, Diderot, d'Holbach), and also had a powerful impact in the German lands (Herder, Lessing), likewise in the 18th century. Its key components included rationalism, reason, pragmatism, toleration, and a belief in the perfectibility of the human person and society through the discovery and application of certain natural laws. In the political sphere, it emphasized popular sovereignty, although it also gave birth to the notion of "Enlightened Despotism" (q.v.). In art and literature it followed classical models, and sought the application of symmetry, harmony, and perfection to all creative manifestations. Enlightenment entered Hungary (q.v.) in the mid-18th century in conjunction with the birth

of the Hungarian National Revival Movement (q.v.) that was in the
hands of the common nobility (q.v.). It manifested itself primarily in
literature and in efforts to up-date the Magyar (Hungarian) language
(q.v.). Its earliest political manifestation was the ill-fated Jacobin
Conspiracy of 1794–95 (q.v.) under the leadership of the defrocked
abbot Ignác Martinovics (q.v.). Its most important result was the
birth of Hungarian Political Nationalism (q.v.) connected with the
Hungarian Reform Period (1825–48) (q.v.). The most eminent
pioneers of Hungarian Enlightenment were Mátyás Bél (q.v.),
György Bessenyei (q.v.), and Ferenc Kazinczy (q.v.).

**ENTAILED ESTATE [FIDEI COMMISSUM, HITBIZO-
MÁNY].** An estate that is indivisible, cannot be mortgaged, and
has to be inherited within a single family. Normally, it is the oldest
male heir who inherits the estate and is the sole owner, but has the
obligation to support all other members of the family. The purpose
of this arrangement was to keep a large estate intact within a specific
noble family. This legal custom came to Hungary from Spain via
the Spanish Habsburgs (q.v.) in the 17th century, and was officially
approved for the aristocracy (q.v.) in 1687, and for the common
nobility (q.v.) in 1723. This system survived right up to the end of
World War II (q.v.), at which time the largest Hungarian entailed
estate (c.300,000 acres or 158,000 hectares) was owned by Prince
Pál Esterházy (1901–89), whose ancestor of the same name, Prince
Pál Esterházy (1635–1713) (q.v.), had transformed his property into
an entailed estate in 1695. All Hungarian entailed estates were
expropriated at the time of the post–World War II (q.v.) land reform
(q.v.) in March 1945. The system of entailed estates is related to an
older Hungarian legal custom called *aviticitas (ősiség)* (q.v.).

EÖTVÖS, BARON JÓZSEF [JOSEF] (1813–71). Poet, novelist,
political philosopher, and one of the great liberal statesmen of 19th-
century Hungary. Although coming from an aristocratic family with
close Habsburg (q.v.) connections, Eötvös turned into an advocate of
Hungarian nationalism and progressive social reform very early in
his life. As a member of the Upper House (q.v.) of the Hungarian

Diet (q.v.), Eötvös became a champion of social and political reform during the 1830s and 1840s. In the mid-1840s, he was one of the leaders of the so-called Centralists (q.v.), who advocated an end to county autonomy and the resulting privileges of the provincial nobility. Eötvös explored his ideas both in political essays (e.g., *Jewish Emancipation in Hungary*, 1841; *Reform*, 1846), as well as in social novels (e.g., *The Village Notary*, 1845; *Hungary in 1514*, 1847). Named minister for culture and education after the March Revolution of 1848 (q.v.) (April 7–September 11), Eötvös had little time to implement his reform ideas before leaving Hungary (q.v.) because of the radicalization of the revolution that he disliked. Returning from his self-imposed exile at the end of 1850, he devoted the next ten years of his life to exploring the future of the Habsburg Empire (q.v.) and Hungary's position therein in a number of political essays. He believed that separating Hungary (q.v.) from Austria (q.v.) would be a folly that would lessen Hungary's importance in Europe, and could also lead to its dismemberment, because of its many non-Magyar nationalities (q.v.). His most important work of political philosophy was *The Influence of the Dominant Ideas of the 19th Century upon the State (A XIX. század uralkodó eszméinek befolyása az álladalomra)* (2 vols., 1851-54).

During the 1860s Eötvös played a significant role in the preparation of the Austro-Hungarian Compromise of 1867 (q.v.), while after the compromise he resumed his former position as the minister for culture and education in the new Hungarian government (1867–71). In that capacity he was responsible for introducing Hungary's first comprehensive Law of Education (1868), its unusually liberal Law of Nationalities (1868), as well as the Law of Jewish Emancipation (1868) (q.v.), which granted full citizenship rights to the country's Jewish population. Baron József Eötvös was one of Hungary's most learned liberal statesmen, who served as a source of inspiration for many 20th-century liberals. For a decade and a half Eötvös had also served as the vice president (1856–66), and the president (1866–71) of the Hungarian Academy of Sciences (q.v.).

EÖTVÖS, BARON LORÁND [ROLAND] (1848–1919). One of Hungary's great physicists, who, like his father, Baron József Eötvös (q.v.), had served both as Hungary's minister for culture and education (1894–95), as well as the president of the Hungarian Academy of Sciences (q.v.) (1889–1905). Educated at the Universities of Königsberg and Heidelberg in Germany (q.v.), the unusually gifted Eötvös was immediately appointed to the professorships of theoretical (1872) and then of experimental physics (1878) at the University of Budapest (q.v.).

During the next five decades he conducted extensive research and worked out a new method for measuring surface tension. He recognized the relationship between surface tension and molecular weights of liquids at different temperatures, which he formulated into the so-called "Eötvös Law" (1876), which later helped Albert Einstein (1879-1955) in working out his Theory of Relativity. Loránd Eötvös also devoted much time to the study of gravity and then designed the Eötvös Torsion Pendulum (1896) to measure the change in gravity within the earth. During his tenure in office in 1894-95 he worked out a plan for the Eötvös College (q.v.), named after his father, which soon became the main center for the education of Hungary's intellectual elite.

EÖTVÖS COLLEGE [EÖTVÖS KOLLÉGIUM]. Founded in 1895 by the then minister for culture and education, Baron Gyula Wlassics (1852–1937), on the basis of a plan by his predecessor, Baron Loránd Eötvös (q.v.), the Eötvös College was modeled on the French Ecole Superior of Paris. It was intended to be a school for the intellectual elite, who, while attending the University of Budapest (q.v.), would also attend special seminars and tutorials at Eötvös College. In contrast to Hungary's other institutions of higher learning, all of which emphasized German learning and German mentality, the students at Eötvös College were also given a large dose of French culture and learning. This French influence was further increased during the 1930s and early 1940s, when German culture became tainted with Nazism. With the triumph of communism after World War II (q.v.), the college was accused of being a hotbed of bourgeois mentality and of Western imperialism. Thus, in 1950 it was disbanded and transformed into a dormitory for the University of Budapest. Following the collapse of communism in 1989–90 (q.v.), the Eötvös College was resurrected once more, but in the mid-1990s it was still only a shadow of its former self.

EÖTVÖS LORÁND UNIVERSITY see **UNIVERSITY OF BUDAPEST.**

EPIGRAPHY. A historical subdiscipline that deals with deciphering, classifying, and interpreting inscriptions and various other forms of writings, especially as related to the classical period and the Middle Ages. In Hungary, epigraphy became part of the "Auxiliary Sciences of History" (q.v.), which was taught officially at the University of Budapest already in the 19th century. Following World War II (q.v.), epigraphy and most other related auxiliary sciences of history were removed from the basic curriculum of future historians, and they were not restored again until the mid-1980s.

ERA OF REFORM see **HUNGARIAN REFORM PERIOD.**

ERDEI, FERENC (1910-71). Economist, sociologist, and—along with József Darvas (q.v.) and Gyula Ortutay (q.v.)—a member of that group of the Hungarian Populists (q.v.) who became enamored with communism. Erdei made his name with his first sociography entitled *Drifting Sands (Futóhomok)* in 1937. It was soon followed by several equally important works on Hungarian peasant society: *Peasants(Parasztok)* (1938), *Hungarian village (Magyar falu)* (1940), *Hungarian peasant society (Magyar paraszt-társadalom]*(1941), and *Hungarian Homesteads(Magyartanyák])* (1942). After being active in the March Front (q.v.), in 1939 Erdei became one of the founders of the National Peasant Party (q.v.). Thereafter, he progressively moved in the direction of communism, expounding his views on agricultural collectivism at the second Szárszó Conference (q.v.) in 1943. After World War II (q.v.), Erdei served in various ministerial positions in the communist government (1948–56), while during the revolution of 1956 (q.v.) he was a member of the delegation that negotiated with the Soviets. Following the revolution, he switched from politics to scholarly life, serving as the director of the Agricultural Research Institute (1957-71), as well as the general secretary (1957–64, 1970–71) and vice president (1964–70) of the Hungarian Academy of Sciences (q.v.). In 1965 he was elected a member of Hungary's Presidential Council (q.v.). Erdei had a major role in the "socialist transformation of Hungarian agriculture," even though in his later years he too lessened his dedication to communism. Most of his writings were published posthumously in his *Collected Works (Összegyűjtött Művei)* (5 vols., 1973–88).

ERDÉLY see TRANSYLVANIA.

ESTATES [FEUDAL ESTATES, RENDEK]. The constitutionally separate upper layers of feudal society. In Hungary (q.v.) this layering process began in the 13th century and reached full development by the 16th century. The three main Hungarian estates were the nobility (q.v.), the upper clergy (q.v.), and the burghers of the Royal Free Cities (q.v.). Of these three estates the nobility was the largest and the most diverse, composed of the titled aristocracy (q.v.), the landed middle nobility (q.v.), and the common nobility (q.v.) whose members owned only small peasant plots.

ESTERHÁZY FAMILY [ESTERHÁZY DE GALÁNTHA]. One of Hungary's most influential and wealthiest families during the 17th through the early 20th centuries. Allegedly descendants of the Salamon Clan of the conquering Magyars (q.v.), the Esterházys began to rise to prominence only in the 16th century, when they became anti-Turkish fighters in the service of the Habsburgs (q.v.) of Vienna (q.v.). They soon broke into three branches: Fraknó, Csesznek, and Zólyom—each of which reached at least the rank of a count between 1626 and 1715. The westernmost branch of the Esterházy family—centered on the fortress of Fraknó (Forchtenstein) and on the towns of Kismarton (Eisenstadt) and Eszterháza (Fertőd)—was the most successful of the three branches.

In 1687 Paul Esterházy rose to the rank of a prince of the Holy Roman Empire (q.v.). In 1712 this title was extended to all the firstborn males, and then in 1783 to all male and female members of his line. The most important members of the Fraknó branch of the Esterházy family included Count Miklós Esterházy (1582–1645) (q.v.), Prince Pál Esterházy (1635–1713) (q.v.), Prince Miklós József Esterházy (1714-90) (q.v.), and Prince Miklós Esterházy (1765–1833) (q.v.). The most significant member of the Csesznek branch was Count János Esterházy (1901-57) (q.v.), who was the most prominent spokesman of the Hungarians in interwar Czechoslovakia (q.v.).

ESTERHÁZY, COUNT JÁNOS (1901–57). Coming from the Csesznek branch of the family, Count János Esterházy was a highly respected representative of the Hungarian minority (q.v.) in newly created Czechoslovakia (q.v.) after World War I (q.v.). He was the president of the League of Hungarian Community (1931), the executive president both of the National Christian Socialist Party (1932-36) and the United Hungarian Party (1936-39), and after Czechoslovakia's dissolution in 1939, the president of the Hungarian Party (1939-45) in Slovakia (q.v.). After having served in the Czechoslovak Parliament in Prague (1935–38), he became the sole Hungarian representative in the Slovak Parliament of the German puppet state during World War II (1939-45) (q.v.). In that capacity he was the only one among the sixty-two parliamentarians to vote against the so-called "Jewish Law" that deprived Slovak Jews of all of their civil rights. Count János Esterházy was a humanitarian voice of his people in Czechoslovakia and Slovakia. Yet, after World War II he died as a political prisoner of the new communist regime.

ESTERHÁZY, COUNT MIKLÓS [NICOLAUS] (1582–1645). Born a Protestant, Miklós Esterházy threw in his lot with the Habsburgs, converted to Catholicism, and then allied himself with Cardinal Péter Pázmány (q.v.) and the forces of the Hungarian Counter-Reformation (q.v.). Although a Hungarian patriot like his Protestant rivals—Prince Gábor Bethlen (q.v.) and Prince George

Rákóczi I (q.v.) of Transylvania—Esterházy refused to follow the anti-Habsburg independence line represented by the latter. He viewed the struggle between the Habsburg Empire (q.v.) and the Ottoman Empire (q.v.) as a duel between Christianity and Islam, and he simply could not ally himself with the latter against the former. Thus, he never wavered from his unquestioned faithfulness to the Habsburg dynasty (q.v.), which earned for him and for his offspring the latter's gratitude.

In 1613 Emperor Matthias (q.v.) elevated Nicolaus Esterházy and his brothers to the rank of baron (q.v.), while in 1626 he was awarded the title of a count (q.v.). At about the same time Esterházy also gained control over the fortress Fraknó (Forchtenstein) in Western Hungary (q.v.), which became the center of his family's power. A year earlier the Hungarian Diet (q.v.) had elected him the palatine (q.v.) (1625–45), which was the highest office in Hungary (q.v.) next to the king. This office was also borne by his most illustrious son, Prince Paul (1635–1713) (q.v.), who was granted the title of prince of the Holy Roman Empire (q.v.).

ESTERHÁZY, PRINCE MIKLÓS [NICOLAUS] (1765–1833). The grandson of Prince Miklós József (1740–90), Prince Miklós Esterházy was the holder of many high offices, including that of the captain of the Hungarian Royal Nobles' Guard (q.v.). Yet, just as in the case of his grandfather, his fame rests primarily on his being a great patron of the arts. Following the death of his grandfather in 1790, he continued to support Franz Josef Haydn (1732–1809) as well as Johann Nepomuk Hummel (1778–1837) in their musical endeavors. He also commissioned Ludwig van Beethoven (1770–1827) to compose the *Mass in C Major* specifically for his court.

ESTERHÁZY, PRINCE MIKLÓS JÓZSEF [NICOLAUS JOSEF] (1714-90). Grandson of Prince Pál (1635–1713) (q.v.), Prince Miklós József Esterházy held many civil, military, and diplomatic offices in the period of the War of Austrian Succession (1740–48) (q.v.) and the Seven Years' War (1756–63) (q.v.). Yet, he is known less for his military and diplomatic feats than for his affluent lifestyle and for being one of the greatest patrons of art and music in Hungary (q.v.) and the Habsburg Empire (q.v.). In addition to the construction of the Esterházy Palace at Eszterháza (Fertőd) (1764–69), known as the "Hungarian Versailles," Prince Miklós József also founded and supported an opera company, a theater group, a symphony, and a music school. Franz Josef Haydn (1732–1809) was his court musician and court composer at his palaces at Eszterháza and Kismarton (Eisenstadt), and for three decades Haydn was also the conductor of his court symphony (1760–90).

ESTERHÁZY, PRINCE PÁL [PAUL] (1635–1713). The son of Count Miklós Esterházy (1582-1645) (q.v.), who gained the title of a prince of the Holy Roman Empire both for himself (1687) and for the firstborn males of his family (1712). Although he was a poet and a composer, Prince Pál Esterházy's fame rests primarily in the political and military arenas. After distinguishing himself in the anti-Turkish wars of the 1660s and 1670s, he was elected Hungary's palatine (1681–1713) (q.v.). He participated both in the Second Siege of Vienna (1683) (q.v.) and in the Liberation of Buda (1686). Moreover, in 1687 he had a significant role in making the Hungarian Diet accept the hereditary right of the Habsburgs (q.v.) to the Hungarian throne. He did speak up occasionally against Emperor Leopold's (q.v.) absolutism, but on the whole Prince Pál Esterházy remained faithful to the Habsburg cause. In 1695 he transformed his huge landholdings into an entailed estate (q.v.), and had a beautiful Renaissance palace constructed at Kismarton (Eisenstadt). He founded the first symphony orchestra there, published a unique collection of Hungarian Baroque music in 1711, and made the Castle of Fraknó (Forchtenstein) into a major gallery for art and weapons collections.

ESZTERGOM [STRIGONIUM, GRAN]. A city of 32,000 inhabitants on the Danube River (q.v.), which is the seat of the first Archbishopric (1001) and of the Primate or Prince Primate (q.v.) of Hungary, and thus the country's ecclesiastical center. Esztergom had become Hungary's administrative center in the late 10th century under Prince Géza (q.v.). Yet, already in the 11th century it had to

share this position with Székesfehérvár (q.v.), which became the
coronation city and the burial place of Hungary's medieval kings. In
that age of "traveling kingships" (i.e., impermanent capitals), several
other centers also emerged a competitors , among them Óbuda (q.v.),
Temesvár (q.v.), Visegrád (q.v.), and Buda (q.v.). But by the 14th
century it was the city of Buda (today part of Budapest) that had
established itself as Hungary's main capital. As a result the
monarch transferred the ownership of the royal castle of Esztergom
to the Archbishop of Esztergom already in the 13th century. In the
19th century, Esztergom became the site of Hungary's largest
cathedral, built on top of the ruins of the former royal palace.

ETELE see ATTILA.

ETELKÖZ [ETELKÜZÜ, ATALKUZU]. One of the homelands
of the Hungarians in the 9th century, before their conquest of
Historic Hungary (q.v.). It was probably located between the Don
and the Lower Danube, in the area of present-day Ukraine (q.v.) and
northeastern Romania (q.v.). The majority of the Hungarians of the
Árpádian conquest (995–96) (q.v.) left Etelköz either because of a
well-developed military plan to conquer the Carpathian Basin (q.v.)
or because of the military defeats they suffered at the hands of the
Pechenegs (Patzinaks) (q.v.) and the Bulgars (q.v.).

EVANGELICAL [LUTHERAN] CHURCH. The Evangelical
Church is based on the teachings of Martin Luther (1483–1546),
who was responsible for the Protestant Reformation. Luther
disregarded the importance of church traditions and believed the Bible
to be the sole source of Christianity. His teachings first spread
through the north German and Scandinavian states, and then to
Hungary (q.v.), where it was first diffused among the German
burghers (q.v.), Transylvanian Saxons (q.v.), and Slovaks (q.v.) of
Northern Hungary (q.v.). But the Lutheran faith was unable to
compete with the teachings of John Calvin (1509–64), which
captivated a much larger segment of Hungary's population, giving
birth to the Reformed (Calvinist) Church (q.v.). During the 16th

through the 18th centuries, the Habsburg rulers of Hungary tried to prevent the spreading of Luther's teachings, along with those of Calvin, but they failed to eradicate this creed. The Evangelical (Lutheran) faith became an "accepted"religion in 1848, which was reaffirmed in 1868, immediately after the Austro-Hungarian Compromise (q.v.). The structure of the Evangelical Church in Hungary consists of congregations *(presbitérium)*, which are united into dioceses *(egyházmegye)*, and these, in turn, into church districts *(egyházkerület)*. At the end of the 20th century, the Hungarian Evangelical Church has eight dioceses, which are organized into two church districts. The chief executive bodies of the Evangelical Church are the Church Synod *(Szinódus)* and National Church Assembly *(Országos Egyház Közgyűlés)*. Today about 4.2 percent of Hungary's population is of the Evangelical/Lutheran denomination.

EVLIYA CHELEBI [EVLIYA ĆELEBI] (1611-79). A learned Ottoman Turkish traveler, whose ten-volume travelogue is a mine of information about the 17th-century Ottoman Empire (q.v.) and its conqueredprovinces, including Hungary (q.v.). The section dealing with Hungary was translated and published in two volumes by Imre Karácson (1863-1911) in 1904-08. There is a current project centered at Harvard University, which plans to publish all ten volumes in a bilingual (Osmanli Turkish and English) edition. The volume dealing with Hungary is being translated and edited by Gustav Bayerle (b.1931) of Indiana University.

EYALET [VIYALET] see **PASHALIK.**

- F -

FAJSZ [FALITZI, FALICS] (mid–10th c.). One of Árpád's (q.v.) grandsons who was the ruling prince of the Hungarian tribal federation in the mid-10th century (c.948–c.955), but who appears to have had little influence over the individual tribal leaders. Fajsz is mentioned only in one of the contemporary sources, in Constantine Porphyrogenitus's (q.v.) *On the Administration of the Empire (De administrandoimperio).*

FAMILIARITAS. A unique feudal relationship that developed in late medieval Hungary (q.v.) between a feudal lord and his retainers, who were members of the common nobility (q.v.). Such retainers were known as the *familiaris (familiárisok),* who served the lord in military and other capacities. In return, they were supported and protected by him as if they were members of his family *(familia).* This unique Hungarian version of feudalism was based on bilateral agreements, lasted only for a specific period of time, and could be terminated by either of the two parties at will. A chain of permanent feudal interrelationships that characterized Western European feudalism never developed in Hungary.

FASCISM. The ideology of fascism triumphed in Italy (q.v.) in 1922 (Mussolini) and in Germany (q.v.) in 1933 (Hitler). It began to manifest itself in Hungary (q.v.) in the late 1920s. During the 1930s this ideology produced a number of small political parties, but it was unable to gain political muscle until after the German occupation of Hungary (March 19, 1944) (q.v.), and especially after the October 15, 1944, takeover by Ferenc Szálasi (q.v.) and his Arrow Cross Party (q.v.). In Hungary, the ideology of fascism was driven less by its traditional components of racism, anti-Semitism, corporatism, and imperialism, and more by the country's legitimate national complaints stemming from its mutilation after World War I (q.v.). The resulting "Trianon Complex" (q.v.) was perhaps the most

279

powerful psychological force in interwar Hungary (q.v.). It was also the number one motivating factor in its decision to tolerate rightist nationalist movements, and to accept—however grudgingly—an alliance with Mussolini's Italy and Hitler's Germany.

FEBRUARY PATENT (1861). Issued on February 26, 1861, this Imperial document amended the October Diploma (q.v.) of the previous year, and it was meant to serve as the new constitution of the reorganized Austrian Empire (q.v.), including Hungary (q.v). It created a bicameral legislature with limited powers, to be known as the "Imperial Council," with an electoral system designed to give a disproportionate influence to the German urban elements. The council consisted of 343 elected members, of whom only 120 represented the "Lands of the Hungarian Crown" (i.e., Hungary, Croatia, and Transylvania) (q.v.). Its powers embraced all affairs that had not been accorded to the provincial diets under the October Diploma. Under this document, the emperor had reserved for himself absolute control over foreign and military affairs, and the individual governments were responsible only to him alone.

FEDERATION OF FREE DEMOCRATS [SZABAD DEM-OKRATÁK SZÖVETSÉGE = SZDSZ]. One of the two coalition parties that took charge of Hungary (q.v.) in July 1994. Growing out of the liberal dissident movement (q.v.) of the 1980s, and officially founded in 1988, the Federation of Free Democrats (FFD) was the main opposition party during the first post-communist government under the control of a coalition led by the Hungarian Democratic Forum (1990–94) (q.v.). In May 1994 the FFD once more came in second, just behind the Hungarian Socialist Party (q.v.)—the former reform communists—with which it joined in a somewhat uneasy coalition. The FFD is a party of the Westward looking intellectuals and middle classes, that is, of the so-called Urbanists (q.v.). It is in favor of multiparty democracy, parliamentarism, and the transformation of Hungary's economy in the direction of market capitalism.

FEDERATION OF YOUNG DEMOCRATS [FIATAL DEM-OKRATÁK SZÖVETSÉGE = FIDESZ]. One of post-communist Hungary's opposition political parties that grew out of the dissident movement among the university students during the 1980s. Ideologically the Federation of Young Democrats (FYD) stands somewhere between the liberal Federation of Free Democrats (FFD) (q.v.) and the conservative Hungarian Democratic Forum (HDF) (q.v.). During the HDF regime (1990–94) the Young Democrats appeared to be closer to the FFD, but since the Socialist-FFD coalition came to power in June 1994, they moved closer to the HDF. This is so partially because in early 1994 the FYD leadership lost much of its former popularity. Thus, having become a smaller party, they were obliged to move closer to some of the other losing parties. In 1995 the FYD added "Hungarian Citizens' Party" *(Magyar Polgári Párt)* (q.v.) to its name.

FEDERATION OF FREE DEMOCRATS—HUNGARIAN CITIZENS' PARTY see **FEDERATION OF FREE DE-MOCRATS.**

FEHÉRVÁR [FEJÉRVÁR] see **SZÉKESFEHÉRVÁR.**

FÉJA, GÉZA (1900–78). One of the prominent exponents of Hungarian Populism (q.v.) during the 1930s and early 1940s, Féja is known primarily for his sociographical expose *Stormy Corner (Viharsarok)* (1937), which describes the misery of Hungarian peasants and rural proletariat. As a disciple of Dezső Szabó (q.v.), he was a representative of the so-called "Third Road" *(Harmadik út)* (q.v.) orientation on the Hungarian ideological spectrum. Following World War II (q.v.) Féja was unable to return to literary activities until after the Hungarian Revolution of 1956 (q.v.).

FELVIDÉK [ÉSZAK-MAGYARORSZÁG] see **NORTHERN HUNGARY.**

FEMALE QUARTER [QUARTA PUELLARIS, LEÁNY-NEGYED]. The daughter's or daughters' share of the inheritance under traditional Hungarian law. This tradition was introduced to Hungary (q.v.) via the coming of Christianity. By the early 13th century it became so widespread that it was incorporated into the Hungarian Golden Bull (q.v.). Under this law, irrespective of their numbers, the daughters collectively could inherit only one-quarter of the total property. Initially this applied to the whole estate, but by the 14th century it became a custom that purchased property was divided equally among all of the children, irrespective of their sexes. Because of the law of *aviticitas* (q.v.), and later the law of entail (q.v.), it became an accepted custom that the daughters' share was satisfied through money or other movable property, without infringing on the unity of the landed property.

FÉNYES, ELEK (1807–76). A pioneer statistician and geographer who produced Hungary's most significant statistical works in the 19th century. Being a supporter of the Hungarian national reform movement, during the revolution of 1848–49 (q.v.) he was entrusted with establishing Hungary's first National Statistical Office. Following the defeat of the revolution, he was imprisoned, and after his release, permitted only to fill various lesser offices. During the Age of Absolutism (q.v.), he published a great number of maps, atlases, textbooks, and various commemorative volumes—partially to make a living through publishing. Fényes's most important statistical works, still in use today, include: *The Current Status of Hungary and its Annexed Provinces from a Statistical and a Geographical Perspective (Magyarországnak s a hozzákapcsolt tartományoknak mostani állapotja, statistikai és geográphiai tekintetben)* (6 vols., 1836-40); *Statistics of Hungary (Magyarország statistikája)* (3 vols., 1841-43); *Description of Hungary (Magyarország leírása)* (2 vols, 1847); *The Hungarian Empire from a Statistical, Geographical, and Historical Perspective (A magyar birodalom statistikai, geográphiai és történeti tekintetben)* (vol. I, 1848);*The Geographical Dictionary of Hungary (Magyarország geográphiaiszótára)* (4 vols., 1851); *Hungary during the Pre-March*

Period (Ungarn im Vormärz) (1851); *Description of the Ottoman Empire (A török birodalom leírása)* (1854); *Statistics of the Austrian Empire (Az ausztriai birodalom statistikája)* (1857); *Hungary in 1859 from a Statistical, Landownership, and Topographical Perspective (Magyarország 1859-ben statistikai, birtokviszonyi és topográphiai szempontból)* (8 parts, 1859-60); and *Statistical and Geographical Description of the Austrian Empire (Az ausztriai birodalom statistikája és földrajzi leírása)* (1867).

FERDINAND   I (1503–64). Holy Roman Emperor (r.1556–64), king of Hungary and Bohemia (r.1526–64), and archduke of Austria (r.1521–64), Ferdinand was the son of Philip the Fair of Burgundy and Johanna the Mad of Spain. He was also the brother of Emperor Charles V (r.1519–56). Following the Battle of Mohács (q.v.) and the death of King Louis II (q.v.) in 1526, a group of Hungarian nobles elected Ferdinand king of Hungary (December 1, 1526). This election was based partially on the Habsburg-Jagellonian family agreement of mutual succession (1515), and partially on the belief that Ferdinand would be better able to withstand the mounting Turkish pressure upon Hungary than his rival, King John I Zápolya (q.v.), elected king by another group of noblemen only a few weeks earlier. This double election placed Hungary (q.v.) into an impossible situation, for the rivalry between the two kings made it even more difficult to ward off Ottoman (q.v.) expansion (q.v.). During the 1530s both kings of Hungary were forced to become tribute-paying vassals of Sultan Süleyman (r.1520–66) (q.v.). In 1538 they concluded the Treaty of Várad (q.v.), in which they agreed that after King John's death, Ferdinand would become the sole ruler of Hungary. This agreement, however, was never implemented.

Following the Turkish conquest of Buda (q.v.) in 1541, and the subsequent incorporation of the central part of Hungary into the Ottoman Empire (q.v.), all of Ferdinand's efforts to dislodge the Turks failed. Hungary remained tripartitioned into Royal Hungary (q.v.), Turkish Hungary (q.v.), and Transylvania (q.v.) for about a century and a half. Ferdinand was forced to recognize the Ottoman conquest of Central Hungary in 1547, at which time he also agreed to pay the Turks 30,000 gold pieces every year. This agreement made the Hungarian nobility (q.v.) very bitter, but they were unable to do anything about the status quo. Thereafter Ferdinand went to work to reorganize the administration of the country's northeastern section under his control, hereafter known increasingly as Royal Hungary. Hungary's capital was transferred from Buda to Pozsony (Pressburg) (q.v.), which became the center of its governing institutions. These included the Royal Council *(királyi tanács)* (q.v.), the War Council *(hadi tanács)* (q.v.), the Viceroyalty Council *(helytartóság)* (q.v.), and the Treasury *(kamara)*(q.v.)—all of which functioned under the direction of the palatine *(nádor)*(q.v.). During the next few decades, however, much of the country's administration was gradually transferred to Vienna (q.v.), where it was handled by the comparable Imperial institutions.

FERDINAND II (1578-1637). Holy Roman Emperor (r.1619–37), king of Hungary and Bohemia (1619–37), and archduke of Austria (1619–37). He was grandson of Ferdinand I (q.v.), nephew of Maximilian I (II) (q.v.), and cousin of both Rudolph I (II) (q.v.) and of Matthias II (I) (q.v.). Ferdinand received a strict Catholic education under the guidance of the Jesuits (q.v.), as a result of which he became a bigoted Catholic and fought all his life against the Protestants. After the death of his father in 1598, he inherited the inner Austrian provinces of Styria, Carinthia, and Craina, and would have stayed an archduke, had Rudolph and Matthias not remained childless, which made him the head of the House of Habsburg (q.v.). In 1619–20 Ferdinand broke the opposition of the Austrian Protestant estates, defeated the Czechs (q.v.) at the Battle of the White Mountains (1620), and got his empire embroiled in the lengthy, bloody, and costly Thirty Years' War (1618–48).

After his armies achieved some important victories under the leadership of General Wallenstein (1583–1634), Ferdinand issued the Edict of Restitution (1629), according to which the Protestants were obliged to return all properties seized from the Catholics since the Religious Peace of Augsburg (1555). This decision, however, turned the allied German Protestant princes, and even his Catholic Bavarian relatives, against Ferdinand, all of whom were afraid of the expansion of Imperial powers. Soon they also received support from Protestant Sweden and Catholic France, which similarly feared Habsburg preeminence. These developments, along with the assassination of the able military commander Wallenstein (1634), led to a series of reverses and then to the compromise Peace of Prague (1635). In Hungary (q.v.), Ferdinand's efforts at breaking the power of the Protestants (q.v.) and of the Feudal Estates (q.v.) were thwarted by Prince Gabriel Bethlen (q.v.) of Transylvania (q.v.). In 1626 Bethlen pushed the Habsburg armies out of Hungary and then concluded the Treaty of Pozsony (December 20, 1626), which basically reestablished the *status quo ante bellum.*

FERDINAND III (1608–57). Holy Roman Emperor (r.1637–57), king of Hungary and Bohemia (r.1637–57), and archduke of Austria (r.1637–57). As the son of Emperor Ferdinand II (q.v.), he inherited from his father the Thirty Years' War (1618-48), which ended all Habsburg (q.v.) efforts at establishing central control over the Holy Roman Empire (q.v.). This was codified in the Peace of Westphalia (1648), which ended that bloody religious and dynastic war and pushed the Habsburgs into a secondary position behind the emerging Bourbons of France. The Habsburgs' efforts at breaking the power of the Hungarian Protestants (q.v.) and the Hungarian Estates (q.v.) were similarly thwarted, partially by the outcome of the Thirty Years' War, and partially because of Prince George Rákóczi I's (q.v.) successful military efforts (1644-45) that ended in the Peace Treaty of Linz (September 16,1645).

FERDINAND IV (1633–54). Ferdinand was crowned king of Hungary (1647) and Bohemia (1646) in his father's, Ferdinand III's (q.v.), lifetime. But as he died before his father, Ferdinand IV never actually ruled anywhere.

FERDINAND V [I] (1793–1875). Emperor of Austria as Ferdinand I (r.1835–48), king of Hungary and Bohemia as Ferdinand V (r.1835-48), and archduke of Austria (r.1835-48). He was the son of Holy

Roman Emperor Francis II (Austrian Emperor Francis I) (q.v.), and a man of limited mental capacities. Consequently, much of the actual governing was done by the *Kamarilla* (q.v.), composed of his ministers, especially Prince Metternich (q.v.) and Count Kolowrat (q.v.), and of Ferdinand's uncle, Archduke Francis Charles (1802–78). In his capacity as king of Hungary, Ferdinand sanctioned all of the reform acts of the Hungarian Diet (q.v.) during the 1830s and 1840s, including the April Laws (q.v.) of 1848, which established an independent and responsible Hungarian government for the first time since the mid–16th century. After the Hungarian reform movement developed into a violent confrontation with the Habsburgs (q.v.), the *Kamarilla* forced Ferdinand to resign (December 2, 1848), replacing him with his nephew, Francis Joseph (q.v.), who ruled for the next sixty-eight years. Following his resignation, King Ferdinand lived quietly for more than a quarter of a century, residing mostly in Prague (q.v.).

FEUDALISM. The two important components of feudalism were: (1) the system of interrelationships and mutual obligations among various feudal lords (i.e., lords and vassals), whose ranks stretched from the king down to the lowest members of the nobility; and (2) the system of agricultural production that forced the peasants into a dependent status, binding them to the estates and to the person of the landowning nobility. In Western Europe the feudal system evolved during the 6th through the 8th centuries and disappeared gradually during the Age of the Renaissance in the 14th and 15th centuries. In East Central Europe (q.v.), the first component of feudalism—the system of subinfeudation—never really developed, although there were certain signs of it in the system of *familiaritas* (q.v.) in 14th-century Hungary. The second component—the binding of the peasant masses to the soil—did develop, but it did so only at the turn of the 15th to the 16th centuries. In Hungary, this act of enserfment took place in 1514, following the Dózsa Peasant Revolution (q.v.), when all of Hungary's peasants were bound to the soil. Serfdom did not disappear in Hungary until the revolution of 1848 (q.v.), although Joseph II's (q.v.) peasant reforms of 1783 and

1785 did grant the serfs a limited right of movement. Marxist historians disagree with the above interpretation, for they view the whole socioeconomic system that existed between the Classical Period and the Age of Capitalism as being part of feudalism. In their view feudalism is not limited to the period of bonded serfdom.

FIDESZ see FEDERATION OF YOUNG DEMOCRATS.

FIFTEEN YEARS' WAR [LONG WAR] (1591–1606). One of the longest and most destructive wars fought on Hungarian soil between the Habsburg (q.v.) and the Ottoman Empires (q.v.). Driven by the need for continued conquest, the Ottomans began a new onslaught in 1591, first against the Croatian (q.v.) and Trans-Danubian (q.v.) territories of the Hungarian Kingdom (q.v), and then against Austria (q.v.). The Habsburgs received some help from the Pope and the North Italian states, and later also from Prince Sigismund Báthory (q.v.) of Transylvania (q.v.). In 1596 the Turks gained a major victory over the Habsburgs and the Transylvanian-Hungarian forces at Mezőkeresztes in north-central Hungary, but they were unable to take advantage of this victory. The war continued with increasing violence, especially in Transylvania, which was systematically looted and destroyed by all of the combatants: the Turks, the Habsburg forces under George Basta (q.v.), and the Wallachian invaders under Michael the Brave (r.1593–1601). Finally, in 1604 Stephen Bocskai (q.v.), the future prince of Transylvania, initiated a national uprising. With the support of his *hajdú* (q.v.) forces, he compelled the Habsburgs to conclude the Peace of Vienna (June 23, 1606) (q.v.), which restored Hungary's autonomy and Transylvania's independence, and at the same time assured religious freedom for all Protestants (q.v.). As a follow-up, the Habsburgs also concluded the Peace of Zsitva-Torok (November 11, 1606) with the Turks (q.v.), which left Transylvania in Bocskai's hands, permitted each combatant to retain the territories under its control, recognized the equality of the two emperors, and terminated the tribute payment by the Habsburgs to the Turks.

FIFTY-SIXERS   see   **FREEDOM   FIGHTERS.**

FILLÉR.   A monetary unit in the category of the penny, hundred of
which makes up the *forint* (q.v.). The *fillér* was also used as a unit
of such earlier currencies as the *pengő* (q.v.) and the *korona* (q.v.).

FINNO-UGRIC   LANGUAGES.   This term signifies a group of
related agglutinative languages (q.v.), which are part of the Uralic
branch of the larger Ural-Altaic (q.v.) linguistic family. Structurally
and grammatically, the Finno-Ugric languages are very different
from the Indo-European languages, to which the Germanic,
Romance, and Slavic languages (q.v.) belong. The best known of
the Finno-Ugric languages are the Hungarian (Magyar), Finnish, and
Estonian. Hungarian, however, has also been heavily influenced by
Turkic languages (q.v.), which belong the to Altaic branch of the
Ural-Altaic family, whose original homeland is Central Asia (q.v.).

FIUME [RIJEKA].   An Adriatic port city of Croatia (pop. 140,000),
which during the 19th and early 20th century used to be the main
seaport of Hungary (q.v.). Alternatingly part of the Roman,
Carolingian, Holy Roman (q.v.), and Habsburg Empires (q.v.), as
well as of Venice and Croatia (q.v.), in 1779 Fiume was attached to
Hungary, which was made official by the Hungarian Diet in 1807.
After World War I (q.v.) the city was contested by Yugoslavia and
Italy (1918–24), ruled by Italy (1924–45), became part of
Yugoslavia (1945–91), and then of independent Croatia (1991). In
the period between the 1880s and 1914, Fiume was a major ports of
exit for Hungarian mass emigration (q.v.) to the United States.

FIVE-YEAR   PLANS.   Commonly used central economic plans in
communist countries. In the period between 1950 and 1985,
Hungary (q.v.) had been subjected to six of these plans. They did
result in the country's industrialization and collectivization (q.v.),
but without taking into consideration the economic, social, and
human price of these mass regimentations. In addition to the Five-

Year Plans, Hungary also had two Three-Year Plans (q.v.) during the years 1947–49 and 1958–60.

FOCK, JENŐ (b.1916). A communist politician and former prime minister of Hungary (1967–75). Fock had become involved in Hungary's (q.v.) underground communist movement in the 1930s, and then joined the party and the government apparatus after World War II (q.v.). Following the Hungarian Revolution of 1956 (q.v.), he moved up to become the secretary of the Central Committee of the Hungarian Socialist Workers' Party (1957–61) (q.v.), a deputy prime minister (1961–67), and then the prime minister of Hungary (April 1967– May 1975). Following his resignation and partial withdrawal from politics, Fock served as the president of the Federation of Technical and Scientific Associations (1980–89). Fock's eight-year tenure as prime minister is connected with the introduction of the New Economic Mechanism (NEM) (q.v.) in 1968, which tried to jump-start Hungary's economy by introducing elements of market economy into socialism. This daring move could only be carried out with Soviet approval, and the limits of Hungary's freedom of actions were demonstrated by the almost simultaneous Soviet invasion of Czechoslovakia (q.v.), in which Hungary was also forced to participate. Even with these limitations, the NEM—which was halted for a while in 1972—did result in visible improvements that laid the foundations of the highly touted "goulash communism" (q.v.) of the late 1970s and early 1980s.

FŐISPÁN [SUPREMUS COMES] see **LORD LIEU-TENANT.**

FORCED LABOR SERVICES [MUNKASZOLGÁLAT]. Labor brigades composed of persons who were judged to be politically unreliable, either because of their origin or because of their political views during World War II (q.v.). This system was officially introduced in Hungary (q.v.) in 1939, and starting with 1940, persons in such categories (e.g., Jews, communists, unreliable nationalities) were drafted into these labor battalions, whose purpose was to aid the military efforts of the regular units of the Hungarian Armed Forces. Following the invasion of the Soviet Union by the 2d Hungarian Army (April 11, 1942), most of these labor battalions were also taken to the Russian Front, where most of them perished. They fell victim to the "Winter War of 1942-43" in conjunction with the Battle of Stalingrad (November 1942–February 1943). They shared the fate of the 6th German Army under Field Marshal Paulus (1890–1957) and the 2d Hungarian Army under General Gusztáv Jány (1883–1947).

FORINT [FLORIN]. Hungary's monetary unit that replaced the *pengő* (q.v.) in 1946, and that is divided into hundred *fillérs* (q.v.). Derived from a highly decorated gold coin *(florenus, fiorino)* struck in 13th-century Florence (Firenze), the *forint (florin)* spread through much of Europe during the Renaissance (q.v.) and appeared under various related names and in many diverse values. In Hungary the first gold *forint* was struck under King Charles Robert (q.v.) in 1325. In the Holy Roman Empire (q.v.) it was Emperor Ferdinand I (q.v.) who made it into the universal currency in 1559. Originally struck of gold, in the 17th century the *forint* was increasingly made of silver, which was usually divided into sixty *Kreutzers (krajcár)* (q.v.). The *forint/florin* went through many transformations before being stabilized by an Central European coinage agreement of 1857. On the basis of this agreement five-hundred grams of silver were to produce forty-five *forints,* each of which was to be divided into hundred *krajcárs [Kreutzer].* This standardized *forint* survived until 1892, when it was replaced by the gold *korona* (crown) (q.v.), divided into hundred *fillérs.,* which remained in force until 1925. The *korona,* in turn, gave its place over to the *pengő* (1925–46), and the *pengő* to the still exiting *forint* in 1946.

FORTRESS SYSTEM [VÉGVÁRI RENDSZER]. A parallel system of fortifications on both sides of the Habsburg-Ottoman frontier in the 16th and the 17th centuries, built for the purposes of defending the region's population and securing the most important roads and crossings against the enemy's incursions. The roots of this system reach back to the first Turkish incursions into Hungary (q.v.) in the 15th century, but the system was not fully developed until after Hungary's trisection into "Royal Hungary" (q.v.), Turkish Hungary (q.v.), and Transylvania (q.v.) after 1541. In the course of time the region of the fortresses acquired a life of its own. It was an area of perpetual warfare, but also a region where one could detect signs of increased fraternizations between the garrisons of the two opposing forces. The system stretched from the Dalmatian (q.v.) coast of Croatia (q.v.), northward through Lake Balaton (q.v.), to Lower (q.v.) and Upper Hungary (q.v.). Then it turned in a horseshoe fashion eastward and southward down to the Middle Danube (q.v.) in the area to the east Belgrade (q.v.). Some of the most important fortifications included Kanizsa, Szigetvár (q.v.), Fehérvár (q.v.), Győr (q.v.), Eger (q.v.), Várad (q.v.), Gyula, and Temesvár (q.v.). Following the expulsion of the Turks during the Liberation Wars (q.v.)—which were accompanied and followed by the Thököly Uprising (q.v.) and the Rákóczi War of Liberation (q.v.)—the Habsburgs (q.v.) ordered the destruction of most of the smaller fortresses that were not part of cities, for fear that they would serve as centers of more anti-Habsburg uprisings.

FORTY-EIGHTER PARTY [NEGYVENNYOLCAS PÁRT] (1868–74). Founded after the Austro-Hungarian Compromise of 1867 (q.v.) to espouse the ideas of the revolution of 1848 (q.v.), the Forty-eighter Party was basically an independence-oriented political organization that wished to assert Hungary's (q.v.) separate identity and, ultimately, its separation from Austria (q.v.). In 1875 the party's moderate members joined the new Liberal Party (q.v.), while its left wing formed the Independence Party (q.v.). It leaders included József Madarász (1814–1915), Dániel Irányi (1822-92), and Ignác Helfy (1830–97)—all of whom continued to be active in the Independence Party.

FŐSZOLGABÍRÓ see **SZOLGABÍRÓ [IUDEX NOBILIUM].**

FRAKNÓI [FRANKL], VILMOS (1843–1924). Titular Bishop of Arbe (1892) and one of Hungary's great positivist historians, Fraknói served as the secretary (1879–89) and then as the associate president (1889-92) of the Hungarian Academy of Sciences (q.v.). He specialized on the premodern period and, in particular, on the role of the Hungarian Catholic Church (q.v.) and its religious and educational institutions. He did much of his research in the archives of the Eternal City, where in 1892 he founded the Hungarian Historical Institute of Rome. Fraknói was a pedantic, productive, and highly respected historian, whose writings reflect his conservatism and his dedication to his church. His most important works include: *Hungary's Ecclesiastic and Diplomatic Relations with the Holy See (Magyarország egyházi és diplomáciai összeköttetései a szentszékkel)* (3 vols., 1900-03), *Cardinal Péter Pázmány and his Age (Pázmány Péter és kora)* (3 vols., 1868–72), and *The Age of the Hunyadis and the Jagellonians (A Hunyadiak és a Jagellók kora)* (1896). He also wrote major biographies of King Matthias Corvinus (q.v.), King Louis II (q.v.), Archbishop János Vítéz (q.v.), Cardinal Tamás Bakócz (q.v.), and Palatine István Werbőczy (q.v.), as well as several works on Hungarian culture and education in the Middle Ages.

FRANCIS I [FRANCIS OF LORRAINE, FRANZ VON LOTHRINGEN] (1708–65). Holy Roman Emperor (r.1745–65), husband of the last true Habsburg (q.v.), Empress Maria Theresa (q.v.), and as such, the founding father of the Habsburg-Lorraine dynasty (q.v.). Francis became emperor by virtue of his marriage, that is, he was elected Holy Roman Emperor only because German law did not permit the election of a female to the imperial throne. Through his election, he gained the imperial title, but not real power. The actual governing was done by Maria Theresa, who was "empress" only by virtue of the fact that she was married to an emperor. Having few powers and obligations, Charles devoted his time and efforts to the arts, the sciences, business activities, and to the development of his own private estates. Following his death, two-thirds of his property was used to pay off much of the national debt, and one-third went into a "family living fund," which remained the common property of the Habsburg-Lorraine dynasty until 1919. Francis also produced sixteen legitimate children with his wife, and many illegitimate ones with other women. Two of his sons— Joseph II (q.v.) and Leopold II (q.v.)—became emperors, while several of his daughters became wives of other rulers. The latter included Maria Antoinette (1755–93), the wife of King Louis XVI (r.1774–92) of France, who perished during the French Revolution.

FRANCIS II [I] (1778-1835). Holy Roman Emperor as Francis II (r.1792–1806), Emperor of Austria as Francis I (r.1804–35), king of Hungary and Bohemia as Francis I (r.1792–1835), and archduke of Austria (1792–1835), he was the son of Emperor Leopold II (q.v.), nephew of Emperor Joseph II (q.v.), and grandson Emperor Francis I (q.v.) and his wife, Empress Maria Theresa (q.v.). Francis rose to the throne in the midst of the French Revolutionary Wars, in which he was forced to fight France, while also having to deal with the Jacobin Conspiracy (q.v.) in his empire. Following a series of losses to the French, Francis was forced to cede various Italian and south German territories, and also to relinquish his imperial title when Napoleon dissolved the thousand-year-old Holy Roman Empire (q.v.) in 1806. Sensing the inevitable, Francis had reorganized his German and non-German possession into the Austrian Empire (q.v.) already in 1804, and also had himself crowned the emperor of Austria (August 11). With additional territorial losses in the war of 1809, which was sanctified by the Treaty of Schönbrunn (October 14, 1809), Francis was obliged to give his daughter, Marie Louise, to Napoleon in marriage (April 1810). He also agreed to support his son-in-law's invasion of Russia (1812) (q.v.). After Napoleon's disastrous Russian campaign, however, Francis promptly joined the anti-French coalition and contributed significantly to the series of French defeats in 1813–14. Following Napoleon's exile, Francis hosted the Congress of Vienna (1814–15) (q.v.), which resulted in his reacquisition of all former possessions. In 1815 he joined the Quadruple Alliance and the Holy Alliance, which were meant to keep the status quo in post-revolutionary Europe. In 1820–21

Francis was involved in putting down several revolutionary upheavals in Italy (q.v.).

During the last three decades of his reign, Emperor Francis was largely under the influence of Prince Klemens von Metternich (q.v.), whose conservative philosophy dominated not only the Austrian Empire (q.v.), but also much of continental Europe. In Hungary (q.v.), he took advantage of the Napoleonic wars to govern by decrees and to impose a form of absolutism. This absolutism increased after the Napoleonic Wars, when all manifestations of liberalism and nationalism were suppressed, including the budding patriotism of the conservative Hungarian nobility (q.v.). After the Diet of 1811–12, Francis refused to call another one until 1825. Even then, he convened it only because of major economic problems and increased pressures by the Hungarian Estates (q.v.). The Reform Diet of 1825 (q.v.), however, proved to be a watershed. It started the series of political and social reforms that initiated the Hungarian Reform Period (1825–48) (q.v.) and led to the transformation of Hungarian society. Driven by powerful ideological forces, neither Emperor Francis nor Prince Metternich was able to stop this reform that culminated in the Hungarian Revolution of 1848–49 (q.v.).

FRANCISCANS [FRANCISCAN ORDER, ORDO FRAT- RUM MINORUM = OFM]. A Catholic religious order founded by St. Francis of Assisi (c.1182–1226) in 1210 for the purposes of spreading the faith. The Franciscans believed in complete poverty and initially lived off begging. Yet, almost from the very beginning they were wracked by disagreements about the role of poverty. In 1517 the two extremes finally broke apart into the strict Observants [OFM] and flexible Conventuals or Minorites [OFM Conv.]. Moreover, in 1525 the Observants again broke into two, with one of the branches establishing itself as the Capuchin Order [OFM Cap.].

The Franciscans settled in Hungary (q.v.) in the 1230s, where they played a significant role through the 14th and 15th centuries. They were close to the center of political power and continued to expand into some of Hungary's southern defensive banats (q.v.), including Bosnia (q.v.) and northern part Serbia (q.v.). In the 15th century, they were in the forefront of Hungary's defensive struggle against the Ottoman Turks (q.v.). One of their members, St. John of Capistrano (1386-1456), was a close associate of the famed anti-Turkish crusader, János Hunyadi (q.v.). Although the relative significance of the Franciscans declined during Hungary's Turkish occupation (16th-17th c.) (q.v.), the Franciscans continued to play a major role in Hungary's cultural and religious life until after World War II (q.v.). In 1950, when most of the religious orders were disbanded, the Franciscans survived, but only with two secondary schools (Esztergom and Szentendre) under their control. Following the collapse of communism (1989-90) (q.v.), they also began a process of rebuilding.

FRANCIS FERDINAND (1863–1914). A nephew of Emperor Francis Joseph (q.v.) who, after the suicide of the latter's son, Archduke Rudolph (q.v.), became the heir to the Austro-Hungarian throne. Francis Ferdinand was an ambitious politician who made every effort to increase his influence upon the domestic and foreign policy of the Dual Monarchy (q.v.). He had strong anti-Hungarian feelings, and felt that Hungarian power had to be cut down to reorganize and to revitalize the empire. For this reason he gathered around himself the most prominent spokesmen of the national minorites (e.g., Iuliu Maniu, Milan Hodža, Alexander Vajda-Voievod, etc.) and used them to push the unwilling emperor in the direction of a trialistic solution that would have transformed Austria-Hungary into a "triune" state with the addition of a South Slavic (q.v.) unit. In foreign policy Francis Ferdinand was thought to stand for aggressive militarism, although in actuality he only tried to preserve the unity of the Habsburg Empire (q.v.). But his desire to implement his plan for a South Slavic component within the Dual Monarchy, which would have pulled the rug from under the Serbian dream for a Greater Serbia, aroused the animosity of the Serbian nationalists, and thus contributed to his assassination by members of a Serbian secret society (June 28, 1914).

Francis Ferdinand was a headstrong, diligent, and determined man, but at the same time he was very conservative and bigoted, which made him unpopular in the empire. His determination is demonstrated by his morganatic marriage (q.v.) to Countess Sophie Chotek (after 1909 Princess of Hohenberg) (1900), which obliged him to renounce the right of succession for his offspring. Had he survived, his accession to the throne would have brought him into conflict with the Hungarians. But had he been able to carry out his reorganization plan, followed by the federalization of the empire, he may have been able to avert the dismemberment of the Habsburg state and the political fragmentation of Central Europe (q.v.).

FRANCIS   JOSEPH (1830–1916). Emperor of Austria (r.1848-1916), king of Hungary (r.1848/67–1916), and joint ruler of Austria-Hungary (r.1867–1916). He was the nephew of King Ferdinand V (Austrian Emperor Ferdinand I) (q.v), who was forced to resign as a result of his inability to deal with the revolution of 1848–49 (q.v.). Viewed as the heir to the throne already during Ferdinand's reign, Francis Joseph was reared by his strong and assertive mother, Archduchess Sophie of Wittelsbach (1805–72), who had married Ferdinand's brother, Archduke Francis Charles (1802–78). Although Francis Joseph ascended the throne on December 2, 1848, he was not crowned king of Hungary (q.v.) until 1867, following the Austro-Hungarian Compromise (q.v.) of that year. In 1849 he relied on Russian military intervention to put down the Hungarian Revolution, and then with the help of Prince Schwarzenberg (q.v.) and Alexander Bach (q.v.), he initiated the Age of Absolutism (q.v.). Although personally not involved in the retributions that followed the Hungarian Revolution, he was still held responsible by Hungarian public opinion for its excesses. It took Francis Joseph many decades to live down the image of a tyrant created by General Haynau's (q.v.) actions.

The military reverses suffered by the Habsburg forces in Italy (q.v.) in 1859 compelled Francis Joseph to relax his absolutism in Hungary and to make a compromise with the nation's moderate leaders. After some false starts with the October Diploma (q.v.) and the February Patent (q.v.), he finally did so by concluding the Austro-Hungarian Compromise of 1867. Under the terms of this agreement, the Austrian Empire (q.v.) was transformed into the dualist state of Austria-Hungary (q.v.), where Francis Joseph bore the double title of emperor of Austria and king of Hungary. The new dualist empire had two governments, two parliaments, and two citizenships, but the two states still shared foreign affairs, most military affairs, and some financial matters. This agreement was far from perfect, but Francis Joseph still viewed it as the best of the possible alternatives, and he continued to uphold it until the end of his life. His primary aim was to preserve the empire, and to this end he joined in a military partnership with Imperial Germany (1879) (q.v.). And this partnership remained the cornerstone of his foreign policy to the very end. Sadly enough, it was this partnership that took him into World War I (q.v.), which ended with the dissolution of his empire.

Although gaining much respect and affection in the course of his nearly seven decades of rule, Francis Joseph was not fortunate in his personal life. He married for love (1854), but his marriage soon turned into a loveless coexistence. His only son, Archduke Rudolph (q.v.), with whom his relationship was strained, committed suicide in 1889. His brother, Emperor Maximilian of Mexico (r.1864–67), died in front of a firing squad in 1867. His wife, the artistically inclined Elizabeth (q.v.), who could never understand his devotion to his empire, was assassinated by an Italian anarchist in 1898. Francis Joseph ruled longer than any other monarch in European history save Louis XIV (1643–1715) of France, who, however, began his reign at the age of three. Fate was not very good to Francis Joseph, but his death on November 21, 1916, saved him from witnessing the dissolution of empire barely two years later.

FRANCIS OF LORRAINE see **FRANCIS I.**

FRANGEPÁN [FRANKOPAN] FAMILY. One of the most influential families of Medieval Hungary (q.v.), who emerged onto the national scene in the late 12th century, when King Béla III (q.v.) appointed one of their ancestors, Bertalan, the *comes (ispán)* (q.v.) of Modrus County. From the 13th through the 17th centuries, the

Frangepáns had played an especially significant role in the region of Croatia (q.v.), Dalmatia (q.v.), and Slavonia (q.v.), often serving as the *bans* (q.v.) of those provinces. They also held other important national and ecclesiastical offices until they died out in 1671.

The most noted members of the Frangepán family included: (1) Ferenc János (d.1391), *ban* of Croatia-Dalmatia-Slavonia and the brother-in-law of Emperor Sigismund (q.v.); (2) Miklós (d.1432), *ban* of Croatia-Dalmatia-Slavonia, who assumed the name and coat-of-arms of the Italian Frangipani family; (3) Márton (d.1479), who served both of the great rivals, King Matthias Corvinus (q.v.) and Emperor Frederick III (r.1440–93), and got away with it; (4) Ferenc Kristóf (d.1527), *ban* of Croatia-Dalmatia-Slavonia, who was one of the ablest military commanders and anti-Turkish fighters of his times; (5) Count Ferenc Frangepán (d.1543), archbishop of Kalocsa (1528) and the bishop of Eger (1538), who in 1526 became an adviser of King John Zápolya (q.v.), but then served as one of the architects of the Peace of Várad (q.v.) that hoped to reunite Hungary under King Ferdinand (q.v.); and (6) Count Ferenc Kristóf Frangepán (1620–71), the last member of the family, who became involved in the Wesselényi Conspiracy (q.v.) and was executed for high treason.

FRATER GYÖRGY see MARTINUZZI, GYÖRGY.

FREEDOM FIGHTERS [FIFTY-SIXERS]. A term applied to those who left Hungary (q.v.) after the revolution of 1956 (q.v.), irrespective of whether they were actively involved in the revolution or not. Their numbers were around 200,000, of which about 40,000 emigrated to the United States. About two-thirds of them were young males, most with transferable technical skills, who merged easily into the receiving societies. They also lacked the political baggage of their immediate predecessors, the post-World War II (q.v.) Displaced Persons (q.v.), for they were not in the category of "ex-enemies" and their participation in the anti-communist uprising classified them as "heroes." For these reasons, most of them did very well in their new countries—be these in Western Europe, North America, or Australia.

FREEDOM OF MOVEMENT FOR THE PEASANTRY [SZABAD KÖLTÖZÉSI JOG]. Although there were increased efforts to limit the free movement of the peasants (from estate to estate) during the 14th and 15th centuries, the Hungarian peasants retained this right until after the Dózsa Peasant Revolution of 1514 (q.v.). A law passed by the Hungarian Diet (q.v.) as a result of that revolution bound the peasants to the soil and thereby transformed them into bonded serfs (q.v.). They remained in this unfree position until the peasant reforms of Joseph II (r.1765/80–90) (q.v.), which restored the right of free movement. Yet, not until the serf emancipation (q.v.) of 1848 did they really regain their complete personalfreedom.

FREE ELECTIONISTS [SZABAD KIRÁLYVÁLASZTÓK]. Members of those political groups, who, after the dissolution of Austria-Hungary (q.v.), wished to reestablish the monarchical system of government in Hungary (q.v), but not by restoring the Habsburgs (q.v.) to the Hungarian throne. Most of them wanted a "Hungarian" on the throne, preferably one with some link to the Árpáds (q.v.) or to one of the other dynasties. Although active during the interwar period (q.v.), the Free Electionists were really fringe groups, with no realistic hopes of ever achieving their goal.

FREE HUNGARY MOVEMENT (1941–42). A pro-Hungary political movement initiated in the United States by the exile politician Tibor Eckhardt (q.v.) on September 27, 1941. Its goal was to represent Hungary (q.v.) in the West, in light of the fact that the Hungarian government was forced into a coalition with Hitler's Germany (q.v.). The movement was not very successful, and it was undercut by the political emigration of the surrounding Successor States (q.v.), as well as by the left-leaning Hungarian political emigration under the leadership of Rusztem Vámbéry (q.v.), Oscar Jászi (q.v.), and Count Michael Károlyi (q.v.). It was disbandedon July 9, 1942, and its role was taken over by the American Hungarian Federation (q.v.), the primary umbrella organization of the Hungarians in North America.

FREE MASONRY. Founded in the 18th century as an organization to advance the cause of universal human brotherhood, the roots of Free Masonry reach back to the 13th and 14th centuries, and more specifically to the brotherhood of those stone masons who were building the great Romanesque and Gothic cathedrals of Medieval Europe. Revived as an association of proponents of the ideas of Enlightenment (q.v.), 18th-century Free Masonry included such diverse personalities as Voltaire, King George IV of England, Frederick the Great of Prussia, as well as Benjamin Franklin, George Washington, and Thomas Jefferson of the United States. In Hungary (q.v.) the first Free Mason organization was founded in 1770 by such noted exponents of Hungarian National Revival (q.v.) and liberalism as Gergely Berzeviczy (q.v.), Ferenc Kazinczy (q.v.), Count Ferenc Széchényi (q.v.), Ferenc Kölcsey (q.v.), and the executed leader of the Hungarian Jacobins (q.v.), Ignác Martinovics (q.v.). Following the Jacobin Conspiracy of 1794–95 (q.v.), Free Masonry was abolished and was not revived until 1868. During the Dualist Period (q.v.), Hungarian Free Masons became closely associated with the ideas and activities of Bourgeois Radicalism (q.v.). Thus, after World War I (q.v.), it was suppressed both by Béla Kún's (q.v.) communist and Admiral Horthy's (q.v.) conservative regimes. Free Masonry was revived in 1945, suppressed in 1950, and then revived again in 1989.

FRIEDRICH, ISTVÁN (1883–1958). An industrialist, who in the immediate post-World War I (q.v.) period became Hungary's (q.v.) prime minister in one of the brief transitional governments (August 7–November 24, 1919), and then the minister for defense in another one (November 24, 1919–March 15, 1920). In the fall of 1921 Friedrich was involved in guerrilla wars that tried to preserve Hungary's western frontier lands (Burgenland) (q.v.) by creating a separate little state called the *Lajtabánság* (Banat of Lajta) (q.v.), as well as in King Charles IV's (q.v.) second attempt in to regain his Hungarian throne. For this reason he was briefly placed under arrest. Although usually in opposition, Friedrich remained a member of the Hungarian Parliament (q.v.) right up to 1939.

- G -

GÁBOR SISTERS. Zsazsa (b.1917), Magda (b.1919), and Éva (1921-96) are Hungarian-American film actresses, whose beauty has enchanted Hollywood for several decades following World War II (q.v.). Although they all played in a number of movies, they were better known for their unusual beauty, than for their acting talents. The most famous among them, Zsazsa, was elected Miss Hungary in the mid-1930s. She married a Turkish diplomat in 1938 (the first of her nine husbands), and then emigrated to the United States in 1941. For several decades, she was the *par excellence* Hungarian beauty in the eyes of the American public and represented Hungary more than probably anyone else.

GALICIA [HALICH, HALICS, HALICZ, GÁCSORSZÁG]. A province that today is largely part of Ukraine (q.v.), with a small section in Poland (q.v.). In the 9th century it was part of Kievan Russia (q.v.). With the gradual disintegration of that state in the 12th century, it became part of the Principality of Galicia-Volynia. In the early 13th century, Hungarian rule was extended over the province, and King Andrew II (q.v.) even assumed the title "King of Galicia." Hungarian pretensions ended with the Mongol conquest (q.v.) in the mid-13th century. In the 14th century the province became part of the expanding Lithuania, and then, with the Union of Krewo (1386), a component of the Polish-Lithuanian Common-wealth (q.v.). After the partitions of Poland (1772–95), Galicia was attached to the Habsburg Empire (q.v.). After World War I (q.v.) it became part of resurrected Poland (q.v.), but following World War II (q.v.) most of it was attached to the Soviet Union. Since Ukraine's separation in 1991, it is part of the independent Ukrainian State.

GALILEI CIRCLE [GALILEI KÖR] (1908-19). A progressive association of Hungarian university students established in

November 1908 on the basis of the ideology of Bourgeois Radicalism (q.v.). Before World War I (q.v.) the Galilei Circle became involved in propagandizing the working classes in and around Budapest (q.v.). The Galileists did this both through sociographical publications, as well as by organizing workers' study circles. They were especially critical of the unequal distribution of agricultural wealth in Hungary (q.v.), that is, of the existence of large estates with their millions of exploited peasants. This prompted them to establish close contacts with the Social Democratic Party (q.v.) and to toy with the ideology of Marxism.

In 1917, several members of the Galilei Circle—including Ilona Duczynska, Otto Korvin, and Imre Sallai—began illegal antiwar activities and established Workers' Councils [Soviets] (q.v.) on the Russian model. They were soon arrested, convicted and imprisoned (January–October 1918). Following the collapse of Austria-Hungary (October 31, 1918) (q.v.), the Circle resumed its activities and a number of its members participated in the founding of the Communist Party of Hungary (q.v.). Subsequently some of them also assumed various political roles in Béla Kun's (q.v.) Hungarian Soviet Republic (q.v.). Thus, after the fall of the Kun Regime, the radical members of the Galilei Circle either emigrated or were convicted of various political crimes.

GARAI FAMILY. One of the most powerful aristocratic families in 14th- and 15th-century Hungary (q.v.). The members of the Garai family came to prominence in the mid–13th century, when they received large land grants from Prince Béla, the second son of King Béla IV (q.v.). By the 14th century their lands stretched over twelve counties in south-central Hungary, their power being centered on the town of Gara in Valkó (later Verőcze) County, from where they took their name. During the Age of the Anjous (q.v.), the members of the Garai family served in many important royal and ecclesiastical offices. The most prominent among them are Miklós Garai (d.1386), the ban of Macsó (1359–75) and the palatine of Hungary (1375–85); his son of the same name, Miklós Garai (1366–1434), the ban of Macsó (1387–90), ban of Croatia-Slavonia (1397–1401), and the palatine of Hungary (1402-33); and the latter's son, László Garai (d.1459), the ban of Macsó (1419–47) and the palatine of Hungary (1447–58). During the reign of Louis the Great (q.v.), the Garais were powerful military lords and top administrators, while during the Age of Sigismund (q.v.) and János Hunyadi (q.v.), they were among the kingmakers of Hungary. Their opposition to Matthias Corvinus (q.v.) led to their decline and fall and their gradual disappearance form the history. The last known male member of the family, a certain László, died in 1528.

GATE TAX [PORTALIS, KAPUADÓ]. First introduced to Hungary (q.v.) in 1336 by Charles I (q.v.), this tax replaced the revenue formerly derived from the minting and then the reminting of coins into lower grade. The gate tax had to be paid only by the peasant classes, and initially only by those well-to-do peasants who had large gates that could be negotiated by a fully loaded hay wagon. Initially this tax had no relationship to the number of persons or families living behind that gate. In various altered forms, this tax survived right until the revolution of 1848-49 (q.v.) In the 16th and 17th centuries, the gate tax was also used by the Turks (q.v.) in the section of Hungary that was part of the Ottoman Empire (q.v.).

GENDARMERIE [CSENDŐRSÉG]. A national police force whose members were under military orders and were treated as if they were members of the national army. The first gendarme unit was established in revolutionary France in 1791, which then was copied by several European and non-European states, including Canada (Canadian Mounted Police). The first gendarme unit in the Austrian Empire (q.v.) was established in 1814, and in Hungary (q.v.) proper in 1849. It functioned until 1867 under the name of *zsandárság* and served as a tool of Habsburg absolutism in Hungary. Disbanded at the time of the Austro-Hungarian Compromise of 1867 (q.v.), it was reestablished in 1881 under the name of *csendőrség*. It survived until 1945, when it was disbanded by the post–World War II regime. Those of its members who failed to emigrate were persecuted indiscriminately, partially because of their stout support of the old regime and partially because of their role in having aided the collection of the Hungarian Jews (q.v.) following the German occupation of Hungary (q.v.).

GENEALOGY. As a discipline, genealogy is the study of family origins and the relationship among various families and individuals. Its research goals are aided by such other disciplines as archeology, history, biology, statistics, sociology, and other related studies. The sources of genealogical research include birth certificates, birth registers, property deeds, trial documents, final testaments, official genealogical tables, memorials, inscriptions, headstones, folklore, and oral traditions. In Hungary (q.v.), ever since the mid–19th century, the discipline of genealogy had been classified as one of the Auxiliary Sciences of History (q.v.). It was cultivated on a high level by scholars such as Iván Nagy (1824–98), Albert Nyáry (1828–86), László Fejérpataky (1857–1923), Antal Áldásy (1869–1932), Béla Kempelen (1874–1952), Imre Szentpétery (1878–1950), and others, right up until the end of World War II (q.v.). Calling it a "reactionary" discipline, the new communist regime abolished the study of genealogy at all universities, and its study was not resumed until the mid-1980s. Next to the University of Budapest (q.v.), which had a special chair for the Auxiliary Sciences of History (q.v.) ever since the early 19th century, the study of genealogy was centered on the Hungarian Heraldic and Genealogical Association *(MagyarHeraldikaiésGenealógiaiTársaság)* (q.v.) founded in 1883, abolished after World War II (q.v.), and resurrected in 1983.

GENTRY [DZSENTRI]. This English term was imported to Hungary after the Austro-Hungarian Compromise of 1867 (q.v.), and it was applied to those members of the Hungarian middle nobility (q.v.) who, after losing their estates and flooding the ranks of the state and county bureaucracy, still tried to live the life of the well-to-do landed nobility. Toward the end of the Dualist Period (q.v.) and during the interwar years (q.v.), this term was also applied to those members of the lower nobility (q.v.) who had likewise moved into bureaucratic occupations, as well as to such non-noble elements who performed administrative duties, were members of the intelligentsia, or managed to make themselves owners of landed estates. The members of this socially heterogeneous gentry class dominated Hungary up to 1945. They were conservative ideologically and very traditional in outlook. They practiced social customs that were reflective of a much earlier age, which made interwar Hungary (q.v.) into the home base of a "Neo-Baroque society" (q.v).

GERARD, SAINT [SZENT GELLÉRT] (c.980-1046). Catholic bishop and one of the pioneers of Hungarian Christianity. Born into a Venetian patrician family, Gerard ended up in Hungary in 1015 while on the road to Jerusalem. He became a close associate of King St. Stephen (q.v.), who entrusted the education of his son, the future St. Emeric (q.v.), to Gerard. In 1030 he was commissioned to organize the bishopric of Marosvár (later Csanád), and then was appointed its first bishop. In 1037 Gerard visited his homeland, but then returned to Hungary. Following King Stephen's death in 1038, Bishop Gerard withdrew from public life. In 1046 he fell victim to the pagan uprising led by Vata (q.v.) on a hill within today's Budapest (q.v.), now known as Gerard's Hill *[Gellérthegy]* (q.v.).

GERARD'S HILL [SZENT GELLÉRTHEGY]. A picturesque steep hill in the middle of Budapest (q.v.), on the right or Buda side of the Danube (q.v.), with several mineral springs rising at its foot that feed a number of well-known spas. Originally known as the Mountain of Pest *(Mons Pestiensis)*, people began to refer to it as St. Gerard's Hill already in the 15th century. According to general belief, it was on top of this hill where Bishop St. Gerard (q.v.) was martyred in 1046. Until the Turkish conquest (q.v.), a small chapel crowned its peak, but in the 16th century the Turks replaced it with a wooden palisade, which survived into the 18th century. In 1815 its place was taken by an astronomical observatory, and then in 1851 by the still existing fortification, known as the Citadella. The latter was built at the orders of General Haynau (q.v.) to control the "rebels" following the defeat of the Hungarian Revolution of 1848–49 (q.v.). Starting with the 16th century, the Germans began to call it "Block Mountain" *(Blocksberg),* probably after the wooden Turkish stockade. Following the Austro-Hungarian Compromise of 1867 (q.v.), the Citadella lost its military significance and Gerard's Hill became an exclusive residential quarter for the well-to-do citizens of Budapest. In 1904 the St. Gerard memorial was built on the hill's eastern side, while in 1947 the huge "Statue of Liberty" was erected on its top to commemorate the Soviet "liberation" (occupation) of Hungary.

GERMAN CONFEDERATION [DEUTSCHE BUND] (1815-66). A confederation of thirty-nine German states formed at the Congress of Vienna (1814–15) (q.v.), which replaced the defunct Holy Roman Empire (q.v.). Although most of its inhabitants were Germans, it did have a minority of Czechs (Bohemia), Danes (Holstein), and Italians (South Tyrol, Trentino). About half of the Austrian Empire (q.v.) and about two-thirds of Prussia were inside the German Confederation. Each component state had extensive autonomy, and two of them—Austria and Prussia—were great powers in their own right. Each of the states was represented at the Diet of Frankfurt, chaired by the Austrian Emperor (and King of Hungary), who was the permanent president of the Confederation. The policies of the component states were coordinated by a largely powerless diet, which, after the revolutions of 1848, became the Frankfurt Parliament that promoted the idea of German unity. During the 1860s, Prussia challenged Austria's preeminence and assumed the leadership in the German unification process. The Austro-Prussian War of 1866 led to the defeat and expulsion of Austria, and to the foundation of the Prussian-led North German Confederation (1866–71). This act served as a catalyst in transforming the Austrian Empire into Austria-Hungary (q.v.). The Franco-Prussian War of 1870–71, which ended in France's defeat, brought about the unification of the German states into the new German Empire (q.v.), which overnight became continental Europe's number one power.

GERMAN EMPIRE (1871–1918). Unified by Prussia after its victory in the Franco-Prussian War (1870–71), the new German Empire overnight became the most powerful continental state. It was dominated by the militarily oriented Junker class, whose members were descendants of the Teutonic Knights (q.v.). Led by Otto von Bismarck (1815-98), the German Empire hosted the Congress of Berlin (1878), joined with Austria-Hungary (q.v.) in the Dual Alliance (1879) (q.v.), joined with Austria-Hungary and Italy (q.v.) in the Triple Alliance (1882) (q.v.), and then undertook to gain its "place in the sun" by initiating a quest for colonies in 1885. The aggressiveness of the new German Empire was countered by a coalition of such old colonial powers as Britain, France, and Russia (q.v.), which coalesced into the Triple Entente (1894–1907) (q.v.). This polarization of Europe, combined with a growing military and naval race, and a series of international crises, eventually led to the outbreak of World War I (q.v.). The loss of the war by the German Empire and Austria-Hungary resulted in the former's mutilation and in the latter's complete dissolution. The German Empire was replaced by the smaller Weimar Republic (1918–33) and then by Hitler's Third Reich (1933–45), both of which affected small interwar Hungary's (q.v.) position in the world.

GERMAN OCCUPATION OF HUNGARY (1944). The successful German support for Hungary's (q.v.) goal to regain some of the territories lost after World War I (q.v.) compelled the Hungarian government to become allied to Germany (q.v.) in World War II (q.v.). This was an uneasy alliance, from which Prime Minister Kállay (q.v.) tried to extricate the country as early as 1942. By early 1944 Hungary's withdrawal from this alliance was imminent, which prompted Hitler to order the military occupation of the country. It took place on March 19, 1994, while Regent Horthy (q.v.) was on a state visit to Germany. This German occupation was followed by the introduction of severe measures against the Hungarian Jews (q.v.), by the rise of the fascist Arrow Cross Party (q.v.) to power (October 15, 1944), and by the Hungarian Holocaust (q.v.) that resulted to the death of several hundred thousand Jews.

GERMANS IN HUNGARY. Hungarians have had close contacts with Germans even before the Árpádian conquest of Hungary (q.v.) when they became allies of the East Frankish ruler and later Holy Roman Emperor Arnulf (r.888/96–901). During the three-quarters of a century following their conquest of the Carpathian Basin (q.v.), these contacts were mostly antagonistic, for the Hungarians repeatedly raided German territories. From the late 10th century onward, however, the relationship alternated between antagonism and friendship. This was so, partially because of Hungary's need for German cultural influences and partially because of the Holy Roman Empire's (q.v.) repeated efforts to gain control over the country.

Hungary's Christianization began in the late 10th century and it brought a great number of German clergymen, military leaders, administrators, and soldiers of fortune to Hungary. Many of these were granted estates and became members of the Hungarian upper nobility (q.v.). Large-scale migration of Germans, however, was not undertaken until the mid–12th century, when they began to settle in Western Hungary *(Burgenland)* (q.v.), north-central Hungary *(Zipserland, Szepesség)* (q.v.), several sections of Transylvania (q.v.), and in some of Hungary's important urban centers, such as Esztergom (q.v.), Pozsony (q.v.), and Buda (q.v.). These medieval settlers were generally artisans and miners who were brought in because of their urban skills and technical know-how.

Following the expulsion of the Turks (q.v.) in the late 17th and early 18th centuries, however, a new wave of German migration began, motivated by the large landowners' need for cultivators, and the Habsburg Imperial Government's desire to repopulate the lands that had been depopulated by the Liberation Wars (q.v.). This time most of the German settlers were peasants, who settled on some of Hungary's best agricultural lands and established prosperous agricultural centers throughout the country. During the six centuries of their migration, the German immigrants came from many diverse sections of the Holy Roman Empire. Yet, those who settled during the Middle Ages were generally known in Hungary as Saxons (q.v.), while those coming in the 18th–century came to be known as Swabians (q.v.). With the rise of Hungarian nationalism (q.v.) in the

19th century, most of the urban Germans (except the Saxons of Transylvania) became Magyarized and came to constitute a significant portion of the modern Hungarian urban middle classes. Even so, as late as 1910, over 10 percent of Historic Hungary's (q.v.) population was still German (1.9 out of 18.3 million). Moreover, even after Hungary's dismemberment at Trianon (q.v.), there still remained nearly half a million Germans out of a population of eight million. This situation changed only after World War II (q.v.), when most of the Germans fled or were expelled. By 1960 only 50,000 Hungarian citizens claimed to be of the German mother tongue. The role of the Germans in Hungarian history is extremely important. During the Middle Ages they were the primary urbanizers and the importers of modern technology, while during more recent times, the Magyarized Germans constituted a significant portion of the nation's administrative and scientific intelligentsia.

GERMANY. A generic terms for the powerful country or group of countries inhabited by Germans immediately to the west of Hungary (q.v.). In the course of the past one thousand years this generic term was used to refer to the Holy Roman Empire (10th c.–1806) (q.v.), the German Confederation (1815–66) (q.v.), the German Empire (1871–1918), the Weimar Republic (1918–33), Hitler's Third Reich (1933–45), and post-World War II Germany. Between 1949 and 1989, Germany consisted of two parts: West Germany (German Federal Republic) (GFR, BRD) and East Germany (German Democratic Republic) (GDR, DDR).

GERŐ, ERNŐ (1898–1980). The second most important communist leader in post-World War II Hungary (q.v.), who was feared and detested almost as much as "Hungary's Little Stalin," Mátyás Rákosi (q.v.). After serving in the Hungarian Red Army in 1919, Gerő fled abroad and spent most of the interwar years in the Soviet Union (q.v.). Returning in 1945, he became one of Hungary's three top communist leaders who—along with Rákosi and Mihály Farkas (1904–65)—ruled the country with iron hands (1948–53, 1954–56). In the weeks before the Hungarian Revolution of 1956 (q.v.), Gerő

had replaced Rákosi as the head of the Hungarian Workers'
(Communist) Party (q.v.) and then had a major role in calling in the
Russian troops and thus suppressing that revolution. Having
become an embarrassment to Khrushchev, he spent the next four
years in the Soviet Union. After his return in 1960, he was
confronted with the many illegalities committed during the Rákosi
Regime and was stripped of all his party functions. Gerő spent his
remaining years as a translator for various publishing houses.

GESTA [DEEDS]. A relatively simple medieval historical work
whose name is derived from *gesta rerum* or *res gestae* (past deeds).
Written in Latin, the *gesta* is related to the chronicle (q.v.), although
it is more of a literary work than the latter. In contrast to the
chronicle, the *gesta* is organized more along thematic lines and it
usually reproduces various heroic legends connected with the origins
of a nation or ethnic group. At times it is difficult to distinguish
between a medieval *gesta* and a chronicle, and this is also true in the
case of Hungarian traditions. The first Hungarian *gesta,* the so-called
Ancient Gesta (Ősgeszta) (q.v.) was written in the 11th century,
and portions of it were later copied by Anonymus (q.v.), Kézai (q.v),
and other chroniclers in the 12th through the 15th centuries.

**GESTA HUNGARORUM [DEEDS OF THE HUNGARI-
ANS].** The name of three medieval Hungarian chronicles, including
the lost *Ancient Gesta (Ősgeszta)* (q.v) and the still existing *Gesta
Hungarorum* by Anonymus (q.v.) and by Kézai (q.v.).

GESTAPO [GEHEIME STAATSPOLIZEI]. Secret State Police
of Hitler's Third Reich (1933–45). Its founding director was
Hermann Göring (1893–1946), who was replaced in 1934 by
Heinrich Himmler (1900–45). It was the primary instrument of the
political persecutions, mass deportations, and executions connected
with Hitler's New Order in Europe. The Gestapo also had a
significant role in Hungary (q.v.), especially after the country's
German occupation on March 19, 1944, when the members of this

force became involved in the collection and extermination of the Hungarian Jews (q.v.).

GÉZA, PRINCE (c.940–97). Ruling prince of Hungary (r.970–97), son of Prince Taksony (q.v.), and father of the future King St. Stephen (q.v.). He was responsible for reasserting princely powers, following the disintegration of central control after the Árpádian conquest (q.v.) of Hungary (q.v.). He extended his control over the Hungarian Tribal Federation (q.v.) that had been weakened by the marauding expeditions of the previous seven decades, and established marriage alliances with the Kabars (q.v.) and with the powerful tribe of Prince Gyula (q.v.) of Transylvania (q.v.). He married the latter's daughter Sarolta, the mother of the future King St. Stephen. Géza made the city of Esztergom (q.v.) his capital and also established friendly relations with Western Europe. Thus, he signed a treaty of friendship with Holy Roman Emperor Otto I (r.936–73) and was baptized in 973 under the name of Stephen. He never became a true believer, for to him Christianization was a purely political act. Yet he still supported the spread of Christianity and laid down the foundations of the Catholic Church administration in his country. He founded the Bishopric of Veszprém (q.v.), undertook the construction of the Abbey of Pannonhalma (q.v.), and had his only son and successor reared as a faithful Catholic. In 996 he gained for the latter the hand of the Bavarian Princess Gisella (q.v.) in marriage. Many of Prince Géza's achievements in the spread of Western Civilization in Hungary were later incorrectly attributed to his son, King St. Stephen.

GÉZA I (c.1040–77). King of Hungary (r.1074–77), son of King Béla I (q.v.), and successor to his cousin, King Salamon (q.v.), whom he eventually defeated with the help of his brother and successor King St. Ladislas (q.v.). After the death of his father in 1063, Géza received the "dukátus" (duchy) (q.v.), while his cousin Salamon gained the kingship. Initially the two cousins got along fairly well and even fought side by side against the Czechs (q.v.), the Venetians, the Pechenegs (q.v.), and the Byzantines (q.v.), but after

1071 their relationships changed because Géza decided to gain the royal crown for himself. Their rivalry resulted in Salamon's defeat and deposition and the elevation of Géza to the Hungarian throne. As the king of Hungary, Géza was able to force Emperor Henry IV (r.1056–1106) out of the country and free Hungary from the Salamon-created vassalage to the Holy Roman Empire (q.v.). In 1075 Géza received a crown from Byzantine Emperor Michael VIII Dukas (r.1071–78), which later became the lower half of the Holy Crown of Hungary (q.v.). He died after only three years of rule and was buried in the city of Vác.

GÉZA II (1130-62). The son of King Béla II the Blind (q.v.) and the king of Hungary (r.1041-62), who ascended the throne at the age of eleven. During the next five years the country's government was in the hands of his mother, the Serbian Helena (Ilona) and her brother Ban Belos (q.v.). King Géza's sixteen years of de facto rule proved to be a stable one, because he was supported by most of Hungary's upper classes. In 1146 he defeated the invading forces of Marquis Henry (Markgraf Heinrich Jasomirgott) of Austria (q.v.), and in 1147 he saw the German and French knights of the Second Crusade through Hungary (q.v.). He also led several campaigns into Kievan Russia (1148-52) (q.v.) to aid his brother-in-law, Iziaslav II (r.1146–54), in the latter's struggle for the Kievan throne. During the 1150s, King Géza became embroiled in wars against the Byzantine Empire (q.v.) as well as in the struggle between the Papacy and the Holy Roman Empire (q.v.). Initially he helped Emperor Frederick Barbarossa (r.1152–90), but then switched to Pope Alexander III (r.1159–81). He also supported Serbia's aspirations to throw off Byzantine rule, but then was forced to fend off his own brothers' (Stephen's and Ladislas's) desire to his throne. After his victory, both of his brothers fled to Byzantium. It was during Géza's reign that the Saxons (q.v.) had settled in Northern Hungary (Zipserland) (q.v.) and Transylvania (q.v.).

GHETTO. In Medieval and Early Modern Europe the Jews were restricted to certain sections of the cities, which were called ghettos, named after the 13th-century Jewish quarter of Venice that used to house a cannon foundry. During Christian holidays, the Jews could not leave the ghettos, and when they left, they usually had to wear a sign of their Jewish identity, such as a distinct headgear or a specific mark on their clothing. In medieval Hungary (q.v.) there were major Jewish quarters in several cities, such as Buda (q.v.), Kismarton, Pozsony (q.v.), and Sopron (q.v.). These Jewish ghettos were officially disbanded after the Jewish Emancipation Law of 1868 (q.v.), although some Jewish quarters did survive right up to World War II (q.v.). Following the German occupation of Hungary (q.v.) on March 19, 1944, the Budapest Jews were forced into ghettos and then most of them were taken to German extermination camps.

GIESSWEIN, SÁNDOR (1856–1923). A Catholic priest, political writer, and the cofounder and leader of both the Christian Socialist Movement and of the Catholic People's Party, the forerunner of the Christian Democratic People's Party (q.v.). While working through the ranks to reach the post of a papal prelate (1909), Giesswein was inspired by Pope Leo XIII's (r.1878-1903) encyclical, *Rerum novarum* (1891), which prompted him to spread the ideology of Christian Socialism (q.v). In 1904 he became the first president of the Federation of Christian Socialist Associations *(Keresztény-szocialista Egyesületek Szövetsége}*, while in 1905 he was elected to the Hungarian Parliament (q.v.) on the Christian Socialist ticket. Giesswein was also involved in such diverse activities as the propagation of the Esperanto language and getting the budding feminist movement started. In the last phase of World War I (q.v.), he became a vocal opponent of the war, which compelled him to establish contacts with such left-leaning organizations as the Galilei Circle (q.v.). During 1918–19 Giesswein became a member of Count Michael Károlyi's (q.v.) Hungarian National Council, and in the early 1920s he continued to serve as a member of the Parliament (q.v.). He spoke up repeatedly against the White Terror (q.v.) perpetrated by various paramilitaristic nationalist organizations. Giesswein wrote extensively both on religious and on social issues. His most important works on Christian Socialism include *Workers'*

Protection (Munkásvédelem) (1901); *The War and Social Sciences (A háború és a társadalomtudomány)* (1915); and *At the Threshold of a New Age (Új Idők küszöbén)* (1918).

GISELLA, QUEEN [GIZELLA] (c.980/85–c.1060/65). Wife of King St. Stephen (q.v.), mother of Prince St. Emeric (q.v.), daughter of Prince Henry II of Bavaria, and sister of Holy Roman Emperor Henry II (r.1002–24). Having married the future King Stephen in 996, Gisella is credited with a major role in the Christianization of Hungary. As none of her five children survived her, she returned to Bavaria (1045) a few years after her husband's death (1038) and became the abbes of the Convent of Passau. Her tomb is still in existence in the *Frauenkirche* of that city. According to Hungarian tradition, Queen Gisella was responsible for the foundation of the Orthodox Convent of Veszprémvölgye (c.1018), allegedly for the Byzantine wife of her only son, Emeric.

GLATZ, FERENC (b.1941). One of the most gifted Hungarian historians, who during the transitional period from communism to democracy was Hungary's minister for culture and education (1989-90) and since May 1996 is the president of the Hungarian Academy of Sciences (q.v.). Glatz has spent most of his scholarly life (since 1968) at the Institute of History (q.v.) of the Hungarian Academy of Sciences, becoming its associate director in 1986 and its director in 1988. Since 1975 he has also been teaching at the University of Budapest (q.v.), and in 1990 became the founding director of the newly established European Institute *(Europa Institut),* which organizes conferences, receives visiting scholars, and grants research scholarships. Glatz has been associated with the official journal of the Hungarian Historical Association—*Centuries (Századok)*—ever since 1963, and in 1979 he became the founding editor of the popular and very influential periodical *História.*

Glatz's primary area of interest are historiography, philosophy and methodology of history, cultural politics, and the administration of the historical profession. In the latter respect he seems to be an heir to Sándor Szilágyi (q.v.) and Sándor Domanovszky (q.v.), who represented, respectively, much of the moving force in dualist-age and interwar Hungarian historical studies. Ferenc Glatz's most significant works include: *East Central Europe in World War II (Ostmitteleuropa im zweiten Weltkrieg)* (1978); *Historian and Politics (Történetíró és politika)* (1980); *Society, Politics and Administration in the Habsburg Monarchy, 1830-1918 (Gesellschaft, Politik und Verwaltung in der Habsburgermonarchie,1830-1918)* (1988); *National Culture—Cultured Nation, 1867-1987 [Nemzeti kultúra— kulturált nemzet, 1867-1987]* (1988); *Historiography in an Age of Change [Történetírás korszakváltásban]* (1990); *Scholarship, Culture, Politics: Selected Speeches and Writings of Count Kunó Klebelsberg, 1917-1932 (Tudomány, kultúra, politika. Gróf Klebelsberg Kunó válogatott beszédei és írásai, 1917-1932)* (1990). Glatz is also the editor-in-chief of an ongoing major multivolume Hungarian historical atlas collection entitled *Atlases for Hungarian History. A Narrative Map-History of Hungary (Atlaszok Magyarország történetéhez. Magyarország története térképeken elbeszélve)* (1995–).

GOLDEN BULL OF HUNGARY [BULLA AUREA] (1222). Issued by King Andrew II (q.v.) of Hungary (q.v.) only seven years after the similar, but more limited, English Magna Carta, the Hungarian Golden Bull is the foundation stone of Hungarian constitutionalism. The issuance of this document was forced upon the king by the free landowners (*servientes regis* = royal servants) (q.v.), who subsequently evolved into the common nobility (q.v.) of Hungary. They utilized the weakening of royal power and the growing dissension among the various groups of magnates (q.v.) to force King Andrew to guarantee constitutionally their rights and privileges. With this act, the freemen were trying to undercut the growing power of the magnates—many of them now of foreign origin—by extracting from the king the promise that he could no longer grant large estates and whole counties to foreigners, nor appoint them to important royal offices. By thus asserting themselves, the freeholders came to limit the powers of the formerly all-powerful kings and of the ever more powerful magnates.

At the same time, however, they also codified and perpetuated their own privileged position as a noble class. These constitutionally guaranteed privileges included, among others, the freedom from taxation (unless they voted to tax themselves in instances of national crises), their unique position before the court of law, their right to own large intangible properties, and their obligation to fight for the king only within the borders of Hungary. In addition to these guarantees for the privileges of the lower nobility, the Golden Bull also contained terms that were helpful to the commoners. Thus, it prevented the king from minting coins more than once a year (to slow down the debasement of the currency), forbade the church from collecting the tithe (q.v.) in money, and also prohibited the magnates from living off the population during their frequent travels in the country. The final (31st) paragraph also formulated the Law of Resistance *(ius resistendi),* which proclaimed that, should the king or his successors ever violate the terms of the Golden Bull, the nobility will have the right to rise up against them.

Although slightly altered in the course of the next few decades by substituting ecclesiastical sanctions for *ius resistendi,* the Golden Bull remained the cornerstone of the Hungarian Constitution (q.v.) for many centuries. At the diet of 1687—in wake of the Habsburg victories against the Turks (q.v.)—the Hungarian nobility gave up its right of "free election" and granted the male line of the Habsburg dynasty (q.v.) hereditary succession to the Hungarian throne.

GOLDEN HORDE [KÖK ORDA, BLUE HORDE]. The westernmost segment of the great Mongol Empire, which, after the death of its founder, Genghis Khan (d.1227), was divided into four subempires. Located to the west of the Ural Mountains and centered on the city of Saray on the lower Volga, the Golden Horde was meant to be ruled by Genghis Khan's oldest son, Juchi. But because of Juchi's early death, it was the latter's son, Batu Khan (q.v.), the conqueror of the Eastern Slavs (q.v.) and the one who invaded Hungary (q.v.) in 1241–42, who became the actual organizer of this sub-empire. The khans of Saray ruled the Russians and many of the other Eastern Slavs until the second half of the 15th century, when the disintegration of the Golden Horde permitted Ivan the Great (r.1462-1505) of Moscow to throw off the Mongol yoke. Its successor states were later integrated into the Russian Empire (q.v.), the last one being the Crimean Khanate (q.v.), which was annexed in 1783. During the 16th and the 17th centuries, the Crimean Tatars (q.v.) launched many devastating invasions into Hungary and autonomous Transylvania (q.v.).

GOLDZIHER, IGNÁC [IGNATZ] (1850–1921). One of the most prominent Hungarian Orientalists whose works are still being used today throughout the world. After receiving his doctorate at the University of Leipzig in Germany, Goldziher became a lecturer (1872) and then professor of Semitic studies (1894) at the University of Budapest (q.v.). In addition to being perhaps the best known contemporary practitioner of Semitic studies, Goldziher also became the founder of modern Islamic studies in Hungary. His most important works, many of them written and published in German, include: *Myth among the Hebrews (Der Mythos bei den Hebräern)* (1876); *Islam [Az iszlám]* (1881); *Islamic Studies (Mohammedanische Studien)* (2 vols., 1889–90); *Poetic Traditions of the Heathen Arabs (A pogány arabok költészetének hagyománya)* (1893); *Studies on Arabic Philology (Abhandlungen zur arabischen philologie)* (2 vols., 1897–99); *Lectures on Islam (Vorlesungen über den Islam)* (1910); *The Essence and Development of Judaism (A zsidóság lényege és fejlődése])* (2 vols., 1919). Many of his works have also appeared in English and French translations.

GÖMBÖS, GYULA [JULIUS] (1886–1936). A military officer and nationalist politician who rose to prominence during the post-World War I revolutions (1918–19) and later served as the prime minister of Hungary (1932–36) (q.v.). Being a professional military man, the end of World War I (q.v.) found Gömbös a captain on the Hungarian General Staff. During the Károlyi Regime (q.v.) at the end of 1918 and early 1919, he served in the ministry of defense. After the establishment of the Hungarian Soviet Republic (q.v.) under Béla Kun (q.v.), Gömbös became active in the counter-revolutionary movement and was one of the founders of the MOVE (Hungarian National Defense Association) (q.v.) and of the Counterrevolutionary Committee in Vienna. Gömbös soon rose to be the state secretary of the Counterrevolutionary Government of Szeged (q.v.), and then became the emissary of the same government in Vienna (q.v.). As a close associate of Admiral Horthy (q.v.), who in 1920 was elected the regent of Hungary (q.v), he became very active in interwar Hungarian politics. In 1921 Gömbös had a significant role in the struggle against the Austrians to retain Burgenland (q.v.) for Hungary, as well as in defeating King/Emperor Charles's (q.v.) effort to regain his Hungarian throne. In 1923 Gömbös left the ruling party coalition and became the cofounder of the ephemeral Hungarian National Independence(Race Protective) Party *(Magyar Nemzeti Függetlenségi [Fajvédő] Párt)* (q.v.).

In 1928 he compromised with Prime Minister Bethlen (q.v.), returned to the governmental party and was soon appointed minister for defense (1929–32). Following his appointment to the prime ministership (October 1, 1932), Gömbös proclaimed his political program consisting of ninety-five theses, which included the strengthening of central governmental authority (including the power of the regent), a broad social reform program, the peaceful revision of the terms of the Treaty of Trianon (q.v), and a plan for an anti-Bolshevik military alliance that was to stretch from Poland (q.v.), via Hungary (q.v.), Yugoslavia (q.v.), and Bulgaria (q.v.), to Turkey. When his goals for this alliance were thwarted by the Little Entente (q.v.), he turned to the likewise revisionist Italy (q.v.) and signed the Rome Protocols (March 1934) that provided for an Italian-Hungarian-Austrian cooperation. Gömbös also moved progressively closer to Germany (q.v.). But his unrealistic dreams for an Italian-German-Hungarian tripartite arrangement were undermined by Germany's strength and rapid rise that soon overshadowed even Mussolini's Italy. In 1935 Gömbös split with the conservative faction of the governmental party led by former Prime Minister Bethlen (q.v.), which shook his position somewhat. Only his growing kidney disease and imminent death prevented his dismissal by Regent Horthy. He died on October 6, 1936, in a Munich hospital.

GÖNCZ, ÁRPÁD (b.1922). Writer, translator, and since 1990 the president of Hungary (q.v.). Like his fellow playwright, President Václav Havel of Czechia (Czech Republic (q.v.), Göncz rose to the presidency as a result of the unexpected collapse of communism (q.v.) in the course of 1989-90. A graduate of the School of Law of the University of Budapest (1939-44) (q.v.) and of the Agricultural University of Gödöllő (1952-56), before 1956 Göncz had worked in various intellectual and physical occupations. His involvement in the revolution of 1956 (q.v.) had earned for him a life sentence, of which he served over six years until the general amnesty of 1963. Following his release, Göncz devoted himself to literary and human rights activities. In 1988 he was one of the founders of the liberal political party, Federation of Free Democrats (FFD) (q.v.), while in May 1990 he became one of the FFD's representatives in the first post-communist Hungarian Parliament (q.v.). He was elected the president of the Parliament, and then in August of that year the president of Hungary. Göncz was reelected to the presidency in 1994.

GÖRGEY, ARTÚR [ARTHUR] (1818–1916). Revolutionary general, minister for defense, and several times commander-in-chief of the Hungarian armed forces during the revolution of 1848-49 (q.v.). As a member of Hungary's common nobility (q.v.), Görgey became a professional officer in the Hungarian Royal Nobles' Guard (q.v.) and then in the Habsburg Imperial Army (1837–45). In 1845 he resigned his commission and enrolled to study chemistry at the University of Prague (1845–48). After the outbreak of the Hungarian Revolution (q.v.) in March 1848, he joined the revolutionary armies and soon rose in ranks. By November of that year he became a general and the commander of the Army of the Upper Danube. This was done at Kossuth's (q.v.) urging, who recognized Görgey's ability as a military strategist. Görgey's skills as a military leader were further demonstrated in the winter and spring campaigns of 1848–49. Yet, the two leaders soon parted ways, for Görgey resented

Kossuth's growing radicalism and unwillingness to compromise with the Habsburg dynasty (q.v.). He also disapproved of the Kossuth-inspired dethronement of the Habsburgs (April 14, 1849), which led to Russian military intervention and to Hungary's ultimate defeat.

Although an opponent of radicalism in Hungary's political leadership, between May 7 and July 5 Görgey served as the country's minister for defense, after which he became the commander-in-chief of the main Hungarian Army at Vác. By this time, however, the Russian invasion under the leadership of Prince Ivan Paskievich inflicted a series of defeats upon the Hungarian armies. This led to Kossuth's resignation (August 11) and for two days (August 11–13) to Görgey's accession to the leadership of Hungary. Realizing the hopelessness of the situation, Görgey surrendered to the Russian Army at Világos (q.v.) on August 13, 1849. Being defended by Czar Nicholas I (r.1825–55), who counseled moderation to Emperor Francis Joseph (q.v.), in contrast to many other revolutionary generals, Görgey only suffered incarceration at Klagenfurt. He returned to Hungary after the Austro-Hungarian Compromise of 1867 (q.v.), and then spent the next half a century trying to clear his name against Kossuth's accusations of treason. Görgey died at the age of ninety-eight in seclusion at Visegrád (q.v.), only a few months before the death of Francis Joseph (q.v). He had published his war memoirs under the title *My Life and Deeds in Hungary* (*Mein Leben und Wirken in Ungarn*) (1852).

GOTHIC ART AND ARCHITECTURE. Originating in 12th-century France, the Gothic style spread through much of Europe and replaced its Romanesque predecessor in the 13th century. Most of the greatest European cathedrals were built in the Gothic style, which was replaced only gradually by the Renaissance and Baroque style in the 15th through the 18th centuries. In Hungary the Gothic style began to spread in the mid-13th century, climaxed in the 15th, and produced such major cathedrals as those of Buda (q.v.), Pozsony (q.v.), Kassa (q.v.) and Sopron (q.v).

GOULASH COMMUNISM [GULYÁS KOMMUNIZMUS]. The latter period of the Kádár Regime (q.v.), which embraced the 1970s and 1980s. This was communism with a human face, which introduced political and economic liberalization measures that made Hungary (q.v.) the envy of the Soviet Bloc (q.v.). The quality of life of Hungary's population improved progressively, for which reason the regime and Kádár personally became increasingly popular. Some of these improvements were the result of the introduction of elements of market economy, while others were derived from the large Western debts assumed by the country at this time. The period of Goulash Communism began to wind down during the late 1980s, at the time when Gorbachev was trying desperately to save the Soviet Union (q.v.). It came to an end in 1989–90, when the whole communist system and ideology collapsed throughout the world.

GRAND DUKE [GROSSHERZOG, NAGYHERCEG]. A title between the king and the prince (duke) and roughly equivalent to the title "archduke" (q.v.) borne by the members of the Habsburg family (q.v.) since 1453. The first to have the title of grand duke were the members of the Medici family of Florence (1569). The same title was also held by the members of the Russian czarist family from the 18th century on. Today only the rulers of Luxembourg have the title of grand duke, although the exiled members of the former Russian ruling family, the Romanovs, also use it.

GRAND MASTER [GROSSMEISTER, NAGYMESTER]. The title of the elected leaders of the chief knightly orders starting with the 12th century, such as the Teutonic Knights (q.v.) and the Knights of Malta.

GRAND VIZIER [NAGYVEZÉR, VEZĪR-I AZAM]. The highest office next to the sultan (q.v.) in the Ottoman Turkish Empire (q.v.), whose incumbent was the ruler's alter ego. As the presidents of the Divan (Imperial Council) (q.v.), the grand viziers headed the empire's civil administration; and as the commanders-in-chief of the Ottoman Armed Forces, they were also in charge of all military policies and operations. Following the age of Süleyman the Magnificent (r.1520-66), the grand viziers likewise commanded all major military campaigns.

GREAT HUNGARIAN PLAIN [ALFÖLD]. The large flat area in the central part of the Carpathian Basin (q.v.). Since Hungary's dismemberment at the Treaty of Trianon (q.v.), the Great Hungarian Plain consists of the eastern half of Hungary on the left side of the Danube (q.v.), and sections of Romania (q.v.) and Serbia (q.v.). Traditionally, it comprised the central part of Historic Hungary (q.v.) and stretched between the Danube River in the west and the Bihar Mountains in the east, on the borders of historic Transylvania (q.v.). The Great Hungarian Plain or *Alföld* is basically a grassy flat land very similar to the American prairies and to the southern Russian and Ukrainian steppes.

GREATER HUNGARY see **HISTORIC HUNGARY.**

GREAT HUNGARY see **MAGNA HUNGARIA.**

GREAT MORAVIA see **MAGNA MORAVIA.**

GREEK CATHOLICS see **BYZANTINE CATHOLICISM.**

GRÓSZ, KÁROLY (b.1930-96). Communist politician, prime minister of Hungary (1987-88) (q.v.), and János Kádár's (q.v.) immediate successor as the secretary general of the Hungarian Socialist Workers' Party (q.v.). Grósz came to power at the time of the imminent collapse of communism, and he was forced to witness the collapse of communist power as well as of the political party that represented it. With the rise of the first post-communist government in 1990, Grósz withdrew from politics and died in 1996.

GROVE, ANDREW S. [ANDRÁS GRÓF] (b.1936). President of Intel Corporation, one of the inventors of microprocessing, and also one of the most successful of the Hungarian Freedom Fighters (q.v.), who immigrated to the United States after the Hungarian Revolution of 1956 (q.v.). Educated at the City College of New York and having received his Ph.D. at the University of California at Berkeley, Grove joined Intel Corporation in 1968 and made it into the number one producer of microprocessors in the world. His major published works include: *Physics and Technology of Semiconductor Devices* (1867) and *High-Output Management* (1982).

GUBERNIUM [FŐKORMÁNYSZÉK].   The chief governmental agency of Transylvania (q.v.) under Habsburg (q.v.) rule in the period between 1691 and 1867. The centrally appointed governors who headed the *gubernium* were almost exclusively pro-Habsburg Hungarian aristocrats who carried out the wishes of the monarchs. This office was terminated at the time of the Austro-Hungarian Compromise of 1867 (q.v.), when Transylvania was reintegrated once more into the Kingdom of Hungary (q.v.).

GYŐR [RAAB].   Hungary's sixth largest city with a population of about 135,000, located halfway between Budapest (q.v.) and Vienna (q.v.). Győr became an administrative center already at the time when King St. Stephen (q.v.) established the Hungarian county system in the early 11th century. In 1271 it was raised to the rank of a Royal Free City (q.v.) and, after the conquest of Central Hungary by the Turks (q.v.) in the 16th century, it became one of the most significant Christian fortifications in the chain of fortresses between the Ottoman (q.v.) and the Habsburg Empires (q.v.). For a brief period during the Fifteen Years' War (q.v.) it fell under Turkish control (1594-98), but then it was reconquered and continued to fulfill its function as an important defensive fortress of the Habsburg realm. In the 19th century Győr developed into the most important commercial city of Trans-Danubia (q.v.), and into the second most significant grain processing center in Hungary (q.v.). It does have a law college and a teachers' training college since the 19th century, but—much to the sorrow of its citizens—it still lacks a university .

GYŐRFFY, GYÖRGY (b.1917). One of the most prominent of Hungarian medievalists who has contributed significantly to the reinterpretation of Hungarian origins and Hungarian history during the reign of the Árpád dynasty (q.v.). After teaching and researching at his alma mater, the University of Budapest (q.v.) (1940–50), Győrffy spent nearly four decades (1949-88) at the Institute of History (q.v.) of the Hungarian Academy of Sciences (q.v.). He wrote his most important works in the subdisciplines of historical geography, historical criticism, and ethnogenesis, among them his ongoing monumental *Hungary's Historical Geography during the Árpádian Age (Az Árpádkori Magyarország történeti földrajza)* (3 vols., 1963–87), and a significant portion of the first volume of the still unfinished ten-volume *History of Hungary (Magyarország története)* (1984). Győrffy's other important works include: *The Pechenegs and the Hungarians (Besenyők és magyarok)* (1940), *Our Chronicles and Hungarian Protohistory (Krónikáink és a magyar őstörténet)* (1948), *About Hungarian Ancestors and the Hungarian Conquest (A magyarok elődeiről és a honfoglalásról)* (1958), *King Coloman (Kálmán király)* (1969), *King Stephen and his Achievements [István király és műve)* (1987), and *Oriental Elements among the Hungarians (A magyarság keleti elemei)* (1990). A much abbreviated version of his biography of King Stephen was published in English under the title *King Saint Stephen of Hungary* (1994).

GYOSZ [GYÁRIPAROSOK ORSZÁGOS SZÖVETSÉGE, NATIONAL ASSOCIATION OF INDUSTRIALISTS]. The GYOSZ was established in 1902 and survived until 1947. While it functioned, it was one of the most powerful interest groups in Hungary (q.v.), which included all prominent members of the country's industrial and financial aristocracy. In 1928 the GYOSZ gained the right to send two representatives in the Upper House (q.v.) of the Hungarian Parliament (q.v.).

GYPSIES [CIGÁNYOK, ROMA]. A nomadic ethnic group that originated in northern India and then gradually wound its way through the Middle East to the European continent. They first appeared in Eastern Hungary (Transylvania) (q.v.) in the early 15th century (1416), while also spreading through much of the continent. Initially the Gypsies were thought to be of Egyptian origin, hence their name: Gypsy. Although they call themselves "Rom" or "Roma" (man, human), in Europe they are known under well over a dozen different names (e.g., Bohemian, Cigán, Ciganin, Cigány, Cikán, Cygan, Cyganski, Gipsy, Gitan, Gitano, Gypsy, Jedupak, Roma, Romanichel, Tsigane, Zigeuner, Zingaro, etc.). There may be as many as three million Gypsies in the world, of whom one million live in Europe. Of the latter, the largest numbers live in Romania (q.v.), Hungary (q.v.), Slovakia (q.v.), the former Soviet Union (q.v.), and Spain. In 1971 Hungary had about 320,000 Gypsies, but the great majority of these simply viewed themselves as Hungarians. 71 percent spoke primarily Hungarian (Magyar), 21.2% one of the Gypsy dialects, 7.6 percent Romanian, and 0.2 percent some other language. Those Gypsies who still know their native language known as Romany, speak several distinct dialects, some of which are barely comprehensible to each other.

The Gypsies have pursued a nomadic lifestyle throughout much of their history. In Hungary, they began to accept a sedentary lifestyle only in the 1940s. Their integration into Hungarian society, however, was very slow and painful. Yet, by the 1990s, Hungarian Gypsies *(Romungro)* could be found in virtually every class and occupation. After the fall of communism, a distinct Gypsy ethnic consciousness resurfaced throughout East Central Europe (q.v.). Many of the partially assimilated Gypsies organized themselves into separate Gypsy interest groups (e.g., the Roma Parliament). In Hungary, the Gypsies have been connected with the so-called "Hungarian Gypsy music," primarily because many of them are natural-born musicians and violin players. But Hungarian Gypsy music is neither real Gypsy nor original Hungarian folk music. Rather, it is a 19th-century romantic popular music that came to be connected to the Gypsies only by virtue of the fact that they became its primary conveyers throughout the country.

GYULA. The title of the de facto ruling prince of the conquering Hungarians (Magyars) (q.v.) of the 9th century. The *gyula* was nominally second to the sacred ruler called *kende (kündü)* (q.v.), but by virtue of his control of administration and command of the armed forces, he was supreme in both military and judicial matters. Following the successful conquest of Hungary (q.v.) and the subsequent death of Prince Kurszán (q.v.) in 904, who had held the position of *kende*, these two offices were merged and Prince Árpád (q.v.) became the sole leader of the Hungarians. By this act he established the unquestioned dominance of the Árpád dynasty (q.v.) which ruled Hungary for over four centuries.

GYULA (10th c.). The name of at least three Hungarian tribal chiefs in Transylvania (q.v.), which is derived from the office of the *gyula* (q.v.) that may have been borne by several of their ancestors. Gyula I (late 9th–early 10th c.) probably part of the Árpádian conquest (q.v.) of Hungary (q.v.), is often identified with Prince Kurszán (d.904) (q.v.). Gyula II (mid 10th c.) married his daughter, Sarolta, to Prince Géza (q.v.) and thus became King St. Stephen's (q.v.) grandfather. In 952–53 he visited Constantinople (q.v.), where he converted to Byzantine Christianity (q.v.) and was given the title of a Byzantine patrician. Gyula III (late 10th–early 11th c.) was King Stephen's uncle, who rebelled against his nephew and was roundly defeated by him (1003). His defeat ended the power of the family of the Gyulas in Transylvania, which province was then integrated into the Kingdom of Hungary.

GYULAFEHÉRVÁR [ALBA IULIA, WEISSENBURG, KARLSBURG]. A former Hungarian Royal Free City (q.v.) at the confluence of the Maros and the Ompoly Rivers in Transylvania (q.v.), which after World War I (q.v.) was awarded to Romania (q.v.). During much of the 16th and 17th centuries, when Transylvania was an autonomous vassal state of the Ottoman Empire (q.v.), Gyulafehérvár served as the province's capital city. There its Hungarian ruling princes held their court, and there many of them were buried.

- H -

HABSBURG DYNASTY [HABSBURGS] (1273–1918). The family that has ruled longer than any other European dynasty, whose roots reach back to the 10th century to the castle of Habichtsburg (Hawk's Castle) in eastern Switzerland. The members of this dynasty were Holy Roman Emperors (1273–91, 1298–1308, 1438–1740, 1745–1806), Austrian emperors (1804–1918), kings of Hungary (q.v.) and Bohemia (q.v.) (1526–1918), kings of Spain and the Spanish Empire (1516–1700), kings of Portugal and the Portuguese Empire (1580–1640), and rulers of dozens of other principalities and provinces within the Holy Roman Empire (q.v.), Italy (q.v.), the Low Countries, the Balkans (q.v.), and various portions of East Central Europe (q.v.). The might of the Habsburgs at the height of their power is best expressed by Emperor Charles V's (1519–56) (q.v.) proud dictum: "The sun never sets in my empire." But the complexity of their realm is even more visible in the number and variety of their titles—divided into "Great," "Middle," and "Small" categories—which together numbered more than 150. Thus, upon the dissolution of the Holy Roman Empire and the loss of their Holy Roman Imperial title in 1806—over a century after they had been shorn of their Spanish and Portuguese possessions—Francis I (II) (q.v.) still introduced his Imperial edicts with the following "Great" titles: "We, Francis the First, by the Grace of God Emperor of Austria, King of Jerusalem, Hungary, Bohemia, Dalmatia, Croatia, Slavonia, Galicia and Lodomeria, Archduke of Austria, Duke of Lorraine, Salzburg, Würzburg, Frankonia, Styria, Carinthia and Craina, Grand Duke of Cracow and Transylvania, Margrave of Moravia, Duke of Sandomir, Mazovia, Lublin, Upper and Lower Silesia, Auschwitz and Sátor, Teschen and Friaul, Prince of Berchtesgaden and Mergentheim, Princely Count of Habsburg, Görz and Gradisca, Margrave of Upper and Lower Lusatia and Istria, Lord of Volhynia, Podolia and Brescia, Triest, Freudenthal, Eulenburg and Windisch Mark, Great Voievod of Voivodina, Serbia, etc., etc." At times, as the dynasty's fortunes changed, some of these titles were dropped or replaced by others. This happened in 1867, after the Habsburgs had been pushed out of Germany (q.v.) and·Italy, and the Austrian Empire (q.v.) was transformed into Austria-Hungary (q.v.).

HABSBURG HUNGARY see **ROYAL HUNGARY.**

HABSBURG IMPERIAL ARMIES see **AUSTRO-HUN-GARIAN ARMED FORCES.**

HABSBURG LANDS. In the late 18th century the Habsburg Empire (q.v.) included the following part: The German-speaking Hereditary Lands *(Erbländer)* (q.v.), the Hungarian Crown Lands *(Ungarn, Kroaten und Siebenbürgen)* (q.v.), the Bohemian Crown Lands *(Böhmen, Mähren und Schlesien)* (q.v.), Galicia (q.v.), Bukovina (q.v.), the Italian Duchies of Milan and Mantua, the United Austrian Netherlands (Holland and Belgium), and a number of smaller fiefs in the German part of the Holy Roman Empire (q.v.), known as "Front Provinces" *(Vorlände).*

HABSBURG-LORRAINE DYNASTY [HABSBURG-LOTH-RINGEN] (1780–1918). Continuation of the Habsburg dynasty (q.v.), whose last male member, Charles VI (King Charles III) (q.v.), died in 1740. Charles's daughter Maria Theresa (q.v.) married Francis of Lorraine (q.v.) and the two families fused. Yet, because of the historical importance of the Habsburgs, their name remained the dominant part of this new dynasty's name, whose members ruled until the dissolution of Austria-Hungary (q.v.). Thus, in common usage, they were, and still are, referred to simply as the Habsburgs.

HABSBURG, OTTO VON see **OTTO VON HABSBURG.**

HABSBURGS see **HABSBURG DYNASTY.**

HALICH [HALICS, HALICZ] see **GALICIA.**

HAJDÚ [HAJDUK]. Originally, landless peasants who escaped from the creeping serfdom in 15th-century Hungary (q.v.). Initially the *hajdús(hajdúk)* served as armed guards who accompanied Hungary's cattlemen and cattle herds in their trek to the Holy Roman Empire (q.v.). Taking advantage of the opportunities offered by the growing number of Turkish wars—like the Cossacks in contemporary Muscovite Russia (q.v.) and the Polish-Lithuanian Commonwealth (q.v.)—the escaped peasants *(hajdús)* congregated in armed groups and elected their own captains. During Hungary's Turkish occupation (q.v.) in the 16th and 17th centuries, their ranks were inflated by the dispossessed members of the lower nobility (q.v.), persecuted Protestants, unpaid soldiers from the frontier fortifications, urban poor, and even some *Székelys* (q.v.) from Transylvania (q.v.). These *hajdús* developed their own fighting methods, which consisted primarily of rapid forays and sudden raids upon their targets. Many of them also became temporary mercenaries, who served specific towns, various members of the landed nobility, and at times even the kings of Hungary and the princes of Transylvania. Because of their unreliability, occasionally all three governments of trisected Hungary (Royal Hungary, Turkish Hungary, and Transylvania) (q.v.) tried to exterminate them, but without success. In 1604–06, most of the *hajdús* enlisted into the services of Prince Stephen Bocskai (q.v.) in his successful war against the Habsburgs (q.v.). In return for this, Bocskai settled about 10,000 of them on his Trans-Tisza (q.v.) estates, which resulted in the foundation of six *hajdú* towns. Similarly to the Cossacks in the Russian Empire, the *hajdú* inhabitants of these towns soon attained a kind of seminoble status. They were free from all state and feudal taxes, and their only obligation was to serve in the military.

Between the mid–18th century and 1945, the terms *hajdú* and *hajdúk* were also applied to various liveried attendants with certain police powers in the counties, towns, and larger landed estates. In the 16th century, on the other hand, the term *hajdú* in its plural form—*hajdúk*—was transferred to the Balkans (q.v.), where it came to denote those Robin Hood-like outlaws, whose primary targets were the Turkish occupiers of their lands.

HAJDÚ TOWNS AND DISTRICTS. Following Prince Stephen Bocskai's (q.v.) successful war against the Habsburgs (q.v.) in 1604-06, he settled about 10,000 of his *hajdú* followers on his estates located on the left bank of the upper Tisza River (q.v.) to the west and northwest of the city of Debrecen (q.v.). They were settled mainly in six newly founded towns, including Hajdúböszörmény, Hajdúdorog, Hajdúhadház, Hajdúnánás, Hajdúszoboszló, and Hajdúvámospércs, to which later the town of Polgár was added. In the 17th century many other new *hajdú* towns were also founded by members of the wealthy landed nobility, all of which enjoyed the so-called "*hajdú* liberties." This meant that the citizens of these towns were free from all taxes and feudal obligations. But in return for this they were obliged to perform military services. During the 18th century, these newer *hajdú* towns all lost their special status and their inhabitants sank back into the ranks of the peasantry. In 1790 the original *hajdú* towns were organized into a separate administrative district, which was governed by an elected captain and sent its own representatives to the national diet (q.v.). The *hajdú* district retained its special status and administrative system until 1876, when it was merged into the newly organized Hajdú County.

HAJNÓCZY, JÓZSEF (1750–95). One of the leaders of the Hungarian Jacobins (q.v.), a strong critic of Hungarian feudal society, and thus a supporter of Joseph II (q.v.). In 1786 Joseph II appointed Hajnóczy the vice lord lieutenant of Szerém County. But not being a member of the Hungarian nobility (q.v.), after Joseph's death (1790) Hajnóczy lost his office, which made him an even more vocal exponent of reform. Hajnóczy supported the progressive wing of the Hungarian National Revival Movement (q.v.) and at the same time agitated for radical social reform in a series of political pamphlets. He criticized the Hungarian feudal constitution (q.v.), and demanded complete social and legal equality of the peasants, taxation of the Hungarian nobility, secularization of all church property, and freedom of expression for everyone. In 1794, the defrocked radical monk, Ignác Martinovics (q.v.), enlisted him into the ranks of the "Society for Freedom and Equality" and thus dragged this basically scholarly man into his naively organized conspiracy. This resulted in Hajnóczy's arrest (August 16, 1794) and his execution (April 27, 1795). Some of his relevant writings were published by Kálmán Benda (1913–94) in *The Papers of the Hungarian Jacobins (A magyar jakobínusok iratai)* (3 vols., 1952–57).

HANÁK, PÉTER (b.1921). One of Hungary's prominent historians and intellectuals who began as a Marxist and ended up as a dedicated Western liberal. Hanák is a penetrating thinker and a brilliant stylist, wherefore most of his writings read like creative fiction. After over four decades of association with the Institute of History (q.v.) and the Eötvös University of Budapest (q.v.), in 1991 Hanák took charge of the Historical Section of the English-language Central European University (q.v.) founded by George Soros (q.v.). In addition to hundreds of short essays, Hanák is the author of a number of major works. He is the editor and primary author of the seventh volume of the ongoing ten-volume *History of Hungary [Magyarország története]* that deals with the period between 1890 and 1918 (1978). Some of his other important works include: *Hungary in the [Habsburg]Monarchy(MagyarországaMonarchiában)* (1975), *How did our Ancestors Live? (Hogyan éltek elődeink?)* (1980), *Hungary in the Danubian Monarchy (Ungarn in der Donaumonarchie)*(1984), *Oscar Jászi's Danubian Patriotism (Jászi Oszkár dunai patriotizmusa)* (1985) *A Millennium (Egy ezredév)* (1987), and *Clinging to Utopia (Ragaszkodás az utópiához)* (1993).

HARACH [HARÁCS, HARAÇ]. Originally called *cizye,* the *harach* was the most important head tax paid by non-Muslims in Islamic states. It was introduced into Turkish Hungary (q.v.) in 1578, after which the heads of all families were obliged to pay it irrespective of their economic and social status. The collection of the *harach* ended only with the expulsion of the Turks in the late 17th century. It is reflective upon the nature of this tax that the Hungarian version of the term *harács* in its verbal form *(harácsolni)* came to mean extorting and looting.

HARASZTHY, ÁGOSTON [AUGUST] (1812-69). One of the first prominent Hungarian settlers in the United States, known as the "father" of the California viticulture (wine industry). Although a member of the Hungarian common nobility (q.v.), Haraszthy was so disenchanted with conditions in Hungary that he took a tour of the United States (1840–42) with the intention of possible immigration. He was so impressed that he returned home only to publish his *Travels in North America (Utazás Éjszak-Amerikában)* (1844) and to sell his property. In 1844 he emigrated permanently, along with his family. Initially he went to Wisconsin to found Haraszthyville (now Sauk City), but by 1849 he was already in California.

First he resided in San Diego, serving as the county sheriff and then as a state representative, but by 1852 he resettled in Sonoma Valley to experiment with grape growing and wine making. In 1857 the California Agricultural Society asked him to examine the state's wine production, the result of which was his path-breaking *Report on Grapes and Wines of California* (1859). In 1862 California's governor dispatched him on a fact-finding mission to Europe. He returned with 100,000 vines embracing 1,400 varieties of grapes. Upon his return, he wrote the first American handbook on viticulture, *Grape Culture, Wines, and Wine-making* (1862).

In spite of his successes, Haraszthy was dissatisfied with his achievements. In 1868 he departed for Nicaragua, where he bought a sugar plantation and also built several sawmills. His goals and plans were cut short by his death in 1869. Of his three sons, one remained in Nicaragua and two made their fortunes in California. Like many of the educated Europeans of those days, Haraszthy too liked to pass himself off as one of higher social standing. Thus, first he promoted himself to a "Colonel" and then to a "Count." Haraszthy's use of these titles was so commonplace that they reappeared even in the *Congressional Records* on the occasion of the 100th anniversary of his death.

HARTVIK LEGEND. A collection of legends about King St. Stephen (q.v.) compiled by Bishop Hartvik (c.1050-c.1103) of Magdeburg. In 1088 Hartvik settled in Hungary (q.v.), where he was appointed the bishop of Győr (q.v.) and became a close associate both of King St. Ladislas (q.v.) and of King Coloman (q.v.). Around 1100, at Coloman's request, he collected all of the earlier legends about King St. Stephen and shaped them into a uniform narrative, known after him as the *Hartvik Legend.*

HĀS [HASS, HÁSZ] ESTATES. Large fiefs, domains of the sultan, princes of blood, and prominent governors *(beylerbeys, sanjak beys)* that yielded more than 100,000 *akćes* (q.v.) of income per year. In Turkish Hungary (q.v.), as elsewhere in the Ottoman Empire (q.v.), the most valuable lands and the largest settlements were all declared*hās* property immediately after the conquest (e.g., Buda, Kecskemét, Cegléd, Nagykőrös, etc.). The citizens of these *hās* towns possessed a great deal of internal autonomy and paid their taxes to the Turks (q.v.) in pre-agreed lump sums.

HAVASALFÖLD see WALLACHIA.

HAYNAU, BARON JULIUS JAKOB (1786–1853). Austrian general who was commander-in-chief of the Habsburg Imperial Armies (q.v.) at the time of the defeat of the Hungarian Revolution of 1848-49 (q.v). Born as the illegitimate son of Prince William, the elector of Hessen, Haynau became a professional soldier and served in the Austrian Army until his retirement in 1847 with the rank of a colonel. Upon the outbreak of the revolutions in the Austrian Empire (q.v.), he volunteered for military service and was sent to Italy (q.v.), where he excelled in putting down the revolutionaries. The excesses he perpetrated in Brescia made his name known and hated all over Europe. At the end of May 1849 Haynau was promoted to a general and replaced Prince Felix Windischgraetz (q.v.) as the military commander in Hungary (q.v.). In cooperation with the invading Russian Army, he defeated the Hungarian revolutionaries, but the Hungarian commander, Görgey (q.v.), chose to capitulate to the Russians. This made Haynau seek revenge against those who fell into his hands. Thus, in addition to imprisoning thousands, he ordered the execution of Hungary's first prime minister, Count Lajos Batthyány (q.v.), as well as thirteen Hungarian military leaders (twelve generals and one colonel) on October 6, 1849. His violent deeds as Hungary's military commander displeased the Viennese political leaders, who forced him to resign (July 1850). For a while Haynau withdrew to his Hungarian estates in Szabolcs County, but then decided to take a West European tour. His reception in Paris, Brussels, and London, however, was most unfriendly, and in London he was even assaulted by some workers. But he was feted in Berlin and made an honorary citizen of Vienna (q.v.). Haynau's name is among the most hated names in Hungary, being in the category of that of Caraffa (q.v.).

HEDVIG, SAINT [SAINT JADWIGA] (c.1371-99). The younger daughter of King Louis the Great (q.v.), who inherited her father's Polish throne (1384–99), while her older sister, Maria (q.v.), gained the Hungarian crown. In 1386 Hedvig married Grand Duke Jagello (r.1386–1434) of Lithuania and unified Poland (q.v.) and Lithuania into a single Polish-Lithuanian Commonwealth (q.v.). She thus became the progenitress of the Jagellonian dynasty (q.v.) that ruled Poland-Lithuania until 1672, and Hungary during 1440-44 and 1490-1526. Her efforts in the Christianization of Lithuania resulted in her canonization by the Catholic Church.

HELTAI, GÁSPÁR (c.1490/1510-74). Protestant reformer, preacher, writer, printer, and the author and publisher of the first synthesis of Hungarian history in the Magyar language (q.v.). In 1536 Heltai fell under the influence of the humanist Bishop Brodarics (q.v.) and studied theology, but in the early 1540s converted to Lutheranism (q.v.). In 1543–44 he studied at the University of Wittenberg, then for the next three decades (1544–74) served as the pastor of the Saxon Congregation of Kolozsvár (q.v.). In the meanwhile, in 1559 he converted to Calvinism (q.v.), and then sometime after 1564 to Unitarianism (q.v.). While engaged in the search for the right religion, in 1550 Heltai founded a printing press in Kolozsvár, which then served as the most important instrument for the systematization of the Hungarian language in a written form. He used his press to publish dozens of important books in Hungarian, German, and Latin in a number of disciplines. But his most important publication is his own *Chronicle of the Deeds of the Hungarians (Chronica az Magyaroknac dolgairól)* (1575). Although called a chronicle, this is the first real synthesis of Hungarian history written in stylistically sophisticated Hungarian language.

HELYTARTÓTANÁCS see VICEROYALTY COUNCIL.

HERALDRY. The study of coats of arms (q.v.), their history, and the legal regulations that apply to them. In Hungary, heraldry has been part of the Auxiliary Sciences of History (q.v.) ever since the mid–19th century. Its practitioners usually also pursue the study of genealogy (q.v.).

HEREDITARY KINGSHIP. The constitutional right of the members of a specific family to succeed to a throne through inheritance. In Hungary, the members of the Árpád dynasty (q.v.) had hereditary rights (c.896-1301) to the Hungarian throne. But the rulers from several of the succeeding and often rival dynasties—such as the Czech Přemyslides, the Bavarian Wittelsbachs, the Neapolitan Anjous (q.v.), the Czech-German Luxemburgs (q.v.), and the Austrian Habsburgs (q.v.)—while claiming the throne on the basis of hereditary rights via the female line, were able to ascend only through elections. The Hungarian Hunyadi (q.v.) and Zápolya (q.v.) families could make no such claims. The Habsburgs survived as "elected kings" of Hungary for 161 years (1526-1687), before they were able to have the Hungarian Diet (q.v.) accept them as hereditary rulers in the male line (1687). The Pragmatic Sanction of 1723 (q.v.) extended this right also to the female line.

HEREDITARY LANDS [ERBLÄNDER, ÖRÖKÖS TARTO-MÁNYOK]. By the 19th century, the Hereditary Lands of the Habsburg dynasty consisted of the following largely German-speaking provinces of the Habsburg Empire (q.v.): the Duchy of Austria, below and above the Enns; the Duchy of Styria; the Duchy of Carinthia; the Princely County of Tyrol; the Duchy of Carniola, the Counties of Istria, Vorarlberg, Gorizia-Gradisca;and the City of Triest. The other major components of the contiguous segment of the Habsburg Empire included the Hungarian Crown lands (q.v.), the Bohemian Crown lands (q.v.), Galicia (q.v.), Bukovina (q.v.), and for a while the Italian provinces of Milan and Mantua.

HERZL, THEODORE [TIVADAR] (1860–1904). A Budapest-born Hungarian Jewish intellectual, who is considered to be the "father" of the Zionist movement and thus the "spiritual father" of modern Israel. In 1878 Herzl moved to Vienna (q.v.), where he became a journalist, working for the *Wiener Allgemeine Zeitung (Viennese Universal News)* and then for the *Neue Freie Presse (New Free Press)*. In addition to news articles, he also wrote plays and essays. But his name became widely known only in 1896 when he published his book *The Jewish State (Der Judenstaat),* written under the influence of the growing anti-Semitism manifested in the Dreyfus Affair (1894–96) in France. Although Herzl was initially in favor of assimilation, by this time he became convinced that the only solution to the Jewish question was the foundation of a Jewish homeland. After elaborating his ideas in his book, Herzl organized the first World Zionist Congress in Basel (1897), which accepted his views and goals. He was also elected as the first president of the newly founded World Zionist Organization. In that capacity he contacted several of the most influential European rulers—e.g., those of Austria-Hungary (q.v.), Germany (q.v.), Ottoman Empire (q.v.)—to explore the possibilities for the foundation of a Jewish homeland in Palestine or in some other region of the world. Herzl's efforts made Zionism (q.v.) into a worldwide movement, but it took Hitler and the Holocaust (q.v.) to make his dream into a reality forty-four years after his death. Following Herzl's relocation to Vienna, several other members of his family remained in Budapest. They changed their name to Heltai and several of them became prominent Hungarian intellectuals. The best known among them was his nephew, Jenő Heltai (1871-1957), who became one of

Hungary's best-loved writers, playwrights, and literary interpreters of its urban culture in the late-dualist (q.v.) and interwar periods.

HÉTSZEMÉLYES TÁBLA see SEVEN-PERSON COURT

HIGHER NOBILITY [ARISTOCRACY, MAGNATES, FŐ-NEMESSÉG]. The segment of the Hungarian nobility that owned large estates, held high offices, and, starting with the 15th century, acquired hereditary titles such as baron, count, marquis, duke, or prince. Until 1848 the holders of these titles were hereditary members of the Upper House (q.v.) of the Hungarian Diet (q.v.), where they could represent themselves. Between 1885 and 1918, this right of hereditary representation was limited to a few top families, and the members of the Upper House also included appointed representatives of the top intellectual, financial, and industrial worlds. The high dignitaries of the Catholic Church also counted among the higher nobility and likewise held seats in the Upper House. In 1792 this right was extended to the bishops of the Orthodox Christians (q.v.), and in 1885 also to the ecclesiastical leaders of the Evangelical (q.v.), Jewish (q.v.), Reformed (q.v.), and Unitarian Churches (q.v.).

HISTORIC HUNGARY (10th c. - 1918). Also known as "Greater Hungary," "Lands of the Hungarian Crown," "Hungarian Crown Lands," "Crown Lands of St. Stephen," and "Lands of the Holy Crown of Hungary," this geographical entity was basically identical with the Carpathian Basin (q.v.). It included, in addition to present-day Hungary, all of Slovakia (q.v.), Carpatho-Ruthenia (q.v.), Transylvania (q.v.), and portions of the Great Hungarian Plain (q.v.) attached to Romania, the Banat of Temesvár (q.v.) that had been divided between Romania and Yugoslavia, Voivodina (q.v.), Slavonia (q.v.), Croatia (q.v.), and the Western fringes of Austria known as Burgenland (q.v.).

HISTORICAL INSTITUTE see INSTITUTE OF HISTORY.

HISTORICAL STUDIES see **HUNGARIAN HISTORICAL STUDIES.**

HOLOCAUST IN HUNGARY. The destruction of about half a million Hungarian citizens classified as Jews (q.v.) after the German occupation of Hungary (q.v.) on March 19, 1944. Those from the provinces (about 350,000) were collected and shipped off to German death camps between May 15 and June 27. Most of those in Budapest, after having been forced into ghettos (June 17–24), were deported only after the overthrow of Regent Horthy (q.v.) on October 15, 1944. Many of these Budapest deportees (perhaps 150,000) also perished in the death camps. Those who survived either returned to Hungary or emigrated to Palestine/Israel, or to the United States.

HOLY CROWN, DOCTRINE OF [SZENTKORONATAN]. An ideological-constitutional system connected with the Holy Crown of Hungary (q.v.), which by the 15th century made that crown into the symbol and representative of royal power, the country, and then the Hungarian statehood itself. This doctrine was first codified in the *Tripartitum* (q.v.) of 1514, which asserted that the king and the noble estates are all inseparable parts of the Holy Crown, and that all power emanates from the "nation"—*Natio Hungarica* (q.v.)—which is transferred upon the king only by virtue of his being crowned by the Holy Crown. These rights include legislative powers, judicial powers, the right of ennoblement, and the right to grant titles and property. In the 18th century, the Doctrine of the Holy Crown was augmented by the infusion of the religious-mystical principles of *Regnum Marianum* (Mary's Kingdom), which claimed that ever since King St. Stephen (q.v.), Hungary had been under the protection of Virgin Mary. The social and constitutional changes that followed the revolution of 1848–49 (q.v.) gradually extended the membership in the Holy Crown from the nobility (q.v.) to the other members of the modern nation. Moreover, with the growth of nationalism, Historic Hungary (q.v.) was increasingly referred to as the Lands of the Hungarian Holy Crown. The Doctrine of the Holy Crown survived Historic

Hungary's collapse after 1918. During the interwar years it was used to bolster Hungarian revisionism (q.v.).

HOLY CROWN OF HUNGARY [SAINT STEPHEN'S CROWN]. This is the most important item among Hungary's royal regalia, which goes back to the early 11th century. According to the traditional view, its upper part was given by Pope Sylvester II (r.999–1003) to King St. Stephen (q.v.) in A.D. 1000, which then was combined with another crown given by Byzantine Emperor Michael Dukas (r.1071–78) to King Géza I (q.v.) of Hungary in 1074. In the course of time the Holy Crown became the most important symbol of Hungarian statehood, giving birth by the 15th century to the Doctrine of the Holy Crown (q.v.), after which all laws were passed not in the name of the king, but in the name of the Holy Crown. In 1514 this doctrine was incorporated into István Werbőczy's (q.v.) legal system known as the *Tripartitum* (q.v.), and remained in force right up to 1945. No ruler was accepted as legitimate unless crowned by the Holy Crown of Hungary. The last monarch to be crowned with it was King Charles IV (Emperor Charles I) (q.v.) in 1916. After World War II (q.v.) the Holy Crown fell into American hands and was kept at Fort Knox until 1977, when it was returned to Hungary. In 1990 its image was put back into the Hungarian flag, but without any of its former legal and constitutional significance. Today the Holy Crown is a cherished display piece in the Hungarian National Museum in Budapest.

HOLY ROMAN EMPERORS (962–1806). The rulers of the Holy Roman Empire (q.v.) who were elected to their office for life by the princes of the most prominent states within the empire. Known as the "Electors" *(Kurfürsten),* their number was set in the 13th century at seven. These included four secular rulers (palatine of the Rhine, prince of Saxony-Wittenberg, marquis of Brandenburg, and king of Bohemia), and three church leaders (archbishops of Mainz, Cologne, and Trier). Their rights and privileges were specified in the Golden Bull of 1356, issued by Charles IV (r.1346–78). In 1623 the electoral title of the palatine of the Rhine was transferred to the duke

(later king) of Bavaria, but then the palatine of the Rhine regained it
in 1648, which raised the number of the electors to eight. In 1692
the prince (later king) of Hanover also joined the ranks of the
electors, raising their number to nine. In 1803, the archbishops of
Cologne and Trier lost their titles and their places were taken over
by the rulers of Salzburg, Würtemberg, Baden, and Hessen-Kassel.
Thus, during the last three years of the Holy Roman Empire, the
number of electors rose to eleven. In the periods 1437–39, 1556–
1740, and 1745–1806, the Holy Roman Emperors, coming from the
Habsburg dynasty (q.v.), were also kings of Hungary (q.v.).

HOLY ROMAN EMPIRE (962–1806). A medieval state that at
onetime embraced the German, Czech, and much of Italian-speaking
Central Europe. Established in 962 by Otto the Great (r.936–73) and
Pope John XII (r.955–63) as a continuation of the Carolingian
Empire of Charlemagne (r.771-814) and his successors, it survived
until the early 19th century. In theory the Holy Roman Empire was
the restored Roman Empire of Classical times, and its purpose was
to unite all of Western Christendom into a single political entity.
In practice, however, it was largely a confederation of German and
German-dominated states, whose rulers recognized only a vague
supremacy of the Holy Roman Emperor. Until 1250 it was under
the rule of the Hohenstaufen dynasty. They were followed by several
alternating dynasties, of which the Habsburgs survived the longest
(1273–91, 1298–1308, 1437–1740, 1745–1806).

All of the emperors were elected monarchs, and none of them
were able to carry through the centralization of the empire. Thus, the
Holy Roman Empire remained a loose collection of hundreds of
near-independent principalities and lesser political entities, which
finally fell victim to Napoleon's restructuring of Europe. During the
10th through the 15th centuries, the Holy Roman Emperors made
numerous unsuccessful efforts to incorporate Hungary (q.v.) into
their realm, just as they had done with Bohemia (q.v.). With the
election of the Habsburgs to the Hungarian throne in 1526,
however, they succeeded partially, for in their capacity as kings of
Hungary they bound the Hungarian State to the empire. Thus, while

Hungary never became legally part of the Holy Roman Empire, its powerful presence was a constant factor in Hungarian history.

HÓMAN, BÁLINT [VALENTINE] (1885-1951). One of Hungary's great medievalists and an interwar minister for culture and education (1932–38, 1939–42), who died as a political prisoner of the communist regime. After having served as the director of the National Széchényi Library (q.v.) (1922-23) and of the Hungarian National Museum (1923-32), and having been professor of medieval Hungarian history at the University of Budapest (q.v.) (1925-32), in 1932 Hóman became Count Klebelsberg's (q.v.) successor in the Ministry for Culture and Education. By that time he was one of Hungary's great historians who, together with Gyula Szekfű (q.v.) had authored the eight-volume *Hungarian History (Magyar történet)* (1928-34), which is still the most readable and balanced synthesis to date. But his involvement in politics pushed him to the right and he lost himself in the quagmire of political ideologies. During his early years Hóman was a representative of the Positivist School of Hungarian historiography (q.v.), but later he tried to move in the direction of the idea-driven German *Geistesgeschichte* School that had been popularized in Hungary by Szekfű and several Hungarian philosophers. In addition to his volumes in the multivolume *Hungarian History* that he coauthored with Szekfű, Hóman's most important works include: *Hungarian Monetary History (Magyar pénztörténet)* (1916), *Hungary's Financial Affairs and Economic Policy in the Age of Charles Robert (A magyar királyság pénzügyei és gazdaságpolitikája Károly Róbert korában)* (1921), *The New Paths of Hungarian Historiography (A magyar történetírás új útjai)* (1931), *Saint Stephen (Szent István)* (1939), and *History of the Hungarian Middle Ages (Geschichte des ungarisches Mittelalters)* (2 vols., 1940–43). Hóman's most important scholarly studies were published in his three-volume collected *Works (Munkái)* in 1938 under the titles: *Hungarian Middle Ages (Magyar középkor), Historiography and Source Criticism (Történetírás és forráskritika),* and *Cultural Policy (Művelődéspolitika).*

HONORATIOR CLASS. The class of the non-noble intelligentsia before the revolution of 1848–49 (q.v.) that resulted in the abolishment of most of the legal privileges of the nobility (q.v.). The honoratior class included professors, teachers, attorneys, physicians, engineers, and administrators who lacked the patent of nobility. They derived their collective name from the fact that they were compensated for their work by *honoraria,* that is, by unspecified sums of money. Although they lacked the privileges of the nobility (including freedom from taxation and the right to vote in local and national elections), by virtue of their education they were still treated as if they were members of the common nobility (q.v.). During the Hungarian Reform Period (q.v.) (1825-48), virtually all members of the *honoratior* class became exponents of the social and political transformation of Hungary (q.v.).

HONVÉD [HONVÉDSÉG, HONVÉD ARMY]. The name of a member of the Hungarian Army (q.v.) and of the Hungarian National Army itself during the following periods: the Hungarian Revolution of 1848-49, the Age of Dualism (1867-1918) (q.v.), the Interwar Period (1920-45) (q.v.), the immediate post-World War II years (1945-48), and the Post-Communist Period since 1990 (q.v.).

HORKA [HARKA]. One of the chief dignitaries of the conquering Hungarians (q.v.), who was third in importance after the *kende* (q.v.) and the *gyula* (q.v.). According to Constantine Porphyrogenitus (q.v.), the *horka* was the chief judge among the Hungarians. Some scholars believe that *horka* may have been the title of the chief of the Kabar tribes (q.v.), who joined the Hungarians at the time of the Árpádian conquest (q.v.) of the Carpathian Basin (q.v.).

HORN, GYULA (b.1932). Prime minister of Hungary (q.v.) since July 1994, Horn is a former communist politician who made his name as the country's foreign minister (1989-90) during the transitional period from communism to capitalism. In that capacity he opened the Iron Curtain's (q.v.) floodgates by permitting thousands of East German tourists to leave Hungary via Austria (q.v.) to West Germany (q.v.). This act shook the very foundations of the already tottering communist regimes in East Central Europe (q.v.), leading within two months to the breaching of the Berlin Wall (November 9, 1989). A man with technical education, Horn joined the Hungarian foreign ministry in 1959, after which he served in various administrative and diplomatic posts, eventually becoming state secretary (1985–89) and then the head of the foreign ministry. In 1990 Horn was elected president of the newly organized Hungarian Socialist Party (q.v.), which unified the former reform communists (q.v.). For the next four years he served as the Socialist Party's spokesman in the Hungarian Parliament (q.v.), while in 1994 he led his party to political victory. Since assuming power, Horn lost much of his popularity, largely because of his inability to extricate Hungary from its economic and social malaise. For his role in having precipitated the collapse of the Berlin Wall and thus the reunification of Germany (q.v.), in 1990 the German government honored him with its most prestigious award, the so-called "Charles Prize" named after Frankish Emperor Charlemagne (Karl der Große).

HORSE NOMADS [EQUESTRIAN NOMADS]. This term is not identical with the term nomad, as used regularly. The latter term applies to stone age people of Australia, New Guinea, and portions of Africa and the Americas, many of whom have preserved their simple nonsedentary way of life into the 20th century. The "horse nomads," on the other hand, were highly skilled, mostly Turkic (q.v.) and Mongol (q.v.) peoples of the Eurasian steppes, whose primary occupation was animal husbandry and military conquest, based to a large degree upon their effective use of the horse and the fighting methods developed in connection with the horse. Their nomadism is connected with the fact that they did not build permanent cities like the people of the Middle East, Western Europe, India, or China. Rather, they alternated regularly between their summer and winter quarters, both of which were needed for their large herds. They were the ones who invented the saddle, the stirrup, the powerful reflex bow, the curved saber, as well as the unique fighting methods from horseback, all of which made them virtually invincible, until they decided to settle down. The best examples of such horse nomads, who built huge and powerful empires, were Attila's Huns (q.v.), Baian's Avars (q.v.), Genghis Khan's Mongols (q.v.), and to some degree even the Ottoman Turks (q.v.). Although on a much smaller scale, the Conquering Magyars (Hungarians) (q.v.) also belonged in the category of horse nomads, along with such Turkic invaders as the Khazars (q.v.), Bulgars (q.v.), Pechenegs (q.v.), and Cumans (q.v.).

HORTHY, NICHOLAS [MIKLÓS] (1868-1957). Admiral Nicholas Horthy de Nagybánya was Hungary's regent (q.v.) during the interwar period (1920–44) (q.v.) when Hungary (q.v.) was a kingdom without a king. After going through the Naval Academy in Fiume (q.v.), Horthy served for over three decades in the Austro-Hungarian Navy (1886–1918), reaching the rank of a rear admiral and becoming its last commander-in-chief. For a while he was also Emperor Francis Joseph's (q.v.) aide-de-camp (1909–14). During the postwar revolutions that followed the collapse of Austria-Hungary (q.v.) and the dethronement of the Habsburgs (q.v.), Horthy became the commander of the anti-Bolshevik "National Army," on the strength of which the Parliament elected him regent of Hungary. In that capacity he prevented King Charles IV (Emperor Charles I) (q.v.) from reclaiming his throne in 1921, and thus made his regency a permanent one.

Being a traditional nationalist, Horthy became an upholder of Hungary's conservative social system and also a proponent of revisionism (q.v.), aimed at recovering the territories lost after World War I (q.v.). A staunch anti-communist and anti-radical, Horthy also rejected the rightist ideologies of Fascism and Nazism. Yet, because of the Italian and German help in recovering some of the lost territories, he was unable to keep the country from joining the Axis powers during World War II (q.v.). At the same time, while permitting the passage of anti Semitic laws (q.v.) to appease the Germans, he did protect the Jews until after the Germany occupation of Hungary (q.v.) on March 19, 1944. Starting with 1942, Horthy tried unsuccessfully to take his country out of the war through secret negotiations with the Western Allies. His announcement of Hungary's withdrawal from the war on October 15, 1944, ended in a fiasco. He was arrested and taken to Germany, permitting Hungary to fall under the control of the Arrow Cross Party (q.v.) under the leadership of Ferenc Szálasi (q.v.). After the war he refused to get involved in emigré politics, but settled in remote Portugal, where he died in 1957. His remains were repatriated to Hungary in 1992.

HORTHY REGIME see HORTHY, NICHOLAS and INTER-WAR PERIOD.

HORVÁTH, MIHÁLY (1809-78). One of Hungary's great 19th-century historians of the National Liberal School. Born into an impoverished noble family, Horváth spent much of his youth tutoring the children of well-to-do aristocratic (e.g., those of the Keglevich and Erdődy families), while studying for the priesthood. Being a prolific writer, he wrote important works while already in his twenties. He became a member of the Hungarian Academy (q.v.) in 1841, largely on the basis of his *History of Industry and Commerce in Hungary (Az ipar és kereskedelem története Magyarországon)* (1840). In 1844 Horváth was appointed a professor at the Theresianum (q.v.) in Vienna, four years later he was named the bishop of Csanád, and in May 1849 he became the minister of culture and education in the revolutionary Hungarian government.

After the defeat of the Hungarian Revolution, Horváth was forced into exile, and for nearly two decades he lived in Belgium, France, Italy, and Switzerland. He returned to Hungary at the time of the Austro-Hungarian Compromise of 1867 (q.v.). In the same year he became the vice president of the newly organized Hungarian Historical Association (q.v.), and two years later he was elected to the Hungarian Parliament (q.v.). Although Horváth wrote many works on diverse topics, he is best known for his three major syntheses: *Twenty-Five Years from the History of Hungary, 1823-1848 (Huszonöt év Magyarország történetéből, 1823-1848)* (3 vols., 1865), *History of the Hungarian War of Independence in 1848 and 1849 (Magyarország függetlenségi harczának történet 1848-ban és*

1849-ben) (3 vols., 1865), and *History of Hungary (Magyarország történelme)* (8 vols., 1871-73). His smaller historical studies were later collected and published in his *Shorter Historical Works (Kisebb történelmi munkái)* (4 vols., 1968). Mihály Horváth had a major impact upon the development of Hungarian historical studies in the 19th century, and his views influenced even 20th-century historians.

HOSPES [GUEST, SETTLER]. The collective name of the free Western settlers (Saxons, Valoons, French, Italians, Bavarians, Austrians, etc.) in medieval Hungary (q.v.). Initially, this term applied to settlers from all walks of life, including clergymen, knights, artisans, and peasants. Later, however, it came to be used primarily in conjunction with the burghers of the newly founded cities. The *hospes* usually brought their own legal codes with them (e.g., Magdeburg Law), which then served as foundation stones for the development of Hungary's municipal law codes. The term *hospes* was also used during the 13th and 14th centuries in reference to that segment of the agricultural class that possessed rights and privileges almost equal to those of the urban burghers.

HUMANISM. Humanism was the main spiritual-intellectual trend of the Age of the Renaissance (q.v.), which liberated the individual from the religious limitations of the Middle Ages, and which tried to restore the dominance of the spirit and art of the Greco-Roman World to a position of dominance. In order to achieve this goal, the humanists immersed themselves into the writings of the Greek and Roman literati and promulgated the latter's more critical worldview. They believed in the free development of the individual and in the right of every person to seek worldly happiness. They also tried to harmonize the views of the pagan philosophers of the Classical Age with the teachings of Christianity. For these reasons they came into conflict with medieval religiosity and with the leaders of the official church that still emphasized otherworldliness, even though many of them already lived a worldly existence. Humanism emerged in the 14th-century urban centers of Northern Italy, with their powerful burghers and forward-looking intelligentsia, who became the advocates and carriers of social and intellectual modernization. Although the humanists wrote in classical Latin, their activities also advanced the cause of national literatures and national histories. Humanism entered Hungary (q.v.) along with the spirit of the Renaissance during the reign of Matthias Corvinus (q.v.) in the second half of the 15th century and continued to flower during the age of the Jagellonians (q.v.) up to 1526. Its most prominent exponents included the Italian expatriates Antonius Bonfini (q.v.) and Marzio Galeotto (1427–97), and the native Hungarians Johannes Vitéz (q.v.), Janus Pannonius (q.v.), István Werbőczy (q.v.), and Tamás Bakócz (q.v.). The development of Hungarian humanism was cut short by the Battle of Mohács (q.v.) and the subsequent Turkish conquest and trisection of Hungary. Yet, it still survived in the Latin and Hungarian (Magyar) language writings of some 16th-century Catholic historians and Protestant theologians. The most prominent among these late humanists were the historians Miklós Oláh (q.v.), Johannes Sambucus (q.v.) (1531–84), and Miklós Istvánffy (q.v.), as well as the Protestant theologians Gáspár Heltai (q.v.), Gáspár Károli (q.v.), and Miklós Szenczi-Molnár (q.v.).

HUNGARIAN ACADEMY OF SCIENCES [MAGYAR TUDOMÁNYOS AKADÉMIA]. Founded in 1825 at the initiative of Count István Széchenyi (q.v.) for the purposes of cultivating the Hungarian language and Hungarian history, during the post–World War II (q.v.) period the academy had become the center of most scholarly and scientific research in Hungary (q.v.). During the early years of its existence, the academy invited scholars and literary men to its membership and offered various prizes for significant literary and scholarly works. In 1859 its activities were divided into three sections, each headed by a prominent writer or scholar who functioned under an elected president, a vice president, and an executive secretary. The three sections were: I. Language and Literature, II. Philosophy and Historical Sciences, and III. Mathematics and Natural Sciences.

After World War II the academy was reorganized, politicized, and also redirected toward basic research. In the period between 1946 and

1965 the number of its sections were increased from three to ten, each of which functioned with two to four dozen specialized committees. During the same period the academy gained control over a series of basic research institutes, which by 1990 numbered nearly sixty. It also supported about equal number of research centers at the nation's major universities, oversaw eighteen scholarly and scientific associations, and published nearly ninety scholarly and scientific periodicals. At the time of the its reorganization in 1949, the Academy also gained control over the granting of top research degrees established on the Soviet model, called "Candidate of Sciences" *(Tudományok Kandidátusa)* and "Doctor of Sciences" *(Tudományok Doktora)*. These new degrees ranked above the university diplomas and university doctorates, the latter of which was even abolished briefly (1951–59). For over four decades this system was controlled by the Committee on Scientific Qualifications *(Tudományos Minősítő Bizottság)* (1952-94), ending in 1994, when the "Candidate of Sciences" degree was abolished and the "Doctor of Sciences" degree was retained only for honorary purposes. The granting of research degrees returned to the universities, whose doctorates were upgraded to the level of an American Ph.D.

In 1949 over half of the academy's earlier members (122 of 224) were demoted or purged, including its former president, Archduke Joseph August of Habsburg (q.v.). Their places were taken by new members, many of whom were elected for political reasons. After going through a series of changes concerning the categories of membership, in 1991 the Academy's 473 members were divided into "Full Members" (185), "Corresponding Members" (92), "External Members" (32), and "Honorary Members" (164)—with the possibility for further reorganization looming on the horizon.

In 1992 the Széchenyi Academy was established within the confines of the Hungarian Academy of Sciences, specifically for the purpose of honoring artists and writers. The Hungarian Academy of Sciences has its own central library and archives (founded in 1826), controls five dozen specialized libraries connected with its research institutes, and operates its own publishing house (established in 1875, reorganized in 1950).

HUNGARIAN AMERICAN COALITION [HAC] (1991). The newest, but most active and pragmatic, of the American Hungarian umbrella organizations, whose primary goal is to air the problems of the Hungarian minorities in the surrounding states of Slovakia (q.v.), Romania (q.v.), Ukraine (q.v.), Little Yugoslavia (q.v.), and Croatia (q.v.). Although officially founded on August 20, 1991, its origins reach back to 1989, when about two dozen Hungarian organizations decided to create such a high-level coalition to deal with the increasingly critical problem of the minorities. In addition to airing the latter complaints to the appropriate U.S. governmental agencies, the HAC also sponsors annual human rights workshops at various American colleges and universities for the purposes of increasing political activism among young Hungarian American intellectuals.

HUNGARIAN ASSOCIATION [MAGYAR TÁRSASÁG] (1952). Founded in Cleveland, Ohio, it is one of the most comprehensive and durable Hungarian cultural-political associations in the world. Its original intention was to serve the Cleveland Hungarian community, which has been the largest compact Hungarian community outside of Hungary ever since the early 20th century. In the course of time, however, the Hungarian Association became the parent organization of many other institutions and world federations, including the St. Stephen Free University (1953), the Hungarian School (1958), the annual Hungarian Congresses held in Cleveland with the participation of representatives from all over the world (1961), the Árpád Academy for the recognition of Hungarian scientific and cultural achievements abroad (1966), the Transylvanian World Federation (1968) organized for the protection of Hungarian minorities in Romania, and then during the 1970s and 1980s several world federations for Hungarian artists, librarians, Orientalists, teachers, engineers, physicians, and so on—all under the aegis of the Cleveland Hungarian Association. Until 1992 the Cleveland Hungarian Association was under the leadership of its founding president, János Nádas (q.v.). Since his death the presidency has passed to his brother, Gyula Nádas (b.1905). The scientific and scholarly activities of the Hungarian Association, including the leadership of the Árpád Academy (q.v.), was in the hands of their close associate, Professor Ferenc Somogyi (q.v.).

HUNGARIAN CITIZENS' PARTY [MAGYAR POLGÁRI PÁRT] see FEDERATION OF YOUNG DEMOCRATS.

HUNGARIAN CONQUEST [HONFOGLALÁS] (896). This refers to the conquest of the Carpathian Basin (q.v.) or Historic Hungary (q.v.) by the Hungarian tribes in the late 9th century. The official date is 896, but the actual conquest took place over a period of about fifteen years between 892 and 907. Although there are many controversies about the nature of the Hungarian conquest, it is generally agreed that it was initiated by Prince Álmos (q.v.), the leader of the Magyar tribe (q.v), and then completed by his son Árpád (q.v.), the founder of the dynasty that had ruled Hungary for four centuries (896-1301). More recently, it also became accepted that while Árpád was the executor of the conquest, the sacred ruler or *kende* (q.v.) was Prince Kurszán (q.v.). Based on the chronicle *Gesta Hungarorum* by Anonymous (q.v.), Hungarian tradition holds that Árpád's conquering Hungarians were convinced that they were simply reconquering their ancient homeland that had been ruled by their ancestors, including King Attila (q.v.) and the Huns (q.v.). While the direct link between the Huns and the Hungarians is now rejected by most scholars, there are those who believe that the Árpádian conquest (q.v.) was the "Second Conquest" (q.v.). They hold that Hungarian tribes known as "Wangars" did indeed live in the Carpathian Basin at least since about 670, when they invaded and resurrected the declining Avar Empire (q.v.). They came to be known as the "Late Avars" (q.v.). Other scholars identify the first conquest with even earlier migration, while still others speak of several Hungarian conquests going back at least to Hunnic times.

HUNGARIAN CONSTITUTION. In contrast to the written Constitution of the United States (1788), and similarly to the "Historical Constitution" of England, the traditional Hungarian

Constitution consisted of various legislations and royal decrees that reached back to the time of King St. Stephen (q.v.) in the early 11th century. Its most important foundation stone, however, is the Hungarian Golden Bull *(Bulla Aurea)* (q.v.) promulgated in 1222, seven years after the English Magna Carta. The laws and decrees of the first five hundred years were collected and published by István Werbőczy (q.v.) in his so-called *Tripartitum* (q.v.) of 1514, which —with occasional minor amendments—served as the basis of Hungarian constitutionalism right up to the revolution of 1848-49 (q.v.). Amended by the laws of 1848, which ended all features of feudalism (q.v.), by the terms of the Austro-Hungarian Compromise of 1867 (q.v.), as well as by the forced adjustments following the collapse of the Austro-Hungarian Empire in 1918, the traditional Hungarian Constitution survived right up to 1945. After a period of chaos and partial disregard, on August 20, 1949, it was replaced by Hungary's first "Socialist Constitution" (Act 1949:XX), which survived for four decades. This constitution was revised in conjunction with the fall of communism (Act 1989:XXXI and Act 1990:XL), and it has been in a process of further revision ever since.

HUNGARIAN COUNTY SYSTEM [COMITAT, MEGYE, VÁRMEGYE]. Usually referred to in medieval documents by the Latin term *comitatus,* the origin of the Hungarian counties is obscure. Its Hungarian name *megye* (county) or *vármegye* (fortified county) is believed to have come from the South Slavic *medja* (border). Nowadays it is generally believed that evolution of the Hungarian county was the result of the combination of several factors, including the place of settlement of the original clans, the construction of fortresses at a relatively early stage of history, the population density of a particular area, and the coming of Frankish influences in conjunction with the implantation of Christian Church administration in the 11th century. Although King St. Stephen (q.v.) is credited with the establishment of the counties, he was probably responsible only for laying out the foundations of the county system. In the course of the 11th through the 13th centuries two distinct types of counties evolved: the royal county *(királyi* *megye)* and nobles' county *(nemesi megye).* The first in time was the royal county system that embraced much of Hungary, most of which was in royal possession. The royal counties served administrative, military, economic, and judicial functions. By the 13th century, most of the royal lands had been transferred to private hands. Thus, the significance of the royal counties also declined, and their places were gradually taken over by the autonomous nobles' counties. Toward the end of the 13th century, the provincial nobility —known as the "royal servants" *(servientes regis)* (q.v.)— gained so much power that they began to elect their own administrative officers, who thus assumed the powers of the formerly centrally appointed *ispán (comes)* (q.v.). The latter continued to represent the king in the autonomous nobles' counties, but the de facto administration went into the hands of the elected *alispán (vice comes)* (q.v.). During the 14th century, many of the powerful local magnate families extricated themselves from under the authority of the nobles' counties and established direct relationships to the king.

The development of the autonomous nobles' counties continued unabated, and by the 16th century they had developed their own complex autonomous administrative system. Nominally under the royally appointed *főispán (comes),* the actual administration of the county was in the hands of the elected *alispán (vice comes),* who in turn was aided by a number of *szolgabírós* (district administrators) (q.v.), and by numerous lesser administrators. Starting with 1526, the counties came to be represented at the national diet via elected representatives—usually two from each county. With the introduction of this system, the direct representation of the lower nobility ended. The upper nobility continued to represent themselves at the diet. From the 16th through the early 19th centuries, the autonomy of the Hungarian counties became so entrenched that they were almost states within a state. This extensive county autonomy permitted the Hungarian nobility (q.v.) to withstand the growing pressures of centralization and Germanization. Although the legal privileges of the nobility were abolished in 1848, the nobles' county survived almost intact until 1870. At that time the counties lost their right of separate legal jurisdiction, but their structural makeup remained unchanged right up to the end of World War II (q.v.).

HUNGARIAN-CROATIAN UNION see CROATIA, PACTA CONVENTA, LADISLAS I., COLOMAN.

HUNGARIAN CROWN LANDS [HISTORIC HUNGARY, LANDS OF THE HUNGARIAN CROWN, CROWN LANDS OF SAINT STEPHEN]. In the 19th century the Lands of the Hungarian Crown consisted of the Kingdom of Hungary (q.v.), Kingdom of Croatia (q.v.), Grand Duchy of Transylvania (q.v.), the Military Frontier District (q.v.), and the City of Fiume (q.v.). Following the Austro-Hungarian Compromise of 1867 (q.v.), Transylvania and the Military Frontier were reintegrated into Hungary, while Croatia and Fiume retained their separate identities within Hungary. These Lands of the Hungarian Crown together made up Greater or Historic Hungary (q.v.).

HUNGARIAN CULTURAL NATIONALISM. This refers to the national revival movement in the period between the mid–18th century and 1825, when Hungarian national consciousness was expressed primarily in literary form. At that time the main goal of the exponents of Hungarian nationalism was to develop the Magyar language (q.v.) into a modern tool of literary expression. They wanted to use that language to write about ancient glories and thus arouse the people's awareness about their identity.

HUNGARIAN DEMOCRATIC FORUM [MAGYAR DEM- OKRATA FÓRUM = MDF] (1987/89). Founded in 1987 as an independent cultural-social-political movement by a group of mostly Populist Hungarian intellectuals who met at Lakitelek (q.v.) in September 1987, two years later (October 1989) the Hungarian Democratic Forum (HDF) transformed itself into a political party. Gaining popularity by virtue of its Populist (q.v.) coloration and because of the universal unpopularity of the communists, it went on to win the elections and formed the first post-communist government (May 1990) under the leadership of Prime Minister József Antall (q.v.). Taking power in the midst of a national euphoria, the HDF faced huge expectations, but it was unable to live up to most of them. Thus, although engaged in the dismantlement of communism and in the building of a democratic-capitalist system, its leaders and its policies proved to be ineffective, and the party rapidly lost its popularity. By the next elections four years later (1994), the HDF was barely able to send its representatives to the Parliament. It was also forced to see the return of the same reform communists (q.v.) to power, from whom it assumed control in 1990. At the moment, the HDF is one of the four opposition parties in the Hungarian Parliament (q.v.).

HUNGARIAN DIET [DIÉTA, ORSZÁGGYŰLÉS]. The name of the feudal parliament that functioned from the 13th century until 1848. Its roots go back to the Golden Bull of 1222 (q.v.) which acknowledged the representation of the upper clergy and the secular aristocracy. By 1267 the members of the lower nobility *(servientes regis)* (q.v.) also held their own meeting, and in 1298 they joined the members of the aristocracy in the first general assembly *(congregatio generalis)*. In the 14th century these meetings became increasingly frequent, and in 1447 the diet reserved for itself the right to elect Hungary's king. The nobility did not renounce this right until the diet of 1687, when they did so in favor the the Habsburgs (q.v.) under the impact of the Liberation Wars (q.v).

In the 14th and the 15th centuries all members of the Hungarian nobility (q.v.) represented themselves in the diet, but after 1526 only the upper nobility (aristocracy) could do so. The lower nobility was able to participate only through its elected county representatives. The Act of December 1608 recognized the de facto separation of the two branches of the nobility and made this separation into a law by officially recognizing the distinction between the Upper House (q.v.) for the aristocracy, and the Lower House (q.v.) for the representatives of the lower nobility (q.v.). This structure of the feudal diet remained unchanged until the revolution of 1848–49 (q.v.), when it relinquished its place to the Hungarian Parliament (q.v.), whose members were elected on the basis of a broad representation.

HUNGARIAN DISSIDENT MOVEMENT see **DISSIDENT MOVEMENT.**

HUNGARIAN EMIGRATION see **EMIGRATION FROM HUNGARY.**

HUNGARIAN ESTATES [MAGYAR RENDEK]. The Hungarian estates consisted of the nobility (q.v.), the clergy (see ecclesiastical society), and the citizens of the Royal Free Cities (q.v.). The nobility and the clergy were divided into several widely divergent layers. After 1606, the upper nobility or aristocracy (q.v.) and the upper clergy (q.v.) were separated into the Upper House (q.v.) of the Hungarian Diet (q.v.), while the lower or common nobility (q.v.) and the burghers were represented in the Lower House (q.v.). The representation of the burghers, however, was limited, sporadic, and developed only gradually. The development of the Hungarian Estates began in the early 13th century and was completed at the turn of the 16th and 17th centuries. Their privileges, and thus the Hungarian Estates themselves, were abolished in early 1848.

HUNGARIAN FREEDOM FIGHTERS' FEDERATION [MAGYAR SZABADSÁGHARCOS SZÖVETSÉG = MSZSZ] (1957). Generic name for a series of parallel, yet rival organizations founded after the defeat of the Hungarian Revolution of 1956 (q.v.) by the so-called Fifty-sixers (q.v.) of Freedom Fighters (q.v.). The most significant of these associations included the following: (1) the Hungarian Freedom Fighters' Federation (HFFF) established by General Béla Király (q.v.) in early 1957 in Vienna, which subsequently moved to New York and then gradually withered away as General Király switched the focus of his activities from politics to academics; (2) the Hungarian Freedom Fighters' World Federation (HFFWF) founded by General Lajos Dálnoki-Veress

(1889-1976) in Germany in 1957, which subsequently established branches throughout the world, and then after Dálnoki-Veress's death in 1976, transferred the center of its activities to the United States; (3) the Hungarian Freedom Fighters (National Guardian) World Federation (HFF[NG]WF) established by the Pongrátz brothers (Gergely and Ödön) jointly with the Hóka brothers (Mihály and Ernő) in New York in 1957, which drew its inspiration from the heroism of the anti-Soviet street fighters of Budapest and thus represented not the acknowledged leaders but the common combatants of the revolution; and finally (4) the Hungarian Freedom Fighters Movement (HFFM) founded in Cleveland, Ohio, around periodical *Scythian Horn (Szittyakürt),* whose founders combined the views of the above-mentioned street fighters with various far-fetched ideas about Hungarian national origins.

Because of the multiplicity of such federations and their even more numerous local branches, their relationship to each others is confusing even to one who is active in Hungarian emigré circles. But it appears that of the still functioning federations the HFFWF founded by General Dálnoki-Veress has the most followers and enjoys the greatest recognition. The primary goal of these federations was always to keep the Hungarian cause alive in the West and to promote the struggle against the Soviet occupation of Hungary (q.v.). With the collapse of communism (q.v.), their activities declined significantly. In 1990 a number of their leaders repatriated and became active in Hungarian domestic politics.

HUNGARIAN GOLDEN BULL see GOLDEN BULL OF HUNGARY.

HUNGARIAN HERALDIC AND GENEALOGICAL ASSO-CIATION [MAGYAR HERALDIKAI ÉS GENEALÓ-GIAI TÁRSASÁG] (1883). Founded for the study and cultivation of heraldry (q.v.), diplomatics (q.v.), sfragistics (q.v.), genealogy (q.v.), and the other Auxiliary Sciences of History (q.v.), the association ceased to exist in 1949, as a result of the communist regime's perception that these were all "feudalistic disciplines." It was reestablished only in 1983 after the relaxation of the regime and the renewed interest in genealogy and its related fields. The Associations's official periodical was the *Turul* (Mythical Eagle), which was published between 1883 and 1944, and then resurrected in the early 1990s. The appearance of works such as Iván Bertényi's *Little Hungarian Heraldry (Kis magyar címertan)* (1983) and *New Hungarian Heraldry (Új magyar címertan)* (1993), István Kállay's *The Auxiliary Sciences of History (A történelem segédtudományai)* (1986), and Péter Gunst's *The History of Hungarian Historical Studies (A magyar történetírás története) (1995)*, is an indication that the discipline is alive and it is bound to grow in the future.

HUNGARIAN HISTORICAL ASSOCIATION [MAGYAR TÖRTÉNELMI TÁRSULAT] (1867). Founded in the year of the Austro-Hungarian Compromise (q.v.), until after World War II (q.v.) the Historical Association was the main center of the Hungarian historical discipline. Thereafter, it was rapidly replaced by the Institute of History (q.v.) and a number of other related research centers. This situation has not even been altered by the post-communist reforms in the Hungarian scholarly world. The Historical Association still publishes its main periodical *Centuries (Századok),* initiated in 1867. During its heyday it had also published *Historical Repository (Történelmi Tár)* (1878–1935) for short historical sources, and the *Hungarian Historical Biographies (Magyar történelmi életrajzok)* (1885–1917), and supported many other scholarly endeavors, including the publication of the archives of prominent historical families, such as the Zichy (q.v.) and the Teleki (q.v.) clans. The Historical Association's original goals included not only the advancement of historical scholarship, but also the popularization of history among the population at large. Its presidents and vice presidents included some of the most prominent Hungarian historians of the past century and a quarter. The post-World War II transformation of the Hungarian Academy (q.v.) with its many research institutes, however, pushed the Historical Association into the background, from which it never recovered.

HUNGARIAN HISTORICAL STUDIES. The development of historical studies in Hungary (q.v.) went through the same stages as Western historiography. It began with the heroic epics on national origins, reaching back to preliterate times. Some of these epics were lost, while others were incorporated into medieval works. It continued with the medieval chronicles in the period between the 11th and the 15th centuries, the best known of which are the *Ancient Gesta* (q.v.), the *Gesta Hungarorum* by Anonymous (q.v.) and then by Kézai (q.v.), the *Viennese Illuminated Chronicle* by Márk Kálti (q.v.), and finally the *Chronica Ungarorum* by Thuróczy (1435–88/89) (q.v.). These chronicles were followed by humanist historical works of the 15th through the early 17th centuries, starting with those of Antonio Bonfini (1427–1503) (q.v.), Miklós Oláh (1493–1568) (q.v.), István Szamosközy (1565–1612), and Miklós Istvánffy (1538–1615) (q.v.). The humanists were followed by the Baroque School, which produced several major political biographies—such as those of Miklós Bethlen (1642–1716) and Prince Ferenc Rákóczi (q.v.), and the so-called "source collectors" of the late 17th through the 18th century, the most prominent of whom were Péter Bod (1712– 69) (q.v.), Mátyás Bél (1684–1749) (q.v.), István Kaprinay (1714–86), György Pray (1723–1801), and István Katona (1732– 1811). The first major modern syntheses on Hungarian historical evolution were written in the late 18th through the early 19th century by scholars such as Benedek Virág (1754–1830), Ignác Aurél Fessler (1756–1839), Ádám Pálóczi-Horváth (1760-1820), Ésiás Budai (1766–1841), János K. Engel (1770–1814), and István Horvát (1784–1846). Their activities were followed by the birth of the National Liberal School, represented especially by the major syntheses of Mihály Horváth (1809–78) (q.v.) and László Szalay (1813–64).

  This orientation, in turn, was replaced in the last third of the 19th century by the Hungarian Positivist School, which produced some of Hungary's greatest historians, including Arnold Ipolyi (1823–86) (q.v.), Ferenc Salamon (1825–92), Sándor Szilágyi (1827–99) (q.v.), Gyula Pauler (1841–1903) (q.v.), Vilmos Fraknói (1843–1921) (q.v.), Ignác Acsády (1845–1906) (q.v.), Henrik

Marczali (1856–1940) (q.v.), László Fejérpataky (1857–1923), Dávid Angyal (1857–1943) (q.v.), and Károly Tagányi (1858–1924). The strength of this school lay in introducing scientific source criticism into Hungarian historical research, in publishing major critically evaluated source collections (e.g., the *Monumenta Hungariae Historica* series), in establishing the institutional infrastructure of Hungarian historical research (e.g., various related associations and commissions), and in producing major syntheses, which, although heavily factographic and dry, were also very reliable. In its later stages the Positivist School was paralleled by the National Romantic School that reached into the interwar period and was represented by the works of such scholars as Kálmán Thaly (1839–1909), Jenő Csuday (1852–1938), and István Rugonfalvi-Kiss (1881–1957). In addition to disregarding modern source criticism and the comparative method, the latter were characterized by a strong anti-Habsburg bias and by a Hungarocentric view of history, which was unable to perceive Hungarian developments within the context of European history.

This was precisely one of the strengths of the next historical orientation, the so-called *Geistesgeschichte* School, that was inspired especially by the writings of Wilhelm Dilthey (1834-1911). As opposed to Marxist and other materialist orientations, the latter school emphasized the essential common identity of human developments, all motivated primarily by the dominant ideas of the age. Both Positivism and National Romanticism survived right up to World War II (q.v.), but the dominant historical orientation during the interwar period, and for a while even beyond, was the *Geistesgeschichte* School, whose greatest practitioner, and perhaps the greatest Hungarian historian of all times, was Gyula Szekfű (1883–1955) (q.v.). His eight-volume *Hungarian History (Magyar történet)* (1928–34), coauthored with Bálint Hóman (1885–1951) (q.v.), a noted medievalist, who also tried to move from Positivism to the *Geistesgeschichte* orientation, is the most brilliant synthesis of Hungarian history produced up to this date.

In addition to the above-mentioned schools, the interwar period (q.v.) also saw the development of an Ethnohistory School represented by Elemér Mályusz (1898-1989) (q.v), the Hungarian *Kulturgeschichte* or Civilization School represented by Sándor Domanovszky (1877–1955) (q.v.), a New Legal and Constitutional History School represented by Ferenc Eckhart (1885–1957) (q.v.), a Universal History School represented by István Hajnal (1892–1956), as well as a proto-Marxist School that stretched from Ervin Szabó (1877–1918) to Erik Molnár (1894–1966) (q.v.).

World War II represents a watershed in Hungarian historical studies in that the interwar historical schools were barely able to survive beyond the end of that world conflict. By 1948 Hungary came under the monolithic rule of the Communist Party (q.v.), and this also applied to the discipline of history. For the next four decades the study of history was in the grip of the deterministic ideology of Marxism as interpreted momentarily by the leaders of the Soviet Union (q.v.) and its Hungarian exponents. Historical objectivity was thrown out the window, and its place was taken by Marxist partisanship. Until its collapse in 1989-90, Marxist historical scholarship went through three stages: the period of "vulgar Marxism" (1948–1964), the period of "mature Marxism" (1964–79), and the period of "lip service Marxism" (1979–90). The most important exponents of the first period were Erik Molnár, József Révai (1898–1959) (q.v.), Erzsébet Andics (1902–86), and Aladár Mód (1908–73); the second period was characterized by the scholarly activities and leadership of Zsigmond Pál Pach (b.1919) (q.v.), Iván T. Berend (b.1930) (q.v.), and György Ránki (1930-88) (q.v.); while the third period witnessed the emergence of Ferenc Glatz (b.1941) (q.v.) and his generation of "Westernizers" under the guidance of the then already Westernized György Ránki.

The collapse of communism pushed many of the old guard out of power and placed leadership into the hands of Glatz and his generation, jointly with some surviving members of the pre-Marxist generation, such as Domokos Kosáry (b.1913) (q.v.), who became the Hungarian Academy's (q.v.) first post-communist president.

HUNGARIAN JACOBINS [MAGYAR JAKOBÍNUSOK]. The Hungarian Jacobins were members of two revolutionary secret societies founded during the early 1790s and then united in 1794 under the leadership of Ignác Martinovics (q.v.). Martinovics, however, turned into a spy informer and thus most members of the society were arrested, convicted, and imprisoned. Seven of the top leaders, including Martinovics himself, were beheaded in 1795 on the "Field of Blood" under the walls of the fortress of Buda (q.v.). The Hungarian Jacobins took their name and ideas from the most radical segment of the French parliamentarians in the National Convention (1792–95), whose leaders were M. Robespierre, J. P. Marat, and A. L. Saint-Just. The most prominent leaders and members of the Hungarian Jacobins, who were implicated in the Jacobin Conspiracy of 1794–95, included Ignác Martinovics, József Hajnóczy (q.v.), and Ferenc Kazinczy (q.v.).

HUNGARIAN LANGUAGE see MAGYAR LANGUAGE.

HUNGARIAN LIFE, PARTY OF [MAGYAR ÉLET PÁRT-JA] (1939–44). The continuation of the National Unity Party (q.v.), which lost its parliamentary majority in 1939. The Party of Hungarian Life was similarly a governmental coalition party and it remained in power until the Arrow Cross Party (q.v.) took over the government in a coup d'état on October 15, 1944.

HUNGARIAN LINGUISTIC REVIVAL see HUNGARIAN NATIONAL REVIVAL.

HUNGARIAN MINORITIES. These national minorities are those 3.6 to 3.8 million Hungarians (Magyars) in the surrounding states —including Romania (2.2 to 2.5 million), Slovakia (800,000), Serbia (400,000), Ukraine (200,000), Croatia (20,000), Slovenia (10,000), and Austria (10,000) —who live on territories that used to be part of the Kingdom of Hungary (q.v.) before its dismemberment after World War I (q.v.), sanctioned by the Treaty of Trianon (q.v.) in 1920.

HUNGARIAN NATIONAL COUNCIL [MAGYAR NEM-
ZETI BIZOTTMÁNY] (1947–58). The Hungarian National
Council (HNC) was a kind of parliament-in-exile supported by the
U.S. Government via the Free Europe Committee. During its
existence it had usually over seventy members, made up mostly of
exiled politicians. Its actual leadership, however, was in the hands of
its Executive Committee—a kind of government-in-exile— manned
by about a dozen prominent personalities, under the presidency of
Msgr. Béla Varga (1903–96), the president of the last pre-
communist Hungarian Parliament (1946–47). In 1958 the HNC was
dissolved and replaced by the less significant Hungarian Committee
(Magyar Bizottság) (1956–90), which had lost most of its financial
support as well as its semiofficial governmental status.

HUNGARIAN NATIONAL REVIVAL MOVEMENT. This
movement embraced the century between 1760 and 1848, which
combined the periods of Hungarian Cultural Nationalism (q.v.) and
Hungarian Political Nationalism (q.v.). Although manifestations of
Hungarian national consciousness are evident throughout the
Turkish period in the 16th and 17th centuries, not until the
influences of French and German Enlightenments in the mid–18th
century did the Hungarian National Revival Movement begin. It
started in the Viennese palace of the Hungarian Royal Nobles' Guard
(q.v.), and then it gradually spread into Hungary (q.v.). The initial
manifestations of this national revival were largely literary,
linguistic, and cultural, but at the diet of 1825 they became
political. Whereas the cultural phase of this revival movement
updated and modernized the language, and dug into the Hungarian
historical past, the political phase formulated concrete demands for
national recognition. Moreover, it also pushed the idea of
nationhood and national consciousness down to the level of the
simple folk, who hitherto had been left out of the notion of the
"Hungarian Nation" *(Natio Hungarica)* [q.v.).

HUNGARIAN NOBILITY see NOBILITY, COMMON NO-
BILITY, LOWER NOBILITY, UPPER NOBILITY.

HUNGARIAN PARLIAMENT [ORSZÁGGYŰLÉS, NEM-ZETGYŰLÉS]. The Hungarian legislative assembly since the eruption of the Hungarian revolution in March 1848, when the feudal assembly, the Hungarian Diet (q.v.), was replaced by a representative parliament. The Hungarian Parliament functioned during 1848–49, 1861, and from 1865 until the present. Its Hungarian name was *országgyűlés* (State Assembly), except between 1920–26 and 1945–47, when it was called *nemzetgyűlés* (National Assembly). The Parliament was bicameral during 1848-49, 1861, 1865-1918, and 1926–1945. Its more representative Lower House *(képviselőház)* (q.v.) was counterbalanced by the Upper House *(felsőház)* (q.v.), which before 1918 was called the House of Lords *(főrendház)*.

HUNGARIAN PEOPLE'S REPUBLIC [MAGYAR NÉP-KÖZTÁRSASÁG] (1949-89). Hungary's official name between August 18, 1949 and October 23, 1989.

HUNGARIAN POLITICAL NATIONALISM. This term refers to the period between 1825 and 1848, also known as the Hungarian Reform Period (q.v.), when Hungarian national consciousness moved from the cultural to the political phase. This move manifested itself in the growing demand for meaningful political reform, economic modernization, and for the recognition of Hungary's (q.v.) unique position within the Austrian Empire (q.v.). The radicalization of Hungarian Political Nationalism was one of the causes of the revolution of 1848–49 (q.v.).

HUNGARIAN POPULISM see POPULISM IN HUNGARY.

HUNGARIAN PROTESTANTISM see PROTESTANTISM IN HUNGARY.

HUNGARIAN REFORMATION see PROTESTANTISM IN HUNGARY.

HUNGARIAN REFORM PERIOD (1825–48). The period between 1825, which is the date of the first Hungarian Reform Diet (q.v.), and the March Revolution of 1848 (q.v.). The Reform Period was characterized by the rise of Hungarian political nationalism (q.v.) and by the gradual dismemberment of the country's feudal social structure by the liberal-minded nobility (q.v.). Its last phase coincided with the German *Vormärz* (Pre-March) period.

HUNGARIAN REVISIONIST LEAGUE [MAGYAR REVÍ ZIÓS LIGA] (1927-45). An organization founded for the purposes of advancing the cause of the revision of Hungary's frontiers as established by the Treaty of Trianon (q.v.) in 1920. The Revisionist League was a newer version of the Land Protection League *[Területvédő Liga]* (1919-20), that tried to prevent Hungary's mutilation. The establishment of the Revisionist League on July 22, 1927 under the leadership of the celebrated novelist and playwright Ferenc Herczeg (1863-1954) was prompted by the activities of the British journalist and publisher Lord Harold Sidney Rothermere (1868-1940), who took up the cause of Hungarian Revisionism (q.v.). The League tried to advance its goals through propaganda activities in Britain, France, the United States, as well as in Germany and Italy. While they found a number of sympathetic ears, the first world leader to openly support Hungary's revisionist aims was Benito Mussolini (1883-1945) of Italy.

HUNGARIAN REVISIONIST MOVEMENT (1920-45). A movement born in 1920, which tried to undo the mutilation of Historic Hungary (q.v.) sanctioned by the Treaty of Trianon (q.v). The movement began immediately after the signing of the peace treaty, but it did not go into high gear until receiving the open support of Lord Harold Sidney Rothermere (1868–1940) who—after the death of his brother, Lord Alfred Charles William Northcliffe (1865–1922)—became the new king of British journalism. Rothermere spoke up against Trianon in an article in his flagship paper, the *Daily Mail* (June 21, 1927). This support prompted the Hungarians to establish the Hungarian Revisionist League (q.v.) and to go on the offensive. They initiated a major propaganda campaign in Britain, France, the Unites States, Germany, and Italy, which resulted in a number of favorable hearings and promises for help. As an example, the British Parliament established a Study Committee under the chairmanship of Robert Grower, which by 1933 resulted in a parliamentary resolution that demanded the revision of Hungary's frontiers. Similarly sympathetic voices were heard in a number of other countries as well. Senator William E. Borah spoke up for Hungarian revisionism in the United States, and he also appealed directly to Prime Minister Laval of France. Yet, the only head of state that came out openly and strongly in favor of the revision of Hungary's frontiers was Benito Mussolini (1883–1945). This explains Hungary's gravitation toward Italy (q.v.) during the early 1930s. Then, when Italy linked up to Germany (q.v.) in the Berlin-Rome Axis in 1936, Hungary too followed suit and established a closer relationship with Germany.

The Revisionist Movement achieved some of its aims in the course of 1938–41, when Hungary regained portions of Northern Hungary (1938) (q.v.) and all of Carpatho-Ruthenia (1939) (q.v.) from Czechoslovakia (q.v.), most of Northern Transylvania (1940) (q.v.) from Romania (q.v.), and portions of Southern Hungary or Northern Voivodina (1941) (q.v.) from Yugoslavia (q.v.). These gains, however, came at the price of an alliance with Germany and Italy, which ultimately led the country into World War II (q.v.) on the losing side. It also resulted in the loss of these territories once more in 1944–45, which losses were then sanctioned by the Peace Treaty of Paris (q.v.) in 1947.

HUNGARIAN REVOLUTION OF 1848-49. Known in Hungary (q.v.) as the "March Revolution" and the "Hungarian War of Liberation," this upheaval lasted from March 15, 1848, until October 2, 1849. The March Revolution was the capstone to the Hungarian Reform Period (q.v.) that began in 1825 and culminated in the elimination of the vestiges of feudalism by the diet of 1847–48. It placed Hungary on the path of political and economic modernization by establishing an elected modern representative

Parliament (first session: May 29, 1848) and a responsible Hungarian government under Prime Minister Count Lajos Batthyány (q.v.). The Viennese *Kamarilla* (q.v.) that ran the Imperial Government (q.v.) in the name of the feebleminded King Ferdinand V (q.v.), however, approved the Hungarian autonomy only reluctantly and with the secret understanding that it would be undone as soon as feasible. To achieve their goal, they began to incite the national minorities (q.v.) against the Hungarians, and also sowed the seeds of dissension among the ranks of Hungary's political leaders. The growing radicalization of the revolution and the likelihood of a military confrontation with the Habsburgs (q.v.) resulted in the resignation of the moderate Batthyány Government (September 28, 1848) and in the creation of the National Defense Committee (q.v.) under the leadership of the much more radical Lajos Kossuth (q.v.). The open warfare that ensued did bring the Hungarians a number of major military victories during the winter and spring of 1849, but with the defeat of the revolutions throughout Europe, the hope for a Hungarian victory became increasingly unlikely. A peaceful solution sought by the moderate elements was made impossible by the radicals' dethronement of the Habsburgs and the election of Kossuth to be the regent of Hungary (April 14, 1849). The subsequent Russian military intervention (June 18) made the Hungarian defeat inevitable. After Kossuth's resignation (Aug. 11), General Artúr Görgey (q.v) surrendered to the Russians (August 13) at Világos (q.v.). Sporadic fighting continued for a while, but by October 2, 1849, General Klapka (q.v.) surrendered the fortress of Komárom and the Hungarian War of Liberation came to an end.

HUNGARIAN REVOLUTIONS OF 1918-19. Also known as "Post–World War I Revolutions," this term refers to the radical social and political changes that took place after the collapse of Austria-Hungary (q.v.) in October 1918. At first, power fell into the hands of liberal-socialist coalition under the leadership of Count Mihály Károlyi (q.v.) (October 31, 1918–March 21, 1919), and then into the hands of the communists under Béla Kun (q.v.) (March 21–August 1, 1919). The latter established the Hungarian Soviet

Republic (q.v.) and introduced the Red Terror (q.v.), which eventually undermined even its modest popularity. This nine-month socialist-communist revolution was replaced by the conservative-nationalist regime of Admiral Miklós Horthy (q.v.), first as the commander-in-chief of the Hungarian Armed Forces (August 15, 1919) and then as the elected regent of Hungary (March 1, 1920).

HUNGARIAN REVOLUTION OF 1956. An anti-Soviet and anti-communist uprising that erupted on October 23, 1956, and resulted in a few days of freedom for Hungary (October 23-November 4, 1956). The roots of this revolution reach back to Hungary's (q.v.) subjugation by the Soviet Union (q.v.) after World War II (q.v.) and the imposition of a monolithic communist rule (1948) under Mátyás Rákosi (q.v.). This dark period of communist terror ended in 1953, when Stalin's death brought about the replacement of Rákosi with the more humane Imre Nagy (q.v.). After two years of relaxation (1953–55) Rákosi reasserted his control (1955–56), only to lose it again in wake of Nikita Khrushchev's de-Stalinization campaign that also brought about the relaxation of Soviet control over the satellite states. The Polish Revolt of June 1956 was the first sign of a break in this control. Next came the Hungarian Revolution which shook the very foundation of the Soviet Empire, and for a while appeared to have initiated a withdrawal of Soviet power from East Central Europe (q.v.).

The revolution erupted spontaneously in Budapest (q.v.) in the afternoon of October 23, when a peaceful demonstration in support of the Poles had turned violent because of shootings by members of the secret police. This action brought Imre Nagy back into power (October 24), which in turn resulted in the formation of a new coalition government, the end of one-party rule, the beginning of the Soviet (q.v.) withdrawal from Hungary, and the proclamation of Hungary's independence and neutrality. The revolution would probably have succeeded had the Suez War not distracted the attention of the world, and had Western intervention not emboldened the Russians to affect a similar intervention in Hungary. President Eisenhower's proclamation of sympathy without practical help also encouraged the Soviets. The result was the return of the Soviet Armed Forces (November 4, 1956) and the gradual defeat of the revolutionaries during the next few weeks. Another result was the exodus of about 200,000 Hungarians, the so-called Freedom Fighters (q.v.) to the West, 40,000 of whom ended up in the United States. The defeat of the revolution was followed by a period of repression by the new Kádár Regime (q.v). But by the early 1960s, a political and economic liberalization movement had began, which produced the so-called "Goulash Communism" (q.v.) of the 1970s and early 1980s. During those years Hungary became the envy of its neighbors and the pioneer in the undoing of communism right up to the collapse of that system in 1989–90.

HUNGARIAN REVOLUTIONARY GOVERNMENT OF WORKERS AND PEASANTS [MAGYAR FORRADAL-MI MUNKÁS-PARASZT KORMÁNY] (1956–89). The official name of the Soviet-supported communist government established in early November 1956 under the leadership of János Kádár (q.v.) to oppose the national government under the prime ministership of Imre Nagy (q.v.). This government remained in power until 1989, even though Kádár himself was pushed out of power in 1988. His successors were forced to prepare the ground for the transfer of power to the first post-communist government under the leadership of the Hungarian Democratic Forum (q.v.) and Prime Minister József Antall (q.v.). After the period of reaction and retribution following the defeat of the revolution of 1956, this government initiated in 1962 a policy of gradual political and economic liberalization that lasted until its demise in 1989–90, which produced the much-envied "Goulash Communism" (q.v.) in Hungary (q.v.).

HUNGARIAN ROYAL NOBLES' GUARD [MAGYAR KIRÁLYI NEMESI TESTŐRSÉG] (1760). The Royal Guard had existed in Hungary ever since King St. Stephen (q.v.) in the early 11th century, but not until the reign of Maria Theresa (q.v.) in the 18th century did it acquire a unique characteristic and significance. She established the Hungarian Royal Nobles' Guard in 1760 in Vienna (q.v.) specifically for the sons of the Hungarian nobility (q.v.). She did this partially to reward the nobility for their support in the Seven Years' War (q.v.), and partially to gain their affection and support for her dynasty. Moreover, she also wanted to raise their appreciation for Western culture and learning during their stay in Vienna. The Hungarian Royal Nobles' Guard consisted of 120 young noblemen, two from each county, all of whom were obliged to serve for five years. During their stay in Vienna they became acquainted with Western social customs, with the philosophy of the Enlightenment (q.v.), as well as with the ideology of modern nationalism. Thus, although this was not Maria Theresa's intention, the members of the Royal Nobles' Guard were responsible for initiating the Hungarian National Revival Movement (q.v.).

The most influential among the early guardsmen were György Bessenyei (q.v.) and Sándor Kisfaludy (q.v.), the first of whom is generally viewed as the "father" of this revival movement. In the fall of 1848, following the outbreak of the Hungarian Revolution (q.v.), most of the guardsmen joined the Hungarian revolutionary armies. As a result, the Royal Guard was dissolved in 1850. It was reestablished again after the Austro-Hungarian Compromise of 1867 (q.v.), but this time its members did not have to come exclusively from the ranks of the nobility. The Hungarian Royal Guard (not Nobles' Guard) survived in this more modern form the collapse of Austria-Hungary (q.v.), right up to the end of World War II (q.v.).

HUNGARIANS see MAGYARS.

HUNGARIAN SOCIALIST PARTY [MAGYAR SOCIAL-ISTA PÁRT] (1989). Founded on October 7, 1989 by the reform communists, following the dissolution of the Hungarian Socialist Workers' Party (q.v.), the Hungarian Socialist Party (HSP) became one of the main opposition parties of the first post-communist government (1990–94). Having won the most number of votes in the election of 1994, since July of that year the HSP has been the majority party of the ruling coalition that unites it with the Federation of Free Democrats (q.v.).

HUNGARIAN SOCIALIST WORKERS' PARTY [MAGYAR SZOCIALISTA MUNKÁSPÁRT] (1956-89, 1989). The name of the reorganized Communist Party of Hungary (q.v.) following the defeat of the Hungarian Revolution of 1956 by the Soviet Army. Its predecessors included the Hungarian Workers' Party (1948–56), the Hungarian Communist Party (1944–48), and the Communist Party of Hungary (1918–44)—the latter of which functioned largely illegally ever since the fall of the Hungarian Soviet Republic (q.v.) on August 1, 1919. The Hungarian Socialist Workers' Party was the dominant force in Hungary for thirty-three years—thirty-two of them under the leadership of János Kádár (q.v.). The party dissolved itself in October 1989, after which its moderate majority established the Hungarian Socialist Party (q.v.), while the radical and numerically insignificant minority reestablished itself under the original name of the Hungarian Socialist Workers' Party.

HUNGARIAN SOVIET REPUBLIC [MAGYAR TANÁCS-KÖZTÁRSASÁG (1919). The first Hungarian communist regime under the leadership of Béla Kun (q.v.) that came into power four and a half months after the collapse of Austria-Hungary (q.v.). It was preceded by the "bourgeois liberal" (or liberal-socialist) regime of Count Mihály Károlyi (q.v.), which resigned power on March 21, 1919, in face of the impossible territorial and other terms imposed by the victorious allies upon Hungary (q.v.). The leaders of the Hungarian Soviet Republic were associated with the attempted communization of Hungary, and they were also responsible for the accompanying Red Terror (q.v.). The latter strengthened the various counterrevolutionary movements and also produced the almost equally violent White Terror (q.v.). The Hungarian Soviet Republic collapsed on August 1, 1919, after which its leaders fled abroad.

HUNGARIAN TRIBAL FEDERATION. This federation of seven Hungarian tribes came into being in the course of the 6th through the 9th centuries, while the Hungarians or Magyars (q.v.) were subjects of the Khazar Empire (q.v.). The Hungarian Tribal Federation included the Magyar, Nyék, Kürtgyarmat, Tarján, Jenő, Kér, and Keszi tribes—under the leadership of the Magyar tribe, which gave its name to the whole federation and to the resulting nation. The unity of the federation was sealed by a so-called "blood oath" (q.v.) in Etelköz (q.v.), where the tribal leaders accepted Álmos (q.v.) and his son Árpád (q.v.), the leaders of the Magyar tribe, as the head of the tribal federation. They vowed that they would only be led by Álmos, Árpád, and their heirs and successors. This event took place sometime before their conquest of the Carpathian Basin (q.v.) in the late 9th century, at which time they were also joined by three related Kabar tribes (q.v.). The Hungarian Tribal Federation survived the conquest through much of the 10th century. Only in the late 10th and early 11th centuries were the powers of the individual tribal leaders cut down and then the tribes molded into a single nation.

HUNGARIAN TRUTH AND LIFE PARTY [MAGYAR IGAZSÁG ÉS ÉLET PÁRTJA] see HUNGARIAN WAY MOVEMENT.

HUNGARIAN WAR OF LIBERATION see HUNGARIAN REVOLUTION OF 1848-49.

HUNGARIAN WAY MOVEMENT [MAGYAR ÚT MOZGALOM] (1992). This movement grew out of the Hungarian Democratic Forum (q.v.) and was founded by the populist-nationalist István Csurka (q.v.) in late 1992, who was being forced out of the HDF because of his extremist views. After having been ejected, Csurka also founded the Hungarian Truth and Life Party *(Magyar Igazság és Élet Pártja)* (MIÉP), which proved to have so little appeal that it did not even make it to the Hungarian Parliament (q.v.) in 1994. The Hungarian Way Movement and the MIÉP both advocate a kind of populist nationalism that idealizes the peasants, distrusts the urbanites, and believes in the existence of a kind of world conspiracy that tries to undermine the health and well-being of Hungary (q.v.) and the Hungarian nation.

HUNGARIAN WORKERS' PARTY see **COMMUNIST PARTY OF HUNGARY.**

HUNGARIAN WORLD FEDERATION [MAGYAROK VILÁGSZÖVETSÉGE] (1938). The federation was founded in 1938 at the Second Hungarian World Congress in Budapest (q.v.), after nine years of existence as the "Central Office of the Hungarian World Congress" *(Magyarok Világkongresszusa Központi Irodája)*, which had been established in 1929, at the First Hungarian World Congress, likewise in Budapest. The goal of the federation was to unite all Hungarians throughout the world in a joint effort to advance the cause of Hungary (q.v.), and in particular the cause of Hungarian revisionism (q.v.). After World War II (q.v.), the World Federation was reorganized to fit the needs of the new regimes that came into being under the watchful eyes of the Soviet Union (q.v.). The idea of revisionism was cast out and the federation was reoriented to represent the interests of the communist government.

With the start of the liberalization movement in the mid-1960s, the World Federation undertook an offensive to discredit the staunchly anti-communist emigrés and to gain the sympathy of those exiles who were willing to engage a dialogue with the changing regime. One of the important milestones in the reaching-out process was the establishment of the "Mother Tongue Movement" in 1970, which organized conferences for Hungarian educators, supported various Hungarian cultural efforts abroad, and also spread the idea that Hungary was indeed a changing country. These ideas were spread both through word of mouth, and through various publications. The latter included the World Federation's *Hungarian News (Magyar Hírek)* and the Mother Tongue Movement's *Our Language and Culture (Nyelvünk és Kultúránk).*

Following the collapse of communism in 1989-90 (q.v.), the World Federation went through a period of turmoil. In December 1991, its leadership was replaced by a group of populist writers and intellectuals under the presidency of Sándor Csoóri (q.v.). Thereafter the federation reoriented itself primarily toward the problems of the hitherto disregarded Hungarian minorities (q.v.) in the neighboring states. This reorientation still holds true in 1997, even though the federation's work was made more difficult in 1994, when the first post-communist government was replaced by the reform communists under the leadership of the Hungarian Socialist Party (q.v.).

Since coming to power, the new leadership's most impressive shows were the Third Hungarian World Congress in August 1992 and the Fourth Hungarian World Congress in June 1996, both of which differed from their predecessors by the multitude of emotional political controversies that erupted at its sessions. The Hungarian World Federation's post-communist publications include the ephemeral *World Federation (Világszövetség)* (1991–92), the much more solid quarterly *Hungarian Observer (Magyar Figyelő)* (1992–), and the recently initiated monthly *World News (Világlap)* (1996–). Since 1992, the World Federation is also in charge of a "Duna TV" (Danubian TV), whose programs are broadcast via satellite. As most of its other cultural programs, its television broadcasts are also geared primarily to the Hungarian minorities in the surrounding states of Slovakia (q.v.), Ukraine (q.v.), Romania (q.v.), and the countries of former Yugoslavia (q.v.).

HUNGARIST MOVEMENT [HUNGARISTA MOZGALOM] see ARROW CROSS PARTY.

HUNGARO-CROATIAN COMPROMISE [LAW XXX OF 1868, NAGODBA] (1868). This agreement followed the Austro-Hungarian Compromise of 1867 (q.v.) and it established a kind of dualism within dualism (q.v.), whereby Croatia-Slavonia (q.v.) saw her long standing autonomy reestablished within the Kingdom of Hungary (q.v.). Fully autonomous in internal matters under the leadership of its own elected diet (q.v.) that functioned in Croatian under the governance of a ban (q.v.) appointed by the king of Hungary (i.e., the emperor of Austria), Croatia-Slavonia also had her representatives in the Hungarian Parliament (forty in the Lower

House (q.v.) and three in the Upper House (q.v.)), as well as in the annual Hungarian Parliamentary Delegations that coordinated the relationship between Austria (q.v.) and Hungary (four from the Upper House and one from the Lower House). Croatia-Slavonia's interests in the Hungarian government were represented by a Croatian Minister without Portfolio, and the Croatian delegates in the Hungarian Parliament (q.v.) had the right to use their own language in parliamentary debates and hoist their own flag next to the Hungarian flag. Moreover, the laws that had relevance to Croatia-Slavonia also had to be published in Croatian. The Hungaro-Croatian Compromise also dealt with Croatia-Slavonia's contributions to the common budget, the Hungarian and the Austro-Hungarian Armed Forces (q.v.), and with other matters of common concern. The latter were usually dealt with in a proportional manner, although at times they were more generous to Croatia-Slavonia than the proportional relationship would have warranted. The compromise was amended several times during the period of its existence (i.e., 1873, 1880, 1889, 1897, 1906, 1913).

HUNGARY [REPUBLIC OF HUNGARY, MAGYAR-ORSZÁG]. Hungary today is a small country of 36,000 square miles with 10.2 million inhabitants. Before 1918, it was a country of 126,000 square miles with a population of 21.5 million (which today would amount to about 30 million). This Greater or Historic Hungary (q.v.), in turn, was part of the still larger Austro-Hungarian Empire (q.v.), which was a state of 261 square miles with a population of fifty-three million, placing her populationwise in between contemporary Germany and France. With the exception of the period of the Ottoman conquest (q.v.), Historic Hungary had survived intact ever since its foundation in the 9th and 10th centuries. During the 11th through the 15th centuries, the Kingdom of Hungary was actually much larger, for its rulers usually controlled significant additional territories in the Balkans (q.v.) and in present-day Poland (q.v.) and Ukraine (q.v.). At times, the Hungarians also expanded northward and westward, as was the case under Coloman (q.v.), Louis the Great (q.v.), and Matthias Corvinus (q.v.).

HUNGARY, KINGDOM OF see **HISTORIC HUNGARY.**

HUNKY [HUNKEY, HUNKIE] IMAGE. This is a derogatory term applied to the simple and largely illiterate peasant immigrants of the turn of the 19th to the 20th century. Although derived from "Hungarian," it ultimately came to cover most of the simple immigrants of Eastern and Southeastern Europe of whatever nationality. The term Hunky came into use primarily because some of the earliest of these economic immigrants were Slovaks (q.v.) and Ruthenians (Rusyns) (q.v.) from Hungary (q.v.), who, being Hungarian citizens, were routinely referred to as Hungarians. Once this image had been established, it was automatically transferred to most other contemporary immigrants from the Austro-Hungarian Empire (q.v.), as well as to those from various multinational regions of the Russian Empire (q.v.) and the Balkans (q.v.).

HUNOR AND MAGOR [MAGYAR]. According to the chronicler Kézai (q.v.), these two brothers were the forefathers of two alleged sister nations: the Huns and the Magyars or Hungarians. Their parents were Nimród (Menroth) of biblical fame and his wife Eneth. This view had been perpetuated in Hungarian lore—including the "Legend of the Wondrous Stag" (q.v.)—until it came to be accepted as truth by most Hungarians.

HUNS. Turkic people of Central Asiatic origin who crossed the Volga in A.D. 372 and then conquered much of Eastern and Central Europe. By the early 5th century they established the center of their realm in today's Hungary (q.v.), subjugated most of the German and Slavic tribes (q.v.), and then systematically attacked and extorted vast monetary tributes from both Roman Empires. They reached the climax of their power under Attila (r.433-53) (q.v.), whose empire stretched from the borders of the two humbled Roman Empires to the beyond the Caucasus Mountains and into Central Asia (q.v.). Following Attila's death in 453, his empire fell victim to the fratricidal wars among his sons. Many Huns were killed, others were absorbed by their former subjects, and still others went back to the east and then merged into such later invaders as the Avars (q.v.), Bulgars (q.v.), and Magyars (q.v.) or Hungarians. According to Hungarian lore, one group of Huns under Attila's youngest son Irnák—known to the Hungarians as Csaba (q.v.)—settled in Transylvania (q.v.). In the 9th and 10th centuries they joined forces with the invading Magyars and then became the frontier guards of the Hungarian Kingdom. Their late descendants are still there today, the Hungarian-speaking *Székelys [Szeklers]* (q.v.) of that former Hungarian province, which became part of Romania (q.v.) in 1920.

HUNNIC EMPIRE. There existed several Hunnic empires in Asia both before and after the Christian Era, but this term usually refers to the Empire of Attila (q.v.) in the mid-5th century (r.433-53). Although this empire centered on Hungary (q.v.), it embraced a huge territory that stretched from the the two Roman Empires in western and southern Europe to beyond the Caucasus and into Central Asia (q.v.). It was a multinational and multilingual state, in which the Huns constituted only the ruling core element. The majority of its inhabitants consisted of various Germanic, Slavic, and related Turkic tribes. The kings of the German tribes played an especially significant role in the leadership of the Hunnic Empire, which explains why Attila became one of the heroes of a number of German and Scandinavian heroic epics. Attila's Hunnic Empire is usually compared to such other horse-nomadic (q.v.) empires as those of Genghis Khan (c.1167-1226) and Tamerlane (Timur Lenk) (d.1405), as well as the Ottoman Empire (q.v.) during its rise to prominence in the 14th through the 16th centuries.

HUNNIC-HUNGARIAN CONNECTIONS. The belief that the Huns (q.v.) and the Hungarians (q.v.) were related peoples has been part of Hungarian traditions at least since the time of the Árpádian conquest (q.v.) of Hungary (q.v.). The members of the Árpád dynasty (q.v.) regarded themselves as the direct descendants of Attila (q.v.), and they viewed their conquest of Hungary as the legitimate reclaiming of possessions held by their ancestors. These traditions came to be expressed in the "Legend of the Wondrous Stag" (q.v.) as well as in Kézai's *Gesta Hungarorum* (q.v.) and other medieval Hungarian chronicles. Moreover, this view was also current among Western chroniclers in the late 9th and early 10th century, when they first came into contact with the Hungarians, whom they equated with the Huns. In the 19th century, however, modern scholarship began to undermine this belief, largely on the basis of linguistic considerations that contrasted the Finno-Ugric (q.v.) language of the Hungarians with the Turkic (q.v.) language of the Huns. While this anti-Hunnic view is still most popular among modern Hungarian linguists and historians, the pro-Hunnic view has also its supporters. Moreover, it has reemerged recently in the works of prominent scholars who claim at least partial connections between the Huns and the Hungarians. These scholarly arguments about the validity or invalidity of Hunnic-Hungarian relationship, however, appear to have had little impact upon popular beliefs. Many Hungarians still view the Huns as their ancestors, and they still regard Attila as one of their national heroes.

HUNYADI FAMILY see **HUNYADI, MATTHIAS CORVINUS.**

HUNYADI, JÁNOS [JOHN] (c.1407–1456). Military leader, Hungarian national hero, and the regent of Hungary (r.1446-53), who was one of the most effective and celebrated anti-Turkish fighters in the mid–15th century. Of obscure origin—some claim that he was the illegitimate son of Emperor Sigismund (q.v.)—Hunyadi received his initial training in the art of war in the armies of some of the great Hungarian and Serbian generals of those years. In 1430 he accompanied Sigismund to Italy, in 1433 to Switzerland, and in 1437 to Bohemia (q.v.). In the meanwhile, he also studied the art of war in the armies of some of the best Italian condottieri and Hussite mercenaries, including Filippo Visconti (1392–1447) of Milan. Between 1439 and 1446 Hunyadi served as the ban of Szörény, one of Hungary's southern defensive banats (q.v.), and simultaneously also as the voievod of Transylvania (q.v.) (1441–46). During this period he built up a powerful private army that consisted of feudal levies and of Czech mercenaries. After the death of King/Emperor Albert (q.v.) in 1439, he supported the election of Vladislav (Úlászló) of Poland (q.v.) as king of Hungary, after which he became the king's close adviser. In 1442 Hunyadi won a series of victories against the advancing Turkish armies, while in 1443 he led a successful invasion into the Balkan (q.v.) territories of the Ottoman Empire (q.v.). These victories emboldened King Vladislav, who organized the Crusade of Varna (q.v.) in 1444, which, however, turned into a defeat. The king died at the battlefield and Hunyadi was barely able to escape with his life.

Upon returning to Hungary, after a brief captivity in the hands of Vlad II of Wallachia (q.v.), Hunyadi resumed his position in the leaderless country. In 1445 he became one of the country's seven "chief captains" and also a member of the National Council, while in 1446 he was elected regent (q.v.) of Hungary. Hunyadi led another crusade against the Turks in 1448 (which failed because of the treachery of George Brankovich of Serbia), but then he resumed the country's centralization and preparation for an inevitable showdown with the Turks (q.v.). To advance his anti-Turkish crusade, he made peace with Holy Roman Emperor Frederick III (r.1440–93) and agreed to accept Ladislas V Posthumous (q.v.) as Hungary's king. In 1453 he resigned as the country's regent and accepted appointment as Hungary's captain-general (1453–56). After the Ottoman Turkish conquest of Constantinople (q.v.) in the same year, Hunyadi resumed his military preparations. In 1454 he inflicted a major defeat on the Turks, and two years later he won his greatest victory by defeating Sultan Mehmet the Conqueror (July 21–22, 1456) at Belgrade (Nándorfehérvár)(q.v.). Hunyadi's victory was so complete that it resonated throughout the Christian World and delayed Hungary's conquest by seven decades. In commemoration of this victory, Pope Calixtus III (r.1455–58) ordered the tolling of the church bells at noon (Angelus) throughout Western Christendom, a tradition that survived for centuries. Hunyadi did not live long enough to enjoy the fruits of his victory. He died of the plague on August 11, 1456, and was buried at Gyulafehérvár (q.v.) in Transylvania.

HUSSITISM. A pre-Protestant religious reform movement inspired by and named after the Czech Catholic priest Jan Hus (c.1370-1415). It questioned the orientation of the contemporary church toward worldliness and demanded its return to the original teachings of Christianity. It was partially a religious and partially a social reform movement that subsequently also assumed certain anti-German tendencies. This anti-German tendency was the result of the dominance of the German element in the towns and cities of the Medieval Czech Kingdom (Bohemia) (q.v.), and in particular the Germans' preeminence at the University of Prague founded in 1348. The most important Czech centers of this movement were Prague (q.v.), Pilsen (Plžen), and Tábor. After Jan Hus's burning at the stake in 1415 at Constance, the movement split into two different branches. The moderate *Utraquists* or *Calixtins,* who demanded communion in two species, were opposed by the radical *Táborites,* who rejected most of the teachings of the Catholic Church and wanted to end all vestiges of feudalism. Emperor Sigismund (q.v.), also King of Hungary (q.v.), led a number of crusades against them, but the radical *Táborites* managed to survive into the 1430s. Only after concluding a compromise with the moderate *Utraquists* (Compacta of Prague) was Sigismund able to destroy their power in the Battle of Lipany in 1434.

Hussitism in a moderate form survived throughout the 15th and 16th centuries, and then gradually merged into Protestantism. Its influence was also felt in Hungary (q.v.), partially because of the spread of this movement into the country, and partially because of the repeated Hungarian efforts to crush this movement under Sigismund and Matthias Corvinus (q.v.). Many of the ex-Hussites fighters became mercenaries in King Matthias "Black Army" (q.v.), which then he used to conquer Moravia (q.v.), Silesia (q.v.), and Lower Austria (q.v.), including the city of Vienna (q.v.).

HUSZÁR, GÁL (d.1575). A Calvinist clergyman and a pioneer of Hungarian book printing. Huszár first appeared on the Hungarian cultural scene in 1553 in the west Hungarian town of Magyaróvár, having been driven there by the wrath of Primate-Archbishop

Miklós Oláh (q.v.) of Esztergom (q.v). Soon after his arrival, Huszár established a school in that city, but within five years he had to flee again. After spending some time in Vienna (q.v.), Kassa (q.v.), Debrecen (q.v.), Komárom (q.v.), Nagyszombat (q.v.), and Komját, he finally ended up at the Calvinist College of Pápa. Huszár spent his most fruitful years in the city of Debrecen, where he wrote and published a good number of Protestant theological works. Upon his departure from Debrecen, he left his printing press there, making that city into one of the important centers of book printing in 16th and 17th-century Hungary. Gál Huszár's most important works include: *About Jesus Christ's Holy Supper (Az Úr Isus Christusnac Szent Vachoraiarol)* (1558), *Divine Adorations and the Psalms (Isteni dicséretek és psalmusok)* (1560), and *Prayers and Praises of God appropriate for Christian Congregations (A keresztyén gyűlekezetbe való isteni dicséretek és imádságok)* (1574]. While Huszár himself was a dedicated Calvinist, the impact of his printing activities was universal. It aided the continued development of the Hungarian (Magyar) language (q.v.) as a tool of literary expression.

- I -

ILLÉSHÁZY, ISTVÁN (c.1541–1609). One of late-16th-century Hungary's most powerful lords, who in 1608 was elected the country's first Protestant palatine *(nádor)*(q.v.). Although coming from the ranks of the lower nobility, between the 1570s and 1603 Illésházy acquired one of the largest landholdings in northwestern Hungary. For three decades he served the Habsburgs (q.v.) faithfully in many important governmental posts, which they rewarded by land grants and by raising him in 1587 to the rank of a baron (q.v.). Yet, because of the dynasty's need for more financial resources to pursue their war against the Turks (q.v.), in 1603 the Habsburgs accused Illésházy of high treason with the intention of depriving him of his properties. As a result the hitherto pro-Habsburg lord joined Prince Bocskai's (q.v.) anti-Habsburg "War of Liberation." Yet, even while fighting them, Illésházy still favored a compromise with the Habsburg dynasty. Thus, after the compromise Peace of Vienna in 1606 (q.v.), he regained all his estates and in 1608 was elected Hungary's palatine. His election was pushed through by the Hungarian Diet (q.v.) in spite of Habsburg supported for the candidacy the noted historian Miklós Istvánffy (q.v.). Although not in Istvánffy's category as a historian, Illésházy was also an author of some note, writing in Latin in the style of the late humanists (q.v.).

ILLYÉS, GYULA (1902–83). Writer, poet, sociographer, translator, editor, and the most respected representative of the Populist (q.v.) current in Hungarian literature and politics. In the decades before his death he became the unofficial "sage of the nation," who was watched over and respected even by Hungary's (q.v.) communist regime (q.v.). Born on a feudal estate in Trans-Danubia (q.v.), in his younger days Illyés became attracted to radical social movements largely because of his firsthand knowledge of the misery of the Hungarian rural masses. But being unable to coordinate his Hungarian patriotism with the ideology of Marxism, he became an advocate of the so-called "Third Road" (q.v.) or "Third Alternative" that sought to find a midcourse between capitalism and socialism. His most influential work is the *People of the Puszta (Puszták népe)* (1936), in which he describes the world of the exploited Hungarian peasants. This book placed him immediately into the forefront of the Hungarian Populism. Although Illyés never became a communist, he approved of many of the social and political changes in post–World War II (q.v.) Hungary. Hoping to gain his approval, the regime courted him and showered him with rewards. At times, however, it also castigated him for his dissensions. Illyés's relationship with the Kádár Regime (q.v.) improved in proportion to its liberalization initiated in the 1960s, and its increased attention to national issues, including the problems of the Hungarian minorities (q.v.) in the surrounding states. During the last two decades of his life, Illyés's influence pervaded all aspects of Hungarian life.

IMPERIAL COURT see IMPERIAL GOVERNMENT.

IMPERIAL GOVERNMENT [IMPERIAL COURT]. Often referred to simply as "Vienna," the Imperial Government of the Habsburg Empire (Austrian Empire, Austria-Hungary) (q.v.) was headed by the emperor, who was also king of Hungary (q.v.). To a lesser or greater degree, this government controlled Royal Hungary (q.v.) in the 16th and 17th centuries, and then all of Historic Hungary (q.v.) from the 17th through the early 20th century, up to the end of the empire in 1918. Although there were governmental organs and institutions in Hungary throughout this period, they were generally subservient to, and depended upon, the Imperial Government in Vienna. This dependence was much less during the immediate post-Mohács (q.v.) period and during the age of Austro-Hungarian Dualism (1867–1918) (q.v.), when Hungary gained a position of partnership within the Austro-Hungarian Empire (q.v.).

IMRE see EMERIC.

IMRÉDY, BÉLA (1891-1946). A rightist politician, banking expert, and the prime minister of Hungary (1938-39) just before the outbreak of World War II (q.v.). After earning his law degree at the University of Budapest (q.v.), Imrédy went into banking and by 1928 he was the director of the Hungarian National Bank. Between 1932 and 1935 he served as Hungary's minister for financial affairs. Upon becoming the prime minister (May 14, 1938), he cooperated with Germany (q.v.) in the dismemberment of Czechoslovakia (q.v.), hoping to regain some of the Hungarian-inhabited regions of Slovakia (q.v.), that is, former Northern Hungary (q.v.), lost by the Treaty of Trianon (q.v.). Imrédy's prime ministership saw the passage and preparation of two Jewish Laws (q.v.) that limited the civil and political rights of Hungary's Jewish citizens. He also took Hungary into the Anti-Commintern Pact (January 13, 1939). Forced to resign (February 16, 1939) because of his own alleged Jewish background, Imrédy continued to pursue rightist politics. In 1940 he established the Party of Hungarian Renewal *(Magyar Megújulás Pártja)* and then allied himself with the Hungarian National Socialist Party. Following Hungary's German occupation (March 19, 1944), Imrédy was one of the German-supported candidates for the prime ministership, but he had to settle for the Ministry of Economic Affairs (May 23–August 7, 1944). Imrédy continued to support the German war effort to the very end. After the war he was tried and executed as a war criminal (February 28, 1946).

INDEPENDENCE FRONT [FÜGGETLENSÉGI FRONT] (1944–54). The commonly used name of the Hungarian National Independence Front (HNIF) *(Magyar Nemzeti Függetlenségi Front),* organized on December 3, 1944 by all of the anti-Fascist parties in Hungary, including the Citizens' Democratic Party, the Communist Party, the Peasant Party, the Smallholders' Party, and the Social Democratic Party. The Independence Front was formed to aid the rebuilding and the democratic transformation of Hungary (q.v.). Following the elections of 1945, however, it lost its usefulness to the communists, wherefore it was pushed into the background. In early 1949, the Independence Front was reorganized into a new

Hungarian National Independence Front, and then put to work to mobilize mass support for the communist takeover of power. In the fall of 1954, it was replaced by the Patriotic People's Front (q.v.).

INDEPENDENCE PARTY [FÜGGETLENSÉGI PÁRT] (1868/74–1918). The most significant opposition party in the Hungarian Parliament (q.v.) during the Age of Dualism (1867-1918) (q.v.). Its roots reach back to the revolution of 1848–49 (q.v.) and more specifically to the anti-Compromise faction of the Hungarian Parliament of 1865–68. It came into being in 1868 under the name of "Forty-Eighter Party" *(Negyvennyolcas Párt)*. In 1874, just before the birth of the dominant Liberal Party (q.v.), it assumed the name of "Independence Party."

INDEPENDENT SMALLHOLDERS' PARTY see SMALL-HOLDERS' PARTY.

INSTITUTE OF HISTORY [TÖRTÉNETTUDOMÁNYI IN-TÉZET] (1949). The Institute of History is one of several dozen research institutes of the Hungarian Academy of Sciences (q.v.). It was established in 1949, at the time of the Academy's reorganization, by integrating the earlier Teleki Institute (founded in 1941) into the Academy of Sciences. It is divided into several chronological and topical sections, each of which is headed by a prominent historian. The institute itself is under the leadership of a director and two assistant directors. During the half century of its existence, its membership consisted of fifty to sixty historians, whose primary function was to conduct research on a number of major common projects as well as on topics of interest to them personally. Many members of the institute also had (have) teaching positions at one of Hungary's universities. Former directors of the Institute of History include Eric Molnár (1949–66) (q.v.), Zsigmond Pál Pach (1967–85) (q.v.), György Ránki (1986–88) (q.v.), Ferenc Glatz (1988–96) (q.v.), while its recently appointed current director is Zoltán Szász (1996–). In the course of its first four decades, the Institute of History was Hungary's primary center of historical research. During the 1970s and 1980s, it was also in the forefront of the liberalization of historical research through a progressive introduction of Western standards and Western methodology. Much of these achievements were connected with the activities of György Ránki in his capacity of the assistant director (1962-76), executive director (1976–86), and director (1986–88) of the institute, and also the first holder of the Hungarian Chair (1979–88) at Indiana University in Bloomington, Indiana, United States.

INSTRUCTIONS. These were given to the elected parliamentary deputies by the nobility of each county (q.v.), which told them how to vote on specific issues. They were obligatory instructions, which made the functioning of the national diet (q.v.) very difficult and cumbersome, but which could not be violated. During the Hungarian Reform Period (q.v.), when the diet was the scene of an ongoing struggle between the reformers and the reactionaries, several reform-minded deputies resigned, rather than to follow the unacceptable instructions of their counties. This was the path taken by Ferenc Kölcsey (q.v.), one of the important reform leaders, in 1835, when he was unable to change the mind of his constituents. This archaic system of instructions survived until early 1848, when it was abolished, along with the Hungarian Feudal Diet (q.v.).

INTELLECTUAL EMIGRATION/IMMIGRATION. This term refers to one of the smallest, but intellectually most powerful, waves of Hungarian immigration to America, which took place during the late 1920s and 1930s, largely as the result of the spread of Nazism in Central Europe (q.v.). At that time, scores of internationally renowned scientists, artists, and literary men left Hungary (q.v.) and Central Europe and settled in the United States. Among them were such scientists as Theodore von Kármán (q.v.), Leo Szilárd (q.v.), Edward Teller (q.v.), and Eugene Wigner (q.v.), mathematicians such as John von Neumann (q.v.), George Pólya (1888-1985), and Gábor Szegő (1895-85), musicians such as Béla Bartók (q.v.), Antal Doráti (1906-88), Eugene Ormándy (q.v.), Fritz Reiner (1888-1963), George Széll (1897-1970), Sir George Solti (b.1912), social scientists such as Oscar Jászi (q.v.) and the Polányi brothers (q.v.), writers like Ferenc Molnár (q.v.), film stars like Béla Lugosi (q.v.), and many hundreds of others of similar caliber.

INTERNATIONAL ASSOCIATION OF HUNGARIAN STUDIES [NEMZETKÖZI MAGYAR FILOLÓGIAI TÁRSASÁG] (1977). Established in 1977, the International Association of Hungarian Studies (IAHS) is the top multidisciplinary international association for scholars involved in any aspect of Hungarian studies. Based in Budapest under the auspices of the Hungarian Academy of Sciences (q.v.), it has about a thousand members from about thirty-five countries. Its periodicals include the English-language *Hungarian Studies,* and the Hungarian-language *Hungarológiai Értesítő (Hungarological Proceedings).* The IAHS holds congresses every five years, its past congresses having met in Budapest (1981), Vienna (1986), Szeged (1991), and Rome (1996).

INTERWAR HUNGARY see INTERWAR PERIOD.

INTERWAR PERIOD [INTERWAR YEARS] (1918/20-44/45). Broadly speaking, this is the period between the the end of World War I (q.v.) and the end of World War II (q.v.). In a more limited sense it refers to the regency of Admiral Miklós Horthy (q.v.) that stretched from March 1, 1920, to October 15, 1944. The interwar period was characterized by the ideology of conservative nationalism and a powerful revisionism (q.v.) that tried to restore Hungary's (q.v.) historic frontiers, mutilated after World War I and then sanctioned by the Treaty of Trianon in 1920 (q.v.). The first year and a half of this period was taken up by various liberal-socialist-communist revolutions and a counterrevolution (October 31, 1918-March 1, 1920), while last few months (October 15, 1944–April 4, 1945) were marked by the violent reign of the Arrow Cross Party (q.v.) and Hungary's physical destruction by a series of desperate battles between the Germans and the Soviets.

IPOLYI, ARNOLD (1823–86). Cultural historian, folklorist, and Catholic bishop of Nagyvárad (q.v.), Ipolyi is best known as the pioneer of Hungarian mythological studies. Although he performed his priestly functions, he was always more interested in historical research than in theology and religious liturgy. He was continuously active in various scholarly societies, including the Hungarian Historical Association (q.v.) and the Kisfaludy Literary Society. The National Archeological and Cultural Society named its highest prize after him. Ipolyi's most important works include *The History of Monumental Medieval Art in Hungary (A középkori emlékszerű művészet története Magyarországon)* (1863), *The Remnants of Medieval Plastic Art in Hungary (A középkori szobrászat emlékei Magyarországon)*(1863), *A Survey of the Cultural History of the City of Besztercebánya (Besztercebánya városa műveltségtörténeti vázlata)* (1874), and his very influential *Hungarian Mythology (Magyar mythológia)* (1854), which made his name known throughout the Hungarian scholarly world.

IRON CURTAIN (1946–89). The barbed wire-enforced line that for forty-three years had divided the Western World from the Soviet Bloc (q.v.) and consigned such East Central European (q.v.) countries as Poland (q.v.), Czechoslovakia (q.v.), and Hungary (q.v.), as well as the Balkans (q.v.), to the Communist World. The Iron Curtain was the product of the Cold War that arose after World War II (q.v.) between the Soviet Union (q.v.) and the United States. Its existence was first recognized by Winston Churchill, who mentioned it in his speech at Westminster College (Fulton, Missouri) on March 5, 1946. This Iron Curtain was first breached by the Hungarians on August 20, 1989, when, in conjunction with a "Pan European Picnic" cosponsored by Archduke Otto von Habsburg (q.v.) and the reform communist politician Imre Pozsgay (q.v.), they permitted thousands of East German tourists to cross the Austro-Hungarian border in the vicinity of Sopron (q.v.). This was the first step in the collapse of communism (q.v.), which ended in the complete dismantlement of the Iron Curtain.

IRREDENTISM see **HUNGARIAN REVISIONIST MOVEMENT.**

ISABELLA [IZABELLA] (1519–59). The daughter of King Sigismund I (r.1506–48) of Poland and wife of King John Zápolya (q.v.), one of Hungary's two rival monarchs in the period after the Battle of Mohács (1526) (q.v.). Following King John's death in 1540, Isabella became one of the guardians and coadjutors of her minor son, John Sigismund (q.v.). Following Sultan Süleyman's (q.v.) conquest of Buda (q.v.) in 1541, she transferred her court to Gyulafehérvár (q.v.) in Transylvania (q.v.). In 1551, György Martinuzzi (q.v.), the other guardian and de-facto administrator of the eastern half of the Kingdom of Hungary (q.v.), forced Isabella to resign and to transfer all powers to the rival king, Ferdinand of Habsburg (q.v.). He did this in the hope that the latter would be able to reestablish the unity of Hungary. Although Isabella left for Poland (q.v.), Martinuzzi's dream of the reunified Hungary was not realized. In 1556, Isabella was recalled by a powerful group of Hungarian nobles (q.v.), who were dissatisfied with Ferdinand's rule and feared Turkish retributions. She remained coadjutor of the "Eastern Kingdom" until her death in 1559, when John Sigismund took over personally.

ISLAMIC CIVILIZATION. The civilization based on the religion of Islam founded in the early 7th century by Prophet Mohammed (d.632) and centered through most of the Middle Ages on the city of Baghdad. In the mid–13th century, its spiritual leader, the Caliph (q.v.), moved to Cairo, and then in 1518 to Istanbul (q.v.). Islamic Civilization influenced the Hungarians (q.v.) both before and after their conquest of the Carpathian Basin (q.v.)—largely through their frequent contacts and interaction with various peoples of the Islamic faith. It also impacted upon them during the Ottoman conquest (q.v.) of Hungary (q.v.) in the 16th and 17th centuries.

ISMAELITES [IZMAELITÁK]. As used in medieval Hungary, this term referred to all peoples of the Islamic faith—be they Arabs,

Khazars (q.v.), Pechenegs (q.v.), Cumans (q.v), Volga Bulgars
(q.v.), or any other ethnic group. Many of the Ismaelites were
individual immigrants, who accepted service in the Hungarian Royal
administration. From their ranks came most of the tax collectors,
toll collectors, customs officers, and administrators of the Royal salt
mines. Starting with the 12th century, some of the Ismaelites came
to be known as *szerecsen (Saracen),* while in the 13th century they
were also called *böszörmény (Musulman, Muslim).*

ISPÁN see COMES NO. 1.

ISRAELITES [IZRAELITÁK] see JEWS IN HUNGARY.

ISTANBUL see CONSTANTINOPLE.

ISTVÁN see STEPHEN.

ISTVÁNFFY, MIKLÓS [NICOLAUS] (1538–1615). One of
Hungary's great humanist (q.v.) historians and statesmen, who is
generally known as the "Hungarian Livy." After serving as the
secretary of Hungary's primate, Miklós Oláh (q.v.), Istvánffy
transferred to the Imperial Court of Rudolph II (q.v.) in Prague
(q.v.), where he reached the rank of a vice palatine. In 1608 Istvánffy
was the Habsburg Imperial Court's candidate for the post of
Hungary's palatine *(nádor)*(q.v.), but he lost the election to István
Illésházy (q.v.), largely because of his known pro-Habsburg leanings
at the time when an important segment of the Hungarian nobility
(q.v.) had its disagreements with the Habsburg dynasty (q.v.). This
loss virtually incapacitated him psychologically for the rest of his
life. Istvánffy's most important scholarly work is his *History of
Hungarian Events in 34 Books [Historiarum de rebus Ungaricis libri
XXXIV],* written in classical Latin and first published posthumously
in 1622. This work covers the period between 1490 and 1606, using
the style and approach of the Roman historian Livy (Titus Livius)
(59 B.C.–17 A.D.). Its appearance placed Istvánffy immediately into
the forefront of Hungary's authors of the late humanist period.

ITALY. A country of sixty million people on a territory of 116,600 square miles, which occupies what used to be the heartland of the Roman Empire. As a unified country, Italy is new, having come into being only in 1861. Prior to that, for well over a millennium, it was only a "geographical expression," its territory being the homeland to about a dozen or so rival states. But these individual states have played a significant role in the history of Europe, as well as in the development of Hungary (q.v.). Of these Italian states the three that had the greatest impact on Hungary were the Papal States, the Republic of Venice, and the Kingdom of Naples. From Rome came Hungary's Christian Civilization at the turn of the first to the second millennium, when Pope Sylvester II (r.999-1003) sent what became the Holy Crown of Hungary (q.v.) to the future King St. Stephen (q.v.). A few centuries later, from Northern Italy came the culture of the Renaissance and Humanism. The best Hungarian humanist scholars all studies at such Italian universities as those of Padua and Bologna—the latter of which had been the home of a special Hungarian college *(natio)* ever since 1265. During the late Middle Ages, the Republic of Venice was one of Hungary's source of Western culture, learning, and religion. Yet, at the same time it was an ongoing rival for the control of Dalmatia (q.v.) and such important Dalmatian cities as Zara (q.v.), Spalato, and Ragusa (q.v.). In the 14th century, Naples was both the home base and the object of conquest of the Hungarian Anjou dynasty (q.v.).

In the 19th century, Italy was an important source of inspiration for Hungarian nationalism. Many of Hungary's defeated "forty-eighters" (q.v.) ended up in Italy, and a good number of them also cooperated with Cavour (1810-61) and Garibaldi (1807-82) in the two Italian leaders' efforts to unify Italy, while at the same time undercutting the hated Austrian Empire (q.v.). In the interwar period (q.v.) Italy was again an important source of influence and support for Hungary, largely because of all the great powers, only Mussolini's Italy was willing to supported Hungary's demand for a revision of its ethnically unjust frontiers that had been imposed upon the defeated nation at the Treaty of Trianon in 1920 (q.v.).

- J -

JACOBINS, JACOBIN CONSPIRACY see **HUNGARIAN JACOBINS.**

JAGELLONIAN DYNASTY. A dynasty of Lithuanian origins that ruled Poland-Lithuania (q.v.) (1386–1572), Hungary (q.v.) (1440–44, 1490–1526), and Bohemia (q.v.) (1471–1526) for nearly three centuries. It had derived its name from Jagello or Jogailla (c.1350–1434), the grand duke of Lithuania (r.1377–92), who through his marriage to Jadwiga (Hedvig) (q.v.), the daughter of King Louis the Great (q.v.) of Hungary (q.v.) and the heir to the Polish throne, also became the king of Poland (1386–1434). His son Władysław VI (Vladislav I, Úlászló I) (q.v.) was the first Jagellonian on the Hungarian throne (r.1440–44), who died at the Battle of Varna (1444). The Jagellonians returned to the Hungarian throne in 1490 in the person of Vladislav II (Úlászló II) (q.v.) and Louis II (q.v.), the latter of whom perished at the Battle of Mohács in 1526 (q.v.). In the period between 1490 and 1526, the Jagellonians controlled much of East Central Europe (q.v.), including the Polish-Lithuanian Commonwealth (q.v.), the Czech Kingdom (q.v.), and the Kingdom of Hungary, along with its vassal states in the Balkans (q.v.). This so-called "Jagellonian System"—rivaled by the emerging Habsburg Empire (q.v.)—is viewed by Polish historians as the climax of Polish power. The Hungarians, on the other hand, regard the last two Jagellonians as ineffective rulers, whose vacilating domestic and foreign policies prepared the ground for Hungary's demise.

JAKÓ, ZSIGMOND (b.1916). The "grand old man" of Hungarian Transylvanian historical studies, Jakó started out as an exponent of the Hungarian Ethnohistory School (see Hungarian Historical Studies) initiated by Elemér Mályusz (q.v.). Following Northern Transylvania's (q.v.) reannexation by Romania (q.v.) in 1945, he became the master of Transylvanian-Hungarian social, economic, and cultural history. Having studied at the Universities of Budapest, Vienna (q.v.), and Innsbruck, in 1941 Jakó became an archivist at the Transylvanian National Museum (1941-50), and taught at the Hungarian (1942-59), and then at the joint Romanian-Hungarian (1959-81) University of Kolozsvár (Cluj) (q.v.). Jakó's best known works are *Bihar County before the Turkish Conquest (Bihar megye a török pusztítás előtt)* (1940), *Peasant Obligation Lists of the Castle Estates of Gyula (A gyulai vártartomány urbáriumai)* (1944), *Transylvanian Phoenix: The Heritage of Miklós Misztófalusi-Kis (Erdélyi féniks. Misztótfalusi Kis Miklós öröksége)* (1970),*Writing, Book, Intelligentsia (Írás, könyv, értelmiség)* (1976), *Students of the College of Nagyenyed, 1662-1848 (Nagy-enyedi diákok, 1662-1848)* (1979), *History of the Latin Script (A latin írás története)* (1987), *Minutes of the Convent of Kolozsmonostor, 1289-1556) (A kolozsmonostori konvent jegyzőkönyvei, 1289-1556)*, 2 vols. (1990). Jakó was also the founding editor of the annual *Studies in Cultural History (Művelődestörténeti tanulmányok)* (1979–), which brought many of Romania's best Hungarian historians together.

JANISSARIES [JANICSÁROK, YENIÇERILER]. The elite infantry of the Ottoman Empire (q.v.) in the period between the mid–14th and the early 19th century. Initially, the ranks of the Janissaries came from captured Christian children, but then, starting with the 15th century, from the special levy or tax on children *(devshirme).* Those conscripted were divided into two groups based on their abilities. The most capable went into the Palace School of Istanbul (q.v.), where they were converted to Islam and were trained to be the administrative and military leaders of the empire. The rest were farmed out to Turkish families in Anatolia (q.v.), where they learned Turkish and were converted to Islam. At the age of eighteen they were collected and taken to military camps for training. Thereafter they were assigned to Janissary units throughout the empire. They became dedicated fighters for Islam. Theoretically they could rise to the very top of Ottoman leadership. Starting with the early 17th century, the Janissaries gained the right to marry and to establish families. Thereafter they became a hereditary group of military nobility, whose fighting effectiveness declined, but who became a drain on the empire's resources and also hindered its modernization. Their increasingly negative role ended in 1826, when they were exterminated through a concerted effort of Sultan Mahmud II (r.1808–39). The Janissaries had played a significant role in the conquest and rule of Hungary (q.v.) in the 16th and 17th centuries. Relatively few Hungarians became Janissaries, because by the time of the Turkish conquest (q.v.), the system of *devshirme* ceased to expand to newly conquered territories. But the pashas of Buda (q.v.) and many other regional commanders usually came from their ranks.

JANUS PANNONIUS [JÁNOS CSEZMICSEI] (1434–72). A great humanist poet and the bishop of Pécs (q.v.). Educated in Italy (q.v.) with the support of his influential uncle Johannes Vitéz (q.v.), Janus became one of the close collaborators and advisers to King Matthias Corvinus (q.v.). But disagreeing with Matthias's Western conquests, he turned against the king. After the failure of the conspiracy, he fled to and died in Croatia (q.v.). Janus Pannonius was the first prominent representative of Hungarian profane literature, who left a major impact upon the development of Hungarian literary culture in general. In 1985 the restructured and expanded University of Pécs (q.v.) was named in his honor.

JÁNY, GUSZTÁV (1883-1947). The commander-in-chief of the Second Hungarian Army that perished on the Soviet front in the winter of 1942-43. Jány graduated from the Austrian Imperial Military Academy at Wiener-Neustadt in 1905, after which he served in the Hungarian *Honvéd* Army (q.v.) and was eventually promoted to the rank of a colonel-general. In the period between 1932 and 1936 he was the director of the Ludovika Military Academy in Budapest (q.v.), after which he commanded the Hungarian army units stationed at Szombathely (1937-38) and Budapest (1940-42). Following the destruction of the Second Hungarian Army in the vicinity of Stalingrad, Jány voluntarily retired from the army. At the end of 1944 he fled to Germany (q.v.), but then returned in 1946, only to be convicted and executed as a war criminal (1947).

JÁSZI, OSCAR [OSZKÁR] (1875–1957). A social scientist, publicist, politician, and one of the best-known exponents of parliamentary liberalism and progressive sociological studies in early-20th-century Hungary (q.v.). Jászi was the founder and leading spirit of Hungary's first and most influential liberal sociological periodical, the *Twentieth Century (Huszadik Század)* (1900-19), which he also edited for most of its two decades (1906-19). He likewise had a role in the foundation of the Hungarian Sociological Association *(TársadalomtudományiTársaság)*(1901), as well as in two of its affiliates, the Free College of Sociology *[Társadalomtudományok Szabadiskolája]*(1905–17, 1918–19) and the Galilei Circle *(Galilei Kör)* (1908–18)—the latter of which was geared to the university students. In 1914 Jászi became the founding president of the National Bourgeois Radical Party *(Országos Polgári Radikális Párt)*(1914–19), and after the collapse of Austria-Hungary (q.v.), a member of the Hungarian National Council, as well as the minister of minority affairs (October 31, 1918–January 19, 1919).

Being unable to cooperate with Béla Kun's (q.v.) Hungarian Soviet Republic (q.v.), Jászi left Hungary in May 1919. Until 1925 he lived in Vienna (q.v.), where he became one of the leaders of the Hungarian Political Emigration and the Editor of the Viennese *Hungarian News (Bécsi Magyar Újság)* (1921-25). In 1925 he emigrated to the United States, where he was appointed professor of sociology at Oberlin College in Ohio (1925-57). Following his immigration, Jászi withdrew from active politics, although he corresponded with many Hungarian political emigrés throughout the world. Moreover, during World War II (q.v.), he was one of the leading members of the American Federation of Democratic Hungarians *(Demokratikus Magyarok Amerikai Szövetsége)* (1941-45). In 1947 Jászi visited Hungary briefly, but he was unable to come to terms with the then emerging communist regime (q.v.) He died in 1957 in Oberlin and his remains were returned to his homeland in 1991. Oscar Jászi was the most prominent Hungarian exponents of bourgeois radicalism and liberal socialism, as well as the most sophisticated prophet for the need of nationality peace in multiethnic East Central Europe (q.v.). Although Jászi had authored over a dozen major books on various sociological, aesthetic, and political topics, in the West he is best known for his *The Dissolution of the Habsburg Monarchy* (1929), which he wrote and published in the United States. His most important earlier political works include: *The Nationality Question and Hungary's Future (A nemzetiségi kérdés és Magyarország jövője)* (1911), *The Evolution of National States and the Nationality Question [A nemzeti államok kialakulása és a nemzetiségi kérdés)* (1912), *The Monarchy's Future (A monarchia jövője)* (1918), *Hungary's Future and the Danubian United States (Magyarország jövője és a Dunai Egyesült Államok)* (1918), and *Hungarian Calvary - Hungarian Resurrection (Magyar kálvária - magyar feltámadás)* (1920).

JAZYGES [JÁSZ, JÁSZOK]. A nomadic ethnic group of Alanic origin that settled in Hungary (q.v.) in the course of the 13th and 14th centuries. They were, and remained, in close association with the Cumans (q.v.) and settled on the Great Hungarian Plain (q.v.) in close proximity to the latter in an area known as *kunság és jászság* (Cumania and Jazygia). It is located between the Danube (q.v.) and the Tisza (q.v.) Rivers, roughly to the east of Budapest (q.v.). The Jazyges were allegedly close relatives of the Ossets of the Caucasian region, who were an Alanic people. In spite of all the attempts to enserf them, the Jazyges—like the Cumans—were able to retain some of their regional autonomy up to 1876, when all of the autonomous territories were merged into the regular Hungarian county system (q,v.). The capital of the Jazyg Autonomous Territory was Jászberény, the site of the famous Horn of Lehel (q.v.).

JELKY, ANDRÁS (1730-83). A noted Hungarian traveler and soldier of fortune, who started out as a simple tailor, but ended up as a wealthy and respected citizen of Buda (q.v.). Jelky left Hungary in 1754, was captured in Holland and shipped off to the Dutch colonies in East India. He survived several shipwrecks, was sold into slavery, and lived in the jungles of Java and Ceylon (Sri Lanka). In 1761 he went into business in Jakarta, made his fortune, and then joined the Dutch colonial government. In 1770 he was sent off as an envoy to Japan. He returned to Hungary in 1778, where died four years later. Jelky wrote the story of his life and adventures in German under the title *The Lifestory of Mr. A. Jelky, a born Hungarian (Geschichte des Herrn A. Jelky, eines geborenen Ungarn)* (1779).

JELLACHICH, COUNT JOSIP [JELAČIĆ, JELLASICS, JELLASCHICH] (1801–59). A Habsburg Imperial general, ban of Croatia (1848–59), and one of the most ardent opponents of the Hungarian Revolution of 1848-49 (q.v.). Being an exponent of early Croatian nationalism, known as Illyrianism, Jellachich was selected by the Viennese *Kamarilla* (q.v.) to implement its anti-Hungarian and antirevolutionary plans. In March 1848 he was named ban of Croatia, without consulting the Hungarian Diet (q.v.). In that capacity he led Croatian and Serbian Frontier Guard armies against the Hungarians, but was repeatedly defeated. He did not participate in the final phase of the Hungarian Revolutionary War, but returned to Zagreb (q.v.) to govern Croatia (q.v.) as its ban and its military administrator. In 1854, Jellachich was raised to the rank of a count (he had been a baron earlier), in gratitude for his contributions to the preservation of the Austrian Empire (q.v.).

JESUITS [JESUIT ORDER, SOCIETAS JESU, S.J.]. A Catholic religious order founded in 1534 by St. Ignatius of Loyola (1491-1556) specifically for the purposes of fighting the Protestant Reformation (q.v.). The Jesuits are organized like a military order under the control of a general, who resides in Rome and has often been referred to as the "Black Pope." (The reason is that, as opposed to the Pope, who is always in white, the Jesuit General, is always in black.) In the 16th and 17th centuries the Jesuits became the chief exponents of the Counter-Reformation (q.v.) and gained control of many institutions of higher learning. By the 18th century they became so powerful politically that in 1773 the Pope was forced to disband the order. Reestablished in 1814, they concentrated their efforts on higher education. The Jesuits settled in Hungary in 1561, where they successfully re-Catholicized much of the country. Their most prominent leader during the Counter-Reformation was Cardinal Péter Pázmány (q.v.), the archbishop of Esztergom and Hungary's primate, who founded the Jesuit University of Nagyszombat (Tyrnau) (q.v.), which later was transferred to the capital and became the still functioning University of Budapest (q.v.). The Hungarian Jesuits had a major influence upon Hungarian Baroque (q.v.) culture and learning, including linguistics (János Sajnovics), historical studies (Gábor Hevenesi, István Katona, György Pray), and astronomy (Miksa Hell). The Hungarian Jesuit Order was disbanded between 1773 and 1853, as well as between 1949 and 1989.

JESZENSZKY, GÉZA (b. 1941). Hungary's foreign minister in the first post-communist Hungarian government (1990-94). A historian by training, in 1976 Jeszenszky joined the teaching staff of the Karl Marx University of Economics (q.v.) in Budapest (q.v.), and later spent two years (1984-86) as a visiting Fulbright Professor at the University of California at Santa Barbara. While retaining his university post, in 1987 he became a founding member of the Hungarian Democratic Forum (HDF) (q.v.), which in 1989 transformed itself into the political party that came to dominate Hungary's first post-communist government. While continuing to teach at the renamed University of Economics, since 1994 Jeszenszky also serves as his party's deputy in the Hungarian Parliament (q.v.). When the HDF split in the spring of 1996, Jeszenszky went with the more liberal minority that established the Hungarian Democratic People's Party (q.v.). Jeszenszky's most important historical work is *The Lost Prestige (Az elveszett presztizs)* (1986), which analyzes the reasons for the decline of Hungary's image in the period prior to World War I (q.v.).

JEWISH EMANCIPATION. The first attempt at Jewish emancipation was made in 1849, when on July 28 of that year the Hungarian Parliament (q.v.) extended full citizenship rights to all of the Hungarian Jews (q.v.). This law, however, came to nothing because of the defeat of the Hungarian Revolution of 1848–49 (q.v.). The Jews were finally given full Hungarian citizenship rights by the Law of Jewish Emancipation (Act 1867:VII), which followed the Austro-Hungarian Compromise of 1867 (q.v.). After 1867, the Jews of Hungary were officially classified as "Hungarians of the Jewish faith" and only practicing Jews were considered Jews until the Nazi-inspired Jewish Laws (q.v.) of 1938-41.

JEWISH LAWS. These were the anti-Semitic legislations passed in interwar Hungary (q.v.). The first of them is know as the "numerus clausus law" of 1920, which empowered the Ministry of Education to set nationality and ethnic quotas for entrance into Hungarian universities and law academies. This quota system was directed primarily against the Jews (q.v.), partially because of their overwhelming presence in the professions, and partially as a reaction to their leadership position in the Bolshevik-inspired Hungarian Soviet Republic (q.v.). As a result of this law, a significant number of Hungarian students (Jewish and non-Jewish) found it necessary to study at Austrian, German, and Swiss universities. Much more significant were the three anti-Semitic laws passed between 1938 and 1941 in response to the growth of the Fascist ideology and increasing pressures from Nazi Germany (q.v.). The "First Jewish Law" (May 29, 1938) proclaimed that no more than 20 percent of the membership of the journalistic, legal, medical, and engineering professions can be of the Jewish faith. (This law still defined a Jew as a person of the Jewish faith.) Their numbers were similarly limited in business, commerce, and finance. The "Second Jewish Law" (May 2, 1939) reduced this quota to 6 percent (their actual ratio in Hungary's total population), and added the theater and film industry, and the state monopolies to the categories to which the law applied. At the same time this "Second Jewish Law" forbade Jews to be in leadership positions in the professional associations, and in industrial and commercial establishments. (This law defined a Jew as one having one Jewish parent or two Jewish grandparents, irrespective of their religion.) The "Third Jewish Law" (August 8, 1941) forbade marriage or sexual contact between Jews and non-

Jews. (This law defined a Jew as one of the Jewish faith, or one who had at least two grandparents born into the Jewish faith.) These anti-Semitic laws were passed under the influence of the growing anti-Semitic propaganda emanating from Nazi Germany and from the various local Fascist groups. Some lawmakers went along with this trend simply to prevent Hungary's military occupation by Germany.

JEWS IN HUNGARY. Jews have lived in Hungary (q.v.) even before the series of Hungarian conquests (q.v.) of the Carpathian Basin (q.v.) between the 7th and the 9th centuries. A number of them also came with Prince Árpád's (q.v.) Conquering Magyars (q.v.) in the late 9th century, many of whom may have been descendants of the Khazars (q.v.) who had been converted to Judaism a few decades earlier. The number of Jews in Hungary was relatively small until the 13th century when, in wake of the devastations caused by the Mongol conquest (q.v.), King Béla IV (q.v.) encouraged their immigration from the south German territories. He permitted them to settle in such towns as Sopron (q.v.), Vasvár, Esztergom (q.v.), Óbuda (q.v.), and the Castle Hill of Buda (q.v.). He also assured them of their privileges in the Edict of 1251. The 14th century saw the further influx of Jews from Austria (q.v.), Styria, Bohemia (q.v.), and Moravia (q.v.), most of whom settled in such western border towns as Kismarton, Pozsony (q.v.), Sopron, and Kőszeg. Others moved further inward into Győr, Tata, Szakolca, Vrebó, and Galgóc. Following the Battle of Mohács (q.v.) in the early 16th century, many of these Jews moved back to German and Czech territories. Their places, especially in Turkish Hungary (q.v.), were taken by Sephardic Jews, who had been expelled from Spain by Ferdinand and Isabella in the late 15th century, and who then worked their way through the Ottoman Empire (q.v.) and the Balkans (q.v.) into Hungary. They settled in Buda, Székesfehérvár (q.v.), and in many smaller towns along the Danube (q.v.) and the Tisza (q.v.) rivers. Most of these Sephardic Jews disappeared during and after the Liberation Wars (q.v.) in the late 17th century.

The next wave of Jewish immigration took place in the 18th century, when many of Hungary's landed aristocrats (e.g., the

Batthyány, Esterházy, Pálffy, and Zichy families) established Jewish settlements on their estates. The majority of these new settlers came from Moravia (q.v.). Almost at the same time, Northern Hungary also witnessed the immigration of the first Jews from Poland (q.v.) just before that country's partitions. In 1735-38 there were officially 11,621 Jews in the Kingdom of Hungary. During the last third of the 18th century their number increased rapidly, and by 1785 it reached 75,000. This was primarily the result of the mass immigration of Yiddish-speaking Orthodox Jews from Galicia (q.v.), which had been attached to the Habsburg Empire (q.v.) in the First Polish Partition of 1772. In the 19th century this increase was even more rapid. In 1869 the number of Hungary's Jewish citizens was 553,641, in 1910 it reached 938,458, and by 1918—the year that signaled the end of Historic Hungary (q.v.)—it was around one million in a population of slightly over 19 million for Hungary proper, or 21 million for Greater Hungary, including Croatia-Slavonia (i.e. around 5 percent). Following Historic Hungary's dismemberment in 1920, there remained 473,000 Jews in a population of eight million. As a result of the territorial revisions in 1938–41, by the end of 1941, Hungary's Jews had almost doubled to 911,000 out of a population of 14,669,000. Perhaps more than half of these Jewish citizens of Hungary (up to 500,000) perished in the Holocaust (q.v.) after Hungary's German occupation (q.v.).

The Jews were given full citizenship rights by the Law of Jewish Emancipation (q.v.) in 1867, after which they rapidly assimilated into the Hungarian nation. This sweeping emancipation initiated a rapid process of assimilation, as a result of which, by the turn of the century, the majority of the Jews living in urban areas had become assimilated Hungarians. By the time of World War I (q.v.), the assimilated Hungarian Jews constituted a very significant portion of the Hungarian intelligentsia, being represented far above their numbers in literature, journalism, law, medicine, business, and the sciences. Many of them also became exponents of Hungarian nationalism, notwithstanding the presence of some anti-Semitic manifestations that accompanied the integration of the Jews into Hungarian national life. This mutually beneficial relationship was shaken by the post–World War I revolutions (q.v.) and the counter-revolutions largely because of the belief that the Jews were somehow connected with Marxism and the communist revolutionary movement. This resulted in the rebirth of a more intense anti-Semitism, which, however, was still tolerable throughout the interwar period (q.v.). It became increasingly less tolerable in the late 1930s and early 1940s, when the growth of Nazi influences made life progressively more difficult for those who were classified as Jews. The years 1938-41 also witnessed the promulgation of three anti-Semitic "Jewish Laws" (q.v.), which deprived the Jews of their full Hungarian citizenship rights, but at the same time saved them from extermination as was the case in the surrounding states. The situation changed after Hungary's German occupation (q.v.) on March 19, 1944, which resulted in the Jews being collected and deported to various German death camps. This Hungarian Jewish Holocaust (q.v.) destroyed the majority of the Hungarian Jews. Many of those who survived (most of them in Budapest) remained in Hungary, but a significant number of them emigrated to Palestine or, after 1948, to the state of Israel. Today there are close of a 100,000 Hungarians who claim to be Jewish, although few of them practice their religion. A significant number of Hungarian Jews live in Israel, and a lesser number in North America.

JOHN I see JOHN ZÁPOLYA.

JOHN II see JOHN SIGISMUND.

JOHN SIGISMUND [JÁNOS ZSIGMOND, JOHN II] (1540-71). King of Hungary (r.1540–51, 1556–70) and the first prince of Transylvania (r.1556-71), was the son of John Zápolya (John I) (q.v.) and Isabella (q.v.), the daughter of king Sigismund I (r.1506-48) of Poland (q.v.). He was elected king of Hungary's eastern half soon after his birth, and just before the death of his father. The actual power, however, was in the hands of György Martinuzzi (q.v.) until 1551, and then Queen Izabella until 1559. Between 1551 and 1556 John Sigismund gave up the throne to his rival, King

Ferdinand I (q.v.) of the Habsburg dynasty (q.v.), and moved to Poland. But when Ferdinand proved unable to defend Hungary (q.v.) against the Turks (q.v.), he returned to Hungary. John Sigismund's election as prince of Transylvania in 1556 finalized Hungary's trisection into Royal Hungary (q.v.), Turkish Hungary (q.v.), and Transylvania (q.v.) for the next century and a half. He relinquished his Hungarian royal title to his rival, Maximilian (q.v.), in the Agreement of Speyer (q.v.) in 1570. During his de facto reign in Transylvania (1559-71), John Sigismund changed religion three times. He left Catholicism (q.v.) for Lutheranism (q.v.), then Lutheranism for Calvinism (q.v.), and finally Calvinism for Unitarianism (q.v.), and thereby established the system of four "accepted" religions in Transylvania.

JOHN ZÁPOLYA [JÁNOS SZAPOLYAI, JOHN I] (1487–1540). King of Hungary (r.1526-40), and the rival of King Ferdinand I (q.v.) of Habsburg (q.v.) in the period of disunity following the Battle of Mohács (q.v.). Ever since 1505, during the rule of the weak Jagellonian kings (q.v.), John Zápolya had been the so-called National Party's candidate for the Hungarian throne. Although unable to become Hungary's (q.v.) palatine *(nádor)* (q.v.) like his father, in 1511 he was appointed voievod of Transylvania (q.v.) and thus became one of the country's most powerful leaders. He was late in arriving with his armies to the Battle of Mohács (q.v.) in 1526. This saved him from defeat and perhaps death—as was the fate of King Louis II (q.v.). In November of that year a group of Hungarian nobles (q.v.) elected him the king of Hungary, while in December another group of nobles elected his rival, Ferdinand, the archduke of Austria (q.v.). This dual election threw Hungary into a turmoil, from which it never recovered. After two years of civil war, King John was forced to flee to Poland (q.v.). He returned in 1529 to resume his struggle against his rival, this time with the help of the Turks (q.v.), at the expense of becoming the vassal of Sultan Süleyman (q.v.) (q.v.). This struggle inflicted a heavy damage upon Hungary, which by 1538 compelled both of the kings to sign the Treaty of Várad (Nagyvárad) (q.v.) that stipulated that King John's death would be followed by the country's reunification under King Ferdinand. But John's marriage to Isabella (q.v.), the daughter of King Sigismund (r.1506–48) of Poland in 1539, and the subsequent birth of his son, John Sigismund (q.v.), made him renounce the terms of this treaty. He left his throne to his son under the regency of his wife, which threw Hungary into another civil war and ultimately led to the country's trisection. King John Zápolya was a weak and vacillating ruler, who pursued a selfish policy, which placed his family's interests before those of his country. His refusal to reunite the country under Ferdinand's leadership sealed Hungary's fate and left a permanent scar upon the nation.

JÓKAI, MÓR [MAURUS] (1825–1904). Hungary's most popular novelist and writer of romantic fiction, who had grown into a kind of "national institution" already in his lifetime. A friend of the great national lyricist Sándor Petőfi (q.v.), Jókai was also a member of the group of young intellectuals known as the March Youth *(márciusi ifjak)* (q.v.), who, on March 15, 1848, were responsible for starting the Hungarian Revolution of 1848–49 in the city of Pest (today part of Budapest) (q.v.). Later in life Jókai became a supporter of the Austro-Hungarian Compromise of 1867 (q.v.), as well as of the constitutional rule by Emperor Francis Joseph (q.v.). He wrote many scores of romanticized historical novels, primarily on the Age of the Ottoman Turkish Conquest of Hungary (q.v.) and on the revolution of 1848-49 and its impact. Many of his works had been translated into dozens of languages, including English. While they are out of vogue today in the English-speaking world, in Hungary Jókai is still the most widely read novelist.

JOSEPH I (1678–1711). Holy Roman Emperor (r.1705-11) and king of Hungary (r.1687/1705-11) and Bohemia (1705-11), he was the son of Holy Roman Emperor and King Leopold I (q.v.). His reign coincided with the War of Spanish Succession (1701-14) and with the Rákóczi War of Liberation (1703-11) (q.v.). Joseph's Imperial Armies, under the command of Eugene of Savoy (q.v.), scored major victories against the French and their allies, but his early death in

1711, which elevated his brother Charles VI (King Charles III) (q.v.) to the Habsburg (q.v.) throne, altered the alliances and assured the Spanish throne to the French Bourbons. Joseph I died a few weeks before the Peace of Szatmár (q.v.), which ended the Rákóczi War, but he lived long enough to see the end of the uprising in Hungary. Joseph I was an intelligent and reasonable monarch, who could have become a great ruler had he survived longer on the Habsburg throne.

JOSEPH II (1741–90). Holy Roman Emperor (r.1765–90) and king of Hungary (r.1780–90) and Bohemia (r.1780–90), he was the son of Queen Maria Theresa (q.v.) and Holy Roman Emperor Francis I of Lorraine (q.v.). Dedicated to a policy of socioeconomic and political reform, modernization, and centralization, Joseph II represented the climax of enlightened despotism (q.v.) in Central Europe (q.v.). He became Holy Roman Emperor already in 1765, but he did not really begin to rule until the death of his mother in 1780. In his efforts to modernize the Habsburg Empire (q.v.) he came to clash with the powerful Hungarian nobility (q.v.), who were trying to defend their feudal privileges. In order to be able to attack these outdated privileges, Joseph refused to have himself crowned king of Hungary (thus in Hungary he was called the "Hatted King"), and he also took Hungary's Holy Crown (q.v.) to Vienna (q.v.).

Joseph's most important reforms included the extension of state control over the Catholic Church (q.v.), the issuance of the Edict of Toleration (q.v.), the dissolution of many of the Catholic religious orders he deemed superfluous, the establishment of an Educational Fund from the appropriated church properties, the ending of the feudal autonomy of the counties (q.v.), the administrative restructuring of the whole empire, the naming of Royal Intendants to take the place of the local nobility, the partial elimination of serfdom (q.v.) by granting the peasants the right of free movement, the introduction of the ideas of the Enlightenment into public education, and the introduction of German as the administrative language of his empire—all of which together came to be known as Josephinism (q.v.). In Hungary, his centralizing policies—including the introduction of German administrative language—were used by the conservative nobility as a pretext to rouse the nation against Joseph's modernizing reforms. Disregarding the fact that many of the peasants called him the "good emperor," the nobility proclaimed him the enemy of the Hungarian nation and began to prepare for a showdown. The growing dissatisfaction of the nobility led to a kind of nobles' uprising in Hungary and to a mounting unrest in his Austrian and his Czech lands. By 1789, when forced to face the threat of the French Revolution, the very unity of his realm was in danger. Joseph's problems were further augmented by his misdirected war against the Turks (1788-91). Given these realities and close to death, in early 1790 Joseph revoked many of his reforms—with the exception of those concerning the peasants and religious toleration.

Joseph II was a dedicateddisciple of the Enlightenment, but he lacked pragmatism and the magic touch to implement his reforms with sufficient finesse. His methods were authoritarian. Thus, in spite of his good intentions, most of his policies failed. In Hungary, Joseph's name has a bad ring to it, because it is usually associated with forced Germanization. Nonetheless, he was an enlightened, but a misunderstood man, who was too much ahead of his times.

JOSEPH ANTON, ARCHDUKE [PALATINE JOSEPH, JÓZSEF NÁDOR] (1776–1847). The son of Leopold II (q.v.) and the royal viceroy (r.1795–1847) and palatine (r.1796–1847) of Hungary (q.v.), who founded the Hungarian branch of the Habsburg dynasty (q.v.). Being able to make himself liked by the Hungarian nobility (q.v.), Palatine Joseph was also able to secure more help for the dynasty in its struggle against Napoleon. His influence was decisive in Emperor Francis's (q.v.) decision to convene the Hungarian Diet (q.v.) in 1825, which initiated the Age of Reform (q.v.) in Hungary that ultimately culminated in the elimination of feudalism and the revolution of 1848-49 (q.v.). While trying to tone down the demands of the radicals, Palatine Joseph repeatedly supported moderate reforms and the modernization of Hungary. He also supported the Hungarian National Museum, the National Széchényi Library (q.v.), the Hungarian Academy of Sciences (q.v.), and the general beautification of the twin cities of Buda and Pest (later Budapest) (q.v.). Palatine Joseph's death in 1847 prevented him from witnessing the collapse of the whole system of reform he had nurtured for a half a century. In the palatine's office he was followed by his oldest son, Archduke Stephen (1817–67), who turned out to be Hungary's last viceroy and palatine (1847-48).

JOSEPH AUGUST, ARCHDUKE [JOSEPH HABSBURG, JÓZSEF FŐHERCEG] (1872–1962). Grandson of Palatine Joseph (q.v.), Hungary's last field marshal and first post–World War I (q.v.) regent (October 27–29, 1918, August 7–23, 1919). When King Charles IV (Emperor Charles I) resigned on October 27, 1918, he appointed Archduke Joseph as Hungary's regent *(homo regius),* but the revolution that erupted on October 31 prevented him from exercising his office. For a while he withdrew from politics, but after the collapse of the Hungarian Soviet Republic (q.v.) in early August 1919, he became regent once more, and used his office to name a government and to appoint Admiral Horthy (q.v.) as the commander-in-chief of the new National Army. In 1920 he lost out to Horthy in the election for Hungary's regency. Thereafter, Archduke Joseph withdrew from politics and devoted his time and efforts to cultural and scholarly matters. Among others, he served as the president of the Hungarian Academy of Sciences (1935-45) (q.v.). In 1944 Archduke Joseph left Hungary (q.v.), emigrated to the United States, and then resettled in Germany (q.v.), where he became involved in Hungarian emigré politics. Archduke Joseph's most important published work is *The World War, as I Saw It (A világháború, amilyennek én láttam)* (1927).

JOSEPHINISM [JÓZEFINIZMUS].   The Austro-Hungarian or Habsburg version of Enlightened Absolutism connected with the reign of Joseph II (q.v.) in the late 18th century. Its main goals included the elimination of the archaic feudal institutions that survived in the Habsburg lands, the introduction of religious toleration, and the modernization of the whole social, economic, and administrative system of the Habsburg Empire (q.v.). The Hungarian supporters of Josephinism came the intelligentsia, many of whom came from the ranks of the common nobility (q.v.). They expected the policies of Josephinism to push Hungary in the direction of a modern parliamentary state, and therefore many of them would even have been willing to accept German as Hungary's, main administrative language. A number of the adherents of Josephinism participated in the movement of the Hungarian Jacobins (q.v.).

JÓZSEF, ATTILA (1905-37). One of Hungary's most highly valued 20th-century poets, who is known as the "bard of the working classes." Coming from an "underclass"working family, and being reared by a single mother whose husband had forsaken her, József had a very difficult childhood. He was moved constantly between his broken home and various foster families and institutions, until finally in 1919 his much older brother-in-law became his mentor and guardian. In 1924 he enrolled at the University of Szeged (q.v.), but his rebellious poems made in impossible for him to stay. After spending some time at the Universities of Vienna and Paris among left-leaning emigré intellectual circles (1925-27), József returned home and lived the remaining years of his life on the fringes of Hungary's (q.v.) avant garde literary life and underground political world. But unable to fit into either one of them fully, he committed suicide at the end of 1937. Because of his brief association with the illegal Communist Party (q.v.), József was given little recognition by the official circles of interwar Hungary (q.v.). But, precisely for the same reason, the post-World War II communist regime proclaimed him to be the greatest Hungarian poet ever. He was, indeed, a great poet, who expressed the social misery of Hungary's lower classes better than anyone else. Yet, his overall influence upon the Hungarian mind was, and still is, less encompassing than that of the 19th-century Petőfi (q.v.) and early-20th-century Ady (q.v.). By a strange turn of fate, however, the University of Szeged (q.v.)—that did not want him in 1925—was renamed after him in 1961.

JULIANUS (d.1237). A Dominican friar who in 1235 was sent by King Béla IV (q.v.) to the East to find fellow Hungarians who remained back in the original homeland. Brother Julianus did find some of these Hungarians in the vicinity of the Middle Volga and was even able to converse with them in the Magyar language (q.v.). He returned to Hungary (q.v.) in 1236 and brought with him the news of the impending Mongol invasion (q.v.). Julianus set out again in 1237, but this time he was unable to go beyond Suzdal in Russian Mesopotamia By that time the Mongols had conquered *Magna Hungaria* (q.v.), the land of the Eastern Hungarians. After his initial visit, Julianus related his experiences to his superior, Brother Ricardus, who wrote it down and sent it to the Pope. Following his second excursion, Julianus reported his experiences in his "Letter about the lives of the Tatars." Ricardus's report appeared under the title *Facts about Greater Hungary (De facto Hungariae Magnae)*.

JUNIOR KINGSHIP [IFJABB KIRÁLYSÁG]. This title refers to the autonomous rule of a younger member of the royal dynasty over a segment of the country, and is very similar to the *dukátus [ducatus]* (q.v.). The junior kingship was the result of the rivalry between King Béla IV (q.v.) and his son, the future King Stephen V (q.v.). Based on an agreement between them concluded at Pozsony (q.v.) in the fall of 1262, Béla IV retained control over the country's western half with the title *rex senior Hungariae* (senior king of Hungary), while Stephen gained control over the eastern half with the title *iunior rex Hungariae* (junior king of Hungary). King Béla's death in 1270 ended this dual kingship, but it did not end internal dissension. It continued on and on, leading to disintegration and to the rise of oligarchs (q.v.) or regional lords, who tore Hungary apart.

JURÁTUS [JURATI]. Know also as the "Parliamentary Youth" *(országgyűlési ifjak)*, they were lawyer-candidates working as interns at the Hungarian Feudal Diet (q.v.) during the Age of Reform (q.v.) in the years before the Revolution of 1848–49 (q.v.). Employed by the elected deputies, the *jurati* aided the cause of the liberal nobility in its strive to modernize Hungary (q.v.). Many of the *jurati* came from the ranks of the impoverished lower nobility (q.v.).

- K -

KABARS [KAVARS]. Three fragmented tribes of the Khazars (q.v.), who joined Prince Árpád's (q.v.) Conquering Magyars (q.v.) when they occupied the Carpathian Basin (q.v.) in the late 9th century. The Kabars allegedly rebelled against central authority and had to flee the Khazar Empire (q.v.) about the same time when the Hungarians also terminated their allegiance to the Khazar Khagans. This alliance between the Hungarians and the Kabars resulted in a bilingualism among the ruling classes of the new Hungarian Tribal Federation (q.v.), which survived well into the 10th century. In this new federation the Kabars always fought in the front of the armies, which seems to indicate that they constituted a dependent auxiliary tribe of that federation. Some believe that the Kabars became rapidly assimilated into the Hungarians. Others, however, claim that they preserved their separate identity for a long time. In fact, they may still be around as components of the *Székelys* (q.v.) of Transylvania (q.v.). This view, however, is undercut by the traditions of the *Székelys* themselves, which holds that they are the descendants of Attila's Huns (q.v.) — unless the Kabars themselves were part of the Hunnic remnants that had moved back east after Attila's death.

KÁDÁR, JÁNOS (1912–89). Hungary's communist leader and party chief for over three decades following the Hungarian Revolution of 1956 (q.v.). Originally called János Csermanek (his mother's name) because of his illegitimate birth, Kádár grew up in a very poor family, became an industrial worker in the late 1920s, and then in 1930 joined both the Communist Youth Movement (q.v.) and the Communist Party of Hungary (q.v.). After serving in various underground activities, in 1943 he became the leader of Hungary's small and illegal Communist Party. Following Word War II (q.v.), Kádár lost his party position to the returning Muscovites (q.v.) under the leadership of Mátyás Rákosi (q.v.). Yet he still served in many important party and governmental positions right up to his own arrest for "Titoism" in 1951. Being freed in 1954 as a result of the post-Stalinist thaw, Kádár resumed his party activities, which after the revolution of 1956 (q.v.) led to his becoming the secretary of the Hungarian Workers' (Communist) Party (October 25, 1956).

Although initially supportive of the revolution and the revolutionary government headed by Imre Nagy (q.v.), by early November Kádár had turned his back on them and with Soviet support established a rival government. He also reestablished the Communist Party under the name Hungarian Socialist Workers' Party (q.v.). In the course of the next three decades Kádár held many governmental and party positions, but as the man in control of the party, he was in charge of the country within the limits permitted by his Soviet masters. During the period between 1956 and 1962 Kádár's rule was characterized by retributions, imprisonments, deportations, and executions, including the Soviet-directed execution of Imre Nagy in 1958, which had earned for him the universal condemnation of the world.

After 1962, however, Kádár began a policy of political and economic liberalization that eventually evolved in the the much-touted "goulash communism" (q.v.) of the 1970s and 1980s. As a result Kádár became increasingly popular, both at home and abroad, in spite of his participation in the invasion of Czechoslovakia (q.v.) in 1968. Although never able to get rid of the stigma stemming from Prime Minister Nagy's execution, by the late 1970s and early 1980s he was viewed as a kind of benevolent "grand old man" of communism. Kádár's fortunes began to change in the 1980s, partially as a result of Gorbachev's *perestroika* and and rapid disintegration of the Soviet Union (q.v.), and partially because of the winding down of Hungarian goulash communism.

After 1985 Kádár rapidly lost his grip on the leadership of the party and had to witness the decline of his popularity. In May 1988 the increasingly feeble Kádár was pushed out of power, replaced by the colorless Károly Grósz (q.v.). He withdrew from public life and died a year later without having given account of himself and his deeds. He lived just long enough to learn about the rehabilitation and official reburial of his rival and victim, Imre Nagy. Kádár's place in history is secure, but it is too early to assess the relative size of his merits and demerits. Although in light of the major economic difficulties that beset post-communist Hungarian society, his "gulyás communism" appears to look better and better to the average Hungarian. Kádár's books number about two dozen, all of which contain speeches and essays on party politics.

KÁDÁR REGIME (1956–88/89). The three decades that followed the Hungarian Revolution of 1956 (q.v.) under the leadership of János Kádár (q.v.), which was characterized by a short period of reaction (1956–62), and then by a lengthy period of liberalization (1962-88) that produced the much-touted "goulash communism" (q.v.) in Hungary (q.v.). Although officially ending with Kádár's resignation in May 1988, sometimes the period is extended to include the year that embraced the ephemeral leadership of his successor, Károly Grósz (q.v.), until the fall of 1989.

KÁLLAY, MIKLÓS [NICHOLAS] (1887–1964). A prominent Hungarian politician and a prime minister of Hungary (1942–44). After having served in several governments during the 1930s, in March 1942 Regent Horthy (q.v.) appointed Kállay Hungary's prime minister with the specific instructions to end the exclusively German orientation and to try to take the country out of the war. Kállay began secret negotiations with the Western powers, but fearing German retributions, he was unable to fulfill their conditions. Yet, because the Germans had learned about these secret contacts, they decided to preclude the possibility of a separate peace by occupying Hungary. Soon after the country's occupation (March 19, 1944), Kállay was arrested and taken to a German concentration camp. After being liberated in 1945, he settled in Italy (q.v.), and then in 1951 emigrated to the United States, where he became a member of the Hungarian National Committee (q.v.). He was a strong supporter of the unsuccessful "Liberation of Captive Nations Policy" initiated by the United States in the early 1950s, and was disappointed when nothing came of it. While active in emigré politics, Kállay also wrote and published his memoirs under the title

Hungarian Premier: A Personal Account of a Nation's Struggle in the Second World War (1954).

KÁLMÁN see COLOMAN.

KALOCSA. The center of the second Hungarian archbishopric, founded by King St. Stephen (q.v.) in 1009, only eight years after that of Esztergom (q.v.). Even today, the archbishop of Kalocsa is second in position behind the archbishop of Esztergom, the latter being also the primate (q.v.) of Hungary (q.v.).

KÁLTI, MÁRK [MÁRK DE KÁLT] (14th c.) A clergyman and chronicler who is generally regarded to be the compiler of the so-called Viennese *Illuminated Chronicle (Chronicon Pictum Vindobonense)* (1358) (q.v.). Having been always in upper levels of church leadership and in proximity of the Royal Court, Kálti was in a good position to compile a major chronicle based on earlier chronicles and on his own observations of history in action. His *Illuminated Chronicle* is the most beautiful and best-preserved of the many medieval Hungarian chronicles. (See also Hungarian Historical Studies.)

KAMARA see TREASURY.

KAMARILLA. The informal but powerful group of advisers who gathered around Prince Metternich (q.v.) and Count Kolowrat (q.v.), who dominated the State Council *(Staatskonferenze)* under the reign of the incompetent Ferdinand V (q.v.) in the decade and a half before the Revolution of 1848-49. Under the presidency of the king's uncle, Archduke Ludwig (1784-1864), and with the heavy presence of Metternich and Kolowrat, the members of the Kamarilla were in charge of the domestic and foreign policy of the Austrian Empire (q.v.), and therein also of Hungary (q.v.).

KÁPOLNA, UNION OF (1437). A defensive union among the three "historic" nations of Transylvania (q.v.)—the Magyars (q.v.), the

Magyar-speaking *Székelys* (q.v.), and the German-speaking Saxons (q.v.)—which served as the foundation stone for the system of government that evolved in that province after the post-Mohács (q.v.) period, when after Hungary's trisection, Transylvania became an autonomous vassal state of the Ottoman Empire (q.v.). This union was rooted in the chaotic social and political conditions of Hungary (q.v.) under the rule of Sigismund (q.v.), who was unable to defend the country's southeastern frontiers from the repeated raids by the Ottoman Turks (q.v.) and their allies, the voievods of Wallachia (q.v.). These raids made the lives of the peasant masses so unbearable that they rose in rebellion against their lords and the the wealthy burghers of the Transylvania towns. This, in turn, prompted the latter to come together in a defensive Union at Kápolna (September 16, 1437) to defeat the rebels and impose their will on the population.

A few months after their triumph, the three nations renewed their union at Torda (February 2, 1438) (q.v.), which then became a permanent foundation stone of the Transylvania constitutional system. The Vlachs (later renamed Romanians) were left out of this union, partially because of their small numbers in contemporary Transylvania, and partially because they were simple peasants who lacked the nobility to speak up for them. Not being among the historic nations of Transylvania, they could not share in its political power until after the Hungarian Revolution of 1848-49 (q.v.) and the Austro-Hungarian Compromise of 1867 (q.v.), which introduced a limited form of representation to the whole of Hungary.

KARLOWITZ, PEACE TREATY OF (1699). This treaty ended the Liberation Wars (q.v.) and pushed the Turks (q.v.) out of most of Historic Hungary (q.v.), except the Banat of Temesvár (q.v.), which was regained only with the Peace Treaty of Passarowitz in 1718 (q.v.). Although most of Hungary had been reconquered by the Habsburgs armies (q.v.), it was not fully reunited. Its southern fringes were made into the Military Frontier District (q.v.) under a separate military administration, while Transylvania (q.v.), with portions of the Partium (q.v.), was made into a Grand Duchy directly under the Habsburg emperors. These regions were not reunited with Hungary until the second half of the 19th century, in consequence of the Austro-Hungarian Compromise of 1867 (q.v.).

KARMAN, THEODORE VON [TÓDOR KÁRMÁN] (1881–1963). One of the greatest Hungarian-American scientists, who was an important pioneer of aerodynamics and one of the "fathers" of American space technology. He was responsible for analyzing the so-called "Karman vortex street" and for devising a new "Law of Turbulence." After some earlier visits, in 1930 Karman settled permanently in the United States, where he was appointed director of the Guggenheim Aeronautical Laboratory at the California Institute of Technology (1930–49). While there, he also organized the Institute's Jet Propulsion Laboratory, a federally funded center for research on rocketry and space technology. Karman's work in aerodynamics was used for the design of supersonic aircrafts, which initiated supersonic flights.

KAROLI [KÁROLYI], GÁSPÁR (c.1529–1591). Protestant clergyman, writer, and translator-publisher of the first complete Hungarian Bible. With the financial support of such wealthy aristocrats as Sigismund Rákóczi (q.v.), the future prince of Transylvania, and Lord Chief Justice István Báthory (1555-1605), Karoli undertook this task in 1586 in the town of Vizsoly. The Bible was published in July 1590 in about 700-800 copies. It came to be known as the "Vizsoly Bible," and because of its wide use, its language contributed greatly to the consolidation of the Hungarian (Magyar) literary language (q.v.).

KÁROLY see CHARLES.

KÁROLYI, COUNT GYULA [JULIUS] (1871–1947). A conservative politician and prime minister of Hungary (1919, 1931-32). During the period of the Hungarian Soviet Republic (q.v.), Károlyi established a counterrevolutionary government in the city of Arad (q.v.) (May 5–30, 1919), which he soon transferred to Szeged (q.v.)

(May 31–July 12), where he relinquished his place to Dezső Ábrahám (July 12–August 12). After years away from active politics, in 1927 Károlyi returned to the recently reestablished Upper House (q.v.), served as Hungary's foreign minister (1930-31), and finally as its prime minister (1931-32) during the great economic crisis that stemmed from the worldwide depression. Following his resignation he withdrew from politics once more, but remained one of Regent Horthy's (q.v.) close confidants right up to the end. During the World War II (q.v.) Károlyi supported Prime Minister Kállay's (q.v.) clandestine efforts to take Hungary out of the war.

KÁROLYI, COUNT MICHAEL [MIHÁLY]   (1875-1955). A liberal politician, a prime minister of Hungary (Oct. 31, 1918–Jan. 11, 1919), and then the president of the first Hungarian Republic (Jan. 11–Mar. 21, 1919). As a member of Hungarian Parliament (q.v.) since 1901, Károlyi went through several anti-Habsburg (q.v.) political parties before organizing his own during World War I (q.v.). He was against Austria-Hungary's (q.v.) participation in the war, and also supported the broadening of suffrage rights. Just before King Charles IV (Emperor Charles I) (q.v.) resigned his throne, he appointed Károlyi Hungary's prime minister (October 31, 1918), a position he held until assuming the country's presidency (January 11, 1919) for a two-month period until March 21, 1919.

When unable to deal with the consequences of the war, including the loss of over two-thirds of Historic Hungary's (q.v.) territory, Károlyi resigned and transferred political power to the communists under the leadership of Béla Kun (q.v.). He left Hungary in July 1919 and did not return until after World War II (q.v.). After visits to the United States and the Soviet Union (q.v.), and after a temporary stay in France, he finally settled down in England. During the interwar years (q.v.), Károlyi became increasingly tied to the international communist movement, becoming an ardent supporter of the Soviet Union, and even of Joseph Stalin. During World War II he was involved in an attempt to organize the left-leaning Hungarian emigration into a kind of United Front against Hungary's ruling regime, an act that pitted him against the patriotic majority among Hungarian-Americans (q.v.). Károlyi returned home in 1946 and was promptly appointed his country's ambassador to France (1947). He resigned this position in 1949, primarily because not even he was able to collaborate further with Mátyás Rákosi's (q.v.) Stalinist regime. Károlyi stayed in France until his death in 1955, but his remains were returned to Hungary in 1962.

KÁROLYI, COUNT SÁNDOR [ALEXANDER] (1669–1743). A prominent aristocrat who, during the Rákóczi War of Liberation (1703-11) (q.v.), joined the anti-Habsburg *kuruc* (q.v.) forces and by 1710 became their commander-in-chief. Although a close confidant of Prince Rákóczi (q.v.), after a series of *kuruc* defeats in 1710-11, he judged the Hungarian cause to be hopeless and began to champion the idea of a compromise peace. Thus, on April 30, 1711—while Prince Rákóczi was in Poland (q.v.)—he concluded the Peace of Szatmár (q.v.), which ended the war and forced Rákóczi and his associates into exile. In return for this act, King Charles III (Emperor Charles VI) (q.v.) rewarded him with large estates and awarded him the title of a count. Károlyi continued to serve the Habsburgs up to his death, rising to the rank of a field marshal, even though he did not speak a word of German. During the same time he devoted a great deal of attention to the development of his estates, including the bringing of German settlers to his vacant lands. In the meanwhile, he also wrote his memoirs, corresponded with Prince Rákóczi, and tried to help as many of his former *kuruc* comrades as possible. Even so, his name is still viewed with a degree of suspicion by patriotic Hungarians. Károlyi's memoirs appeared under the title *Memorable Events of my Life... [Magam életének...emlékezetes folyásai]*, 2 vols. (1866).

KÁROLYI REGIME see KÁROLYI, COUNT MICHAEL.

KASSA [KASCHAU, KOŠICE]. One of the most prominent cities of former Upper Hungary (q.v.), which after World War I (q.v.) was given to Czechoslovakia (q.v.) and renamed Košice. In 1938 Kassa was returned to Hungary (q.v.) by the First Vienna Award (q.v.), but after World War II (q.v.) it was reannexed to Czechoslovakia (q.v.). Since 1993 it has been part of independent Slovakia (q.v.), with a current population of over 100,000. First noted in contemporary documents in 1230, by 1347 Kassa had become a Royal Free City (q.v.). Growing in significance during the Turkish occupation of Central Hungary (q.v.), in the mid-16th century it had became the military and the financial center of Upper Hungary. By 1660 Kassa had its own college, and in the early 18th century it had also played a prominent role in the Rákóczi War of Liberation (q.v.). The city's Gothic cathedral was built in the early 15th century and it is one of the most important representatives of Hungarian Gothic architecture (q.v.). In 1906 the remains of Prince Ferenc Rákóczi (q.v.) were reinterred the the cathedral, after nearly two centuries in Turkey (q.v.). In 1910 Kassa had a population of 44,211, of which 33,350 (75 percent) were Hungarians and only 6,547 (15 percent) Slovaks. In the course of the past half a century, however, this ratio had been completely reversed.

KAZINCZY, FERENC (1759–1831). A writer and perhaps the most significant personality of the Hungarian Linguistic Revival Movement (q.v.) of the late 18th and early 19th centuries. Stemming from a family of nontitled common nobility (q.v.), Kazinczy studied law, worked in various administrative offices, became an enthusiastic supporter of Joseph II's (q.v.) enlightened reforms, and founded (with János Batsányi and Dávid Baróti Szabó) one of the first Hungarian literary journals, the *Magyar Museum* (1788–93). But unhappy with the turn of events in the 1790s, Kazinczy became involved in the ill-fated Jacobin Conspiracy of 1794-95 (q.v.), after which he was arrested and convicted to death. His death sentence was commuted to imprisonment, which later he described in his *Diary of My Captivity (Fogságom naplója)* published only a century after his death. He was freed in 1801, after which he threw himself into the cause of the Hungarian (Magyar) language (q.v.). He corresponded with and encouraged virtually everyone who in any way was involved in the Hungarian National Revival Movement (q.v.). Kazinczy himself coined many thousands of new words to modernize and update the Magyar language, which had remained archaic because of having been pushed into the background by Latin (q.v.), and later by German (q.v). In 1828 Kazinczy published his *Memoirs of My Life [Pályám emlékezete]*, which is perhaps the best of his written works. His letters, published in thirteen volumes (1890-1960), are among the most important sources of the Hungarian Linguistic Revival Movement.

KEMÉNY, JOHN [JÁNOS] (1607–62). Prince of Transylvania (r.1661-62) and a rival of Prince Michael Apafi (q.v.). Born into a family of wealthy noblemen, Kemény grew up in the Transylvanian Court of Prince Gabriel Bethlen (q.v.). After Bethlen's death he became a supporter of the Rákóczi family (q.v.) and served both George Rákóczi I (q.v.) and George Rákóczi II (q.v.) faithfully. During the 1650s he was the commander-in-chief of George Rákóczi II's armies during the latter's invasion of Moldavia (1653) (q.v.) and Poland (1657) (q.v.). In the Polish war, Kemény and his armies were defeated and captured by the Crimean Tatars (q.v.) in the service of the Ottoman Empire (q.v.). Having been ransomed in 1659, Kemény returned to Transylvania (q.v.), but in light of the chaos that followed Prince Rákóczi's death (1658), he became a supporter of a pro-Habsburg policy. Thus, he opposed Ákos Barcsay (q.v.), who was made prince of Transylvania by the Turks (q.v.).

After Barcsay was forced to resign (December 31, 1660), the Transylvania estates elected Kemény as their ruling prince (January 1, 1661). The Ottomans refused to accept his election, which forced Kemény to seek the support from the Habsburgs (q.v.). But the Habsburg Imperial Forces (q.v.), commanded by Field Marshal Montecuccoli (q.v.), proved to be unable to deal with the Turks (q.v.). They withdrew from Transylvania, leaving Kemény to his fate. In the meanwhile, the Turks forced the Transylvanian Diet to elect their own candidate to the throne in the person of Michael Apafi (September 14, 1661), who tried, but was unable to come to terms with his rival. Kemény continued the struggle without much hope. He was defeated and killed by the forces of Küćük Mehmet Pasha in the Battle of Nagyszőlős (January 22, 1662). Kemény's

Auto-biography (Önéletírás), written during his Tatar captivity, is an important historical source for that period, and it is also an significant Hungarian-language literary work.

KENDE [KÜNDE, KÜNDÜ]. The title of the chief of sacred prince of the Conquering Magyars (Hungarians) (q.v.) in the 9th and early 10th centuries in a system of dual kingship (q.v.) that had evolved among them under the influence of the Khazars (q.v.). The title of the second in command, but the de facto leader, was *gyula* (q.v.). It is generally believed that at the time of the Árpádian Conquest (q.v.) in the late 9th century, the *kende* was Prince Kurszán (q.v.), while the position of *gyula* was held by Prince Árpád (q.v.), who subsequently managed to combine the two offices within his own family. The office of the *kende* ended with Kurszán's death in 904.

KENÉZ. The title of the leaders of the Vlach (Romanian) (q.v.) clans that began to settle in eastern Hungary (Transylvania) (q.v.) in the 13th century. In the 14th and 15th centuries the Vlach leaders who established new village settlements in Hungary (q.v.) were also known by this name. They collected taxes and feudal dues, served as local judges and administrators, and many of them eventually became members of the Hungarian nobility (q.v.). The role of the Vlach *kenéz* -es was very similar to that of the German *soltész* -es (q.v.) in Upper Hungary (q.v.).

KERTÉSZ, STEPHEN [ISTVÁN] (1904–86). Hungarian diplomat, political scientist, and historian, who was one of the post-World War II (q.v.) pioneers of Hungarian studies in the United States. After filling various diplomatic posts at the International Court in The Hague (1938–42), the Hungarian Embassy in Bucharest (1943–44), and the Paris Peace Conference (1946–47), and after serving as the Hungarian Ambassador to Italy (1947–48), Kertész cut his ties with communist Hungary (q.v.) and emigrated to the United States. Following a brief period at Yale University (1948-50), he was appointed to the University of Notre Dame (1950–74), where he developed a program devoted to Hungary and

East Central Europe (q.v.), and also published a number of significant works on that region. The latter include *Diplomacy in a Whirlpool* (1953), *The Fate of East Central Europe* (1956), *East Central Europe and the World* (1962), *Between Russia and the West: Hungary and the Illusions of Peace-Making, 1945-47* (1984), and *The Last European Peace Conference: Paris 1946* (1985).

KÉZAI, SIMON [SIMON DE KÉZA] (late 13th c.). Author of the chronicle Gesta *Hungarorum (Deeds of the Hungarians)* (q.v.) written between 1282–85, which covers Hungarian history until the year 1280. Based on some of the earlier Hungarian chronicles, Kézai's work has preserved the Hungarians' perception of their own history, including their belief that they are connected with Attila's Huns (q.v.), and that the Hunnic conquest of the 5th century was really the first Hungarian conquest of the Carpathian Basin (q.v.). While this view is disputed by many modern scholars, it is held by others. Moreover, this Hunnic-Hungarian connection is also part of Hungarian national traditions and consciousness.

KHAGAN [KÁGÁN]. The title of a sovereign nomadic ruler among the Turkic peoples (q.v.) of Central Asia (q.v.), the Near East (q.v.), and Eastern Europe (q.v.). It is related to the title *khan,* and at one time the two were coequal. Later the *khan* became the title of a lesser ruler. The Khazar Empire (q.v.) of the 7th through the 10th centuries had two rulers, and in this dual kingship (q.v.) the Khagan was the higher or sacred ruler. The title of the ruler of the Avar Empire (q.v.) of the 6th-9th centuries was also Khagan.

KHALIF [KHALIFA] see **CALIPH.**

KHAN [KÁN]. The lower of two titles among some Turkic peoples, such as the Avars (q.v.) and Khazars (q.v.) of old. Later, it was also the title of the rulers of the Mongol Empire (e.g. Genghis Khan), as well as of the rulers of some of its successor states, such as the Khanate of the Golden Horde (q.v.).

KHAZAR EMPIRE (c.630-965). Established around A.D. 630 by the Turkic Khazars (q.v.), after they had freed themselves from under the control of the West Türk Empire that stretched over Central Asia (q.v.) and Eastern Europe (q.v.). Within a century the Khazars established a powerful state that had lively commercial relationships with the Islamic World as well as with the Byzantine Empire (q.v.). In the middle of the 7th century the Khazars conqueredthe Onogur-Bulgar state of Prince Kuvrat (d. c.642) and his sons in the region of the Crimea (q.v.). This resulted in the emigration of the proto-Bulgars in several directions. One group under Asparuch moved into the Balkans (q.v.) and the Carpathian Basin (q.v.) and laid the foundations of the medieval Bulgarian Empire. Another group moved northeast to the Middle Volga region and established Magna Bulgaria in the vicinity of Magna Hungaria (q.v.).

The Khazar political system was built on the principle of dual kingship (q.v.), at the top of which was the sacred Khagan (q.v.) with minimal political power, with the real power being in the hands of his second in command, the khan (q.v.). In the 860s the Khazar upper classes converted to Judaism and thus may have formed the basis of some of the East European Jewry of later years. In the 10th century the Khazar Empire was weakened by the persistent attacks by the related Pechenegs (q.v.), and then in 965 it was overthrown by Prince Svyatoslav of Kiev (q.v.). During the 9th century, for an undetermined period of time, the Hungarian tribes were also vassals of the Khazar Empire. Upon liberating themselves, they moved westward and settled in the Carpathian Basin (q.v.) that probably already had a large Hungarian-speaking population from some of the earlier invasions and settlements.

KHAZARS. Turkic speaking people who founded and ruled the Khazar Empire (q.v.) in the 7th through the 10th centuries. The Khazar ruling classes are known to have converted to Judaism in the 860s. Some of the Khazar tribal fragments who rebelled against central authority—known as the Kabars (q.v.)—joined Prince Árpád's Conquering Hungarians (q.v.) and became part of the Hungarian Tribal Federation (q.v.).

KHUEN-HÉDERVÁRY,   COUNT   KÁROLY   [KARL]   (1849–1918). A conservative politician, who served as the ban of Croatia (1883-1903) and the prime minister of Hungary (1903, 1910-12). He is known primarily for his undiplomatic methods in undercutting the nationalist movement in Croatia-Slavonia (q.v.), where his name and memory are intensely disliked. But he also used similar strong-hand methods against the opposition parties in the Hungarian Parliament (q.v.). In addition to the above mentioned offices, Khuen-Hédervárý also held other ministerial posts, included that of the "Hungarian Minister Attached to the Person of the King" (1904–05).

KIEV [KIJEV, KIIV]. A city on the Middle Dnieper River, the current capital of Ukraine (q.v.), which began as the political center of the Poliani tribes in the 7th century, and then by the 860s became the capital of of Kievan Russia (q.v.). In the 9th century Kiev was within the confines of the Khazar Empire (q.v.), and then in the middle of that century it came under the rule of the Hungarian Tribal Federation (q.v.), led by Prince Álmos (q.v.). In 1240 the city was sacked by the Mongols (q.v.), in the 14th century it was conquered by the Lithuanians (q.v.), and starting with 1384 it became part of the Polish-Lithuanian Commonwealth (q.v.). In 1661 Kiev and its region was acquired by Muscovite Russia (q.v.) and remained under Russian rule up to the disintegration of the Soviet Union (q.v.) at the end of 1991. Members of the Hungarian Árpád dynasty (q.v.) and the Kievan Rurik dynasty had a close relationship and frequently intermarried from the 11th through the 13th centuries. A part of the Kievan State, the province of Galicia (Halich) (q.v.), was a frequent target of Hungarian military expansion in the Middle Ages.

KIEVAN   RUSSIA   [KIEV   RUS',   KIEVAN   STATE]   (860s–1240). The East Slavic state founded in the 860s under the leadership of a group of Varangians (Scandinavians). It fell under the rule of the Scandinavian Rurik dynasty in 878 (or 882), grew into a significant state in the 10th and early 11th centuries, accepted Byzantine Christianity (q.v.) in 988, disintegrated into a loose confederation of states after 1054, and then fell victim to the Mongol conquest (q.v.)

between 1237 and 1240. Starting with the reign of Yaroslav the Wise (r.1015–54), members of the Árpád dynasty (q.v.) frequently intermarried with those of the Rurik dynasty. This included not only its mainline in Kiev (q.v.), but also many of its branches, among them those of Galicia (q.v.),Volhynia, and Lodomeria.

KINIZSI, PÁL (d.1494). The only one of King Matthias Corvinus's (q.v.) generals who became a folk hero. Kinizsi's romanticized exploits have been incorporated into Hungarian folklore. The son of a simple miller, Kinizsi rose to prominence because of his military leadership abilities. During the 1460s and 1470s he participated in most of King Matthias's wars, and in the 1480s he was entrusted with the defense of Hungary's (q.v.) southern frontiers against the Turks (q.v.). After King Matthias's death, Kinizsi refused to support the latter's illegitimate son and designated heir, Johannes Corvin (q.v.), but switched side to King Vladislav II (q.v.). Kinizsi died fighting against the Turks at the Fortress of Szendrő (Smederevo) in the vicinity of Belgrade (q.v.). Although a folk hero, in reality Kinizsi was a cruel man who frequently devised unique torture methods against his Turkish captives. Some of these were later applied to the leaders of the Dózsa Peasant Revolution (q.v.), who were defeated and captured in 1514.

KIRÁLY, BÉLA K. (b.1912). Military leader, historian, politician, and one of the important personalities in the Hungarian Revolution of 1956 (q.v.). Király was a professional army officer who graduated both from the Ludovika Military Academy (1935) and the Hungarian War Academy of Budapest (1942). Following World War II (q.v.) he joined a new People's Army (q.v.), rose to he rank of a brigadier general, served as the commander of the Hungarian Infantry (1949–50), and then served as the director of the Miklós Zrínyi Military Academy (1950–51). Arrested on trumped-up political charges in 1951, Király was condemned to death, but managed to survive until 1956, when he was freed by the revolutionaries. Imre Nagy's (q.v.) revolutionary government appointed him military commander of Budapest (q.v.) and also the commander of the newly organized

Hungarian National Guard. After the revolution he immigrated to the United States, where he earned a Ph.D. in history from Columbia University (1963), and then served as a professor of history at the City University of New York. During this period he published widely and at the same time initiated several scholarly publication series, mostly as joint ventures with Brooklyn College and Columbia University Press.

In 1989 Király returned to Hungary (q.v.) and was elected, member of the first post-communist Hungarian Parliament (1990-94) (q.v.). The new government also promoted him to the rank of a retired "colonel-general"—currently the top rank in the Hungarian Armed Forces. Király's most important written works include *Hungary in the Late Eighteenth Century* (1969), *Ferenc Deák* (1975), and *The First War among Socialist States (Az első háború a szocialista országok között)* (1981). Also important are his reminiscences, *From the Honvéd Army to the People's Army (Honvédségből a néphadseregbe)* (1986), and *From Revolution to Revolution (Forradalomtól forradalomig)* (1990). Many of the volumes published by Atlantic Research and Publications, Inc., were coedited by Király himself.

KISBARNAKI-FARKAS, FERENC [FRANZ FARKAS VON KISBARNAK] (1892–1980). A Hungarian general who after World War II (q.v.) became one of the leaders of the Hungarian emigration. Immediately after the war, Kisbarnaki-Farkas established the Hungarian Freedom Movement (Magyar Szabadság Mozgalom) in Germany (q.v.), which, for a while, was one of the two most significant and most widespread organizations of the Hungarian emigrés. Then, in August 1947, he called together the surviving members of the prewar Hungarian Parliament (q.v.) at Altötting, Bavaria, where he held a "Hungarian Parliament in Exile" and had himself elected the new "regent of Hungary." While these Quixotic efforts proved to be meaningless, Kisbarnakl-Farkas still remained one of the most visible and most consulted leaders of the Hungarian emigration. He was involved in the leadership of many of their chief international organizations, served as the grand master of the

Military Order of Vitéz (q.v.) (1957–80), and also presided over the Hungarian Scout Association in Exile (q.v.) (1946-80). His two important works are *The History of the Parliament of Altötting (Az altöttingi országgyűlés története)* (1969), and *Reflections on the Tatár Pass (A Tatárhágó visszanéz)* (1952)—the latter being his reminiscences about Hungary's military actions in World War II.

KISFALUDY, SÁNDOR (1772-1844). Sándor Kisfaludy and his brother, Károly, were the best representatives of that segment of the Hungarian common nobility (q.v.), which had intellectual curiosity and literary ambitions, and thus became involved in the Hungarian Linguistic and National Revival Movements (q.v.). Sándor was the pioneer of the two, who became acquainted with the ideas of Enlightenment (q.v.) and nationalism while a member of the Hungarian Royal Nobles' Guard (q.v.) in Vienna (1792–96). He continued to serve in the Habsburg Army (q.v.) until 1799, when he resigned, returned home, married his great love, Róza Szegedy (1800), and began to publish his literary works which almost overnight made him into one of the most significant exponents of the rising Hungarian literature. These works included his lyrical *Grieving Love (A kesergő szerelem)* (1801) and *Happy Love (A boldog szerelem)* (1807), as well as his collection of epics, *Legends from Hungarian Past (Regék a magyar előidőkből)* (1907)—all of which were published under the pen name of "Himfy." Although continuing to publish historical epics and dramas, and although very popular among the rising literati during the first two decades of the 19th century, Sándor Kisfaludy could not keep up with the pace of literary changes and he was gradually left behind by others, including his own much younger brother, Károly Kisfaludy (q.v.).

KISFALUDY, KÁROLY (1788-1830). Similarly to his brother, Sándor (q.v.), Károly Kisfaludy was also one of the most noted representatives of the Hungarian Linguistic Revival Movement (q.v). Like his brother, he started his career in the Habsburg Army (1806–11) (q.v.), where he too fell under the influence of rising Hungarian nationalism. But unlike his brother, who subsequently settled into the life of a well-to-do Hungarian landowning gentry (q.v.), Károly broke with his family's way of life and lived like an impoverished intellectual. He began to write under Sándor's influence, but soon moved beyond him by championing new forms and new literary trends. By 1821 Károly Kisfaludy had become the leading spirit of the "Aurora Circle" that congregated around the literary yearbook *Aurora,* which he edited in Pest (now part of Budapest) (q.v.) that was fast becoming the intellectual center of Hungary (q.v.). Károly Kisfaludy consciously neglected to publish the older pioneers of Hungarian literary revival (including his own brother), and he purposely looked for new talents within the ranks of the impoverished nobility and the commoners.

Károly Kisfaludy wrote lyrical poetry, epics, and critical essays, but his greatest success was in writing plays, including comedies, social dramas, and historical dramas. His initial plays included the comedy *The Suitors (A kérők)* (1817), the historical dramas *Voievod Stibor (Stibor vajda)* (1918) and *The Tatars in Hungary (A tatárok Magyarországon)* (1819), and the social dramas *Friendship and Generosity (Barátság és nagylelkűség)* (1820) and *Irene* (1820). Károly Kisfaludy was the first Hungarian writer who lived for literature and from literature. His impact upon the development of modern Hungarian literature and the Hungarian national spirit was enormous. His disciples honored him by establishing and naming after him the Kisfaludy Association *(Kisfaludy Társaság)* (1836–1952), which for well over a century was Hungary's most respected and influential literary society.

KISZ see **COMMUNIST YOUTH ORGANIZATIONS.**

KLAPKA, GYÖRGY [GEORGE] (1820–92). One of the better known generals of the Hungarian Revolution of 1848–49 (q.v.). In 1842 Klapka was admitted into the ranks of the Hungarian Royal Nobles' Guard (q.v.) in Vienna (q.v.), where he became acqualnted with Artúr Görgey (q.v.), a future commander-in-chief of the Hungarian Armies during the revolution. He joined the revolutionary armies with the rank of a captain, but by April 1849 he was promoted to a general. During the last phase of the revolution he was the commander of the fortress of Komárom, which he surrendered only on October 2, 1849—several weeks after the surrender of the Hungarian Armies at Világos (q.v.). Moreover, he gave up only on the condition that all his men be permitted to go free. Klapka emigrated to Turkey (q.v.), then to Italy (q.v.), and still later to Switzerland. At the time of the Austrian-Italian-French War of 1859, he was involved in organizing the Hungarian Legion in Italy. In 1864 he supported Garibaldi's anti-Austrian military actions, and two years later also those of the Prussians. In 1861 Klapka was briefly considered for Winfield Scott's position as the commander-in-chief of the Union Armies, but his price was too high. Following the Austro-Hungarian Compromise of 1867 (q.v.), he returned to Hungary (q.v.) and was elected to the Parliament as a member of Kálmán Tisza's (q.v.) left-center party group. He recorded his reminiscences in several volumes, including *The National War in Hungary and Transylvania (Der Nationalkrieg in Ungarn und Siebenbürgen)* (1851), *My Life and Experiences (Életem és élményeim)* (1881), and *From My Reminiscences (Emlékeimből)* (1886).

KLEBELSBERG, COUNT KUNÓ (1875–1932). Hungary's most highly regarded minister for culture and education (1922–31), President of the Hungarian Historical Association (q.v.) (1917–32), and the originator of the ideology of "neo-nationalism" that emphasized the unique "state-forming abilities" and cultural preeminence of the Hungarians among the peoples of the Carpathian Basin (q.v.). In his capacity as minister for culture and education Klebelsberg established a system of village schools, reformed and expanded Hungary's secondary education system, established the University of Szeged (q.v.), built a new campus for the University of Debrecen (q.v.), founded Hungarian Historical Research Institutes in Vienna (q.v.), Berlin, and Rome, and reorganized the whole Hungarian scholarly infrastructure. In his capacity as the president of the Historical Association, he initiated a number of major research projects and publications, the most important being the *Sources on* *the Recent History of Hungary (Fontes Historiae Hungaricae Aevi Recentoris)*, of which forty-four volumes appeared (1921–44), and the proposed but unfinished twenty-nine volume *Handbook of Hungarian Historical Sciences (A magyar történettudomány kézikönyve)* (1923-34). Although he did have ulterior motives, namely to undercut the injustices of Trianon (q.v.), his cultural policy and all publications associated with his name always remained on a high ethical and scholarly level. Klebelsberg's most important works include *Neo-Nationalism (Neónacionalizmus)* (1928), *Speeches, Articles, Parliamentary Proposals, 1916–1926 (Beszédei, cikkei, törvényjavaslatai, 1916-1926)* (1927), *In World Crisis (Világváltságban)* (1931), and *Scholarship, Culture, Politics (Tudomány, kultúra, politika)*, ed. Ferenc Glatz (1990).

KODÁLY, ZOLTÁN (1882–1967). Composer, researcher of folk music, and widely known developer of the "Kodály Method" of music education. In contrast to the even better-known Béla Bartók (q.v.), Kodály limited his collecting activities to Hungarian folk music. Between 1907 and 1942 he was a professor at the Liszt Music Academy in Budapest (q.b.), but after 1925 he devoted most of his time to composing and to the elaboration of his method of music education. Between 1946 and 1949 he was the president of the Hungarian Academy of Sciences (q.v.), after which he directed the Academy's Institute of Folk Music (1950-67). During the final decades of his life, Kodály received recognitions and honors — including numerous honorary doctorates — from many countries and universities. His method of music education is practiced and emulated all over the world.

KÖLCSEY, FERENC (1790–1838). One of the most important and influential literati of the Hungarian Reform Period (q.v.), who was active as a writer, as a reform politician, as well as a defense lawyer for Hungarian patriots. Kölcsey became an early disciple and supporter of the pioneer prophet of Hungarian Linguistic Revival (q.v.), Ferenc Kazinczy (q.v.), who was also his relative. It was under Kazinczy's influence that he began to write. He wrote poetry

—including the Hungarian national *Hymn* (1823)—and he also wrote philosophical studies and critical literary essays. In 1832 Kölcsey was elected as Szatmár County's representative to the Hungarian Diet (q.v.), where he soon became one of the most influential representatives of the progressive "Reform Generation" (q.v.), which included such personalities as Széchenyi (q.v.), Wesselényi (q.v.), Kossuth (q.v.), Deák (q.v.), Eötvös (q.v.), and others. Unwilling to comply with the obligatory "instructions" (q.v.) of his county, which went against his progressive political beliefs, Kölcsey resigned his position in 1835 and devoted the remaining three years of his life to the defense of Hungarian patriots accused of political treason.

KOLKHOZ [KOLHOZ, TERMELŐSZÖVETKEZET]. Collective farms that, starting with 1928, were the results of forced land collectivization in the Soviet Union (q.v.). After 1948 the kolkhozes were also introduced into Hungary (q.v.), resulting in the destruction of the traditional peasant class and the customary system of agriculture based on small privately owned lands. Many of the kolkhozes survived even the collapse of communism (q.v.), largely because by that time very few rural Hungarians were willing to engage in small-scale farming.

KOLLONICH, COUNT LEOPOLD [KOLLONITSCH, LIPÓT] (1631–1707). Cardinal archbishop of Esztergom, primate of Hungary (q.v.), and Habsburg imperial statesman. Having started out as an officer in the Habsburg Imperial Army (q.v.), in 1660 Kollonich joined the priesthood and rose rapidly in the ranks. Within six years he became the bishop of Nyitra (1666), then bishop of Wiener-Neustadt (1670), bishop of Győr (1685), archbishop of Kalocsa (1691), and finally the archbishop of Esztergom (q.v.), and thus the primate of Hungary (q.v.) (1696). In 1686 Kollonich was also made member of the College of Cardinals. In 1672 he was likewise appointed to the directorship of the Hungarian Royal Treasury (q.v.), of which he was relieved in 1684, but only because of the strong protest by the Hungarian Diet (q.v.).

In spite of this setback, Kollonich remained Emperor Leopold's (q.v.) chief advisor on Hungarian affairs. In 1688, for example, he was entrusted with the preparation of a plan for the integration of reconquered Hungary (q.v.) into the Habsburg Empire (q.v.). The result was his *Reorganization Plans for the Kingdom of Hungary (Einrichtungswerk des Königreichs Hungarn),* which called for the extension of Habsburg absolutism, breaking the backs of the Hungarian nobility (q.v.), and settling Germans (q.v.) in the country's depopulated areas. Some of his proposals for social and economic reforms were progressive, but most of them were never implemented, because they would have placed Hungary (q.v.) on the level of the German-speaking Hereditary Provinces (q.v.). Kollonich's name and memory are disliked in Hungary, not only because of his primary loyalty to the Habsburgs (q.v.), but also because of his participation in the persecution of the Hungarian Calvinists (q.v.) and their clergymen, most of whom ended up as galley slaves on the Adriatic Sea (q.v.).

KOLOWRAT-LIEBŠTEINSKI, COUNT ANTON (1778-1861). One of the two most prominent Habsburg statesmen during the post-Napoleonic period, who was the primary rival of the powerful Prince Metternich (q.v.). Born in Prague, in 1806 Kolowrat became the lord mayor of his native city and in 1811 the leader *(Oberstburggraf)* of the Bohemian estates. In 1826 Emperor Francis I (q.v.) appointed him the head of the Political Section, and in 1827 also the head of the Financial Section of the State Council *(Staatsrat)* in Vienna (q.v.). As a member of the Imperial Government (q.v.), Kolowrat represented moderation and reform. But after Emperor Francis's death in 1835 his influence declined and thereafter he was less able to counteract Metternich's antireform tendencies. Following the outbreak of the Viennese Revolution (March 13, 1848) and the fall of Metternich (March 21, 1848), Kolowrat became Austria's (q.v.) first constitutional prime minister. Unable to stem the revolutionary tide, he soon resigned (April 4) and withdrew from political life. Kolowrat is known to have been a supporter of Czech cultural and national revival, and as such his activities also aided the Hungarian national revival movement (q.v.).

KOLOZSVÁR [KLAUSENBURG, CLUJ, CLUJ-NAPOCA]. A city of over 200,000, which used to be one of the most important towns and occasional capitals of Transylvania (q.v.) in the course of the 16th through 20th centuries. It was founded in the late 12th century upon the ruins of a Dacian and Roman fortress. Established in the 1170s jointly by Hungarians and Saxon settlers (q.v.), by the 14th century Kolozsvár had become a prominent walled city where the Hungarians and the Saxons alternated as elected mayors.

In the 16th century the Hungarians had become the majority and pushed the Saxons out of power. King Matthias Corvinus (q.v.) was born in Kolozsvár, and in the 16th and 17th centuries about eighty Transylvanian diets were held there. Although representing the three "nations" (Hungarians, Hungarian-speaking Székelys, and the Saxons), all of these diets functioned in Hungarian at that time when the diets of Royal Hungary were still conducted in Latin. During these centuries Kolozsvár was an important Hungarian cultural center, with schools, theaters, literary societies, and since 1872 a new university. Following World War I (q.v.), the city was detached from Hungary and attached to the much enlarged Romania (q.v.). In 1940 it was returned to Hungary, but after World War II (q.v.) it was again made part of Romania. In 1910 Kolozsvár had a population of 60,808, of which 50,704 (80 percent) were Hungarians and only 7,562 (12 percent) Romanians. The systematic Romanianization of the last five decades had reversed this ratio completely.

KÖPECZI, BÉLA (b.1921). Historian, literary historian, and cultural politician, who during the latter half of the Kádár Regime (q.v.) served both as assistant secretary and secretary of the Hungarian Academy of Sciences (q.v.) (1970-82), as well as Hungary's (q.v.) minister for cultural affairs (1982-88). A product of the intellectually exclusive Eötvös College (q.v.), Köpeczi is a man of wide learning, with an emphasis upon French culture. As a historian, his primary area of research is the Age of Prince Ferenc Rákóczi II (q.v.) and

French-Hungarian connections. His most important works include *Ferenc Rákóczi II (II. Rákóczi Ferenc)* (1955), *The Rákóczi War of Liberation and France (A Rákóczi-szabadságharcés Franciaország)* (1966), *The Rákóczi War of Liberation and Europe (A Rákóczi-szabadságharcés Európa)* (1970), *Rákóczi Mirror: Diaries, Reports, Memoirs about the War of Liberation (Rákóczi tükör. Naplók, jelentések, emlékiratok a szabadságharcról)* (1973), *"Hungary, the Enemy of Christianity." The Thököly Uprising in European Public Opinion ("Magyarországa kereszténység ellensége". A Thököly-felkelés az európai közvéleményben)* (1976); *Prince Ferenc Rákóczi II's Memoirs about the War in Hungary (II. Rákóczi Ferenc fejedelem emlékiratai a magyarországi háborúról)* (1978), *The Hungarians and the French from Louis XIV to the French Revolution (Magyarok és franciák, XIV. Lajostól a francia forradalomig)* (1988), and *The Exiled Rákóczi (A bujdosó Rákóczi)* (1991). Köpeczi also served as the editor-in-chief of the Hungarian Academy's three-volume *History of Transylvania (Erdély története)* (1986), which created an angry reaction in Romania, and which later also appeared in an abbreviated form in French, German and English.

KOPPÁNY (d.997/98). One of the prominent princes of the Árpád family during the reign of Grand Prince Géza (q.v.), who, after the latter's death in 997, claimed both the Hungarian throne and the hand of Géza's widow, Sarolta. He based his claim on the principle of seniority (q.v.) and on the practice of levirate (q.v.). To enforce his claim, he launched an attack from his tribal fief in the Somogy region of Trans-Danubia (q.v.) against Géza's son and heir, the future King St. Stephen (q.v.). Being soundly defeated—in line with the traditions of the age—Koppány was quartered and his remains were nailed onto the gates of Esztergom (q.v.), Győr (q.v.), Veszprém (q.v.), and an unknown fortress in Transylvania (q.v.). According to 11th-century Hungarian traditions, Koppány was an enemy of Christianity. Had he succeeded, he would have returned the Hungarians to their pagan traditions.

KÖPRÜLÜ GRAND VIZIERS. Members of a family of Albanian origin, who rose to be the grand viziers (q.v.) and at certain moments the de facto leaders of the Ottoman Empire (q.v.) during the latter half of the 17th century. They planned and directed several major anti-Habsburg (q.v.) campaigns to and through Hungary (q.v.) in the period between the early 1660s and the 1690s. They were also involved in trying to save the empire after its defeats in the Liberation Wars (q.v.). The most prominent members of the Köprülü dynasty included the grand viziers Mehmet (r.1656–61), Ahmet (r.1661–76), Mustafa (r.1689–91), and Hüseyin (r.1699–1702), although there were several others as well in the lower levels of command. The goal of the Köprülüs was to resuscitate the once mighty Ottoman state. Although able military leaders, they ultimately failed, because the old Ottoman spirit was already gone and the main institutions of the empire were in the process of decay. Their cooperation with Thököly (q.v.) and the *kuruc* (q.v.) rebellions in Hungary was also a failure. Moreover, it brought more misery than success to Hungary and the Hungarians. The 20th-century descendants of the Köprülü grand viziers became prominent historians and statesmen, among them Mehmet Fuat Köprülü (1890-1966), the founder of the Institute of Turkology (1924) and foreign minister of Turkey (1950–54).

KORONA [CROWN]. Hungary's (q.v.) monetary unit between 1892 and 1926, after which it was replaced by the *pengő* (q.v.). The *korona* was divided into hundred *fillérs* (q.v.) and it was worth about twenty cents in U.S. currency. Its predecessor, the *forint* (q.v.), divided into hundred *krajcárs* (q.v.), had been Hungary's primary currency ever since the 16th century. Although replaced by the *korona* in 1892, the *forint* continued to be accepted at a ratio of two *koronas* for one *forint* until the end of Austria-Hungary (q.v.) in 1918.

KOSÁRY, DOMOKOS [DOMINIC G.] (b.1913). A noted historian, the best-known disciple of Gyula Szekfű (q.v.), and between 1990 and 1996 the president of the Hungarian Academy of

Sciences (q.v.). Kosáry began his career as an exponent of the *Geistesgeschichte* School (see Hungarian Historical Studies) but after World War II (q.v.) he perforce switched over to a moderate form of Marxism, from which he distanced himself since 1990. He taught at Eötvös College (1938–49) and the University of Budapest (1946-49), and has also been associated with the Hungarian Historical Institute (1941–45), the East European Institute (1945–49), the Agricultural University of Gödöllő (1954–57), the Archives of Pest County (1960–68), and Institute of History (q.v.) of the Hungarian Academy of Sciences (1968-89).

Kosáry's primary area of research is 18th and 19-century social and cultural history, and historical bibliography. His most lasting works include: *A History of Hungary* (1941; reprinted 1971), *Introduction into the Sources and Literature of Hungarian History (Bevezetés a magyar történelem forrásaiba és irodalmába)* (3 vols., 1951-58), *Culture in Eighteenth-Century Hungary (Művelődés a XVIII. századi Magyarországon)* (1980), *The History of the Hungarian Press, 1848-1892* (1985), *The Press during the Hungarian Revolution of 1948-1849* (1986), *The Enlightenment in Europe and in Hungary (A felvilágosodás Európában és Magyarországon)* (1987); *Reconstruction and the Rise of a Bourgeois Way of Life, 1711-1867 (Újjáépítés és polgárosodás, 1711-1867)* (1990), and *The Görgey Question (A Görgey-kérdés)* (1994), which first appeared in a briefer version in 1936.

KOŠICE see KASSA.

KOSSUTH, LOUIS [LAJOS] (1802–94). Perhaps the best known 19th-century Hungarian statesmen, who had a preeminent leadership role in the Hungarian Revolution of 1848–49 (q.v.). Coming from a family of lower nobility (q.v.), Kossuth made his name at the Hungarian Reform Diets (q.v.) of the 1830s, when he published the *Dietary Proceedings (Országgyűlési Tudósítások)* (1932–36) and the *Parliamentary Proceedings [Törvényhatósági Tudósítások]* (1836–37). With these publications he popularized the struggle for social and political reform in Hungary (q.v.). Because of his radical views and unchecked language, he was arrested in 1837 and then imprisoned until 1840. He devoted his time in prison to learning English, the language of the idealized republic across the sea [United States]. In January 1841 he founded and edited the *Pest Journal (Pesti Hírlap)*, which became the herald of the liberal reformers. He advocated the elimination of the nobles' privileges and fought for his country's sovereignty. But while advocating Hungary's national sovereignty, he paid little attention to the demands of the national minorities (q.v.), such as the Slovaks (q.v.), Romanians (q.v.), Croats (q.v.), and Serbs (q.v.).

His lack of national tolerance, coupled with his views about taking Hungary out of the Habsburg Empire (q.v.), brought him into direct conflict with the "father" of the Hungarian Reform, Count István Széchenyi (q.v.). His irreconcilable views began to alienate, not only the conservative political leaders, but also the more moderate segments of the Hungarian reformers. In 1844 Kossuth was forced out of the editorship of his journal, after which he founded the Protective Association *(Védegylet)* to advance the cause of Hungarian industry and manufacturing against its more advanced Austrian rival. At the diet of 1847-48, Kossuth was accepted as the leader of the Opposition. The news of the February Revolution in France prompted him to demand the approval of the "Opposition Manifesto" *(Ellenzéki Nyilatkozat)* that he had prepared during the previous year. In the new Hungarian government that was headed by Count Batthyány (q.v.), Kossuth became the minister of finance. But by July of that year he concerned himself less with financial matters than with the eventual showdown with Austria (q.v.). At his urging, the Hungarian Parliament (q.v.) established the National Defense Council *(Országos Honvédelmi Bizottság)* (September 1848), which body assumed full power following the resignation of the Batthyány government in late October.

Having been elected president of the National Defense Council, for all practical purposes Kossuth became the dictator of Hungary. He was responsible for radicalizing the situation by openly challenging the Habsburgs, even though his government was forced to flee to Debrecen (q.v.) by the end of the year. Unwilling to listen to voices of moderation, represented, among others, by General Artúr Görgey (q.v.), on April 14, 1849, Kossuth pushed through the dethronement of the Habsburgs (q.v.) as well as his own election as the "Governing President" *(kormányzóelnök)* of Hungary. These acts triggered the Russian military intervention (June 15), which, in turn, doomed the Hungarian Revolution. When sensing the inevitability of the doom, Kossuth transferred his "Governing Presidency" to General Görgey (August 11). But when the latter surrendered to the Russian forces at Világos (August 13), he accused his successor of treason.

Kossuth fled to Turkey, and after a year and a half at Kütahya, went on a tour of the United States (December 4, 1851–July 14, 1852). He hoped to garner enough support to be able to continue his fight against the Habsburgs. He did generate a great deal of enthusiasm, but gained very little practical help. Thus, he returned to Europe a disappointed man.

Kossuth devoted the next fifteen years of his life to various anti-Habsburg schemes, while also elaborating plans for the reorganization of Central Europe (q.v.)—among them his plan for a Danubian Confederation. But after the Austro-Hungarian Compromise of 1867 (q.v.), even he realized that he was chasing unattainable goals. All he could do thereafter was to criticize his former comrades, who had opted to follow the path of realism and came to terms with Austria.

In 1860 Kossuth settled in Italy (q.v.) and, after having relinquished all hopes to return to Hungary, in 1879 he began to assemble his writings under the title *My Papers from the Emigration (Irataim az emigráczióból)*. He died in 1894 in Turin (Torino), Italy, but his remains were immediately repatriated and given an official burial, in spite of the displeasure of Emperor/King Francis Joseph (q.v.).

Kossuth's death only increased his popularity among the common people of Hungary. This was the result of the erroneous view that Kossuth alone was responsible for the dismantlement of feudalism and for the emancipation of the serfs. This over-simplified view became the essence of the patriotism of the common folk, both at home and abroad, including the hundreds of thousands of peasants who emigrated to the United States at the end of the 19th and early 20th centuries. There are several major collections of Kossuth's writings, including The *Papers of Louis Kossuth (Kossuth Lajos Iratai)*(13 vols., 1880-1913), and *The Complete Works of Louis Kossuth (Kossuth Lajos összes munkái)* (in progress; 15 volumes have appeared since 1948).

KOSSUTH EMIGRATION. The group of political emigrés who left Hungary (q.v.) after the unsuccessful Hungarian Revolution of 1848–49 (q.v.). Most of them first went to the Ottoman Empire (q.v.), and from there to Italy, France, England, or the United States. Several thousand of the Kossuth immigrants ended up in the United States, and even Kossuth (q.v.) himself visited the new republic across the sea between December 1851 and July 1852. Because of their social background, few of the Kossuth immigrants could fit into America's society of self-made men. They tried their hands at everything, but after a while—especially after the Austro-Hungarian Compromise of 1867 (q.v.)—many of them repatriated to Hungary. They had a significant role in the Union Armies during the Civil War, partially because of their belief in human freedom, and partially because the military way of life appealed to them much more than did civilian life, which usually involved the type of work that was alien to their background. The Kossuth emigrés established Hungary's image as a land of freedom-loving gentry-nobility, an image that appealed to most Americans, notwithstanding their attachment to democracy. This image was altered and then destroyed by the simple turn-of-the-century economic immigrants, whose presence turned the Hungarian gentry image into the image of a Hunky (q.v.).

KOVÁCS, IMRE (1913-80). One of the best known Hungarian Populist (q.v.) intellectuals who rose to prominence with the publication of his sociographical work, *The Silent Revolution (A némaforradalom)*(1937), which was a very powerful indictment of the remnants of feudalism in interwar Hungarian society. In the same year he was one of the founders of the March Front (q.v.) that demanded a thorough social and political transformation of Hungary (q.v.), while in 1939 he participated in the establishment of the National Peasant Party (q.v.). During World War II (q.v.), Kovács was an active member of the underground Resistance Movement (q.v.). After the war, in 1945 he became the general secretary, and then in 1946 the president of the National Peasant Party. Being pushed out of power by the crypto-communists, Kovács left Hungary in 1947 and two years later emigrated to the United States. He joined the staff of the Free Europe Committee (1949), where—with some intermissions—he stayed until his retirement.

In addition to being involved in emigré politics, Kovács wrote profusely for various emigré periodicals in Europe and North America. These include the *New Horizon (Új Látóhatár)*(Munich), the *Literary Gazette (Irodalmi Újság)* (London-Paris), the *Canadian Hungarians (KanadaiMagyarság)* (Toronto), as well as others. He also edited *The New Hungarian Quarterly* (1961-63) and the Free Europe Committee's *News from Hungary (Magyarországi Hírek)* (1963-78). In addition to the already mentioned *The Silent Revolution,* Kovács's most significant works include: *Emigration [Akivándorlás]* (1938), *In the Shadow of the Soviets (Im Schatten der Sowjets)* (1948), *Facts about Hungary* (1958), *The Conquest of Hungary (Magyarországmegszállása)* (1979); *The March Front (A Márciusi Front)* (1980), and his posthumous *Populism, Radicalism, Democracy: Publicistic Essays (Népiség, radikalizmus, demokrácia. Publicisztikai írások)* (1992).

KRAJCÁR [KREUTZER]. Small monetary unit in the category of the penny. Between the late 18th century and 1892, hundred *krjacárs* made up a single *forint* (q.v.). After 1892 the *krajcár* was replaced by the *fillér* (q.v.). During much of the 19th century, two *krajcárs* were worth about one U.S. cent.

KRISTÓ, GYULA (b.1939). One of the most prominent and most prolific medievalists of Hungary (q.v.) who is also a noted practitioner of several auxiliary sciences of history (q.v.). A product of the University of Szeged, Kristó stayed home and became the founder of a "School of Medieval History" at his alma mater, where he also served as the dean of humanities (1987–89) and as the president (1982–85) of the university. A prolific researcher and writer, Kristó has authored well over two dozen works, some of them pushing back the frontiers of early Hungarian history. They include: *The Provincial Lordship of Matthew Csák (Csák Máté tartományi hatalma)* (1973), *The History of the Eleventh Century Principality in Hungary (A XI. századi hercegség története Magyarországon)* (1974), *The Century of the Golden Bulls (Az aranybullák évszázada)* (1976), *Feudal Disunity in Hungary (Feud-ális széttagolódás Magyarországon)* (1979), *From Levedi's Tribal Federation to St. Stephen's State (Levedi törzsszövetségtől Szent István államáig)* (1980), *The Wars of the Age of the Árpáds (Az Árpád-kor háborúi)* (1986),*The Árpádian Rulers (Az Árpád-házi uralkodók)* (1988), *The Evolution of the Counties in Hungary (A vármegyék kialakulása Magyarországon)* (1988), *The Wars of the Age of the Anjous (Az Anjou-kor háborúi)* (1988), *Archives of the Anjou Period (Anjou-kori oklevéltár)* vols. I and II (1990–92), *The Rise and Decline of the Árpád Dynasty (Az Árpád-ház tündöklése és hanyatlása)* (1992), and *The Carpathian Basin and the Ancient History of the Hungarians to 1301 (A Kárpátmedence és a magyarság régmultja 1301-ig)* (1993). Kristó also served as the editor-in-chief and the primary author of the recently published *Medieval Hungarian Historical Encyclopedia, 9th-14th Century (Korai Magyar Történeti Lexikon, 9–14. század)* (1994).

KÜKÜLLEI, JÁNOS [JOHANNES DE KÜKÜLLE] (c.1320–93). A chronicler who had served King Louis the Great (q.v.) in various clerical and administrative offices, including that of his personal chaplain (1358–82). Küküllei authored the history of the reign of King Louis under the title *Chronicle of King Louis (Chronicon de Ludovico rege)* during the 1380s. Although the original work did not survive the ravages of history, it was preserved as part of István Thuróczy's (q.v.) *Chronicle of the Hungarians (Chronica Hungarorum)* (1488).

KULAK [KULÁK]. A derogatory term for the well-to-do peasants in the Soviet Union (q.v.), which after 1945 was also introduced to Hungary (q.v.). After 1948 all Hungarian peasants who owed more than 25 *holds* (10 hectares) of land were labeled *kulaks*, lost their lands, and suffered various other forms of persecution. After being forced off their lands, they were compelled to work as wage earners in *kolkhozes* (q.v.) or in industry and mining. The *kulaks* were legally rehabilitated in 1989.

KUN [CUMANI, COMANI, KIPCHAK, POLOVTSI] see **CUMANS.**

KUN, BÉLA (1886–1938). One of the founders of the Communist Party of Hungary (q.v.) and the leading figure of the Hungarian Soviet Republic (q.v.) in 1919. Born and educated in Transylvania (q.v.)—then still part of Hungary (q.v.)—Kun became associated with the socialist movement in his high school days. In 1914 he was drafted and sent to the eastern front. Captured by the Russians in 1916, he found his way to the Bolsheviks and soon became one of their political organizers in Petrograd (St. Petersburg, Leningrad) and Moscow. Kun returned home in November 1918 at the specific orders of Lenin, and he immediately went to work to prepare a communist takeover of Hungary. After the establishment of the Hungarian Soviet Republic (March 21, 1919), he assumed the posts of the commissar for foreign affairs and the commissar for military affairs. He was often personally involved in the actions of the Hungarian Red Army that tried to preserve much of Historic Hungary (q.v.). During the same period he was also accused of complicity in the so-called "Red Terror" (q.v.). After the fall of the Soviet Republic (August 1, 1919), Kun emigrated to Vienna (q.v.), and then in 1920 to Bolshevik Russia, where he became active in the newly founded Third Communist International or Commintern. Between 1921 and 1936 he was a member of its Executive Committee, and for a while (1928-35) also of its Presidential Council. In 1936 Kun fell victim to the Stalinist purges. He was arrested, allegedly because of his close association with Bucharin, and then executed in August 1938.

KÚRIA [MAGYAR KIRÁLYI KÚRIA, HUNGARIAN RO-YAL CURIA] see CURIA.

KURSZÁN [KUSAN, CUSA, CUSAN, CURZAN] (d.904). The name of the chief or sacred prince among Conquering Hungarians of the late 9th century who held the title of *kende* (q.v.) Although the de facto power was in the hands of Prince Árpád (q.v.), who held the title of *gyula* (q.v.), Prince Kurszán also had a significant role in the conquest of the Carpathian Basin (q.v.). He was killed by the Bavarians in 904, after which his lands and his title were assumed by Árpád, who combined the titles of *kende* and *gyula* into the common title of grand prince.

KURUC [KURUCOK, CRUCIATUS, CRUSADERS]. Although first used in conjunction with the peasant rebels of the Dózsa Peasant Revolution (q.v.) of the early 16th century, the term *kuruc* is basically the collective name of those Hungarians who rebelled against Habsburg absolutism in the late 17th century under the leadership of Imre Thököly (q.v.). Although suffering defeat, along with their Turkish supporters, during the so-called "Liberation Wars" (q.v.), the *kuruc* movement was resurrected in the Rákóczi War of Liberation (1703–11), which resulted in the compromise Peace of Szatmár (q.v.) of 1711.

Because of their anti-Habsburg stance, the *kuruc* fighters often became idealized and romanticized in Hungarian history, and their struggel fraequently assumed the aura of a war for independence. Their association and alliance with the declining Ottoman Turkish Empire (q.v.), however, has often been viewed as a betrayal of the Western Christian World, and contemporary European public opinion often portrayed them as the enemies of Christianity.

KUTHEN [KÖTÖNY, KÖTÉNY] (d.1241). Ruling prince of the Cumans (q.v.), who in 1238 suffered a major defeat at the hands of the Mongols (q.v.) under the leadership of Batu Khan (q.v.) and then in 1239 asked to be admitted to Hungary (q.v.). King Béla IV (q.v.) permitted Kuthen and his Cumans to settle in his country, but compelled them to accept Christianity. When in the spring of 1241 the Mongols launched their invasion of Hungary with some Cumans in their ranks, the Hungarians wrongly suspected Kuthen to be in Mongol pay and massacred him and his retainers. After Kuthen's death, his Cumans began a systematic destruction of the country and then moved down to the Balkans (q.v.). This Cuman devastation weakened Hungary at the very moment when it was facing the invading Mongols.

- L -

LABANC. The collective name of those Hungarians who supported the Habsburgs (q.v.) in the wars of the late 17th and early 18th century. The latter included the Thököly Uprising of 1678–85 (q.v.), the Liberation Wars of 1683–99 (q.v.), and the Rákóczi War of Independence of 1703–11 (q.v.). The *labanc* fighters—whose name is derived from the disheveled wigs *(loboncos)* of the Imperial military officers—were opposed by the *kuruc* (q.v.) armies, who fought against the Habsburgs, at times with the support of the Ottoman Turks (q.v.). Even though many of the *labanc* were just as dedicated Hungarians as their *kuruc* opponents, their pragmatism was—and still is—oftehn viewed in some circles as a betrayal of the country. As opposed to the term *kuruc*, therefore, the term *labanc* has a very negative connotation in Hungary.

LABOR SERVICE see **FORCED LABOR SERVICE.**

LACKFI [LACZKFI, LACZKFY] (14th c.). The most prominent magnate family of the Age of the Anjou dynasty (q.v.) in Hungary (q.v.), who took their roots back to the Hermann clan of the time of King St. Stephen (q.v.). The first prominent member of the family was "Lack the Son of Dénes" (Dénes fia Lack) (d.1357), the count of the Székelys (q.v.) (1329–42) of Transylvania (q.v.), whose offspring, in turn, called themselves "Lackfi" = "Son of Lack."

From among Dénes's sons, István (d.1355) served as the voievod of Transylvania (q.v.) (1344-50), ban of Croatia–Slavonia (q.v.) (1351-53), lord chief treasurer of Hungary (1343-44, 1353-55), as well as King Louis's commander-in-chief in his Italian campaigns; Dénes (d.1355) served as King Louis's envoy to the Papal Court (1344), the bishop of Tinnin (1348-49) and Zagreb (1349-50), and the archbishop of Kalocsa (1350-55); and Miklós (d.1368) served as the voievod of Transylvania (1367-68), and one of

King Louis's most prominent generals in his Italian and Lithuanian campaigns.

From among István's sons, Dénes (d.1366) was the ban of Szörény (1355-56), the voievod of Transylvania (1359-66), and the ban of Northern Bulgaria (1365-66); Imre (d.1375) was the "master of the horse" (1359-67), ban of Croatia-Slavonia (1368), voievod of Transylvania (1369-72), and palatine (q.v.) of Hungary (1372-75); and István Jr. (d.1397) was the count of the Székelys (1367-70), ban of Croatia-Slavonia (1371-72, 1383-84), voievod of Transylvania (1372-76), and palatine of Hungary (1387-92). István Lackfi was also a member of the Governing Council during King Sigismund's (q.v.) ill-fated Crusade of Nicopolis (q.v.) in 1396. During Sigismund's absence he switched his support to Ladislas of Naples (1377–1414), a claimant to the Hungarian throne. For this he was later arrested and beheaded(1397) at King Sigismund's orders. The family died out with Miklós's son, László, sometime during the 1420s.

LADISLAS I [ST. LADISLAS, SZENT LÁSZLÓ] (c.1040– 95). King of Hungary (r.1077-95), son of King Béla I (q.v.), brother of King Géza I (q.v.), and uncle of King Coloman (q.v.). Coming to the throne at the time of the outbreak of the Investiture Controversy, Ladislas initially sided with the Papacy. When Pope Urban II (r.1088-99) refused to recognize his conquest of Croatia (1089-91), however, he switched over to Emperor Henry IV (r.1056-1106). During the 1080s and early 1090s, he devoted much of his time to Hungary's defense against the pagan Cumans (q.v.), as well as to the consolidation of central power and private property rights in his kingdom. His three law codes (late 1080s and early 1090s) are among the foundation stones of Hungarian constitutionalism.

King Ladislas is credited with completing the foundations of the Catholic Church (q.v.) in Hungary (q.v.) by establishing the Bishoprics of Várad (q.v.) (1080s) and Zagreb (q.v.) (1091), by founding the Abbeys of Somogyvár and Szentjobb (1091), and by arranging the canonization of King St. Stephen (q.v.), Prince Emeric (q.v.), and Bishop Gerard (q.v.) in 1083. Having no sons, King

Ladislas's final years were occupied with the problem of succession to the throne. Of his two nephews, he preferred the younger and healthy Álmos to the crippled Coloman (q.v.), but in order to avoid a civil war, he ultimately accepted the latter's right to succeed him. His daughter Piroska (Irene) (c.1088-1132) later married Byzantine Emperor John II Comnenos (r.1118-43).

King Ladislas was canonized a century after his death (1192) and came to be revered as Hungary's primary Christian knight in its fight against paganism. His cult reached its climax under the rule of King Louis the Great (q.v.) and King/Emperor Sigismund (q.v.) in the 14th and 15th centuries. King Ladislas was buried in the Abbey of Várad (q.v.), where his tomb became a site of pilgrimages. He is generally viewed to be among Hungary's most revered monarchs.

LADISLAS II [LÁSZLÓ] (c.1131-63). King of Hungary (r.1162–63), son of King Béla II (q.v.), and brother of Kings Géza II (q.v.) and Stephen IV (q.v.). As the second son of King Béla the Blind, Ladislas was named the Prince of Bosnia (q.v.) in 1137. But unwilling to accept the preeminence of his older brother, in 1158 or 1160 he rebelled against Géza II, and then fled to the Byzantine court. Following King Géza's death in 1162, Ladislas reappeared in Hungary (q.v.) and had himself crowned king in rivalry with his nephew King Stephen III (q.v.). He died of poison the very next year and was buried at the royal capital of Székesfehérvár (q.v.).

LADISLAS III [LÁSZLÓ] (c.1199-1205). King of Hungary (1204-05), and son of King Emeric (q.v.), who was barely six years old when he died, ruled nominally only for a few months. Although crowned king in his father's lifetime, following the latter's death, Ladislas was forced to flee to Austria (q.v.), where he died within a few months, leaving the throne to his assertive uncle, Andrew II (q.v.). Ladislas was buried at the royal capital of Székesfehérvár (q.v.), next to several other Hungarian kings.

LADISLAS IV [LADISLAS THE CUMAN, KUN LÁSZLÓ] (1262–90). King of Hungary (r.1272–90), son of King Stephen V (q.v.), and grandson of King Béla IV (q.v.). Because of his close association with the pagan Cumans (q.v.), he is generally known as "Ladislas the Cuman" (Kun László) and is one of Hungary's (q.v.) least respected rulers. Ladislas came to the throne at the age of ten with little preparation for ruling. After assuming personal power in 1277, he associated himself primarily with his mother's people, the half-civilized Cumans. This practice ultimately brought upon him the wrath of the Catholic Church (q.v.), resulting in his excommunication by archbishop Ladomér in 1287.

King Ladislas's greatest shortcoming was his inability to deal with the squabbling regional lords, which undermined central power, destroyed normal civil life, and produced feudal anarchy in Hungary. His most significant foreign policy act may have been his decision to support Emperor Rudolph of Habsburg (q.v.) (r.1273-91) against King Ottokar II of Bohemia (r.1253-78) in the Battle of Marchfeld (August 26, 1278), which ended in Rudolph's victor and in Ottokar's defeat and death. This Hungarian-supported victory may have been the single most important element in the rise of the Habsburgs to power (q.v.) and in the creation of the Habsburg Empire (q.v.). King Ladislas was killed by some Cuman ruffians, allegedly hired by the members of the Borsa clan. He was buried in the Abbey of Csanád.

LADISLAS V [LADISLAS POSTHUMUS, UTÓSZÜLÖTT LÁSZLÓ] (1440–57). King of Hungary (r.1440/53–57), son of King/Emperor Albert (q.v.), and grandson of King/ Emperor Sigismund (q.v.). Although crowned in 1440, Ladislas was not really accepted as Hungary's king until 1453, and even then, he ruled mostly as an absentee king from Prague (q.v.). His influence in Hungary (q.v.) was minimal, as the country's fate was still in the hands of its former regent, János Hunyadi (q.v.). In 1452 King Ladislas fell under the influence of Hunyadi's number one rival, Ulrik Cillei (q.v.), who after Hunyadi's death (August 11, 1456), tried to take control over the country. This resulted in Cillei's killing (November 9, 1456) by Hunyadi's supporters, and then in King Ladislas's vengeance against the Hunyadi family. He had

Hunyadi's oldest son, László (1433–57), beheaded, and his younger son, Matthias Corvinus (q.v.), taken captive to Prague. Soon thereafter, Ladislas fell victim to the bubonic plague, which permitted Matthias's election as the new king of Hungary (1458).

LAJTA [LEITHA]. A 135 mile (210 kilometer) long tributary of the Danube (q.v.) that originates to the north of the Semering to the southwest of Vienna (q.v.) and empties into the Danube at Mosonmagyaróvár in Hungary (q.v.). For nearly ten centuries the section of the Leitha on a straight line between Vienna and Buda (Budapest) (q.v.) served as the border between Austria (q.v.) and Hungary (q.v.). Thus, one tended to speak of the two parts of the Habsburg (Austro-Hungarian) Empire (q.v.) as being composed of Cis-Leithania [this side of the Leitha] (q.v.) and Trans-Leithania (that side of the Leitha) (q.v.).

LAJTABÁNSÁG [BANAT OF LAJTA] (1921). An ephemeral and nominal ministate that existed for about five to six weeks in what used to be Western Hungary (q.v.), but is now the province of Burgenland (q.v.) in Austria (q.v.). It was named after the river Lajta (Leitha) (q.v.), which used to be the border between Austria and Historic Hungary (q.v.). It was proclaimed an "independent state" by Lieutenant Colonel Pál Prónay (1875–1944/45), the leader of an army of Hungarian freebooters, on October 4, 1921, and collapsed somewhere between November 6 and 15 of the same year. Prónay and his supporters were trying to save that region for Hungary after the collapse of Austria-Hungary (q.v.) and the signing of the Treaty of Trianon (q.v.) (June 4, 1920), while the political situation was still fluid. The capital of Lajtabánság was the town of Felsőőr (Oberwarth). Prónay evacuated the area starting November 6, 1921, largely under pressure by Regent Nicholas Horthy (q.v.), who was afraid of Western, Yugoslav (q.v.), and Czechoslovak (q.v.) military intervention. Although Prónay never officially proclaimed himself the ban (q.v.) of Lajtabánság, he did establish a military government and also had stamps printed and commemorative medals struck.

LAKITELEK (1987-1988). A town on the Tisza River (q.v.), which was the site of two gatherings of dissident Hungarian Populist (q.v.) intellectuals, who saw the gradual collapse of communism and decided to prepare for it. At the first gathering (September 27, 1987) they established the Hungarian Democratic Forum (HDF) (q.v.) as a loose movement, while at the second gathering (September 3, 1988) they transformed it into an independent social organization. This was followed (March 11-12, 1989) by the Forum's conversion into a political party, which assumed power in May 1990 as the dominant political force in Hungary's (q.v.) first post-communist government. Lakitelek is now the site of a "People's College," an "Emigration Archives," and the Antológia Publishers, all of which are run by the HDF's current president (March 1996), Sándor Lezsák (q.v.).

LAND REFORM. This generally refers to the redistribution of landownership, more specifically to the transfer of lands from the large estate owners to the small peasants. A first land reform was attempted by the Károlyi Regime (q.v.) after World War I (q.v.), which was to transfer all lands above 500 *holds* (200 hectares) to peasant ownership, with provisions for the compensation of the former owners. The Béla Kun's (q.v.) Hungarian Soviet Republic (q.v.) altered these plans and called for the nationalization of all lands above 100 *holds* (40 hectares], with the goal of establishing collective farms or kolkhozes (q.v.). Because of the brevity of these regimes neither of these plans could be fully implemented, and whatever was implemented was immediately undone by the subsequent regimes.

The Horthy Regime (q.v.) was the first to introduce a limited land reform in 1920, which transferred a mere 948,000 *holds* out of a total of 16.6 million *holds*—that is, 5.7 percent of the total agricultural lands—to the poor peasants and to the members of the newly established military Order of Vitéz (q.v.). The first thorough land reform was carried out after World War II (q.v.) by Hungary's postwar coalition government (March 17, 1945), at which time all of the large- and medium-size estates were appropriated and distributed to the poor peasants. This land reform law confiscated all estates above 1,000 *holds* (400 hectares), all lands above 100 *holds* (40 hectares) of estates below 1,000 *holds*, all vineyards and orchards above 20 *holds* (8 hectares), and all forests above 10 *holds* (4 hectares). This was done without any compensation to the former owners, and with minimal obligations on the part of the peasants. This system, however, did not survive for long. After the rise of a monolithic communist system in 1948, the individual ownership of land was proclaimed to be antisocialist, and in the 1950s most of the peasants were forced into agricultural collectives *(kolkhozes)* (q.v.) and state farms. This situation was reversed only after the collapse of the communist regime in 1989-90, which resulted in the return of much agricultural land into private hands.

LANDS OF THE HUNGARIAN CROWN see **HISTORIC HUNGARY**.

LÁSZLÓ, GYULA (b.1910). An archeologist, classical historian, graphic artist, museologist, and past professor of Hungarian archeology at the University of Kolozsvár (q.v.) (1940–44) and the University of Budapest (q.v.) (1944–51, 1957–80). László is best known for his "Theory of Double Conquest," which claims that the so-called "Late Avars" (q.v.) were in fact early Hungarians. But in addition to this theory about Hungarian origins, László wrote a number of path-breaking books on Hungarian archeology and society of the preconquest period, based largely on his own excavations.

The most significant among László's two dozen books and 600 articles include: *The Art of the Conquering Hungarians (A honfoglaló magyarok művészete)* (1943), *The Life of the Conquering Hungarian People (A honfoglaló magyar nép élete)* (1944), *Upon the Path of Hunor and Magyar (Hunor és Magyar nyomában)* (1967), *Hungary's Art at the Time of the Barbarian Invasions (A népvándorláskori művészet Magyarországon)* (1970), *From Vértesszőlős to Pusztaszer. Life in the Carpathian Basin until the Foundation of the Hungarian State (Vértesszőlőstől Pusztaszerig. Élet a Kárpát-medencében a magyar államalapításig)* (1974), *Studies in Archeology (Régészeti tanulmányok)* (1977), *The "Double*

Conquest" (A "kettős honfoglalás") (1978), *Our Ancient History (Őstörténetünk)* (1981), *Árpád's People (Árpád népe)* (1988), and *About Our Ancestors (Őseinkről)* (1990).

LATE AVARS [WANGARS]. The conquerors who entered the Avar Empire (q.v.) around A.D. 670, mixed with the Avars (q.v.), and strengthened their state, which then survived into the early 9th century. During the past two decadesthese "Late Avars" have been identified by Gyula László (q.v.) as the "Early Hungarians" who preceded the Árpádian conquest (q.v.) of Hungary (q.v.) by 120 years, and who later merged with the latecomers. This theory is known as the "Double Conquest" (q.v.), which is based partially on archeological, anthropological, ethnographic, and linguistic evidence, and partially on ancient Hungarian traditions found in medieval chronicles that hold that the Árpádian Conquest (q.v.) was only the last of two or several earlier conquests of the Carpathian Basin (q.v.) by the Hungarians (q.v.). According to some of these views, these series of conquests reach back at least to the Age of Attila (q.v.).

LATIFUNDIUM [LATIFUNDIA]. The Latin name of large landed estates that first developed in the Roman Empire. This term was popularized in Hungary (q.v.) in the 18th century, when, in wake of the expulsion of the Turks (q.v.), the Habsburgs (q.v.) granted large estates to their faithful supporters of whatever nationality. Following the Austro-Hungarian Compromise of 1867 (q.v.), estates in excess of 10,000 *holds* [4,000 hectares] were usually referred to by this name.

LATIN CHRISTIANITY see CATHOLIC CHURCH.

LATIN LANGUAGE IN HUNGARY. Latin had been introduced into Hungary (q.v.) in the late 10th and early 11th centuries along with Catholicism. It soon became the country's primary literary language, as well as the language of the court and the royal documents. By the 13th and 14th centuries Latin had also become the language of the evolving feudal nobility (q.v.) as well as of the feudal diet (q.v.). Laws, decrees, and regulations were written in Latin, as were most of the chronicles, historical epics, and various sacred writings. The climax of Latinism was reached during the Age of Hungarian Humanism (q.v.) in the late 15th and early 16th centuries under Matthias Corvinus (q.v.) and the Jagellonian kings (q.v.). The coming of the Reformation (q.v.), however, emphasized the vernacular and, consequently, by the mid–16th century Latin increasingly had to share its place with the Magyar language (q.v.). Although Latin remained the primary administrative language of Royal or Habsburg Hungary (q.v.), in Transylvania (q.v.) its place was taken over by the Magyar language. Following the expulsion of the Turks (q.v.), the use of Latin expanded to most other parts of reunified Hungary. By the late 18th century, however, it found a new rival in the expanding German language. This process occurred almost simultaneously with the Hungarian National Revival Movement (q.v.), which aided the expansion of the Magyar language. Thus, after eight centuries of dominance, Latin was gradually relegated to a secondary position. The result was that by 1844 Magyar had replaced Latin as the language of the Hungarian diet, as well as the primary language of the Hungarian nobility. Latin, however, continued to survive through the second half of the 19th century, largely via the continued use of hundreds of Latin terms that have become part of the spoken and written Magyar. Most of these were not weeded out until well into the 20th century.

LÁZÁR, GYÖRGY (b.1924). A communist bureaucrat of working-class background who rose through the party ranks and then held the second longest tenure in Hungary's (q.v.) history as the country's prime minister (1975–87). Lázár's tenure coincided with the last phase of the Kádár Regime (q.v.), which is still viewed by many as the age of "goulash communism." (q.v.). But it survived largely on Western credits that more than doubled Hungary's loan obligations from less than eight billion to over sixteen billion U.S. dollars. Although Hungary had become the darling of the West under the system of "advanced socialism" *(fejlett szocializmus)* connected with Lázár's prime ministership, the lack of meaningful structural changes continued to undermine the system, which then collapsed under its own weight. While known for its improving relations with the West, the Lázár Regime is also remembered for its insensitivity to the problems of the Hungarian minorities (q.v.) in the neighboring states, and for its start of the Bős-Nagymaros (Gabčikovo) hydroelectric project on the Danube (q.v.), which brought an ecological disaster upon the northwestern part of Hungary.

LEBEDIA   see LEVEDIA.

LEGEND OF THE WONDROUS STAG [CSODASZAR-VAS MONDA]. A fraction of the legend of Hungarian origins, which was first committed to writing in the late 13th century by the chronicler Simon Kézai (Simon de Kéza) (q.v.). According to this legend, the two sons of King Nimród by the name of Hunor and Magor (Magyar) (q.v.) and two hundred of their retainers went on a hunt. Suddenly, a beautiful white stag appeared before them, which drew them into the swamps of Maeotis, located on the Crimean Peninsula (q.v.). There they encountered several hundred maidens, among them the two daughters of King Dúl of the Alans. They promptly mated with these maidens, and from them originated the two sister nations, the Huns (q.v.) and the Hungarians [Magyars] (q.v.). They grew and prospered, but after a while they became so numerous that they had to leave their original homeland. The Huns were the first to leave, after which they established a large empire that reached the apogee of its power under Attila (q.v.) in the mid-5th century. Several hundred years later the Hungarians also followed the Huns, and eventually conquered the Carpathian Basin (q.v.) that used to be the center of the great Hunnic Empire (q.v.).

LEGITIMISM [LEGITIMIZMUS]. The recognition of the right of succession by members of a ruling dynasty. In Hungary this term became current in 1921, following King Charles IV's (q.v.) second unsuccessful attempt to regain the Hungarian throne, which led to the dethronement of the Habsburg dynasty (q.v.) (November 6, 1921). This legitimist movement tried to restore the Habsburgs (q.v.) in the person of Charles's son, Archduke Otto (q.v.). Legitimism was especially popular among the aristocracy (q.v.), the members of the Catholic clergy (q.v.), an a significant portion of the gentry-based bureaucracy and upper middle class. Hungary remained a "kingdom without a king" throughout the interwar period (q.v.), and not until after World War II (q.v.) (Act 1946:I) was the institution of the monarchy abolished.

LEHEL [LÉL] (d.955). One of the chief commanding generals of the Hungarian armies that invaded the German lands in the mid–10th century. Allegedly, a descendant of one of the conquering chiefs, Lehel disregarded the views of Prince Fajsz (q.v.), who exercised very little power over the individual tribes, and then, along with several other tribal leaders, descended upon Germany (q.v.). In contrast to his earlier campaigns, on this occasion he was trapped and defeated by Emperor Otto the Great (r.936/62–73) at the Battle of Augsburg, also known as the Battle of Lechfeld (955) (q.v.). Following that battle, Lehel and several other Hungarian generals were captured and hanged in the city of Augsburg. According to a Hungarian legend, before his death Lehel was permitted to blow his war horn once more, which then he used to kill Emperor Otto's rebellious son-in-law, Conrad, who had betrayed him. This same legend also claims that Lehel's instrument, which was damaged in this killing, is still in existence in the city of Jászberény in Hungary (q.v.). There does in fact exist a carved ivory horn in Jászberény, which is known as the "Horn of Lehel" (Lehel kürtje). It is a 10th-century Byzantine work, but it is rather unlikely that this was the one used by Lehel after the Battle of Augsburg.

LEITHA see **LAJTA.**

LÉL see **LEHEL.**

LENIN BOYS [LENIN-FIÚK]. The "storm troopers" of the Hungarian Soviet Republic (q.v.) in 1919 under the command of József Cserny (1892–1919), but ultimately under the authority of

Tibor Szamuely (q.v.). During their brief reign of terror (March-
August, 1919), the Lenin Boys consisted of 200 to 400 dedicated
Bolsheviks who made it a point to root out all anti-revolutionary
activities. They were the executors of the so-called "Red Terror"
(q.v.) in Hungary. After the fall of the Hungarian Soviet Republic,
those who failed to emigrate were executed (about twenty of them)
or given long prison sentences.

LEO IV [LEO THE WISE]. Emperor of Byzantine Empire (r.886-
912), who ruled at the time of the Árpádian Conquest of Hungary
(q.v.). He came into contact with the leaders of the Conquering
Magyars [Hungarians] (q.v.) on many occasions, and also wrote
about them in several of his works. The most significant of these is
his *Tactics (Taktika),* which describes the fighting methods of the
Magyars, whom he repeatedly calls "Türks." Leo has also preserved
much other contemporary information about the Hungarians.

LEOPOLD I [LIPÓT] (1640–1705). King of Hungary (r.1657–1705)
and Holy Roman Emperor (r.1658–1705). As the younger son of
Ferdinand III (q.v.), Leopold was reared to be a priest. The early
death of his older brother, Ferdinand IV (q.v.), however, forced him
to give up his original plans so as to assume the leadership of the
Habsburg Empire (q.v.). Being in constant rivalry with Louis XIV's
France, Leopold tried to live peacefully with the Ottoman Turks
(q.v.). Thus, even though the Habsburg forces won an important
victory against the Ottomans at the Battle of St. Gotthard (1664) and
the Treaty of Vasvár (1664), he agreed to permit them to retain all
their Hungarian lands. These unwarranted concessions, combined
with Leopold's attempts to introduce absolutism to Royal Hungary
(q.v.), resulted in an anti-Habsburg conspiracy led by the Hungarian
palatine, Ferenc Wesselényi (q.v.), and supported by several top
aristocrats. Having been revealed to Leopold, the Wesselényi
Conspiracy (q.v.) was suppressed and the conspirators punished.

Leopold's continued support of absolutism and his persecution
of the Protestants (q.v.), however, soon led to a general anti-
Habsburg uprising (1678–85) under the leadership of Imre Thököly

(q.v.). The Habsburgs' (q.v.) successful defense of Vienna (q.v.) in 1683 and the subsequent victories against the Ottoman Turks, resulting in the reconquest of most of Hungary (q.v.), did help Leopold's cause. But the subsequent treatment of Hungary as if it were simply a Habsburg colony led to an even more violent uprising that culminated in the Rákóczi War of Liberation (1703–11) (q.v.). Although physically frail and possessing only modest intellectual capacity, Emperor Leopold still gained much for the Habsburgs. In addition to the acquisition of Transylvania (q.v.) (1691) and the reconquest of Hungary (1699), he forced the Hungarian nobility (q.v.) to give up their right of free election and make the Habsburgs into Hungary's hereditary kings (1687). Leopold died in the midst of two wars—the War of Spanish Succession (1701–14) and the Rákóczi War of Liberation—but it was his successors who had to deal with these wars. The first of them ended in the loss of Spain (Treaty of Utrecht in 1713 and the Treaty of Rastatt in 1714), and the second in significant concessions to the Hungarian nobility (Treaty of Szatmár of 1711) (q.v.).

LEOPOLD II [LIPÓT] (1747–92). King of Hungary (r.1790–92) and Holy Roman Emperor (r.1790–92). Leopold was a younger son of Maria Theresa (q.v.) and of her husband, Holy Roman Emperor Francis of Lorraine (q.v.). He succeededto the throne only because his brother, Emperor Joseph II (q.v.), had no sons. Before ascending the Holy Roman Imperial and the Hungarian thrones, Leopold was the ruler of the Grand Duchy of Tuscany, where he was known for his enlightened reforms. At the time of his accession, the Habsburg Empire (q.v.) was in a war with the Ottoman Empire (q.v.), close to a war with France, and faced open rebellions in the Austrian Netherlands (Belgium) and in Hungary (q.v.). Except for France, Leopold pursued a policy of compromise. He concludedpeace with the Ottomans at the Treaty of Sistovo in 1791, and ended the rebellions in Hungary and the Netherlands through moderate appeasements. Knowing that he could not avoid the challenge from revolutionary France, he concluded a military alliance with Frederick

William II (r.1786–97) of Prussia (q.v.), but then died before the outbreak of the war.

Leopold appears to have been just as enlightened as his brother, but in contrast to Joseph II (q.v.), he was also a pragmatic man, who always took into consideration the existing realities. His death robbed the Habsburg Empire of a potentially great ruler and substituted instead a man of modest capacities. His son and successor, Francis II (I) (q.v.), was the last Habsburg to wear the crown of the Holy Roman Empire, and also the first to be known as the emperor of Austria. His brother, Archduke Joseph Anton (q.v.), became the palatine (q.v.) of Hungary (r.1795–1847) and the progenitor of the Hungarian branch of the House of Habsburg.

LEVEDIA [LEBEDIA]. One of the earlier homelands of the Magyars (Hungarians) (q.v.), which they held before occupying Etelköz (q.v.) around A.D. 830. Levedia was allegedly named after the Hungarian prince Levedi, who led the Hungarians to Etelköz. Levedia was probably an outlying part of the Khazar Empire (q.v.), and it was located on both sides of the Don River, embracing the region between the Lower Volga and the Azov Sea (q.v.), immediately to the north of modern Stavropol. Levedia may have been occupied by the Hungarians for at least two centuries before they moved on to Etelköz (c.830) and then to the Carpathian Basin (q.v.) (c.895–96).

LEVENTE [LIÜNTIKA] (d.920s). The oldest son and successor of Prince Árpád (q.v.). He was probably in charge of the Kabar tribes (q.v.) at the time of the conquest of the Carpathian Basin (q.v.). Following Árpád's death in or around 907, Levente probably became the head of the Hungarian Tribal Federation (q.v.).

LEVENTE MOVEMENT. A paramilitary organization founded in 1921 for rural youth between the ages of 12 and 21. The purpose of the levente movement was to indoctrinate the nation's young with patriotism and revisionism (q.v.). Its obligatory nature made it very unpopular. Thus, during the 1930s its leaders tried to adopt some of the methods of the scouting movement (q.v.), which was basically an organization for the middle- and upper-class youth of interwar Hungary (q.v.). In 1939, membership in the levente organization was made obligatory for all young males, and on a voluntary basis even for girls between the ages of 10 and 19. Following the assumption of political power by the Arrow Cross Party (q.v.) in October 1944, many of the levente youth were drafted into special battalions to fight to the end. The movement was disbanded by the first postwar regime in the spring of 1945.

LEVIRATY [LEVIRATE, LEVIRÁTUS]. A custom going back to biblical times, when a man's widow with no sons was obliged to marry her dead husband's brother to produce a male heir. This custom prevailed in Hungarian tribal society, amended in such a way that the widow was obliged to marry the eldest male member of the extended family (e.g., the brother, cousin, or even the father of her deceased husband). Based on this tradition Koppány (q.v.) wanted to marry Sarolta, the widow of Grand Prince Géza (q.v.), and thus inherit the throne, in place of Géza's son Vajk/Stephen (future King St. Stephen) (q.v.). On a limited scale, this system survived in Hungary into the modern period, although increasingly in conflict with the teachings and practices of the Catholic Church (q.v.).

LEZSÁK, SÁNDOR (b.1949). A poet, writer, and country school teacher, who in 1987 was one of the founders of the Hungarian Democratic Forum (HDF) (q.v.), and since March 1996—when the MDF split into two—he became its president. A member of the HDF's upper leadership ever since the start, in 1993 Lezsák served for a few months as the party's acting president, and in 1994 he was elected to the Hungarian Parliament (q.v.). Lezsák is also the founding-president of the People's College *(Népfőiskola)* (1991), the "Emigration Archives," and the Antológia Publishers *(Antológia Kiadó)* of Lakitelek (q.v.), as well as of the Lakitelek Foundation that supports these institutions. In addition to a few books of verses, Lezsák is known primarily as the scriptwriter of the rock opera *Attila, the Sword of God (Attila, Isten kardja).*

LIBERAL PARTY [SZABADELVŰ PÁRT] (1875–1906). The political party that governed Hungary for three decades during the Age of Dualism (q.v.). It was born in 1875 from the fusion of the Deák Party (q.v.) and the so-called "Left Central Opposition" under the leadership of Kálmán Tisza (q.v.). The Liberal Party was a strong supporter of the Austro-Hungarian Compromise of 1867 (q.v.) and tried to uphold this dualism (q.v.) through a tight party control over its parliamentarians. For this reason, the latter came to be known as the *Mameluks* (slaves) (q.v.)—a term borrowed from the Mamluk Sultans of Egypt.

The Liberal Party supported Austria-Hungary's occupation of Bosnia (q.v.) in 1878, the Dual Monarchy's close cooperation with Imperial Germany (q.v.) as expressed in the Dual Alliance of 1879 (q.v.), as well as the continued preeminence of the Magyars (q.v.) within the Kingdom of Hungary (q.v.). Its most influential guiding spirit was Kálmán Tisza, who served as prime minister for a decade and a half (r.1875–90). Others included Baron Béla Wenckheim (q.v.) (r.1875), Count Gyula Szapáry (q.v.) (r.1890–92), Sándor Wekerle (q.v) (r.1892–95), Baron Dezső Bánffy (q.v.) (r.1895–99), Kálmán Széll (q.v.) (r.1899–1903), Count Károly Khuen-Héderváry(r.1903) (q.v.), and Count István Tisza (q.v.) (r.1903–05). During the 1890s and early 1900s the Liberal Party lost its popularity, partially because of its insensitivity to social issues, and partially because it was unable to fulfill the growing aspirations of Hungarian national independence within the context of dualism.

In 1905 the Liberal Party lost the elections for the first time in three decades, after which it fell apart. Many of its former members came together in the National Social Circle *(Nemzeti Társaskör)* (1906–10), which they transformed in 1910 into the National Labor Party (NLP) *(Nemzeti Munkapárt)* (q.v.) (1910–17). Led by Count Tisza, for the next seven years the NLP became the main governmental party within the ruling coalition, which lasted almost to the very end of the Austro-Hungarian Empire (q.v.).

LIBERATION WARS (1683–99). Lasting for over sixteen years, the Liberation Wars were the accidental by-products of the Second

Siege of Vienna (q.v.), which ended in Turkish defeat and initiated the collapse of Ottoman rule (q.v.) in Hungary (q.v.). Following the victory at Vienna (q.v.), the Habsburg imperial generals Charles of Lorraine (1643–90), Louis of Baden (1677–1707), and later Eugene of Savoy (q.v.) (1663–1736) pushed into Hungary, and by 1686 liberated the ancient Hungarian capital of Buda (q.v.). This was followed by the victorious Second Battle of Mohács (1687), and then by the similarly victorious Battle of Zenta (1697). Two years later the exhausted Turks (q.v.) signed the Treaty of Karlowitz (January 26, 1699) (q.v.), wherein they relinquished all of Historic Hungary, with the exception of the Banat of Temesvár (q.v.).

The Liberation Wars were destructive, not only to the Turks, but also to Hungary and its population. After sixteen years of plunder by the opposing Habsburg (q.v.) and Ottoman (q.v.) armies, the country was destroyed, devastated, denuded, and depopulated. The Habsburgs tried to solve this problem through a policy of colonization, which awarded large estates to foreigners and altered the country's ethnic composition. This policy planted the roots of the national minority problems of the 19th century, and Hungary's dismemberment in the 20th century. Moreover, it also produced an immediate reaction on the part of the Hungarian nobility (q.v.), many of whom felt cheated out of their lands, which resulted in the protracted and destructive military struggle known as the Rákóczi War of Liberation (q.v.).

LITHUANIA see **POLISH-LITHUANIAN COMMON-WEALTH.**

LIBRARIES see **NATIONAL SZÉCHENYI LIBRARY, CORVINA LIBRARY.**

LITTLE ENTENTE [KISANTANT] (1920–21). A political and military alliance established by Czechoslovakia (q.v.) and Yugoslavia (q.v.) (August 14, 1920), soon joined by Romania (q.v.) (April 23, 1921), for the purposes of upholding the territorial reorganization of Central Europe (q.v.) as specified by the post-

World War I treaties (q.v.). Dedicated to fight against Hungarian revisionism (q.v.), with the strong support of France, it fell apart in wake of the Munich Agreement (September 29, 1938), which began the dismemberment of Czechoslovakia.

LITTLE YUGOSLAVIA. The new South Slavic (q.v.) state that came into being in the course of 1991–92 as a result of the disintegration of Yugoslavia (q.v.) that had been established after World War I (q.v.). With the secession of Slovenia (q.v.), Croatia (q.v.), Bosnia-Herzegovina (q.v.), and Macedonia, Little Yugoslavia today consists only of Serbia (q.v.), Montenegro, and the former Hungarian territory of Voivodina (q.v.). Given the war in Bosnia, the future size and status of Little Yugoslavia is still uncertain.

LÓFŐ. One of the upper segments of *the Székely [Szekler]* (q.v.) society of Transylvania (q.v.) during the Middle Ages and the Early Modern Period. In the 15th and 16th centuries, the *lófő* nobles still possessed considerable landed property, but by the 18th and 19th centuries, most of them became relatively poor.

LÓRÁNTFFY, ZSUZSANNA (c.1600-60). Although an offspring of a prominent Hungarian magnate family, Zsuzsanna Lórántffy became part of Hungarian history only by virtue of her marriage (1616) to György Rákóczi I (q.v.), the future ruling prince of Transylvania (r.1630–48). Being a devout Calvinist (q.v.), she had a significant role in influencing her husband's anti-Habsburg policies, as well as in his support of various Protestant causes. Lórántffy was especially supportive of the Calvinist College of Sárospatak, located on her patrimonial estates. Following the death of her husband in 1648, she left Transylvania (q.v.), settled down in Sárospatak and made the local college into the most prestigious school among all Hungarian Protestant colleges. She invited and appointed a number of well-known foreign professors, including the famous Czech educator and social philosopher, John Amos Comenius (q.v.). Being opposed to some of the orthodox tendencies within the Hungarian Reformed Church (q.v.), she favored the participation of the common folk in its leadership. She also supported the education of the Vlach (Romanian) settlers in southeastern Transylvania, for in 1657 she founded a school for them at Fogaras.

To advance the cause of Protestant learning, to spread the Calvinist faith, and to aid the Reformed clergy in their debates against their Catholic rivals, in 1651 Zsuzsanna Lórántffy established a printing press at Sárospatak. She herself debated and wrote extensively, although only one of her works ever appeared in print under the title *Moses and the Prophets (Mózes és a próféták)* (1641). Another of her writing, *About the origins of the Holy Spirit (A Szentlélek származásáról),* remained unpublished and disappeared. In light of her many activities on behalf of the Hungarian Reformed Church, Zsuzsanna Lórántffy is viewed as "one of the brightest lights" of Hungarian Calvinism.

LORD CHIEF JUSTICE [IUDEX CURIAE REGIAE, OR-SZÁGBÍRÓ]. The highest national officer after the palatine (q.v.) in medieval and early modern Hungary (q.v.). This office came into being in the 12th century, when the palatine's office gained national significance and many of its judicial and economic functions in running the royal estates devolved upon the palatine's second-in-command. By the early 13th century, the lord chief justice became the highest judge in the Royal Court, who represented the king in the latter's absence. In the 14th century, he was considered the highest justice in the Kingdom of Hungary (q.v.). Yet, he still could not make legal decisions contradicting those of the king or the palatine. During the 18th and the 19th centuries, he performed functions that in effect made him into the vice palatine. The office of the lord chief justice lost its functions in 1884, after which it became an honorific title until 1945.

LORD CHIEF TREASURER [MAGISTER TAVERNICO-RUM, TÁRNOKMESTER, FŐKINCSTARTÓ]. Initially an officer of the Royal Court, but later the holder of one of the top offices of the realm. During the age of the Árpáds (q.v.), the lord chief treasurer handled the income from the Royal possessions and

Royal monopolies *(regale)* (q.v.). But after the establishment of Royal Treasury (q.v.) (14th–19th c.], the lord chief treasurer became a kind of superior justice dealing with the judicial matters concerning a segment of the Royal Free Cities (q.v.). From the early 16th century onward, he was the third in rank after the palatine (q.v.) and the lord chief justice (q.v.). Thus, in the absence of the first two, he chaired the Upper House (q.v.) of the Hungarian Diet (q.v.) as well as the Seven-Person Court (q.v.). After the Austro-Hungarian Compromise of 1867 (q.v.), the office of the lord chief treasurer became purely ceremonial.

LORD LIEUTENANT [COMES, SUPREMUS COMES, FŐISPÁN]. He was the monarch's representative at the head of each autonomous county. Originally called *ispán (comes)* (q.v.), in the 15th century the lord lieutenant's title was changed to *főispán (supremus comes,* chief lord lieutenant). His most important function was to carry out the royal decrees and to lead the military *banderia* (q.v.) of the county nobility (q.v.). With the development of the "nobles' county" (q.v.) in the 16th century, however, the role of the *főispán* declined and it was increasingly assumed by the *alispán (vice comes,* vice lord lieutenant] (q.v.), who was the representative of the local nobility. During the Age of Dualism (q.v.), the royally appointed *főispán* was the trustee of the government. In 1950 this office was abolished and replaced by system of communist councils *(soviets)* (q.v.), and then in 1990, by a system of self-governing councils *(önkormányzat)* (q.v.).

LORRAINE, PRINCE CHARLES [LOTHARINGIAI KÁROLY] (1643–90). Habsburg Imperial general during the first half of the Liberation Wars (q.v.). He was the commander-in-chief of the Habsburg Imperial Armies (1683-88), who participated in the lifting of the Second Siege of Vienna (q.v.) in 1683, led the liberation of Buda (q.v.) in 1686, and had a significant role in the expulsion of the Turks (q.v.) from much of Hungary (q.v.).

LOUIS I [LOUIS THE GREAT, NAGY LAJOS] (1326–82). King of Hungary (r.1342–82) and Poland (r.1370–82), son of King Charles I Robert (q.v.), and father of Queen Maria (q.v.) of Hungary (q.v.) and Queen Jadwiga (q.v.) of Poland (q.v.). King Louis, the second member of the Hungarian branch of the Anjou dynasty (q.v.), expanded his country's influence from the Adriatic (q.v.) and the Black Seas (q.v.) in the south, to the Baltic Sea (q.v.) in the north. In 1338 Louis was named by his father the prince of Transylvania (q.v.) and in 1342 he ascended the throne of Hungary (q.v.). He devoted much of his life to the extension of Hungary's political and military influence.

In 1345 King Louis reasserted his country's control over Croatia (q.v.), and after an earlier unsuccessful attempt in 1358, he also acquired from Venice all of Dalmatia (q.v.), along with its islands, including the Republic of Ragusa (Dubrovnik) (q.v.). He reasserted Hungary's rule on the Adriatic in another long war with Venice toward the end of his reign (1377–81). Between 1343 and 1378, King Louis pursued at least seven wars against Serbia (q.v.), which ultimately resulted in making Prince Lazar's domain a Hungarian vassal state. In 1357 he also gained control over western Bosnia (q.v.), and in 1366 the ban of Bosnia became his vassal. Louis followed a policy of expansion also toward Wallachia (q.v.) (1344–75) and northern Bulgaria (q.v.) (1365–69), forcing the rulers of these states to become his vassals. In the east he fought against the Crimean Tatars (q.v.), and in several campaigns (1345–70) also tried to make Moldavia (q.v.) a vassal state, but there he achieved only limited success.

King Louis had an unusually good relationship with his uncle, Casimir the Great of Poland (r.1333–70). He participated in a number of Casimir's wars against the Lithuanians and the Tatars (1351–55). In 1370, after Casimir's death, Louis inherited the Polish throne, but by remaining an absentee ruler, he never became popular in that country. Yet, he still pursued his wars against the Lithuanians, and in 1372 also extended Hungary's control over Halich (Galicia) (q.v.).

King Louis was related both to the Luxemburgs (q.v.) of Bohemia (q.v.) and to the Habsburgs (q.v.) of Austria (q.v.). Relations among these dynasties were generally friendly, although there were also occasional conflicts. His least successful efforts were his campaigns to the Kingdom of Naples, where, in 1345, his young brother, Andrew (q.v), had been murdered with the complicity of his own wife, Johanna (q.v.). In 1347–48 and 1350 King Louis personally led two punitive campaigns to Italy (q.v.), but Johanna managed to escape his wrath with the support of the Popes of Avignon. After his first Italian campaign, Louis assumed the title "King of Sicily" and also revived the title "King of Jerusalem," which had been first assumed by Andrew II (q.v.) in the early 13th century. The latter title survived until the very end of the Habsburg Empire (q.v.) and of Historic Hungary (q.v.) in 1918.

The final years of King Louis's reign were occupied with the problem of succession. He had no sons, and of his three daughters, only two survived. Wishing to retain the unity of his realm, he wanted to have Maria (q.v.) acknowledged both in Hungary and in Poland. For this reason he confirmed the unique privileges of the Polish nobility in the Charter of Kassa in 1374, in which he also exempted them from all taxes, save a nominal levy on landed property. His aim, however, was not realized. The Polish estates decided to elect his younger daughter, Hedvig (Jadwiga) (q.v.), and thus ended the Hungarian-Polish personal union.

King Louis's reign saw the influx of late medieval Italian and French culture and the principles of knighthood into Hungary, along with some of the early influences of the Italian Renaissance. It was under his rule that the idealization of Hungary "knight king"—St. Ladislas (q.v.)—had reached its climax. In 1351 he reaffirmed the terms of the Golden Bull of Hungary (q.v.), and in 1367 established Hungary's first university at Pécs (q.v.). The latter was Central Europe's (q.v.) fourth institution of higher learning, following Prague (1348), Cracow (1364), and Vienna (1365), but predating Heidelberg (1386). King Louis himself usually acted like a medieval knight. Most of the time he led his armies personally, and often became engaged in one-to-one combats. King Louis's reign saw the conquest of much of the Balkans (q.v.) by the Ottoman Turks (q.v.), as well as their first incursion into Southern Hungary (1375). But Louis did not seem to have taken the Turkish threat seriously. His last years were taken up by his skin disease, which drove him into an ever deeper religiosity. He died in the fall of 1382 and was buried in Székesfehérvár (q.v.). He was a popular king and one of Hungary's greatest rulers, whose memory has been preserved as that of a generous and fair knight who was always willing to fight for what he judged to be a just cause.

LOUIS II [LAJOS, LUDOVIK] (1506–26). King of Hungary (r.1516-26) and Bohemia (r.1516-26), son of King Vladislav II (q.v.), and the last of the Jagellonians (q.v.) on the Hungarian throne. Having been crowned king of Hungary (q.v.) and Bohemia (q.v.) already as a child (in 1508 and 1509), Louis succeeded his father in 1516. He married Maria of Habsburg (1505–58), the granddaughter of Emperor Charles V (r.1519–56) and the sister of the future King Ferdinand I (q.v.) already in 1515, but the marriage was not consummated until 1521 when Louis came of age.

During Louis's minority, the government of Hungary (q.v.) was under the control of Archbishop Tamás Bakócz (q.v.), Lord Chief Treasurer János Bornemisza (d.1527), and Marquis George of Brandenburg. Unable to comprehend the Turkish danger from the Balkans (q.v.), the young king paid little attention to Hungary's southern defenses, and he was also lax in ending the anarchy that pitted Hungary's regional lords against one another. He fought bravely at the Battle of Mohács (q.v.) in 1526, but was unable to stem the Turkish tide and lost his life in this attempt. King Louis's remains were buried at Székesfehérvár (q.v.). His death was followed by the dual election of Ferdinand of Habsburg (q.v.) and John Zápolya (q.v.) to throne. This, in turn, resulted in the country's trisection, accompanied by the loss of Hungary's full independence for several centuries.

LOUIS THE GREAT see LOUIS I.

LOWER HOUSE. The feudal Lower House of the Hungarian Diet (q.v.) was established in 1606, when, for the first time, the Hungarian aristocracy (q.v.) and common nobility (q.v.) began to meet separately. Hereafter, the members of the upper nobility (q.v.) and the representatives of the common nobility (q.v.) congregated separately in the two houses of the diet. In 1848, the Lower House *(alsó tábla)* and the Upper House *(felső tábla)* were replaced by a unicameral Parliament (q.v.). With the reestablishment of the bicameral legislature (1885–1918 and 1926–45), the Lower House *(alsóház)* was also reestablished under a different name.

LOWER HUNGARY [ALSÓ-MAGYARORSZÁG]. As used during the Turkish period (q.v.) in the 16th and 17th centuries, this term referred to the western half of Northern Hungary (q.v.), that is, to the western half of today's Slovakia (q.v.). Contrary to common assumption, therefore, it is not equivalent to Southern Hungary (q.v.). To the east of Lower Hungary was Upper Hungary (q.v.), from which it was divided by the eastern borders of the counties of Liptó, Zólyom, and Nógrád. Starting with the mid-16th century, Lower Hungary was under the control of its own captain general *(főkapitány)*, who was stationed at Érsekújvár, located to the north of the fortress of Komárom on the Danube (q.v.). During the 19th century, the term Lower Hungary gradually lost its currency.

LOWER NOBILITY [KISNEMESSÉG]. The lowest rank of the Hungarian nobility whose members usually lived in the provinces, owned little or no property, and survived almost on the level of the peasant masses. Many of them were involved in subsistence farming and worked their lands themselves without the benefit of serf ownership. At various times, they went under different names, including *"bocskoros nemesség"* (sandaled nobility), *"hétszilvafás nemesség"* (nobility with seven plum trees), and *"kisnemesség"* (small nobility). They were referred to by these names because they were generally so poor that they could not even buy boots for themselves, nor did they own property that held more than a half a dozen (seven) plum trees. During the Hungarian Reform Period (q.v.), the members of the lower nobility were among the staunchest opponents of reform, because they felt that if they were to lose their legal privileges, they would be hardly distinguishable from the peasantry. Their fears turned out to be correct, for after serf emancipation (q.v.) in 1848, most of them did, in fact, merge into the ranks of the free peasantry. The lower nobility was officially part of the common nobility *(köznemesség)* (q.v.), but it represented the lowest level of that nobility, whose upper level consisted of well-to-do nontitled nobles, the so-called propertied nobility *(birtokos nemesség)* (q.v.). The latter usually controlled political life in the autonomous Hungarian counties (q.v.) and pressured the lower nobility to vote the way they wanted them to vote.

LUCRUM CAMERAE [KAMARAHASZNA]. One of the important sources of Royal income during the 11th through the early 14th centuries, derived from the obligatory exchange of older coins for newer ones that had lower silver or gold content. King Charles Robert (q.v.) abolished this obligatory exchange and instituted the gate tax (q.v.) as a primary source of royal income.

LUGOSI, BÉLA (1883-1956). One of the best known Hungarian-American actors and film stars, who made his name widely known by starring in dozens of Dracula (q.v.) films, which made his name virtually synonymous with that of Count Dracula (q.v.). After performing in the theaters of Szeged (q.v.) and Budapest (q.v.), Lugosi left Hungary in 1919 after the collapse of the Hungarian Soviet Republic (q.v.), with which he sympathized. After a brief spell in Berlin, in 1921 he emigrated to the United States, where he tried to make it on the New York stage. After some modest successes, he was discovered by fellow Hungarians in Hollywood, who gave him a role in Bram Stoker's *Dracula,* a role from which he was never able or willing to escape.

LUKÁCS, GYÖRGY [GEORGE] (1885-1971). A noted literary critic, essayist, and philosopher, who, during the first half of the 20th century, was perhaps the most sophisticated exponent of

Marxist philosophy in Hungary (q.v.) and throughout much of the world. Born into a wealthy banking family, Lukács studied in Hungary and in Germany (q.v.), gaining his doctorate in law at the University of Kolozsvár (q.v.) in 1906. For the next eleven years he moved back and forth between Hungary and Germany, living and working in Budapest, Berlin, and Heidelberg. Lukács was drawn to Marxism from the philosophical point of view, wherefore in 1918 he joined the newly established Communist Party of Hungary (q.v.), and soon after became a member of the government of the Hungarian Soviet Republic (q.v.).

After the fall of the Hungarian Soviet Republic, Lukács fled abroad and eventually settled in the Soviet Union (q.v.), where he became involved in the work of the Third Communist International and also produced works of literary criticism as a member of the Marx-Engels Institute and the Institute of Philosophy of the Soviet Academy of Sciences. Returning home after a quarter century of exile, in August 1945 Lukács became a member of the Provisional Parliament and was also appointed professor of philosophy at the University of Budapest (q.v.). In the meanwhile, however, he had become disenchanted with the excesses of applied Marxism (i.e., Stalinism), which pushed him increasingly into the opposition and into the camp of Imre Nagy (q.v.). During the Hungarian Revolution of 1956 (q.v.), he was named minister of culture and education in the Nagy government. After the defeat of the revolution, Lukács was Arrested briefly imprisoned (1956-57). He lived in obscurity until the mid-1960s, when he was rehabilitated and permitted to publish. By that time he had become so popular among progressive Marxist intellectuals that he had risen to the position of a sage, creating a virtual "school" around himself.

During his younger days Lukács was a staunch critic of Hungary's social system controlled by the old landed nobility and the new financial aristocracy (which included his own father). At the same time he also viewed with skepticism all manifestations of Populism (q.v.) that tended to idealize the peasants. Initially he believed that Marxism represented a solution for all of society's ills. He developed a special version of Marxist esthetics, wherein he drew a connection between creative art and social struggle. Later, however, he became less certain of the all-embracing power of Marxism, especially in light of the perversion of that ideology when applied to actual practice—as happened under Stalin in the Soviet Union (q.v.) and under Rákosi (q.v.) in Hungary (q.v.).

Lukács's most important works, many of them originally written in German, include: *The History of the Development of the Modern Drama (A modern dráma fejlődésének története)* (1911), *The Soul and the Forms (A lélek és a formák)* (c.1911), *The Theory of the Novel (A regény elmélete)* (c.1914-15), and *History and Class Consciousness (Történelem és osztálytudat)* (1923)—the latter being labeled "revisionist" by some orthodox Marxists. Lukács's later works include: *The Literary Theories of Marx and Engels (Marx és Engels irodalomelmélete)* (1949), *The History of Esthetics (Adatok az esztetika történetéhez)* (1953), and the *Dethronement of the Intellect (Az ész trónfosztása)* (1954), the latter of which explores the ideological history of modern irrationalism. During the last years of his life, Lukács was working on his intended magnum opus, which was to be the history of esthetics. But he was never able to finish it. He only published its first volume under the title *Uniqueness of Esthetics (Az esztétikum sajátossága)* (1957).

LUTHERAN CHURCH see **EVANGELICAL CHURCH.**

LUXEMBURG [LUXEMBOURG] DYNASTY. A family of Holy Roman Emperors and Czech and Hungarian kings, who rose to prominence in the early 14th century, when Henry VII (r.1308-13) was elected Holy Roman Emperor. His son, John, was elected the king of Bohemia (q.v.) (r.1310-46), but turned into an absentee king who died at the Battle of Crécy (1346) fighting against the English in the Hundred Years' War. John's son, Charles IV, King of Bohemia (r.1346-78) and Holy Roman Emperor (r.1347-78), was one of the greatest Czech rulers of all times. Of Charles's two oldest sons, Wenceslas (Václav) became the king of Bohemia (1378-1419) and Holy Roman Emperor (1378-1400), until he was deposed for incompetence. At the same time, Sigismund was elected king of

Hungary (r.1387-1437), his deposed brother's successor as Holy Roman Emperor (r.1410-37), and after his brother's death, the king of Bohemia (r.1419-37). As Sigismund had no sons, after his death, the power of the House of Luxemburg passed on to the House of Habsburg (q.v.) through the marriage of his daughter, Elizabeth, to Albert of Habsburg (q.v.). Although only for a brief period, Albert ascended to all three of the thrones he had inherited from his father-in-law.

- M -

MAGNA HUNGARIA [GREAT HUNGARY, EARLY HUNGARY]. One of the earlier homelands of the Hungarians (Magyars) located to the east of the Middle Volga, close to the confluence of the Kama River, but to the east of Magna Bulgaria. The name "Magna Hungaria"—which really means "Earlier Hungary" and not "Greater Hungary"—was first used by Frater Julianus (q.v.), who visited that area in 1235–36, but then was forced to flee because of the Mongol invasion (q.v.). Julianus and several other Dominicans (q.v.) encountered Hungarian speaking peoples already in the Caucasus region. But they found a whole Hungarian-speaking nation in Magna Hungaria, an area that nowadays is generally identified with Bashkiria to the west of the Ural Mountains. Most scholars believe that before the 5th century A.D. all Hungarians used to reside in Magna Hungaria. According to this view, some stayed there, while others gradually migrated south from the 6th through the 9th centuries. Other scholars hold that the Hungarians of Magna Hungaria originally lived just north of the Caucasus Mountains and moved up there only in the second half of the 7th century, along with the Bulgarians who founded Magna Bulgaria around A.D. 670.

MAGNA MORAVIA [GREAT MORAVIA, EARLY MORAVIA]. A small state that existed according to the traditional view —for about eight decades in the northwestern corner of what became Historic Hungary (q.v.), that is, in today's western Slovakia (q.v.), with its center in the city of Nyitra (Ńitra). It came into being during the late 820s and then ceased to exist in 907. Its first known ruler was Prince Mojmir I (r.833-46), who was followed by Prince Rastislav (r.846–70), the one responsible for inviting in 863 the brothers St. Cyril and Methodius (q.v.) to bring Byzantine Christianity (q.v.) and literacy to his people. They did this by creating the Cyrillic (originally Glagolitic) alphabet (q.v.), which became the alphabet of all of the Orthodox Slavs (q.v.). Rastislav was followed by Svatopluk I (870–94), and then by the latter's two feuding sons, Mojmir II (894–902) and Svatopluk II (902–07).

During the 880s Orthodox Christianity was pushed out of Moravia by Catholicism represented by the Bavarians, while during the next decade and a half Moravia's remaining power declined rapidly. It was given a fatal blow by the invading Magyars (q.v.) of the Árpádian Conquest (q.v.), who defeated the allied Moravian-Bavarian Army in 907. A conscious or unconscious misinterpretation of the meaning of the Latin word "magna" by 19th-century romantic historians led to its translation as "great," which in turn led to the birth of the notion of the "Great Moravian Empire." In reality, Magna Moravia or Moravia Magna was a tiny Slavic state on the frontiers of Germandom, whose adjective "magna" ("great") has exactly the same meaning and connotation as "great" or "grand" in such words as "grandfather" and "great grandfather" (German: *Grossvater;* French: *Grandpere].* It simply means that it predated another Moravia (q.v.) that had been formed in the 10th century a bit to the west of it, and which is still in existence today within the Czech Republic (q.v.).

A more recent scholarly view about Moravia Magna—espoused by historians Imre Boba, Péter Püspöki-Nagy, Charles R. Bowlus, and Martin Eggers—is that it was not located in today's western Slovakia, but rather on the Southern Morava River in present-day Serbia (q.v.). While this view is as yet not fully accepted, descriptions by contemporary Latin and Byzantine (q.v.) sources do seem to fit the southern location much better than the northern one.

MAGNATES. This was one of several terms in medieval times to refer to the upper nobility or aristocracy (q.v.). This word first appeared in the mid–12th century, when it replaced such older Latin terms as *optimes, proceres, and maiores.* In the 13th century it was used only occasionally as a synonym for *barones* (barons) (q.v.), but then it reappeared again in the mid–15th century in reference to the upper layers of the aristocracy. With the rise of hereditary titles in the late 15th century, it came to be used as a collective term to refer to the holders of such titles as baron, count, marquis, and prince.

MAGYAR [MAGYARS, MAGYAROK]. This is the name by which the Hungarians call themselves. This word is derived from the name of the ruling tribe (Magyar or Megyer) of the Hungarian Tribal Federation (q.v.) at the time of the Árpádian Conquest of Hungary (q.v.). Although variants of the term Hungarian are more commonly used abroad, some nations (e.g., the Slovaks, Turks, and at times even the Germans) do refer to the Magyars with a version of their native name.

MAGYAR CONQUEST see **HUNGARIAN CONQUEST.**

MAGYAR LANGUAGE [HUNGARIAN LANGUAGE]. Being named after the leading tribe of the Conquering Magyars (q.v.), the Magyar language belongs to the Uralic branch of the Finno-Ugric (q.v.) family of languages, which, in turn, are probably part of the still broader Ural-Altaic languages (q.v.). It is therefore in a different linguistic category than most of the European languages, the majority of which belong to the Indo-European (Indo-Germanic) linguistic family. Not counting the languages of some minor Eurasian peoples, the closest relatives of the Magyar language are Finnish and Estonian, but within the Ural-Altaic category it is also related more remotely to the various Turkic languages (q.v.). This is also true because of the Magyars' close association with various Turkic peoples (q.v.) before and after the Árpádian Conquest (q.v.). The latter included the Huns (q.v.), Bulgars (q.v..), Khazars (q.v.), Kabars (q.v.), Pechenegs (q.v.) and the Cumans (q.v.), which made the Magyars, but especially their leading classes, fully bilingual.

The most important feature of the Magyar language is its agglutinative character (q.v.), which means that it relies very heavily on the use of prefixes and suffixes that are glued to the original root word. As a result of its long association (1,100 to 1,500 years) with various Germanic, Latin (q.v.), and Slavic languages (q.v.), the Magyar language has also been enriched through word borrowings

---

from all of these languages. But these borrowed words are still used according to the laws of the Magyar language. Although the Hungarians had their own runic script (q.v.) before the Árpádian Conquest, following their acceptance of Christianity around A.D. 1000 they switched over to the Latin liturgical language and to the Latin alphabet. As opposed to English, however, which uses twenty-six letters with many more sounds, the Hungarians have forty-one (or forty-three) letters, which cover most of the sounds in the Magyar language. (It does not use "q" and "w"—which have the same sounds as "k" and "v"—except for foreign words.)

The Hungarians have stretched the Latin alphabet to fit their language by creating new "letters" through the use of various accent marks (á, é, í, ó, ö, ő, ú, ü, ű) and by doubling up letters (cs, gy, ly, ny, sz, ty, zs, dzs). At times the use of accent marks are there only to help pronunciation. At other times, however, they alter the meaning of the words completely (e.g., sor = row, sör = beer; bor = wine, bőr = skin; sas = eagle, sás = reed, tar = bare, tár = open wide). Today the Magyar language is spoken by about 15 million people, 10.5 million in Hungary, and 4.5 million abroad, most of them in the surrounding states of Slovakia (q.v.), Ukraine (q.v.), Romania (q.v.), Serbia (Little Yugoslavia) (q.v.), Croatia (q.v.), Slovenia (q.v.), and Austria (q.v.)—all or portions of which used to be part of Historic Hungary (q.v.) before 1918. A smaller segment of the Hungarians living beyond Hungary's frontiers are scattered in various Western states, the majority of them in the United States.

MAGYARIZATION   [HUNGARIANIZATION]. The process of natural or directed assimilation of non-Magyars into the Hungarian nation. This phenomenon was the direct result of 19th-century nationalism, when—because of adverse circumstances stemming from the Ottoman Turkish conquest (q.v.) and the Habsburg settlement policies (q.v.) in the 18th century—the Magyars found themselves in minority in their own country. With the rise of modern nationalism, many of the non-Magyar urban dwellers (Germans, Jews, Serbians, Slovaks, Romanians, etc.) became naturally assimilated into the dominant nationality of Hungary (q.v.). After the Austro-Hungarian Compromise of 1867 (q.v.), but especially during the two decades prior to World War II (q.v.), there was also an unsuccessful semiofficial assimilation policy via the use of schools and administrative methods. The nature and level of that policy, however, were mild as compared to the forced assimilation and ethnic cleansing policies directed against the Magyars by the post-World War I (q.v.) and post–World War II (q.v.) regimes of Romania (q.v.), Czechoslovakia (q.v.), and Yugoslavia (q.v.).

MAGYAR NATION [HUNGARIAN NATION]. The nation that was formed out of the conquering tribes that gained control over the Carpathian Basin (q.v.) in the late 9th and early 10th centuries, plus various earlier and later settlers with whom they mixed. These included various proto-Magyar groups and related Turkic peoples who arrived before and after the Árpádian conquest (q.v.), as well as various non-Magyar nationalities found there or who emigrated later.

MAGYARORSZÁG [HUNGARY]. The name by which the Hungarians call their homeland. It is a combination of two terms: *Magyar* = Hungarian, and *ország* = country. Thus it means "Hungarian Country" or "Land of the Hungarians." In light of the major territorial changes that have taken place in the course of the past millennium—especially since Historic Hungary's (q.v.) dismemberment following World War I (q.v.)—the term *Magyarország* has been used to refer to territories that were significantly different in shape and size. Today's Hungary is located in the central lowlands of the Carpathian Basin (q.v.) on about 36,000 square miles. Before its collapse in 1918-20, Historic Hungary's (q.v.) territory was three and a half times as large (126,000 square miles) and embraced all of the Carpathian Basin (q.v.) and a portion of the Adriatic Sea (q.v.) coast.

MÁLYUSZ, ELEMÉR (1898–1989). One of Hungary's greatest 20th-century historians and the founder of the so-called "Ethno-history School," which flourished during the 1930s and early 1940s and influenced the thinking of many intellectuals until the end of

World War II (q.v.). After working in the Hungarian National Archives, in 1930 Mályusz was appointed to the University of Szeged (q.v.), and then in 1932 to the Chair of Medieval Hungarian History at the University of Budapest (q.v.). Originally Mályusz was an early student of Gyula Szekfű (q.v.), who become the transplanter and most prominent exponent of the German *Geistesgeschichte* School (see Hungarian Historical Studies), which emphasized the preeminence of universal ideas and the Spirit of the Age in shaping human history. Later, however, Mályusz turned against this orientation, largely because of Szekfű's emphasis upon "universal" rather than the "national" spirit, and because of his simultaneous preference for a *labanc* (pro-Habsburg) (q.v.) interpretation of Hungarian history. In Mályusz's view, national creativity emanated from the "unconscious life and cultural activities of the people as a whole." Therefore, one should not try to find outside sources for all spiritual and cultural manifestations in Hungarian history.

After writing many shorter studies on this topic, Mályusz summarized his views in a book entitled *Hungarian Historical Studies (Magyar történettudomány)* (1942). But his career as an ethnohistorian came to an end in 1945, when he was only forty-seven years old. Thus, he was never able to develop his views fully, nor to make the Ethnohistory School into a real alternative to the much better developed and represented *Geistesgeschichte* orientation. Mályusz lived for over four more decades beyond his period of greatness, but throughout that period he was forced to function on the peripheries of the dominant Marxist historiography.

Most of Mályusz's later works deal with medieval chronicles or with the social history of the later Middle Ages. These include: *Archives of the Age of Sigismund (Zsigmondkori oklevéltár)* (3 vols., 1951-58), *The Thuróczy Chronicle and its Sources (A Thuróczy-krónika és forrásai)* (1867), *Ecclesiastical Society in Medieval Hungary (Egyházi társadalomközépkori Magyarországon)* (1971), and *The Reign of King Sigismund in Hungary (Zsigmond király uralma Magyarországon)* (1984), which also appeared in German in 1990.

MAMELUKS [MAMLUKS]. Originally the mameluks were those who composed the slave armies of the Egyptian sultans between the mid-13th and the early 16th century, some of whom became sultans themselves. In Hungarian history this term was applied mockingly to those members of the Hungarian Parliament (q.v.) who, after the Liberal Party's (q.v.) rise to power, slavishly followed the dictates of their leaders, especially those of Kálmán Tisza (q.v.), who was Hungary's prime minister between 1875 and 1890.

MARCH FRONT [MÁRCIUSI FRONT]. An informal association of progressive Hungarian intellectuals and writers during the 1930s, which in 1937 called for a radical land reform and a rapid democratization of interwar Hungary (q.v.). The members of the March Front included those who represented the Populist Movement (q.v.), as well as others who sympathized with socialism and even communism. Because of these internal ideological differences, the March Front was dissolved in 1939.

MARCH REVOLUTION see **HUNGARIAN REVOLUTION OF 1848-49.**

MARCH YOUTH [MÁRCIUSI FIATALOK, MÁRCIUSI IFJAK]. Young intellectuals who were primarily responsible for starting the Hungarian Revolution (q.v.) on March 15, 1848. Their most important members included the poet Sándor Petőfi (q.v.), the novelist Mór Jókai (q.v.), and the historian Pál Vasvári (1826-49).

MARCZALI, HENRIK [HENRY] (1856-1940). One of Hungary's greatest historians who was the most outstanding synthesizer of the Hungarian Positivist School (q.v.). Marczali was also one of the implanters of the German scientific method and scientific historical scholarship to Hungary (q.v.). He himself was the product of the best Austrian, German, and French masters, and he produced several epoch-making works long before his appointment as a professor of Hungarian history at the University of Budapest (q.v.) (1895–1924). During his long scholarly career Marczali trained several generations of outstanding historians, and he wrote probably more books and articles than any other Hungarian historian, not excluding his best-known students, Gyula Szekfű (q.v.) and Bálint Hóman (q.v.). Marczali edited and published some of the most important source collections of medieval Hungarian History: *Sources of Hungarian History in the Age of the Árpáds (A magyar történet kúfői az Árpádok korában)* (1880) and the *Handbook of Hungarian Historical Sources (A magyar történet kútfőinek kézikönyve)* (1901). He likewise authored the still useful three-volume *History of Hungary in the Age of Joseph II (Magyarországtörténete II. József korában)* (1881-88), which subsequently appeared in an abbreviated English version under the title *Hungary in the Eighteenth Century* (Cambridge, 1910). These works pay considerably more attention to economic, social, and cultural issues than was customary among Positivist historians, and they also treat in detail the institutional structure of Hungarian society. This also holds true for most of Marczali's other synthetic works, among them the three large volumes (on the periods up to 1301 and between 1711–1815) that he wrote for the ten-volume *Millennial History of Hungary* (1895–98) edited by Sándor Szilágyi (q.v.). This is likewise true for the six volumes on the 16th through the 19th centuries that he contributed to the twelve-volume *Great Illustrated History of the World (Nagy Képes Világtörténet)* (1898–1904) that he himself edited. Just before the outbreak of World War I (q.v.) Marczali published two other significant interpretative works: his one-volume *History of Hungary (Magyarországtörténete)* (1911), and his German language synthesis of Hungarian constitutional developments entitled *Hungarian Constitutional Law (Ungarisches Vervassungsrecht)* (1911).

Throughout his scholarly career Marczali's philosophical and political outlook was that of a 19th-century liberal. As such, he rejected all radical ideologies—be they on the Left or on the Right. Yet, his sympathies for the Károlyi Regime (q.v.) at the end of World War I (q.v.) still got him into trouble with the interwar political system. This resulted in his forced retirement at the age of sixty-eight. Being pushed out of the center of Hungarian historical scholarship made Marczali a bitter man. This bitterness was further aggravated by the fact that interwar Hungary's (q.v.) most successful historians were all his former students, and they all thrived during his own period of isolation. In spite of his late-life misfortunes, Marczali's fame and name remain unchanged. He represents the Hungarian Positivist Historical School better than anyone else. In point of fact, in retrospect, only his most gifted student, Gyula Szekfű, achieved a status comparable to that of the old master. His works are still read today, and they usually make a better reading than those produced by most post–World War II (q.v.) historians.

MARGARET, SAINT [SZENT MARGIT] (1242–70). Daughter of King Béla IV (q.v.), who was born in the midst of the Mongol Invasion (q.v.) and was offered to the church by her parents in return for the liberation of Hungary (q.v.). From the age of three she was reared in the Dominican Convent of the city of Veszprém (q.v.). In 1252 she was transferred to the new Dominican Convent established on the Island of the Hares on the Danube (q.v.) between Buda (q.v.) and Pest (q.v.), today called St. Margaret's Island in Budapest (q.v.). There she lived the life of dedication, poverty, and charity, which acquired for her the fame of a saint during her lifetime. After her death, her convent, that was dedicated to Virgin Mary, became a place of pilgrimage. Margaret was beatified soon after her death, but she was not canonized by the Catholic Church until 1943 — even though the Hungarians viewed her as a saint for many centuries.

MARIA THERESA [MÁRIA TERÉZIA] (1717–80). Ruling queen of Hungary and Bohemia (r.1740–80), archduchess of Austria (r.1740–80), daughter of Emperor Charles VI (King Charles III) (q.v.), and wife of Emperor Francis I (q.v.). Thus, although often called "Empress Maria Theresa," her highest title was "queen of Hungary." She was an empress only by virtue of the fact of being married to an emperor. Maria Theresa was the first female member of the Habsburg dynasty (q.v.) to rule, which she was able to do on the basis of the Pragmatic Sanction (q.v.) promulgated by her father, the last male member of the dynasty.

Despite all her father's efforts, her accession to the throne was contested by Bavaria (q.v.), Prussia (q.v.), and France, which resulted in the War of Austrian Succession (q.v.) (1740–48), in the course of which she lost Silesia (q.v.) to Frederick the Great's Prussia. During the war, the German electors, unwilling to select a female ruler, elected her husband, Francis of Lorraine (q.v.), to the Holy Roman Imperial throne (1745). In 1772 Maria Theresa participated with Frederick the Great of Prussia and Catherine the Great of Russia in the First Partition of Poland, which gained for her Galicia (q.v.). Two years later (1774) she also acquired Bukovina (q.v.) from the Ottoman Empire (q.v.). Earlier she participated in the Seven Years' War (q.v.), and then, jointly with her son, Joseph II (q.v.), also in the War of Bavarian Succession (1778–79). Neither of these wars brought her significant gains.

Maria Theresa wished to strengthen the internal cohesion of her empire by increasing the loyalty of the difficult-to-control Hungarian nobility (q.v.), who had supported her in her time of need at the beginning of the War of Austrian Succession. Thus, she made every effort to bind them to Vienna (q.v.) and to the Imperial Court (q.v.). It was for this reason that she established the Hungarian Royal Nobles' Guard (q.v.) and the St. Stephen Order, and it was also for this reason that she was generous in granting aristocratic titles to her supporters. She wanted to tie Hungary economically to the Hereditary Lands (q.v.), which she did by making that country increasingly dependent upon Austrian industries. This policy was often called a form of economic colonialism.

Maria Theresa was a kind person, but a very religious one, which limited her acceptance of the ideas of the Enlightenment (q.v.). Thus, while her Urbarium of 1767 (q.v.) limited the powers of the feudal lords over the peasants, her Poor Laws of 1775 contained some enlightened reforms concerning poor houses, work houses, and orphanages, and her Ratio Educations of 1777 (q.v.) displayed a number of forward-looking educational ideas, she continued to limit the religious freedom of the Protestants (q.v.) and the Jews (q.v.). She also exercised a form of censorship in face of the rapid influx of "revolutionary" ideas. Following the death of her husband in 1765, her son acquired the title of Holy Roman Emperor and became her coruler. But as they did not see eye to eye—Joseph II being much more radical and forward-looking—this partnership was a rocky one until the very end.

While engaged in running the empire of the Habsburgs (q.v.), Maria Theresa bore sixteen children, the majority of whom are buried next to her in the Habsburg Tomb in Vienna. Although not a child of the Enlightenment, she was a good person and an able ruler, who is remembered fondly even today.

MARQUIS [MARKGRAF, ŐRGRÓF]. An aristocratic title between that of a prince and a count. Originally a Marquis or Markgraf was an administrator of a frontier province ("March" or "Mark") of the Carolingian Empire during the reign of Charlemagne (r.768-814). In addition to administrative authority, however, he also possessed military and judicial powers. Later this office became a hereditary aristocratic title, which spread through several Western and Central European states (q.v.). It was transplanted to Hungary (q.v.) in the 18th century, following the granting of large landed estates to foreign favorites of the Habsburg dynasty (q.v.), including the Pallavicini family of Italian origin.

MARTINOVICS, IGNÁC [IGNATZ] (1755–95). Catholic priest and abbot who became an atheist philosopher and then the leader of the ill-fated conspiracy of the Hungarian Jacobins (q.v.). Having entered the Franciscan Order (q.v.) at the age of sixteen, Martinovics obtained a doctorate in theology and philosophy at the University of Buda(Budapest) (q.v.), even though he was much more attracted to technology and the natural sciences. In 1781 he joined the Habsburg Army (q.v.) as a chaplain and two years later became of professor of natural sciences at the newly established University of Lemberg (Lvov, L'viv) (1783). He authored several books on mathematics and chemistry, and also invented various kinds of threshing and cutting machines. During the 1780s he fell under the influence of d'Holbach's philosophy of atheism, and in 1788 he summarized his

views on this question in an anonymous French language work
entitled *Philosophical Essays (Mémoires philosophiques).*

Being a devotee of radical social reforms represented by the
French Revolution, in 1791 Martinovics became a secret agent of
Emperor Leopold II (q.v.), allegedly to advance the cause of
Enlightenment. He spied and informed regularly against the
conservative Hungarian nobility (q.v.), who were still trying to
preserve their class and economic privileges in face of Imperial
centralism. At this time Martinovics also authored many pamphlets
in defense of Leopold's policies, hoping that this would land him in
an influential job. Following the Leopold's death, however, he was
dismissed by Emperor Francis (q.v.). This angered his vanity and
pushed him in the direction of a group of radical intellectuals who
congregated around the person of a progressive legal scholar, József
Hajnóczy (q.v.) (1750–95). Although they were only asking for the
continuation of Joseph II's (q.v.) enlightened reforms, to increase his
own importance, Martinovics described this group as a Jacobin
organization, whose members were trying to emulate the French
Revolution. In the spring of 1794 Martinovics was instrumental in
enlisting Hajnóczy and many of his disciples into two secret
societies: the Society of Reformers *(Reformátorok Társaság)*and the
Society of Liberty and Equality *(Szabadság és Egyenlőség
Társasága).*

Having learned about these activities, Emperor Francis had
Martinovics and the members of the two secret societies arrested and
convicted. The totally amoral Martinovics tried to save himself by
informing on his political friends and offering to continue his
spying activities for Vienna. This time, however, his offer was
rejected. On May 20, 1795, he and four of his much worthier
coconspirators were beheaded on the Field of Blood in Buda
(Budapest) (q.v.). For many years, the Hungarian public viewed
Martinovics as a national hero. The revelation of his multiple
double-spying activities by historian Fraknói (q.v.) in 1880,
however, destroyed most of his heroic halo. Even so, driven by
political considerations, Marxist historians of the 1950s tried to
restore his prestige.

MARTINUZZI, GYÖRGY [FRATER GYÖRGY, BROTHER GEORGE] (1482–1551). Hungarian statesman and Catholic cardinal who played a decisive role in Hungary's (q.v.) fate at the time of country's trisection following the Battle of Mohács (q.v.). Of Croatian noble origin, Martinuzzi was reared in the court of Johannes Corvin (q.v.). In 1504 he joined the household of the widow of Palatine István Zápolya (Szapolyai) (d.1499), and then switched over to her son, John Zápolya (q.v.), the future king of Hungary. In the meanwhile he had joined the Paulist Order (q.v.) where, because of his education and good connections, he was soon named the abbott of the Polish Monastery of Czestochowa. In 1528 Martinuzzi became a close adviser to King John I, who sent him on various diplomatic missions and also had him appointed the bishop of Várad (Nagyvárad) (q.v.) (1534).

Martinuzzi worked feverishly for the reunification of Hungary (q.v.) and had a decisive role in the Treaty of Várad (q.v.) (1538) between the two rival kings that foresaw a unification under Habsburg (q.v.) rule. The belated birth of King John's son, however, ended this dream. At King John's death in 1540 Martinuzzi became young John Sigismund's (q.v.) guardian, and in 1541 defendedthe city of Buda (q.v.) in his name against King Ferdinand's (q.v.) forces. Sultan Süleyman's (q.v.) occupation of the city in that very year, however, altered Martinuzzi's views. He again came to view the Habsburgs as the only real hope for Hungary. Thus, while waiting for the right opportunity, he organized the country's eastern section into a separate political entity and thus laid the foundations of an independent Transylvanian state (q.v.).

In 1551 Martinuzzi compelled young John Sigismund and his mother, Izabella (q.v.), to renounce the throne, after which he immediately relinquished Transylvania to King Ferdinand (q.v.). In return for this, Ferdinand named him the voievod of Transylvania and arranged for his appointment as the archbishop of Esztergom (q.v.), with the rank of a cardinal. But the forces that had been dispatched by King Ferdinand to assume control over Transylvania proved to be insufficient. Thus, to gain time, Martinuzzi began to negotiate with the Turks (q.v.). This was interpreted by the commander of Ferdinand's forces, Giovanni Castaldo (1500-62), as a sign of Martinuzzi's impending treason and thus the general had him murdered. This was most unfortunate, for Martinuzzi's death ended all chances for Hungary's reunification until the decline of Ottoman Turkish power in the late 17th and early 18th centuries.

MARIA [MARY] (c.1370/71–95). Queen of Hungary (r.1382–95), and the daughter of the King Louis the Great (q.v.), who had inherited her father's Hungarian throne, while her younger sister Hedvig/Jadwiga(q.v.) gained the Polish throne. Because of Mary's youth, after ascending the throne, it was her mother, Elizabeth of Bosnia, who ruled in her place. Many of the magnates under the leadership of Palatine Miklós Garai (q.v.) supported her, but others switched their allegiance to the Neapolitan branch of the Anjou dynasty (q.v.) in the person of King Charles III of Naples (r.1381-86). In August 1385 they offered him the Hungarian crown and asked him to come to Hungary (q.v.).

Charles's coming to Hungary coincided with Mary's marriage to Sigismund of Luxemburg (q.v.), the son of Holy Roman Emperor and Czech King Charles IV (r.1346-78) and brother of Emperor/King Wenceslas (Václav) (r.1378-1400/19). In November of that year, the Hungarian Diet compelled Mary to resign and elected in her place the Neapolitan ruler under the name Charles II (q.v.). Charles's rule, however, proved to be very brief (December 31, 1385-February 24, 1386), for he was murdered within two months. Following his death, Mary once more ascended the Hungarian throne, but this time along with her husband Sigismund, to whom she deferred in all matters. She died in 1395 and was buried in Nagyvárad (q.v.).

MARY see MARIA.

MÁTÉ [MÁTUS, MATTHEW] see CSÁK, MÁTÉ.

MATTHIAS I see MATTHIAS CORVINUS.

MATTHIAS II [MÁTYÁS] (1557–1619). King of Hungary (r.1608–19), Holy Roman Emperor (r.1612–19), son of King/ Emperor Maximilian (q.v.), and brother of King/Emperor Rudolph (q.v.). After serving as the governor of the Netherlands and the viceroy of Lower and Upper Austria (q.v.), in 1606 Matthias was elected the head of the House of Habsburg (q.v.) in place of his deranged brother Rudolph. In the same year he negotiated the Peace of Vienna (q.v.) with Prince István Bocskai (q.v.) of Transylvania (q.v.). Two years later, with the full support of the Hungarian, Austrian, and Moravian nobility, he forced his brother to renounce the Hungarian, Czech, and Austrian thrones, although permitting him to retain the thrones of Bohemia (q.v.) and the Holy Roman Empire (q.v.).

Having been crowned king of Hungary in November 1608 after significant concessions to the Hungarian nobility (q.v.) and the Protestants (q.v.) in Hungary, Matthias went to work to restore order in the country. He did the same after his official accession to the Czech throne in 1611, but with much less success. In 1612 Matthias made an effort to conquer Transylvania (q.v.) so as to reunite it with the rest of Hungary, but the defeat of his armies ended this dream for a while. The final years of Matthias's reign were filled with an increasingly emotional struggle against the Czech nobility, which ultimately led to their election of the Protestant Frederick of Palatinate to the Czech throne and to the outbreak of the Thirty Years' War (1618–48). Matthias died without offspring. His several thrones, therefore, were inherited by his cousin, Ferdinand II (q.v.) of Styria, whose Jesuit education and bigot Catholic upbringing assured the continuation of the religious struggle in the Habsburg Empire (q.v.).

MATTHIAS CORVINUS [MATTHIAS I, MÁTYÁS HU-NYADI] (1440/43-90). King of Hungary (r.1458-90) and son of the great national leader, János Hunyadi (q.v.). Matthias was one of the greatest personalities of late medieval Hungarian history (q.v.), whose reign represents the last moment of greatness for an independent Hungary (q.v.). In wake of the period of chaos that followed the death of King Sigismund (q.v.)—a period when János Hunyadi's regency and personal role represented the only element of stability—Matthias Hunyadi (later to be known as Matthias Corvinus) was elected king of Hungary (January 24, 1458. His election took place with the support of the country's common nobility (q.v.), who had also supported his father against the irresponsible and increasingly oppressive magnates (q.v.).

Aware of the dangers of feudal decentralization, after his election Matthias immediately went to work to decrease the power of the magnates (q.v.) and to disband the baronial leagues (q.v.) that had undermined royal power and endangered Hungary's position in face of the grave threat from the Ottoman Turks (q.v.). With the support of the common nobility and the burghers of the increasingly significant Royal Free Cities (q.v.), Matthias reasserted centralization, strengthened royal power, and rebuilt the institutions of royal administration and royal justice (e.g., Chancellery, Royal Treasury, Judicial System). He also established one of the first standing armies of Europe—the famous Black Army (q.v.)—which he used to bolster his power at home and to expand Hungarian influences abroad. To achieve these goals, he introduced a more efficient taxation system, which increased his revenues significantly. At the same time, he also protected the tax -paying population from the exactions of the local authorities. His elimination of the feudal anarchy and local arbitrariness increased the tax-paying potential of the peasants, who were able to produce more and did so more effectively. His reign likewise favored the cities, urban life, artisanship, industry, and commerce, all of which prospered. Consequently, those involved in these urban endeavors were likewise able to pay more taxes.

Even though Matthias had a powerful army at his disposal, he never went beyond simple defensive wars against the Turks (q.v.). Rather, he concentrated most of his resources on the West, primarily against the Czech Kingdom (q.v.) and the Arch Duchy of Austria (q.v.). His wars ultimately yielded him Moravia (q.v.) and Silesia (q.v.) (1478), the Czech royal crown (1469), as well as the eastern provinces of the Habsburgs (q.v.), including the city of Vienna (q.v.). Matthias's Western-oriented conquests and his lack of sufficient attention to the Turkish danger were often criticized even by his closest supporters, such as Johannes Vitéz (q.v.) and Janus Pannonius (q.v.). But he pursued this policy primarily because of his dream of being elected Holy Roman Emperor (q.v.) and then using the resources of the whole empire to turn against the Turks. His acquisition of the title "king of Bohemia" was also meant to secure this goal by gaining control over the vote of the Czech king in the imperial elections.

Matthias's marriage to Beatrix of Aragon (q.v.), the daughter of King Ferdinand of Naples, in 1476, increased the influx of Renaissance (q.v.) culture and humanist learning (q.v.) in Hungary. His royal court at Buda (q.v.) became a center of East Central European humanism as well as the camping ground of many Italian artists and scholars (e.g., Bonfini, Callimachus, and Galeotti). He also supported native Hungarian humanists (e.g. Johannes Vitéz, Miklós Váradi, and Janus Pannonius) and sent many young Hungarians for further studies to Italian universities and dukal courts. In 1467 Matthias founded the University of Pozsony (Academia Istropolitana) (q.v.), in 1473 he sponsored a printing press in Buda (the sixth oldest in the world), and during the same period he likewise established the Corvina Library *(Bibliotheca Corviniana)* (q.v.), which became the greatest royal library in East Central Europe (q.v.). The brilliance of Matthias's court was made known through many commissioned books, some of which were historical works that glorified him and his family and "established" his descent from some of the greatest rulers of the ancient world. King Matthias also supported Renaissance architecture, which became evident especially at his capital city of Buda and at the palace fortress of Visegrád (q.v.), which became his favorite second home.

As Matthias never produced legitimate children, his last major undertaking was the effort to assure the Hungarian throne for his illegitimate son, Johannes Corvin (q.v.). It was for this reason that he promulgated the Palatine Law of 1485, which gave unusually comprehensive powers to his favorite, Palatine Imre Zápolya (Szapolyai) (q.v.) (d.1487), the uncle of the future King John II (q.v.). He also obliged his most immediate favorites and supporters—including his private secretary and future primate of Hungary, Tamás Bakócz (q.v.)—to swear allegiance to Johannes Corvin. Yet, when he died unexpectedly in Vienna, none of these arrangements helped. He was betrayed by all of his alleged friends and supporters, and his son never made it to the throne. Under the new king, Vladislav II (q.v.), Hungary began its rapid decline, which ended on the bloody fields of Mohács (q.v.) thirty-six years later.

King Matthias Corvinus was one of the most highly regarded and beloved rulers of Hungary, who came to be known among the common people as "Matthias the Just." This image, which has been preserved in many folk tales and legends, is probably derived from Matthias's success in restraining the power of the squabbling magnates and in creating an era of stability and prosperity for Hungary. In light of what came after him, his achievements appear even greater. The Age of Matthias Corvinus was the last great period in the history of an independent Hungary. His life and times have been chronicled by his court historian, Antonio Bonfini (q.v.).

MÁTYUSFÖLD [TERRA MATHAEI, MATHVSFELDE, MATUŠOVA ZEM]. A region in the northwestern section of Historic Hungary (q.v.)—today Slovakia (q.v.)—along the Vág (Váh) River. It was centered on the fortress of Trencsén (Trenčín), which was the heart of the regional lordship of Máté Csák (q.v.) in the late 13th and early 14th centuries until 1321. *Mátyusföld* was first mentioned in documents with the Latin term *terra Mathaei* in 1384, and then with the archaic German term *Mathvsfelde* in 1545. It survived as an unspecific regional designation without any legal or administrative significance into the 20th century.

MAXIMILIAN I [II] [MIKSA] (1527–76). King of Hungary and Bohemia (r.1564–76), Holy Roman Emperor as Maximilian II (r.1564–76), and son of Ferdinand I (q.v.). Maximilian grew up in Spain, but in 1542 his father appointed him viceroy of Hungary (q.v.), and in 1553 Maximilian was crowned king, even though Ferdinand was still alive. This was to make certain that the elective throne of Hungary would be retained by the Habsburgs (q.v.). After his father's death, Maximilian ascended the thrones of Hungary (q.v.), Bohemia (q.v.), and the Holy Roman Empire (q.v.), while his cousin, Philip II (r.1556–98), ruled Spain, the Netherlands, and the Spanish Empire. Maximilian's short reign was spent in fighting against the Turks (q.v.) and against John Sigismund (q.v.) of Transylvania (q.v.). He came to terms with the Turks in the Treaty of Adrianople in 1568, wherein he recognized the Turkish occupation of much of Hungary and agreed to pay an annual tribute of 30,000 gold. Two years later he also came to terms with John Sigismund in the Treaty of Speyer (q.v.), according to which the latter relinquished his royal title and was guaranteed his rule over Transylvania (q.v.) and the Partium (q.v.) for himself and his descendants. Maximilian also tried to acquire Poland (q.v.), but he was bested by Stephen Báthory (q.v.) of Transylvania.

MEDICAL UNIVERSITIES IN HUNGARY see UNIVERSITIES, MEDICAL.

MEGYE see HUNGARIAN COUNTY SYSTEM.

MELIUS-JUHÁSZ, PÉTER (1536–72). One of the most noted pioneers of Hungarian Protestantism (q.v.) and the first bishop (1561/62–72) of the Hungarian Reformed Church (q.v.) centered on the city of Debrecen (q.v.). His Magyar-language literary activities spanned the whole spectrum of Christianity. They include polemical writings against Catholic theologians, but also debates with Ferenc Dávid (q.v.), the founder of Hungarian Unitarianism (q.v.). Melius-Juhász is also the author of the first Hungarian language book on botany, agriculture, and medical sciences, which was published posthumously by his widow under the title *Herbarium* (1578).

MERSEBURG, BATTLE OF (933). The first Hungarian defeat at the hands of the Germans (q.v.) during the Hungarian Dukal Age (q.v.). In 933 an invading Hungarian army was defeated by Henry the Fowler (r.918–36). But this defeat of a relatively small force failed to end the Hungarian military excursions to the West. They continued until another major defeat at the hands of Otto the Great (r.936–73) in the vicinity of the city of Augsburg (q.v.) in 955.

MÉSZÁROS, LÁZÁR (1796-1858). A general and a minister of defense (April 1848–May 1849) in the Hungarian revolutionary government of 1848 (q.v.). Following the resignation of Prime Minister Batthyány in early October, Mészáros became a member of the Kossuth-led National Defense Committee (q.v.), and then in July of 1849, the commander-in-chief of the Hungarian Honvéd Armies (q.v.). Following the Hungarian surrender at Világos (q.v.), Mészáros emigrated to Turkey (q.v.), then to the United States, and finally to England, where he died in 1858. His remains were returned to Hungary in 1991. His memoirs appeared posthumously under the title *Lázár Mészáros's Life, Foreign Correspondence, and Memoirs (Mészáros Lázár élettörténete, külföldi levelezése és emlékiratai)* (2 vols., 1866–67)

METTERNICH, PRINCE KLEMENS LOTHAR (1773–1859). Foreign minister (1809–21), state chancellor (1821–26), and president of the Imperial Council (1826–48) of the Austrian Empire (q.v.), Prince Metternich was perhaps the dominant statesman in post-Napoleonic Europe. He had entered Austrian diplomatic service in 1801. After serving in Dresden and Berlin, in 1806 he was appointed the Austrian ambassador to Paris. In 1809 he became Austria's foreign minister, and from that moment he retained control over Austria's foreign policy and much of its domestic policy for nearly four decades. Initially he supported a conciliatory policy toward Napoleon, but after the latter's Russian fiasco (1812) and military defeat at Leipzig (1813), he turned against Napoleon and was instrumental in his undoing.

Metternich engineered the First Treaty of Paris (May 30, 1814) with the returning Bourbons, and he also orchestrated the political agenda of the Congress of Vienna (q.v.) (1814–15), which reorganized post-Napoleonic Europe on the basis of the principle of legitimacy. To uphold this principle, Metternich was also instrumental in the establishment of the Quadruple Alliance (q.v.) (1815) and the Quintuple Alliance (1818), which represented the power behind the Holy Alliance, inspired by Czar Alexander I (r.1801–25). Being a shrewd and able statesman, Metternich enlisted all means for the preservation of the Old Order in face of the revolutionary tendencies and ideologies of his age. The Metternich System began to be undermined already in the 1820s in conjunction with the Greek Revolution (1821–29) and the gravitation of both England and France out of the alliance system. But Metternich was still able to perpetuate his conservative order in the central and eastern part of Europe right up to 1848.

With respect to Hungary (q.v.), he was a powerful opponent of the Hungarian Reform Movement (q.v.) in the period between 1825 and 1848. Yet, not even he was able to stop the wheel of history. His antiliberal and archconservative system collapsed in March 1848, when revolutions broke out in many parts of the Austrian Empire and the German Confederation (q.v.). Fearing for his life, Metternich fled to England, and then lived in Belgium before returning to Vienna in 1851. Following his return, he never entered active politics, but still gave occasional advice to young Emperor Francis Joseph (q.v.). Metternich worked on his memoirs and correspondence, but they were published only two decades later under the title *From Metternich's Collected Papers [Aus Metternichs nachgelassenen Papieren* (8 vols., 1880-84). Although one of the really great statesmen of 19th century Europe, his anti-progressive stance made Metternich's name disliked by most liberals and most nationalities of the former Habsburg Empire (q.v.).

MEZŐVÁROS [AGRICULTURAL TOWN] see **OPPIDUM.**

MIDDLE NOBILITY see **COMMON NOBILITY.**

MILES [FIGHTER, SOLDIER, ARMED KNIGHT]. At the time of the Árpádian conquest (q.v.) of Hungary (q.v.) all adult males were fighters. Following their settling down, social differentiations began, and by the time of King St. Stephen (q.v.) in the early 11th century, even laws began to distinguish among commoners *(vulgaris),* fighters *(miles),* and the aristocratic counts *(comes).* In the course of the next two centuries, this differentiation became greater and more complex. Thus, by the 13th century, some of the *miles* had sank into the ranks of the peasantry, while others became members of the "royal servants" *(servientes regis)* (q.v.), who made up the common nobility *(nobiles, köznemesség)* (q.v.).

MILITARY FRONTIER DISTRICT [MILTÄRGRENZE, HATÁRŐRVIDÉK]. Following the conquest and trisection of Historic Hungary (q.v.) in the 16th century, each of the two competing states—the Habsburg (q.v.) and the Ottoman Turkish Empires (q.v.)—established a series of frontier fortifications to deal with the state of permanent war that existed between them even in times of official peace. The administration of these frontier fortresses was placed under the direction of the Court Military Council *(Hofkriegsrat, Udvari Haditanács)* established in 1556. Following the expulsion of the Turks (1699), the Habsburg Imperial Government established the Croatian-Slavonian Military District, which stretched from the Adriatic Sea (q.v.) to the Tisza River (q.v.). They settled this district with Croatian and Serbian families, whose primary function— in addition to agricultural activities—was to be in a constant state of readiness for war.

Following the Treaty of Passarowitz (q.v.) (1718)—which regained the Banat of Temesvár (q.v.) and pushed Habsburg power into northern Serbia (q.v.)—the Habsburg government also created the Military District of the Banat in South-Central Hungary, which was inhabited mostly by newly settled Swabians (q.v.) and Vlachs (q.v.). Then in the 1760s they also established several military districts in Eastern and Southern Transylvania (q.v.), that involved Hungarian Székelys (q.v.) and Romanian Vlachs. Those who were settled there, or remained in these military districts, received free lands. Their tax obligations were also reduced by two-thirds, and in times of war they were free from all taxes. In return for this, all healthy adult males were obliged to participate in military training on a regular basis, and in case of a war, they were the first to be mobilized. With the decline of Turkish danger, the military districts lost their usefulness. Those in Transylvania were disbanded in 1851, while those in Croatia-Slavonia were liquidated between 1871 and 1885. Following their dissolution, the military districts were integrated into the regular civil administration system of the Kingdom of Hungary (q.v.).

MILLENNIUM (1896). Within its Hungarian context, this term refers to the events of 1896, when Hungary (q.v.) held its official festivities commemorating the one-thousand years of the Árpádian conquest (q.v.). The date itself is arbitrary, for the conquest began earlier and ended later. But given contemporary realities and the state of preparations, that year was judged to be the most acceptable. The millennial festivities were preceded by the rebuilding of the Hungarian capital into a modern metropolis. Some of the most worthy projects included the building of the Millennial Monument at the entrance of the City Park, the reconstruction of the Andrássy Boulevard that connected the Inner City with this Millennial Monument, the construction of the first subway in Europe under the Andrássy Boulevard, the building of the second largest Parliament building in Europe *(Országháza)*(1885–1904), the reconstruction of the Royal Palace (1881-1902), and the construction of the so-called Fishermen's Bastion (1901-05) on Castle Hill. These activities also included the building of the third bridge to connect the two parts of the city, the building of the Francis Joseph Bridge (now Liberty Bridge) (1896), the construction of a replica of the Vajdahunyad Castle (János Hunyadi's castle) (1896-1904) in a totally reconstructed City Park, as well as numerous other monumental building projects that are still the pride of Budapest today.

    The Millennium also involved the construction of several millennial monuments on Hungary's borders, which, however, were all dismantled barely two decades later, along with the frontiers of Historic Hungary (q.v.). The festivities and exhibits about Hungarian achievements lasted for a whole year. In retrospect the Millennium of 1896 represented the climax of Hungarian prestige and pride in the modern world, which could not be duplicated at the time of the Millecentennial of 1996.

MINDSZENTY, CARDINAL JÓZSEF [JOSEPH] (1892-1975). Cardinal archbishop of Esztergom (q.v.), who was the last to hold the title "Prince Primate of Hungary" (q.v.). Born into a simple family under the name József Pehm, Mindszenty joined the Catholic priesthood in 1915. After several other church offices, in 1944 he was named the bishop of Veszprém (q.v.), in which capacity he opposed the anti-Semitic policies of the Arrow Cross Party (q.v.). He was arrested (November 27, 1944) and held in captivity until the end of the war (April 1945). In August of that year, Pope Pius XII (r.1939–58) appointed him the archbishop of Esztergom (q.v.), and the next year made him a cardinal of the Catholic Church. Mindszenty openly opposed the antireligious policies of the communists. Thus, soon after the communist takeover (q.v.), he was arrested, convicted, and imprisoned (1949). Liberated by the Hungarian Revolution of 1956 (q.v.), his freedom lasted only for a few days. After the Russian invasion (November 4), he found asylum at the American Embassy in Budapest (q.v.). He stayed there until his official expulsion from Hungary on September 28, 1971, which was also approved by the U.S. State Department, because his presence there was becoming politically burdensome.

Cardinal Mindszenty settled in Vienna (q.v.), making his home at the Pázmáneum (q.v.), which had been a center for Hungarian theological learning for several centuries. He traveled frequently, visiting Hungarian communities around the world. During these travels, Mindszenty preached both his brand of anti-communism, as well as the need for Hungarian survival. His *Memoirs* (1974), which appeared in several languages one year before his death, reveal him to have been a conservative churchman, who rejected, not only the radical political ideologies, but also many other manifestations of modernism. In 1975 Cardinal Mindszenty was buried temporarily at Mariazell in Austria (q.v.). In 1991 his remains were returned to Hungary and interred next to Hungary's other prince primates in the Cathedral of Esztergom (q.v.).

MINING TOWN [CIVITAS MONTANA, BÁNYAVÁROS].
These were privileged walled cities founded in the 13th and 14th centuries, mostly by invited German settlers (q.v.), specifically for the purposes of opening up mines so as to increase the precious metal (gold and silver) and salt production in Hungary (q.v.). Most of these towns were located in Northern Hungary (q.v.) and in Transylvania (q.v.), and many of them were "Royal Free Cities" (q.v.), meaning that they were under direct royal administration and exempt from the control of the local authorities. As such, they enjoyed extensive autonomy. They elected their own officials under their own laws, which they imported from the Holy Roman Empire (q.v.). Some of the smaller mining towns, however, were under the authority of regional lords.

MINORITIES see **NATIONAL MINORITIES IN HUNGARY.**

MINSZ (1948-50) see **COMMUNIST YOUTH ORGANIZATIONS.**

MOHÁCS, BATTLE OF (1526). This battle had perhaps the greatest impact upon Hungarian history, for it resulted in the country's trisection and in the establishment of Ottoman Turkish (q.v.) and Habsburg (q.v.) rule for many centuries to come. The battle took place on August 29, 1526. It was fought by the Hungarian Royal Army of about 24,000 to 25,000 men, led by the young and inexperienced King Louis II (q.v.), against the Ottoman Turkish Army of about 110,000 to 130,000 fighters, under the command of Sultan Süleyman (q.v.). Following his accession to the throne, Süleyman offered a peace treaty to Hungary (q.v.), but he received no response. Thus, after capturing Belgrade (1521), Rhodes (1522), and the fortress of Szörény (1526), he undertook a campaign against the land of the Magyars.

Hungary in 1526 was far removed from the powerful country it had been under Matthias Corvinus (q.v.) in the late 15th century. The disintegration of central power under the Jagellonian dynasty (q.v.), the rise of competing war lords and aristocratic leagues, the Dózsa Peasant Revolution of 1514 (q.v.) and the subsequent enserfement of the peasantry (q.v.), the Protestant Reformation and its negative impact upon Hungarian unity, the reign of an inexperienced youth, who was unable to end the private wars among the powerful lords, and the general miscalculations concerning the strength of the Ottoman Army all combined to make this encounter a totally hopeless one.

The battle lasted only a few hours, but it ended in the virtual annihilation of the Hungarian Royal Army, of whose ranks about 20,000 died. The dead included King Louis and most of his advisers and commanders. In wake of this unexpectedly quick victory, Sultan Süleyman occupied Buda (q.v.) temporarily, but then—as yet unprepared for a lasting occupation—withdrew from Hungary. This withdrawal gave the Hungarians another fifteen years to solve their country's problems. But they were unable to take advantage of this respite. The double election of John Zápolya (q.v.) and Ferdinand of Habsburg (q.v.), the resulting rivalry between the two kings, and the continued struggle between several groups of magnates (q.v.) only worsened the situation. It was these post-Mohács problems that turned the Battle of Mohács into the worst national calamity that had ever befallen Hungary during its first six centuries of existence in the Carpathian Basin (q.v.).

MOHI [MUHI], BATTLE OF (1241). One of the greatest defeats in Hungarian history, when King Béla IV's (q.v.) armies were totally annihilated by the invading Mongols (q.v.) on April 11, 1241. In consequence of this defeat—which was the result of delayed mobilization, mistakes in selecting the battlefield, ineffective leadership, and the numerical inferiority of the Hungarian armies— all of Hungary was overrun and destroyed by the Mongol armies. But as they stayed only until 1242, King Béla IV was given the chance to rebuild his country.

MOLDAVIA [MOLDOVA, MOLDOVLACHIA, VLACHO-BOGDANIA]. The northeastern province of present-day Romania, which in the 11th through the 13th centuries was inhabited by Cumans (q.v.) and was known as Cumania. In addition to the Cumans, it may also have been inhabited by some Vlach (q.v.) shepherds who were gradually moving up from the Balkans. In 1226 or 1227 King Andrew II (q.v.) of Hungary established the Bishopric of Milkó in the region later known as Moldavia. His intention was to Christianize the pagan Cumans. But the Mongol invasion (q.v.) of the mid–13th century scattered these Cumans and also ended the Bishopric of Milkó. For the next century the area was a no man's land, although nominally part of the Mongol Empire. But the Hungarian victory of 1345 pushed the Mongols back beyond the Dniester River, after which King Louis the Great (q.v.) established a defensive banat called "Our Moldavian Land" *(terra nostra Molduana)*. At the same time he appointed a certain Vlach leader by the name of Dragos as the voievod (q.v.) of Moldavia, who governed it until 1359, when he was pushed out by a rival, Voievod Bogdan.

The date of 1359 can be viewed as the start of Moldavia's existence as a relatively independent state, even though for the next century and a half it was usually obliged to accept either Hungarian or Polish overlordship. This situation ended at the turn of the 15th to the 16th century, when Moldavia came under Ottoman Turkish (q.v.) rule and remained so until 1878. In the 16th and 17th century Moldavia was an autonomous Turkish province, ruled by native Vlach princes, while between 1711 and 1821, following the deposition of the native rulers, it had to accept the rule of the Greek Phanariots (q.v.). After the Greek Revolution of 1821–29, while Moldavia still remained part of the Ottoman Empire (q.v.), Russian influences increased significantly. In 1862, under the leadership of Prince Alexander Cuza (r.1859-66), Moldavia was united with the other Vlach principality of Wallachia (q.v.), and then it was renamed Romania (q.v.). The Principality of Romania gained its full independence at the Congress of Berlin (q.v.) in 1878, and then three years later (1881) it became the Kingdom of Romania.

The Republic of Moldova formed after the dissolution of the Soviet Union in 1991 has been carved out of what used to be the eastern part of medieval Moldavia, known in those days as

Bessarabia. Bessarabia had been annexed to the Russian Empire by the Treaty of Bucharest in 1812. It returned to Greater Romania in 1918, and then went back to Russia (Soviet Union) (q.v.) in 1945.

MOLNÁR, ERIK (1894–1966). The "father" of Hungarian Marxist historical studies in the period after World War II (q.v.). Molnár became converted to Marxism as a prisoner of war in Russia during World War I (q.v.). After returning home, he became a radical publicist and popular historian, writing historical and sociological essays for various leftist periodicals under such assumed names as Erik Jeszenszky, István Pálfai, and Lajos Szentmiklósy. He was especially concerned with the application of Marxism to the evolution of early Hungarian society. During World War II (q.v.) he published a two-volume work on this topic entitled *The Society of Árpádian Hungary (Az Árpádkori társadalom)*(2 vols., 1943). After the war, he continued these efforts, publishing such additional works as *The History of Hungarian Society from the Ancient Period to the Age of the Árpáds (A magyar társadalom története az őskortól az Árpádokig)* (1945), *The History of Hungarian Society from the Age of the Árpáds to Mohács (A magyar társadalom története az Árpádkortól Mohácsig)* (1949), and *The Ancient History of the Hungarian People (A magyar nép őstörténete)* (1953).

In the period between December 1944 and November 1956, Molnár also served in a number of governmental posts, including that of the minister of welfare (1944–47), minister of propaganda (1947–48), minister of foreign affairs (1948, 1952–53), and minister of justice (1950–52, 1954–56), as well as Hungary's ambassador to the Soviet Union (1948–49) and the president of the Hungarian Supreme Court (1953–54). During the same period, Molnár had a determining role in the reorientation of Hungarian historical studies (q.v.), both through his officially promulgated and mass-produced works, and via his position as the director of the Institute of History (q.v.) of the Hungarian Academy of Sciences (q.v.) (1949-66) and the president of the Hungarian Historical Association (q.v.) (1958-66). Before his death, Molnár also served as the editor-in-chief of the first major and somewhat credible Marxist synthesis of Hungarian history intended for public consumption, *History of Hungary [Magyarország története]* (2 vols., 1964). His last years were filled with a debate concerning the alleged continued presence of nationalistic elements in Hungarian Marxist historical studies, which he tried to eradicate.

MOLNÁR FERENC (1878–1952). The best-known Hungarian playwright outside of Hungary (q.v.). Molnár's plays have been translated into two dozen or more languages. He made his name in the first decade of the 20th century both in prose and in drama. With his novel, *The Boys of Pál Street (Pál útja fiúk)* (1907), Molnár produced one of the jewels of world literature. Yet, he became known to the world primarily through his popular plays, such as *Liliom (Lily)* (1909), *The Swan (A hattyú)* (1920), *Glass Slippers (Az üveg cipő)* (1924), *The Play is the Thing (Játék a kastélyban)* (1926), *Olympia* (1928) and others. Being a true urbanite and a keen observer of bourgeois lifestyles, Molnár wrote witty stories and applied to them to the stage with unmatched craftsmanship. Although not as highly regardedin Hungary as in the West, to the world at large Molnár represents the best of Hungarian literature. Perhaps precisely because of his popularity outside of Hungary, in 1930 Molnár moved in Switzerland, and then in the late 1930s to New York. He died there in 1952, and did so without having produced anything that could have rivaled his earlier works that grew out of his native soil.

MONGOLS [TATARS, TARTARS]. A group of tribes to the north of China, who under the leadership of Genghis (Chingis) Khan (d.1227)—originally called Temüdjin—established a huge Eurasian Empire that at the height of its power occupied an area roughly equal to the former Soviet Union (q.v.), plus portions of the Middle East. Originally the name "Mongol" was the name of Genghis Khan's own tribe, but after his conquests it was applied to the people of his empire as a whole. "Tatar" was the name of the rival tribe, but for some reason it too was accepted as one of the commonly used collective names of Mongols. "Tartar," on the other hand, is simply a corruption of "Tatar," which is derived from the biblical "Tartarus" mountain. In 1206 Genghis Khan was officially proclaimed the ruler of the whole Mongol/Tatar realm, after which he continued to expand his empire at an even greater speed.

The Mongols' first intrusion into Europe took place in 1223, which resulted in the defeat of the Cumans and Russian/East Slavic princes at the Battle of Kalka River close to the Sea of Azov (q.v.). In 1236 the Mongols defeated and destroyed Magna Bulgaria on the Middle Volga, and by 1240 they conquered Kiev (q.v.) and the whole of Kievan Russia (q.v.). In 1241 they continued their thrust into Europe, defeating the Poles, the Germans, the Czechs, and the Hungarians. The Hungarian defeat at the Battle of Mohi (Muhi) (q.v.) on April 11, 1241, was followed by the destruction of much of the country, and then by the Mongol withdrawal from Hungary (q.v.) in 1242. Batu Khan (q.v.) left because he wished to be considered as a successor to the Great Khan Ugudey (Ögödey), who died in December 1241.

Batu never made it back to Mongolia. He settled down on the Lower Volga, where he founded the city of Saray, which became the center of the Empire of the Golden Horde (q.v.), which in turn was one of the component states of the Mongol Empire as a whole. The Mongols dominated Russia and the Eastern Slavs until the late 15th century, when they fragmented into several smaller khanates. One of these, the Khanate of Crimea (q.v.), became a vassal state of the Ottoman Empire (q.v.) in 1475, and in that capacity it continued to pose problems for Hungary and for Transylvania (q.v.) right up to the end of the 17th century.

MONGOL CONQUEST see **MONGOL INVASION OF HUNGARY.**

MONGOL INVASION OF HUNGARY (1241-42). The Tatar Mongol armies under the leadership of Batu Khan (q.v.) invaded Hungary (q.v.) in the spring of 1241. The main Mongol army under the personal leadership of Batu Khan (q.v.) crossed the Carpathians (q.v.) at Verecke Pass on March 12, 1241, and on April 11 defeated King Béla IV's (q.v.) army at the Battle of Mohi (Muhi) (q.v.).

King Béla fled via Pozsony (q.v.) to Austria (q.v.), where he sought the protection of Duke Frederick II of the Babenberg dynasty (q.v.). Instead of getting help, Duke Frederick forced Béla to cede three western Hungarian counties to Austria. (Béla did get back at Frederick in 1246, when he defeated and killed the latter and thus ended the Babenberg line in Austria.) By May 1241 King Béla was in Zagreb (q.v.), from where he sought help from Pope Gregory IX (r.1227-41), Holy Roman Emperor Frederick II (r.1212-50), as well as King Louis IX (St. Louis) (r.1226-70) of France. Although no help came, Béla undertook efforts to prevent the Mongols from crossing into Trans-Danubia (q.v.). This too proved to be futile, because in January 1242 the Mongol armies cross over the frozen Danube, after which they took control over all of Western Hungary and also invaded Croatia (q.v.) and Dalmatia (q.v.). In March 1242 King Béla found refuge on one of the Dalmatian islands.

The situation appeared desperate, when suddenly, at the news of Great Khan Ögödey's death, the Mongol armies withdrew, because Khan Batu's hope to succeed Ögödey as the great khan. The Mongol invasion left Hungary in shambles. Its population decimated, most of its towns and villages destroyed, and its social and economic development thrown back by decades. These new realities compelled King Béla to urge the magnates (q.v.) to build stone fortresses to serve as impregnable strongholds in case of a new Mongol invasion. During the next few decades, many scores of fortresses were built. But as it turned out, these were used less against the Mongols, and more to shore up the power of the feudal nobility (q.v.). Ultimately, many of these nobles with newly built stone fortresses transformed themselves into regional warlords and undermined the central power in Hungary. Thus began the country's political disintegration, which was not reversed until the second and the third decades of the 14th century under the new Anjou dynasty (q.v.).

MONTECUCCOLI, PRINCE RAIMONDO (1609–80). A Habsburg Imperial field marshal and author of books on military strategy. Born into an Italian noble family, he joined the Habsburg Imperial Armies (q.v.) in the late 1620s, fought in the Thirty Years' War

(1618–48), rose in ranks rapidly, and by 1648 became a member of the Habsburg Imperial War Council (q.v.). In 1651 Montecuccoli was given the rank of a prince, in 1655 he was granted Hungarian estates, in 1658 he was appointed a field marshal, and in 1660 he was named the commander-in-chief of the Habsburg Imperial Armies (q.v.) in Hungary (q.v.). In that capacity, in 1661 he invaded Transylvania (q.v.) to aid Prince John Kemény (q.v.) against the Turks (q.v.). But having achieved very little, he left Kemény to his face the Turks alone. This caused much uproar in Hungary, which involved him in a controversy with the most highly regarded Hungarian military commander of that age, Count Miklós Zrínyi (q.v.), who also happened to be the author of heroic epic and works on military strategy.

In the course of the next three years, Montecuccoli did very little to stem the Turkish tide, which resulted in the loss of Várad (Nagyvárad) (q.v.) in the Partium (q.v.), Érsekújvár in Upper Hungary (q.v.), and Zerinvár in lower Trans-Danubia (q.v.). During the 1664 Ottoman invasion of Hungary, he defeated the Turks at the Battle of St. Gotthard (Szentgotthárd) (August 1), but in the Peace Treaty of Vasvár (August 10) he still relinquished all of the territories conquered by the Turks. This made him very unpopular in Hungary, which only increased his antipathy toward the Hungarians. After 1664 Montecuccoli lived mostly in Austria (q.v.) and devoted his time to writing works on military tactics. In addition to his unwarranted concessions to the Turks, Montecuccoli is best remembered for his alleged statement: "The three most important prerequisites for a successful war are: money, money, and money."

MORAVA [DÜRNKRUT], BATTLE OF (1278). This battle was a showdown between King Ottokar II (r.1253-78) of Bohemia (q.v.) and the new Holy Roman Emperor Rudolph of Habsburg (q.v.), ending in the former's defeat and death, and in the planting of Habsburg power in Austria (q.v.). The battle took place on August 26, 1278, and Habsburg victory was assured by the presence of a large Hungarian army under the leadership of King Ladislas IV (q.v.), who was trying to recoup some earlier Hungarian losses against King Ottokar. This Habsburg-Hungarian victory ended the career and aspirations of the powerful Czech king and at the same time secured the Babenberg (q.v.) possessions for the Habsburgs (q.v.). As such, it determined the fate of the nations and states of East Central Europe (q.v.) for many centuries to come.

MORAVIA. The Margravate of Moravia was the smaller of the two core lands of the medieval Czech Kingdom (q.v.), the larger one being Bohemia (q.v.). In the 10th century it was ruled from the fortress of Libice by the Slavnik dynasty. But in 995 the Slavniks were defeated and exterminated by the Přemyslide dynasty (q.v.) of Bohemia, who then unified the two provinces into a single state. With occasional exceptions—such as its 15th-century conquest by King Matthias Corvinus (q.v.) of Hungary—Moravia remained part of the Czech state. In the early 16th century Moravia fell under Habsburg rule, where it remained until 1918, when it became part of the new Czechoslovak (q.v.) state. Following the disintegration of Czechoslovakia at the end of 1992, Moravia remained part of the Czechia (Czech Republic) (q.v.).

MORAVIA MAGNA see MAGNA MORAVIA.

MORGANATIC MARRIAGE. A marriage of a man of higher rank with a women of inferior rank, which precludes both the wife and their common offspring from inheriting their father's rank and possessions. The best known example of such a marriage was that of Archduke Francis Ferdinand (q.v.), the heir to the Austro-Hungarian throne, and Countess Sophia Chotek, in 1900, which was staunchly opposed by Emperor Francis Joseph (q.v.). Although in 1909 Countess Chotek was given the title "Princess of Hohenberg," none of their three children had the right of succession. They were compelled to assume the name and title of their mother. Francis Ferdinand's assassination a Sarajevo (q.v.) in 1914 prevented him from trying to change the implications of this morganatic marriage for his children. Given his personality, he may have tried to do so after ascending the throne. But in light of the constitutional traditions of the Habsburg Empire (Austria-Hungary) (q.v.), he may not have been able to carry it through.

MÓRICZ, ZSIGMOND (1879–1942). Novelist, writer, the greatest representative of critical realism in Hungarian prose, and—along with Ady (q.v.) and Dezső Szabó (q.v.)—one of the spiritual fathers in interwar Hungarian Populism (q.v.). Coming from a simple peasant family, Móricz knew the meaning of poverty and privation. Thus, his political views were always left of center, and he himself was generally a vocal exponent of progressive social and political reforms. Given his background, Móricz naturally became closely associated with the progressive literary periodical, the *West (Nyugat)* (q.v.), as well as with the post–World War I (q.v.) Károlyi Regime (q.v.). This made him less than fully acceptable to the Horthy Regime (q.v.) that ruled interwar Hungary (q.v.). For this reason, during the regime's early phase (q.v.) he was often subjected to political molestations. But his name and fame as a noted novelist saved him from serious repercussions. His death in 1942 also saved him from having to make compromises with the post–World War II (q.v.) communist regime, which did enjoy the propaganda services of Móricz's overenthusiastic daughter, Virág Móricz (b. 1909).

MOVE [MAGYAR ORSZÁGOS VÉDERŐ EGYESÜLET, HUNGARIAN NATIONAL DEFENSE ASSOCIATION] (1918-44). An antirevolutionary, anticommunist, and nationalist association organized in November 1918 by about a thousand demobilized professional army officers who saw their world collapsing and who wished to stem the tide of this collapse. From late 1918 through 1921, the MOVE became a powerful force under its second elected leader, Gyula Gömbös (q.v.), who made it into an active nationalist organization that supported many of the freebooter detachments that were involved in the White Terror (q.v.) and in various military efforts to preserve more of Hungary's historic territories, such as the creation of the *Lajtabánság* (q.v.). The MOVE had also played a significant role in the establishment and stabilization of the Horthy Regime (q.v.), as well as in sabotaging

King Charles IV's (q.v.) two efforts to regain his Hungarian throne. Although its significance declined after 1921, the organization survived throughout the interwar years (q.v.). But after the stabilization of Admiral Horthy's (q.v.) conservative political system, its activities were transferred onto the social scene. It always represented the views and ideas of right radicalism, and for this reason some of its members displayed considerable sympathy for National Socialism (q.v.) and for various political organizations connected with that ideology.

MUNKÁCSY, MIHÁLY [MICHAEL] (1844–1900). The most highly regarded Hungarian painter of the late 19th century, Munkácsy became known throughout the Western World. Having lost his parents early in life, Munkácsy had a very hard childhood, which made him a sickly child and affected his whole life. While in his early twenties, he studied with some of the best artists in Vienna (q.v.) and Munich, then in 1867 he went to Paris with a Hungarian state scholarship. There he became acquainted with the work of Courbet, which decided his own orientation for life. In the early 1870s, when already well known in Europe, he settled in the French capital and married the widow of Baron Marches. He took several world tours to popularize his work (including rips to the United States), and at times he would also visit his homeland. In preparation for the Hungarian Millennium (q.v.), he was commissioned to paint the huge fresco entitled "The Hungarian Conquest" *(Honfoglalás),* which is still to be seen in the Reception Room of the Hungarian Parliament (q.v.). Although Munkácsy's monumental paintings and his traditional style are out of vogue today, he is still the best known Hungarian artist abroad.

MUSCOVITE RUSSIA. The Russian state that was formed in the early 14th century upon the ruins of Kievan Russia (q.v.), around the little town of Moscow, under the Danilovich branch of the Rurik dynasty (q.v.). Initially Muscovite Russia was under the over-lordship of the Golden Horde (q.v.), ruled by the grand dukes of Moscow. They threw off the Mongol yoke in the late 15th century, and then in the middle of the 16th century (1547) they assumed the title of czar. Thereafter, Muscovite Russia was known as the Czardom of Muscovy up to the early 18th century, when Peter the Great (r.1682/89-1725) transformed it into the Russian Empire (q.v). Contacts between Muscovite Russia and Hungary (q.v.) were minimal until the Liberation Wars (q.v.) and the Rákóczi War of Liberation (q.v.) in the late 17th and early 18th centuries.

MUSCOVITES. The appellation of those Hungarian communist leaders who spent all or most of the interwar years (q.v.) in exile in the Soviet Union (q.v.) and then returned at the end of World War II (q.v.) to take control over Hungary (q.v.). The most notorious of these Muscovites were Mátyás Rákosi (q.v.), Ernő Gerő (q.v.), and József Révai (q.v.), but their ranks also included the reform-minded Imre Nagy (q.v.).

- N -

NÁDAS, JÁNOS [JOHN]. (1903-92). One of the most prominent and vocal leaders of the post-Word War II (q.v.) Hungarian emigration (q.v.) in the United States, who was the founding president of the Hungarian Association (q.v.) of Cleveland, Ohio, as well as of a host of other organizations and activities connected with that association. Most significant of these activities were the annual Hungarian Congresses *(Magyar Találkozók)* undertaken in 1961, whose proceedings were published in the yearbooks entitled *Chronicle (Krónika)* (1962–). Nádas's first involvement in politics took place in Budapest (q.v.) within the Party of Hungarian Life (q.v.), and he remained dedicated to it all his life. He was already involved in emigré politics in the Hungarian refugee camps in Austria (q.v.). But only after immig-rating to the United States in 1950 did he make himself into the chief spokesman of the conservative branch of the Hungarian immigrants. Nádas was basically an organizer, not a writer. Thus, although his name appears as the coeditor of the above-mentioned annual proceedings of the Hungarian Congresses, the actual editing was done by his close friend and collaborator, Professor Ferenc Somogyi (q.v.). Following Nádas's death, his role was taken over by his younger brother, Gyula (Julius) Nádas (b.1905).

NÁDASDY FAMILY. An old Hungarian aristocratic family, a number of whose members had played significant roles in Hungary's (q.v.) history during the 16th through the 18th centuries. The first of these was Tamás Nádasdy (1499–1562), who supported Ferdinand of Habsburg's (q.v.) royal aspirations after the Battle of Mohács (q.v.) and then served him in many different capacities. In 1553 he was given the rank of a baron and ended his life as Hungary's palatine (1554–62). His marriage to Orsolya Kanizsai (d.1571) made him the lord of one of the largest estates in Hungary. Tamás Nádasdy's son,

Baron Ferenc Nádasdy (1555-1604), was one of the fiercest anti-Turkish fighters of the late-16th century, who was known to his contemporaries as the "Black Bey of Hungary." During the Fifteen Years' War (q.v.), which ended with the Peace Treaty of Zsitva-Torok in 1606 (q.v.), Ferenc Nádasdy served as the captain of Trans-Danubia (q.v.) and also as one of the top commanders of the Habsburg forces fighting against the Turks (q.v.). He was married to the infamous Countess Erzsébet Báthory (q.v.) who, after her husband's death, came to be known as the "Blood Countess of Hungary." Their grandson, Count Ferenc Nádasdy (1625–71), whose father had gained the title of count in 1625, also reached high offices. He became lord steward in 1646 and lord chief justice in 1664. In the following years, however, he became involved in the anti-Habsburg Wesselényi Conspiracy (q.v.), which resulted in his execution for high treason in 1671. His sons survived their father's execution. Count Ferenc Nádasdy (c.1660-1718) became an imperial general and by 1708 was appointed a vice field marshal of the Habsburg Imperial Army (q.v.), while Count László Nádasdy (1662-1729) joined the Catholic clergy and ended his life as the bishop of Csanád (1710–29). His grandson, Count Ferenc Nádasdy (1708–83), on the other hand, became one of the most noted Habsburg generals of the 18th century. He fought in the War of Austrian Succession (q.v.) and also in the Seven Years' War (q.v.), when he rose to the rank of a field marshal. During the last three decades of his life he also served as the ban of Croatia (q.v.) (1756–83).

NÁDOR   [NÁDORISPÁN,   COMES   PALATINUS]   see **PALATINE.**

NAGY, FERENC (1903–79). A Smallholders' Party (q.v.) politician and one of the post–World War II (q.v.) prime ministers of Hungary (q.v.). Nagy came from a simple peasant family and had only six grades of primary education. He joined the Smallholders' Party in 1924, but being dissatisfied with the way it was led, in 1930 he joined forces with Zoltán Tildy (q.v.) and others in establishing the Independent Smallholders' Party (q.v.), for which he served for the next decade and a half as its secretary (1930–45). In 1939 Nagy was elected as his party's representative to the Hungarian Parliament (q.v.). Following Hungary's German occupation in 1944 (q.v.), he was arrested and imprisoned (April 12–October 15). After the Arrow Cross Party (q.v.) came to power (October 15), he went underground and survived. Following World War II Nagy immediately resurrected the Independent Smallholders' Party and was soon elected its president (August 1945). At the same time he became a member of the Provisional National Assembly (April-November 1945), as well as of the first elected Parliament (November 1945). In the course of 1945-47 he held several ministerial positions, including the prime ministership (February 4, 1946–June 1, 1947).

With the imminence of the communist takeover and the possibility of a political trial, Nagy left for Switzerland and then resigned his post. He emigrated to the United States, where he became a founding member of the Hungarian National Council (1947–58) (q.v.), as well as of its sequel the Hungarian Committee (1958–90). In 1947 Nagy also participated in the establishment of the International Peasant Union, and later became its vice president (1948–64) and then its president (1964–70). During the same period, he was on the lecture tour, speaking to audiences at about 400 universities. In 1970 he withdrew from politics and died nine years later, just when preparing to visit Hungary. His book, *The Struggle behind the Iron Curtain* (1948), contains his political memoirs and is an important source for post–World War II Hungarian history.

NAGY, IMRE (1896-1958). Communist politician, prime minister, and one of the martyrs of the Hungarian Revolution of 1956 (q.v.). Coming from a poor peasant family, initially Nagy was trained to be a locksmith. Having served in World War I (q.v.), Nagy became a Russian prisoner of war, where he was converted to communism and joined the Bolshevik Party. He returned home in 1921 to engage in underground activities. In 1929 he returned to the Soviet Union (q.v.), where he became associated with the Institute of Agricultural Sciences and the Central Statistical Office. Toward the end of 1944, Nagy repatriated to Hungary (q.v.) and became one of the top leaders

of the Hungarian Communist Party (q.v.). During the postwar years
he served in various ministerial positions, including the minister of
agriculture (December 1944–November 1945), minister of interior
(November 1945–March 1946), minister of food production
(December 1950–January 1952), minister of collectivization
(January–November 1952), deputy prime minister (November 1952–
July 1953), and prime minister (July 1953-April 1955).

During the late 1940s and early 1950s, Nagy disagreed with
Rákosi's (q.v.) merciless policy of collectivization and regimentation
that was reminiscent of Stalin's rule in Soviet Russia (q.v.). For
this reason he fell out of favor with Rákosi and during the periods
between 1948–50 and 1955–56 he was shoved aside. In April 1955
he was stripped of all his offices and expelled from the Communist
Party (q.v.). Nagy reemerged again at the time of the Hungarian
Revolution of 1956 (q.v.), which overthrew the Rákosi Regime
(q.v.) and introduced a short period of freedom. Between October 24
and November 4, he served as the prime minister of the
Revolutionary Government. Following the Russian invasion and a
brief period of asylum at the Yugoslav Embassy, Nagy was taken for
internment to Romania (q.v.). In 1958 he was repatriated, brought to
trial, convicted, and then—under Soviet pressure—executed for high
treason (June 30, 1958). Allegedly, his execution was carried out
because of his unwillingness to denounce the Revolution of 1956.
By his execution, Nagy was made into a Hungarian national martyr
and a rallying point for the opponents of the regime. His official
reburial on June 16, 1988, signaled the beginning of the end for the
discredited communist rule in Hungary.

NAGYATÁDI-SZABÓ,   ISTVÁN (1863–1924). Peasant politician
and one of the founders (1909) and the president of the Independence
and Forty-Eighter Agricultural Party. In 1908 he was elected to the
Hungarian Parliament (q.v.), where he remained until his death. In
1918 his party merged with the large estate owners' Agricultural
Party to form the National Smallholders' and Agricultural Party
under Nagyatádi-Szabó's presidency (see Small-holders' Party).
Between 1918 and 1924 he served in several Hungarian governments

in various ministerial posts, among them four times as the minister of agriculture (1918, 1919, 1919–20, 1922–24). Nagyatádi-Szabó was a compromiser who was forced into various governmental coalitions by his own weakness. In the course of these political mergers, he usually watered down the goals of his own party.

NAGY, IVÁN (1824–98). A noted historian and perhaps Hungary's most prominent genealogist. A jurist by training, between 1855 and 1870 Nagy was employed in the Library of the University of Budapest (q.v.), between 1870 and 1878 he served as the editor of the Proceedings of the Hungarian Parliament (q.v.), and after 1883 he was elected one of the vice presidents of the Hungarian Heraldic and Genealogical Association (q.v.). Iván Nagy's multivolume work, *Hungary's Families with Coats-of-Arm and Genealogical Tables (Magyarországcsaládaiczímerekkel és nemzedékrendi táblákkal)* (13 vols., 1857–68), is still the most comprehensive and useful among such major genealogical undertakings for developments in the centuries before the 1850s. Because this work was found to be indispensable, it was reprinted in its entirety in 1987.

NAGYSZENTMIKLÓS, TREASURES OF [NAGYSZENT-MIKLÓSI KINCS]. Also known as "Attila's Treasure" *(Attila kincse)*, this collection of twenty-three golden vessels was found in 1799 and was taken to the Art History Museum *(Kunsthistorisches Museum)* of Vienna (q.v.). The origin of this treasure is still being debated. Some hold it to be the product of 7th- or 8th-century Avar (q.v.) culture, others believe it to be of 9th-century Bulgarian (q.v.) origin, while still others view it as the work of 10th-century Hungarian (q.v.) goldsmiths. The artistic decorations and inscriptions upon the plates, cups, goblets, bowls, and pitchers point to a culture of Turkic (q.v.) origins, which fits well with all of the above-mentioned peoples. In all probability, some of the pieces were made earlier than others, which would permit the incorporation of all of these provenances. Their final owner, however, must have been a 10th-century Hungarian of very high position.

NAGYSZOMBAT [TIRNAVIA, TYRNAU, TRNAVA]. A small city in former Northern Hungary (q.v.)—now part of Slovakia (q.v.)—which, after the conquest of Esztergom (q.v.) by the Turks (q.v.) in 1543, became Hungary's ecclesiastical center and remained so until 1820. For nearly three centuries, Nagyszombat had served the seat of the archbishop of Esztergom who was also the prince primate of Hungary (q.v.). In the 17th century, under the Prince Primate Cardinal Pázmány (q.v.), the city became the center of Hungary's Counter-Reformation (q.v.). This movement relied heavily on the printing press established there in 1577, as well as on the Jesuit University founded there (University of Nagyszombat, q.v.) by Cardinal Pázmány in 1635. Pázmány's University was later transferred to Buda (q.v.) (1777), and then to Pest (q.v.) (1784), and subsequently developed into the still existing University of Budapest (Eötvös Loránd University) (q.v.).

NAGYVÁRAD [VÁRAD, VARADINUM, WARDEIN, GROSSWARDEIN, ORADEA, ORADEA MARE]. Founded by King St. Ladislas (q.v.) around 1080, Nagyvárad became one of medieval Hungary's most important cities under the name of Várad (Fortress). A number of 11th- through 15th-century Hungarian kings were buried there. Várad became a bishopric soon after its foundation, while in the second half of the 15th century, under the humanist Bishop János Vitéz (q.v.), it developed into one of the important centers of Hungarian Humanism (q.v.). In 1514 it played a gruesome role in the Dózsa Peasant Revolution (q.v.), and in 1538 it was the site of the unimplemented Treaty of Várad (q.v.), wherein Hungary's two rival kings agreed to reunite the country under the rule of the Habsburg dynasty (q.v.). Located in what later became Partium (q.v.), after the year 1557, for over a century, it was ruled by the princes of Transylvania (q.v.). Between 1660 and 1692 it fell under Turkish occupation (q.v.). At the turn of the 19th and 20th centuries, the city—now called Nagyvárad (Great Várad)—developed into an important industrial and cultural center, which was often referred to as the "Paris on the Szamos," the reference here being to the river that crosses it on its way to the Tisza (q.v.). It was a center of a progressive literary movement, which was best exemplified by Hungary's greatest 20th-century poet, Endre Ady (q.v.). Transferred to Romania (q.v.) after World War I (q.v.), Nagyvárad returned to Hungary during World War II (q.v.), but then it was lost again in 1945, along with its mostly Hungarian population.

NARODNIKS [POPULISTS]. The designation of the Russian Populists in the second half of the 19th century, whose ideas contributed to the Great Reforms (1861–81). They were involved in various secret societies and "movements to the people" and later they also founded the Social Revolutionary Party. The exponents of Hungarian Populism (q.v.) in the 1930s and their later disciples were often referred to as *narodniks(narodnikok)*.

NATIO HUNGARICA [HUNGARIAN NATION]. This was the medieval concept of a nation, which until 1848 included only the members of the Hungarian nobility (q.v.). Thus, before the revolution of 1848 (q.v.), "Natio Hungarica" should not be equated with the nation as a whole in the modern sense of that term. Similarly limited notions of a "nation" also existed in such other nearby feudal states as Poland (q.v.) ("Natio Polonica") and the Czech Kingdom (q.v.) ("Natio Bohemica").

NATIONAL DEFENSE COMMITTEE [ORSZÁGOS HON-VÉDELMI BIZOTTMÁNY] (1848–49). Hungary's highest executive body during the middle phase of the revolution of 1848–49 (q.v.). Established on September 16, 1848, the National Defense Committee (NDC) was manned by six members of the Hungarian Parliament (q.v.) under Lajos Kossuth's (q.v.) presidency. Its goal was to establish an Army of National Defense (Honvéd Army) (q.v.) to protect the achievements of the revolution. After the resignation of the moderate government under Lajos Batthyány (q.v.) (October 2, 1848), the NDC was expanded and fell under the control of the uncompromising Kossuth (q.v.). Although nominally responsible to the Hungarian Parliament (q.v.), in practice the Kossuth-chaired NDC assumed all executive powers and disregarded the legislature.

The NDC retained its powers until its dissolution in April 1849, which coincided the dethronement of the Habsburgs (q.v.) (April 14, 1849) and the simultaneous election of Kossuth as the "governing president" *(kormányzóelnök)* of Hungary (April 14, 1849).

NATIONAL FOLK AND FAMILY PROTECTION FUND [ORSZÁGOS NÉP- ÉS CSALÁDVÉDELMI ALAP] (1940-45). Established in 1940 and generally known only as the ONCSA, the primary function of this fund was to support large families, especially agricultural families with many children. Most help was to be repaid in money, labor, or in kind, but under conditions that would not burden these families too much. The ONCSA was the last important social welfare measures of the Horthy Regime (q.v.).

NATIONAL FEDERATION OF AMERICAN HUNGARIANS [AMERIKAI MAGYAROK ORSZÁGOS SZÖVETSÉGE = AMOSZ]. The largest Hungarian American umbrella organization founded in 1984, after a split within the ranks of the much older American Hungarian Federation (AHF) (q.v.). In 1996, the AMOSZ, under the leadership of László Pásztor (q.v.), had over a hundred member organizations, about twice as many as the AHF.

NATIONAL LABOR PARTY [NEMZETI MUNKAPÁRT] (1910-17). The political party founded by Count István Tisza (q.v.) in 1910, in wake of the 1906 collapse of the Liberal Party (q.v.) that had dominated much of Hungarian politics during the previous three decades. The National Labor Party (NLP) was a conservative nationalist party that supported Austro-Hungarian dualism (q.v.) against the Hungarian firebrands who wanted separation from Austria (q.v.). It was the ruling governmental party during the prime ministerships of Count Károly Khuen-Héderváry(q.v.) (1910–12), László Lukács (1912–13), and Count István Tisza (1913–17). Following Tisza's resignation in 1917, the NLP fell apart.

NATIONAL MINORITIES IN HUNGARY. The relatively small number of Slovaks (q.v.), Romanians (q.v.), Serbs (q.v.), Croats (q.v.), and Germans (q.v.) who remained in Hungary (q.v.) after its dismemberment by the Treaty of Trianon (q.v.) in 1920. Their numbers were and are so small that, even though favored by the Hungarian government, their position cannot influence the treatment of the much greater number of Hungarian minorities in the Successor States (q.v.).

NATIONAL MINORITIES IN THE SUCCESSOR STATES. The Hungarian minorities that had been transferred to the newly created or much enlarged states after World War I (q.v.) by the Treaty of Trianon (q.v.) of 1920. This treaty transferred 1,664,000 Hungarians to Romania (q.v.), 1,072,000 to Czechoslovakia (q.v.), 465,000 to Yugoslavia (q.v.), and 26,000 to Austria (q.v.)— that is, about 3.5 million Hungarians altogether. The position of these Hungarians changed almost overnight from that of a "ruling nation" to that of a "minority nationality." This required a great deal of psychological adjustment on their part, especially in light of the fact that their transfer took place in violation of the very same principle of national self-determination that gave birth to these new states. Given their long tradition of social and cultural preeminence and the obligatory terms of minority protection signed by the Successor States, these Hungarian minorities still managed relatively well during the interwar years (q.v.). The majority of them were returned to Hungary for a few years as a result of the partial triumph of Hungarian Revisionism (q.v.) in 1938–41. After World War II (q.v.), however, when they were moved into a minority status once more, their position worsened progressively. By the 1970s they had become the subjects of the most oppressive policy of denationalization, especially in Ceausescu's Romania (q.v.). The fall of communism in 1989-90 gave them a brief period of respite, but during the 1990s they are once more subjected to an increasingly oppressive policy of assimilation in several of the surrounding states, especially in Romania (q.v.) and Slovakia (q.v.).

NATIONAL MINORITY LAW [ACT 1868: XLIV]. One of the first liberal minority laws in Europe that guaranteed many rights to the national minorities of Hungary (q.v.) within the confines of the Austro-Hungarian Empire (q.v.). Although it proclaimed the concept of a "single and indivisible political nation" to which all citizens of Hungary belonged irrespective of their ethnic background, and although it made the Magyar language (q.v.) the official language of the Kingdom of Hungary, this law also guaranteed the use of all other languages on the middle and lower levels of administration and jurisprudence. It likewise guaranteed the rights of the various nationalities to use their own mother tongues on the primary and the secondary levels of education, that is, in the elementary schools and the high schools.

NATIONAL MINORITY QUESTION. The question that had plagued Hungary (q.v.) and the Austro-Hungarian Empire (q.v.) during the late 19th and early 20th centuries, which ultimately led to their dismemberment after World War I (q.v.). Given the rise of modern nationalism, the goal of an increasing number of nationalities and ethnic groups was self-expression and self-determination, which was also embodied in President Wilson's Fourteen Points. Although implemented after World war I (q.v.), the principle of national self-determination was also violated at the same time. With the creation of the several Successor States (q.v.), whose borders were drawn unfairly in their favor, about one-third of the Hungarian (Magyar) nation (q.v.) was placed under foreign rule, within the borders of states that were just as multinational as Historic Hungary (q.v.) had been. Thus, the national minority question continued to plague the Carpathian Basin (q.v.), except now in the form of Hungarian minorities clamoring for recognition and self-determination. This question is still with us in the 1990s. Its problems are exemplified by the bloody ethnic struggles in former Yugoslavia (q.v.), by the bisection of Czechoslovakia (q.v.), and by the increasingly emotional issue of the mistreatment of the Hungarian minorities in most of the surrounding states.

NATIONAL PEASANT PARTY [NEMZETI PARASZT-PÁRT]. Founded in 1939, the National Peasant Party (NPP) grew out of the Hungarian Populist Movement (q.v.) and viewed itself primarily as the representative of the poor peasantry. It achieved very little results during World War II (q.v.), but after the war it became active for a few years. Unable to compete with the much more popular Smallholders' Party (q.v.), it remained a minor political force until its forced merger with the Communist Party in 1949. During the Revolution of 1956 (q.v.), the NPP resurfaced again briefly, but this time under the name Petőfi Party *(Petőfi-Párt),* named after the 19th-century Hungarian poet, Sándor Petőfi (q.v.).

NATIONAL RECKONING BOARD [NEMZETI SZÁMON-KÉRŐ SZÉK] (1944). In the period between October 26 and early 1945, the National Reckoning Board was the highest court cum secret police of the Szálasi-government (q.v.). It was headed by the gendarmerie colonel, Norbert Orendi (d.1946), whose goal was the total extermination of the opponents of the Arrow Cross Regime (q.v.). Members of the National Reckoning Board were responsible for arresting then executing the prominent leaders of the anti-Arrow Cross Committee of Liberation of the Hungarian National Uprising, including Endre Bajcsy-Zsilinszky (q.v.) and Major General János Kiss (1883-1944). They were arrested on November 22 and executed on December 8 and 24, 1944, respectively.

NATIONAL SOCIALISM [NAZISM]. German ideology, related to Italian Fascism (q.v.), that advocated chauvinism, racism, anti-Semitism, and an almost irrational hatred of communism. During the 1930s and early 1940s, it also had a significant impact on Hungary (q.v.), the most important results of which included the country's involvement in World War II (q.v.) on the German side, and in particular, the development of various Hungarian clone movements during that period. The climaxing of this impact was the assumption of governmental power by the Arrow Cross Party (q.v.) during the last few months of the war, which led to the country's near total destruction.

NATIONAL SZÉCHÉNYI LIBRARY [ORSZÁGOS SZÉ-
CHÉNYI KÖNYVTÁR] (1802). Hungary's national library and
the depository of the largest collection of books and other printed
materials found in the country. Established in 1802 by Count Ferenc
Széchényi (q.v.), the father of the great reformer Count István
Széchenyi (q.v.), today the library has close to six million units,
including over two million books, 2.5 million pamphlets and other
smaller printed material, 250,000 volumes of periodicals, 625,000
manuscripts, 185,000 maps, 150,000 music scores, and many other
items connected with the Hungarian past. Ever since 1804 the
Széchényi Library received obligatory copies of all works printed in
the country. It collects all printed and manuscript materials related to
Hungary and to the Hungarians in all languages. Until the mid-
1980s the National Széchényi Library was located in the building of
the Hungarian National Museum and in several other temporary
buildings on the Pest side of Budapest (q.v.). Since 1985 it has
occupied the largest structure of the reconstructed royal palace on top
of Castle Hill in the Buda section of Budapest.

NATIONAL UNITY PARTY [NEMZETI EGYSÉG PÁRT-
JA] (1932–39). Successor of the United Party (q.v.), which had been
formed in 1922 from several parties as the party of the ruling
Horthy Regime (q.v.). After the rise of Gyula Gömbös (q.v.) to the
prime ministership (1932-36), he reshaped the United Party to aid
him in his efforts to move Hungarian politics to the Right. During
Béla Imrédy's (q.v.) tenure in office (1938–39), the National Unity
Party lost its majority. Imrédy's successor, Prime Minister Pál
Teleki (q.v.), reorganized and renamed it once more into the Party of
Hungarian Life *(Magyar Élet Pártja).* The latter party dominated
Hungary until the Arrow Cross (q.v.) takeover in the fall of 1944.

NATIONAL WORK PARTY [NEMZETI MUNKAPÁRT]
(1910–17). A political party founded by Count István Tisza (q.v.),
after the disintegration of the Liberal Party (q.v.), for the purposes of
upholding the system of dualism (q.v.) between Austria (q.v.) and
Hungary (q.v.). Most of its members came from the ranks of the

defunct Liberal Party. Its primary rival was the Independence Party (q.v.), but it was opposed also by various other anti-Habsburg (q.v.) elements in the Hungarian Parliament (q.v.). As a so-called "governmental party," the National Work Party supported the prime ministership of Count Károly Khuen-Héderváry (q.v.), László Lukács (r.1912-13), and Count István Tisza. Following Tisza's resignation in June of 1917, the National Work Party fell apart.

NEAR EAST. The area at the meeting of Europe, Asia and Africa, which during medieval times was occupied by the Byzantine Empire (q.v.) and the heartlands of the Islamic Civilization (q.v.), and in early modern and modern times by the Ottoman Empire (q.v.). According to some scholars, the Proto-Magyars (Early Hungarians) may have had some connections with the Trans-Caucasian Near East. During the rule of the Árpád dynasty (q.v.), Hungary had intimate political and economic contacts with the Byzantine Empire, and to a lesser degree with the Islamic World. In more recent times, on the other hand, it was influenced by the Ottoman Turkish rule.

NÉKOSZ see **PEOPLE'S COLLEGES.**

NÉMETH, LÁSZLÓ (1901–75). Novelist, essayist, social thinker, and one of the most prominent representatives of Hungarian Populism (q.v.) on an intellectual level. Németh was educated as a physician, and he practiced both medicine and dentistry, but he made his name known primarily as a literary man and a social thinker. Between 1932 and 1937 he edited and published his own journal, entitled *Witness (Tanú),* filling it with his own essays, wherein he elaborated his ideas on social reform. He professed his belief in the essential leadership position of the nation's intelligentsia as well as the need to emphasize quality over quantity.

In 1940 he published a collection of essays called *The Revolution of Quality (Minőség forradalma),* and in 1942 a two-volume work entitled *In Minority (Kisebbségben).* These two works contained Németh's best essays on his social philosophy. They displayed an imposing intellectual capacity and a wide learning that had an impact on most of his contemporaries. In philosophizing about the nature of his nation, Németh distinguished between what he called the "deep Magyars" *(mély magyarok)* and the "diluted Magyars"*(híg magyarok)*—the latter presumably being those partially assimilated Hungarians, who were not fully one with the nation. This was a questionable, and in those days of rampant racism, even a dangerous philosophy, which Németh later repudiated.

Another concern of his was the fate and position of the Hungarian nation within East Central Europe (q.v.). He castigated the ever-present hatred and rivalry among the peoples of the Danube Basin (q.v.), and saw no other solution except each-other's acceptance and toleration. During World War II (q.v.), Németh participated in both of the epoch-making Szárszó Conferences (q.v.) in 1942 and 1943, which were gatherings of Populist intellectuals who exchanged views and ideas concerning Hungary's path during and after the war.

Following World War II, initially Németh taught in provincial schools, but then, starting with 1949, he lived and worked in Budapest (q.v.). He devoted himself to literary translations and to writing plays, novels, and occasional essays. He stayed out of the Hungarian Revolution of 1956 (q.v.), and following the revolution, he even made his uneasy peace with the Kádár Regime (q.v.). Németh, however, never really found his place in the new world of communism, even though, during his later years, he was awarded numerous honors and recognitions. Although he was an intellectually demanding novelist, Németh made his greatest impact with his earlier essays on social philosophy.

NÉMETH, MIKLÓS (b.1948). Hungarian economist, politician, and a former prime minister. A product of the Budapest University of Economic Sciences (q.v.) and of Harvard University, Németh taught at his alma mater in Budapest (1971–77), worked for the National Central Planning Bureau (1977–81), and then was appointed one of the economic experts of the Hungarian Socialist Workers' Party's (q.v.) upper hierarchy (1981–88). Soon after Kádár's forced retirement, Németh was named Hungary's prime minister (November

26, 1988–May 23, 1990), who was obliged to preside over the dismantling of the communist system and the transfer of power to the Hungarian Democratic Forum (q.v.). After his term in office ended, Németh withdrew from politics and became one of the vice presidents of the London-based European Bank for Reconstruction and Development. Recently there were some rumors that Miklós Németh may return to Hungary and to Hungarian political life.

NEOACQUISITION COMMISSION [NEOACQUISITICA COMMISSIO]. A special Imperial commission established in 1684 by Emperor Leopold I (q.v.) for the purposes of regulating property rights in territories that were regained after a century and a half of Turkish occupation (q.v.). The commission was especially active between 1690 and 1707, when most of the reclaimed lands were parceled out either to the descendants of their original owners, or—when legal proof of original ownership was unavailable or unreliable—to various foreign favorites of the Habsburgs (q.v.). The commission's activities contributed significantly to the bitterness that embraced post-Liberation Hungary (q.v.), which ultimately led to the eruption of the Rákóczi War of Liberation (q.v.) in 1703. The Neoacquisition Commission was disbanded in the 1740s.

NEOBAROQUE SOCIETY [NEOBAROKK TÁRSADA-LOM] (1920–44). An expression first used by historian Gyula Szekfű (q.v.) to characterize the social structure and mentality of interwar Hungary (q.v.) under the regency Admiral Horthy's (q.v.). To him many of the features of that society (e.g., extreme class consciousness, the use of titles, importance of family connections and genealogy, etc.) appeared to reflect the mentality and way of life of the 18th-century Hungarian Baroque period (q.v.). Since Szekfű's coining of this term, interwar Hungary has often been characterized as a neobaroque society.

NESTOR'S CHRONICLE [PRIMARY CHRONICLE] (c.1113-18). The oldest East Slavic (q.v.) chronicle, written in the Monastery of the Caves in Kiev (q.v.), which describes the foundation and development of the Kievan State (q.v.) from c.852 until the early 12th century. Nestor's *Chronicle* has many references to the Magyars (q.v.) of the pre-Conquest period, when they controlled the region of Kiev. It also has much to say about of the post-Conquest relations between Hungary and Kiev, when the Árpáds (q.v.) often intermarried with members of the Rurik dynasty (q.v.).

NEUMANN, JOHN VON [JÁNOS NEUMANN] (1903–57). One of the greatest mathematicians of the 20th century who is often called the "father" of the computer age. Neumann studied at the Universities of Budapest (q.v.) and Zürich, receiving his doctorate in his native city. In 1927 he was appointed to the University of Berlin, in 1929 to the University of Hamburg, in 1930 to Princeton University, and in 1933 to the Institute for Advanced Studies at Princeton. In 1954 he became a member of the U.S. Atomic Energy Commission. Initially Neumann worked with mathematical logic and the theory of sets, and then he switched to quantum mechanics and to the theory of games. He had a most significant role in the development of computers, including the application of binary numbers, memory, program storage, and command system. He also had an important role in establishing the theoretical foundation for the liberation of atomic energy. Neumann published his theoretical studies in German, English, and Hungarian. He never received a Nobel Prize, primarily because he died too young.

NEW ECONOMIC MECHANISM [NEM] (1968). Presented and elaborated at the May 1966 Congress of the Hungarian Socialist Workers' Party (q.v.), and introduced on January 1, 1968, the NEM was an effort to inject elements of market economy into Hungary's (q.v.) socialist system that was floundering. Domestic and foreign political pressures halted the NEM temporarily in 1972. In 1975 it was resumed again, leading to the development of the so-called "goulash communism," which, at least for a while, made Hungary the darling of the West. But because many of these achievements were the results of free-flowing Western loans to Hungary, which were used not for the transformation of the economy, but to keep economically unviable institutions and industries alive, this system of "socialist market economy" or "advanced socialism" was bound to collapse under its own weight. It did so in 1989–90.

NICOPOLIS, CRUSADE OF (1396). An attempt by King Sigismund of Hungary (q.v.), later Holy Roman Emperor (q.v.), to break the power of the Ottoman Turks (q.v.) in the Balkans (q.v.) in wake of the great Ottoman victory at Kossovo Polje (1389) against a Serbian-led South Slavic coalition. In addition to Sigismund's Hungarians, the Crusaders' Army consisted of many Western knights from various German- and French-speaking provinces. Unfamiliar with the Turks (q.v.) and Turkish fighting methods, and unwilling to listen to the Hungarian commanders who were more familiar with these than the Western knights, the latter charged the Turks and were totally annihilated. Most were cut down, many of the top commanders were captured, and King Sigismund himself was barely able to escape with his life. He fled via the Black Sea (q.v.) to Constantinople (q.v.), and from there via the Adriatic Sea (q.v.) to Dalmatia (q.v.), and then back to Hungary.

NIEDERHAUSER, EMIL (b.1923). One of Hungary's top specialists of East and Southeast European history, who is equally at home in most Western and Slavic languages. A member of the Institute of History (q.v.) of the Hungarian Academy (q.v.) since 1949, and a professor of East European History at the University of Debrecen (q.v.) for over three decades (1951–84), Niederhauser produced several generations of historians. At the same time he wrote a number of major syntheses on the whole spectrum of Central and East European history, including the following: *History of Bulgaria (Bulgária története)* (1959), *Serf Emancipation in Eastern Europe (JobbágyfelszabadításKelet-Európában)*(1962), *Russian Culture in the 19th Century (Az orosz kultúra a XIX. században)*(1972), *The Habsburgs (A Habsburgok)* (1977), *The Rise of Nationality in Eastern Europe* (English, 1982), *Storm in the Habsburg Empire (Sturm im Habsburgerreich)*(1990), and *The History of Historical*

Studies in Eastern Europe (A történetírás története Kelet-Európában) (1996).

NITRA [NEUTRA] see NYITRA.

NOBILITY [NOBILIS, NOBLES]. The collective group name of the hereditary ruling classes in the Medieval and Early Modern periods who enjoyed certain rights and privileges not possessed by the majority of the population, most of whom were peasant serfs (q.v.). This type of nobility began to emerge with the rise of the concept of landownership and large landed estates controlled by a limited number of persons or families. The nobility was not a uniform class, but developed several layers, usually depending on the size of their estates and the importance of the offices they held. The relationship among the various layers of nobility resulted in a feudal relationship between the lords and their vassals, each of whom could be a lord and a vassal at the same time. The top layer of the nobility with the largest estates became members of the aristocracy (q.v.) who came to control to various degrees both the lower layers of the nobility and the peasantry on their estates. The latter usually became bound to the estates they worked on and for the use of which they paid feudal dues.

In Hungary from the 10th to the 13th century, the term "nobility" *(nobilis)* was used to refer to the country's top political and administrative leaders. In the 13th century the meaning of this term was expanded to embrace the lower layers of the administrative and military classes, who were known as "royal servants *(servientes regis)*. Thus evolved the common nobility {q.v.), which came to rely heavily upon the king in its efforts to free itself from the controls of the barons (q.v.) who made up the aristocracy. Following the promulgation of the Hungarian Golden Bull (q.v.) in 1222, the common nobility was increasingly able to assert its collective rights against the aristocracy. Until the 15th century, membership in the nobility was conditioned on the ownership of landed estates, inherited from the original clans, or granted by the king. But in the 16th century the process of ennoblement became very common even without the grant of lands by the king. The rights of the nobility were set down and codified by Werbőczy's *Tripartitum* (q.v.) of 1514, which still asserted the unity and uniformity of the noble class. But this uniformity was largely fictional, which became increasingly evident in the course of the next three centuries.

These differences were also acknowledged constitutionally in 1608, when the Hungarian Diet (q.v.) was split into two houses, with the members of the upper nobility (aristocracy) (q.v.) representing themselves in the Upper House (q.v.), and the members of the lower nobility (q.v.) sending their representatives to the Lower House (q.v.). By the 18th and early 19th century the nobility had become divided into several readily recognizable layers: (1) The aristocracy, whose members had large estates and held titles such as prince (q.v.), marquis (q.v.), count (q.v.), and baron (q.v.); (2) the non-titled but propertied nobility (q.v), who controlled the county offices; (3) the nontitled and nonpropertied middle segment of the common nobility (q.v.), who usually functioned as learned bureaucrats or intellectuals; and (4) the semiliterate peasant nobility (q.v.) with small plots of land, who were often referred to as the "sandalednobility" (q.v.) or the "nobility with seven plum trees" (q.v.). The most important factors that differentiatedthem from the peasants were their personal freedom and their right to vote in local and national elections.

In 1848 and in 1867, respectively, the nobility's special legal and constitutional privileges were abolished. Yet, the king would still ennoble persons of achievement. Occasionally, he would still hand out even aristocratic titles (including prince, count, and baron) up to the end of the Austro-Hungarian Empire (q.v.) in 1918.

NOBLES' COUNTY see HUNGARIAN COUNTY SYSTEM

NOBLES' INSURRECTION [NEMESI FELKELÉS]. Obligatory military service of the nobility, derived from their noble status. This obligation was first mentioned in the Golden Bull of 1222 (q.v.), which freed the nobility from all taxes. In theory, this custom survived until the diet of 1847–48, when it was abolished along with their tax-free status. During the Age of the Anjous (q.v.) in the 14th century, the members of the nobility joined and fought in their own county *banderia* (q.v.) under their own flags and leaders. After 1397 the commander-in-chief of these nobles' *banderia* was the palatine (q.v.). Starting with the mid–15th century, however, nobles' insurrection could only be called in case of national emergency, that is, when the Hungarian Royal Army (q.v.) was unable to defend the country. With the birth of the permanent standing armies (mercenary armies) in the 16th century, this military obligation of the nobility lost its practical meaning, although they still retained their tax-free status. The last nobles' insurrection in Hungary (q.v.) took place in 1809 against the invading Napoleonic armies, but it ended in a total debacle.

NOBLES' PRIVILEGES. The rights and privileges of the Hungarian nobility first codified in the Golden Bull of 1222 (q.v.). As these privileges increased in the course of the 13th through the 15th centuries, they were enumerated and systematized in the *Tripartitum* of 1514 (q.v.). The most important nobles' privileges included the following: (1) A nobleman could not be arrested without a legal warrant (except in case of murder, robbery, and other violent crimes); (2) he could only be judged by special nobles' courts manned by his peers; (3) he could not suffer physical punishment; (4) he was free from all kinds of taxes, except if the Hungarian Diet (q.v.) voted to tax itself for special national emergencies; (5) he was obliged to bear arms only within the institution of the nobles' insurrection (q.v.); (6) until 1687 he had the right to rebel against the king, should the king violate the terms of the Hungarian Constitution (q.v.).

NONA [NINTH, KILENCED]. A feudal due introduced by King Louis the Great (q.v.) in 1351. This was really the second tenth (tithe) (q.v.) of all the grain and wine produced by the peasants. The first tenth of the produce—known as the *dézsma* (tithe) (q.v.)—went to the Catholic Church (q.v.), while this newly introduced second tenth—the *nona (ninth)*—was paid by the peasants to their landowners, be they lay persons or churchmen. This meant that now the peasants had to relinquish 20 percent of all their produce. This second tithe was the result of the great plague (Black Death) that hit Hungary in 1349. Having reduced the country's population significantly, the large landowners were offering special privileges (i.e. lower feudal dues) to the peasants who would settle on their estates. The *nona* was introduced specifically to prevent the flight of the peasants from the lands of the lower nobility (q.v.) to the lands of the higher nobility (q.v.), who could offer them better terms.

NON-MAGYAR NATIONALITIES see **NATIONAL MINORITIES IN HUNGARY.**

NORTHERN HUNGARY [FELVIDÉK, FELFÖLD, FELSŐ-MAGYARORSZÁG, ÉSZAK-MAGYARORSZÁG]. Variations of this term have been used to refer to the upper highlands of Historic Hungary (q.v.) ever since the 10th century. During the Turkish period in the 16th and 17th centuries, it constituted the northeastern part of Royal Hungary (q.v.), which was in turn divided into two administrative districts: Upper Hungary (q.v.) in the east and Lower Hungary (q.v) in the west. During the 18th and the 19th centuries, the terms Lower and Upper Hungary gradually lost their currency and relinquished their places once more to Northern Hungary *(Észak-Magyarország).* In the latter part of the 19th century, however, the term Northern Hungary was gradually replaced by the newer term "Upper Region" *(Felföld or Felvidék).* The latter term —especially *Felvidék*—continued to be used as a synonym for Slovakia even after World War I (q.v.), when Hungary had lost that region to the newly created state of Czechoslovakia (q.v.).

NUMERUS CLAUSUS [CLOSED NUMBER]. This term applies to an anti-Jewish quota system introduced in Hungary (q.v.) during the interwar years (q.v.). The first numerus clausus law of 1920 stated that no nationality or ethnic groups can be represented at the universities in higher percentage than their share in the total population. The Jews were singled out because, being largely urban middle class types, they were naturally over-represented at the universities as well as in the various professions. The first of the three Jewish Laws (q.v.) passed 1938 was also largely in this category, having *numerus clausus* implications.

NUMISMATICS   [NUMIZMATIKA].   One of the Auxiliary Sciences of History (q.v.), which deals with the study of medals, coins, and various other forms of monetary units used during the past few millennia. In Hungary (q.v.), this discipline gained recognition during the latter part of the 19th century, along with the development of scientific historiography (see Historical Studies in Hungary).

NYITRA   [NITRA,   NEUTRA].   The alleged capital of Great Moravia (Magna Moravia) (q.v.) in the 9th century, composed of an earthen stronghold and of a small settlement under the castle hill. On nearby Zobor hill there was also an earthen fortress. The Hungarians (Magyars) conquered this region around A.D. 900 and by the early 11th century Nyitra had become the center of one of the royal counties (q.v.). Its original castle on castle hill was built at this time. The Nyitra region originally was part of the Archbishopric of Esztergom (q.v.), but in the late 11th or early 12th century, Nyitra became the center of a new Hungarian bishopric. In 1288 Ladislas IV (q.v.) gave the castle, the town, and the surrounding territory to the bishop of Nyitra. It remained an ecclesiastical property for centuries.   In 1317 it was partially destroyed by Máté Csák (q.v.), but after the restoration of royal power by the Anjous (q.v.), peace returned to the region.   It remained so even after the Ottoman conquest (q.v.), for the Turks never penetrated beyond the Danube River (q.v.).   Thus Nyitra remained part of Royal Hungary (q.v.).   After Historic Hungary's (q.v.) dismemberment following World War 1 (q.v.), Nyitra—now spelled Nitra—became part of Czechoslovakia (q.v.), and later of Slovakia (q.v.).

- O -

OBSTRUCTION   [OBSTRUKCIÓ]. A legally acceptable parliamentary procedure—like filibustering in the U.S. Congress— whereby a minority party or several minority parties were able to prevent the regular functioning of the Hungarian Parliament (q.v.) during a segment of the Age of Dualism (q.v.). Because of the unceasing obstructionism on the part of the opposition parties (e.g., long speeches and consciously provoked debates), the years between 1896 and 1912 constituted a period of incessant crises in Hungary's constitutional government, which ultimately was ended by Prime Minister István Tisza (q.v.) through force.

ÓBUDA [OLD BUDA]. A section of today's Budapest (q.v.) on the right side of the Danube (q.v.), to the north of Buda (q.v.). Originally, Óbuda was a 1st-century Roman settlement under the name of Aquincum (q.v.), which served as the capital of the province of Lower Pannonia. After the decline of Roman power, it was occupied by the Huns (q.v.), Longobards, Avars (q.v.), and various Slavic peoples (q.v.), and for a while in the Middle Ages it was known as Attila's city *(Attila városa,* or *Etzelburg* in the medieval German heroic epic of *Nibelungenlied).*

   Following the Árpádian conquest (q.v.) of Hungary (q.v.), Óbuda may have served as the home base of Prince Kurszán (q.v.), while in 907 Prince Árpád (q.v.) was buried there, next to a spring that arose immediately to the north of the city. After the establishment of Hungary (q.v.) as a Christian kingdom, Óbuda became one of the administrative centers or the Royal estates. It also became the home base of several religious institutions, including a cathedral, a provostship, a Franciscan monastery, a Clarissa convent, a hospital, and many others. King Sigismund (q.v.) established Hungary's second university there in 1389 or 1395 (see

University of Óbuda), and the city flourished right up to the Turkish conquest (q.v.) of Hungary in the early 16th century.

Óbuda was destroyed and depopulated in 1526. It was partially rebuilt in the years after, but it remained only a shadow of its former self throughout the 16th and the 17th centuries. In 1659 the town and its region was given to the Count Zichy family (q.v.), under whose guidance it was made into a respectable urban center. In 1840 it was granted the legal status of an *oppidum* (q.v.), while in 1873 it merged with the cities of Buda and Pest (q.v.) to form the metropolis of Budapest (q.v.)

OCTOBER DIPLOMA (1860). An Austrian Imperial Constitution issued by Emperor Francis Joseph (q.v.) on October 20, 1860, that restored some autonomy to the Austrian Empire's (q.v.) component states that had been deprived of that autonomy in wake of the failed revolutions of 1848-49 (q.v.). In Hungary (q.v.) the October Diploma reestablished the prerevolutionary governmental institutions, restored the old county system, and permitted the use of Hungarian (Magyar) (q.v.) as the country's administrative language, but left foreign affairs, military affairs, and most financial affairs in the hands of the Imperial Government (q.v.). To assure central control, it established the Imperial Council *(Reichsrat)*, whose members were to be elected by the diets (q.v.) of the individual provinces and lands of the empire. These concessions satisfied only the conservative aristocracy, but not Hungary's liberal leadership, which rejected it at the Parliament of 1861.

OLÁH see VLACH.

OLÁH, MIKLÓS [NICOLAUS OLAHUS] (1493–1568). Historian, statesman, churchman, and the archbishop of Esztergom (q.v.). Coming from a noble family, Oláh grew up in the court of King Vladislav II (q.v.). In 1526 he became the personal secretary of King Louis II (q.v.). Then, after the king's death at Mohács (q.v.), he was appointed the personal secretary of the widowed Queen Mary, whom he accompanied to the Netherlands, where the latter became the viceroy (1530–56). After his repatriation, Oláh was appointed successively the bishop of Zagreb (1543–48), the bishop of Eger (1548–53), and the archbishop of Esztergom (1553–68). In 1543 he also became King Ferdinand's (q.v.) chancellor, and then in 1562, the royal viceroy (q.v.) in Hungary (q.v.).

Being a strong supporter of the Counter-Reformation (q.v.), in 1561 Oláh invited the Jesuits (q.v.) to settle in Hungary. He also supported Catholic schools and in 1558 raised the Chapter School of Nagyszombat (q.v.) to the rank of an academy (college). Eight decades later (1635), this same institution was transformed into the University of Nagyszombat (q.v.), the predecessor of the present-day University of Budapest (q.v.). Oláh was a learned humanist scholar who kept up a wide correspondence with many other humanists, and who, while in the Netherlands, belonged to the circle and close friends of Erasmus of Rotterdam (c.1466–1536). Oláh's most important historical work is his *Hungary and Attila [Hungaria et Attila],* which he wrote in classical Latin and had published in Vienna (1563). The main hero of his book is King Matthias Corvinus (q.v.), whom he idealized. His work also supplies a great deal of information about the intellectual and cultural life of royal courts of Buda (q.v.) and Visegrád (q.v.) at the time of King Matthias.

OLD CHURCH SLAVONIC see CHURCH SLAVONIC.

OLIGARCHY [OLIGARCHIA]. This "rule of a few" represented a political system wherein political power was in the hands of a select group of powerful families, such as in the Classical Greek or Renaissance Italian city states. Hungary never officially had a system of oligarchy, but in times of the disintegration of royal power, the control over the state came to be divided among a number of influential feudal families or leagues of families, who were routinely referred to as oligarchs. This was the case at the turn of the 13th to the 14th, and the 15th to the 16th centuries, when powerful baronial families disregarded the weak kings and carved virtual minikingdoms for themselves out of various sections of

Hungary (q.v.). During the first of these periods, the most powerful oligarch was Máté Csák (q.v.), while during the second period, it was John Zápolya (q.v.), the latter of whom was elected as one of Hungary's rival kings in 1526.

OLMÜTZ, CONSTITUTION OF (1849). The Austrian Imperial Constitution promulgated by Emperor Francis Joseph (q.v.) on March 4, 1849, in the Czech city of Olmütz (Olomouc), while the Hungarian Revolution of 1848–49 (q.v.) was still in progress. This document revoked Hungary's April Laws (q.v.), abolished the country's pre-1848 feudal constitution, and separated Transylvania (q.v.), the Partium (q.v.), Croatia-Slavonia (q.v.), Bácska (Bachka) (q.v.), the Banat of Temesvár (q.v.), and all the Military Districts (q.v.) from Hungary proper. The remaining part of the country was simply merged into the Austrian Empire (q.v.).

ÖNKORMÁNYZAT [SELF-GOVERNMENT, AUTONOMY, AUTONOMOUS GOVERNMENTAL ORGAN,]. In the past the term *önkormányzat* referred to the autonomy of individual provinces or institutions. After the collapse of communism (q.v.) and its system of government that had been based on workers' councils *(tanácsok, soviets)* (q.v.), this term came to refer to the local governmental organs that have replaced the workers' councils. The *önkormányzat* is now in charge of all villages, towns, cities, and even sections of the largest cities that have their own mayors. As an example, the city of Budapest has a lord mayor and twenty-two mayors, each heading a district with its own *önkormányzat*.

OPPIDUM [AGRICULTURAL TOWN, MEZŐVÁROS]. Large village-like settlements in medieval and early modern Hungary (q.v.), which, because of their size, enjoyed a degree of autonomy that was more appropriate for walled cities. The *oppidi* evolved mostly from royal, ecclesiastical, or privately owned villages that were located on main trade routes. This process began in the 13th century, and by the 15th century most of them had acquired the right of self-government, including the right to elect their own mayors and other town officials, run their own affairs, and come under a special taxations system. At the same time they still dependedto a large degree upon their feudal lords. After King Matthias Corvinus's (q.v.) death in 1490, the emerging feudal lords and oligarchs tried to deprive the *oppidi* of their well-established rights, but they were never able to achieve this goal. In the 16th century many of the *oppidi* fell under direct or indirect rule of the Ottoman Turks (q.v.), where most of them were declared*hass* estates (q.v.) and thus were able to retain much of their autonomy. Those who fell into the region of "permanent warfare" (q.v.) became depopulated, while others in more protected regions became significantly inflated. Some of the latter acquired a population somewhere between twenty to thirty-thousand. In appearance they were like overgrown villages, although in addition to agriculture, they also became involved in large-scale wine and cattle trade. Following the expulsion of the Turks (q.v.) in the late 17th and early 18th centuries, the condition of many of the *oppidi* worsened, largely because their former or newly acquiredlords tried to push their citizens back into serfdom. Those that survived were able to buy their collective freedom in the early 19th century, after which they developedinto real cities. The best examples of this successful transformation are the cities of Debrecen (q.v.), Kecskemét, and Szeged (q.v.)—all of which have evolved into important cultural centers and university towns in the 20th century.

OPPOSITION PARTY [ELLENZÉKI PÁRT] (1846–48). The political party that united the reform-minded and progressive members of the Reform Diets (q.v.) of the Hungarian Reform Period (q.v.). After many years of informal cooperation among them, the reformers finally established their own political party in 1846 under the leadership of Lajos Kossuth (q.v.). In early 1847 they published their "Opposition Manifesto" *(Ellenzéki Nyilatkozat),* which served as a basis for the reform laws of 1847-48. Its main points included universal and uniform taxation, equality before the law, emancipation of the serfs while simultaneously compensating the landowning nobility, increased participation of the non-noble elements in political rights, and the termination of the legal custom of *aviticitas* (q.v.). The members of the first Hungarian government after the March Revolution (q.v.) came largely from the ranks of the Opposition Party.

ORADEA   [ORADEA   MARE,   VÁRAD]   see   NAGYVÁRAD.

ORBÁN,   VIKTOR (b.1963). A young politician and the founding president of the Federation of Young Democrats (FYD) (q.v.). During the first post-communist Hungarian government (1990–94) under Prime Minister József Antall (q.v.), Orbán was one of the main opposition leaders and a rising star on the Hungarian political scene. Toward the end of that period, however, he made a number of political mistakes that lessened his popularity and penalized his party in the 1994 elections. Because of the inevitable aging process, in 1995 Orbán renamed his party by adding the name Hungarian Citizens' Party *[Magyar Polgári Párt]* to it. The original FYD, therefore, is now called Federation of Young Democrats—Hungarian Citizens' Party (FYD—HCP) (q.v.). On the ideological spectrum it stands somewhere between the populist-nationalist Hungarian Democratic Forum (HDF) (q.v.) and the radical-liberal Federation of Free Democrats (FFD) (q.v.). Ever since the elections of 1994, Orbán has been in search for coalition partners among such other chastised political parties as the HDF (q.v.) and the Christian Democratic Party (q.v.).

ORMÁNDY,   EUGENE   [JENŐ] (1899–1985). One of the greatest Hungarian-born and Hungarian-educated American music conductors. In Hungary, Ormándy was viewed as a *Wunderkind,* who began his career at the age of five, received his degree from the Liszt Academy in Budapest (q.v.) at the age of fourteen, and became a professor at the same institution at the age of seventeen. In 1921 he was appointed a concert master in New York. Between 1931 and 1936 he was the music director of the Minneapolis Symphony Orchestra. In 1936 he moved to Philadelphia to aid Leopold Stokowski (1782–1977), and in 1938 he assumed the directorship of the Philadelphia

Symphony Orchestra, a position he retained for over four decades (1938–80). Ormándy was one of the few all-time great conductors and music directors, who pushed the Philadelphia Orchestra into the very top rank among the great orchestras of the world.

ORTHODOX CHRISTIANITY see **ORTHODOX CHURCH, BYZANTINE CATHOLICISM, BYZANTINE CHRISTIANITY, BYZANTINE EMPIRE**

ORTHODOX CHURCH. The roots of the Orthodox Church reach back to the division of the Roman Empire and the foundation of Constantinople (q.v.) as the capital of the Eastern Roman Empire in the early 4th century. The rivalry between the two capitals—Rome and Constantinople—and the different nature of the influences working upon the Eastern and Western Empires gradually produced two distinct Christian civilizations, which diverged from each other both in their liturgical practices and in their world views. By the 9th and 10th centuries these differences erupted into open ideological controversies and major rivalries for the souls of the heathen people of Central and East Europe (q.v.). In 1054 this rivalry resulted in an official split between the two branches of Christendom, which remained intact until our own days. In addition to the Greeks, who were in charge of the Orthodox Church, the people who converted to Eastern Christianity included most of the South Slavs (q.v.) (Serbs, Bulgarians, Macedonians), the Eastern Slavs (q.v.) (Russians, Ukrainian, and Belorussian), and Romanians (q.v.).

Orthodox Christians refused to accept the preeminence of the Pope and, during the existence of the Byzantine Empire (q.v.), they practiced caesaropapism, which placed both spiritual and temporal powers into the hands of the the Byzantine emperors. In contrast to the Catholic Church, Orthodox Christianity was willing to accept the existence of autonomous "national churches" under their own leaders, although the language of liturgy for the Slavic peoples until the 20th century was the common Church Slavonic (Old Church Slavonic) (q.v.) developed in 9th-century Bulgaria (q.v.). The top ecclesiastical leaders of Orthodox Christianity were the theoretically coequal patriarchs of Constantinople, Antioch, Jerusalem, and Alexandria (later joined by the patriarchs of Bulgaria, Serbia, and Muscovy). In practice, however, the first among equals was the patriarch of Constantinople, who, by virtue of his proximity to the Byzantine emperors, almost evolved into an Eastern Christian Pope. Then, following the conquest of Constantinople by the Turks (1453) and the establishment of a patriarchate in Moscow (1689), this preeminence gradually shifted to the patriarch of Muscovy. In addition to the patriarchs, the Orthodox Christian hierarchy consists of the metropolitans (archbishops), the bishops, and the various arch priests, who are followed by the married lay clergy.

Orthodox Christianity entered Hungary in the 10th century, immediately after the Árpádian conquest (q.v.). In the second half of the 10th century it came into contact and conflict with Latin Christianity that came from the West. Then, in the early 11th century, it was largely pushed out by Catholicism, which under King St. Stephen (q.v.) became Hungary's official religion. From the 13th and 14th century onward, most of the Orthodox Christians in Hungary came from the ranks of the Vlachs (q.v.) and the Rusyns (q.v.), who migrated to Hungary in ever-increasing numbers. In the 17th and 18th centuries they were joined by the Serbians (q.v.), who settled on Hungarian territories left vacant after the expulsion of the Turks (q.v.). Until 1792, Orthodox Christianity was only in the category of "tolerated religions," but in that year it was fully accepted and its bishops and archbishops became ex officio members of the Upper House (q.v.). From the mid–18th century on, both the Romanian and the Serbian Orthodox Churches had their own metropolitan archbishops in Hungary, although in the case of the former, a significant number of them united with Rome and came to form the Romanian Uniate or Byzantine Catholic Church (q.v.).

ORTUTAY, GYULA (1910–78). An ethnographer and cultural politician who started out as a Populist (q.v.) in the 1930s, but after World War II (q.v.) became an exponent of the communist system in Hungary (q.v.). In 1943 Ortutay joined the Smallholders' Party (q.v.), yet after 1945 he helped to destroy the party by aiding its sellout to the communists. Between 1947 and 1950 Ortutay was Hungary's minister for culture and education and in that capacity helped to liquidate Hungary's traditional educational system and proven institutions, including the intellectually exclusive Eötvös College (q.v.). For several decades, while involved in communist party politics, Ortutay was professor of folklore and ethnography (1946–78) at the University of Budapest (q.v.), member of the Hungarian Parliament (1945–53, 1958–78), president of the Patriotic People's Front (q.v.), and member of Hungary's Presidential Council (q.v.) (1958–78).

Although an opportunist in politics, Ortutay did produce respectable scholarly works in the area of folklore and ethnography. In addition to serving as the editor-in-chief of the *Hungarian Ethnographical Encyclopedia (Magyar Néprajzi Lexikon)* (5 vols., 1977–82), his most important works include: *Our Peasants (Parasztságunk)* (1937), *Székely Folk Ballads (Székely népballadák)* (1937), *Hungarian Folk Arts (Magyar népművészet)* (2 vols., 1941), *Hungarian Folk Poetry (Magyar népköltészet)* (1943), *Culture and Politics (Művelődés és politika)* (1949), *Writers, Peoples, Centuries (Írók, népek, századok)* (1960), *Immortal Folk Poetry (Halhatatlan népköltészet)* (1966), *Hungarian Folklore. Essays* (English, 1972), *Shining Clear Lights (Fényes tiszta árnyak)* (1973), and a major synthesis, *Hungarian Ethnography (Magyar néprajz)* (with Iván Balassa, 1979).

OTTO [OTTO WITTELSBACH, OTTO THE BAVARIAN] (1261–1312). Son of the duke of Bavaria (q.v.) and Princess Elizabeth of Hungary (q.v.), and thus a descendant of the Árpáds in the female line, Otto was one of the rival kings of Hungary (r.1305–07) in the period after the dying out of the Árpád dynasty (q.v.). Although King Vencel (q.v.) had transferred his own claim to the Hungarian throne to Otto, the latter was unable to defend his claim against the more aggressive and more capable Charles Robert (q.v.) of the Neapolitan Anjou dynasty (q.v.). After Otto's return to Bavaria via Transylvania (q.v.), Poland (q.v.), and Silesia (q.v.), he never made another attempt to reassert his claim upon the Hungarian throne.

OTTO VON HABSBURG, ARCHDUKE (b.1912). Oldest son of King Charles IV (Emperor Charles I) (q.v.) and of his wife Queen Zita (Empress Zita) (q.v.), and thus the heir of the nonexistent throne of the Austro-Hungarian Empire (q.v.). A noted statesman, political philosopher, and a member of the European Parliament, Otto became the heir apparent upon the death of his exiled father in 1922 on the Island of Madeira. Between 1922 and 1929 Otto lived in Spain, after which he moved to Belgium to study at the University of Louvain. He received his doctorate in law and political science in 1935. Before his university years he was tutored by Austrian and Hungarian teachers. Thus, in addition to French (the language of his mother), he speaks both German and Hungarian as a native. He is also fluent in English and Italian, and on a more modest level he likewise speaks Spanish and Croatian.

During the 1930s there were well-developed plans both in Austria (q.v.) and in Hungary (q.v.) for the restoration of the monarchy under Otto's leadership. The rise of National Socialism (q.v.) and the outbreak of World War II (q.v.), however, prevented the realization of these plans. After the German occupation of Belgium in 1940, Otto and most members of the Habsburg family (q.v.) emigrated to the United States and to Canada. While there, Otto agitated for the restoration of the Habsburg Empire (q.v.) in the form of a Danubian Confederation, but without any tangible results. He returned to Europe in the late fall of 1944, but was not permitted to settle in Austria. Thus he settled in Bavaria (Germany) (q.v.) and in 1951 married Princess Regina Saxon-Meiningen, from whom he has seven children: two boys and five girls.

In 1961, in order to make it possible for his children to enter Austria, Otto resigned his claim to the throne. In 1978 he became a German citizen and one year later was elected as the Bavarian Christian Socialist Union's representative to the European Parliament in Strassbourg. Otto was permitted to enter Austria only in 1966, but was unable to visit Hungary until 1989. After the collapse of communism (q.v.), he and his family became a frequent visitors to the latter country, and in 1990 the Hungarian Smallholders' Party (q.v.) even wanted to nominate him for the country's presidency. Not wishing to get entangled in post-communist politics, Otto tactfully declined this honor, claiming that he could do more for Hungary in his capacity as a European parliamentarian. In 1996, his younger son, George von Habsburg (b.1964), was appointed the Hungarian ambassador extraordinary and plenipotentiary. Archduke Otto is a prolific writer and the author of about two dozen books on various political and historical topics. Most of the latter deal with current political issues, but they also include a biography of one of Otto's most prominent ancestors, the Holy Roman Emperor Charles V (r.1519-56).

OTTOMAN CONQUEST OF HUNGARY. The Ottoman Turks (q.v.) began their incursions into Hungary's (q.v.) southern defensive banats (q.v.) in the late 14th century, but they were unable to penetrate the country on a permanent basis until the early 16th century. They defeated the Hungarian Royal Army under King Louis II (q.v.) at the Battle of Mohács (q.v.) in 1526, after which they conquered much of central Hungary. Although withdrawing for a while, they soon resumed their advance and in 1541 they conquered Buda (q.v.). After the conquest of the Hungarian capital, the Turks incorporated the country's central section into their empire and integrated it into the regular Ottoman administrative system. They also extended their control over Hungary's eastern half by making Transylvania (q.v.) into a tribute-paying vassal state of the Ottoman Empire (q.v.). This situation remained basically unchanged until after the expulsion of the Turks in the late 17th and early 18th centuries. The nearly two centuries of Turkish rule was characterized by a condition of permanent warfare (q.v.) between the Habsburg (q.v.) and the Ottoman Empires, which devastated and depopulated the country. As such, the Turkish rule was indirectly responsible for the settlement of a large number of foreigners—especially Romanians and Serbians—in formerly Hungarian-inhabited terri-tories. These ethnic changes undermined the position of the Magyars

(Hungarians) in their own country and ultimately led to Hungary's mutilation after World War I (q.v.).

OTTOMAN EMPIRE [TURKISH EMPIRE] (c.1300–1922). An Islamic empire that grew out of a *gazi* principality founded around 1300 by a certain Turkish emir called Othman or Osman (d.1326), who gave his name both to the empire he created and to its inhabitants. Initially centered on the Anatolian city of Bursa (1326–61), then on the southern Balkan city of Adrianople (Edirne) (1361–1453), after the conquest of Constantinople (q.v.) in 1453, the former Byzantine capital became the Ottoman Empire's new capital under the name of Istanbul. The Ottoman Empire reached the apogee of its power under Sultan Süleyman the Magnificent (r.1520-66) (q.v.). At the end of his rule it embraced all of the Balkans (q.v.), most of Hungary (q.v.), all of Anatolia (Asia Minor) (q.v.), the region around the Black Sea (q.v.), most of the Near East (q.v.) and North Africa, much of the Arab Peninsula, and both shores of the Red Sea. The Ottoman Empire's success depended on its system of political and social meritocracy and on its people's religious zeal. It began to decline through internal decay at the turn of the 16th and 17th centuries, and then started to contract with the Liberation Wars (q.v.) of the late 17th century. It disintegrated completely after World War I (q.v.).

The Turks defeated the Hungarians at the Battle of Mohács (q.v.) in 1526, after which they incorporated much of central Hungary into their empire and made its eastern half, the autonomous principality of Transylvania (q.v.) into a vassal state.

OTTOMANS [OTTOMAN TURKS] see **TURKS, OTTO-MAN EMPIRE.**

- P -

PACH, ZSIGMOND PÁL (b.1919). One of the prominent Marxist economic historians who, after Erik Molnár (q.v.), became the director of the Institute of History (q.v.) of the Hungarian Academy of Sciences (q.v.), and who therefore also dealt extensively with the ideological aspects of Hungarian historical studies (q.v.). Pach's directorship (1967–85) saw the gradual maturation of Hungarian historical scholarship from "vulgar Marxism" to "lip service Marxism"—a phenomenon that was connected to a large degree with the activities of one of Pach's favorite student, György Ránki (q.v.). Next to ideological matters, Pach's primary area of research was the economic history of Hungary (q.v.) and East Central Europe (q.v.) during the 15th through the 19th centuries. Because of his close connection with the leadership of the Hungarian Socialist Workers' Party (q.v.), Pach's role was significant in the defense of the relative freedom of action of the historians at the Institute of History. His most important works include *West European and Hungarian Agricultural Developments in the 15th-17th Centuries (Nyugat-európai és magyarországi agrárfejlődés a XV-XVII. században)* (1963), *Historical Ideology and Historical Scholarship (Történet-szemlélet és történettudomány)* (1977), *History and National Consciousness (Történelem és nemzettudat)* (1987), and *The Region of East Central Europe at the beginning of the Modern Age (A közép-kelet-európai régió az újkor kezdetén)* (1991).

PACTA CONVENTA (1102). A document that allegedly set down the terms of the Hungarian-Croatian Personal Union (q.v.) at the turn of the 11th and 12th centuries. In point of fact, both Upper and Lower Croatia (q.v.) were conquered by King Ladislas (q.v.) in 1091 and King Coloman (q.v.) in 1097, following the death of the last independent Croatian ruler, King Zvonimir (r.1076–89). The often cited Pacta Conventa is known to us only from a 14th-century document, and many historians view it as a later fabrication. At the same time, its existence is widely known and accepted, and the terms incorporated into this document did approximate the relationship between the two countries for about eight centuries, right up to the dissolution of the Habsburg Empire (q.v.) and Historic Hungary (q.v.) in 1918.

PALATINE [PALATINUS, COMES PALATINUS, NÁDOR, NÁDORISPÁN]. The highest office in medieval Hungary (q.v.) immediately after the king. It was established by King St. Stephen (q.v.) in the early 11th century on the basis of Frankish models developed in the Carolingian Empire. At the beginning, the palatine handled only the affairs of the Royal Court, but by the 12th century he developed into the ruler's alter ego, who was placed in charge of all central administrative, judicial, and military matters. Starting with the 13th century, the palatine became increasingly the representative of the noble estates. His role was incorporated into the Golden Bull of 1222 (q.v.), which extended his jurisdictional power over all persons in the land, with the exception of the nobility if it involved capital punishment. His constitutional competence was circumscribed by the Palatine Law of 1485 promulgated by Matthias Corvinus (q.v.), which made him the guardian of a minor king and the commander-in-chief of the Hungarian Armed Forces. Later the palatine also came to preside over the Seven-Person Court *(Hétszemélyes Tábla)* (q.v.) (1535) and the Viceroyalty Council *(Helytartótanács)* (q.v.) (1723).

PALEOGRAPHY. One of the Auxiliary sciences of history (q.v.) that deals with the origins and development of writing and with the deciphering of ancient and medieval scripts and texts. In Hungary, the pioneers of this subdiscipline—especially as it relates to medieval Hungarian history—were László Fejérpataky (1857–1923) and Antal Áldásy (1869–1932). (*see* Hungarian Historical Studies.)

PÁLFFY FAMILY. One of Hungary's great aristocratic families that rose to prominence during the reigns of King Louis the Great (q.v.)

(r.1342–82) in the person of a certain Pál Kont and his immediate offspring. Thereafter, his descendants called themselves Pálffy (= "Paulson" or "Son of Paul"). They produced prominent personalities throughout the next six centuries. One branch of the family rose to the rank of a baron (q.v.) in 1581, another to that of a count (q.v.) in 1599, and still another one to that of a prince (q.v.) in 1807. Several members of the family held high offices, including the office of the palatine (q.v.), through these centuries. The best known among the Pálffys is Count Miklós (Nicolaus) Pálffy (1657–1732), primarily because he was the commander-in-chief of the Habsburg Imperial Army (q.v.), who in 1711 concluded the Peace of Szatmár (q.v.) with Count Sándor Károlyi (q.v.), the commander-in-chief of the Hungarian *kuruc* Army of Prince Ferenc Rákóczi (q.v.). One of his late descendants, Count Fidél Pálffy (1895-1946), became a follower of Ferenc Szálasi (q.v.), joined the Arrow Cross Party (q.v.), and was executed in 1946 as a war criminal. Some members of the Pálffy family still live in Austria (q.v.).

PANNONHALMA. The first Benedictine Abbey founded in Hungary (q.v.) in 996 by Prince Géza (q.v.), named after St. Martin and located in north-central Trans-Danubia (q.v.) on top of Mount St. Martin. At the time of King St. Stephen (q.v.) in the early 11th century, Pannonhalma became the a chief abbey and thus the center of all of the Benedictine monasteries in Hungary. The Abbey of Pannonhalma was granted a foundation charter by King Stephen in 1002. In the course of its millennial history, Pannonhalma had developed into one of the most important centers of Christian learning in Hungary. Since the collapse of communism in 1989–90, it is in the process of renewal.

PANNONIA. Originally a province of the Roman Empire, which coincided roughly with today's Trans-Danubia (q.v.) and the northern segment of Croatia (q.v.). The Romans lost Pannonia in the 5th century, but its name survived beyond the Hungarian conquest (q.v.). The Árpáds (q.v.) occasionally called themselves also the "kings of Pannonia." The name remained current right up to our own times, and it has been used to refer to the section of Historic Hungary (q.v.) to the west of the Danube River (q.v.).

PANNONIUS see **JANUS PANNONIUS.**

PAN-SLAVISM. An ideological and political movement born in the early 19th century, which advocated the necessary cooperation and union of all Slavic peoples (q.v.). Its originator was the Slovak Lutheran clergyman Ján Kollár (1793–1852), who elaborated his romantic views in his epic *The Daughter of Slava (Slávy dcéra)* during the 1820s and 1830s, while serving as the pastor of a Slovak Lutheran congregation of Buda (q.v.). Initially, Pan-Slavism was a movement of the small Slavic peoples of the Austrian Empire (q.v.). But after the Crimean War (1853–56), which the Russians lost badly, it also expanded to the Russian Empire (q.v.). Thereafter, Pan-Slavism became increasingly a tool of Russian imperialism as that huge country tried to expand its influence into the Balkans (q.v.), toward Constantinople (q.v.) and the Straits. Russian-encouraged Pan-Slavism also had a major part in stirring up problems in Austria-Hungary (q.v.) and in engineering the assassination of Francis Ferdinand (q.v.) in 1914. This act served as the immediate cause of World War I (q.v.), which led to the disintegration of Austria-Hungary and to the fall of the Romanov dynasty in Russia (q.v.).

PAN-TURANISM. A Romantic ideological movement born in the early 20th century, which advocated the cooperation of all so-called Turanian peoples (q.v.). It started in Hungary (q.v.) as the Turanian Movement (q.v.), which was triggered by the fear of Slavic encirclement. From Hungary this ideology spread to Turkey (q.v.) and to other Turkic peoples (q.v.) in the Caucasian and Central Asiatic sections of the Soviet Union (q.v.). In contrast to Pan-Slavism (q.v.), however, Pan-Turanism never developed into a meaningful political movement, and its influence was usually limited to a few Romantic dreamers.

PARIS, PEACE TREATY OF (1947). The treaty that was imposed upon Hungary (q.v.) by the victorious powers after World War II (q.v.), which basically reestablished the artificial borders created by the Treaty of Trianon (q.v.) following World War I (q.v.). It deprived Hungary of all territories regained between 1938 and 1941, and imposed the additional loss of three villages to Czechoslovakia (q.v.), across the Danube (q.v.) from Bratislava (Pozsony) (q.v.). Hungary was forced to pay reparations to the Soviet Union (200 million dollars), as well as to Czechoslovakia (q.v.) and Yugoslavia (q.v.) (50 million dollars each). The Treaty of Paris (February 10, 1947) also limited the size and nature of the Hungarian armed forces (65,000) and provided for the free navigation of the section of the Danube under Hungarian control.

PARLIAMENT see **HUNGARIAN PARLIAMENT.**

PARTIUM [RÉSZEK]. A segment of Hungary to the east of the Tisza River (q.v.), which during the 16th century was progressively attached to autonomous Transylvania (q.v.), but without ever becoming part of it. Constitutionally, the Partium always remained part of Royal Hungary (q.v.), even when under Transylvanian or indirect Ottoman Turkish rule (q.v.). Its area was first defined in the Treaty of Speyer (q.v.) (1571) between Emperor Maximilian (q.v.) and Prince John Sigismund (former King John II) (q.v.). Most of the Partium was reattached to Hungary in 1733, and the remaining part in 1836. During the country's administrative reorganization in 1876, several counties were carved out of it, while other segments were attached to existing counties. After World War I (q.v.), a significant portion of the former Partium was attached to Romania (q.v.), along with all of Historic Transylvania.

PASHA [PAŠA]. High honorific rank and title in the Ottoman Empire (q.v.) comparable to that of a field marshal or a military governor. There were three levels of pashas, who were distinguished from one another by their banners (i.e., one-horse-tail pasha, two-horse-tail pasha, three-horse-tail pasha). The very top pashas held the title of vizier (q.v.) and were usually members of the Imperial Council or Divan (q.v.). Virtually all of the top military leaders and administrators of Turkish Hungary (q.v.) had the title of pasha.

PASHALIK. A military-administrative province of the Ottoman Empire (q.v.) under the administration of a pasha (q.v.). At one time or another the *pashaliks* were also known as *vilayets* (q.v.) or *eyalets*. During Turkish times the section of Hungary under Ottoman rule was gradually made part of five separate pashaliks. The main province was the Pashalik of Buda (1541–1686), which consisted of eighteen separate districts or sanjaks (q.v.). A decade later the Turks (q.v.) established the Pashalik of Temesvár (q.v.) (1552–1716/18) in the southeast, and five more decades later the Pashalik of Kanizsa (1600–90) in the southwest. Toward the end of the Turkish rule came the creation of the Pashalik of Várad (Nagyvárad)(q.v.), which, however, survived only for three decades (1660–92). A portion of southwestern Hungary, primarily the area known as Slavonia (q.v.), was incorporated into the Pashalik of Bosnia that had already been established in the 15th century (c.1463–1878) .

PASSAROWITZ, TREATY OF (1718). The treaty that ended the Austro-Turkish War of 1716-18 and regained all of the remaining parts of Historic Hungary (q.v.), including the Banat of Temesvár (q.v.) and Szerémség (q.v.). For about two decades the Turks also lost Northern Serbia (q.v.) with Belgrade (q.v.), as well as Little Wallachia, or the former Banat of Szörény (q.v.).

PASSIVE RESISTANCE [PASSIVA RESISTANTIA]. The practice of withdrawing from public life and of refusing to cooperate with authorities. This policy became very popular in Hungary (q.v.) after the defeat of the Hungarian Revolution of 1848–49 (q.v.). The defeated Hungarians had no power to oppose the introduction of absolutism (q.v.), but most of them, including their acknowledged leaders, refused to cooperate with the Habsburgs (q.v.). This passive resistance continued under the leadership of Ferenc Deák (q.v.) until, in wake of Austria's defeat in the Austro-Prussian War of 1866, Emperor Francis Joseph agreed to negotiate. These negotiations resulted in the transformation of the Austrian Empire (q.v.) into the dualist state of Austria-Hungary (q.v.).

PÁSZTOR, LÁSZLÓ (b.1921). One of the politically most active Hungarian-American leaders, who since 1984 has been the president of the National Federation of American Hungarians (NFAH) (q.v.), currently the largest Hungarian umbrella organization in the United States. Earlier, Pásztor was the secretary general of the Hungarian Freedom Fighters' Federation (1964–69), director of the Heritage Groups (Nationalities) Division of the Republican National Committee (1969–73), and chairman of the board (1974–79) and then executive president (1979–84) of the American Hungarian Federation (AHF) (q.v.). The split of the AHF in 1984 resulted in Pásztor's establishing the NFAH, which he has headed ever since. As a Freedom Fighter (q.v.), Pásztor's political activism during the last four decades centered on the struggle against communism and on defending the interests of the Hungarian minorities (q.v.) in the Successor States (q.v.). This political activism took place largely within the ranks of the Republican Party.

PATRIOTIC PEOPLE'S FRONT [HAZAFIAS NÉP-FRONT] (1954–89). A broadly based social organization founded in 1954 "to unite all the working classes of the Hungarian people" for the purposes of "building socialism." It replaced the Hungarian National Independence Front—known simply as the Independence Front *(Függetlenségi Front)* (q.v.)—which was founded in 1944 and then reorganized in 1949. In effect, the Patriotic People's front was another tool in the hands of the Communist Party (q.v.) for their reengineering of society. It failed totally in the revolution of 1956 (q.v.), but it was reorganized and placed in the service of "socialist reconstruction." During the Kádár Regime (q.v.), the leaders of the People's Front were involved in marshaling popular support for creation and implementation of various new laws and regulations.

The collapse of communism (q.v.) also led to the dissolution of the Patriotic People's Front.

PATRONAGE, RIGHT OF [IUS SUPREMI PATRONA-TUS, FŐKEGYÚRI JOG]. The monarch's right to influence the appointment of holders of high church offices. During the Middle Ages, the Popes made every effort to limit such privileges claimed by the most secular rulers in Europe, but this effort was never fully successful. Moreover, it led to the bloody Investiture Controversy of the late 11th through the mid-13th century. In light of the resulting decline of papal prestige, the Council of Constance (1414-17) recognized the right of the king of Hungary—who also happened to be the Holy Roman Emperor—to control the appointment of high ecclesiastical personnel. Thus, in the course of the next five centuries, no high church office in Hungary could be filled and no papal decree could be published without the prior approval of the reigning monarch. As an example, following the First Vatican Council of 1870, Emperor Francis Joseph (q.v.) refused to permit the publication of the papal decree that announced the acceptance of the Dogma of Papal Infallibility.

PAULER, GYULA (1841-1901). One of Hungary's great Positivist historians who is generally credited with having introduced the philosophy of Positivism (q.v.) into Hungarian historical studies (q.v.). The son of a great jurist, Tivadar Pauler (1816-86), and the father of a noted philosopher, Ákos Pauler (1876-1933), Gyula Pauler is a good example of the traditional a 19th-century Hungarian intellectual. He studied law, but was more attracted to history and archival research than to legal matters. Based on his scholarly achievements, in 1874 he was appointed director of the Hungarian National Archives *(Magyar Országos Levéltár),* and was called upon to reorganize that institution by combining the collections of the Royal Court (q.v.), the Royal Curia (q.v.), the Viceroyalty Council (q.v.), the Hungarian and the Transylvanian Chanceries (q.v.), the Transylvania Gubernium (q.v.), the Hungarian and Transylvanian Treasuries (q.v.), and various other major administrative and judicial bodies of Historic Hungary (q.v.). He did this by studying the functioning of some of the major Western European archives.

Initially Pauler wrote mostly works on the philosophy of history, such as *The Influence of Positivism upon the Writing of History (A postitivizmus hatásáról a történetírásra)* (1871), and *August Comte and Historiography (Comte Ágost és a történelem)* (1875). Subsequently, however, he produced the most reliable, detailed and pedantic syntheses on the medieval history of Hungary. The best-known among his later works are *The History of the Hungarian Nation in the Age of the Árpádian Kings (A magyar nemzet története az Árpádházi királyok korában)* (2 vols., 1993), and *The History of the Hungarian Nation until St. Stephen (A magyar nemzet története Szent Istvánig)* (1900).

PAULIST ORDER [ORDO SANCTI PAULI, PÁLOS REND]. The only major Catholic religious order founded in Hungary (q.v.). It was established around 1250 by St. Eusebius (d.1270), and received papal approval in 1256. The heyday of the Paulist Order coincided with the age of the rule of the Anjou (q.v.) and the Hunyadi dynasties (q.v.) in the 14th and the 15th centuries. It survived the Turkish conquest (q.v.), but then was abolished by Joseph II (q.v.) in 1786. Its Polish branch continued to function and the Paulists were replanted in Hungary in 1934. Abolished again in 1949, the Paulist Order resurfaced once more in 1989.

PÁZMÁNEUM. A theological school and Catholic seminary founded in 1623 in Vienna (q.v.) by Primate-Archbishop Péter Pázmány (q.v.) specifically for the purposes of educating Hungarian priests. The Pázmáneum had served the cause of priestly education well for three and a half centuries. In 1971, it also became the haven for Cardinal Mindszenty (q.v.) after his exile from the American Embassy in Hungary (q.v.).

PÁZMÁNY, CARDINAL PÉTER (1570–1637). Primate of Hungary (q.v.), cardinal-archbishop of Esztergom (q.v.), and the most powerful exponent of the Counter-Reformation (q.v.) in his homeland. Coming from a Protestant family, Pázmány converted to Catholicism while still in his teens. In 1587 he joined the Jesuit Order (q.v.), after which he studied at Kolozsvár (q.v.), Cracow, Vienna (q.v.), and Rome, and then taught at the Jesuit University of Graz, Austria (q.v.). In 1607 Pázmány became an associate of Primate-Archbishop Forgách (r.1607–15), and then in 1616 he followed the latter at the head of the Hungarian Catholic Church (r.1616–37). In 1629 he was also made member of the College of Cardinals.

Being totally dedicated to the re-Catholicization of Hungary, Pázmány was responsible for the foundation of several institutions of higher learning. These included Jesuit seminaries in Nagyszombat (q.v.) and Pozsony (q.v.), a major seminary—the still existing Pázmáneum (q.v.)—in Vienna (1623), and a Jesuit University of Nagyszombat (q.v.) (1635), which subsequently became the University of Budapest (q.v.).

As an ardent advocate of Counter-Reformation, Pázmány's policies and interests were tied closely to those of the Habsburg dynasty (q.v.). In 1618 it was he who crowned Ferdinand II (q.v.) the king of Hungary. Yet, during the last few years of his life, he too began to appreciate the importance of a Hungarian-led Transylvania (q.v.) as a rival force to Habsburg absolutism. Pázmány was responsible for the re-Catholicization of many aristocratic families (e.g., Forgách, Thurzó, Esterházy, Zrínyi, etc.). His views had a major impact upon the views of these aristocrats, among them also the most prominent mid-17th-century national leader of Hungary, Count Miklós Zrínyi (q.v.).

A prolific writer, Pázmány authored many significant theological works. These include also polemical essays against Protestantism, which he wrote while debating important theological questions with such Protestant reformers as István Magyari (d.1605) and Péter Alvinczy (1570-1634). Pázmány wrote these works in the vernacular Magyar language (q.v.), which had a major impact upon the development of the modern Hungarian literary language. His complete works were later published in seven volumes (1894-1905) and his collected letters in two volumes (1910-11).

PEASANT COUNTY [PARASZTVÁRMEGYE]. A defensive association founded and manned by the Hungarian peasants in 16th- and 17th-century Turkish Hungary (q.v.). In areas under Turkish rule and in the frontier regions where normal civil life could not be defended by the nobles' counties (q.v.), the peasants organized themselves under their own leaders and undertook to deal with all aspects of civil life, administration, and self-defense. After the withdrawal of Turkish power in the late 17th and 18th centuries, these peasant counties were gradually integrated into the regular nobles' counties.

PEASANT NOBILITY. The impoverished members of the common nobility (q.v.)—often known also as the "sandaled nobility" (q.v.) or "seven plum trees nobility" (q.v.)—whose everyday life approximated that of the peasantry. The two things distinguished them from the free peasants was their freedom of movement and their right to vote in local and national elections. (See also Common Nobility.)

PECHENEGS [PATZINAKS, BESENYŐK]. Extinct Turkic people who during the 10th and the 11th centuries controlled the Pontic Steppes (q.v.) to the north of the Black Sea (q.v.). In the 9th century they lived between the south Urals and the Volga River. In the 860s they had a role in the destruction of the Khazar Empire (q.v.), while during the latter part of that century they pushed the Hungarian Tribal Federation (q.v.) across the Carpathian Mountains (q.v.) into the Carpathian Basin (q.v.). In the 10th century their power extended from the Volga in the east to the lower Danube (q.v.) in the west. In the 11th century they were defeated and replaced by their Turkic relatives, the Cumans (q.v.). In the same period, some of the Pechenegs crossed the Carpathians and settled in small groups on the Great Hungarian Plain (q.v.). They were gradually absorbed by the Hungarians. A number of other Pecheneg groups moved down into the Balkans (q.v.) to serve as Byzantine frontier guards, only to be assimilated by the local Bulgarian population.

PENGŐ. Hungary's monetary unit between 1926 and 1946, which consisted of 100 *fillérs* (q.v.). It replaced the *korona* (q.v.), which had became unusable because of the rapid inflation after World War I (q.v.). Following World War II (q.v.), the *pengő* fell victim to the greatest hyperinflation in human history. Thus, on August 1, 1946, it was replaced by the *forint* (q.v.), at the exchange rate of 400,000 quadrillion or four sextillion *pengős* for a single *forint*.

PEOPLE'S ARMY [NÉPHADSEREG]. A Soviet type of armed force that combines military training with the socialist ideological indoctrination of its members. The Hungarian People's Army was established in 1948 in consequence of the communist takeover of political power in Hungary (q.v.). It had replaced the earlier Honvéd Army (q.v.) that used to be completely depoliticized. The People's Army, in turn, was replaced by the new Honvéd Army in 1990.

PEOPLE'S COLLEGES [NÉPI KOLLÉGIUMOK]. These so-called colleges were really dormitories established after World War II (q.v.) specifically for the purpose of making it possible for the children of poor peasants and workers to attend institutions of higher learning. The members of these "colleges" drew their inspiration largely from the Hungarian Populist Movement (q.v.) of the 1930s, and now they were to be trained in the principles of democracy and self-government. In 1946 about 200 of these "colleges" with over 10,000 students united into the National Federation of People's Colleges *(Népi Kollégiumok Országos Szövetsége = NÉKOSZ)* (1946-49). In 1949 all people's colleges were dissolved and integrated into the network of regular college and university dormitories. This was done because Hungary's communist rulers felt that these "colleges" had become impediments to their efforts to gain control over the minds of the young.

PERMANENT WARFARE. This phenomenon characterized the military frontier region between the Habsburg (q.v.) and the Ottoman Empires (q.v.) during the 16th and the 17th centuries. In its center lay the fortress system (q.v.) that stretched for hundreds of miles from central Croatia (q.v.) in a wide arch to the eastern section of Upper Hungary (q.v.). The region in the vicinity of this fortress system constituted the area of "permanent warfare."

PERSONALITY CULT. This officially sponsored and uncritical adulation of the national leader climaxed in the Soviet Union (q.v.) in the years following World War II (q.v.), when Stalin's glorification reached such absurd levels that it went far beyond the deification that used to be accorded to the Russian czars. Stalin's glorification was equaled only by the deification of Nicolae Ceausescu (1918–89) in Romania (q.v.) during the 1970s and 1980s, who was virtually canonized, along with all members of his family. The Hungarian version of this personality cult developed in the period between 1948 and 1953. It centered around the person of the communist leader Mátyás Rákosi (q.v.), but it never reached the level of the Stalinist and the Ceausescu cults. During his years in power Rákosi was depicted as the great, wise, and almost infallible "father" of his nation. The Rákosi-cult was undermined by Stalin's death in 1953, and then totally destroyed by the Hungarian Revolution of 1956 (q.v.).

PERSONAL UNION [PERSZONÁLUNIÓ]. A confederation of two or more states, whose unity is represented primarily by the person of their common ruler, who may have different titles in both or all of the confederated states. Hungary (q.v.) was in such personal unions with Poland (q.v.) in the late-14th and mid-15th centuries, with the Czech Kingdom (q.v.) in the 15th and early 16th centuries, with the Holy Roman Empire (q.v.) in the first half of the 15th century, and with the Habsburg Empire—i.e., with Austria, various Germanic lands, the Czech lands, and several other Slavic lands—in the period between 1526 and 1918. If such personal unions last for a long period of time, they tend to become real unions—as was the case between Hungary and Croatia (q.v.) from the late 11th century to 1918, and between Poland and Lithuania (q.v.) from the late-14th to the mid-18th centuries.

PEST. The eastern half of today's Budapest (q.v.). Established in the late 3rd century by the Romans as Contra-Aquincum, across the Danube (q.v.) from Aquincum (q.v.), after the Árpádian Conquest (q.v.) Pest became part of the holdings of the ruling family. In the 10th century it was settled by Ismaelite (q.v.) merchants, and by the 13th century it became a noteworthy commercial town. During the 14th century, Pest's relative importance declined as compared to the new capital of Buda (q.v.) on the other side of the Danube, but in the next century its prominence increased once more. In 1541 Pest was conquered by the Ottoman Turks (q.v.) and declined to the position of a secondary town. Following the expulsion of the Turks in 1686, it was rebuilt and repopulated once more, and in 1703 it became a Royal Free City (q.v.). By the early 19th century Pest overtook and surpassed both of the two capital cities—Buda and Pozsony (q.v.)— as Hungary's industrial and commercial hub. In 1848 Pest became connected with Buda via the newly constructed Chain Bridge (q.v.), while in 1873 it was made part of the new metropolis of Budapest (q.v.), formed by the unification of Buda, Pest, and Óbuda (q.v.).

PETER [PETER ORSEOLO] (c.1010-46 or 59). King of Hungary (r.1038–41 and 1044–46), son of the doge of Venice, and nephew of King St. Stephen (q.v.). Peter became the heir to the Hungarian throne after the death of Stephen's only son, Prince Emeric (q.v.), in 1031. Upon ascending the Hungarian throne, Peter tried to follow the policies of King Stephen, but being a foreigner, he was disliked and overthrown by the latter's brother-in-law, Aba Sámuel (q.v.). Peter regained his throne three years later, but at the price of making Hungary (q.v.) a vassal state of the Holy Roman Empire (q.v.). This resulted in his second deposition by the sons of King Stephen's cousin, Vazul (q.v.). Caught while trying to flee, Peter was blinded and killed (1046). According to another source, although blinded, he continued to live in King Andrew I's (q.v.) royal court until 1059.

PETITION PARTY [FELIRATI PÁRT] (1861). The rival of the Resolution Party (q.v.) at the Hungarian Parliament of 1861, which was convened to deal with the terms of the October Diploma (q.v.)

of 1860 and the February Patent (q.v.) of 1861. The Parliament rejected the terms of both of these Imperial constitutional plans and wished to negotiate only on the basis of the April Laws (q.v.) of 1848. The disagreement between the two parties had to do with the way they were to communicate their views to Emperor Francis Joseph (q.v.). Led by Ferenc Deák (q.v.), the Petition Party wanted to appear conciliatory by presenting its views in the form of a "Petition to the Emperor." The Resolution Party, led by Count László Teleki (q.v.), on the other hand, wished to do so in the form of a "Resolution of the Hungarian Parliament." Ultimately it was the Petition Party that won the day, but the displeased emperor still dissolved the legislature. At the Parliament of 1865-67, the members of the Petition Party organized themselves into the new Deák Party (q.v.), which in 1875 reshaped itself into the Liberal Party (q.v.) that governed Hungary through much of the Dualist Period (q.v.).

PETŐFI CIRCLE [PETŐFI-KÖR] (1954–56). A Budapest-based association of Hungarian intellectuals named after the 19th-century poet Sándor Petőfi (q.v.) that was established in 1954 within the communist-controlled Federation of Working Youth *(Dolgozó Ifjúság Szövetsége* = DISZ) (q.v.). Its foundation having been made possible by the political thaw that followed Stalin's death, the Petőfi Circle became increasingly critical of the communist terror the had embraced Hungary (q.v.) between 1948 and 1953. By 1956 the Circle was openly in favor of liberal political reforms. The intellectual debates during its mass meetings had a significant impact upon the course of events that led to the anticommunist Hungarian Revolution of 1956 (q.v.). After the defeat of the revolution, many of the Petőfi Circle's leaders fled to the West, while others were arrested and imprisoned.

PETŐFI, SÁNDOR (1823–49). One of the greatest and perhaps the most popular of Hungary's (q.v.) lyrical poets who participated in the Hungarian Revolution of 1948–49 (q.v.). He was a member of the March Youth (q.v.), served as an officer in the Hungarian

Honvéd Army (q.v.), and became the adjutant of General Joseph Bem (q.v.) in the latter's Transylvanian campaigns.

Being the son of a simple village innkeeper, Petőfi was the spokesman of the lower classes. He wrote for the common folk, in the language of the common folk, and in favor of a major social revolution. He was at once a Hungarian nationalist and a social revolutionary who directed his popular lyrics against the Habsburgs (q.v.) and against the socially oppressive members of the Hungarian nobility (q.v.). Many of his short lyrical poems are so popular that they are recited and sang as if they were folk songs. Petőfi disappeared and presumably died on July 31, 1849 at the Battle of Fehéregyháza, in the vicinity of the Transylvania town of Segesvár. He died fighting against the invading Russian forces under the command of Prince Paskievich. Some of his most popular poems have been translated into about fifty languages, and over 200 of his poems have been set to music in several languages.

Ever since Petőfi's death, there have been stories that he did not die near Segesvár, but was captured and taken as a captive to Russia. In the decades following the revolution, several of these pseudo-Petőfis have turned up in Hungary. More recently, there were also stories to the effect that they have located his grave in Siberia. None of these claims, however, were ever proven conclusively.

PHANARIOTES	**[FANARIOTÁK].** Originally the wealthy Greek merchants of the Phanar (light house) section of Constantinople (q.v.), from whose ranks came the ruling princes of Moldavia (q.v.) and Wallachia (q.v.) (1711–1821). The richest Phanariotes purchased these thrones from the Ottoman Sultans (q.v.), and then tried to regain their investment with profit by overtaxing the local Vlach (Romanian) (q.v.) population. Thus, their rule was extremely unpopular in the region that later became Romania (q.v.). Because the Phanariotes had a virtual stranglehold over the economic life of the declining Ottoman Empire (q.v.), by the 18th century most members of the Greek money aristocracy were referred to as Phanariotes. The oppressive Phanariote rule in the two Danubian Principalities (q.v.)—common name for Wallachia (q.v.) and

Moldavia (q.v.)— drove many thousands of Vlach peasants and shepherds over to Transylvania (q.v.). This influx altered the ethnic composition of that province in favor of the Romanians and set the stage for future nationality conflicts and territorial partitioning.

PIARISTS [ORDO SCHOLARUM PIARIUM, KEGYES-REND]. A Catholic teaching order founded in 1597 by St. Joseph of Calasansa (1556–1646), which received papal approval in 1621. The Piarists settled in Hungary (q.v.) in 1665, where initially they were governed by Polish (1665–91) and German (1691–1721) superiors. Having become independent in 1721, they rapidly increased their influence by establishing a growing number of school. In 1781 they survived Joseph II's (q.v.) disbandment of over 700 religious orders, and by the early 20th century they controlled twenty-four preparatory schools and five primary schools. The Piarists survived even the communist-ordered dissolution of the Hungarian religious orders in 1949, although they were able to retain only two of their secondary schools. Moreover, their showcase school in the nation's capital was nationalized and appropriated for use by the University of Budapest (q.v.). Since the collapse of communism (q.v.), the Piarists are gradually regaining some of their schools and other property. The order's influence in modern Hungary was great, because many of the country's top Catholic political leaders were educated in their schools, including the country's first post-communist leader, Prime Minister József Antall (q.v.).

PIAST DYNASTY (10th c.–1370). The first ruling dynasty of Poland (q.v.), whose members intermarried both with the Árpád (q.v.) and the Anjou dynasties (q.v.) of Hungary (q.v.). The last Piast was King Casimir the Great (Kazimierz) (r.1333-70), who left his throne to his nephew, King Louis the Great of Hungary (q.v.).

PLACETUM REGIUM [LAW OF ROYAL APPROVAL, KIRÁLYI TESZVÉNYJOG]. The right of the ruler to veto the open proclamation of papal decrees and to censor all official documents going to the Pope from his country. Although in the case of Hungary (q.v.) some historians take this right back to King St. Stephen's (q.v.) "apostolic kingship," the first known royal decree to refer to this right was that of King Sigismund (q.v.) in 1404. It was the same decree that also codified the Right of Royal Patronage (q.v.). The *ius placetum* was confirmed by Joseph II (q.v.) in 1781, renounced by Francis Joseph (q.v.) in 1850 and 1855, and then reinstated by him in 1870. He did so specifically for the purposes of preventing the publication of the newly enacted Dogma of Papal Infallibility.

POLAND. Hungary's immediate neighbor to the north from the 10th to the late 18th century when Poland was partitioned. Poland was "discovered" by the advancing Germans in 962. It was a small West Slavic (q.v.) state under the Piast dynasty (q.v.), which accepted Christianity in 966 and then fought successfully against forced incorporation into the German-led Holy Roman Empire (q.v.) Poland's fortunes declined in the second half of the 12th century, but changed for the better in the late 14th, when—through a personal union with Lithuania in 1386—it became the leader of the large Polish-Lithuanian Commonwealth (q.v.). At the Union of Lublin in 1569 the two countries were merged into the Kingdom of Poland, which for a while became the largest and most powerful state in East Central Europe (q.v.), located between the Habsburg (q.v.), the Ottoman (q.v.), and the rising Muscovite-Russian (q.v.) states.

The combination of internal decay and external pressures resulted in the decline of Polish power, leading to its partitioning (1772–95) and disappearance as a state (1795) for about a century and a quarter. It was resurrected in 1918 as a smaller and more compact state, but fell victim to Nazi Germany (q.v.) in 1939. Resurrected once more in 1945 and shifted to the west by nearly half a country, Poland today is midsize European state with an area of about 120,000 square miles and a population of thirty-eight million.

The relationship between Hungary and Poland has always been a very close one. The two countries were immediate neighbors from the 10th through the 18th centuries, they were often ruled by the members of the same dynasties (i.e., Anjou and Jagellonian), and the southern section of Poland became part of the Austrian Empire (q.v.) and then of Austria-Hungary from the late 18th through the early 20th centuries. Only since the creation of Czechoslovakia (q.v.) in 1918 did the two states and nations cease to be immediate neighbors.

POLÁNYI FAMILY. One of the great intellectual families of early-20th-century Hungary (q.v.), whose members were involved in various contemporary progressive intellectual and political movements. The literary salon of "Cecil Mama" (Cecilia Whol Polacsek, 1862–1939) in early-20th-century Budapest (q.v.) was the gathering place of such prominent intellectuals as Oszkár Jászi (q.v.), Ervin Szabó (q.v.), and György Lukács (q.v.). Her three gifted offspring all became prominent intellectuals in their own right and all made their mark after their emigration from Hungary in the interwar years (q.v.).

The oldest of them, Laura Polányi (1882– 1959), became a noted historian and bibliographer. She left her homeland in 1932 and emigrated to the United States in 1939. Her brother, Károly (Karl) Polányi (1886–1964), departed from Hungary after the collapse of the Károlyi Regime (q.v.) in 1919 and became an internationally known economic theorist and social philosopher. After some years in Vienna, he emigrated to England (1933), and after World War II (q.v.) to Canada and the United States. The youngest of the three siblings, Mihály (Michael) Polányi (1891– 1976), became a celebrated physicist and later, social philosopher who first settled in Berlin (1919–33) and then (1933) in Manchester, England. His son, the Canadian John Charles Polányi (b.1929), won the Nobel Prize in chemistry in 1986.

POLES. The largest West Slavic (q.v.) nationality, situated between the Germans (q.v.) and the Russians (q.v.), who in the Middle Ages had created one of the most lasting states in East Central Europe (q.v.). For about nine centuries the Poles have been the friends and immediate neighbors of the Hungarians (q.v.), and at times they— or at least some of them—were part of single political configurations (1370–82, 1440–44, 1490–1526, 1772–1918).

Polish-Hungarian friendship manifested itself even in 1939, when Hitler's attack against Poland was followed by the flight of many Poles to Hungary, and from there to the West. These two nations were also the first to rebel against Soviet domination in 1956.

POLISH-LITHUANIAN COMMONWEALTH (1386–1795). The dualistic state that had been created by the Union of Krewo (1386), when the heir to the Polish throne, Jadwiga (q.v.)—the younger daughter of Louis the Great of Hungary (q.v.)—married Grand Duke Jagello of Lithuania (q.v.). This marriage resulted in a personal union (q.v.) between the two countries under the new Jagellonian dynasty (q.v.), which ruled Poland-Lithuania until 1572. This personal union was transformed into a real union by the Union of Lublin (1569), when the two countries were merged into the Kingdom of Poland.

This much enlarged state became a significant power in the 16th and 17th centuries, which for a while was a serious rival for Muscovite Russia (q.v.) for the leadership among the Slavs (q.v.). Undermined by the weakness of its political institutions and surrounded by antagonistic great powers, it was dismembered in the late 18th century in three separate partitions (1772, 1793, and 1795). The Polish-Lithuanian Commonwealth always had a very close and friendly relationship with partitioned Hungary (q.v.), including autonomous Transylvania (q.v.), whose ruling prince, Stephen Báthory (q.v.), was elected to the Polish throne in 1576.

POLITICAL EMIGRATION see **EMIGRATION FROM HUNGARY.**

PONTIC STEPPES. The flat grassland to the north of the Pontus (Black Sea) (q.v.), which has been the homeland and grazing ground of many horse nomads (q.v.), including the Huns (q.v.), Avars (q.v.), Bulgars (q.v.), Khazars (q.v.), Magyars (Hungarians) (q.v.), Pechenegs (Patzinaks) (q.v.), Cumans (Polovtsi) (q.v.), and the Tatars (Mongols) (q.v.). The Pontic Steppes were also important in the early history of the Hungarians, for two of their pre-conquest homelands—Levedia (q.v.) and Etelköz (q.v.)—were located there.

PONTUS see BLACK SEA.

POPULISM [POPULISTS, POPULIST MOVEMENT, NÉPISÉG, NÉPI MOZGALOM]. A literary-political movement in interwar Hungary (q.v.), which rejected both capitalism and communism as acceptable alternatives. The Populists tried to devise their own "Third Road" (q.v.) ideology, and also to find their own "Special Hungarian Path" to the future. Having been inspired by the misery of Hungary's peasant masses, the primary goal of the Populist Movement's main protagonists was the uplifting of the peasants through sweeping social and educational reforms. Many of these advocates themselves came from the ranks of the peasants and they wished to dismantle Hungary's class society.

Although contemporaneous with its German "völkish" counterpart, Hungarian Populism was different in that it rejected outright racism, as well as the call for a totalitarian political order. The movement's original inspirers included the poet Endre Ady (q.v.), the novelist Zsigmond Móricz (q.v.), and the essayist Dezső Szabó (q.v.). Some of the early manifestations of Populism were the establishment of the right-radical Miklós Bartha Society (1925–44), the left-oriented Sarló Movement (q.v.) (1928–33), and the liberal Szeged Youth Movement (Szegedi Fiatalok) (1931-38). Populism became an official movement in 1931 at a meeting of young Populist writers in the city of Debrecen (q.v.). This was followed by the appearance of several Populist periodicals, including László Németh's (q.v.) highly intellectual *Witness (Tanú)* (1932– 36), the sociologically oriented *Response (Válasz)* (1934–38, 1946– 49), and the *People of the Orient (Kelet Népe)* (1935-42), which expounded the views of peasant radicalism.

The second half of the 1930s witnessed the appearance of a series of influential sociographies from the hands of Populist writers, who described the ills of Hungarian society, especially as related to the lives of the peasants. The most significant of these works included Gyula Illyés's (q.v.) *People of the Puszta (Puszták népe),* Géza Féja's (q.v.) *Stormy Corner (Viharsarok),* Ferenc Erdei's (q.v.) *Drifting Sands (Futóhomok),* Imre Kovács's (q.v.) *Silent Revolution (Néma forradalom),* Zoltán Szabó's *The Situation at Tard (A tardi helyzet),* and József Darvas's (q.v.) *The History of a Peasant Family (Egy paraszt család története).*

In 1935 many of the Populists joined hands in the "New Spiritual Front" *(Új Szellemi Front)* to support the social reform goals of Prime Minister Gyula Gömbös (q.v.). But being disappointed in their expectations, they moved to the left into the "March Front" (Márciusi Front) (q.v.) (1937–38), wherein they demanded the democratic transformation and social reorganization of their homeland. Other manifestations of the Populist Movement included the foundation of the National Peasant Party (Nemzeti Parasztpárt) (q.v.), the establishment of the "Hungarian Life Publishers" (Magyar Élet Kiadó) (1939–50), and the two national gatherings (1942–43) of Populist intellectuals at Szárszó (q.v.).

During World War II (q.v.) Hungarian Populism became polarized. The right radicals included such writers as József Erdélyi, István Sinka, and Kálmán Sértő, while the left radicals were represented by Ferenc Erdei (q.v.), Péter Veres, Pál Szabó, and Gyula Ortutay (q.v.). A number of the most prominent Populists remained in the center, among them László Németh (q.v.), Gyula Illyés (q.v.), Géza Féja (q.v.), and János Kodolányi. After World War II the Populist Movement was gradually pushed into the background and by 1949 completely suppressed. It was revived briefly during the Hungarian Revolution of 1956 (q.v.), and then during the last years of the communist regime and the foundation of the Hungarian Democratic Forum (q.v.) . But their renewed activities again polarized Hungarian society into the Populists versus the Urbanists (q.v.), as they did during the 1930s.

PORTE [PORTA]. The unofficial name of the government of the Ottoman Empire (q.v.) that was in charge of much of Hungary (q.v.) during the 16th and 17th centuries. The term was derived from the Latin term for gate *(porta)* and refers to the main gate of the Imperial Palace *(Topkapi Sarayi)* in Istanbul (q.v.).

POSITIVISM see **HUNGARIAN HISTORICAL STUDIES.**

POST-COMMUNIST PERIOD [POST-COMMUNISM]. The period since the collapse of communism (q.v.) in 1989–90. Initially this period was characterized by euphoria and unrealistic expectations, followed by disenchantment with the results of the transition from communism to capitalism, and then by the partial return of the heirs of communism to political power. The post-communist period is also characterized by a multiplicity of political parties, vicious political infighting, growing personal antagonisms, pauperization of the masses, and the simultaneous rise of a *nouveau riches* entrepreneurial class. No less is it characterized by the reemergence of nationalism and ethnic rivalries, leading to controversies and potential conflicts with the even more nationalistic neighbors of Hungary (q.v.). The latter include the Romanians, the Slovaks, and the Serbs, who control large blocks of Hungarian minorities (q.v.). Hungary's relationship with such other neighbors as the Austrians (q.v.), Slovens, Croats (q.v.) and the Ukrainians (q.v.) is much more amiable, perhaps precisely because they are in charge of relatively small number of Hungarians.

POST–WORLD WAR I REVOLUTIONS (1918-20). The revolutions that followed in wake of the collapse of Austria-Hungary (q.v.). These included the "liberal-socialist revolution" of Count Mihály Károlyi (q.v.), the "communist revolution" of Béla Kun (q.v.), and the "counterrevolution" under the leadership of Admiral Miklós Horthy (q.v.).

POST-WORLD WAR I TREATIES (1919-20). The five treaties that were imposed upon the defeatedstates after World War I (q.v.) These included the Treaty of Versailles with Germany (June 28, 1919), the Treaty of St. Germain with Austria (September 10, 1919), the Treaty of Neuilly with Bulgaria (November 27, 1919), the Treaty of Trianon (q.v.) with Hungary (June 4, 1920), and the Treaty of Sèvres with Turkey (August 20, 1920). The latter, however, was never implemented and was replaced by the Treaty of Lausanne (July 24, 1923). The Treaty of Trianon is viewed by most Hungarians as one of the greatest tragedies in the history of their nation.

POZSGAY, IMRE (b.1933). One of Hungary's top "reform communists" (q.v.) who was perhaps more responsible than anyone else for the quick collapse of the communist regime and for the transfer of power to the Hungarian Democratic Forum (q.v.). Pozsgay started out as a faithful communist and rose to power through the ranks of the communist bureaucracy and the Hungarian Socialist Workers Party (q.v). He served as the minister of culture (1976–80), minister of Culture and Education (1980–82), general secretary of the National Committee of the Hungarian People's Front (q.v.), and a state minister (1988–89). At the same time, he was also a member of the Party's Central Committee (1980–89), the Party's Politburo (1988–89), as well as of the Party's Presidential Council when it was transformed into the Hungarian Socialist Party (q.v.) (1989).

During the 1980s, Pozsgay moved progressively in the direction of Populist nationalism and became a champion of the revived Populist Movement (q.v.). He supported the Populists' gatherings at Lakitelek (q.v.), and in a sense was responsible for their ability to form themselves into the Hungarian Democratic Forum (q.v.). He was also the first to declare that the Hungarian Revolution of 1956 (q.v.) was not a "counterrevolution," but rather a popular uprising. Yet, in 1989 his Populist friends sabotaged Pozsgay's candidacy for the presidency of the new Hungarian Republic. Thus, having fallen out with his former fellow communists, and having been rejected by the Populists in Hungary's first post-communist government, Pozsgay was pushed into the background, where he still remained in the mid-1990s.

POZSONY [POSONIUM, ISTROPOLIS, PRESSBURG, BRATISLAVA]. For nearly a millennium Pozsony had been a

Hungarian Royal Free City (q.v.), and for over three centuries (1526–1848) it had served as the capital of Historic Hungary (q.v.). Pozsony was also the site of the crowning of Hungary's kings for three centuries (1526–1830). The Hungarians had conquered the region around Pozsony in 892 and soon made it into an important royal stronghold. The fortress was constructed in the 11th century, and was greatly expanded in the 15th through the 18th centuries. In 1467 King Matthias Corvinus (q.v.) established Hungary's third university—Academia Istropolitana (q.v.)—in that city, which, however, did not survive very long.

After the Battle of Mohács (q.v.) and the subsequent Turkish conquest (q.v.) of central Hungary, the capital was moved from Buda (q.v.) to Pozsony, where it remained until the Revolution of 1848 (q.v.). During the Middle Ages the majority of Pozsony's inhabitants were German settlers (q.v.), but there were also large Hungarian and Jewish contingents in the city. The Slovaks (q.v.) began to move into Pozsony only in the 19th century, and even as late as 1918 they constituted only about 15% of the city's population (i.e., 12,000 out of 80,000). Yet, the Treaty of Trianon (q.v.) awarded Pozsony to newly created Czechoslovakia (q.v.), which promptly renamed it Bratislava and made it into the capital of the country's eastern half, Slovakia (q.v.). Thereafter, the ethnic composition of the city's population was altered both by immigration and expansion, i.e., by the incorporation of nearby villages. Since 1993, Pozsony, under the name of Bratislava, has been the capital of independent Slovakia.

PRAGMATIC SANCTION (1713/23). The "Austrian Pragmatic Sanction" is an imperial decree issued by Emperor Charles VI (King Charles III in Hungary) (q.v.) in 1713 that proclaimed the right of the female members of the Habsburg dynasty (q.v.) to succeed to the throne of the Austrian provinces or Hereditary Lands (q.v.). The "Hungarian Pragmatic Sanction" of 1723, which was ratified by the Hungarian Diet (q.v.), extended this right of female succession to the Kingdom of Hungary (q.v.), but only to the descendants of Charles III (VI), Joseph I (q.v), and Leopold I (q.v.). At the same time it also proclaimed Hungary's separate constitutional position within the Habsburg Empire (q.v.), the continued preeminence of the Hungarian constitution in Hungary (q.v.), and the special privileges of the Hungarian nobility (q.v.). It was on the basis of these documents that Maria Theresa (q.v.) ascended the Habsburg and Hungarian thrones in 1740. The collapse of Austria-Hungary (q.v.) in 1918 ended the constitutional force of these two documents, as did the Hungarian Law of 1921, which stripped the Habsburgs (q.v.) of the right of succession.

PRAGUE [PRAHA, PRAG, PRÁGA]. The capital of Bohemia (q.v.) and its Successors States (Czechoslovakia and the Czech Republic), as well as one of the former capitals of the Holy Roman Empire (q.v.). Prague was first made into an Imperial city by Charles IV (r.1346–78), who in 1348 founded the first university in Central Europe (q.v.), the University of Prague, where many Hungarian students were also enrolled. In the 14th and 15th centuries, Prague was the largest and most prominent city in Central Europe (q.v.) to the north of Venice and Constantinople (q.v.). Neither Austria's Vienna (q.v.), nor Poland's Cracow, nor Hungary's Buda (q.v.), nor any of the German cities were in its class. In 1457–58, the future King Matthias Corvinus (q.v.) was imprisoned there, and after his election to the Hungarian throne, he made major efforts to conquer the city, along with Bohemia (q.v.). Matthias was able to conquer only Moravia (q.v.) and Silesia (q.v.) , although he did conquer Vienna in 1485. Under Emperor Rudolph II (King Rudolph I) (q.v.) at the turn of the 16th and 17th centuries, Prague once more became the capital of the Holy Roman Empire. Thus, the affairs of Royal Hungary (q.v.) and Transylvania (q.v.) were also decided in, or influenced from, that city.

PREMONSTRATENSIANS [ORDO CANONICUS REGU-LARIS PRAEMONSTRATENSIS]. A Catholic religious order founded in 1220 by St. Norbert (c.1080–1134), afterwards archbishop of Magdeburg, based on the rules of St. Augustine (354–430). The order penetrated Hungary (q.v.) in the 12th century and established numerous monasteries there, several of which also fulfilled notarial functions by issuing and authenticating official documents. The period of Turkish conquest (q.v.) and the Reformation (q.v.) was unkind to the Premonstratensians. They lost all their Hungarian possessions and regained some of them only after the Liberation Wars (q.v.) at the turn of the 17th and 18th centuries. Having been abolished by Joseph II (q.v.) in the 1780s, the Premonstratensians were reestablished in 1802, after which they devoted their attention to teaching. The center of their activities were the monasteries of Jászó and Csorna, but they also controlled several secondary schools in Hungary. The order was abolished again in 1949, but then reestablished once more in 1989. During the 1990s, the Premonstratensians regained some of their property and resumed their educational activities.

PŘEMYSLIDE DYNASTY (c.905–1306). The original ruling dynasty of Bohemia (q.v.) and the Czech Kingdom (q.v.). The Přemyslides and the Árpáds frequently competed with each other, but also intermarried. The last member of the Přemyslide dynasty was Wenceslas III (r.1305–06), who was related to the Árpáds (q.v.) in the female line and thus became one of the rival kings of Hungary under the name of Vencel (r.1301–05) (q.v.). Vencel had to compete with Charles Robert (q.v.) of the Anjou dynasty (q.v.). The latter ultimately outperformed and outlived all his competitors and established his family in Hungary.

PRESIDENTIAL COUNCIL OF THE HUNGARIAN PEOPLE'S REPUBLIC (1949–89). During the existence of the Hungarian People's Republic (q.v.), the Presidential Council *(Elnöki Tanács)* took the place of the President of the Republic (1946-49) (q.v.), although these functions were de facto exercised by the council's president *(Elnöki Tanács elnöke)*. Established in 1949, the Presidential Council consisted of twenty-one persons, including its president, two vice presidents, one secretary, and seventeen regular members. Abolished in 1989, it was replaced once more by the office of the President of the Republic (q.v.), elected by the members of the Hungarian Parliament (q.v.). During its existence, the Presidents of the Presidential Council were: Árpád Szakasits (q.v.) (1948/49–50) (q.v.), Sándor Rónai (1950–52), István Dobi (1952–67), Pál Losonczi (1967–87), Károly Németh (1987–88), and Brunó F. Straub (1988–89).

PRESIDENT OF THE HUNGARIAN REPUBLIC (1946–48, 1989–). This office was established on February 1, 1946, after the Hungarian Parliament (q.v.) officially abolished the monarchy and elected Zoltán Tildy (q.v.) (r.1946–48) as the first President of the Republic. The office was replaced on August 23, 1949 by the Presidential Council (q.v.), de facto by the President of the Presidential Council. The last President of the Republic and the first President of the Presidential Council was Árpád Szakasits (q.v.) (r.1948–50).The office of the President of the Republic was resurrected on October 17-20, 1989, when Mátyás Szűrös (b.1933) (q.v.) was elected as the Provisional President (1989–90). He was replaced by Árpád Göncz (q.v.) who is the first permanent post-communist President of the Hungarian Republic (1990–).

PRIMATE [PRINCE PRIMATE]. The title of the heads of the Catholic Church hierarchy in Hungary (q.v.) and in many other European countries. The primates are usually archbishops as well as members of the College of Cardinals. Hungary's primate had always been the archbishop of Esztergom (q.v.), which is the first archbishopric established by King St. Stephen (q.v.) in 1001. The archbishop's position as primate was made official by the Pope in 1394, thereby gaining the right to be the one to crown Hungary's kings. In 1715 the archbishop of Esztergom was given the title "Prince of the Holy Roman Empire," after which all archbishops of Esztergom were known as prince primates of Hungary right up to 1945, when their princely title was abolished.

PRIMOR. Since the 16th century the title of the high-ranking members of the Hungarian *Székely* (q.v.) nobility of Transylvania (q.v.). Although not nearly as well known as the other aristocratic titles that originated in the West (e.g., baron, earl, count, marquis, duke), the title of "primor" did exist and it ranked somewhere in the vicinity of the English knighthood, identified with the title "Sir."

PRINCE [HERZOG, HERCEG, FÜRST]. An office, and later a title, of German-Frankish origin, roughly equivalent to that of a duke *(dux)*. In Hungary (q.v.), from the 11th century on, this title was held only by the nonreigning members of the royal family. Starting with the 16th century, the title of prince was also awarded to a few members of the Hungarian aristocracy (q.v.), while in the 17th and 18th centuries, some of these aristocrats were also given the title "Prince of the Holy Roman Empire." The latter included the Batthyány (q.v.), Esterházy (q.v.), and Grassalkovich families, as well as the reigning prince primate (q.v.) of Hungary.

PRINCE PRIMATE see PRIMATE.

PROPERTIED NOBILITY [BIRTOKOS NEMESSÉG] see COMMON NOBILITY.

PROTESTANTISM IN HUNGARY. Protestantism had penetrated Hungary (q.v.) in the late 1520s and early 1530s, initially in the form of Lutheranism (q.v.). It was soon followed both by Calvinism (q.v.) and by antitrinitarianism or Unitarianism (q.v.). By the late 16th century, however, it was Calvinism that became the most prominent denomination among the Hungarian Protestants, leading to the development of the Hungarian Reformed Church (q.v.). It became especially important in the country's eastern and north-eastern regions, while Lutheranism and the resulting Hungarian Evangelical Church (q.v.) remained confined to the western fringes. Unitarianism (q.v.), on the other hand, survived only in Transylvania (q.v.). In the 19th and 20th centuries several other smaller Protestant denominations also penetrated Hungary, but they never came to rival the older and more established Protestant churches.

PROVISIONAL NATIONAL ASSEMBLY [IDEIGLENES NEMZETGYŰLÉS (1944–45). It was called together, while the war was still going on, on December 21, 1944, in the city of Debrecen (q.v.), at the initiative of the IndependenceFront (q.v.), to serve as a provisional Hungarian Parliament (q.v.) until regular elections can be held. The members of the Provisional National Assembly (PNA) were selected by the so-called "national committees" that were organized by local activists in Hungary's eastern region already occupied by the Soviet Army. The PNA had 230 members, representing the Communist Party (71), Smallholders' Party (55), Social Democratic Party (38), Peasant Party (16), Citizens' Democratic Party (12), and the labor unions (19). Nineteen delegates had no party affiliations. After all of Hungary had been conquered by the Soviet Army (April 4, 1945), the PNA's membership was expanded to 498. It functioned until the first regular postwar elections of November 4, 1945.

PROVISIONAL PERIOD [PROVISORIUM] (1860-67). The period of transition in Hungarian history between the Age of Absolutism (1849-60) (q.v.), on the one hand, and the Age of Compromise (1867-1918), on the other. After the promulgation of the October Diploma (q.v.) in 1860 and the February Patent (q.v.) in 1861, the Habsburgs (q.v.) gave up their absolutist rule in Hungary (q.v.) and worked hard to achieve a compromise with the Hungarians. This effort resulted in the Austro-Hungarian Compromise of 1867 (q.v.) and in the transformation of the Austrian Empire (q.v.) into Austria-Hungary (q.v.).

PRUSSIA. A German state that unified several dozen other German states into the German Empire (q.v.) in 1871. Prussia was formed by joining the duchies of Brandenburg (that had been part of the Holy Roman Empire) and East Prussia (originally the state of the Teutonic Knights) in 1525, into a single entity. In 1701 Prussia was transformed into a kingdom, and in the course of the 18th and 19th centuries, it grew into one of Europe's great powers. Because both the ruling Hohenzollern dynasty and the landed aristocracy of

Prussia were descendantsof the Teutonic Knights (q.v.), it evolved into an aggressive militaristic state, which militarism was then transferred to the new German Empire. Until the 1870s, Prussia was a persistent rival and enemy of the Habsburg Empire (q.v.). But after the Dual Alliance of 1879 (q.v.) Prussian-led Germany and Austria-Hungary (q.v.) became allies. This alliance set the stage for Hungary's involvement in two world wars on the German side.

PRUSSIANS. Originally a Baltic people, related to the Latvians and the Lithuanians, who have been overcome by the Teutonic Knights (q.v.) in the 13th century, and then assimilated into the German settlers or into other nearby peoples. Starting with the 14th century, the term "Prussian" was progressively transferred to the Germans (q.v.) who conqueredand assimilated the original Baltic Prussians. These German Prussians, being partial descendantsof the Teutonic Knights, inherited the spirit of militarism of their forebearers. Thus, the Kingdom of Prussia (q.v.) that they built in the course of the 15th through the 19th centuries retained much of this militaristic spirit. Moreover, when in 1871 Prussia unified the German states into the new German Empire (q.v.), the Prussian leadership also infused this new empire with this spirit of militarism. Thus, the term "Prussian" also came to be equated with German militarism. In the period between the Austro-Hungarian Compromise of 1867 (q.v.) and the end of World War II (q.v.), Hungary's fate had been tied intimately to the fate of Prussian-led Germany (q.v.).

PÜSKI, SÁNDOR (b.1911). A publisher and prominent exponent of the ideology of Hungarian Populism (q.v.). Himself of peasant stock and extremely sympathetic to the Populist cause, in 1939 Püski foundedthe Hungarian Life Publishers *(Magyar Élet Könyvkiadó)* specifically for the purposes of publishing the works of Populist authors. In that capacity he was one of the organizers of the momentous Szárszó Conferences (q.v.) in 1942 and 1943. His publishing house was nationalized in 1950, and in 1962-63 he suffered political imprisonment. In 1970 Püski emigrated to the

United States. Initially he opened a bookstore in New York, but then in 1975 he resumed his publishing activities under the name Püski Publishers *(Püski Kiadó)*, which in 1989 he relocated from New York to Budapest (q.v.). Since his repatriation to Hungary (q.v.), Sándor Püski has immersed himself once more into Hungarian Populist activities, including publishing the works of Populist authors and organizing conferences reminiscent of the Szárszó Conferences (q.v.) of the early 1940s.

- R -

RÁC. The original Hungarian name for the Serbs (q.v.), derived from the medieval Latin name of their country, Rascia. The latter, in turn, originated from its Serbian version Raška, which is derived from the city of Raš on the Raška river. From the 15th through the 19th centuries the Hungarians called Serbia *Rácország* (Rác Country). In the latter century it was gradually replaced by the currently used Serb, Serbs, Serbian, Serbians *(Szerb, Szerbek)* (q.v.), derived from the Latin term *servus* (servant). The term "Rác" has been preserved in such Hungarian place names as Ráckeve and Rácfürdő.

RÁDAY, PÁL (1677–1733). A prominent Calvinist statesman, who served Prince Francis Rákóczi II (q.v.) both as a personal secretary and as a diplomatic envoy. In the latter capacity he visited many of the capitals of early 18th-century Europe. Ráday joined the Rákóczi War of Liberation (q.v.) at its very outset in 1703. By the following year he was already Prince Rákóczi's personal secretary, in which capacity he became the most prominent publicist of the *kuruc* (q.v.) cause. He authored most of the political and propaganda pamphlets put out by Rákóczi's court, and he was also the chief editor of the *kuruc* newspaper, *Mercurius Veridictus ex Hungaria (Truthful Mercury from Hungary)* (1705–10), which was meant to counterbalance Habsburg political propaganda in Western Europe.

Following the Treaty of Szatmár in 1711 (q.v.), which ended this protracted struggle, Ráday accepted the amnesty incorporated into this treaty. He continued to play an important role in Hungarian politics, participating in all of the national diets during the second and third decade of the century (1715, 1721-23, and 1728-29). He showed considerable political moderation, and spoke up only in conjunction with the religious freedom of the Protestants (q.v.). In 1712, Ráday was elected the first general curator *(egyetemes főgondnok)* of the Hungarian Reformed Church (q.v.), a position he retained until his death in 1733.

In addition to his journalistic work during the Rákóczi War of Liberation, Ráday is also the author of a few theological works. His letters and papers were collected and published in two volumes under the title *Papers of Pál Ráday (Ráday Pál iratai)* (1955-61). Ráday has supported the scholarly activities of a number of literati, including those of the great polyhistor, Mátyás Bél (q.v.). He was likewise responsible for laying the foundations of the Ráday Library in Budapest (q.v.), which today is the most important Protestant library in Hungary (q.v.).

RADNÓTI, MIKLÓS (1909-44). An extremely sensitive and humane poet who, next to Endre Ady (q.v.) and Attila József (q.v.), is perhaps the most highly regarded lyricist of 20th-century Hungarian literature. Coming from a well-to-do Budapest industrial family, Radnóti broke with his family traditions and moved into literature. Starting with 1931, he published about a half a dozen volumes of poetry, which placed him almost immediately into the forefront of Hungarian literature. Being of Jewish origin, during World War II (q.v.), Radnóti was compelled to spend years in forced labor brigades (q.v.). He died in mid-November 1944, while being driven afoot to a German death camp. His last poems—that deal with the meaning of life and death, with his own powerlessness, and with his longing for his home and his family—were excavated from a mass grave immediately after the war. There are those who believe that, had he written in a major Western language, Radnóti would be recognized as one of the great figures of world literature.

RAGUSA [DUBROVNIK]. A former city state in Dalmatia (q.v.), which from the mid-14th through the early 16th century (1358–1526) was under the suzerainty of Hungary (q.v.). Founded in the mid-7th century by the inhabitants of the Latin cities of Epidaurum and Salona that had been destroyed by the Avars (q.v.), Ragusa developed into an important Dalmatian commercial center. During the 11th and 12th centuries, it was fought over by the Venetians,

Normans, and Byzantines (q.v.), while between 1205 and 1358, it acknowledged the suzerainty of the Venetian Republic (q.v.). Transferring its loyalty in 1358 to Louis the Great (q.v.) of Hungary, Ragusa was Hungary's vassal state until the collapse of the Hungarian Kingdom in 1526. During the 16th through the 18th centuries, Ragusa became a tributary state of the Ottoman Empire (q.v.). In the early 19th century (1806/08–14), it was a French dependency, while in 1815 it became part of the Austrian Empire (q.v.). After the collapse of Austria-Hungary (q.v.) in 1918, Ragusa was attached to Yugoslavia (q.v.), while after the downfall of the latter state (1991), it became part of independent Croatia (q.v.).

The original Latin inhabitants of the city were later joined by Slavs (q.v.) and then during the later Middle Ages and Early Modern Period they were submerged in the region's Slavic population. Although the Slavs called the city Dubrovnik, Ragusa had retained its Latin-Italian culture and way of life up to the modern period. For late medieval Hungary, with limited access to the see, the Republic of Ragusa represented an important window to the outside world.

RAJK, LÁSZLÓ (1909–49). One of Hungary's top communist leaders after World War II (q.v.) who in 1949 fell victim to Rákosi's (q.v.) Stalinist purges, even though earlier he himself had been involved in purging rival politicians. Following a brief period of university studies (1929–30), Rajk spent much of the next fifteen years either in underground communist activities or in captivity (1941–44, 1944–45). In 1937–39 he was a member of the International Brigade in the Spanish Civil War, while between 1939 and 1941 he lived in exile in France.

Following his release from imprisonment (September 1944), Rajk became one of the organizers and leaders of the communist wing of the Resistance Movement (q.v.) in Hungary. Arrested by the Szálasi Regime (q.v.) in October 1944, he was taken to Germany, from where he returned in May 1945. After his return, Rajk became a member of the top communist leadership in Hungary, including the powerful Politburo. Yet, his position was not easy, for he had to compete against the better-placed Muscovites (q.v.), such as Rákosi (q.v.), Gerő (q.v.), and Révai (q.v.). After several strictly party positions, in 1946 Rajk became Hungary's minister of interior (March 1946–August 1948), in which capacity he was responsible for liquidating rival political parties and political leaders, thereby creating conditions for the establishment of a monolithic communist rule. But having become a potential rival to Rákosi, he was relieved of his post and made briefly Hungary's foreign minister (August 1948–May 1949).

In May 1949 Rajk was accused of Titoism and disloyalty to the Soviet Union (q.v.). He was arrested, and, after a political sham trial, convicted and executed. Rajk was posthumously rehabilitated in 1955 and officially reburied just before the outbreak of the Hungarian Revolution of 1956 (q.v.). Although hailed as a hero and a victim of the Rákosi Regime (q.v.), during his years in power Rajk was just as vicious in the elimination of political rivals as his own rivals had been in getting rid of him. During the 1980s, his son, László Rajk, Jr. (b.1949), became a leader of the Hungarian Dissident Movement (q.v.) centered on the underground periodical *Speaker (Beszélő)*. In 1988 the younger Rajk also served as one of the founding members of the Federation of Free Democrats (q.v.).

RÁKÓCZI [RÁKÓCZY] FAMILY. An old Hungarian family whose roots reach back to the Bogát-Radván clan in the age of the Árpád dynasty (q.v.). The clan's early landed estates were located in Zemplén County in Upper Hungary (q.v.), and its first known ancestor was a certain Csepán (d.1227). The family rose to prominence in the 16th century, when it acquired new estates in Abaúj County in the lower part of Upper Hungary. In the same century, the Rákóczis broke into two branches, represented by the brothers Ferenc and Zsigmond. The former's descendants remained members of the common nobility (q.v.), but Zsigmond's offspring ascended to the ranks of the aristocracy (q.v.). They acquired the title of baron in 1588, the title of count in 1607, and in the title princes of the Holy Roman Empire (q.v.) in 1645. This branch produced several ruling princes of Transylvania (q.v.), including Sigismund (q.v.), George I (q.v.), George II (q.v.), Francis I (q.v.), and Francis II (q.v.). Both branches died out in the mid– 18th century.

RÁKÓCZI EMIGRATION. The emigration of Prince Ferenc Rákóczi's (q.v.) *kuruc* (q.v.) supporters following the Rákóczi War of Independence(q.v.), who were compelled to leave their country, because they were willing to accept the terms of the Treaty of Szatmár (q.v.). Some of them remained in France, but most of them eventually ended up in the Ottoman Empire (q.v.). The last to die was Kelemen Mikes (1690-1761), who styled himself as Prince Rákóczi's scribe, and who wrote highly imaginative letters to a nonexistent aunt. (See also Emigration from Hungary.)

RÁKÓCZI, FRANCIS [FERENC] I (1645–76). Elected prince of Transylvania (q.v.) in 1652, Francis I never actually ruled. He lost that chance at the time of the demise and death of his father, George II (q.v.). Francis I is known primarily for being the father of the much more famous Francis II (q.v.), for being the first husband of the equally famous Ilona Zrínyi (q.v.), and for being involved in the ill-fated Wesselényi Conspiracy (q.v.). In fact, he was the only one of the conspirators to escape capital punishment, primarily because of the Counter-Reformation (q.v.) merits of his mother, Zsófia Báthory (1629–80), and because of her willingness to pay 300,000 *forints* to the Habsburg Imperial Government (q.v.).

RÁKÓCZI, FRANCIS [FERENC] II (1676–1735). Prince of Transylvania (r.1704-11), leader of the anti-Habsburg Rákóczi War of Liberation (1703–11), and one of the most revered personalities in Hungarian history. Son of Prince Francis Rákóczi I (q.v.) and Ilona Zrínyi (q.v.), Francis Rákóczi II was born into power and wealth. Yet, at a certain moment of history, he was willing to sacrifice all of this for what he thought was the good of his nation. During the long siege of the fortress of Munkács (1685–88) by the Habsburg Imperial forces at the time of the Thököly Uprising (q.v.), young Rákóczi was at his mother's side. Following Ilona Zrínyi's capitulation, he was taken from her and reared by Austrian Jesuits in

Bohemia (q.v.). They pressured him to join the clergy, but without success. Having come of age in 1692, he extricated himself from under the guardianship of Cardinal Kollonich (q.v.) by marrying Princess Charlotte Amalia of Hessen-Rheinfels (1679–1722). Rákóczi then moved to Hungary (q.v.) to take over the affairs of his 2.7 million acre (1.1 million hectares) estates and to become the lord lieutenant (q.v.) of Sáros County.

In Hungary he was shocked at the absolute misery of the common folk. Some of this suffering was the result of the Liberation Wars (q.v.), but much of it was the consequence of Habsburg misrule, leading to the peasant uprising of Hegyalja in eastern Upper Hungary (1697). The rebels tried to enlist the support of the equally embittered Hungarian nobility (q.v.) under the leadership of Rákóczi. Although in sympathy with many of the rebels' complaints, Prince Rákóczi was not yet ready for this undertaking. He fled to Vienna (q.v.) to avoid even the shadow of complicity. The bloody reprisals that followed, however, pushed him further into an anti-Habsburg camp. Thus, on the eve of the War of Spanish Succession, he made contacts with Louis XIV (r.1643–1915) of France for a possible military cooperation against the Habsburgs (q.v.) of Vienna (q.v.). But Rákóczi was betrayed by his French contact and was forced to flee to Poland (q.v.).

He returned to Hungary in 1703 to assume the leadership of a new War of Liberation. Initially, his forces achieved spectacular successes, which by 1704 placed almost all of Hungary under his control. This prompted the Transylvanian Diet (q.v.) to elect him the prince of Transylvania (q.v.) (1704), and the Hungarian Diet (q.v.) of Szécsény to name him "Governing Prince" *(Vezérlő Fejedelem)* of Hungary (1705). Some even wished to elect him king of Hungary, but this idea was rejected by Rákóczi himself, who saw it as untimely. While pushing for Hungary's independence, Rákóczi was also sensitive to the country's social problems. Thus, several of his decrees dealt with the peasant problem. He tried to improve the lot of the serf, but without alienating the nobility.

The Habsburgs had their own problems with France, wherefore they tried to persuade Rákóczi to move toward a compromise solution. But the conditions they offered were never acceptable to him. Thus, by 1707 he agreed to their official dethronement at the Diet of Ónod. Yet, unable to secure meaningful support from Louis XIV and Peter the Great (r.1682/89–1725), Rákóczi's armies were gradually worn down. This was accompanied by a growing desire for peace even among many of his top followers. This was especially true after 1708, when his cause became increasingly hopeless.

In February 1711 Rákóczi left Hungary to seek help in Poland (q.v.) and Russia (q.v.). During his absence, his commander-in-chief, Count Sándor Károlyi (q.v.), concluded the Peace of Szatmár (q.v.) and laid down his arms before the Habsburg Imperial general, Count János Pálffy (q.v.). Having no choice, and not wishing to accept the Imperial amnesty that had been incorporated into the Peace Treaty of Szatmár, Rákóczi remained in Poland. From there he went to France (1713–17), and eventually settled in the Ottoman Empire (q.v.) (1717–35). Between 1718 and 1735 he lived in the city of Tekírdağ (Rodostó) on the shores of the Sea of Marmara. His remains were returned to Hungary in 1906, and then laid to rest in the cathedral of his favorite city, Kassa (q.v.). Rákóczi's sons—József (1700–38) and György (1701–56)—proved to be failures. Reared in Vienna, they both became international soldiers-of-fortune who lived under various names and titles. The former died as an Ottoman-supported claimant to the Transylvanian throne in the midst of the Austro-Turkish War of 1736–39. The latter declined to be a claimant when offered support by Sultan Mahmut I in 1742, and died as a forgotten exile in France.

RÁKÓCZI, GEORGE [GYÖRGY] I (1593–1648). Prince of Transylvania (r.1630–48) and son of Prince Sigismund Rákóczi (q.v.), who already before his election to the throne was the wealthiest Protestant magnate in Upper Hungary (q.v.). George Rákóczi, a prominent supporter of Prince Gabriel Bethlen (q.v.) in his wars against the Habsburgs (q.v.), was elected soon after Bethlen's death as his successor. He restored Transylvania's (q.v.) internal stability by breaking the power of the squabbling lords and by reclaiming princely lands. Some of these estates ended up in the hands of the Rákóczi family. He allied himself with the Swedes and the French in the Thirty Years' War, and fought successfully against King Ferdinand III (q.v.) in defense of the rights of the Hungarian nobility (q.v.) and the Hungarian Protestants (q.v.). In the course of the war of 1644 he took much of Upper Hungary, and only Sultan Ibrahim's (r.1640–48) orders prevented him from joining the Swedes in their anti-Habsburg campaign in Moravia (q.v.). The Peace of Linz (1645) transferred seven additional counties under Rákóczi's control. George Rákóczi I was an able and effective ruler, who supported education, defended Protestantism, and protected the interests of tripartitioned Hungary (q.v.) against the Habsburgs and the Turks (q.v.).

RÁKÓCZI, GEORGE [GYÖRGY] II (1621–60). Prince of Transylvania (r.1648–57/60), son of George Rákóczi I (q.v.), and the man who is responsible for destroying Transylvania's (q.v.) peaceful development by his megalomaniac ambitions to gain the Polish throne. Having been elected prince already in his father's lifetime (1642), and having served as the governor of Transylvania in his father's absence in 1644, George Rákóczi II had all the chances to be a successful ruler. But his monarchical ambitions embroiled him in a series of multicornered wars in Poland (q.v.), which ultimately ended in his defeat and deposition. Initially he was successful in his support of the Ukrainian Cossacks against King John Casimir (r.1648–68) of Poland, and in extending his control over the Vlach principalities of Moldavia (q.v.) and Wallachia (q.v.) in 1653. But his invasion of Poland in 1657—in direct violation of the orders of the Ottoman Sultan—ended in his defeat and in his deposition from the Transylvanian throne.

In line with the Sultan's orders, the Transylvanian Diet (q.v.) elected in his place Ferenc Rhédey (q.v.) (November 1657). But Rhédey renounced his throne in favor of Rákóczi two months later (January 1658), as a result of which the Grand Vizier Mehmet Köprülü (r.1656–61) ordered the diet to elect Ákos Barcsay (q.v.). The diet did so in November of that year, after which the two rival princes fought for nearly two years. Rákóczi was ultimately defeated and killed by the Turks in May 1660. This made it impossible for his son, Francis Rákóczi I (q.v.), to succeed him, although already elected prince some years earlier. The tumultuous final years of George Rákóczi II's reign ended the golden age of Transylvania. But his marriage to Zsófia Báthory (1629–80), the last member of the famous Báthory family (q.v.), made the Rákóczis the wealthiest family in all of Historic Hungary (q.v.).

RÁKÓCZI, SIGISMUND [ZSIGMOND] (1544–1608). The first member of the Rákóczi family (q.v.) to be elected prince of Transylvania (r.1607–08) and the man who laid the foundations of the proverbial wealth of his family. Sigismund Rákóczi spent four decades in the service of the Habsburgs (q.v.), fighting successfully against the Turks (q.v.), for which he was raised to the rank of a baron (1588). Around 1590 he married the widow of the wealthy András Mágóchy and with this marriage gained control over huge estates in Upper Hungary (q.v.), including the fortress of Munkács. His relationship to the Habsburgs soured in 1603, when he was accused of high treason simply because they wished to confiscate his estates. This move forced Rákóczi to break with Vienna (q.v.) and to join forces with Prince Bocskai (q.v.) of Transylvania (q.v.) in the latter's war against the Habsburgs. After Bocskai's death, the Transylvanian Diet (q.v.) elected Rákóczi their prince. But his reign was both short (February 1607–March 1608) and turbulent. It was marred by an incessant struggle against rivals, including Gábor Báthory (q.v.), in whose favor he ultimately renounced the throne.

RÁKÓCZI WAR OF LIBERATION see RÁKÓCZI, FRAN-CIS II.

RÁKOSI, MÁTYÁS (1898–1971). Hungary's top communist leader in the period after World War II (q.v.) who is generally known as Hungary's "Little Stalin." His rule was characterized by a reign of terror and by a personality cult unmatched in Hungarian history. Born into a petty bourgeois family, Rákosi became affiliated with various socially progressive movements before World War I (q.v.), but it was his experiences as a Russian prisoner of war that pushed him into the ranks of the Bolsheviks. Having returned home at the end of the war, he became an active communist party worker and in 1919 participated in the political and military activities of the Hungarian Soviet Republic (q.v.) under the leadership of Béla Kun (q.v.). In August 1919 he fled to Austria (q.v.), and from there to the Soviet Union (q.v.), where he became involved in the work of the Third Communist International (Commintern). In 1924 he was sent home to engage in communist underground activities, but in 1925 he was arrested and spent the next fifteen years in prison. In 1940 he was exchanged with the Soviet Union for Hungarian military flags captured by the invading Russian Imperial forces in 1849.

In Moscow Rákosi rapidly became the acknowledged leader of the Hungarian communist immigration, and he also took charge of various propaganda activities directed at his homeland and at the Hungarian prisoners of war in the Soviet Union. Returning home in January 1945, Rákosi assumed control over the Communist Party of Hungary (q.v.), which he dominated until 1956. During those eleven years he held various ministerial positions—including that of prime minister (1952–53)—but his real power lay in his position as the first secretary of the Communist Party. Rákosi was primarily responsible for purging rival political parties (1947–48), and for getting rid—by removal from power or by execution—of rival communist leaders, among them László Rajk (q.v.) and János Kádár (q.v.). He lost some power to Imre Nagy (q.v.) in the immediate post-Stalin years (1953–55), but then made a short comeback (1955–56) before falling to the forces unleashed by the Hungarian Revolution of 1956 (q.v.). Between July 1956 and his death in 1971, Rákosi lived in the Soviet Union. His remains were returned to Hungary and interred at a secret location. His name is inseparably linked with the worst phase of the communist rule in Hungary.

RÁKOSI REGIME (1947–53, 1955–56). In general, this term refers to the period between the liquidation of the postwar coalition government in 1947 and the outbreak of the Hungarian Revolution of 1956 (q.v.). More strictly speaking, it is also used in conjunction with the reign of communist terror in the years between 1948 and 1953, when Mátyás Rákosi (q.v.), known for his personality cult (q.v.) and for the mass persecution of his political enemies and rivals, held supreme powers in Hungary (q.v.).

RÁMA. The southernmost section of Bosnia (q.v.), on the Neretva (Narente) River, next to Herzegovina (see Bosnia). The province was acquired in 1137 by King Béla III (q.v.), who immediately assumed the title "King of Ráma" and at the same time named his son, Ladislas (the future Ladislas II) (q.v.), the "Prince of Bosnia." Even though Ráma was only the southern tip of Bosnia, within the Hungarian context it was used to refer to the whole of Bosnia. It was in this context that the rulers of Hungary (q.v.)—including the Habsburg emperors (q.v.)—have called themselves for nearly eight centuries the "Kings of Ráma (Bosnia)."

RÁNKI, GYÖRGY [GEORGE] (1930–88). A noted economic historian who started out as a convinced Marxist, but then, during the late 1970s and 1980s, was largely responsible for turning Hungarian historical studies to the West. Having been associated with the Institute of History (q.v.) of the Hungarian Academy of Sciences (q.v.) ever since 1953, Ránki rose to be the institute's deputy director in 1962 and then its executive director in 1976. In 1979 he also assumed control over the Hungarian Chair at Indiana University, which he held until his death, and made it into the most important center of Hungarian studies in North America.

Most of Ránki's published works deal with the economic and industrial development of modern Hungary (q.v.), several of which also appeared in English. He wrote many of them jointly with Iván Berend (b.1930) (q.v.), including all but the last of the following works: *Hungary: A Century of Economic Development* (1974), *East Central Europe in the Nineteenth and Twentieth Centuries* (1977), *Underdevelopment and Economic Growth: Studies in Hungarian Social and Economic History* (1979), *The European Periphery and Industrialisation* (1982), *Economy and Foreign Policy: A Struggle of the Great Powers for Hegemony in the Danube Valley, 1919–*

1939 (1983). His most popular work, which became a bestseller in Hungary, was his *The History of the Second World War (A második világháború története)* (1973), which appeared in several editions. Ránki's role was decisive in the Hungarian historical profession's turning to the West, and in relegating the ideology of Marxism to the peripheries of the historical discipline even before the collapse of communism (q.v.).

RATIO EDUCATIONIS (1777). An edict issued by Maria Theresa (q.v.), which reorganized the Hungarian educational system. It was elaborated by Lord Chief Justice József Ürményi (1741–1825), with the collaboration of the historian Ádám Kollár (1718–83) and the archivist Dániel Tersztyánszky (1730–1800). The *Ratio Educationis* established a uniform system of schooling in Hungary (q.v.), embraced all levels of education, and also brought religious and parochial schools under state control. From the Hungarian point of view it was also important that this law guaranteed the autonomy of the Hungarian educational system. The *Ratio Educationis* of 1777 was amended and replaced by a second one in 1806, issued by Francis I (q.v.), which remained in effect until 1848. Because both of these documents were royal edicts that were not sanctioned by the Hungarian Diet (q.v.) and did not take into consideration the special needs of the Protestants (q.v.), the latter refused to accept them and continued to protest against their terms until 1848, when finally all limitations were removed.

RAVASZ, LÁSZLÓ (1882-1975). A theologian, a publicist, bishop of the Hungarian Reformed Church (1921–48) (q.v.), and father-in-law of the great Hungarian thinker, István Bibó (q.v.). During the interwar years (q.v.), Ravasz was perhaps the most influential Protestant personality in Hungary (q.v.)—outside of Regent Horthy (q.v.) himself. A Transylvanian by birth, Ravasz studied at the Reformed Theological Academy of Kolozsvár (q.v.) and at the University of Kolozsvár (q.v.), where he earned his doctorate in 1907. Thereafter he taught at his first alma mater (1907–21), and edited the *Protestant Review (Protestáns Szemle)* (1914–18), the

Reformed Review (Református Szemle) (1918–21), and the
Reformed Life (Református Élet) (1934–45). After the loss of
Transylvania to Romania (q.v.), Ravasz resettled in Budapest (q.v.),
where in 1921 he became the pastor of Hungary's largest Reformed
congregation. In the same year he was also elected the bishop of the
Trans-Danubian Synod of the Hungarian Reformed Church. By
virtue of his ecclesiastical position—upon the reestablishment of a
bicameral legislature in 1927—Ravasz became a member of the
Upper House (1927–44), where he served as a staunch supporter of
the conservative-nationalist Horthy Regime (q.v.). Following the
communist takeover of Hungary, Ravasz was forced out of his
ecclesiastical office (May 1948), and in 1953 he was also deprived of
his Budapest congregation. Thereafter he lived in retirement as a
barely tolerated member of the déclassé Hungarian intelligentsia.

   László Ravasz was a prolific writer and he published extensively
on various philosophical, theological, and sociological topics.
Many of his important essays appeared in such collective volumes
as *Halfway on the Path of Life (Az ember útjának felén)* (1924), *In
the Shadow of Death (A halál árnyékában)* (1927), *At the Top of
Mount Tabor (A Táborhegy ormán)* (1928), *Alpha and Omega (Alfa
és Ómega)* (2 vols., 1933), *Let there be Light (Legyen világosság)*
(3 vols., 1938), and *Inside God's Sifter (Isten rostájában)* (3 vols,
1941). Ravasz's most important posthumous work is his *Memoirs
(Emlékezéseim)* (1992). Among many other similar projects, Ravasz
also prepared a new Hungarian translation of the Bible, which was
published in the United States in 1971.

RAYAH [REAYA, HERD]. The simple tax-paying Muslim and
non-Muslim population of the Ottoman Empire (q.v.). In contrast to
the serfs of Christian Europe, the rayahs were personally free. They
did not own their lands legally, but the use of these lands was theirs
in perpetuity and inheritable within the family. The rayah class was
separated from the administrative, military, and religious elite of the
empire by a vast chasm. Thus, the term had both condescending and
contemptuous connotations. Social mobility was possible through
the child levy *(devshirme)* system, which channeled gifted rayah

children into the elite classes. As most rayahs in the European possessions of the Ottoman Empire were Christians, contemporary Europeans thought the term rayah referred only to its Christian subjects. In the former Kingdom of Hungary (q.v.), which became trisected after the Turkish conquest of the early 16th century, only the central part directly under the control of the Turks was populated by peasants in this category.

RED TERROR [VÖRÖSTERROR]   (1919, 1948-53). Hungary's first Red Terror took place during the period of the Hungarian Soviet Republic (q.v.) in the spring and summer of 1919, connected with the communist dictatorship of Béla Kun (q.v.). The man in charge of this Red Terror was the leader of the so-called "Lenin Boys" (q.v.), Tibor Szamuely (q.v.), who had perpetrated most of the killings of political enemies or alleged enemies of the communist regime. Hungary's second Red Terror took place under the leadership of the Communist Party chief, Mátyás Rákosi (q.v.), in the period between 1948 and 1953. The latter involved judicial murders, liquidations, concentration camps, and forced resettlement of those who were thought to be enemies of communism and who were judged to be potential rivals of Rákosi.

REFORMATION IN HUNGARY.   The anti-Catholic religious reform movement connected with the names and activities of Martin Luther (1483–1546), John Calvin (1509–64), Ulrich Zwingli (1484–1531), Michael Servetus (1509–53), and others began to penetrate Hungary (q.v.) in the 1520s, gaining most of its early converts among the German burghers of Northern Hungary (q.v.). This process was speeded up after the Battle of Mohács of 1526 (q.v.), which saw the extension of Turkish influence into much of the country. By the end of the 16th century, well over half of Hungary's population—including many of the powerful aristocratic families—had become Lutheran, Calvinist, or Unitarian. In the course of the next two centuries, however, the Habsburg-supported Counter-Reformation (q.v.) was so successful that it regained much of Hungary for Catholicism. Protestantism survived only in the country's northeastern and eastern regions, and even there its freedom of action was limited until the end of the 18th century. (See also Protestantism in Hungary.)

REFORM COMMUNISTS. A collective term applied to those communist leaders who wished to create a "communism with a human face" and who ultimately were responsible for ending the communist rule and easing the transition to post-communism. In Hungary (q.v.) during the late 1980s, the most prominent of these reform communists were Imre Pozsgay (q.v.), Miklós Németh (q.v.), and Mátyás Szűrös (q.v.).

REFORM DIETS. The feudal diets (q.v.) during the Hungarian Reform Period (1825–48) (q.v.), which were responsible for undermining the old social and political order and for ending the remnants of feudalism in Hungary (q.v.). These Reform Diets were in session for various lengths of time during the following periods: 1825–27, 1830, 1832–36, 1939–40, 1843–44, and 1847–48.

REFORM GENERATION. This term was originally applied to the generation of reformers active during the Hungarian Reform Period (q.v.), whose work brought about the dismantlement of feudalism and culminated in the Hungarian Revolution of 1848–49 (q.v.). Subsequently various other "reform generations" were also discovered, although with significant disagreement about their identities. Noted interwar historian Gyula Szekfű (q.v.) identified the Second Reform Generation as consisting of those who were responsible for the Austro-Hungarian Compromise of 1867 (q.v.), and the Third Reform Generation as consisting of those less enlightened intellectuals who labored at the turn of the century. In disagreement with Szekfű, the Marxist historian, Zoltán Horváth (1900–67), identified the Second Reform Generation as being identical with those early-20th-century progressive intellectuals who congregated around such highly respected liberal and forward-looking periodicals as the *Twentieth Century (Huszadik Század)* (1900-19) and the *West (Nyugat)* (1908-41). Others view the Populists (q.v.)

of the 1930s and early 1940s as constituting a new Reform Generation. Still others regard the dissidents-turned-politicians of the 1980s and 1990s, who helped to undermine communism, as the most recent Reform Generation, although one that is irreparably split between the Populists (q.v.) and the Urbanists (q.v.). Apparently, historians can only agree on the identity of the First Reform Generation that preceded the revolution of 1848–49.

REFORMED   [CALVINIST]   CHURCH. Of the three main denominations that took root in Hungary (q.v.) in consequence of the Protestant   Reformation   (q.v.)—Lutheranism, Calvinism,   and Unitarianism—it was the teachings of Jean Calvin (1509–64) that found the greatest number of adherents. In 17th-century Transylvania (q.v.) Calvinism became an official state religion, even though in other parts of the former Hungarian Kingdom (q.v.) it was held in check and even pushed back by the Habsburg-led Counter-Reformation (q.v.). Yet, Calvinism managed to survive and in 1781 it gained full acceptance via Emperor Joseph II's Edict of Toleration (q.v.). The 18th century also saw the development of the Reformed Church's administrative structure that survived unchanged until the 1970s. The country was divided into four districts, each headed by an elected bishop, and each divided further into several sub-districts. Until 1975 the central directing body of the Hungarian Reformed Church was the Calvinist Synod, which met periodically and consisted of the lay and ecclesiastical representatives of the four districts. In between two synods, the affairs of the church were entrusted to an executive body called the Universal Convent *(Egyetemes Konvent).* This system of governance changed in 1975, when the Universal Convent was replaced by the Synodical Council *(Zsinati Tanács).*

During the past four centuries, the Hungarian Reformed Church had established and controlled many educational, social, and cultural institutions. Most of these were disbanded or nationalized after 1949. The collapse of communism in 1989-90 (q.v.), however, permitted the reestablishment of many of these institutions. In 1993 the Hungarian Reformed Church also established its own "Gáspár Karoli

Reformed University" in Budapest (q.v.), named after the first translator of the Bible into Hungarian, Gáspár Károli (q.v.).

REFORM PERIOD see HUNGARIAN REFORM PERIOD.

REGALE [REGÁLÉ]. The collective name for the various sources of royal income in medieval and early modern Hungary (q.v.). The most important of these *regales* included the tariff known as *tricesima (harmincadvám)* (q.v.), the gate tax *(portalis)* (q.v.), the royal monopolies (salt, gold, and silver), and the *lucrum camerae (kamarahaszna)* (q.v.) derived from the annual dilution of the silver content of the coins. Most of these sources of royal income remained in royal hands up to recent times. Some of the less significant sources, however—such as the licensing of inns, mills, butcher shops, fords, ferries and fairs—were gradually transferred in the 13th century into the hands of local feudal lords. Up to 1526 the *regales* represented the chief sources of royal income. After the early 16th century, their importance gradually declined through the introduction of various new taxes. Yet, even as late as the 18th century, the *regales* still constituted over one-fourth of the state income.

REGENT [KORMÁNYZÓ]. The "temporary" leader of a country in charge of its political and military leadership. Hungary's first regent was János Hunyadi (q.v.) during a period of the minority of King Ladislas V (q.v.) (1446-53). The next regent was Mihály Szilágyi (d.1461), Hunyadi's brother-in-law, who was in charge briefly in 1458, following the election of his minor nephew, Matthias Corvinus (q.v.), to the Hungarian throne. During the later phase of the Hungarian Revolution of 1848–49 (q.v.), Louis Kossuth (q.v.) had also served Hungary's regent (April–August 1849), although his official title was "governing president." At the end of World War I (q.v.), Archduke Joseph August (q.v.) became the regent for two brief periods (October 27-31, 1918; August 7-23, 1919). Hungary's last regent was Admiral Miklós Horthy (q.v.), who was elected to this office in 1920, in wake of Austria-Hungary's (q.v.) collapse and

the resignation of King Charles IV (Emperor Charles I) (q.v.).
During Horthy's regency, Hungary was a "kingdom without a king"
(1920–44).

REGESTA [REGESZTA]. The published abstracts of documents,
collected in a book form. Within the Hungarian context, these
regestas are usually the abstracts of medieval documents related to
the history of Hungary (q.v.).

REGNUM MARIANUM [MARY'S KINGDOM]. A commonly
used name for Hungary (q.v.) ever since the late 11th century, based
on the belief that just before his death, King St. Stephen (q.v.) had
placed his country under the protection of the Virgin Mary. This
notion became part of the Hungarian state idea, which was most
vigorously represented by the Jesuits (q.v.) during and after the
Counter-Reformation (q.v.).

RELIGIOUS ORDERS. Religious orders have established themselves in Hungary (q.v.) along with the country's Christianization
(q.v.) at the turn of the 10th to the 11th century. Some came along
with Christianity, others were transplanted later. Still others were
founded in Hungary itself, such as the Paulist Order (q.v.) in the
13th century. The first to settle in Hungary were the Orthodox
Christian (q.v.) Basilites and the Catholic Benedictines (q.v.), who
came in the late 10th or early 11th century, respectively. They were
followed by the Cistercians (q.v.) and the Premonstratensians (q.v.)
in the 12th century, the Dominicans (q.v.), Franciscans (q.v.), and
Augustines (q.v.) in the 13th century, the Jesuits (q.v.) in the 16th
century, the Piarists (q.v.) in the 17th century, and many more
smaller male and female orders in the course of the past three
hundred years. These religious orders were all involved in spreading
of the faith, but most of them also had special functions, such as
teaching, social work, or fighting against Protestantism (q.v.).
Some orders suffered during the reign of Joseph II (q.v.) in the late
18th century, many of them survived and others reemerged soon.
They remained functioning orders until dissolved by the Hungary's

communist government between 1948 and 1950. Of the several dozen religious orders, only three male orders and one female order survived this communist massacre, but even those lost most of their property. These were the Benedictines, the Piarists, the Franciscans, and the Sisters of the Poor. The fall of communism in 1989–90 resulted in the revocation of all limitations upon religious orders. As a result, many of them were reestablished and are now in the process of reclaiming their properties and rebuilding their organizational infrastructures.

REMÉNYI, JOSEPH [JÓZSEF] (1891–1956). An important popularizer of Hungarian literature and culture in the United States, and of American literature and culture in Hungary (q.v.). A professor of comparative literature at Western Reserve University (1926–56) in Cleveland, Reményi authored several novels and short stories in Hungarian, scores of critical literary essays in English, and informative cultural syntheses in both languages. In addition to his novels, Reményi's most important works include *America (Amerika)* (1915) and *American Writers (Amerikai írók)* (1927), written for the Hungarian reading public, and *The Hungarians* (1927) and *Hungarian Literature* (1946), written for the American reading public. A posthumous collection of his critical literary essays appeared under the title *Hungarian Writers and Literature* (1964), edited by one of his disciples, August J. Molnár (b.1927). Reményi's Hungarica Library came to constitute an important foundation stone of the library and archives of the American Hungarian Foundation (q.v.) in New Brunswick, New Jersey.

RENAISSANCE. The Renaissance was a modernizing movement that began in Northern Italian city states in the 14th century and then spread in the course of the 15th and 16th centuries throughout Western and Central Europe (q.v.). It was originally thought to be the rebirth of the values and artistic styles of the Classical World, but ultimately it turned out to be more than that. The Renaissance encouraged the accumulation of wealth, glorified worldliness, physical pleasures, and material well-being, and promoted critical thinking and new discoveries in sciences and technology. It portrayed the intellectual and cultural changes of the rising urban culture of Northern Italy, the Netherlands, and later of England and the German lands (q.v.). As such, it had a greater appreciation of the role of the individual as an active agent in shaping one's personal life and environment. It also emphasized the secular, but still within the context of Christian ideals and infrastructure. In Italy its most prominent representatives included Dante (1265–1321), Petrarch (1304–74), Boccaccio (1313–75), Botticelli (1444-1510), Leonardo da Vinci (1452–1519), Michelangelo (1475–1564), Raphael (1483–1520), Vasari (1511–74), and the members of the Medici and the Borgia families. The most noted exponents north of the Alps counted among their ranks the German Albrecht Dürer (1471–1528), the Dutch Erasmus of Rotterdam (c.1466–1536), and the English St. Thomas More (1478–1535). The flowering of the Renaissance coincided with the discovery of printing, climaxed with the great geographical discoveries, and introduced the scientific revolution that stretched from Copernicus (1473–1543), through Kepler (1571–1639) and Galileo (1564–1642), to Newton (1642-1727) and Leibnitz (1646–1716).

Hungary did not begin to feel the impact of the Renaissance until the second half of the 15th century, which coincided with the reign of Matthias Corvinus (q.v.), and then its development was cut short by the fall of the medieval Hungarian Kingdom at Mohács (q.v.) in 1526. Thus, the Hungarian Renaissance was both late and short. Its most important manifestations were in the area of literature, as displayed in the writings of János Vitéz (q.v.), Janus Pannonius (q.v.), Antonio Bonfini (q.v.), István Brodarics (q.v.), and others. But it was also evident in Matthias Corvinus's (q.v.) Corvina Library (q.v.), as well as in his rebuilding in the Renaissance style of the Royal Palace in Buda (q.v.) and the Royal Castle in Visegrád (q.v.). Following King Matthias's death in 1490, the center of the Hungarian Renaissance architecture was shifted to the country's ecclesiastical center, Esztergom (q.v.), which was the city of the primates (q.v.). The Ottoman conquest (q.v.) had put an end to these developments in the country's central and southern region, but the manifestations of the Renaissance continued in Royal Hungary (q.v.) and in Transylvania (q.v.) This was true in literature (see Humanism in Hungary), as well as in architecture. Thus, the Royal Castle of Pozsony (q.v.), in the city that became Hungary's capital for the next three centuries, was reconstructed in the Renaissance style. And this was also true for a number of aristocratic palaces in Trans-Danubia (q.v.), Upper Hungary (q.v.), and in the more protected parts of Transylvania.

RESISTANCE MOVEMENT (1941–45). The antiwar and anti-Nazi movement, which was first institutionalized in the Hungarian Historical Memorial Committee (HMC) *(Magyar Történelmi Em-lékbizottság)* in February 1942. The HMC was allegedly established to nurture the ideals of the Hungarian Revolution of 1848–49 (q.v.), but in actuality its goal was to unite those progressive intellectuals who opposed Hungary's (q.v.) participation in the war. These included Endre Bajcsy-Zsilinszky (q.v.), Gyula Illyés (q.v.), Zoltán Kodály (q.v.), Gyula Szekfű (q.v.), Péter Veres (q.v.), as well as a number of such crypto-communists as József Darvas (q.v.) and Gyula Kállai (b.1910). The Resistance Movement picked up speed following the German occupation of Hungary (q.v.), after which some members of the HMC organized the Hungarian Front (HF) *(Magyar Front)* (May 1944) to engage in anti-German propaganda and to prepare for a new postwar Hungary. After the Arrow Cross (q.v.) takeover in October of that year, the HF also organized a short-lived military resistance movement, the Hungarian National Uprising's Committee for Liberation (HNUCL) *(Magyar Nemzeti Felkelés Felszabadító Bizottsága),* under the leadership of Endre Bajcsy-Zsilinszky (q.v.) and Major General János Kiss (1885–1944). The members of the HNUCL, however, were soon arrested and executed. On December 3, 1944, various anti-German elements organized the Hungarian National Independence Front (HNIF) *[Magyar Nemzeti Függetlenségi Front]* (see Independence Front) with the cooperation of various liberal and communist groups. Following the war, however, the HNIF lost its usefulness to the communists and it was permitted to stagnate until early 1949, when it was reorganized into a new communist-dominated HNIF. During the same period there also existed the shadowy Hungarian Community *(Magyar Közösség),* a secret organization composed mostly of disenchanted army officers. They first organized against the Germans, and after 1945, against the Soviets. The role of the Hungarian Resistance Movement, and especially the role of the communists within that movement, has been played up significantly after World War II (q.v.).

RESOLUTION PARTY [HATÁROZATI PÁRT] (1861). The rival of the Appeal Party (q.v.) at the Hungarian Diet (q.v.) of 1861 under the leadership of Count László Teleki (q.v.). Both parties stood for the restoration of the April Laws (q.v.) of 1848, but the Resolution Party refused to present its views in the form of an "appeal to the throne"—as did its rival under the leadership of Ferenc Deák (q.v.). Ultimately, it was the Appeals Party that won out, mostly as a result of its realism, and perhaps also because of the unexpected suicide of Count Teleki.

RÉSZEK see PARTIUM.

RÉVAI, JÓZSEF (1898–1959). One of Hungary's top communist intellectuals who, for a while after World War II (q.v.), was the cultural dictator of Hungary (q.v.). Having been captivated by the ideology of Marxism in his youth, Révai joined various socially progressive movements already during his student days. In the fall of 1918 he became one of the founders of the Communist Party of Hungary (q.v.). In 1919 he served the Hungarian Soviet Republic (q.v.), while during the interwar years he lived mostly in emigration (Vienna, 1919–30; Czechoslovakia 1934, 1937–39; Soviet Union, 1934–37, 1939–44). In the post-World War II (q.v.) period he was one of the top members of the communist elite, holding various important party and governmental positions. Thus, in addition to being a member of the Communist Party's Politburo (1945–53, 1956), Révai served as the editor-in-chief of the Party's central organ, the *Free People (Szabad Nép)* (1945–50) and also headed the powerful ministry of propaganda *(Népművelési Minisztérium)* (1949–53). Although a dedicated party activist, Révai was not the typical party hack. He was a gifted intellectual, who produced a number of significant scholarly and philosophical works on modern Hungarian intellectual and ideological history. Among them are his biography of the poet Endre Ady (q.v.) entitled *Ady* (1945), and his critical works on modern Hungarian social history, *Marxism and Hungarianness (Marxizmus és magyarság)* (1946), *Marxism and Populism (Marxizmus és népiesség)* (1947), and *Issues of Our Cultural Revolution (Kulturális forradalmunk kérdései)* (1952). Most of Révai's literary and historical essays were collected and published posthumously under the titles *Selected Literary Essays (Válogatott irodalmi tanulmányok)* (1960), and *Selected Historical Studies (Válogatott történelmi írások)* (2 vols., 1966).

REVISIONISM see **HUNGARIAN REVISIONISM.**

REVOLUTION OF 1848-49 see **HUNGARIAN REVOLUTION OF 1848-49.**

REVOLUTION OF 1956 see **HUNGARIAN REVOLUTION OF 1956.**

REVOLUTIONS OF 1918-20 see **HUNGARIAN REVOLUTIONS OF 1918-20.**

RHÉDEY, COUNT FRANCIS [FERENC] (c.1610--67). Elected prince of Transylvania (q.v.) (r.November 1657–January 1658) who, prior to his election at the orders of the Turkish Sultan, was one of Prince George Rákóczi II's (q.v.) military commanders during his invasion of Poland (q.v.) in 1657. After Rákóczi was deposed by the Turks (q.v.), the Transylvanian Diet (q.v.) elected Rhédey the ruling prince, but the latter retained this position only for two months, renouncing it in favor of Rákóczi. Being a supporter of the Habsburgs (q.v.), in 1659 Leopold I (q.v.) granted him the title of a count. Later, under the rule of Prince Michael Apafi (q.v.), he served as a close adviser of the Transylvanian ruler.

RIJEKA see FIUME.

ROBOT [SOCAGE, CORVÉE]. The *robot* was an obligatory labor service supplied by the peasants to the owners of the estates on which they lived. It was introduced in Hungary (q.v.) in the course of the 14th and 15th centuries, reaching early climax in the first years of the 16th, which also saw the introduction of legal serfdom (q.v.). The Hungarian defeat at Mohács (1526) (q.v.) and the resulting Turkish conquest of much of the country resulted in the relaxation of the *robot*. But this was only temporary, for at the end of that century it began to increase once more, reaching an average of three days per week by the mid–17th century. Starting in the late 18th century, the *robot* was gradually reduced, and then completely abolished by the April Laws of 1848 (q.v.). Yet, in practice, some of its elements remained unchanged into the early 20th century.

ROCOCO. An artistic style that grew out of Baroque (q.v.) and coincided in time with the Late Baroque. In Hungary (q.v.), the Rococo appeared only briefly and in a limited way in the late 18th century. It manifested itself primarily in the internal decorations of some churches and aristocratic palaces, and in wrought iron gates and window gratings. At the same time it also appeared in literature, in the writing of such poets as László Amadé (1703–64) and Ferenc Faludi (1704–79). Its literary manifestations, however, are often categorized as being the products of the Baroque mind.

ROGERIUS (1201/05–66). An Italian-born clergyman and archbishop, who is the author of one of the most important sources of Hungary's devastation by the Mongols (q.v.) in 1841-42. Known as the *Song of Misery (Carmen Miserabile),* he authored this work immediately after the Mongol conquest, which he himself had experienced. Master Rogerius—as he is known to historians—was born in Terra Maggiore, Italy, spent several years in Hungary (q.v.), and died as the archbishop of Spalato (Split). Having first visited Hungary in 1233, Master Rogerius spent the years between 1241 and 1249 in the land of the Magyars (q.v.), first as the dean of Várad (1241–43), and then as the canon of Sopron (1243–49) and Zagreb (1249) (q.v.). Thereafter he was almost immediately (1249) named archbishop of Spalato in Dalmatia (q.v.). The *Carmen Miserabile* was first published in the Brünn (Brno) edition of the appendix of Johannes Thuróczy's *Chronica Hungarorum*, published at in 1488.

ROMA see **GYPSIES.**

ROMAN CATHOLIC CHURCH see **CATHOLIC CHURCH.**

ROMANESQUE. The characteristic style of the 11th though the 13th centuries, just before the rise of the Gothic style (q.v.). Romanesque entered Hungary (q.v.) almost simultaneously with the country's Christianization in the early 11th century and manifested itself primarily in Christian church architecture. Its most important promoters and carriers were the religious orders that had settled in Hungary during the age of the Árpád dynasty (q.v.). The most significant remains of Romanesque architecture are the ruins of the royal palace and royal chapel at Esztergom (q.v.), and the abbey churches of Ják and Lebény. Romanesque art is also present in the miniatures and initials of some of the early Hungarian chronicles produced before the 14th century.

ROMANIA [RUMANIA, ROUMANIA, ROMINIA]. The country to the east of Hungary (q.v.) that was first formed in 1859 through the unification of Moldavia (q.v.) and Wallachia, which in 1862 renamed itself Romania. After World War I (q.v.), Romania doubled it size through the acquisition of Transylvania (q.v.) from Hungary and Bessarabia (today's Moldova) from the disintegrating Russian Empire (q.v.). Between 1940 and 1945, it was forced to return Northern Transylvania to Hungary, and in 1945, Bessarabia to the Soviet Union (q.v.). At the moment Romania is a country of 91,700 square miles with a population of 22 million. Among them are 2.5 million Hungarians, whose subjection to attempted forced assimilation is a constant source of friction between the two countries.

ROMANIANS. The inhabitants of Romania (q.v.), who until 1862 were known as Vlachs (q.v.). They changed their national name in the mid–19th century under the contested assumption that they were the descendants of the Roman legions, who had gained control over that region in the 2nd and 3rd centuries A.D. (See Daco-Roman-Romanian Continuity). Romanians speak a Latin-based language that has been heavily influenced by Slavic (q.v.), Hungarian (q.v.), Albanian, and Turkish (q.v.), which influence is still evident after two centuries of purification. Lacking protracted unified independent statehood, Romanian nationalism became very assertive in the 20th century, which intensified Romania's rivalry with its neighbors.

ROMANTICISM. Romanticism was primarily a literary movement that entered Hungary (q.v.) during the Napoleonic Age and evolved hand in hand with the rising Hungarian National Revival Movement (q.v.). It broke with the rigid classical traditions of the Enlightenment and drew its inspiration from the Middle Ages. In its Hungarian version, Romanticism relied very heavily on the national lores derived from Attila's Hunnic Empire (q.v.), the Árpádian Conquest (q.v.) of Hungary (q.v.), and the traditions of the medieval Hungarian Kingdom.

Hungarian Romanticism's most noted exponents included the poets Sándor Kisfaludy (q.v.), Károly Kisfaludy (q.v.), Ferenc Kölcsey (q.v.), and Mihály Vörösmarty (1800-55) (q.v.), the literary critic József Bajza (1804–58), and the novelists Baron Miklós Jósika (1794–1865), Baron József Eötvös (q.v.), and Mór Jókai (q.v.). The latter two, however, were rather unique in that Eötvös also became the pioneer of Realism in Hungarian literature, while Jókai remained an exponent of Romanticism for a half a century beyond the end of that movement. Around 1830, the Hungarian Romantic Movement became involved in the political goals of the Hungarian Reform Period (q.v.), while after 1845 it joined forces with the new

Populist, and even plebeian (q.v.), literature represented by Sándor Petőfi (q.v.) and his followers.

ROYAL CHANCERY [KIRÁLYI KANCELLÁRIA]. The Royal Chancery was responsible for drafting and issuing royal documents and charters. In addition to the king, the queen, the prelates, and the various national officials (palatine, lord chief justice, *voievod* or governor of Transylvania) also had their own chanceries, which fulfilled both administrative and judicial duties. The first Hungarian Royal Chancery was established by King Béla III (q.v.) in the late 12th century, which functioned until the Battle of Mohács (q.v.) in the early 16th century. Following Hungary's defeat by the Turks (q.v.) and its subsequent trisection, the Hungarian Royal Chancery's role was rapidly assumed by the Habsburg Court Chancery *(Hofkanzlei)* at Vienna (q.v.), which had a dominant role in Hungarian affairs until 1690. In that year, its place was taken over by the newly founded Hungarian Court Chancery *(Magyar Udvari Kancellária)*, which, however, also functioned in Vienna, not in the Hungarian capital.

ROYAL COUNCIL [CONSILIUM REGIUM, KIRÁLYI TA-NÁCS]. The Hungarian Royal Council consisted of the country's highest ranking administrative, military, judicial, financial, and ecclesiastical leaders. Initially the council was a fluid and informal group, but since the early 13th century it became customary to include all of the top members of the religious and civil hierarchy (bishops and comeses), members of the royal family, and high ranking court officials who happened to be in the Royal Court (q.v.) at that time. The king, however, only asked for the members' advice, for he was not obliged to follow their advice. In the late 13th century, the members of the high clergy and those members of the aristocracy who held high offices became ex officio members of the Royal Council. By the turn of the 14th and the 15th centuries, the representatives of individual aristocratic families and the lord lieutenants (q.v.) of individual counties could also be invited to participate in the Royal Council's deliberations. During the 15th century, members of the council began to assume executive functions. After Hungary's 1526 defeat and conquest by the Turks (q.v.), the Royal Council was transformed into the Hungarian Council *(Consilium Hungaricum)*, which then was increasingly subjected to the Habsburg Imperial Government (q.v.), more specifically to the Court Council *(Hofrat, Udvari Tanács)* (q.v.) and especially the Secret Council *(Gehemier Rat, Titkos Tanács)* (q.v.).

ROYAL COUNTY see HUNGARIAN COUNTY SYSTEM.

ROYAL COURT [PALATIUM, AULA REGIS, KIRÁLYI UDVAR]. The Royal Court in medieval Hungary (q.v.) served many purposes. It united within itself the country's top civil, military, and economic leadership. During the Árpádian Age (q.v.), the Royal Court was usually mobile, moving from one temporary capital (Székesfehérvár) (q.v.) to the other temporary capital (Esztergom) (q.v.), and from regional administrative courts *(curtis)* to regional administrative courts. During the Anjou period the Royal Court became increasingly stabilized at Visegrád (q.v.) and Buda (q.v.), but only in the 15th and early 16th centuries did it reside permanently to the latter city. Following the Turkish conquest, the Royal Court was relocated for three centuries to Pozsony (1541-1848) (q.v.), and then for a century to Buda (since 1873, Budapest) (q.v.). Ever since 1526, the Hungarian Royal Court had to do without the permanent presence of the king. The latter usually resided in Vienna (q.v.) or, at times, in Prague (q.v.). The most important administrative units of the Royal Court were the Royal Council (q.v.), the Royal Chancery (q.v.), the Royal Treasury (q.v.), and several of the top judicial courts *(curiae)*. After 1526, and especially after 1541, Hungary's affairs were handled more and more in the Imperial Court of the Habsburgs (See Imperial Government).

ROYAL FREE CITIES [LIBERAE ET REGIAE CIVITAT-ES, SZABAD KIRÁLYI VÁROSOK]. Walled cities that were not subject to the will of the counties and local feudal lords, but were directly under the authority of the king. These Royal Free

Cities developed in the 13th century largely as a result of the settlement of German burghers (q.v.) in the country. Starting with 1445, these cities gained the right to send representatives to the feudal diet (q.v.). They could function under their own urban laws, and their privileges included the right to grant citizenship to incoming settlers and to own serfs in the manner of feudal lords. They were free from paying most of the royal tariffs *(regales)* (q.v.) on goods produced within their walls, and they paid their taxes to the king in one lump sum every year. In case of war, they were also obliged to send a certain number of armed men to join the Royal Army. In the mid–15th century the ranks of the Royal Free Cities included Buda (q.v.), Pozsony (q.v.), Sopron (q.v.), Nagyszombat (q.v.), Kassa (q.v.), Eperjes, and Bártfa, and by the early 18th century also the city of Pest (q.v.). In the 16th century the number of the Royal Free Cities increased to fifteen, and their inhabitants were the only ones who were real burghers in the Western sense of that term. Their unique constitutional privileges ended in 1870, but they still continued to call themselves Royal Free Cities up to the end of World War II (q.v.).

ROYAL HUNGARY [HABSBURG HUNGARY]. The western and northern section of Historic Hungary (q.v.), which after the Ottoman Turkish conquest (q.v.) came under the rule of the Habsburg dynasty (q.v.). Its capital city was Pozsony (q.v.), and some of the other more important cities and cultural centers included Sopron (q.v), Győr (q.v.), Nagyszombat (q.v.), Kassa (q.v.), and Eperjes, as well as Zagreb (q.v.) and Fiume (q.v.) in Croatia (q.v.). Royal Hungary became consolidated after the Turkish conquest of Buda (q.v.) in 1541, its territory remaining practically unchanged until the liberation of the old Hungarian capital 145 years later in 1686. In Royal Hungary the traditional Hungarian legal, constitutional, and administrative system remained unchanged, although the latter fell increasingly under the control of the Imperial Government (q.v.) in Vienna (q.v.). Hungary's reconquest and reunification in the course of the Liberation Wars of 1683-99 (q.v.) ended Royal Hungary as a distinct entity.

ROYALISTS IN HUNGARY. Officially Hungary (q.v.) had been a kingdom from the year 1000, when the future St. Stephen (q.v.) was crowned the country's first Christian king, right up to the end of World War II (q.v.). But there were several short periods in its history when monarchical rule was suspended and the ruling dynasty was deposed—at least temporarily. Such was the case in 1707, 1849, and 1921. The last dethronement deprived the Habsburg dynasty (q.v.) of its Hungarian throne and placed the country under the rule of Regent Horthy (q.v.). But Hungary continued to be called a kingdom ("a kingdom without a king, ruled by an admiral without a navy"). At times of such a dethronement, the country's leading classes were usually split between the royalists and the anti-royalists. This was true during the Hungarian Revolution of 1848–49 (q.v.) as well as during the interwar years (q.v.). But in the latter period the royalists themselves were split between those who wanted the restoration of the Habsburgs and those who wished to elect a native Hungarian to the throne. The latter were the so-called "free electionists" *(szabadkirályválasztók)* (q.v.). Both of these factions were in turn fragmented into supporters of one or another member of the Habsburg dynasty, or of one of several non-Habsburg claimants to the throne. The powerful Catholic Church (q.v.) was on the side of the Habsburgs and supported the dynasty's restoration in the person of Archduke Otto von Habsburg (q.v.). The goals of all royalists, however, remained unfulfilled. This was so, partially because of the opposition of the Successor States (q.v.) and partially because Regent Horthy himself was against monarchical restoration, unless it would have meant the establishment of a Horthy dynasty.

ROYAL TREASURY [CAMERA REGIA, KAMARA, KINCSTARTÓSÁG]. The original Hungarian Royal Treasury —as in the case of all medieval political regimes—was an inner chamber of the royal residence, where the king's collective income from the lands under his control and from the royal monopolies *(regale)* (q.v.) were deposited. Hence the name *camera regia* or simply *kamara* in its Magyarized form. Through the rule of the Árpád dynasty (q.v.), Hungary's financial affairs were practically the private concern of the reigning monarchs. Until the mid-13th century the Royal Treasury was in Esztergom (q.v.), but around 1250 a second *kamara* was established at the new capital of Buda (q.v.). This was followed by the creation of several regional treasuries in such southern provinces as Szerémség (q.v.) and Slavonia (q.v.). Starting with the early 13th century, the person in charge of the Royal revenues was the lord chief treasurer (q.v.), whose Hungarian title until 1376 was *tárnokmester*, and then it became *főkincstartó*.

Under the Anjous in the 14th century Hungary's financial administration was divided into ten districts, with an equal number of Royal Treasuries and Royal Treasurers who watched over various sources of royal revenues and collected the *regales* (q.v.). This reorganization coincided with the introduction of a system of tax farming, according to which each of the Royal Treasuries was rented out to tax farmers for a certain number of years, who were called "treasury counts" *(kamara ispánok)*. The 15th century witnessed the introduction of a degree of centralization, but not until after the fall of medieval Hungary in the early 16th century was there established a real centralized financial and taxation system in the form of the Hungarian Treasury *(Magyar Kamara)* founded by King Ferdinand I (q.v.) in 1528.

For the next three centuries Royal Hungary's (q.v.) taxation and financial system was handled by this Hungarian Treasury, which functioned increasingly under the directives of the Habsburg Imperial Court (q.v.). During the 16th and 17th centuries, Transylvania (q.v.) devised its own system of taxation, while Turkish Hungary (q.v.) was integrated into the financial administrative system of the Ottoman Empire (q.v.). The Vienna-controlled Hungarian Treasury was abolished in 1848 and replaced by a Ministry for Financial Affairs, which functioned during the Hungarian Revolution of 1848-49 (q.v.), as well as after the Austro-Hungarian Compromise of 1867 (q.v.).

RUDOLPH, ARCHDUKE (1858–89). The only son and heir of Emperor Francis Joseph (q.v.) and of his wife, Empress Elizabeth (q.v.), Rudolph committed suicide at Mayerling in company of the seventeen-year-old Baroness Maria Vetsera (1872-89). Rudolph was an artistically inclined individual. He had inherited the somewhat unsettled personality of his maternal ancestors of the Wittelsbach dynasty (q.v.). They produced, among others, King Louis the Mad of Bavaria (1848–86; r.1864–86), who is best known for his expensive castle building projects.

Archduke Rudolph had considerably more progressive political views than his father, who did not wish to engage in any meaningful restructuring of the Austro-Hungarian Empire (q.v.). Moreover, in contrast to Francis Joseph, who was stuck to a pro-German foreign policy, Rudolph would have preferred a pro-French orientation. He was a learned man who was involved in the serious study of ethnography, natural sciences, and literature, and who published regularly in these fields. He was also responsible for initiating the twenty-four-volume portrait of the Habsburg Empire (q.v.) entitled *The Austro-Hungarian Monarchy in Words and Pictures (Österreich-Ungarn im Wort und Bild)* (1886–1902), which appeared simultaneously in German and in Hungarian. Like his mother, Rudolph too sympathized with the Hungarians more than was customary among the Habsburgs. Combined with his desire for social and political reform, this sympathy made him very popular in Hungary (q.v.). And this was all the more so, as his cousin and next heir to the throne, Francis Ferdinand (q.v.), disliked the Hungarians intensely, which feeling was mutual.

RUDOLPH OF HABSBURG [EMPEROR RUDOLPH I] (1218–91). The first of the Habsburgs (q.v.) to ascend the throne of the Holy Roman Empire (r.1273–91), after the long interregnum following the dying out of the Hohenstaufen dynasty. Rudolph used his office both to revive the prestige of the empire, as well as to establish his family in what later became the Arch Duchy of Austria (q.v.). His most powerful rival was King Ottokar II (r.1253–78) of Bohemia (q.v.) who by 1260 gained control of most of the Bavarian march lands to the west of Hungary (q.v.). On August 26, 1278, at the Battle of Marchfeld (Dürnkrut), Rudolph defeated and killed

Ottokar II with the help of King Ladislas IV (q.v.) of Hungary
(q.v.). Four years later in 1282 he gave most of the eastern duchies
he gained from Ottokar to his sons. With this move he established
Austria and Vienna (q.v.) as the power base of the House of
Habsburg for the next six and a half centuries. Later his descendants
ascended the thrones of Hungary and Bohemia and ruled both of these
countries for about five centuries (1437–39, 1453–57, 1526–1918).
Their rule ended only in 1918, with the deposition of King Charles
VI (Emperor Charles I).

RUDOLPH I [II] (1552–1612). King of Hungary (r.1576–1608),
King of Bohemia (r.1576–1611), and as Rudolph II (r.1576–1612)
Holy Roman Emperor. Although born in Vienna (q.v.), Rudolph
grew up in the Spanish Habsburg court in Madrid. He succeeded his
father, Maximilian I (Emperor Maximilian II) (q.v.) in 1576, and in
1583 he transferred his capital to Prague (q.v.). Thereafter, he
devoted most of his time to astronomy, astrology, and alchemy.
Among many other real and pseudo-scientists, he brought the noted
astronomers Tycho Brahe (1546–1601) and Johannes Kepler (1570–
1630) to Prague, where he supported their work in the effort to
perfect the Copernican notion of a heliocentric universe. Being
increasingly incapacitated by mental illness, Rudolph paid little
attention to the affairs of the empire and its component parts. This
showed especially during the Fifteen Years War (1591–1606) (q.v.),
when the Habsburg armies proved ineffective in their fight against
the Turks (q.v.). At the same time, this lack of attention brought
havoc and destruction upon Transylvania (q.v.) and upon other parts
of Historic Hungary (q.v.).

Rudolph's support of the Counter-Reformation (q.v.) turned the
heavily Protestant Hungarian city burghers against him, while his
legal suits against wealthy Hungarian aristocrats—with the intention
of appropriating their estates—brought the country's nobility to an
open rebellion. This rebellion was led by István Bocskai (q.v.), who
in 1605 was elected prince of Transylvania, and in 1606 compelled
Rudolph to accept the terms of the Peace of Vienna (q.v.). The latter
included guarantees for rights of the Hungarian nobility (q.v.) as

well as freedom of worship for the Protestants (q.v.). In light of Rudolph's growing mental illness, the members of the Habsburg family cooperated with the nobility of his various lands to force him to renounce his thrones, while retaining his imperial title until his death. His royal positions were taken over by his brother, Matthias (q.v.), who replaced him on the Austrian, Hungarian, and the Moravian thrones in 1608, and on the Bohemian throne in 1611.

RUNIC SCRIPT [ROVÁSÍRÁS]. Hungarian runic script is often called Székely runic script because it survived longest (i.e., until the 17th century) among the Székelys (q.v.) of Transylvania (q.v.). It appears to be related to Turk runic script of Central Asia (q.v.), although some of its letters may be derived from the Greek alphabet. The original Hungarian runic script did not have any signs for vowels, only for consonants, but the latter often stood also for a single syllable. While the Conquering Magyars (q.v.) used the runic script extensively, following the nation's Christianization in the late 10th and early 11th centuries, it was rapidly displaced by the Latin alphabet. Yet, the runic script survived and was used extensively on monumental architectural pieces as late as the mid–16th century. Recently, attempts have been made to establish a connection between the Hungarian runic script and the ancient Sumerian and Hittite cuneiform alphabets, along with the effort to link the Hungarians to these ancient peoples of the Near East. These efforts, however, never went beyond the level of romantic hypotheses.

RURIK DYNASTY. A ruling family of Scandinavian origin that has ruled Kievan Russia (q.v.) and Muscovy (q.v.) from the late 9th to the late 16th centuries (860s–1598). The members of this dynasty frequently interacted and intermarried with the Hungarian ruling dynasties, especially during the Árpádian age (q.v.).

RUSSIA. A collective name of the large East Slavic (q.v.) state to the northeast of Hungary (q.v.), which until 1992 was the dominant state within the Soviet Union (q.v.). From the late 9th through the mid–13th centuries it was know as Kievan Russia (q.v.), from the early 14th through the early 18th centuries as Muscovy or Muscovite Russia (q.v.), from the early 18th through the early 20th centuries as the Russian Empire (1721–1917), and from 1922 to the end of 1991 as the Soviet Union.

RUSSIAN EMPIRE. The official name of the Russian state between 1721, when Peter the Great (r.1682–1725) was proclaimed an emperor with the Latin term "imperator," and the dethronement of Czar Nicholas II (r.1894–1917) in March 1917. In addition to Peter the Great, the most prominent rulers of the Russian Empire included Elizabeth (r.1741–62), Catherine the Great (r.1762–96), Paul (r.1796–1801), Alexander I (r.1801–25), Nicholas I (r.1825–55), Alexander II (r.1855–81), Alexander III (r.1881–94), and Nicholas II (r.1894–1917). During the 19th century, the birth of Russian Pan-Slavism (q.v.) produced a feeling of endangerment in Hungary (q.v.), which pushed the Hungarians toward a military alliance between Austria-Hungary (q.v.) and the German Empire (q.v.).

RUSSIANS. The largest of the Slavic nationalities (q.v), who in the 1990s number about 150 million. They were primarily responsible for the creation of Muscovite Russia (q.v.), the Russian Empire (q.v.), and the Soviet Union (q.v.). They speak an East Slavic language (q.v.), use the Cyrillic alphabet (q.v.), and are mostly Orthodox Christians (q.v.). Starting with the 19th century, the Russians and Russian imperialism in the Balkans (q.v.) produced a feeling of fear in Hungary (q.v), which pushed the Hungarians in the direction of an alliance with the Germans (q.v.).

RUSYNS [RUTHENS, RUTHENIANS]. The smallest of the East Slavic nationalities (q.v.). They live in Carpatho-Ruthenia (q.v.), and a sizable minority, in the United States. Until the end of World War I (q.v.), they were part of Historic Hungary (q.v.). The Treaty of Trianon (q.v.) of 1920 made them part of Czechoslovakia (q.v.). Between 1939 and 1945, they returned to Hungary (q.v.), in 1945 they were forced to join the Soviet Union (q.v.), and in 1992 they became part of independent Ukraine (q.v.). The separate national identity and national consciousness of the Rusyns is of relatively recent origin. For this reason, both the Russians (q.v.) and the Ukrainians (q.v.) have claimed them as their own. In the period after World War II (q.v.), the Rusyns were simply classified as Ukrainians. But after the collapse of the Soviet Union (q.v.), Rusyn national consciousness has reasserted itself once more.

RUTHENIANS   see   RUSYNS.

- S -

**SACRED DUAL KINGSHIP [SZAKRÁLIS KETTŐS FEJE-
DELEMSÉG].** A system of rule among some eastern peoples,
according to which power is shared by two rulers, the king or the
emperor, whose person is sacred, but exercises little real power. His
"viceroy," who lacks such sacredness of personality, is the real
holder of political and military powers. The best-known modern
example of such a "dual kingship" was the Japanese system until the
Meji Restoration of 1867–68. The *mikado* was the sacred emperor,
whose person was untouchable, and who was viewed as a virtual
"god on earth," but the real powers were in the hands of the *shogun,*
who was nominally second in command. Such dualism existed also
in the leadership of the Hungarians of the Árpádian Conquest (q.v.),
where the sacred ruler was the *kende* (q.v.), but the real military and
political powers were held by the *gyula* (q.v.).

**SAINT STEPHEN'S CROWN see HOLY CROWN OF
HUNGARY.**

SALAMON (1053–87). King of Hungary (r.1063–74), son of King
Andrew I (q.v.), and son-in-law of Holy Roman Emperor Henry III
(r.1039–56). Although claiming the throne immediately after his
father's death in 1060, Salamon ascended the throne only after the
death of his uncle, Béla I (q.v.). Lacking sufficient support, in 1064
he was forced to grant the *Ducatus* (q.v.) to his cousins, the future
kings Géza I (q.v.) and St. Ladislas (q.v.). During much of his reign,
Salamon was compelled to fight the invading Cumans (q.v.) and
Pechenegs (q.v.). In 1071 he conquered Belgrade (q.v.) and its
vicinity from the Byzantine Empire (q.v.). But the festering rivalry
with his cousins led to a civil war and then to his defeat at the Battle
of Mogyoród in 1074. Salamon fled to his brother-in-law, Emperor
Henry IV (r.1056–1106), after which Géza I ascended the throne.

During the next thirteen years, he made several efforts to regain his throne, which in 1081 landed him as a prisoner in the fortress of Visegrád (q.v.). Freed in 1083, Salamon attempted two other invasions of Hungary with the help of the Cumans (q.v.), but he was defeated and then disappeared in 1087. Claiming to be a widow, in 1088 Salamon's wife, Judith, married Prince Władisław Hermann (r.1079–1102) of Poland (q.v.).

SAMBUCUS see **ZSÁMBOKY.**

SANDALED NOBILITY see **LOWER NOBILITY.**

SANJAK [SANCAK, SZANDZSÁK]. One of the smaller administrative units within the Ottoman Empire (q.v.) headed by a sanjak bey. Several sanjaks—at times over a dozen—were combined to make up a *vilayet (eyalet)* (q.v.), also known as a *pashalik* (q.v.) headed by a *pasha* (q.v.). In Turkish Hungary (q.v.), the largest and oldest vilayet was the Pashalik of Buda (1541–1686), which was made up originally of eighteen *sanjaks.*

SARAJEVO, ASSASSINATION IN (1914). The politically inspired murder of Archduke Francis Ferdinand (q.v.), heir to the throne of Austria-Hungary (q.v.), which took place on June 28, 1914, in the capital of Bosnia (q.v.), then a province of the Austro-Hungarian Empire. This assassination is viewed as the immediate cause of World War I (q.v.), which topped off several long-range causes. Among the latter were the economic, colonial, and military rivalry among the great powers represented by two rival alliance systems: the Triple Alliance (q.v.) and the Triple Entente (q.v.).

SARLÓ [SICKLE] MOVEMENT (1928-33). A movement of young, progressive Hungarian intellectuals in Slovakia (Czechoslovakia) (q.v.) during the late 1920s and early 1930s. The movement was formalized in 1928 at a scout camp near Gombaszög in August 1928. Its center was the new Slovak capital, Bratislava (the former Hungarian capital of Pozsony) (q.v.). But because most of its members were university students, it also had branches in such university towns as the Czech capital of Prague (q.v.) and the Moravian capital of Brno (Brünn) (q.v.). It was the first movement among Hungarians anywhere, which gave birth to an intensive study of Hungarian peasant life—part of Populism (q.v.)—with the intention of strengthening Hungarian national consciousness. It also emphasized the need for friendship and cooperation among the small peoples of the Danube Basin (q.v.), and worked out several, often unrealistic, plans toward this end. At its 1931 Congress, several prominent members of the *Sarló* seemed to be veering toward the acceptance of communism, which split the movement into a number of factions and led ultimately to its disintegration in 1933.

SAVA [SZÁVA, SAVE] RIVER. A historically important river that used to constitute the southern borders of Historic Hungary (q.v.) in the region between Zagreb (q.v.) and Belgrade (q.v.). It crossed medieval Slavonia (q.v.), while in more modern times it constituted the southern frontiers of that province. The Sava is paralleled by the Drava River (q.v.) to the north. The region between the two rivers—which includes Szerémség (q.v.), modern Slavonia, and northern Croatia (q.v.)—is also known as "The Land Between the Drava and Sava" *(Dráva-SzávaKöze)*.

SAVOY, PRINCE EUGENE [JENŐ SAVOYAI] (1663–1736). A Habsburg military commander of French birth who entered Imperial military service in 1683. He was involved both in the Liberation Wars (1683–99) (q.v.) and in the Austro-Turkish War of 1716–18, which pushed the Turks (q.v.) out of Hungary (q.v.) and the northern Balkans (q.v.). Prince Eugene had served as one of the Habsburg commanders at the Second Siege of Vienna in 1683 (q.v.), participated in the liberation of the old Hungarian capital of Buda (q.v.) in 1686, and inflicted major defeats on the Turks at Zenta (1697), Pétervárad (1716), and Belgrade (1717). Thereby he contributed significantly to the extension of Habsburg power toward the southeast. He also fought for the Habsburgs (q.v.) in the War of Spanish Succession.(1701–15). In 1704 Eugene of Savoy was appointed president of the War Council (q.v.) of the Habsburg Imperial Court (q.v.), while in 1714–15 and 1724–36 he served as the viceroy of the Austrian Netherlands (Belgium). In return for his services to the Habsburg dynasty (q.v.), Prince Eugene was granted a large estate in Hungary, which embraced the whole of the Csepel Island (q.v.) on the Danube (q.v.), where he built a a magnificent palace in the town of Ráckeve. His equestrian statue in the fortress of Buda (q.v.) commemorates his role in the liberation of that city.

SAXONS   see   TRANSYLVANIAN   SAXONS,   ZIPSERS.

SCHWARZENBERG, PRINCE FELIX (1800Ụ52). The scion of an old Frankish princely family who, between November 1848 and April 1852, was the chancellor and foreign minister of the Austrian Empire (q.v.). He was responsible for King Ferdinand V's (q.v.) resignation and Francis Joseph's (q.v.) accession to the throne (December 2, 1848). Schwarzenberg was also behind the dissolution of the Austrian *Reichstag* (Parliament) and the promulgation of the Olmütz Constitution (March 4, 1849) that applied a highly centralized system of government to the whole Austrian Empire (q.v.), including Hungary (q.v.). This act prompted the Hungarian Parliament (q.v.) to carry through the dethronement of the Habsburgs (q.v.) and the election of Lajos Kossuth (q.v.) as the "governor-president" of Hungary. This in turn assured Russian military intervention, that led to the defeat of the Hungarian Revolution of 1848-49 (q.v.). Following the Austro-Russian victory (August 1949), Schwarzenberg went to work to restructure the Habsburg lands into a unified Austrian Empire. In foreign policy he tried to retain Austria's preeminence within the German Confederation (q.v.). Thus, in November 1850, he forced Prussia (q.v.) to give up the idea of a "Prussian Union" within the German Lands ("Humiliation of Olmütz"), but he was unable to have the whole of the Austrian Empire accepted as a member of the German Confederation. Schwarzenberg's sudden death on April 5, 1952, robbed the young Emperor Francis Joseph of his closest adviser. Thereafter, he was forced to rely on several much less competent personalities, including Minister of Interior Alexander Bach (q.v.), who gave his name to the absolutist period of the 1850s.

SCOUTING. The International Scouting Movement was founded in 1908 by Lord Robert Baden-Powell (1857–1941) for the purpose of developing stout character, good citizenship, mental alertness, and physical fitness among the young of the world, as well as to make them appreciate the beauties of nature. Scouting's organizational system was borrowed from the armed forces, and its headquarters are based in Geneva, Switzerland.

The Hungarian scouting movement began in 1910, and was formalized in 1912 by the establishment of the Hungarian Scout Federation. Its main goals included rearing Hungarian youth in the spirit of humanism, religiosity, and patriotism. The movement was basically limited to students in the exclusive preparatory schools, called "gymnasiums," and as such it excluded the children of peasants and workers who did not attend these schools. The latter were compelled to enroll instead in the "Levente Movement" (q.v.) founded in 1921. During the 1930s, Hungarian scouting fell increasingly under the influence of Hungarian Revisionism (q.v.), which was held against by the post-World War II (q.v.) political systems. It was abolished by the communist regime in 1948, which claimed that it was a "fascist-nationalist" organization.

But Hungarian scouting survived abroad. It was resurrected in Germany (q.v.) in 1945, formalized by the establishment of the Hungarian Scout Federation in Exile in 1948, and then transplanted to the United States (Garfield, New Jersey) in 1951. For over three decades, the nominal leader of the "Hungarian Scouting Federation in Exile" was General Ferenc Kisbarnaki-Farkas (1892–1980) (q.v.), but the actual founder and leader was and is Gábor Bodnár (1920–96) (q.v.). In 1988, the scouting movement was reestablished in Hungary. Since then, it has gone through several birth pains, including internal factionalism. In the mid-1990s, it was in the process of rebuilding its original infrastructure and establishing a working relationship with the still functioning Hungarian Scout

Federation in Exile, which recently has been renamed "Hungarian Scouting Federation in Exteris."

SCYTHIA [SZKÍTIA]. A region to the north of the Black Sea (q.v.) roughly identical with the Pontic Steppes (q.v.). In the period between 700 B.C. and 200 B.C., it was under the control of the so-called Scythians, who may have been a combination of Iranians and Turanians (q.v.). Although gradually replaced by the Sarmatians (200 B.C.–A.D. 200), the Goths (A.D. 200–370), the Huns (A.D. 370-460s), and such other Turkic tribes as the Avars (q.v.), Khazars (q.v), Bulgars (q.v.), Pechenegs (q.v.), and others, the name and traditions of the Scythians survived. Thus, several medieval Hungarian chronicles claim that the Conquering Magyars (q.v.) came from Scythia, were descendants of the Scythians, and thus they are the heirs to the Scythian past and traditions. Although very popular in the past, this view is correct only in its geographical claims, for at least two former homelands of the Magyars (Levedia and Etelköz) were located there. Claims of descent, however, are questionable, although there must have been some link between the Conquering Magyars and various Turanian elements (q.v.) within the Scythian Empire.

SECOND CONQUEST see **DOUBLE CONQUEST.**

SECOND SERFDOM see **SERFDOM.**

SECRET COUNCIL [GEHEIMER RAT, TITKOS TAN-ÁCS]. Perhaps the most influential governmental organ in the Habsburg Empire (q.v.) during the 16th and 17th centuries, surpassing progressively the Court Council (q.v.) in importance and influence. The Secret Council's members were called "True Secret Counselor" *(valódi titkos tanácsos)*. The emperor consulted them on all matters of significance. They gave their views, but the decision was made by the emperor, and the actual implementation of the council's policy was carried out by the central Imperial bureaucracy. Although the Secret Council also dealt with the affairs of Hungary (q.v.), it had no Hungarian members until 1646, when Count Pál Pálffy (1580s–1653) was appointed, who simultaneously became the lord chief justice (q.v.) and three years later Hungary's palatine (q.v.). Thereafter a number of other Hungarians were also appointed, but by that time the Secret Council was so diluted that the emperor consulted only its most influential members. In 1709, the role of the Secret Council was taken over by the Secret Conference *(Geheime Konferenz, Titkos Konferencia),* consisting of these influential personalities. The Secret Council lost its significance in the early 19th century, but the title "Secret Counselor" was retained and awarded as a badge of honor by the Habsburgs (q.v.) until 1918. In 1935, this title was resurrected in Hungary (q.v.) and bestowed upon persons of achievement by Regent Horthy (q.v.) until the end of World War II (q.v.).

SECRET POLICE [OFFICE OF STATE SECURITY, ÁLLAMVÉDELMI HATÓSÁG, ÁVH]. The name of the Hungarian secret police under the control of the Ministry of Interior, and subsequently under the Council of Ministers in pre–1956 communist Hungary (q.v.). The ÁVH was organized in 1948 by merging the "Department of Political Organization" *(Politikai Rendészeti Osztály)* with the Ministry of Interior's Department of State Security *(Államvédelmi Osztály* or *ÁVÓ).* It was disbanded in 1956 and replaced by another version of the secret police, under the control of the regular police forces. The ÁVH's most notorious leader was Major General Gábor Péter (1906–93), who controlled this Stalinist secret police between 1948 and 1952. The terms ÁVH and ÁVÓ were and are still used interchangeably in Hungary. ÁVÓ is also used as a generic term for the secret policy. This is true even for the period since 1956, when the ÁVH had already been disbanded.

SELYE, HANS [JÁNOS] (1907-82). A Canadian-Hungarian physician and psychiatrist who was the internationally known father of the "stress theory." During his young days, Selye lived and studied in Vienna (q.v.), Prague (q.v.), Paris, and Rome, but he developed his scientific theories and made most of his achievements at McGill

University in Montreal (1932–76). Following his retirement, he became the founding president of the International Stress Institute (1976–82). The best known among Selye's forty-odd books are his *Stress* (1949) and *The Stress of Life* (1956). He is also the founding editor of the serial *Annual Reports on Stress* (1951–) and the author of the highly regarded textbook, *Endocrinology* (1949).

SENIORITY [SENIORÁTUS]. The principle according to which it is always the oldest male member of a family or clan that inherits the position of leadership and has the right of succession. In a monarchical system, the principle of seniority was eventually replaced by the principle of primogeniture, that is, succession by the firstborn son. The principle of seniority, however, survived in such countries as the Ottoman Empire (q.v.) for a long period of time. During the 11th and 12th centuries, it was also used in Hungary (q.v.) by several rival claimants to the throne. Moreover, seniority likewise survived in the matter of the inheritance of entailed estates (q.v.). The latter could never be divided among several heirs, and were always inherited and controlled by the oldest male among the heirs. This concept, which was similar to the notion of the indivisibility of the estates of the original clans, resurfaced once more in 17th-century Hungary, this time largely under Spanish-Habsburg influences.

SERBIA [RASCIA]. A South Slavic (q.v.) state that came into existence gradually in the course of the 10th through the 13th centuries, when various tribal states coalesced into the medieval Serbia. Although under relentless pressure from Byzantium (q.v.), Hungary (q.v.), and Bulgaria (q.v.), the Serbian state survived, became a kingdom in the early 13th century, and then reached the apogee of its size and power in the mid-14th century under Czar Dušan (r.1331–55). It rapidly disintegrated after Dušan's death, was defeated by the Turks at the Battle of Kossovo Polje in 1389, and then gradually merged into the Ottoman Turkish Empire (q.v.). Following the Napoleonic Wars, the autonomous Principality of Serbia developed within the Ottoman state under two rival dynasties:

the Obrenovich and Karageorgevich. It finally gained independence at the Congress of Berlin (1878) (q.v.) and doubled its size in the Balkan Wars (1912-13). In 1914 Serbia was involved in the assassination of Archduke Francis Ferdinand (q.v.) at Sarajevo (q.v.), which served as the immediate cause of World War I (q.v.). After the war, Serbia became the leader of the new Balkan Slavic state of Yugoslavia (q.v.), which disintegrated during World War II (1941–45), and then once again in the early 1990s. Serbia now constitutes most of Little Yugoslavia (q.v.).

SERBS [SERBIANS, RASCIANS, RÁCOK]. One of the South Slavic nationalities of about ten to twelve million, who are close ethnic and linguistic relatives of the Croats (q.v.), Slovenes, Macedonian Slava, and the Bosnian Muslims (q.v.). The Serbians differ from their primary rivals, the Croats, only in religion and culture. Whereas the former were Christianized by Rome, are Catholics, use the Latin alphabet, and have been part of the Catholic Kingdom of Hungary (q.v.) for a whole millennium, the later were Christianized by Byzantium (q.v.), are Orthodox Christians (q.v.), use the Cyrillic alphabet (q.v.), and have been part of the Orthodox Christian World up to the 15th century, and then of the Ottoman Turkish Empire (q.v.) for many centuries. In the late 17th and 18th centuries many Serbs settled in the depopulated sections of Southern Hungary, in what is today's Voivodina (q.v.), which fact later served as a pretext to detach those territories from Hungary. After 1918 the Serbians were the dominant nationality in newly founded Yugoslavia (q.v.). Since the early 1990s, they control only Little Yugoslavia (q.v.) that consists of Serbia (q.v.), Montenegro, and the provinces of Voivodina and Kossovo.

SERÉDI, JUSTINIÁN [GYÖRGY SZAPUCSEK] (1884–1945). Cardinal-archbishop of Esztergom and the prince primate of Hungary (r.1927–45). Having become a member of the Benedictine Order (1904) (q.v.) and a priest (1908), Serédi had spent about two decades at Saint Anselm University in Rome (1904–18, 1920–27) —as a student, as an instructor, and then as a professor of canon law. At the same time he was given various high positions in the Vatican, while also serving as the editor-in-chief of the nine-volume *Collected Sources of Canon Law (Codicis Juris Canonici Fontes)*. Following the death of Cardinal-Archbishop János Csernoch (q.v.) in 1927, Serédi was named to the Arch See of Esztergom and then made a cardinal. As the holder of one of the top constitutional offices in interwar Hungary (q.v.), he stood for conservative nationalism and for the retention of the preeminent position of the Catholic Church (q.v.). Thus, he viewed the regency of Admiral Horthy (q.v.)—a Protestant—with much suspicion. He would have preferred the restoration of the Habsburg dynasty (q.v.) in the person of Archduke Otto von Habsburg (q.v.). Serédi was not a believer in contemporary racial theories, but like Pope Pius XII (r.1939–58), he viewed communism as a greater danger than Fascism. This may explain why he agreed to administer the oath of office to the Hungarian Arrow Cross (q.v.) leader, Ferenc Szálasi (q.v.), following the latter's assumption of power in the fall of 1944.

SERFDOM. Serfdom was an important component of feudal social system. A serf was a peasant who owned no land, was bound to the person or to the estate of the feudal lord, and was obliged to pay feudal dues (in kind or in money) and to render labor services *(robot)* (q.v.) to his lord. In Hungary (q.v.), as elsewhere in East Central Europe (q.v.) and Russia (q.v.), bonded serfdom came much later than in Western Europe. But it also disappeared much later. Thus, in Hungary, the peasants were basically personally free until the early 16th century, although during the 15th century their freedom was increasingly curtailed. They were known by the term *jobbágy (iobagio)* and, until their enserfement in 1514, they were basically tenant peasants. They evolved into a uniform peasant class in the 13th century through the fusion of the free peasants, freed slaves, and various servant classes. These free peasants or *jobbágys* cultivated lands that were allotted to them by the nobility, in return for which they paid a rent in kind. In the late 15th and early 16th centuries, their position worsened, while after the Dózsa Peasant Revolution (q.v.) of 1514 they were bound to the soil. Thus began the period that Marxist historians have called "second serfdom" and that Western historians simply call serfdom.

After the introduction of serfdom, the position of the peasant-serfs—who continued to be called *jobbágy*—remained basically unchanged until Maria Theresa's (q.v.) *Urbarium* (1767) (q.v.) and Joseph II's (q.v.) partial emancipation decree (1785). The final emancipation of the serfs, however, came at the time of the Hungarian Revolution of 1848 (q.v.). Although in 1514 all peasants had lost their personal freedom, there were in fact differences among them, depending on the size of their plots and the specific conditions under which they worked. During the period of serfdom or "second serfdom" (1514–1848), there did develop social and economic differences between the landed serfs *(telkes jobbágyok)* and the landless serfs *(zsellérek),* as well as within these subgroups.

SERF EMANCIPATION. The Hungarian serfs were freed from all their feudal obligations by the last Feudal Diet (q.v.) in early 1848, which made them free citizens of Hungary (q.v.). However, voluntary emancipation on the part of the nobility was also possible ever since the diet of 1839–40. The Hungarian serfs were the only ones in East Central Europe (q.v.) who did not have to pay redemption payments for their freedom.

SERVIENTES REGIS [SERVIENS REGIS, ROYAL SERVANTS]. The upper layer of the military cast in the service of the king from the 11th through the 13th centuries, who were also under direct royal jurisdiction. They acquired landed estates via royal grants for military service. In the early 13th century, their position was shaken by the influx of many foreigners and the granting of too many estates and offices to these immigrants, many of whom were soldiers-of-fortune. Thus, the *servientes regis* rose in rebellion and forced King Andrew II (q.v.) to issue the Golden Bull in 1222 (q.v.) and thus guarantee their rights and privileges. Following this event, the *servientes regis* gradually coalesced into a separate estate, and then—jointly with the surviving members of the clan leadership—came to form the backbone of the Hungarian common nobility (q.v.). By the second renewal of the Golden Bull in 1267, the term *servientes regis (royal servants)* came to be equated with the term *nobilis (nobles)*, wherefore the former term went out of use.

SETTLEMENT POLICY OF THE HABSBURGS. From the late 17th through the 19th centuries, Hungary (q.v.) had been subjected to several waves of mass immigrations from the Balkans (q.v.), Germany (q.v.), and Galicia (q.v.). These mass migrations were encouraged and supported by the Habsburgs (q.v.) for economic and for political reasons. They wanted to repopulate the lands left vacant by the Liberation Wars (q.v.), and at the same time they wished to settle those lands by reliable non-Hungarians who would support them against the recalcitrant Magyars (q.v.). These officially-sponsored immigrations were complemented by a constant inflow of Balkan peasants, who were encouraged to settle in Hungary by the country's new landed nobility, most of whom had gained their lands as a result of their support of the Habsburg cause during the Turkish wars, and they had no feelings for Hungary.

The first mass migration from the Balkans took place in 1690, when about 200,000 Serbs, among them about 40,00 fighters, transplanted themselves to scantily populated Southern Hungary (q.v.). They came under the leadership of Arsen Chernovich (Černović), the Serbian Patriarch of Peć (Ipek) who gained territories and special privileges for his people from Emperor Leopold I (q.v.). This was followed by additional immigrations of South Slavs (q.v.) to Southern Hungary, Vlach shepherds (q.v.) to Southern Transylvania (q.v.), and German peasants to Trans-Danubia (q.v.) and to the Banat (q.v.) and Bácska (q.v.) section of south-central Hungary.

In 1766 Empress Maria Theresa (q.v.) established a special Settlement Commission, whose goal was to facilitate the official governmental settlement policy. The commission arranged the influx of tens of thousand of German peasants from the Rhine region who upon entering Hungary were soon to be known as Swabians (q.v.). The acquisition of Galicia in 1772 was followed by the mass influx of Orthodox Jews (q.v.) to northeastern Hungary.

As a result of these migrations Historic Hungary (q.v.) became a thoroughly multinational state. In fact, by 1840, the native Magyars (q.v.) barely constituted 40 percent of the population of their own country. In light of the country's depopulation during the final phase of Turkish rule (q.v.), some of these migrations may have been unavoidable. But it was made much worse by the Habsburg's conscious effort to turn Hungary into a multiethnic and multilingual land. The ultimate result was the partitioning of Hungary after World War I (q.v.).

SEVEN CHIEFS [HÉT VEZÉR]. According to medieval Hungarian chronicles, the "seven chiefs" were the leaders of the seven conquering tribes of the Árpádian conquest (q.v.). There are some disagreements as to the names of these tribal leaders. Anonymus (q.v.) in his *Gesta Hungarorum* (q.v.), for example, lists them as follows: Árpád, Előd, Ond, Kund, Tas, Huba, and Töhötöm. Modern Hungarian historians, however, believe that the most significant leaders of the conquerors included Árpád (q.v.) and Kurszán, the first of whom was the *gyula*, while the second was the *kende*. In addition to these two top leaders, the others were Kund, Lél, Örs, Szabolcs, and Vérbulcsú. These traditions make no specific reference to the chiefs of the three Kabar (q.v.) tribes who joined the Hungarian Tribal Federation (q.v.)

SEVEN HUNGARIAN TRIBES [HÉT MAGYAR TÖRZS]. The commonly used names of the seven tribes of the Árpádian Conquest (q.v.) are: Magyar (Megyer), Nyék, Kürtgyarmat, Tarján Jenő, Kara, and Kaza. These tribes were united within the Hungarian Tribal Federation (q.v.) under the de facto leadership of Prince Árpád (q.v.), who was the head of the Magyar tribe that imposed its own name and will upon the whole nation. In medieval Hungarian chronicles these seven tribes are also referred to as *Hetumoger* (Seven Hungarians), who were joined by three Kabar (q.v.) tribal fragments, thus making a total of ten tribes that constituted the Hungarian Tribal Federation (q.v.). The Turkic name of this tribal federation, *On Ogur* (Ten Tribes), was probably the source of the international name of the Magyars, whose variants include Ungar, Ungherese, Vengr, Hungarian, Hongrois, etc. The "H" in front the the English and French version of this name is probably derived from the common assumption that the Magyars were direct descendants of the Huns.

SEVEN-PERSON COURT [TABULA SEPTEMVIRALIS, HÉTSZEMÉLYES TÁBLA]. A high-level court of medieval origin, which functioned until 1848. After 1535 it became part of the Hungarian Royal Curia or simply the Curia (q.v.). Chaired by the palatine (q.v), the members of the Seven-Person Court included three magnates (q.v.) and three high churchmen. At the time of the promulgation of the Pragmatic Sanction (q.v.) in 1723, the membership of this court was expanded to twenty-one. Being basically a court of appeals, its decisions were permanent, and it was impossible to appeal against them, except in certain rare cases to the king himself.

SEVEN PLUM TREES NOBILITY [HÉTSZILVAFÁS NE-MES] see LOWER NOBILITY.

SEVEN YEARS' WAR (1756–63). A major power struggle among the great powers in which the Habsburg Empire (q.v.) was allied with its traditional enemy, France, supported by Russia (q.v.). England, on the other hand, supported the Habsburgs' main rival, Frederick the Great of Prussia (r.1740–86). Although hard pressed, Russia's withdrawal from the war saved Frederick and prevented Maria Theresa (q.v.) from regaining Silesia (q.v.) that she had lost in the War of Austrian Succession (q.v.). The Treaty of Fontainebleau between England and France (November 1762) and the treaty of Hubertsburg between Austria and Prussia (February 1763) ended the continental phase of the war. The colonial phase — known as the French-Indian Wars — ended in English victory and in the acquisition of French Canada by Britain. These and other related terms were codified by the Treaty of Paris (February 1763) among Britain, France, Spain, and Portugal.

SFRAGISTICS [PECSÉTTAN]. The study of the origins, history, meaning, and use of personal and official seals, especially as they relate to medieval and early modern history. Sfragistics is one of the traditional Auxiliary Sciences of History (q.v.) that has been studied in Hungary since the mid-19th century.

SHAMANISM. A primitive religion in which the shamans (priests) communicate with the deities in a state of stupor or trance. Shamans have allegedly been selected for their role even before their birth, their designation being indicated by certain physical signs, such as having more than the normal number of teeth, toes, or fingers. Before their conversion to Christianity, the Hungarians (q.v.) of the preconquest period also followed a version of shamanism. Some of its practices survived for at least two centuries beyond compulsory Christianization, but did so primarily as an underground religion. In the mid-13th century there were still a number of political trials for the secretly active shamans.

SIGISMUND [ZSIGMOND] (1368–1437). King of Hungary (r.1387–1437) and Bohemia (r.1419–37), and Holy Roman Emperor (r.1410–37), whose life was spent in a constant struggle against Baronial Leagues (q.v.) in Hungary, the Hussites (q.v.) in Bohemia (q.v.), and the Ottoman Turks (q.v.) in the Balkans (q.v.). Sigismund gained the Hungarian throne as a result of his marriage (1385) to Queen Maria (q.v.), who was forced to fight for several years against her Neapolitan Anjou (q.v.) relatives. Having been imprisoned and forced to resign in 1386, Maria's partisans elected her husband, Sigismund, as the king of Hungary. The death of her rival, Charles the Little (q.v.), permitted Maria to reassume the throne in 1386, which was followed by the election of her husband as a coruler (1387). Following his election, Sigismund took charge of Hungary and in 1396 organized the first major crusade—the Crusade of Nicopolis (q.v.)—against the Ottoman Turks (q.v.). In his struggle for royal prestige and power, Sigismund initially relied almost exclusively upon the wealthy and powerful Hungarian barons (q.v.). But in 1397 he decided to enlist the services of the common nobility (q.v.) as well. He did this by inviting their representatives (four from each county) to the Diet of Temesvár (q.v.). These efforts, however, proved futile in face of the ongoing wars among the various Baronial Leagues (q.v.), which forced Sigismund to rely increasingly upon foreigners from the German (q.v.) and Italian states (q.v.).

In 1401 some of the barons took him captive to force him to dismiss his foreign advisers. Sigismund's life and throne were saved only through a deal with the Cillei-Garai League and by marrying Herman Cillei's (q.v.) daughter. Relying on this league, for the next few years Sigismund pursued his goal to gain the crowns of Bohemia and the Holy Roman Empire (q.v.). Because of the Pope's support of his rival, Ladislas King of Naples (r.1386–1414), Sigismund issued the Placetum regium (q.v.) in 1404 so as to limit the powers of the Popes in Hungary. In 1405 he also attempted to enlist the support of the cities.

In 1410, Sigismund gained the Holy Roman Emperorship, but lacked money to pursue his imperial policies. It was for this reason that in 1412 he pawned several of the Zipser towns (q.v.) of Northern Hungary (q.v.) to the king of Poland (q.v.), which Hungary failed to regain until the First Polish Partition of 1772. At the Council of Constance (1414–17) Sigismund was instrumental in restoring unity to the Papacy. His role in the burning of Jan Hus (1415), however, contributed to the outbreak of the protracted and bloody Hussite Wars, as well as to the spread of Hussitism (q.v.) to Hungary. During the 1420s Sigismund led several campaigns both against the Czech Hussites and the Ottoman Turks. In the following decade he made his peace both with the Pope (1433) and with the Hussites (1436), but was unable to deal effectively with the continued intrigues of the Cillei family (q.v.). He died in the midst of the great Transylvanian (q.v.) peasant rebellion of 1437, which resulted in the Union of Kápolna (q.v.) in 1437, involving the three "historic nations" of that province: the Magyars (q.v.), the Székelys (q.v.), and the Saxons (q.v.). Sigismund died in Bohemia and was buried in the city of Várad (q.v.) in Hungary. Following his death, he was succeeded by his son-in-law, Albert (q.v.), the first Habsburg (q.v.) on the Hungarian throne.

SILESIA [SCHLESIEN, SLEZSKO, ŚLĄSK]. A province in the southwestern part of today's Poland (q.v.), to the north of the Czech Republic (q.v.), which in the course of the past millennium had been part of Poland (10th c.–1335), Hungary (1178–90), Bohemia (1335–1526), the Habsburg Empire (1526–1748/63), and then of Prussia and the German Empire (1748/63–1918). After World War I (q.v.) Silesia was divided between Germany (q.v.) and resurrected Poland (q.v.), while after World War II (q.v.) it was made part of the reshaped Polish state. Although Silesia's original population was Slavic (q.v.), starting with the mid-13th century it became heavily Germanized through the influx of German miners and artisans. The latter urbanized the province and transformed it into a manufacturing and industrial region. In the 14th and 15th centuries, Silesia's capital, Breslau (Wrocław), had become one of the two largest urban centers in East Central Europe (q.v.), outshining Vienna (q.v.) and outdone only by Prague (q.v.). Silesia remained a German-speaking industrial and cultural center until after World War I (q.v.) and World War II (q.v.). But the political changes connected with the two world wars resulted in the flight or expulsion of much of Silesia's German population.

SIRMIUM see SZERÉMSÉG.

SLAVERY. Slavery was unknown in Hungary (q.v.) before the coming of Christianity and the accompanying social system. There were a number of slaves prior to that date, but most of those were really prisoners of war resulting from various military encounters. Slavery evolved in the course of the 11th through the 13th centuries, but with the development of feudalism in the 13th through the 15th centuries, these slaves were gradually merged into the peasant class. We also know of sporadic slavery during the 16th and 17th centuries, but again these were the results of the ongoing Ottoman-

Habsburg conflict (q.v.) and the simultaneous absence of the concept of a prisoner of war.

SLAVIC LANGUAGES. One of the important linguistic sub-families of the Indo-European languages. Starting with the sixth-century Slavic diaspora, the basic Slavic language came to be divided into three branches: West Slavic, East Slavic, and South Slavic. Then, in the course of the next several centuries, each of these branches gave birth to several national languages. Today the main West Slavic languages include the Polish, Czech, Slovak, and Sorbian; the main East Slavic languages embrace the Russian, Ukrainian, Belorussian, and Rusyn; and the main South Slavic languages are the Bulgarian, Serbian, Croatian, Slovenian, and most recently the Macedonian. During the existence of Historic Hungary (q.v.), the country's most significant Slavic languages included the Croatian, Serbian, Slovak, and Rusyn.

SLAVIC LITURGICAL LANGUAGE see CHURCH SLAVONIC.

SLAVONIA [TÓTORSZÁG]. Not to be confused with Slovenia (q.v.), Slavonia was a province of medieval Hungary (q.v.), which today constitutes the northern half of Croatia (q.v.), including the region around Zagreb (q.v.). The upper half of medieval Slavonia was located between the Drava (q.v.) and the Sava Rivers (q.v.), and the other half to the south of the Sava, but north of original Croatia on the Adriatic Sea (q.v.). In the late medieval period, after Croatia had become part of Hungary, the two provinces (Croatia and Slavonia) were merged into the autonomous Kingdom of Croatia, and the name Slavonia was applied to a more easterly region between the Drava and the Sava Rivers, to the west of Szerémség (q.v.). In the 18th century, a significant portion of Slavonia, along with northern Croatia, was formed into the Military Frontier District (q.v.) of the Habsburg Empire (q.v.). Then, along with Szerémség, it was merged into the triune Kingdom of Croatia-Slavonia-Dalmatia, which remained part of Hungary until the formation of

Yugoslavia (q.v.) in 1918. Although the traditional Hungarian name for Slavonia was *Tótország* (Tót Country), it had nothing to do with the Slovaks (q.v.), whom the Hungarians used to call Tót (plural: Tótok) until the 20th century. Today Slavonia is officially part of independent Croatia, but since the collapse of Yugoslavia in 1991, sections of it are under the occupation of the Bosnian Serbs.

SLAVS. The largest ethnic-linguistic group (c. 300 million) among the European peoples, whose language belongs to the Indo-European linguistic family and whose "original homeland" coincided with today's Belarus (Belorussia) and eastern Poland (q.v.). In the early and high Middle Ages (after the 6th century), the Slavs came to be divided into the Eastern Slavs (Russians, Ukrainians, Belorussians, Rusyns), Western Slavs (Poles, Czechs, Slovaks, Sorbians), and South Slavs (Croats, Serbs, Slovens, Macedonians, Bulgarians). Later they gave birth to numerous nationalities and subgroups, some of which have already disappeared in recent times (19th–20th c.). For nearly a millennium, Hungarians have cohabited Historic Hungary (q.v.) with the Slovaks, Croats, and Rusyns, and had close historical contacts with the Czechs, Poles, Serbs, and the Bulgarians. These Slavs have all influenced Hungarian culture in one way or another, just as the Hungarians have impacted upon the lives, languages, and cultures of these Slavic peoples.

SLOVAKIA [SLOVENSKO, ÉSZAK-MAGYARORSZÁG, FELVIDÉK]. Slovakia had no separate identity, not even in the form of an autonomous province, until the 20th century. From the early 10th century on until late 1918, it was simply the northern part of Historic Hungary (q.v.), which during the Turkish period (q.v.) was known either as Northern Hungary *(Észak-Magyarország)* (q.v.), or as the combination of Upper Hungary *(Felső-Magyarország)* (q.v.) and Lower Hungary *(Alsó-Magyarország)* (q.v.)—the former being its eastern and the latter its western part. Simultaneously, today's Slovakia was also a significant part of Habsburg-ruled Royal Hungary (q.v.).

The rise of Slovak national consciousness in the 19th century brought the Slovaks (q.v.) into a close emotional and intellectual contact with their better known ethnic-linguistic brethren, the Czechs (q.v.), with whom they hoped to create a joint state. The dismemberment of Austria-Hungary (q.v.), and therein of Historic Hungary in 1918-20, did bring about the establishment of that state in the form of Czechoslovakia (q.v.), in which Slovakia enjoyed a limited degree of autonomy. The dissolution of Czechoslovakia in 1938-39 was followed by the establishment of an independent Slovak state for the first time in history (March 14, 1939–April 3,1945). In reality, the first Slovak Republic, under the leadership of the Catholic pries, Monsignor Jozef Tiso (1887–1947), was a German vassal state with little real independence. Reestablished after World War II (q.v.), Czechoslovakia survived until the end of 1992, when it was officially split into the Czech and the Slovak Republics [Czechia and Slovakia] (January 1, 1993). Thus, after nearly six years of nominal independenceduring World War II, Slovakia now appears to have reached a position of real independence.

SLOVAKS [SZLOVÁKOK, TÓTOK]. The smallest of the three main West Slavic peoples (4.5 million) who today constitute the majority of the population of Slovakia (q.v.). Having never experienced independent statehood until the mid–20th century, Slovak nationalism is rooted in a peasant-based ethnic culture, which has many similarities with Hungarian folk culture. This is so because the Slovaks and their ancestors have lived within the confines of Historic Hungary (q.v.) for over a millennium (c.900 to 1918. Until recently, the Slovaks have been known in Hungary as *Tót* (plural: *Tótok)*—derived from the name of the German tribe *Taut,* which also gave birth to the words *Teuton, Teutonic* (German, Germanic). Since after World War I (q.v.) this term has gradually replaced by *Szlovák* (plural: *Szlovákok).* The word *Tótország* (Tót Country), however, never referred to the largely Slovak-inhabited former Northern Hungary (q.v.). Rather it was the Hungarian name of medieval Slavonia (q.v.), which is now part of Croatia (q.v.).

SLOVENIA. The territory inhabited by the Sloven tribes came under Bavarian and then Frankish rule in the 8th century. It remained part of the largely German-dominatedHoly Roman Empire (q.v.) until the empire's dissolution in 1806. In the meanwhile, however, during the late 13th through the 15th centuries, most of the Sloven provinces had become Habsburg dynastic (q.v.) possessions, and remained so until 1918, when Slovenia was made part of the new state of Yugoslavia (q.v.). Following Yugoslavia's dissolution in the early 1990s, Slovenia established itself as an independent state (June 25, 1991), and as such, it became an immediate neighbor of Hungary (q.v.). Its northeastern section houses a small Hungarian population. Slovenia is often confused with Slavonia (q.v.), a former southern province of Hungary, now part of Croatia (q.v.).

SLOVENS [SLOVENIANS]. Members of the smallest South Slavic nationality that inhabits Slovenia (q.v.). About two million strong, the Slovens speak a language that is more remote from Croatian and Serbian than the latter two are from each other. The Slovens never had an independent state until June 25, 1991.

SMALLHOLDERS' PARTY [KISGAZDAPÁRT]. The name of several peasant-oriented parties in the period since 1909, when the first such party was established under the name Independent Forty-Eighter Peasant Party *(Független Negyvennyolcas Gazdapárt).* In early 1919 this party merged with the Agricultural Party *(Földműves Párt)* of the larger landowners into the National Smallholders and Agricultural Party *(Országos Kisgazda és Földműves Párt),* which in 1922 fused into the government-sponsored United Party *(Egységes Párt)* (q.v.). In 1931 the Smallholders' Party seceded from the United Party and assumed the role of a moderate opposition under the leadership of Tibor Eckhardt (q.v.) (1932–41) and then under Endre Bajcsy-Zsilinszky (1941–44) (q.v.). Toward the end of World War II (q.v.), the leaders of the Smallholders' Party rejected both the German occupation of Hungary (q.v.) and political rule by the Arrow Cross Party (q.v.). After the war the Smallholders' Party emerged as Hungary's most popular political party, gaining an absolute majority of 57 percent in the November 1945 elections. Although by far the most popular among the electorate, the Smallholders' Party was attacked and undermined by the Communist Party (q.v.), which was supported by the Soviet occupation forces. In 1947 the leaders of the Smallholders' Party were either arrested or forced to seek asylum in the West. The remaining crypto-communists voted themselves out of existence by giving power over to the Communist Party. Reestablished in 1989, the Smallholders' Party was never able to regain its former popularity. True, in May 1990, it became a member of the ruling coalition headed by the Hungarian Democratic Forum (HDF) (q.v.), but it was plagued by its inability to relate to modern times and by ongoing party factionalism. Since the fall of the HDF-led post-communist government in 1994, the Smallholders' Party has been in opposition under the continued leadership of József Torgyán (q.v.). But because of Hungary's growing economic problems and the Socialist-led government's apparent inability to deal with them effectively, the Smallholders have become more popular.

SOCIAL DEMOCRATIC PARTY OF HUNGARY [MAGYARORSZÁGI SZOCIÁLDEMOKRATA PÁRT]. Founded in 1890 as a direct successor of the General Workers' Party *(Magyarországi Általános Munkáspárt)* of Hungary (q.v.), the Social Democratic Party was the first mainline Marxist political party in Hungary. During the post–World War I revolutions (q.v.), its left wing united with the newly established Communist Party of Hungary (q.v.). After the collapse of the Hungarian Soviet Republic (August 1, 1919) (q.v.), the Social Democratic Party (SDP) reconstituted itself and functioned throughout the interwar period (q.v.) as a legitimate leftist opposition party under the leadership of Károly Peyer (1881–1956) and Anna Kéthly (1889–1976). This period was characterized by a festering division between the party's right and left wings, the latter of which usually cooperated with the underground communist movement. At the end of World War II (q.v.), the Social Democratic Party fell into the hands of such crypto-communists as Árpád Szakasits (q.v.) and György Marosán (b.1908), who created a united front with the Communist Party. Even so, in the fall 1945 elections, the two Marxist parties were overwhelmed by the victorious Smallholders' Party (q.v.). In 1947 the SDP was purged of all of its moderate leaders, and in June 1948 it merged with the communists to form the Hungarian Workers' Party (q.v.), which imposed a monolithic communist rule over Hungary until 1956. Having gone out of existence in 1948, the SDP was reestablished in 1989. In the elections of 1990, however, it did not gain enough votes to send a representative to the Hungarian Parliament (q.v.), a feat repeated in 1994.

SOCIALIST PARTY see **HUNGARIAN SOCIALIST PARTY.**

SOLTÉSZ [SCHULTEISS]. Persons of German origin who were in charge of bringing German settlers to Hungary (q.v.) during the Middle Ages. They were especially active from the 13th century onward, and were responsible for settling many of the urban Zipsers (q.v.) in former Northern Hungary (q.v.). Later they were also placed in charge of those peasants who were involved in clearing forests and building villages around the walled cities that the German settlers had established. For being overseers, the members of the *soltész* profession received compensation from the feudal lords. A number of them also rose to the ranks of the nobility. Their position was similar to that of the *kenéz* (q.v.), who were bringing Vlach peasants and shepherds from the Balkans (q.v.) to medieval Hungary — including Transylvania (q.v.) and the Banat of Temesvár (q.v.).

SOMOGYI, FERENC (1906–95). An American-Hungarian legal and cultural historian and community leader of great influence. During the 1930s and early 1940s, Somogyi taught at the University of Pécs (q.v.) and served briefly in the Hungarian Parliament (q.v.). He left Hungary after World War II (q.v.) and emigrated to the United States in 1950, where he became one of the top intellectual leaders of the conservative-patriotic Hungarian immigrants of North America. In addition to teaching at Western Reserve University,

Somogyi was in charge of the cultural activities of the Hungarian Association of Cleveland (q.v.), and of the scholarly activities of the Árpád Academy (q.v.). He was a detachedand objective scholar, an influential publicist, and an inspiring public personality, who refused to stray into low-grade emigré politics. He kept the institutions under his control on firm ground, away from extremism, and he influenced hundreds of young Hungarian-Americans in their life careers. In addition to his hundreds of popular articles, his most influential works published abroad include *Mission: History of the Hungarians (Küldetés: A magyarság története)* (1973), and *Faith and Fate: A Short Cultural History of the Hungarian People through a Millennium* (coauthored with Lél Somogyi,1977). Somogyi's most significant works in legal and constitutional history were published in Hungary and include *The Institute of Entail and Feudal Property Law (Az ősiség intézménye és a hűbéri vagyonjog)* (1931), *Testamentary Disposition according to the Civil Law of Our Nobility from 1000 to 1715 (Végrendelkezés nemesi magánjogunk szerint 1000-től 1715-ig)* (1937), *Patrimony and Aviticitas (Családiság és ősiség)* (1938), *Sociopolitical Legislation before Werbőczy (Társadalompolitikai törvényalkotás Werbőczy előtt)* (1943), and *Sociopolitical Legislation after Werbőczy (Társadalompolitikai törvényalkotás Werbőczy után)* (1944).

SOPRON [SCARBANTIA, ÖDENBURG]. A city of about 60,000 on the Austro-Hungarian border, which used to be the "capital" of Western Hungary (q.v.) until that province was attached to Austria (q.v.) after World War I (q.v.) and then renamed "Burgenland" (q.v.). Although Sopron had a significant German-speaking population, in 1921—in the only plebiscite permitted by the victorious Allies for defeated Hungary—the city voted to remain part of Hungary and thus earned the denomination *Civitas Fidelissimus* (Most Faithful City). On August 19, 1989, it was in the vicinity of Sopron where the "Pan European Picnic" took place that was accompanied by the opening of the border for the East German refugees who opted to go to Austria (q.v.) and then to Germany (q.v.). This daring act on the part of the Hungarian political leadership was the beginning of the collapse of communist system in East Central Europe (q.v.).

SOROS, GEORGE [GYÖRGY] (b.1930). A Hungarian-American billionaire, philanthropist, and founding president of the highly successful Quantum Fund (1969), which in mid-1995 was worth about twelve billion U.S. dollars and through which George Soros had became one of the most successful financiers of modern times. (In October 1992, he made a billion dollars in a period of only one week.) Starting with 1981—when he had already made his fortune—Soros began to establish a series of "open society" foundations geared to the countries of East Central Europe (q.v.) and the former Soviet Union (q.v.). The goal of these foundations was, and still is, to undermine totalitarianism and to advance the cause of economic and political liberalism in a part of the world that for many decades had been under the rule of communism. This is also the goal of the Soros-founded Central European University (q.v.), with centers in Budapest (q.v.) and Prague (q.v.). This postgraduate-level institution is geared to the study of human society, economy, and historical evolution from the vantage point of the present and the future. To follow up his earlier philanthropic activities, in 1996 George Soros gave away 350 million dollars (about three times as much as Bill Gates, known as the "world's richest man"), making him by far the world's most generous philanthropist.

SOUTHERN HUNGARY [DÉL-MAGYARORSZÁG, DÉL-VIDÉK]. An ill-defined area on the southern frontiers of Historic Hungary (q.v.) whose outlines changed along with the country's fortunes. During the 18th and the 19th centuries, it was generally thought to include the former territories of the Banat of Temesvár (q.v.), Bácska (q.v.), and Szerémség (q.v.). After Historic Hungary's dismemberment and the establishment of Yugoslavia (q.v.), the term Southern Hungary (Dél-Magyarország) was replaced by the expression "Southern Region" *(Délvidék),* which was used to refer to the province of Voivodina (q.v.).

SOUTH SLAVS see SLAVS.

SOVIETS. This term has two distinct meanings. In its original form it refers to the workers' and peasants' councils established in Russia (q.v.) during the revolutions of 1905 and 1917, and in Hungary in 1919 and in the period between 1950 and 1990. In another sense, it is a synonymous term for the government of the Soviet Union (q.v.). Its Hungarian version, *tanács* (plural: *tanácsok)* was used in the name of the Hungarian Soviet Republic *(Magyar Tanács-köztársaság).* After 1950 it became part of the local government introduced by the communists, which survived until 1990. In that year these councils *(tanácsok)* were replaced by new autonomous bodies known as *önkormányzat* (self-government) (q.v.).

SOVIET UNION [USSR] (1922–91). A successor state of the Russian Empire (q.v.), which came into being officially on December 30, 1922. It was the result of the overthrow of the Czarist Regime and the consolidation of political power in the hands of the Bolsheviks. It disintegrated and went out of existence on December 31, 1991. After World War II (q.v.), the Soviet Union rose to be one of the two superpowers in the world, which extended its control over East Central Europe (q.v.), including Hungary (q.v.). The Hungarians rose in rebellion against Soviet control in 1956. Although defeated, the Hungarian Revolution of 1956 (q.v.) shook up the monolithic nature of the Soviet bloc, and was one of the important factors that led to the decline of Soviet control over the communist world. This loss of control was accompanied by an increasingly backward economy and technology, as well as by a growing demand for national self-determination on the part of its national and ethnic minorities. These factors all combined to lead to the gradual decline and disintegration of the Soviet Union and to the simultaneous loosening of its control over Hungary. Although the Soviet domination was briefer than the Ottoman rule (q.v.), most Hungarians view it as having been just as destructive.

SPAHIS. Members of the Ottoman Turkish (q.v.) feudal cavalry, also known as *timaroits* (q.v.), who held their estates *(timars)* (q.v.) in nonhereditary tenure. They constituted the backbone of the Ottoman Armed Forces and had a significant role in the conquest of Hungary (q.v.). In the course of time, a number of these *spahis* or *timaroits* established close relationship with the local population and were able to transform their nonhereditary *timars* lands into hereditary *chiftlik* estates—especially in the Balkans (q.v.). The *spahis* reappear time after time in Hungarian lore and literature of and about the Turkish period (q.v.) in Hungarian history.

SPEYER AGREEMENT (1570). An agreement between Maximilian I (II) (q.v.) and John Sigismund (q.v.), in which the latter renounced his Hungarian royal title, acknowledged Maximilian as his ruler and overlord, and reasserted that Transylvania (q.v.) and the Partium (q.v.) are integral parts of the Kingdom of Hungary (q.v.). In return for these concessions, Maximilian acknowledged John Sigismund as the prince of Transylvania with hereditary rights in the male line to that province as well as to the Partium, but with the condition that upon the dying out of the Zápolya family (q.v.), Transylvania would revert to the kings of Hungary, that is, to the Habsburgs (q.v.). Soon after the ratification of this Speyer Agreement, John Sigismund died without an heir (March 14, 1571), and the Transylvanian estates refused to abide by its terms. They elected Stephen Báthory (q.v.) as their prince and thus set the stage for the continued warfare between the Habsburg kings of Hungary and the Hungarian princes of Transylvania.

STAHEL, JULIUS H. [GYULA SZÁMWALD] (1825–1912). A major general in the Union Army during the Civil War (1861–65), and the first Hungarian to win a Congressional Medal of Honor (1893). Born as Gyula Számwald in Szeged, Hungary, in 1825, two decades later he moved to Pest (later part of Budapest) (q.v.), where he became a partner in Gusztáv Emich's bookstore and publishing firm. In that capacity he became a friend of the March Youth (q.v.), including Hungary's great revolutionary poet, Sándor Petőfi (q.v.).

Stahel/Számwald participated in the Hungarian Revolution of 1848–49 (q.v.), after which he fled to the German Confederation (q.v.). Returning in the early 1850s, he left again in 1855 for personal reasons. In London he worked as a journalist and changed his name to Stahel. In 1856 he emigrated to the United States, where he pursued journalism until joining the Union Army in 1861. His activities in defending the nation's capital against the South earned him a series of promotions as well as President Lincoln's personal gratitude. Following the Civil War, Stahel served in various diplomatic posts in Japan and China (1865–69, 1877–85). Between 1869 and 1877, he worked as a surveyor of mines, while in 1885 he became an insurance company executive. Following his death in New York in 1912, Stahel's papers, decorations, and many personal belongings were deposited in the Hungarian National Museum and in the National Széchenyi Library (q.v.) in Budapest.

STEPHEN I [ST. STEPHEN, SZENT ISTVÁN] (c.967/75–1038). The last ruling prince (r.997–1000) and the first Christian king (r.1000–38), who is revered as the founder of the Christian Kingdom of Hungary (A.D.1000). The son of Prince Géza (q.v.) and originally known under the name of Vajk, he was given the name Stephen at the time of his baptism and confirmation by St. Adalbert (q.v.) in the middle of the 990s. In 995 or 996, Stephen married Gisella (q.v.), daughter of Prince Henry of Bavaria (r.955– 76, 985–95). Then, after his father's death in 997, he succeeded to the Hungarian throne. Stephen's accession, however, was contested by his older male relative, Koppány (q.v.), on the basis of the principle of seniority (q.v.). Koppány was supported by those Hungarians who were trying to preserve tribal rights and the ancient Hungarian pagan faith, and who resented the influx of Western influences. Stephen defeated Koppány at Veszprém (q.v.) with the help of a detachment of German knights and thereby established his preeminence within the Árpád dynasty (q.v.). Wishing to make his country part of the community of Christian nations, Stephen asked for and received a crown from Pope Sylvester II (r.999–1003), with which he was crowned king on Christmas day in the year A.D.

1000. Although this was done with the simultaneous approval of the Holy Roman Emperor Otto III (r.983–1002), Hungary did not become a vassal state of either the Papacy or the empire.

Following his coronation, King Stephen was forced to defend his royal powers against several powerful tribal leaders, among them his maternal uncle, Gyula (q.v.) of Transylvania (q.v.), as well as against Ajtony (q.v.) of the Trans-Tisza region (q.v.). His defeat of these challengers was followed by the organization of Hungarian state and church administration. This included the establishment of the civil administrative system based on several dozen royal counties (q.v.), each of them headed by an *ispán* or *comes* (q.v.). It also included the creation of two archbishoprics (Esztergom and Kalocsa) and eight bishoprics (Veszprém, Győr, Pécs, Transylvania, Eger, Csanád, Bihar, and Vác). To advance the cause of Christian faith and learning, he founded at least three additional Benedictine monasteries (Zalavár, Bakonybél, and Pécsvárad) besides the already existing Monastery of Pannonhalma (q.v.). He likewise ordered the construction of churches and decreed that groups of settlements (each consisting of at least ten villages) should pool their resources to support a parish priest and a congregation. Although Stephen had opted for Catholicism (q.v.), he also tolerated Byzantine Christianity (q.v.). As a sovereign ruler, he minted coins, issued royal decrees and charters, and ordered the collection of Hungarian laws into two separate law codes (c.1001 and 1030s). He likewise ordered the preparation of a collection of moral teachings, known as St. Stephen's *Admonitions (Intelmek)*, allegedly for the education of his son and heir, St. Emeric (q.v.).

In foreign affairs Stephen pursued a policy of friendship toward the Holy Roman Empire (q.v.), which was easy to do during the first quarter of the 11th century because of his excellent relationship with his brother-in-law, Emperor Henry II (r.1002–24). The death of Henry and the accession of Conrad II (r.1024–39), however, led to the deterioration of this relationship. But Conrad's efforts to conquer Hungary and make it a vassal state of his empire, however, were repeatedly repulsed by King Stephen. He similarly ejected Bolesław the Brave (r.992–1025) of Poland (q.v.) from northwestern Hungary

(1010), and then allied himself with his erstwhile enemy to intervene into the internal affairs of the Principality of Kiev (q.v.). Stephen also drove out the Pechenegs (q.v.) from Transylvania (q.v.), and intervened into the affairs of Bulgaria (q.v.) (1014) as the ally of the Byzantine emperor, Basil II (r.963–1025).

As his only son, Emeric, died in an accident in 1031, Stephen named his Italian nephew, Peter Orseolo (Peter I) (q.v.), the son of the doge of Venice, as his heir to the Hungarian throne. This resulted in an assassination attempt on Stephen's life on the part of his cousin, Vazul (q.v.), who then was blinded and exiled along with this three sons. Among the latter were two future kings of Hungary, Andrew I (q.v.) and Béla I (q.v.).

King Stephen died after forty-one years of reign, and was laid to rest in the Royal Basilica of Székesfehérvár(q.v.). Having laid the foundations of a Christian Hungarian Kingdom, King Stephen had become a legend already in his own lifetime. But his cult grew even more rapidly after his death, leading to his canonization—along with Prince Emeric (q.v.) and Bishop Gerard (q.v.)—barely forty-five years after his death in 1083. At the time of his exhumation, his right arm was found to have been preserved. It soon became an object of adoration. Although later cut into several parts—portions of it ending up in Lemberg (L'viv) (q.v.), Vienna (q.v.), and Ragusa (q.v.)—St. Stephen's hand is still preserved today in Budapest in the cathedral that bears his name. In addition to being revered as a saint, King Stephen is also viewed today as the founding father of Hungary and of Hungarian constitutionalism (q.v.).

STEPHEN II [ISTVÁN]   (1101–31). King of Hungary (r.1116–31) and son of King Coloman (q.v.) and Sicilian-Norman Princess Felicia. Stephen II was forced to fight throughout his reign unsuccessful wars against the Czechs (q.v.), Venetians (q.v.), and Byzantines (q.v.), and at the same time ward off the efforts of his uncle, Álmos the Blind (c.1070–1127), to gain the throne on the basis of seniority (q.v.). Not having any children of his own, Stephen II named as his heir his cousin, the future King Béla II (q.v.), who was the son of his deceased rival. Stephen II's rule represents a tragic and unsuccessful period in Hungary's history.

STEPHEN III [ISTVÁN] (1147–72). King of Hungary (r.1162–72), son of King Géza II (q.v.) and Princess Eufrosonia of Kiev (q.v.), whose relatively short reign was spent in fighting against Byzantine Emperor Manuel I's (r.1143–80) designs upon Hungary (q.v.). Manuel supported several of Stephen III's uncles against him. Two of them—Ladislas II (q.v.) and Stephen IV (q.v.)—were actually acknowledged rival kings of Hungary, claiming the throne on the basis of the principle of seniority (q.v.). Even though Ladislas II died in 1163 and Stephen IV was driven out of the country a few months later, the struggle continued until the childless Emperor Manuel accepted Stephen III's brother—the future King Béla III (q.v.)—as the heir to the Byzantine throne (1163). Following the exiled Stephen IV's death in 1165, the war between Hungary and Byzantium (q.v.) was resumed, this time because Emperor Manuel had put Prince Béla forth as a rival claimant to the throne of Hungary. To gain the support of the Catholic Church (q.v.) and the Papacy, in 1169 Stephen III gave up his right to invest the bishops and abbots in Hungary. He is also known for his support of Hungary's urbanization by granting special rights to Walloon settlers in the royal city of Székesfehérvár (q.v.). Stephen III probably died of poisoning, and was succeeded by his brother Béla, who in the meanwhile—because of the birth of a child to Emperor Manuel—had ceased to be the heir to the Byzantine throne.

STEPHEN IV [ISTVÁN] (c.1133–65). The third son of King Béla II the Blind (q.v.) and Princess Helena of Serbia, and the uncle and rival of Stephen III (q.v.). During his short reign (January-June 1163), all his activities centered on trying to retain his throne against his nephew. After fleeing to Byzantium (q.v.), Stephen became a vassal of Emperor Manuel (r.1143–80). Yet, in spite of the latter's support, he was never able to regain the Hungarian throne. He died of poisoning and was buried at Székesfehérvár (q.v.).

STEPHEN V [ISTVÁN] (1239–72). King of Hungary (r.1270–72), son of King Béla IV (q.v.) and Princes Maria of Nicaea, and a rebellious junior king (q.v.) to his father. Stephen V's short reign signaled the beginning of the decline of Hungary (q.v.) under the last members of the Árpádian dynasty (q.v.). Although crowned king already in his father's lifetime (c.1246), who named him to various important posts—Prince of Slavonia (q.v.), Prince of Transylvania (q.v.), Prince of Styria, and finally the Junior King of Hungary (1262)—Stephen still turned against his father. During the 1260s he initiated a series of wars against Béla IV (q.v.), which weakened the country, but were never really resolved. After his father's death in 1270, Stephen V ascended the throne, but he soon faced similar rebellions on the part of the powerful Baron Joachim Gutkeled, supported by his own wife, Erzsébet the Cuman. Stephen V died in the midst of these struggles and was buried on the Island of the Hares, now known as St. Margaret's Island in Budapest (q.v.).

SUB-CARPATHIA see **CARPATHO-RUTHENIA.**

SUCCESSOR STATES. This term refers to the states—other than Austria and Hungary—that had been carved fully or partially out of former Austro-Hungarian Empire (q.v.) after World War I (q.v.). These include the completely new states of Czechoslovakia (q.v.) and Yugoslavia (q.v.), the much-enlarged Romania (q.v.), and the reestablished Poland (q.v.). In the early 1990s, two of these states were further fragmented. Czechoslovakia was divided into the Czech Republic (q.v.) and Slovakia (q.v.), while Yugoslavia disintegrated into Slovenia (q.v.), Croatia (q.v.), Bosnia (q.v.), Macedonia, and "Little Yugoslavia" (q.v.)—that is, Serbia (q.v.), Montenegro, Voivodina (q.v.), and Kossovo.

SÜLEYMAN [SULIMAN, SOLIMAN, SZULIMÁN] (1594–1566). The greatest sultan of the Ottoman Empire (r.1520–66) who defeated the Hungarians at the Battle of Mohács (q.v.) in 1526, conquered Buda (q.v.) in 1541, and then took control over much of Hungary (q.v.), either directly (see Turkish Hungary), or indirectly by making Transylvania (q.v.) into a vassal state. Süleyman tried to take Vienna (q.v.) unsuccessfully in 1529, and then again in 1566. But on the second occasion he died while besieging the fortress of Szigetvár (q.v.), defended by Count Miklós Zrínyi (q.v.), and he never got to Vienna.

SULTAN. Royal or imperial title in the oriental, especially Islamic, countries. This was one of the many titles of the rulers of the Ottoman Empire (q.v.), who conquered Hungary (q.v.). The early rulers were called emirs (q.v.), but starting with Murad I (r.1360-89) they wore the title sultan until 1922.

SUMMÁS. The collective appellation of landless agricultural workers in the period between serf emancipation in 1848 (q.v.) and the end of World War II in 1945 (q.v.). They generally hired themselves out for seasonal work during harvest time in return for a set price ("summa") that was usually paid in kind. In addition, during their period of employment, they were also supplied with lodging and food. These migrant workers were usually hired in groups and only by the owners or managers of large estates. They represented the lowest strata of the Hungarian peasantry (q.v.).

SÜTŐ, ANDRÁS (b.1927). One of the great Hungarian playwrights, essayists, and novelists, who is also a top ideological leader of the two-and-a-half million Hungarians in Transylvania (q.v.). Many of Sütő's writings deal with the life of his own people, who were thrust into a minority status after World War I (q.v.). Other pieces tackle the question of human intolerance toward religious, ethnic, national, or linguistic differences. Sütő has been one of the recognized spokesmen of Hungarians in Romania (q.v.) ever since the early 1970s, when the Ceausescu Regime increased its assimilative pressures on the Hungarian minorities (q.v.). But Sütő's prominence increased even more since the overthrow of Nicolae Ceausescu in December 1989. This is so, partially because of Sütő's increased international recognition (e.g., the Herder Prize, and other similar prizes) and partially because of his growing involvement in the attempt to expose the Romanian Government's continued anti-Hungarian policies.

SWABIANS   [SVÁBOK]. One of the three main groups of German settlers (q.v.) in Hungary (q.v.)—the other two being the Zipsers (q.v.) and the Transylvanian Saxons (q.v.). The so-called "Swabians" —most of whom actually came from the Palatinate and from Saxony—were settled in Hungary during the 18th century. They were brought in to repopulate the regions that had been depopulated during the series of wars and revolutions in the late 17th and early 18th centuries, such as the Thököly Uprising (q.v.), the Liberation Wars (q.v.), and the Rákóczi War of Liberation (q.v.). The Habsburgs (q.v.) also wanted to have a sizable German-speaking, Catholic population upon whom they could always rely.

The Swabians came in two waves during the 1710s and 1770s–80s. They were settled in south-central Hungary, that is, in Bácska (q.v.) and the Banat of Temesvár (q.v.). Others were settled in the depopulated towns and villages of eastern Trans-Danubia (q.v.). The larger towns included Pécs (q.v.), Buda (q.v.), and Pest (q.v.)— the latter two now being part of Budapest (q.v.). During the late 1930s and early 1940s, many of the Swabians fell under the influence of Hitler's propaganda about alleged German superiority. Thus, after World War II (q.v.)—based on the terms of the Potsdam Agreement (July–August 1945)—a significant number of them were expelled from Hungary. During their two centuries' stay, most of the Swabians retained their German language and culture, and generally represented the wealthier portion of Hungary's peasant and urban population. Many of them also became Magyarized (q.v.) and came to constitute a significant portion of the intellectual and urban middle classes in late 19th- and 20th-century Hungary.

SZABAD, GYÖRGY (b.1924). A prominent Hungarian historian and one of the founding leaders of the Hungarian Democratic Forum (HDF) (q.v.), which was the dominant political party in Hungary's first post-Communist government (1990–94). During the prime ministership of József Antall (q.v.), Szabad served as one of the party's top leaders, as well as the president of the Hungarian Parliament (q.v.). Having been trained as a historian, before becoming involved in politics, Szabad taught at the University of Budapest (q.v.) (1954–90), rising to the rank of a full professor in 1970. He specialized in 19th-century Hungarian political history and his major works include: *On the Path between the Revolution and the Compromise, 1860–61 (Forradalom és kiegyezés válaszútján, 1860–61* (1967), *Hungarian Political Trends, 1849--1867* (1977), *Kossuth's Political Career(Kossuth politikai pályája)* (1977), *The Age of Absolutism, 1849–1867 (Az önkényuralom kora, 1849-1867)* (1979), and *The Question of Independent Hungarian Statehood in Age of Bourgeois Transformation (Magyarország önálló államiságának kérdése a polgári átalakulás korában)* (1986). After the HDF Government lost the elections in 1994, Szabad retained both his leadership in the party, as well as his membership in the Hungarian Parliament. At the time of the party split in March 1995, he opted to join the more liberal Hungarian Democratic People's Party (q.v.)

SZABÓ, DEZSŐ (1879–1945). One of the spiritual founding fathers of interwar Hungarian Populism (q.v.), Szabó was a novelist, essayist, short-story writer, and a very popular publicist. A product of the intellectually elite Eötvös College (q.v.), Szabó initially published in such progressive literary and sociological periodicals as the West *(Nyugat)* and the *Twentieth Century (Huszadik Század)*. But during World War I (q.v.) he switched to a conservative-nationalist-populist orientation. Although a protester and a reformer by inclination, Szabó was very disappointed by the events of 1918–1919, especially with the Red Terror (q.v.) connected with Béla Kun's (q.v.) communist regime. He expressed his displeasure in the novel *The Annihilated Village (Az elsodort falu)* (1919), which made him extremely popular in interwar Hungary (q.v.).

During the 1920s Szabó tried his hand in publishing his own periodicals and lived mostly off his writings. He held regular public meetings and lectures in some of the main cafés of Budapest (q.v.) and began to assemble a group of devoted followers. For a while he played around with ideas of "Hungarian racial purity," "ethnic collectivism," and anti-Semitism, but by the 1930s he turned his fulminations against Nazism and the pro-German elements in Hungarian society. His relationship with the regime of Admiral Horthy (q.v.) soon deteriorated, primarily because of his social radicalism that emphasized the need to uplift the Hungarian peasants. From the mid-1930s to the early 1940s, Szabó aired his social and political views in a pamphlet series entitled *Essays by Matthias Goose (Ludas Mátyás Füzetek)* (80 parts, 1934–1942), each of which was between 60 to 150 pages long. A selection of these essays was also published separately in a three-volume work entitled *The Whole Horizon (Egész látóhatár)* (1939). Having lost his freedom of expression during World War II (q.v.), Szabó also lost some of his popularity. He died a lonely eccentric during the siege of Budapest in early 1945. During the four and a half decades of communist rule, Dezső Szabó's writings could not be published. But after the fall of communism, his popularity surged again, at least momentarily.

SZABÓ, ERVIN (1877–1918). Librarian, sociologist, and one of the Hungarian pioneers of Marxist thought. Szabó was a strong supporter of modern literary tendencies in early-20th-century Hungary (q.v.), and he was the first to translate and to publish a selection of Marx's and Engels's writings (2 vols., 1905–09). In the period of World War I (q.v.), while serving as the director of the Budapest City Library (1911–18)—which was named after him in 1945— Szabó was an antiwar activist. His main works include *Social and Party Struggles in the Hungarian Revolution of 1848–49 (Társadalmi és pártharcok a 48–49-es magyar forradalomban)*(1921), and his *Selected Writings (Válogatott írásai)* (1958).

SZABÓ, IVÁN (b.1934). The founding-president of the Hungarian Democratic People's Party (HDPP) (q.v.), formed in March 1996, when the small "Liberal" wing of the Hungarian Democratic Forum (HDF) (q.v.) split from the mainline "Populist" wing. Iván Szabó has been a member of the HDF ever since its foundation in 1987.

During the first post-communist government of József Antall (q.v.) he served as the minister of industry and commerce (1991-93) and the minister of financial affairs (1993-94). Between 1994 and March 1996, Szabó also served as the leader of the MDF opposition in the Hungarian Parliament (q.v.).

SZAKASITS, ÁRPÁD (1888–1965). A pioneer socialist, crypto-communist, and one of the top leaders and general secretary (1938–42, 1945–48) of the Hungarian Social Democratic Party (q.v.). For nearly two years after the communist takeover of power, he was the president of Hungary (1948–50). Although Szakasits had sold his own party and his own comrades to the communists, he was still arrested in 1950 and imprisoned for life. He was rehabilitated in the spring of 1956, yet he still turned against the anti-Soviet Hungarian Revolution of 1956 (q.v.). Following the defeat of the revolution, Szakasits participated in the consolidation of the Kádár Regime (q.v.), for which he was rewarded with various high positions. In 1958 he became the president of the Federation of Hungarian Journalists, in 1959 he was made a member of the Central Committee of the Hungarian Workers' (Communist) Party (1959–65) (q.v), and in 1960 he was appointed to the presidency of the Hungarian Peace Council. Szakasits may have started out as a convinced socialist, but at the end he was the leading instrument in the communist destruction of the Hungarian Social Democratic Party (q.v.).

SZÁLASI COUP (October 15, 1995). This coup d'etat occurred in wake of Regent Horthy's (q.v.) proclamation of an armistice with the Soviet Union (q.v.). To prevent this armistice from going into effect, with German help, Szálasi (q.v.) forced Horthy to resign and had himself sworn in as Hungary's "national leader"(*nemzetvezető*) and prime minister.

SZÁLASI, FERENC (1897–1946). The founding president of the Hungarian Arrow Cross Party (q.v.), and for a few months at the end of the World War II (q.v.) (October 16, 1944–April 4, 1945), the "national leader" *(nemzetvezető)*—a sort of regent cum prime minister—of Hungary (q.v.). Born into a family of professional soldiers, Szálasi was destined for the military from his early youth. He began his military career in 1915 and became a member of the General Staff in 1925 with the rank of a captain. In 1933 he was promoted to the rank of a major.

It was during the late 1920s that Szálasi began to develop ideas about his calling to lead the nation out of the chaos into which the Treaty of Trianon (q.v.) had thrust her. In 1930 he joined the Federation of Hungarian Life *(Magyar Élet Szövetsége)*, a secret society where he soon assumed the leadership. During the early 1930s he authored a "Military Program" for Hungary, which he offered to virtually every political party. But as this program was really a plan for the creation of a totalitarian state, he found no takers. In 1935 Szálasi retired from the armed forces with the intention of devoting his life to the implementation of his program. He immediately founded the Party of National Will *(Nemzet Akaratának Pártja,* which, however, failed completely in the 1936 elections. Szálasi's assertive political activities following this defeat at the polls landed him briefly in prison (1937–38). But in 1939 he founded a new political organization, the Arrow Cross Party (q.v.), which ultimately became the tool of mass destruction toward the end of World War II (q.v.).

During the war, Szálasi had an on again, off again relationship with the Germans (q.v.), who generally distrusted him. Yet, following the German occupation of Hungary (q.v.) (April 19, 1944), when they found no other willing partner, they overthrew Regent Horthy (q.v.) and helped Szálasi to power (October 15-16, 1944). By that time the war was already lost for Germany (q.v.) and her allies, yet Szálasi initiated Hungary's total economic and military mobilization. By doing so, he became the primary instrument of the country's near-total destruction. Simultaneously, he also introduced Arrow Cross political terror that led to the incarceration and death of many tens of thousands of Jews and other opponents of his Fascist regime. With much of the country already under Soviet control, in December 1944 Szálasi transferred the seat of his shrinking power base to the western border city of Sopron (q.v.). Soon thereafter he fled to Germany. Arrested by the U.S. forces, Szálasi was returned to Hungary, where he was tried and executed as a war criminal.

SZÁLASI REGIME (1944–45). The five-and-a-half months (October 16, 1944–April 4, 1995), when Szálasi (q.v.) was officially (although towards the end only nominally) the "leader" and prime minister of Hungary (q.v.). The first three months of the regime were characterized by the rule of terror on the part of the members of the Arrow Cross Party (q.v.), who completed the Hungarian Holocaust (q.v.). During the last two months, Szálasi and his government were already in Germany (q.v.), waiting for Hitler's new "miracle weapon," which never came. From late December 1944, the actual power was in the hands of a Soviet-sponsored Provisional Government and Provisional National Assembly (q.v.) located in the city of Debrecen (q.v.), which governed over an ever increasing segment of Hungary.

SZAMUELY, TIBOR (1890–1919). A journalist and communist activist and agitator, who during the short life of the Hungarian Soviet Republic (q.v.) was the assistant people's commissar of military affairs, as well as the president of the Summary Courts ("Committees behind the Front") established for the purposes of eliminating the regime's political opponents. As such, Szamuely was responsible for much of the violence of the Red Terror (q.v.). After the overthrow of Béla Kun's (q.v.) communist regime, he fled to Austria (q.v.), but fearing retaliation at the hands of the anti-communist white forces, he committed suicide on the day of his flight (August 2, 1919).

SZÁMWALD, GYULA see **STAHEL, JULIUS H.**

SZAPOLYAI, JÁNOS see **JOHN ZÁPOLYA, JOHN I.**

SZÁRSZÓ CONFERENCES (1942, 1943, 1993, 1996). The first meeting of Hungarian Populist (q.v.) intellectuals, sponsored by the Soli Deo Gloria Protestant student organization at the village of Szárszó, took place between June 29 and July 6, 1942. The second and more important conference occurred a year later between August 23 and 29, 1943. This second conference was organized by the director of the Hungarian Life Publishing House in Budapest, Sándor Püski (q.v.), and co-sponsored by the Protestant Soli Deo Gloria, the National Federation of Catholic Agrarian Youth Associations *(Katolikus Agrárifjúsági Legényegyletek Országos Testülete),* and several other Populist organizations. The there-assembled Populist intellectuals debated Hungary's future in light of the country's impending defeat in World War II (q.v.). But as they were divided by along ideological lines, they could not agree on a common course of action. Some of them were attached to rightist nationalism, while others advocated an alliance with socialism, and even communism. The middle course—that is, the so-called "Third Road" (q.v.) approach—was represented by László Németh (q.v.). On the fiftieth anniversary of this second conference, Püski organized the Third Szárszó Conference (1993), which reflected the renewed split between Populism (q.v.) and Urbanism (q.v.). This was also evident at the Fourth Szárszó Conference organized by Püski in Budapest (q.v.), which mirrored the increasing loss of popularity and political power by the advocates of Populism.

SZATMÁR, PEACE OF (1711). The treaty that ended the Rákóczi War of Liberation (q.v.). It was agreed upon and signed, while Prince Rákóczi (q.v.) was absent in Poland (q.v.), by his commanding general Count Sándor Károlyi (q.v.) and the Habsburg Imperial general Count János Pálffy (q.v.). Given the eight-year-long war that preceded the treaty, and the hopelessness of Rákóczi's cause, it was a reasonable agreement. Should Rákóczi have agreed to its terms, he would have been granted amnesty and could have retained all his possessions, with the exception of those castles that were also military fortresses. The same applied to the properties of his supporters and to the widows of his deceased companions. The treaty also proclaimed a general amnesty for everyone involved in the war. The king promised to uphold the constitutional rights of Hungary (q.v.) and Transylvania (q.v.), as well as the special privileges of the Hajdú (q.v.), Cuman (q.v.), and Jazyg (q.v.) towns and districts. Thereafter, any real or alleged violation of the rights of the Hungarian Estates (q.v.) were to be brought before the king through regular constitutional channels. The treaty also stipulated that should Prince Rákóczi (q.v.) decline to accept its terms and fail to return to Hungary, those terms would still be implemented. Rákóczi declined to go along with the Treaty of Szatmár, wherefore he went into exile and died twenty-four years later in Turkey.

SZDSZ see FEDERATION OF FREE DEMOCRATS.

SZÉCHÉNYI, COUNT FERENC [FRANCIS] (1754–1820). The founder of the Hungarian National Museum (1802) and the National Széchényi Library (q.v.), vice lord chief justice of Hungary (q.v.) (1800), and the father of the great national reformer, Count István Széchenyi (q.v.). In contrast to most other members of his class, during the 1780s, Count Ferenc Széchényi was an all-out supporter of Joseph II's (q.v.) social and political reforms. He remained an advocate of moderate reform even after the violence of the French Revolution had disenchanted many other reformers. Captivated by the ideas of national revival, during the late 18th and early 19th centuries, Széchényi became a strong supporter of Hungarian culture and learning, spending significant sums to aid their development. In 1802 he offered his large collection of books, manuscripts, art works, and other Hungarica material to a proposed new museum and library. Once established, he supported these institutions financially until the very end of his life. It should be noted here that Count Ferenc Széchényi wrote his name with two diacritical marks, while his son, Count István Széchenyi, with only one. This difference also applies to the institutions connected with their names, such as the National Széchényi Library and the Széchenyi Chainbridge in Budapest (q.v.)

SZÉCHENYI, COUNT ISTVÁN [STEPHEN] (1791–1860). The son of Count Ferenc Széchényi (q.v.), the founder of the Hungarian Academy of Sciences (q.v.) (1825), and the initiator, moving spirit, and greatest personality of the Hungarian Reform Period (q.v.) (1825–48). In the years after the Napoleonic Period, Széchenyi crisscrossed much of Western Europe and was very impressed by its social, economic, intellectual, and technological development—especially that of England and France. Based on these experiences, he decided to devote his life to the modernization of Hungary (q.v.) on the West European model. He realized that to achieve this goal, he would first have to convince the members of his own social class, the Hungarian aristocracy (q.v.), about the benefits of modernization. His initial efforts included the introuction of horse racing and scientific horse breeding (1822), the foundation of the First Horse Breeding Association (1825), laying the foundations of the Hungarian Academy of Sciences (1825), establishing the National Casino (1827) in the city of Pest (Budapest) (q.v.), where members of his class could meet to discuss issues of modernization and reforms, and advocating the idea of a capitalist economy based on the use of credit.

Széchenyi promoted his reform ideas through a series of books that he authored, including *About Horses (Lovakrul)* (1828), *Credit (Hitel)* (1830), *Clarity (Világ)* (1831), and *Conditions (Stádium)* (1833)—the last of which was published abroad and then smuggled back to Hungary. In these works Széchenyi pleaded for the termination of the remnants of feudalism, including serfdom (q.v.), and for the introduction of a modern social and economic system, based on broad popular representation and on the principles of capitalism. Although he had many opponents, Széchenyi pushed on with his reform schemes. During the 1830s he introduced steam shipping on the Danube (q.v.) (1831), and established the first Hungarian Commercial Bank (1832), the first rolling mill (1832), and the first Hungarian shipyard at Óbuda (q.v.) (1836). At the same time, he undertook various plans for land reclamations, canal building, regulation of the Danube (1835–37), and the introduction of the silk industry and scientific viticulture. He initiated and pushed through the construction of the Chain Bridge (now called Széchenyi Chain Bridge) connecting the twin cities of Buda and Pest (1841–48), flood control projects on the Tisza River (q.v.) (1845–46), and steam shipping on Lake Balaton (q.v.) (1846).

While engaged in these modernization projects, Széchenyi was also active in politics, both at the Hungarian Reform Diets (q.v.) and in the political debates taking place outside the diets. During the 1840s, he increasingly disagreed with the radicals, who wanted to go far beyond the liberal reforms that he had championed. Thus, whereas Kossuth (q.v.) and his supporters were increasingly thinking about separation from Austria (q.v.), Széchenyi was convinced that such a separation would be a national catastrophe, both from a political and from an economic point of view. It would place the Hungarians at the mercy of their national minorities, who collectively were in majority in Historic Hungary (q.v.), and it would also make the country the permanent economic backwater of Europe. This disagreement led to a number of political debates with Kossuth and his supporters, in which Széchenyi came forth as the supporter of rational and systematic reforms, but at the same time the champion of the unity of a reorganized Habsburg Empire (q.v.), in which Hungary would play a significant role. Széchenyi feared revolution and believed that resorting to violence would have catastrophic results for Hungary. Yet, he still participated in the first revolutionary government headed by Count Lajos Batthyány (q.v.) (April–September 1848), but he did so precisely because it had been sanctioned by King Ferdinand V (q.v.). The coming of violence in the fall of 1848, however, forced him to withdraw from the government and also pushed him toward mental instability.

In September 1848 Széchenyi left for Austria (q.v.) and spent the remaining twelve years of his life in a sanatorium in Döbling in the vicinity of Vienna (q.v.). While recuperating there, he still wrote a number of political works that were critical about post-revolutionary absolutism (q.v.) connected with the early years of the reign of Francis Joseph (q.v.) and of his minister of interior, Alexander Bach (q.v.). His most influential work was the German-language *Reflections upon an Anonymous Review (Blick auf den anonymen Rückblick)* (1859), which was a response to an earlier book that was an uncritical praise of the achievements of the Bach Regime. The resulting police action against him led Széchenyi to commit suicide in the spring of 1860. His self-inflicted death placed him once more into the limelight and served to reemphasize the magnitude of his contributions to Hungary's national development.

Most of Széchenyi's writings appeared in two separate collections: *Count István Széchenyi's Works (Széchenyi István gróf munkái)* (9 vol., 1884–96), and *Count István Széchenyi's Complete Works (Gróf Széchenyi István összes munkái)* (13 vols., 1921–39), neither of which is complete. Although the son of the founder of the Hungarian National Museum and National Library, because Count István Széchenyi left the second diacritical mark off his family name, there is this slight difference in the spelling of their names, as well as the names of institutions connected with them.

SZÉCHÉNYI LIBRARY see **NATIONAL SZÉCHÉNYI LIBRARY.**

SZEGED. One of Hungary's (q.v.) five largest regional cities (pop. 190,000) —the others being Debrecen (q.v.), Pécs (q.v.), Miskolc, and Győr (q.v.). It is also a major university town located in southern Hungary, on the two banks of the Tisza River (q.v.), close to the Serbian/Yugoslav border. Until the late 19th century, Szeged was a typical example of a so-called *oppidum* or "agricultural town" (q.v.) and thus very different from a medieval walled city. In the 20th century it achieved some prominence as the birthplace of the Szeged government (q.v.) and the resulting Szeged Idea (q.v.), as well as of an important branch of the Hungarian Populist Movement (q.v.). Its university was originally the University of Kolozsvár (q.v.), which was transferred to Szeged after the loss of Transylvania (q.v.) to Romania (q.v.) following World War I (q.v.).

SZEGED GOVERNMENT (1919). The government established in the city of Szeged in May 1919 as a rival source of authority to Béla Kun's (q.v.) Hungarian Soviet Republic (q.v.). Composed of gentry politicians and professional army officers, the Szeged government was headed by Count Gyula Károlyi (q.v.) (May-July) and then by Dezső Ábrahám (1875–1973) (July-August). Its minister for defense and the commander-in-chief of its armed forces was Admiral Miklós Horthy (q.v.), who later became the regent (q.v.) of Hungary (q.v.).

SZEGED IDEA [SZEGEDI GONDOLAT]. The name of the not fully distilled and systematized political ideology of the interwar Hungarian political regime under the leadership of Admiral Miklós Horthy (q.v.). It was named after the city of Szeged (q.v.), where it originated in 1919, during Béla Kun's (q.v.) Hungarian Soviet Republic (q.v.). The Szeged Idea was the product of a group of anti-communist gentry politicians, professional military officers, and former government bureaucrats who wished to overthrow the communist rule and who hoped to establish a new regime based on the dual ideas of "Christianity" and "nationalism." Because of the heavy presence of Jews in the leadership of the Hungarian Soviet Republic, the Szeged Idea had both anti-communist and anti-Semitic overtones. The latter, however, was toned down, once Admiral Horthy attained power.

SZEGEDI-KIS, ISTVÁN (1505–72). A prominent Protestant theologian and bishop of the Hungarian Reformed Church who was a contemporary of such other Hungarian reformers as Gál Huszár (q.v.) and Ferenc Melius-Juhász (q.v.). Having studied at the Universities of Cracow and Wittenberg—where he earned a doctorate in 1543—Szegedi-Kis returned home and began to spread the teachings of Zwingli and Calvin. Because of the ever-present persecutions, he was forced to move about frequently. Thus, up to 1554, when he was elected the first bishop of the Synod of Baranya in southwestern Hungary (q.v.), he lived in over half a dozen different towns (Tasnád, Gyula, Cegléd, Temesvár, Mezőtúr, Tolna, Laskó), but each time he was driven out. Between 1561 and 1563 Szegedi-Kis was a captive of the Turks (q.v.) at Pécs (q.v.) and Szolnok. After being ransomed, he settled down on Csepel Island (q.v.) and became the pastor of the

Reformed Congregation of Ráckeve, where he wrote most of his theological works that made his name known throughout Europe.

Initially Szegedi-Kis fought primarily against Catholicism, but by 1570 he joined the polemics against anti-Trinitarianism (q.v.). Most of his important works were written in Latin and published posthumously. These include *True Certainty about the Trinity (Assertio vera de Trinitate)* (1573), *A Mirror of the Roman Pontiffs (Speculum Romanorum pontificium)* (1584; German version, 1586), and *The Main Theses of UnadulteratedTheology (Theologiae sincerae loci communes)* (1585). Although a well-known theologian, Szegedi-Kis is probably more significant as an organizer of the Hungarian Reformed Church.

SZÉKELY, MOSES [MÓZES] (c.1550–1603). For a very brief period, Székely was the Turkish-appointed (March-May, 1603) and then the elected prince (May-July, 1603) of Transylvania (q.v.). Moses Székely rose to prominence in the service of the Báthory family (q.v.). After having been commander-in-chief of several armies, in 1601 he turned against Imperial General George Basta (q.v.) and Voievod Michael the Brave of Wallachia (r.1593–1601) (q.v.), who jointly invadedTransylvania in the service of Emperor Rudolph (q.v.) and then introduced a reign of terror into that province. Basta soon had Voievod Michael killed (August 1601) and then continued his reign of terror. During this period (1601–03) Székely supported the candidacy of Sigismund Báthory (q.v.), but when these efforts failed, he assumed the leadership of the anti-Imperial Party and had himself named and then elected prince of Transylvania. He died a few months later in a battle and was succeeded after a hiatus of a year and a half (1603-05) by István Bocskai (q.v.).

SZÉKELY-HUNGARIANS see **SZÉKELYS.**

SZÉKELYS [SICULI, SZEKLERS]. A Hungarian ethnic group in southeastern Transylvania (q.v.), which until the 20th century had retained a certain degree of separate cultural identity from the rest of the Hungarians (q.v.). Their origin is obscure, but their own oral traditions link them to the Huns (q.v.). Their lore holds that they are descendants of a group of Huns who were settled in Eastern Transylvania by Attila's youngest son, Irnák, whom they called Csaba (see Csaba Legend). This view had been popular with the Hungarians from the beginning of their own history in the Carpathian Basin (q.v.), partially because it was also championed by the Árpádian kings (q.v.) who claimed descent from King Attila (q.v.). The Székelys have also been linked to various other Turkic ethnic groups, such as the Avars (q.v.), Bulgars (q.v.), Khazars (q.v.), Kabars (q.v.), and Cumans (q.v.), as well as the non-Turkic Jazyges (q.v.). Many scholars, however, believe that they are descendants of a tribe of Hungarians who have been settled on the eastern fringes of Hungary in the 10th or 11th century as frontier guards. Thus, having failed to integrate into the main body of the Hungarian nation until relatively recently, they retained many of their own special customs and traditions.

The Székelys used to have their own social class system, their society being divided into the nobility consisting of the higher-level *primors* (q.v.) and the lower-level *lófős* (q.v.), and the common Székely population. In the course of the 14th and 15th centuries, their original clan structure gave way to a territorial autonomy called the "Székely University" (Universitas Siculorum), which was divided into seven districts *(szék)*. The "University" was headed by the Székely Count *(Comes Siculorum),* who was one of the three top leaders of the semi-independent Principality of Transylvania during the 16th and 17th centuries—the other two being the Saxon Count *(Comes Saxorum]* and the Hungarian Count *(Comes Hungarorum).* The latter of these was simultaneously the elected prince of Transylvania. These three "historic nations" were bound into a singly interest group established at the Union of Kápolna of 1437 (q.v.), which dominated Transylvania until the Habsburg (q.v.) conquest in the late 17th century.

Throughout the 16th and 17th centuries, the princes of Transylvania have guarded the special rights and privileges of the Székelys, but by the turn of the 17th to the 18th century the common Székelys have sank down into serfdom and did not receive their freedom until the Hungarian Revolution of 1848–49 (q.v.). The Székely *primors* and *lófős*, on the other hand, were gradually integrated into the ranks of the Hungarian nobility (q.v.), but their titles were never really recognized on par with those of the Hungarian aristocracy (q.v.). During the 1880s, economic conditions forced many common Székelys to emigrate to Moldavia (q.v.).

After World War I (q.v.), the Székely homeland was attached to Romania (q.v.) and the Székelys themselves were subjected to a process of denationalization. But precisely because of these pressures, they relinquished their separate cultural identity and merged with the Hungarians. Thus, while many of them still call themselves Székelys, in recent censuses they have identified themselves simply as Hungarians. After World War II (q.v.), the Székelys gained some autonomy through the establishment of the Maros Hungarian Autonomous Region. This autonomy, however, was abolished in the late 1960s in consequence of reemerging Romanian chauvinism under the leadership of the communist dictator, Nicolae Ceausescu (r.1964–89). Today, there are well over two million Hungarians in Transylvania, about half of whom are probably of Székely origin.

SZÉKESFEHÉRVÁR [FEHÉRVÁR, ALBA CIVITAS, ALBA REGIA, WEISSENBURG, STUHLWEISSEN-BURG]. A city of over 100,000 inhabitants in the center of Trans-Danubia (q.v.) in the western part of Hungary (q.v.), which during the early Árpádian age was a bishopric and the second most important city after the first royal capital of Esztergom (q.v.). Originally known as Alba Civitas (White City or White Fortress), it had a fortified royal residence as early as 1007, when King St. Stephen's (q.v.) only son, Prince Emeric (Imre) (q.v.), was born there. By the 13th century, Székesfehérvár was one of the best fortified cities of Hungary, which not even the Mongols (q.v.) were able to take. Its cathedral—built at the orders of St. Stephen and then continuously expanded by later kings—had served for five centuries (1038–1526) as Hungary's coronation church. The city also became the burial place for Hungary's monarchs and their family members—starting with Prince Emeric in 1031 and King St. Stephen in 1038. In the early 13th century, the city became the site of the annual nobles' convocation that gradually evolved into the Hungarian Feudal Diet (q.v.). In 1543 Székesfehérvár was conquered by the Ottoman Turks (q.v.), who looted the Royal Graves and in 1601 blew up the cathedral. Reconquered in 1688, the city was gradually rebuilt and resettled, and by 1777 it once more became a see of a Catholic bishopric. In 1938 Székesfehérvár celebrated the ninth centennial of St. Stephen's death, precededby the excavation of many of the medieval royal sites. Today it is a major manufacturing center in Hungary.

SZEKFŰ, GYULA [JULIUS] (1883–1955). One of Hungary's greatest historians whose influence during the interwar period (q.v.) was all pervasive. Educated at the University of Budapest (q.v.) as a member of the intellectually exclusive Eötvös College (q.v.), after receiving his doctorate in 1904, he was employed at the Hungarian National Museum, the Hungarian National Archives, the Austrian National Archives, and the Hungarian Ministry of Foreign Affairs. In 1925 Szekfű was appointed to the Chair of Modern Hungarian History at the University of Budapest, where he soon created a new "school" of history, the Hungarian version of the Dilthey-inspired *Geistesgeschichte* School *(szellemtörténet)* (see Hungarian Historical Studies.). During the interwar years, Szekfű was allied with the conservative-nationalist Prime Minister Count István Bethlen (q.v.), and served as the founding editor of his influential *Hungarian Review (Magyar Szemle)* (1927–44).

Initially Szekfű was a champion of Hungary's longstanding membership in what he called the "Christian-German Cultural Community," but his distaste for Hitler and Nazism made him break with this orientation and he became an outspoken opponent of Hungary's rightward turn. Following Hungary's German occupation in 1944 (q.v.), Szekfű went underground. Then, following the war, he joined Hungary's "new democratic course," serving as his country's ambassador to Moscow (1946–48) and a member of the

Hungarian Parliament (1953–55). Yet he felt just as out of place in the world of communism as he had in the world of Nazism.

Through much of his life, Szekfű stood for a kind of "Europeanism" in Hungarian historical thinking. He viewed Hungarian history from a wider European perspective. For this reason, he was more critical about Hungary's historical evolution and discussed the role of the Habsburgs (q.v.) more favorably than was customary among Hungarian historians. This embroiled him in a number of major controversies when dealing with such revered personalities as Prince Ferenc Rákóczi (1913) (q.v.) and Prince Gábor Bethlen (1929) (q.v.). Szekfű's most lasting work is his eight-volume *Hungarian History (Magyar történet)* (1928–33), co-authored with the noted medievalist Bálint Hóman (q.v.). He summarized Hungarian historical evolution from the mid–15th century onward in the spirit of "Europeanism" and with the tools of the then fashionable *Geistesgeschichte* orientation. The latter rejected the role of "laws and objective reality" and emphasized the significance of ideas and "creative spirituality" as shapers of human history. Szekfű's ideas embodied in his great synthesis came to shape Hungarian historical thinking during the interwar years and, to a large degree, even after the war.

The exponents of official Marxist historiography never ceased to fight against Szekfű and his views. In addition to the *Hungarian History*, Szekfű's most influential work was his Three *Generations (Háromnemzedék)* (1920) and its sequel *Three Generations and What Follows (Három nemzedék és ami utána következik)* (1934), in which he presented a moving and very personal analysis of the ills of Hungarian society from the 1830s to the 1930s. Szekfű's ideas permeated the whole intellectual world of interwar Hungary (q.v.). He broke with some of these views during World War II (q.v.), but only grudgingly and only when he saw the world being embroiled in the "new barbarism" represented by Hitler and Nazism. He expressed his disenchantment with the course of events in his *We Lost Our Way Somewhere (Valahol utat vesztettünk)* (1942-43), later reissued as *After the Revolution (A forradalomután)* (1947). Szekfű died a bitter, disillusioned man, but his intellectual presence and his influence never disappeared. This influence gained new strength and new currency after the collapse of communism in 1989–90 (q.v.).

SZÉLL, KÁLMÁN (1845–1915). Prime minister of Hungary (1899–1903) at a very critical juncture in its relationship to Austria (q.v.). Having married the daughter of the poet Vörösmarty (q.v.), who was also the foster-daughter of Ferenc Deák (q.v.), Széll became a close confidant of the architect of Austro-Hungarian dualism (q.v.). He represented the Deák Party (q.v.), the Liberal Party (q.v.), and after the latter's demise, several smaller political groups in the Hungarian Parliament (q.v.) for over four decades (1869–1911). Before becoming prime minister, Széll served as minister of financial affairs (1875–78) and also as the head of several prominent financial institutions. In addition to politics, he was interested in scientific agriculture. He established a model farm on his estate at Rátót, where he spent most of his summers. In 1902 Széll ended temporarily the economic duel between Hungary and Austria through an agreement with Prime Minister Körber of Austria, based largely on the so-called "Széll Formula" that he had devised. After his resignation in 1903, Széll remained a member of the Hungarian Parliament, but devoted most of his time to banking and farming.

SZENCZI-MOLNÁR, ALBERT (1574–1639). A Protestant clergyman, writer, philosopher, theologian, and translator whose *Latin-Hungarian Dictionary* and *Hungarian-Latin Dictionary* (1704) were path breaking in Hungarian scholarship. With some minor revisions, they remained in use until the mid–19th century. Szenczi-Molnár's Latin language grammar of the Hungarian language (1610) made it possible for others to acquaint themselves with the language of the Magyars (q.v.). Both his father and grandfather had been millers, but young Albert opted to become an intellectual. Until 1590 he studied in Hungary (q.v.), after which he went to the Holy Roman Empire (q.v.) and enrolled in sequence at the Universities of Wittenberg, Heidelberg, and Strassbourg (1590–99). Thereafter he moved back and forth between Hungary and the empire, living at various times in Nürnberg, Prague, Altdorf, Amberg, and Marburg, and getting to know both Emperor Rudolph II (King Rudolph I) (q.v.) and his famous astronomer, Johannes Kepler (1571–1630). Back home, Szenczi-Molnár lived and worked mostly in Upper Hungary (q.v.) and later in Transylvania (q.v.), where he received the support of Prince Gabriel Bethlen (q.v.). He was a determined and dedicated scholar who went about his work meticulously. He translated about 150 of King David's psalms to Hungarian (1607), published an improved version of the Protestant Bible (1608) originally translated by Gáspár Karoli (q.v.), and translated several of Calvin's theological works (1624). In doing all this, he advanced the Protestant faith, but also the cause of the Magyar language (q.v.).

SZENT-GYÖRGYI, ALBERT (1893–1986). Physician, biochemist, and the only one of the dozen or so Hungarian Nobel Prize winners, who was awarded his prize—for his discovery of vitamin C—while still in Hungary (q.v.). Having received his M.D. at the University of Budapest (q.v.), and his Ph.D. in chemistry at Cambridge University, Szent-Györgyi served as professor of biochemistry at the Universities of Szeged (q.v.) (1931–45) and Budapest (q.v.) (1945–47). In 1947 he left Hungary for political reasons and continued his research and teaching in the United States, in Boston (1947–62, 1971–86), and at Dartmouth College (1962–71). He was a known liberal who worked against Nazi influences during World War II (q.v.), and also against Soviet influences after the war. Following Szent-Györgyi's death, the Medical University of Szeged, where he had conducted his research for the Nobel Prize, was renamed after him (1987).

SZEPES SAXONS see **ZIPSERS**.

SZEPESSÉG see **ZIPSERLAND**.

SZERÉMSÉG [SIRMIUM, SREM, SRIJEM]. A province of Historic Hungary (q.v.) known in Roman times as Sirmium, which may have been the site of an early bishopric before the Árpádian conquest (q.v.) of Hungary. Located between the Danube (q.v.) and the Sava Rivers (q.v.) to the west of Belgrade (q.v.) and to the east of Slavonia (q.v.), Szerémség was occupied by the Hungarians in the late 9th and early 10th centuries. King St. Stephen (q.v.) made it into a military frontier district. In the 11th and 12th centuries, Hungarian power expanded to the south of the Sava River, and along with it, extended also the borders of the province of Szerémség. In the mid-13th century the Trans-Sava part of Szerémség *(Sirmium ulterior)* was formed into the new defensive Banat of Macsó *(Mačva)*, which it remained until the Turkish conquest (q.v.) of the early 16th century. After World War I (q.v.) Szerémség became part of Yugoslavia (q.v.) as a section of the province of Voivodina (q.v.).

SZIGETVÁR. A small town in southern Trans-Danubia, whose fortress was one of Hungary's main defenses against the Ottoman Turks (q.v.) in the early 16th century. In those days, the fortress of Szigetvár stood on a swampy island surrounded by the waters of Almás River. In 1566 Sultan Süleyman's led his sixth and final campaign to Hungary (q.v.), with the intention to conquer Vienna (q.v.). He never made it to the Imperial city, for he was unable to pass by Szigetvár, which was defended by Count Miklós Zrínyi the Elder (q.v.), whose heroic defense of the fortress prevented the sultan from achieving his goal. The Ottomans did conquer Szigetvár after four weeks of siege (August 5-September 8, 1566), but at the price of tens of thousand of dead and their inability to continue their military campaign. Sultan Süleyman himself died in the midst of the siege (September 5). His body was embalmed and returned to Istanbul (Constantinople) (q.v.), but his internal organs were buried at Szigetvár in a special türbe (mausoleum). It still stands today, but now it serves as the church of the village of Turbék. Count Zrínyi's heroic defense of Szigetvár became part of the heroic legends of Hungary. A century later it was made into a heroic epic by Zrínyi's own grandson, the poet Count Miklós Zrínyi the Younger (q.v.).

SZILÁGYI, SÁNDOR (1827–99). Historian and the leading organizer of the historical profession in late–19th–century Hungary (q.v.). Szilágyi was a leading spirit of the historical profession and of the Hungarian Historical Association (q.v.), the editor-in-chief both of the association's periodical, *Centuries (Századok)* (1875–99), and of its source publication series *Historical Repository (Történelmi Tár)* (1878–99). He likewise edited its monograph series, *Hungarian Historical Biographies (Magyar Történelmi Életrajzok)* (1885–99). During the same period Szilágyi was also the director of the Library of the University of Budapest (q.v.), as well as the editor-in-chief of Hungary's still used ten-volume "Millennial History," entitle *History of the Hungarian Nation (Magyar Nemzet Története)* (1895–98). In addition to these editorial and scholarly-administrative activities, Szilágyi authored at least a dozen major works on the history of Transylvania (q.v.) during the 16th and 17th centuries.

SZILÁRD, LEÓ (1898–1964). A noted physicist and close collaborator of Albert Einstein (1879–1955) who was one of the pioneers of the American effort to produce an atomic bomb during World War II (q.v.). In 1939 Szilárd drafted the letter, signed by Einstein, which encouraged President Franklin D. Roosevelt to proceed with the atomic research. Having emigrated to the United States in 1939, for three years he taught at Columbia University (1939–42), and then became associated with the University of Chicago's atomic research project until the end of his life. Although Szilárd was one of the "fathers" of the atomic bomb, later he turned to the idea of controlling these weapons. In 1959 he shared with his fellow Hungarian, Eugene Wigner (q.v.), the "Atoms for Peace Award." Because of his work in uranium fission, Szilárd was a potential Nobel Prize winner at the time of his death. He is one of a half a dozen prominent Hungarian scientists who had a major role in the development of America's atomic power.

SZOLGABÍRÓ [IUDEX NOBILIUM, SERVANT JUDGE]. An important county official from the 13th century until 1950. Originally the *szolgabírós* were elected judges of the *servientes regis (royal servants)* (q.v.), hence their name: "servant judge." But after the development of the nobles' counties (q.v.) in the 13th century, they became the most important elected county administrators.

Originally, each county had four *szolgabírós,* but starting with the 16th century, their number came to coincide with the number of districts *(járás)* in each of the counties. In 1886 the districts were divided into subdistricts, each of which came to be headed by a *szolgabíró,* while each of the original districts were placed under a *főszolgabíró (chief servant judge).* These offices were all abolished in 1950 and were replaced by the Soviet-style council system (q.v.), which, in turn, was abolished in 1990.

SZÖRÉNY, BANAT OF [LITTLE WALLACHIA, OLTE-NIA]. One of the most important defensive banats (q.v.) of medieval Hungary (q.v.), which later constituted the westernmost part of Wallachia (q.v.) to the west of the Olt River. The Banat of Szörény was established in 1227 by King Béla IV (q.v.) in his capacity as "junior king" (q.v.) after his subjugation of the Cumans (q.v.). For a while the control of this region was contested by Bulgaria (q.v.), but the Banat of Szörény remained under firm Hungarian control throughout the 13th and early 14th centuries. With the foundation of the voivodate of Wallachia (q.v.), Szörény came progressively under its control, although Wallachia itself was a vassal state of Hungary. In 1369, Louis the Great (q.v.) recognized the voievod of Wallachia as the ban of Szörény. Thereafter the Banat of Szörény came to be called Little Wallachia *(Wallachia Minor),* and still later took on the name Oltenia after the River Olt.

SZTÓJAY, DÖME [SZTOJAKOVICS] (1883–1946). A professional military man, major general, and Hungary's prime minister during the first phase of the country's German occupation (q.v.) (March 22–August 29, 1944). Having participated in the counter-revolutionary activities at Szeged (q.v.) in 1919, Sztójay went into diplomatic work. He served as Hungary's military attaché (1923–33) and then as its ambassador (1935–44) in Berlin, where he became a devotee of Nazism. Following the German invasion of Hungary on March 19, 1944, the Germans pressured Regent Horthy (q.v.) to appoint Sztójay as the country's new prime minister. In that capacity, Sztójay was responsible for ordering the collection and deportation of most of the Hungarian Jews (q.v.) to German death camps. In 1946 Sztójay was tried and executed as a war criminal.

SZŰRÖS, MÁTYÁS (b.1933). A reform communist (q.v.) politician, who during the transition from communism to democracy served as Hungary's (q.v.) provisional president (October 23, 1989– May 23, 1990). For the next four years (1990–94), during the Antall Regime, he was the assistant speaker of the Hungarian Parliament (q.v.). Being of peasant background, Szűrös always belonged to the Populist (q.v.) wing of the Hungarian Socialist Workers' Party (q.v.), and after 1989 also to the same wing of its successor, the Hungarian Socialist Party (q.v.). For this reason he is viewed much more favorably by Hungary's Populist intellectuals than most of the other former communist party functionaries.

- T -

TÁBLABÍRÓ [COUNTY JUDGE]. Since the 18th century this was the common name of various county judges whose office had developed in the 17th century. Their judicial functions ceased in the mid–19th century, after which it became a honorific title that was granted as a form of social recognition.

TAKSONY (c.905–70). Ruling prince of Hungary (955–70), grandson of Árpád (q.v.) and son of Zoltán (q.v.). Taksony became ruler after the fateful Battle of Augsburg (q.v.), after which he ended the Hungarian marauding expeditions to the West. Taksony tried to find allies in the East, among such Turkic peoples as the Khazars (q.v.) and the Pechenegs (q.v.), and he also took a wife from among them. According to Anonymus (q.v.), at this time some of the Pechenegs settled in Hungary (q.v.) under the leadership of Tonúzoba, who later may have been buried alive, because of his opposition to Christianization. Taksony was followed on the throne by his son, Géza (q.v.), and then by his grandson, the future St. Stephen (q.v.).

TATARS [TARTARS] see MONGOLS.

TAXED NOBILITY [TAKSÁS NEMES]. A segment of the lower nobility (q.v.) whose members since the 16th century were obliged to pay war tax (q.v.) and tithe (q.v.). Their ranks included the armalists (q.v.) and those immigrants from Turkish Hungary (q.v.) who made their livelihood by working on peasant plots.

TECHNICAL UNIVERSITY OF BUDAPEST see UNIVER-SITY OF TECHNICAL SCIENCES.

TELEKI, COUNT LÁSZLÓ (1811–61). In the period before the Hungarian Revolution of 1848–49 (q.v.), Count Teleki was one of the most progressive members of the Opposition Party (q.v.) in the Upper House (q.v.). He was a supporter of Kossuth (q.v.), who in September 1848 sent him as his representative to Paris. Remaining abroad after the fall of the revolution, Teleki continued his political activities by establishing close relationships with the exiled leaders of the other nationalities of the Habsburg Empire (q.v.) and by displaying an unusual sensitivity to the question of minority rights. In 1859, he was one of the three exiled leaders—the other two being Kossuth and Klapka (q.v.)—who established the Hungarian National Directorate *(Magyar Nemzeti Igazgatóság)*, which hoped to lead an offensive against Austria (q.v.) in wake of the Austro-Italian-French War of that year. In 1860, while visiting Dresden, he was arrested and delivered to the Austrians. But Emperor Francis Joseph (q.v.), who was moving toward a compromise with the Hungarians (q.v.), freed him with the provision that he would refrain from politics. In 1861, however, he was invited to the Upper House and was also elected to the Lower House (q.v.) of the Hungarian Parliament (q.v.). There he became the leader of the radical Resolution Party (q.v.). But as his views went far beyond those espoused by his supporters, he clashed even with his own followers and then committed suicide. Some of Teleki's writings were published in 1961 under the title *Selected Works (Válogatott művei)* in two volumes.

TELEKI, COUNT MIHÁLY (1634–90). The last chancellor of Transylvania (q.v.), close adviser to Prince Mihály Apafi (q.v.), and the man primarily responsible for negotiating the transfer of Transylvania (q.v.) under the rule of the Habsburg dynasty (q.v.). Coming from a Transylvanian-Hungarian noble family, Teleki was initially an opponent of the Habsburgs and was connected with the Wesselényi Conspiracy (q.v.). Moreover, between 1672 and 1678 he was the elected commander of the *kuruc* (q.v.) exiles in Transylvania. But recognizing the changing power relationship between the Ottoman Turks (q.v.) and the Habsburgs, he relinquished his position to Imre Thököly (q.v.) and began negotiations with Emperor Leopold I (q.v.). In a secret agreement of 1685—which gained for him the title of an imperial count (q.v.) and large landed estates—Teleki agreed to transfer Transylvania from under Ottoman to Habsburg rule, but with the provision that the province could retain its autonomy. In light of the Ottoman defeat at the Second Siege of Vienna (q.v.) and the subsequent occupation of Transylvania by Habsburg Imperial forces (1687), however, Teleki's efforts to preserve the province's autonomy foundered. He died in the Battle of Zernyest (August 21, 1690) in the course of his effort to defend Transylvania against the invading *kuruc* and Turkish forces under Thököly's command.

TELEKI, COUNT PÁL (1879–1941). A noted geographer and prime minister of Hungary at the beginning (1920–21) and toward the end (1939–41) of the interwar period (q.v.). Coming from a prominent Transylvanian-Hungarian aristocratic family, Teleki first made his name as a noted geographer, and subsequently served as the director of the Geographical Institute (1909–13), secretary general and president of the Hungarian Geographical Society (1910–23), and as the president of the Turanian Society (1913–16) (see Turanism). In 1919 he was one of the leaders of the anti-communist movement, serving in various ministerial posts in the Szeged government (q.v.).

After the establishment of the Horthy Regime (q.v.), Teleki served as its foreign minister (April 19–September 22, 1920) and its prime minister (July 19, 1920–April 13, 1921). Thereafter, while continuing his membership in the Hungarian Parliament (q.v.) and serving as the chief of the Hungarian Scout Federation (see Scouting), Teleki returned to scholarly activities at the University of Budapest (q.v.). At the same time he was also involved in various revisionist activities, as well as in the ideological education of interwar Hungary's intellectual elite. To advance the cause of Hungarian Revisionism (q.v.), based on solid scholarly research, in the mid–1920s Teleki founded the Hungarian Sociographical Institute *(Szociográfiai Intézet)* (1924) and the Political Science Institute *(Államtudományi Intézet)* (1926), which subsequently were merged into the Teleki Institute (1941–49), which in turn was the forerunner of the Institute of History (q.v.) of the Hungarian Academy of Sciences (q.v.).

In 1938 Teleki returned to active politics, first as Hungary's minister for culture and education (May 1, 1938–February 15, 1939), and then as prime minister (February 16, 1939–April 3, 1941). By this time he was so disenchanted with Hungary's close relationship to Nazi Germany that on December 12, 1940, he concluded a Pact of Friendship with Yugoslavia (q.v.). Then, when he was unable to prevent Hungary from joining the German invasion against that country, he committed suicide.

Teleki's most significant scholarly works include the *Historical Atlas of the Cartography of the Japanese Islands (Atlasz a japán szigetek cartográphiájának történetéhez)* (1909), for which he won a French scholarly prize; *Hungary's Ethnographic Map based on Population Density (Magyarország néprajzi térképe a népsűrűség alapján)* (1919); *Economic Geography of America (Amerika gazdasági földrajza)* (1922); *General Economic Geography (Általános gazdasági földrajz)* (1927); and *About Europe and Hungary (Európáról és Magyarországról)* (1934). Teleki also authored the widely used English language survey, *The Evolution of Hungary and its Place in European History* (1923).

TELEKI FAMILY. A prominent Hungarian-Transylvanian aristocratic family descending from the Garázda Clan. The family received its coat-of-arms from King Sigismund (q.v.) in 1409. Having been involved in Transylvanian politics in the 17th century, the Telekis rose to national prominence and was awarded the rank of an imperial count (q.v.) in 1685. Thereafter the Telekis remained in the forefront of Hungarian and Transylvanian cultural and political movements up to the end of World War II (q.v.). In addition to the separately discussed Mihály (q.v.), László (q.v.), and Pál (q.v.), the most noted members of the family included: Count Sámuel Teleki (1739–1822), the chancellor of Transylvania and founder of the Teleki Library *(Teleki-téka)* of Marosvásárhely (Tirgu Mureś); the Transylvanian statesmen and historians, Count József Teleki (1790–1855) and his son Count Domokos Teleki (1810–1876); the pioneer of women's education in Hungary, Countess Blanka Teleki (1806–62); the revolutionary *honvéd* (q.v.) colonel, Count Sándor Teleki (1821–

92); the Africa-explorer and discoverer of Lakes Rudolph and Stefania, Count Sámuel Teleki (1845–1916); and the geologist and Hungary's minister for culture and education in Hungary's Provisional National Government (December 22, 1944–November 15, 1945), Count Géza Teleki (1911–83), who committed suicide after serving as professor of geology at George Washington University (1955–83).

TELLER, EDWARD [EDE] (b.1908). One of the top Hungarian emigré scientists who immigrated to the United States for political reasons in the 1930s. During World War II (q.v.) he was a prominent member of the so-called "Manhattan Project," which developed the atomic bomb. Later he formulated the theoretical foundations of hydrogen fusion and came to be known as the "father of the hydrogen bomb." Teller had studied physics in Hungary and in Germany, and starting in 1929 he was a researcher and lecturer at several German, Danish, and British universities. Following his immigration in 1935, he taught at George Washington University (1935–41), Columbia University (1941–42), University of Chicago (1946–52), and the University of California at Berkeley (1952–75), serving director of the University's Livermore Laboratories (1954–75). Teller retired in 1975 and became a member of Stanford University's Hoover Institution. In recognition of his scientific achievements, he was awarded the Einstein Prize in 1958 and the Atomic Energy Commission's Fermi Award in 1962. Some of Teller's most important books include: *The Structure of Matter* (1949), *Our Nuclear Future* (1958),*The Legacy of Hiroshima* (1962), *The Constructive Uses of Nuclear Explosives* (1968), *Energy: A Plan for Action* (1975), *Nuclear Energy in the Developing World* (1977), *Energy from Heaven and Earth* (1979), *The Pursuit of Simplicity* (1980), and *Better a Shield than a Sword* (1987).

TEMESVÁR [TEMESCHWAR, TIMIŚOARA]. One of the important centers of medieval Hungary (q.v.), which had a significant royal fortress *(Castrum Temesiense)* in 1212. In the 14th century, Temesvár had also served as the country's provisional capital for both King Charles Robert (q.v.) and for Louis the Great (q.v.). In 1397 Temesvár was the site of the Hungarian Diet (q.v.), which for the first time accepted the representatives of the Royal Free Cities (q.v.). In the 15th century the city served as one of the important power bases for the famed anti-Turkish fighter, János Hunyadi (q.v.), while in 1514 it was the site of the defeat and execution of the leaders of the Dózsa Peasant Revolution (q.v.). Temesvár was conquered by the Ottoman Turks (q.v.) in 1552, after which it remained the administrative center of the Pashalik (q.v.) of Temesvár for 164 years. Reconquered in 1716 and regained legally at the Peace Treaty of Passarowitz (q.v.) in 1718, the city and its region remained under separate Habsburg Imperial administration until 1741. The region's southern fringes were incorporated into the Habsburg Military Frontier District (q.v.). After the defeat of the Hungarian Revolution of 1848–49 (q.v.), the city and its region were placed once more under separate administration (1849–60). After World War I (q.v.), the Treaty of Trianon (q.v.) awarded Temesvár to Romania (q.v.), even though the Romanians constituted only about 11 percent of its population. Renamed Timişoara (derived from the Hungarian Temesvár), Temesvár's ethnic composition was rapidly altered by urban expansion and by a policy of resettlement. Today it is a Romanian city of nearly 250,000, but still with a significant Hungarian minority population.

TEMESVÁR, BANAT OF [TEMESI BÁNSÁG]. A roughly rectangular military-administrative province, centered on the city and fortress of Temesvár (q.v.). Traditionally it was bordered in the west by the Tisza River (q.v.), in the east by historic Transylvania (q.v.), in the north by the Maros River, and in the south by the Danube (q.v.). The province evolved as a separate entity only after 1552 when Temesvár and its vicinity fell under Ottoman Turkish (q.v.) rule. It remained there for 164 years and came to constitute a separate administrative unit *(pashalik)* under the Pasha of Temesvár. After its reconquest in the Austro-Turkish War of 1716–18, which ended with the Peace Treaty of Passarowitz (q.v.) in 1718, the Pashalik of Temesvár (q.v.) was renamed the Banat of Temesvár and was placed under separate Habsburg Imperial administration until 1741. Thereafter it was integrated into the regular Hungarian administrative system, although its southern portions remained part of the Habsburg Military Frontier District (q.v.) until 1867. Much of the province was also placed under separate Habsburg Imperial administration in the period of absolutism (q.v.) (1849–60), following the Revolution of 1848–49 (q.v.). After World War I (q.v.), the Treaty of Trianon (q.v.) divided the province between newly created Yugoslavia (q.v.) and much enlarged Romania (q.v.) —with the city and the larger part of the province placed under Romanian rule.

TEMESVÁR, PASHALIK OF. An important province of the Ottoman Turkish Empire (q.v.), which territorially was identical with the Banat of Temesvár (q.v.). For over a century and a half (1552–1716/18) the Pasha of Temesvár was one of the most important military governors in the Ottoman Empire's European possessions, usually second only to the Pasha of Buda (q.v.). He was in charge of keeping the autonomous Principality of Transylvania (q.v.) in check and under continuous scrutiny.

TEUTONIC KNIGHTS [DEUTSCHE RITTERORDEN]. A German religious order established in the Holy Land in 1190–92, whose members were trained armed knights, and whose purpose was to fight against the Moslems and to regain the Holy Land for Christianity. Being pushed out of the Holy Land, King Andrew II (q.v.) invited them to settle in southeastern Transylvania (q.v.) to serve as Hungary's (q.v.) defenses against the pagan Cumans (q.v.). Instead of fulfilling their obligations, the knights began to carve a state out for themselves, which prompted King Andrew to chase them out of Hungary in 1225. In the following year they accepted the invitation of Conrad of Mazovia and settled among the pagan Prussians (non-Germanic Baltic peoples) (q.v.) in the northwestern corner of fragmented Poland (q.v.). In 1237 they united with a similar German fighting order founded in Riga in 1201, thus creating a powerful military order, which soon carved a state out for itself in the eastern and southern Baltic region.

The Teutonic Knights Christianized, assimilated, and/or exterminated the Prussians, launched numerous invasions against Novgorod and other East Slavic states, cut off Poland (q.v.) from the Baltic Sea, established dozens of urban centers, brought in many German settlers, Germanized much of the region, while at the same time assumed the name of the originally non-German Prussians. In the 14th and early 15th centuries the Teutonic Knights were a military great power, who influenced the history of Poland, Lithuania (q.v.), Russian Novgorod, Denmark, Bohemia (q.v.), Hungary, and even the Holy Roman Empire (q.v.).

The power of the Teutonic Knights began to wane in the 15th century, largely because of the declining religious spirit and the lack of new recruits. In 1466 they relinquished many of their conquests to Poland, while in the 16th century they secularized and created two small principalities: East Prussia under the Hohenzollern dynasty (1525) and Kurland (Courland) under the Kettler dynasty (1561). In the 17th and 18th centuries the Hohenzollerns gained control of Brandenburg in the Holy Roman Empire and united it with East Prussia under the name of the Kingdom of Prussia (q.v.), while in the early 18th century Kurland became part of Peter the Great's Russian Empire (q.v.). The descendants of the Teutonic Knights came to constitute the powerful Prussian landowning nobility, which retained the spirit of militarism of its forebearers. From its ranks came the top political and military leaders of modern Prussia and the German Empire (q.v.) they created in 1871.

In addition to their short 13th-century stay, the influence of the Teutonic Knights upon Hungary was limited to the 14th century, when they played a significant role in the great power politics of the Hungarian Anjous (q.v.). Because of Austria-Hungary's (q.v.) and Hungary's (q.v.) close association with Imperial Germany, however, the descendants of the Teutonic Knights have also influenced Hungary's fate in modern times.

THERESIANUM [COLLEGIUM THERESIANUM]. Founded in Vienna (q.v.) by Empress Maria Theresa (q.v.) in 1749 as an exclusive secondary school for the education of the sons of Catholic nobility. In addition to her desire to cultivate the minds of young provincial noblemen, her primary goal was to indoctrinate the students with faithfulness to the Habsburg dynasty (q.v.). In the course of time the Theresianum acquireda Law Academy, and non-Catholics were also permitted to attend. The requirement that the students should come only from the ranks of the nobility was abolished in 1849. After the collapse of Austria-Hungary (q.v.), the Theresianum joined the ranks of the regular Austrian educational institutions. From the mid-18th century to 1918, many members of the Hungarian nobility (q.v.) were educated at the Theresianum.

THIRD ROAD [HARMADIK ÚT]. The ideological path advocated by the Hungarian Populists (q.v.) in the 1930s. They rejected both communism and capitalism as possible alternatives, and wished to create a socially and economically just society, without the totalitarianism and mass regimentation of the former, and without the social insensitivity and economic exploitation of the latter. The Populists idealized the Hungarian peasants, and viewed them as the only true source for the revitalization of the nation. Therefore, their "Third Road" or "Special Hungarian Path" solution was also filled with the components of an idealized agrarian society made up of independent, well-educated, and well-heeled small farmers.

THÖKÖLY, COUNT IMRE [TÖKÖLI, TÖKÖLLI, TEKELI] (1657–1705). The leader of the Thököly Uprising, and the appointed ruling prince of Upper Hungary (q.v.) (1682–85) and Transylvania (q.v.) (September–October 1690). His father, Count István Thököly (1623–70), had participated in the anti-Habsburg Wesselényi Conspiracy (q.v.), wherefore young Imre Thököly was forced to flee to Transylvania (q.v.). There he became associated with the displaced and disaffected elements—soon to be known as the *kuruc* (q.v.)—who after 1670 had gathered in that principality and in 1672 began systematic raids against the Habsburg territories. In 1678 Thököly was elected the leader of the *kuruc* armies and initiated the series of anti-Habsburg wars that are collectively known as the Thököly Uprising of 1678-85. In 1682 he strengthened his position by marrying Countess Ilona Zrínyi (q.v.), the widow of Prince Ferenc Rákóczi I (q.v.), who brought the immense wealth of the Rákóczi family (q.v.) into the anti-Habsburg struggle. In the same year Sultan Mehmet IV (r.1648–87) named him "king of Hungary," but Thököly declined to use that title and only called himself "prince of Upper Hungary." Failing to realize the imminent decline of the Ottoman Empire (q.v.), Thököly continued to rely on Turkish support. The Turkish defeat at the Second Siege of Vienna (q.v.) in 1683, however, ended his hope of ever freeing Hungary (q.v.) from Habsburg control. His disheartened supporters gradually switched over to the Habsburgs (q.v.), and Thököly became expendable even in the eyes of the Turks (q.v.). After Prince Mihály Apafi's (q.v.) death, Thököly was elected prince of Transylvania, but he was unable to hold on to the principality for more than two months. The Peace Treaty of Karlowitz (1699) sealed his fate and forced him into Turkish exile. He settled in Nicomedia (Izmit) in Asia Minor, along with his wife and about 1,500 of his followers. Although Thököly would have liked to join the Rákóczi War of Liberation (q.v.) in 1703, led by his stepson, but his illness prevented him from doing so. He died two years after the start of the uprising. In 1906 his remains were repatriated to Hungary and laid to rest in the Lutheran Church of Késmárk (Kežmarok). But Thököly did not remain home for long. After World War I (q.v.), his hometown became part of newly created Czechoslovakia (q.v.).

THÖKÖLY UPRISING see **THÖKÖLY, COUNT IMRE.**

THREE EMPEROR'S LEAGUE [DREIKAISERBUND] (1873). A vague agreement among Germany (q.v.), Austria-Hungary (q.v.), and Russia (q.v.) to consult on matters of common interest to them. It was the brainchild of German Chancellor Otto von Bismarck, who wished to prevent Russia from joining with revanchist France, and also wished to keep Austria-Hungary and

Russia from clashing over their interests in the Balkans (q.v.). In 1881, the league was transformed into a more formal agreement, in which each of the three powers agreed to remain neutral in case any one of them would go to war with a fourth power. They also agreed not to permit changes in the Balkans, except when agreed upon by all of them. The agreement lapsed in 1887 when Austria-Hungary declined to renew it because of the Bulgarian crisis in which the Russians were deeply involved. Bismarck then signed the Mutual Reassurance Treaty *(Rückversicherungsvertrag)* with Russia, to prevent her from stumbling into a French alliance. The latter treaty, however, was not renewed in 1890.

THREE HISTORIC NATIONS OF TRANSYLVANIA. Traditionally, this phrase was used to describe the three historic nations— the Hungarians or Magyars (q.v.), Székelys (q.v.), and Saxons (q.v.)— of Transylvania (q.v.) who united into the defensive Union of Kápolna (q.v.) in 1437. Later this union was transformed into the political system that governed the province during the period of Turkish vassalage. The Vlachs (later called Romanians) (q.v.) were left out of this union because they were not among the "historic nations" of Transylvania. Their numbers were few and they lacked a significant nobility that could have made their presence felt.

THREE-YEAR PLANS. Two of the communist-directed economic plans for the rebuilding of Hungary (q.v.) following the major destructions and dislocations caused by World War II (q.v.). The first Three-Year Plan was implemented between 1947 and 1949, and was intended to reconstruct Hungary's infrastructure. The second Three-Year Plan had similar goals following the Hungarian Revolution of 1956 (q.v.). It was introduced in 1958 and completed in 1960. The two Three-Year Plans were complemented by six Five-Year Plans (q.v.) that were began in 1950 and ended in 1985.

THURÓCZY, JÁNOS [JOHANNES THURÓCZI] (c.1435– c.1490). A legal scholar, lord chief justice (q.v.) chronicler, and the author-compiler of the most extensive and most popular late-medieval Hungarian history entitled *Chronicle of the Hungarians (Chronica Hungarorum)* (1488). In writing the first half of his work up to the late 14th century, Thuróczy relied on several earlier Hungarian chronicles. But starting with the age of Sigismund (q.v.), he produced an independent work based on contemporary documents, oral traditions, and on his own experiences in the country's top political leadership. Thuróczy's interpretation reflects the views of his own social class, the Hungarian common nobility (q.v.).

TILDY, ZOLTÁN (1889-1961). A Calvinist minister and a Small-holders' Party (q.v.) politician who in the immediate post-World War II (q.v.) period served as Hungary's prime minister (November 1945–February 1946), and then as its president (1946-48). In 1948 the communists forced him to resign. In 1956 Tildy was involved in Imre Nagy's (q.v.) short-lived Revolutionary Government (October 28–November 4, 1956), after which he suffered imprisonment. Pardoned in 1959, he lived his final two years in obscurity. Tildy is generally remembered as a compliant politician who accommodated the communists during his presidency.

TIMAR. The most common nonhereditary fief (landed estate) in the Ottoman Empire (q.v.) with an annual income potential less than 20,000 *akches (akçes)* (q.v.) per year. The holders of timars—known as *timaroits* (q.v.)—made up the bulk of the Ottoman cavalry, which in turn made up the backbone of the Ottoman armies. Other nonhereditary fiefs included the larger *zeāmet (ziamet),* with an income of between 20,000 and 100,000 *akches (akçes)* per year, and the still larger *has* (q.v.)—held by the sultan, princes of the blood, and such high ranking pashas (q.v.) as the *beylerbeys* (q.v.) and the *sanjak beys* (q.v.)—with a yield in excess of 100,000 akches [akçes] per year. Turkish Hungary (q.v.) was divided into thousands of *timars* and *zeāmets,* and most of its major towns were on *hās* lands.

TIMAROITS. Ottoman feudal lords, holders of a nonhereditary timar estates (q.v.), whose obligations included personal service in the Ottoman cavalry. They were also obliged to furnish fully equipped cavalrymen *(spahis)* (q.v.) to the sultan's campaign for each 5,000 *akches (akçes)* (q.v.) of income earned from the *timars* (q.v.) that had been assigned to them. The timaroits were the most visible Ottoman military and administrative personnel in Turkish Hungary.

TIMIŚOARA   see   TEMESVÁR.

TISZA, COUNT ISTVÁN (1861–1918). A conservative Hungarian statesman and the son of Prime Minister Kálmán Tisza (q.v.) who as Hungary's prime minister (1903–05, 1913–17) was the strongest defender of Austro-Hungarian dualism (q.v.) and of the conservative social order. As a member of the Hungarian Parliament (q.v.) and of the Liberal Party (q.v.) since 1886, István Tisza became convinced that the only assurance for Historic Hungary's (q.v.) territorial integrity and for the continued leadership position of the Magyars (q.v.) within Hungary (q.v.) was the preservation of the Austro-Hungarian Empire (q.v.) and the limitation of the extension of voting rights to the national minorities. Thus, throughout his political life, he supported Austro-Hungarian dualism, fought all political parties that tried to undermine this dualism in the name of Hungarian independence, and argued for the retention of political control in the hands of the propertied and educated classes. Tisza saw the agitation for independence and further democratization as self-defeating. These same concerns for self-preservation and the fear of the Russian Empire (q.v.) made Tisza an opponent of Pan-Slavism (q.v.), as well as a strong adherent of the Austro-Hungarian-German military alliance. In controlling the Parliament, he used strong-hand methods similar to those employed by his father. When nationalistic agitation led to the disintegration of the Liberal Party (1905–06), Tisza temporarily withdrew from politics. It was during this period that he became the number one target of the liberal intellectuals gathered around such periodicals as the *Twentieth Century (Huszadik Század)* and the West *(Nyugat)*. Among the latter were such prominent personalities as the poet Endre Ady (q.v.) and the sociologist Oszkár Jászi (q.v.).

Tisza returned to politics in 1910 under the banner of the newly founded National Work Party (q.v.), becoming the speaker of the Parliament in 1912 and prime minister for the second time in 1913. As prime minister he continued to oppose the extension of voting rights for fear of a takeover by the national minorities (q.v.). For the same reason, he also opposed Austro-Hungary's declaration of war against Serbia (q.v.) in 1914, but then relented and went along with it. Given the turn of events in World War I (q.v.) and Emperor Charles's desperate efforts to find a way out of the war through a separate peace, Tisza was forced to resign in June of 1917. Thereafter he voluntarily went to the front as the commander of the Debrecen Hussar Regiment.

Being the number one target of the radicals, on October 31, 1918, Tisza was assassinated by a group of Bolshevik revolutionaries. Following Historic Hungary's dismemberment, Tisza's role as the defender and upholder of Austro-Hungarian dualism made him into a much more appreciated statesman and even a hero of the interwar Horthy Regime (q.v.). In 1921, the University of Debrecen (q.v.) was named after him. Although born a member of the propertied nobility (q.v.), only in 1897 did Tisza join the ranks of the aristocracy (q.v.). Emperor Francis Joseph (q.v.) permitted his uncle, Lajos Tisza (1832–98), to transfer his own newly acquired (1883) title of "count" (q.v.) upon his nephew.

TISZA, KÁLMÁN (1830–1902). A conservative Hungarian statesman of the Dualist Period (q.v.) and the father of Count István Tisza (q.v.), who still holds the longest tenure among Hungary's prime ministers (1875–90). Coming from a Trans-Tisza (q.v.) Protestant noble family, in 1859 Tisza gained much popularity by his stand against the Habsburg-initiated (q.v.) effort to limit the autonomy of the Protestants (q.v.) in Hungary (q.v.). Following the suicide of his uncle, Count László Teleki (q.v.), in 1861, Tisza became the leader of the Resolution Party (q.v.) in the Parliament (q.v.). As one of the top leaders of the "left-center opposition" in the legislature, Tisza initially opposed the Austro-Hungarian Compromise of 1867 (q.v.). In 1875, however, he engineered a merger between his party and the pro-Compromise Deák Party (q.v.), and thus created the Liberal Party (q.v.) that dominated Hungarian political life until its demise in 1906. Soon after this merger, Tisza assumed the prime ministership of Hungary. During his tenure of fifteen years he supported the compromise with Austria (q.v.) and made major efforts to modernize Hungary's economy as well as the archaic Hungarian administrative system. In doing so, he tried to save the impoverished members of his gentry class (q.v.) by bringing them into the ranks of the state administration. In foreign policy Tisza supported Austria-Hungary's expansion into the Balkans (q.v.) through the occupation of Bosnia-Herzegovina (q.v.), as well as the empire's military alliance with Germany via the Dual Alliance of 1879 (q.v.). His control over the Parliament was so thorough, that he was simply called "The General," while the members of his party were routinely referred to as "The Mameluks"([slaves) (q.v.). Although Tisza lost the prime ministership in 1890, he continued to dominate the Liberal Party, and thus much of Hungarian politics until his death in 1902.

TISZA RIVER. Hungary's second largest and second most important river, immediately after the Danube (q.v.). As it originates in the Northeastern Carpathians (q.v.) and empties into the Danube somewhat to the north of Belgrade (q.v.)—both of these regions having been part of Historic Hungary (q.v.)—for quite a while the Tisza was known as the "most Hungarian river" *(legmagyarabb folyó)*. It cuts across the Great Hungarian Plain (q.v.) and divides the Hungarians into what the historian Szekfű (q.v.) called the Western-oriented "Danube Magyars" and the Eastern-oriented "Tisza Magyars." The former of these were generally Catholic (q.v.) and pro-Habsburg (q.v.), while the latter were mostly Calvinist (q.v.) and anti-Habsburg.

TITHE [DECIMA, DÉZSMA, TIZED]. A form of tax paid to the Catholic Church (q.v.) by the peasants during the age of feudalism. Ten percent of most of the produce, live animals, and manufactured goods had to go to the church as a kind of religious tax. In Hungary the compass of the tithe—known as the *dézsma* or *tized*—was extended progressively after the introduction of bonded serfdom (q.v.) in the early 16th century. Thereafter the collection was increasingly carried out by tax collectors who purchased this right from the church. During the 16th and 17th centuries, the terms *dézsma* or *decima* were also used to refer to the feudal dues collected by the absentee Hungarian lords in Turkish Hungary (q.v.), as well as by the representatives of the Ottoman Sultan (q.v.) and various non-Turkish local authorities. The latter included the *hajdú* towns (q.v.) and the peasant counties (q.v.), especially in the transitional region between Turkish Hungary and Transylvania (q.v.), known as the Partium (q.v). The tithe *(dézsma, decima)* is to be distinguished from the *ninth (none)* (q.v.)—that is, the second tenth of the annual yield—which was collected by the landlords from the same peasants during pre- and post-Turkish times.

TŐKÉS, LÁSZLÓ (b.1953). Bishop of the Hungarian Reformed (Calvinist) Church in Transylvania (q.v.), based in Oradea Mare (Nagyvárad) (q.v.), Romania (q.v.), who is credited with starting the revolution that led to the overthrow of the oppressive communist-chauvinist Ceausescu Regime in December 1989. After graduating from the Reformed Theological School at Cluj (Kolozsvár), Tőkés served as assistant pastor and pastor in several Hungarian Reformed congregations in Transylvania, ending up in 1987 in the former Hungarian city of Timişoara (Temesvár) (q.v.). Because of his vocal opposition to the Ceausescu Regime and to Ceausescu's plans to destroy thousands of Hungarian villages in Transylvania to further the cause of the denationalization and forced assimilation of the Hungarians, Tőkés was haunted by the regime. His defense by his followers and sympathizers in December 1989 led to the bloodbath of Timişoara (December 17-18), which in turn served as the catalyst to the uprising in Bucharest that overthrew Nicolae Ceausescu.

Because of his leading role in the Romanian Revolution, Tőkés was initially given made member in Romania's Provisional Committee of National Salvation. But after the consolidation of power in the hands of the ex-communist Ion Iliescu and the simultaneous reemergence of national chauvinism in Romania, Tőkés lost his position and became once more subject to persecution efforts by the Romanian government. Highly regarded in Hungary (q.v.) and in the West, as well as by the Hungarians of Romania, Tőkés has been elected to various leadership positions in Hungarian organizations dedicated to the preservation of Hungarian national rights, including the Federation of Hungarian Workers in Romania *(Romániai Magyar Dolgozók Szövetsége).* Tőkés summarized his view about the events of Timişoara in a book entitled *The Siege of Temesvár '89 (Temesvár ostroma '89)* (1991).

TOLERATION, EDICT OF [EDICTUM TOLERATIONAE, TÜRELMI RENDELET] (1781). Issued by Joseph II (q.v.), who was driven by the spirit of Enlightenment (q.v.), the Edict of Toleration guaranteed freedom of worship to the Protestants (q.v.) and the Orthodox Christians (q.v.) within the Habsburg Empire (q.v.), including Hungary (q.v.). They were given the right to build churches (but without bells and without entrance to the main street), to employ pastors and teachers on a regular basis, and to serve in state offices. Moreover, they were not compelled to take the Catholic oath, nor were the children of mixed marriages obliged to undergo compulsory Catholic baptism. The primacy of the Catholic Church was still retained, but most of the limitations imposed by the Carolina Resolutio of 1731 (q.v.) were terminated.

TOLLAS, TIBOR [TIBOR KECSKÉSI] (b.1920). The penname of the poet and political activist, who in December 1956 founded and ever since edited the widely read emigré newspaper *NationalGuardian (Nemzetőr),* and who thus has become one of the most recognized spokesman of the anti-communist Hungarian emigration. A graduate of the Hungarian Ludovika Military Academy (1941), Tollas served through World War II (q.v.), and also after the war in the new Hungarian People's Army. In 1947 he was arrested and convicted to ten years of imprisonment. Freed in 1956, he became involved in the Hungarian Revolution of that year (q.v.), and then fled to the West. In addition to the *National Guardian,* which he publishes in

Munich, Germany, since 1957 Tollas has published about a dozen volumes of his own poetry, as well as several collections of prison and revolutionary anthologies. The most influential of these is his own *Botanical Garden (Füveskert)* (1957), which contains a selection of the poems that he and his fellow inmates wrote in prison, and which appeared in numerous editions in at least six languages. Also important is his *Glory to the Defeated of 1956 (Gloria victis 1956)* (1966), which is a collection of poems from throughout the world inspired by the Hungarian Revolution of 1956. Because of his strong patriotism and anti-communism, and because of his oratorical ability employed skillfully during his frequent travels among Hungarians throughout the world, Tollas has become a kind a living symbol of Hungarian nationalism and anti-communism. Communism collapsed in 1989–90, yet the turn of events in Hungary did not proceed according to his liking. Thus, Tollas continues to remain a strong critic of the policies of the post-communist governments in Hungary.

TORDA, UNION OF (1438). This agreement renewed the terms and strengthened of the Union of Kápolna (q.v.) of 1437, which brought the three historic nations of Transylvania (q.v.)—the Hungarians, Székelys, and Saxons—into a single interest group, and laid the foundations of an autonomous political system that developed fully only after the Ottoman conquest (q.v.) of much of Hungary (q.v.). This "Union of the Three Nations" was reaffirmed at the diet of Torda on December 20, 1542, following the conquest of Buda (q.v.) by the Turks (q.v.), and after Hungary's trisection had already become a political reality.

TORGYÁN, JÓZSEF (b.1932). President of the Smallholders' Party (q.v.), who rose to prominence in wake of the collapse of communism in Hungary (q.v.). A man who studied both music and law (earning a J.D. in 1955), Torgyán was a practicing lawyer until 1990, when he switched to politics. In the first post-communist Parliament (q.v.) he was the leader of the Smallholders' contingent as a coalition partner of Prime Minister Antall (q.v.) and the

Hungarian Democratic Forum (q.v.). Although reelected in 1994, the victory by the Socialist Party (q.v.) forced him into opposition. In the early years of the 1990s, Torgyán was viewed by many Hungarians as a soapbox orator. Yet, in light of the growing loss of popularity by the socialist government under Prime Minister Gyula Horn (q.v.), since late 1995 he has risen to the ranks of one of the more popular politicians in Hungary.

TÓT [SLOVAK]. The original name by which the Slovaks (q.v.) of Northern Hungary (q.v.) were known until the early 20th century. In medieval Hungary (q.v.) this term was applied collectively to all of the Slavs (q.v.). This usage survived in many areas until early modern times. Thus, medieval Slavonia (q.v.), which is now part of Croatia (q.v.), was known to the Hungarians as *Tótország* (Land of the Tót people). Moreover, many of the Croats (q.v.), who speak the "kai" dialect, as well as the Slovens (q.v.) of southwestern Trans-Danubia (q.v.), were known by this name. But it is the Slovaks who have retained this name for the longest period of time. The origin of this term probably goes back to the name of a German *Taut* tribe, whose name has also given birth to the terms Teuton, *Teutonic* (German, Germanic).

TRANS-DANUBIA [DUNÁNTÚL]. The western and the most developed part of today's Hungary (q.v.), which is located on the right bank of the Danube (q.v.) and coincides to a large degree with the former Roman province of Pannonia (q.v.). In its center is Lake Balaton (q.v.), which is the largest lake in Central Europe (q.v.), as well as the Central Trans-Danubian Mountain range. The latter consists of the Bakony, Vértes, Gerécse, Pilis, Visegrád, and the Buda Hills. Trans-Danubia's most important cities include Buda (q.v.), Esztergom (q.v.), Székesfehérvár (q.v.), Pécs (q.v.), Veszprém (q.v.), Komárom, Győr (q.v.), Sopron (q.v.), and Kőszeg. It is bordered in the north by Slovakia (q.v.), in the west by Austria (q.v.), and in the south by Croatia (q.v.) and Slovenia (q.v.). Trans-Danubia is largely Catholic, with an admixture of Germans and Slavs, who have generally been loyal to the Habsburgs (q.v.). They have been characterized by the noted historian Gyula Szekfű (q.v.) as the "Danube Magyars." (See Szekfű.)

TRANS-TISZA REGION [TISZÁNTÚL]. The eastern half of the Great Hungarian Plain (q.v.) located between the Tisza River (q.v.) and the mountains of Transylvania (q.v.). Since the Turkish conquest (q.v.), its eastern half was known as the Partium (q.v.), most of which was attached to Romania (q.v.) after World War I (q.v.), along with historic Transylvania. The Trans-Tisza Region is heavily Calvinist (q.v.) and is the home base of the independence-oriented and anti-Habsburg (q.v.) "Tisza Magyars." (See Szekfű.)

TRANSYLVANIA [ERDÉLY, SIEBENBÜRGEN, ARDE-AL]. An eastern province of Historic Hungary (q.v.), which after World War I (q.v.) was attached to Romania (q.v.), along with a section of the Great Hungarian Plain (q.v.) known as the Partium (q.v.). At the beginning of the Christian era, Transylvania had been part of the Kingdom of Dacia, which was conquered by the Roman Empire in A.D. 106. After more than a century and a half of Roman rule, the Romans withdrew their legions and also evacuated the province's population in 271. Transylvania and the surrounding area was then settled by Hunnic, Slavic, Germanic, Avar, and proto-Magyar tribes. Then, at the turn of the 9th to the 10th centuries, it was conquered by the Hungarians (Magyars) (q.v.) of the Árpádian conquest (q.v.) and made part of the new Kingdom of Hungary (q.v.).

Some of the Hunnic and proto-Magyar tribes remained there and evolved into the Hungarian-speaking Székelys (q.v.). Later—along with the Hungarians and the Transylvanian Saxons—they became one of the three privileged nations of Transylvania. Retaining a degree of autonomy within the Hungarian kingdom, Transylvania was off and on under the control of a governor or *voievod* (q.v.), who was always appointed by the king. In the mid–12th century the province's ethnic picture was altered by the coming of the Transylvanian Saxons (q.v.), who transplanted elements of urban culture to the region. Then, at the turn of the 12th to the 13th century, the situation was complicated by the gradual infiltration of groups of Vlach (q,v,) shepherds (q.v.) from the Balkans (q.v.). Although their number grew with time, because they failed to achieve meaningful social mobility, they were not given any recognition until modern times. In 1437, Transylvania's three historic nations—the Hungarians, Székelys, and Saxons—signed the Union of Kápolna (q.v.) and formed the "Union of the Three Nations of Transylvania," which still left a great deal of autonomy for each of them. The Vlachs, who much later renamed themselves Romanians, were so inconsequential in those days that they were not even invited to join this union. Following the Turkish conquest (1526) and the subsequent trisection (1541) of Hungary, Transylvania became the home base of a new Hungarian national monarchy under the rule of John Zápolya (q.v.) and John Sigismund (q.v.). Thus, while the western and northern parts of the country evolved into Royal Hungary (q.v.) under the rule of the Habsburgs (q.v.), its eastern section tried to become a "national kingdom." When the experimentation with this kingdom failed around 1570–71, Transylvania took the path of an autonomous principality under the suzerainty of the Ottoman Empire (q.v.) (1571–1690).

During the two centuries of Hungary's tripartitioning, the political system of Transylvania was so arranged that—while the three privileged nations retained their separate autonomies—the principality was always under the rule of a Hungarian prince. These princes were assisted by the Transylvanian Diet (q.v.), which—in contrast to the Latin-speaking Hungarian Diet—continued to use the Magyar (q.v.) as its official language (q.v.). Moreover, these princes and their governments never ceased to represent the ideals of a Hungarian national state, nor fail to work for the ultimate reunification of Historic Hungary. The Liberation Wars (q.v.) of the late 17th and early 18th centuries brought about the reconquest of all parts of former Hungary, but not its reunification. Historic Transylvania remained under separate Habsburg (q.v.) administration until 1848, and only the Austro-Hungarian Compromise of 1867 (q.v.) integrated it completely into the Kingdom of Hungary.

The fall of the Austria-Hungary (q.v.) after World War I (q.v.) brought about the dismemberment of Historic Hungary and the transfer of Transylvania, along with a significant portion of the Great Hungarian Plain (q.v.), to Romania. The northern half of this territory was returned to Hungary by the second Vienna Award (q.v.) of 1940, but then it was lost again after World War II (q.v.). Ever since that time—but especially during the domination of the communist-chauvinist dictator, Nicolae Ceausescu (r.1964–89)—the Hungarians of Transylvania have been subjected to a process of systematic denationalization; and Transylvania itself to a conscious policy of settling more Romanians there from the old kingdom.

While the Ceausescu Regime collapsed in 1989, national antagonism remains on a high level. In this respect, conditions have barely improved in the 1990s. But the recent election (November 1996) of Emil Constantinescu to the Romanian presidency created much hope and many expectations among the Transylvanian Hungarians. This is true, especially since the newly formed Romanian government also has some Hungarian members.

TRANSYLVANIAN DIET. Following the trisection of Historic Hungary (q.v.) after the Turkish conquest (q.v.) in the early 16th century, Transylvania (q.v.) began to develop into a separate state, first under rival kings (1526–70) and then under autonomous princes (1570–1690). The roots of the Transylvanian Diet reach back to 1542, when at a meeting of the Transylvanian nobility at Torda, they reaffirmed the union of the "Three Nations of Transylvania" (q.v.) and established a Governing Council consisting of twenty-one representatives, that is, seven from each of the historic nations: Hungarians (q.v.), Székelys (q.v.), and Saxons (q.v.). Subsequently, this Governing Council was expanded through the inclusion of representatives from the Partium (q.v.) as well as by the admission of various ex officio members representing Transylvania's legal system and administrative structure. Because of the preponderance of the Magyar-speaking members (i.e., Hungarians and Székelys), the Governing Council and the Transylvanian Diet always functioned in Hungarian. Moreover, its minutes and documents were also published in the Hungarian (Magyar) language, at the very same time when the Hungarian Diet itself functioned only in Latin. The

Transylvanian Diet was abolished in 1848, as a result of Transylvania's reunification with Hungary.

TRANSYLVANIAN SAXONS. This German-speaking ethnic group had immigrated to Hungary (q.v.), more specifically to the southeastern part of Transylvania (q.v.), in the middle of the 12th century under King Géza II (q.v.). Strictly speaking they were not Saxons, for they came from the region of the Rhine and Mosel Rivers, but in the course of time they came to be called Saxons. Their obligations included the foundation of walled cities, the spreading of urban culture, and the defense of Hungary's frontiers against invaders from beyond the southern and eastern Carpathians (q.v.). Although the Saxons came in several separate waves, they soon intermingled with each other and developed their own peculiar social system and language. Their most significant cities were Kronstadt (Brassó, Braśov) and Hermannstadt (Nagyszeben, Sibiu), but the list of their newly founded urban centers also included Schässburg (Segesvár, Śighiśoara], Reussmarkt (Szerdahely, Sibiului), Mühlenbach (Szászsebes, Sebeś], Broos (Szászváros, Oraśtie], Neukirch (Újegyház, Nocrich], Reps (Kõhalom, Rupea), Bistritz (Beszterce, Bistriťa], Heltau (Nagydisznód, Cisnãdie], Karlsburg (Gyulafehérvár, Alba Iulia), and others.

The Saxons were first granted autonomy under the leadership of their own counts *(Gräfe, gerébek)* by King Andrew II (q.v.) in the *Diploma Andreanum* of 1224. For the first two and a half centuries these Saxon counts were appointed by the Hungarian monarchs, but in 1464 King Matthias Corvinus (q.v.) granted the Saxons the right to elect their own leaders. In 1437 the leaders of the Transylvanian Saxons signed the Union of Kápolna (q.v.) with the Magyar (q.v.) and the Székely (q.v.) estates. Although originally a defensive measure against the rebellious peasants, it gradually evolved into a trialistic autonomy that characterized the Transylvanian political system for the next several centuries. In 1486 the Saxons established the Saxon University (i.e., National Council) of Transylvania, which hereafter governed them and also represented them at home and abroad. During the 16th and 17th centuries, the Saxons held one-third of the votes for the election of the princes and the governments of Transylvania—the other two-thirds being in the hands of the Magyars and the Székelys, both of whom were Hungarians. In the second quarter of the 16th century, all Transylvanian Saxons converted to Lutheranism, and since 1552 they had their own national Lutheran Church. The political, religious, and military struggles of the Turkish period were difficult for the Transylvanian Saxons, as was the fact that in 1690 they were placed directly under the control of the Habsburg Imperial Government (q.v.) via the *Diploma Leopold-inum.* Even though this document guaranteed Transylvania's political autonomy and the toleration of the main Protestant denominations (Calvinism and Lutheranism), in effect for the next nine decades, the position of the Protestants became increasingly difficult. The 19th century witnessed the rise of Saxon (German) national consciousness, which both helped and hindered their relationship to the Hungarians (Magyars and Székelys).

Following the Austro-Hungarian Compromise of 1867 (q.v.), the autonomy of the Saxons was again guaranteed by law. This many centuries-long coexistence was shattered by the dismemberment of Historic Hungary (q.v.) by the Treaty of Trianon (q.v.). During the interwar years, the Transylvanian Saxons and Hungarians shared the common fate of their new minority status. Hitler's sins, however, also visited them at the end of World War II (q.v.). Many of the Saxons were expelled by the new Romanian Regime. Those who stayed, were subjected to an increasing and relentless process of Romanianization. During the Ceausescu Regime some of them were permitted to emigrate to Germany (q.v.), but only in return for which large sums of German money flowing into Romania (q.v.). Today the Transylvanian Saxons constitute a dying community whose members appear to have only two options: assimilation into a society that is still basically alien to their Western minds, or emigration to modern Germany.

TREASURY   see   ROYAL   TREASURY.

TRIALISM [TRIALIZMUS]. A proposed alternative to the system of Dualism (q.v.) that had been incorporated into the structure of the Austro-Hungarian Empire (q.v.) via the Austro-Hungarian Compromise of 1867 (q.v.). During the existence of Austria-Hungary, several trialistic solutions were proposed by the leaders of the nonparticipating nationalities. The first of these came in 1870, and it would have made the Czechs (q.v.) into the third dominant partner within the Dual Monarchy (q.v.). Then came another proposal in the early 20th century that would have included the South Slavs (Croats, Slovens, Bosnians, Serbians) (q.v.) in this partnership, an idea that was also favored by the heir to the throne, Archduke Francis Ferdinand (q.v.). Finally, during World War I (q.v.) came another proposal for the transformation of Austria-Hungary into an Austro-Hungarian-Polish Confederation. None of these trialistic proposals was ever tried or implemented. The dissolution of the Dual Monarchy (q.v.) and the rise of several small so-called "national states" after World War I (q.v.) made any further experimentations with this idea completely impractical.

TRIANON HUNGARY. The customary name of the small truncated country that had been carved out of Austria-Hungary (q.v.) and of Historic Hungary (q.v.) after World War I (q.v.). It was less than 30 percent of its original size, its frontiers having been established by the Treaty of Trianon (q.v.)—hence its name. It existed in that form between 1918/20 and 1938, when the temporary success of Hungarian revisionism (q.v.) began to enlarge it by regaining some of the lost territories. The term "Trianon Hungary" is also often applied to post–World War II (q.v.) Hungary, even though the latter is not fully identical with interwar Hungary. The Treaty of Paris of 1947 (q.v.) made the country even smaller.

TRIANON, TREATY OF (1920). The post–World War I treaty signed on June 4, 1920, that established and sanctified the new frontiers of "Trianon Hungary" (q.v.). It deprived the country of 71.3 percent of its territory, 63.3 percent of its population, 61.4 percent of its cultivable lands, 88 percent of its forests, 62.1 percent of its railroad lines, 64.5 percent of its highways, 55.7 percent of its industry, 67 percent of its financial institutions, and 100 percent of its gold, silver, copper, and salt mines. It was a treaty, which, in direct violation of the highly touted principle of national self-determination—which was used as a pretext to partition Historic Hungary (q.v.) and Austria-Hungary (q.v.)—placed fully one-third of the Hungarian (Magyar) nation (q.v.) under foreign rule. Most of these Magyars were located just across the new frontiers in several artificially created states, all of which were extremely multinational in character, and only one of which had a majority nationality that exceeded 50 percent of its population.

The Treaty of Trianon also imposed many other limitations and financial obligations upon truncated Hungary (q.v.). Its unusual harshness and unfairness was the number one reason why Hungarian revisionism (q.v.) was so powerful and emotional during the interwar years. It was also the cause of Hungary's willingness to ally herself with Fascist Italy and Nazi Germany in order to undo these injustices and regain some of the Hungarian-inhabited territories directly adjacent to the new frontiers. Although Hungary's cause was just, her participation in World War II (q.v.) on the wrong side, and her inability to get out of the war in time (like Romania), made it certain that her revisionist gains (1938–41) would be lost again. The impact of the Treaty of Trianon created a national disease that used to be called the Trianon Syndrome. It has abated somewhat since World War II, but it is still an emotional issue with most Hungarians. This is particularly so because of the continued mistreatment of the Hungarian minorities (q.v.) in most of the neighboring countries.

TRICESIMA [THIRTIETH, HARMINCAD VÁM]. Royal duty that was applied to all goods imported to or exported from the country ever since the reign of Charles I (q.v.) in the early 14th century. Initially, this amounted to one percent of the value of the goods, but by 1405 the value of this tariff was raised to 3.3 percent. The earliest offices for the collection of the *tricesima* were set up by Louis the Great (q.v.) in the second half of the 14th century.

TRIPARTITUM [HÁRMASKÖNYV] (1514). An extremely influential collection of Latin-language Hungarian laws prepared in 1514 by Lord Chief Justice István Werbőczy (q.v.), which consists of three parts. Even though this collection was never ratified by the Hungarian Diet (q.v.), it remained the de facto source of Hungarian constitutionalism and legal system right up to 1848. This was all the more so, as in 1628 it was incorporated into the *Corpus Juris Hungarici* (q.v.). The *Tripartitum* reflected the class interests of the Hungarian common nobility (q.v.) from which Werbőczy himself emerged. One of its most significant lasting impacts was that it codified the binding of the Hungarian peasants to the soil (bonded serfdom) (q.v.) and thus excluded a large segment of the population from the concept of the "nation." As a result, until the Hungarian Revolution of 1848–49 (q.v.), the Latin term "Natio Hungarica" ("Hungarian Nation") (q.v.) came to be equated in practice simply with the Hungarian nobility (q.v.).

TRIPLE ALLIANCE (1882). A military agreement among Germany (q.v.), Austria-Hungary (q.v.), and Italy (q.v.), which expanded the Austro-Hungarian-German Dual Alliance (q.v.) signed three years earlier (1879). According to this agreement, in case of a Russian attack on either one of them, Germany and Austria-Hungary would help each other, while Italy would remain neutral. In case of a French attack against Germany or Italy, the two would join forces. The Triple Alliance was renewed every five years until 1915, when Italy opted against renewal and joined the Triple Entente (q.v.) in their war against Germany and Austria-Hungary. Austria-Hungary's participation in the Dual and the Triple Alliances was prompted by her fear of Russian Pan-Slavism (q.v.) and expansionism. Russian expansion into the Balkans (q.v.) intruded upon her vital interests there. Moreover, Russian-sponsored Pan-Slavism was undermining her domestic health in light of her numerous Slavic minorities

TRIPLE ENTENTE (1894–1907). A set of three agreements between France and Russia (1894), France and England (1904), and England and Russia (1907) that brought these three colonial powers together into a single alliance system. The Triple Entente was directed largely against Germany and the German-led Triple Alliance (q.v.). The existence of these two competing alliance systems was a major long-range cause of World War I (q.v.).

TRNAVA   see   NAGYSZOMBAT.

TURANIANS. In common usage— first popularized by Max Müller (1823–1900) of Oxford University—the Turanians are composed of those nations that speak one of the Ural-Altaic languages (q.v.) and whose alleged original homeland is the Turanian Plain in Central Asia (q.v.). Most of the Turanians are either Turkic (q.v.) or Finno-Ugric (q.v.). The latter include the Finns, Estonians, and the Hungarians (q.v.). The common denominators of the Turanians include their agglutinative languages (q.v.) and the fact that most, but not all of them, were known to have been in the category of horse-nomads (q.v.). In wake of Müller's linguistic writings, the term Turanian was popularized in the late 19th and early 20th centuries, at the time of the birth of the various pan movements, including Pan-Turanism (q.v.).

TURANIAN MOVEMENT. This movement was a component of Pan-Turanism (q.v.), which proclaimed the need for cultural, economic, and political cooperation among the Turanian peoples (q.v.). It was a Romantic movement born in late-19th and early-20th-century Hungary (q.v.) as a reaction against the threat of Pan-Slavism (q.v.). Its early exponents included the historian Sándor Márki (1853–1925), the poet Árpád Zempléni (1865–1919), and the economist Alajos Paikert (1866–1948)—the latter of whom became the founder of the Turan Society *(Turáni Társaság)* (1910) as well as of its periodical the *Turán* (1913). In 1920 the Turanian Society split into two: the scholarly Kőrösi Csoma Society *(Kőrösi Csoma Társaság)* and the romantic Turanian Federation of Hungary *(Magyarországi Turáni Szövetség).* The first of these pursued scholarly research on the Turanians, while the latter explored and expounded the rather hazy political goals of Pan-Turanism.

The Turanist Movement found response in the new Turkish Republic under Mustapha Kemal Atatürk (1881–1938), as well as among some of the Turkic peoples in the Soviet Union (q.v.). In Hungary it became increasingly the romantic ideology of a few dreamers, which gradually petered out during World War II (q.v.). Some members of this movement joined forces with the Arrow Cross Party (q.v.). In the decades following the war, the Turanian Movement was resurrected among Hungarian emigrés in South America, North America, and Australia. It came to be connected with a number of unscholarly theories about the alleged Sumerian, Egyptian, Hittite, Etruscan, Mayan, etc., origins of the Hungarians.

TURANISM see **TURANIAN MOVEMENT, PAN-TURAN-ISM.**

TURKEY. The commonly used name both of the Ottoman Empire (q.v.) and of the Republic of Turkey that emerged out of the ruins of the Ottoman state after World War I. The Ottoman Empire used to be a multilingual and multiethnic Islamic state, while modern Turkey is a Turkish-speaking secular republic.

TURKIC LANGUAGES. A group of related languages spoken by various Turkic Peoples (q.v.) of the past and the present. They belong into the Altaic subfamily of the Ural-Altaic languages (q.v.), while Hungarian or Magyar (q.v.) is in the Uralic sub-family.

TURKIC PEOPLES. The collective name of those ethnic groups and nationalities of the past and the present that speak one of the many Turkic languages (q.v.). In the past, these Turkic peoples included such nationalities as the Huns (q.v.), Avars (q.v.), Khazars (q.v.), Pechenegs (q.v.), Cumans (q.v.), and the Ottomans (q.v.), many of whom have intermingled with the Hungarians (q.v.). Today, Turkic-speaking peoples inhabit Anatolia (q.v.), parts of the Caucasus mountain range, and much of Central Asia (q.v.). Some of the most prominent among them are the modern Turks, Azeris, Khazaks, Uzbeks, Turkmens, Kirghiz, Kipchak, and Crimean Tatars (q.v.).

TURKISH CONQUEST [OCCUPATION] OF HUNGARY.
The Turks began to attack Hungary's (q.v.) southern borders in the late 14th century, but they were unable to penetrate the country on a permanent basis until the defeat of the Hungarian Royal Army commanded by King Louis II (q.v.) in 1526 at the Battle of Mohács (q.v.). Following Mohács, the Ottomans withdrew from most of the country and did not resume their conquests until 1541. In that year they took possession of the capital city of Buda (q.v.) and made it into the seat of their power in central Hungary. They expanded their control further in a series of wars, the most significant of which were the campaigns of Süleyman the Magnificent (q.v.) (r.1520-66), the Fifteen Years War (q.v.) (1591-1606) at the turn of the century, and the Austro-Turkish War of 1664. The Ottomans tried again to expand their power in 1683, but their Second Siege of Vienna (q.v.) fizzled and they were soon forced out of all of Hungary.

TURKISH EMPIRE see OTTOMAN EMPIRE.

TURKISH HUNGARY (1526/41–1699/1718). The south-central part of the Kingdom of Hungary (q.v.) conquered by the Turks (q.v.) and then incorporated into the Ottoman Empire (q.v.) after the Battle of Mohács of 1526 (q.v.). This continuously enlarged region was surrounded in a horseshoe fashion by Habsburg-ruled Royal Hungary (q.v.) in the west and the north, and the Principality of Transylvania (q.v.) in the east—which itself was an Ottoman vassal state. Initially, Turkish Hungary embraced only the region between the Danube (q.v.) and the Tisza Rivers (q.v.), and the eastern part of Trans-Danubia (q.v.). By the mid-17th century, however, it doubled its size and included territories east of the Tisza, over half of Trans-Danubia, Slavonia (q.v.), and the southeastern part of Croatia (q.v.). It was reconquered by the Habsburgs (q.v.) in the late 17th and early 18th centuries in two separate wars, the Liberation Wars of 1683-99, and the Austro-Turkish War of 1716-18.

TURKS see OTTOMAN TURKS.

- U -

UKRAINE. A former component republic of the Soviet Union (q.v.), located on the Pontic Steppes (q.v.) to the north of the Black Sea (q.v.), which became an independent state on January 1, 1992. The former 9th-century homeland of the Hungarians, Etelköz (q.v.), was both located on the territory of today's Ukraine. The Republic of Ukraine also holds a portion of the Carpathian Basin (q.v.)—the province of Carpatho-Ruthenia (q.v.)—which has been part of Historic Hungary (q.v.) for a whole millennium, from the late 9th century until after World War I (q.v.)

UNITARIANISM [ANTI-TRINITARIANS]. This is a form of Christianity that rejects the Holy Trinity and asserts that God is one person. In the mid-16th century it was known as anti-Trinitarianism, but subsequently it came to be identified primarily as Unitarianism. One of the best-known early advocates of the anti-Trinitarian ideology was the Spanish physician Michael Servetus (1509/11–53), who espoused his views in his *About the Errors of the Trinity (De Trinitatis Erroribus)* (1531) and *Restitution of Christianity (Christianismi Restitutio)* (1553), for which he was later burned as a heretic at the orders of John Calvin (1509–64).

Anti-Trinitarian ideas had penetrated Hungary (q.v.) and Transylvania (q.v.) in the 1550s, and it was in the latter province where they were distilled and shaped into the official denomination of Unitarianism. The man primarily responsible for this was the Protestant clergyman Ferenc Dávid (q.v.), who began to spread his new faith under the protection of Prince/King John Sigismund (q.v.), especially after he had become the latter's court chaplain in 1564. With John Sigismund's approval, Unitarianism became one of the four legitimate religious denominations of Transylvania—the other three being Catholicism, Calvinism, and Lutheranism. Its position was codified by the Diet of Torda in 1568 and reconfirmed by Diet of Székelyvásárhely in 1571.

UNITED PARTY [EGYSÉGES PÁRT] (1922–32). The governmental party established in February 1922 with the burdensome official name of "Catholic-Christian Smallholders', Peasants', and Citizens' Party" *(Keresztény-Keresztyén Kisgazda, Földmíves és PolgáriPárt)* under the de facto leadership of Prime Minister István Bethlen (q.v.). It remained in power until 1932, when, after losing its majority, it reorganized and renamed itself the National Unity Party *(Nemzeti Egység Pártja)* (q.v.). Notwithstanding its name, the United Party was the party of the conservative landowning classes, which had no inclination for meaningful political and social reforms.

UNIVERSITY EDUCATION see **EDUCATION IN HUNGARY.**

UNIVERSITIES, MEDICAL. As separate institutions, medical universities in Hungary (q.v.) were born only after World War II (q.v.), in consequence of the postwar reorganization of Hungarian higher education. The roots of medical education, however, reach back at least to 1769, when the Medical Faculty (School) of the University of Nagyszombat (q.v.) was established. In the course of time, it became the Medical Faculty of the University of Budapest (q.v.). In 1951 it was made an independent institution and renamed the Semmelweis Medical University *(Semmelweis Orvostudományi Egyetem = SOTE)*. Today, it is Hungary's largest medical school, where training is available in Hungarian, English, and German.

In addition to the Semmelweis Medical University of Budapest, Hungary has four other medical schools: The Medical University of Debrecen *[Debreceni Orvostudományi Egyetem = DOTE]*, founded in 1918 as the Medical Faculty of the University of Debrecen (q.v.) and made independent in 1951; the Medical University of Pécs *(Pécsi Orvostudományi Egyetem = POTE)*, originally established in 1918 as the Medical Faculty of the University of Pozsony (q.v.), and made independent in 1951; the Albert Szent-Györgyi University of

Medicine *(Szent-Györgyi Albert Orvostudományi Egyetem = SZOTE)* in Szeged, originally founded in 1872 as the Medical Faculty of the University of Kolozsvár (q.v.), transferred to Szeged in 1921, and made independent in 1951; and the Graduate Medical University *(Orvostovábbképző Egyetem = OTE)* of Budapest, originally founded in 1910, reestablished in 1956, and made into an independent university in 1974. In the course of the 1980s and 1990s, all of the above universities introduced medical training also in the English language, and some of the in German.

UNIVERSITY OF BUDAPEST [EÖTVÖS LORÁND TUD-OMÁNYEGYETEM = ELTE]. Hungary's oldest existing university founded by Cardinal Péter Pázmány (q.v.) in 1635 as a Jesuit institution of higher learning. For a century and a half— while Central Hungary was under Turkish occupation (q.v.)—it functioned in the city of Nagyszombat (q.v.) in northwestern Hungary. In 1770, just before the dissolution of the Jesuit Order (q.v.), the university was taken over by the state, transferred to Buda (q.v.) (1777), and then to Pest (q.v.) (1784). Its primary language of instruction until 1848 was Latin (q.v.), after which it became Hungarian or Magyar (q.v.). In 1922 the university was named after its founder: Péter Pázmány University *[Pázmány Péter Tudomány-egyetem]*, while in 1949 it was renamed after a prominent Hungarian scientist: Loránd Eötvös University *[Eötvös Loránd Tudomány-egyetem = ELTE]*.   Traditionally, the University of Budapest had four "faculties" or schools: Theology, Philosophy, Law, and Medicine. During its reorganization in the course of 1949–51, Theology and Medicine were made into separate institutions, while Philosophy was divided into the Arts and the Sciences. Today the University of Budapest (ELTE) is Hungary's largest and most prestigious university, which also has the largest library. But the Schools of Medicine and Theology are still separate institutions.

UNIVERSITY OF DEBRECEN [KOSSUTH LAJOS TUDO-MÁNYEGYETEM = KLTE]. The roots of the University of Debrecen can be traced back to the city's Reformed College established in 1538. The modern university, however, was founded only in 1912 with the traditional four faculties or schools: Theology, Philosophy, Law, and Medicine, and with the incorporation of the above-mentioned Reformed College. During the interwar years (1921-45), the university bore the name of the famed statesman, Count Tisza István (q.v.), while following World War II (q.v.) it was renamed after the great Hungarian patriot, Lajos Kossuth (q.v.), the Kossuth Lajos University *[Kossuth Lajos Tudományegyetem]*. In 1940 the university lost its School of Law to the reestablished University of Kolozsvár (q.v.). During the postwar reorganization (1949-52), the university lost its Schools of Theology and Medicine, which became independent institutions, but gained a School of Natural Sciences. The University of Debrecen has the nation's second largest university library.

UNIVERSITY OF ECONOMIC SCIENCES [BUDAPEST UNIVERSITY OF ECONOMICS, BUDAPESTI KÖZ-GAZDASÁGTUDOMÁNYEGYETEM = KÖZGÁZ]. Originally a School of the Technical University of Budapest (q.v.) (1934), the University of Economics achieved independent status in 1948. In 1953 it was renamed the Karl Marx University of Economic Sciences, and then in 1990 the Budapest University of Economics. It is Hungary's most important center for the teaching and research of economic sciences.

UNIVERSITY OF KOLOZSVÁR [FERENC JÓZSEF TU-DOMÁNYEGYETEM]. Founded in 1872 as Hungary's second modern university, under the name Francis Joseph University *(Ferenc József Tudományegyetem),* the university was driven out from Kolozsvár (Cluj) (q.v.) in 1919 after Transylvania's annexation by Romania (q.v.). It found a new home in the city of Szeged (1921–40). Following the return of Northern Transylvania (q.v.) to Hungary (q.v.) in 1940, the Francis Joseph University returned to Kolozsvár for a few years (1940–45). It was reorganized after the war as the Hungarian Bólyai University *(Bólyai Tudományegyetem),* which in 1959 was forcibly merged with the Romanian Babeš University and consequently lost its Hungarian identity.

UNIVERSITY OF MISKOLC. The roots of this university can be found in the Mining School of Selmecbánya established in 1735. In 1770 the school was raised to the rank of an academy, and following the loss of Northern Hungary (q.v.) in 1918, it was moved to Sopron (q.v.). In 1959 it was transferred to Miskolc as the Technical University for Heavy Industry. In 1990 it was reorganized as the University of Miskolc, with new Schools of Law and Political Science, Languages, and most recently, Humanities.

UNIVERSITY OF NAGYSZOMBAT [TRNAVA]. Founded in 1635 as a Jesuit institution by the most powerful exponent of the Hungarian Counter-Reformation (q.v.), Cardinal Péter Pázmány (q.v.), the university functioned in Nagyszombat until 1777. In that year it was transferred to the old capital of Buda (q.v.), and then in 1784 to its sister city, Pest (q.v.). After the unification of these two cities into Budapest (q.v.) in 1873, the original University of Nagyszombat evolved into the current University of Budapest (q.v.).

UNIVERSITY OF ÓBUDA. Hungary's second oldest medieval university, which functioned only for a few decades, was founded either in 1389 or 1395 by King Sigismund (q.v.). Very little is known about this university, except that all four of its schools (Theology, Philosophy, Law, Medicine) were represented at the Council of Constance in 1414. By the time of the reign of Matthias Corvinus (q.v.), however, its seems to have gone out of existence.

UNIVERSITY OF PÉCS [JPTE]. Hungary's oldest and Central Europe's (q.v.) fourth oldest medieval university founded in 1367 by King Louis the Great (q.v.). Predated only by the Universities of Prague (1348), Cracow (1364), and Vienna (1365), the original University of Pécs was the pride of Hungary (q.v.) and the result of King Louis's efforts to bring Western learning into his kingdom. Sadly, the original University of Pécs did not survive beyond the mid–15th century. The current University of Pécs dates back only to 1912, when it was established as the Elizabeth University *(Erzsébet Tudományegyetem)* in the city of Pozsony (q.v.), which had been the capital of Hungary in the course of the 16th through the early 19th centuries. Following World War I (q.v.) and the loss of Northern Hungary (q.v.), along with the city of Pozsony (Bratislava) (q.v.) to the newly created state of Czechoslovakia (q.v.), the University of Pozsony was transferred to Budapest (1921–23) and then to Pécs (1923), the site of Hungary's first university. It functioned there under its original name until after World War II (q.v.). Following the return of Northern Transylvania (q.v.) and the reestablishment of the University of Kolozsvár (q.v.)—the University of Pécs lost its School of Philosophy to Szeged. During the postwar reorganization of Hungarian education (1949–51), it also lost its Schools of Theology and Medicine, both of which became independent institutions. The university's reorganization and growth took place during the 1970s through the early 1990s, when, in addition to the existing School of Law, it gained a School of Economics (1975), a School of Philosophy (Arts) (1982), and a School of Natural Sciences (1991). In 1982 it also assumed the name of the famous local humanist poet, Janus Pannonius (q.v.).

UNIVERSITY OF POZSONY. Originally founded in 1467 as the Academia Istropolitana (q.v.), it barely survived its founder, Matthias Corvinus (q.v.). The University of Pozsony was not resurrected until 1912, but then it functioned only for seven years, before the city's transfer to newly created Czechoslovakia (q.v.). After the loss of Pozsony (Bratislava) (q.v.), the university was transferred to Budapest (1921-23), and then to the city of Pécs (q.v.) (1923). Its original buildings in Pozsony were taken over by the new Slovak University of Bratislava, which was soon renamed after the prominent Czech (Moravian) educator, Jan Komenský (Johannes Comenius) (1592–1670) (q.v.).

UNIVERSITY OF SZEGED [JÓZSEF ATTILA TUDO-MÁNYEGYETEM = JATE]. The origin of this university goes back to 1921, when, after the loss of Transylvania (q.v.) to Romania (q.v.), the Francis Joseph University of Kolozsvár (q.v.) was transferred to Szeged (q.v.). After Hungary (q.v.) had regained Northern Transylvania (q.v.) in 1940, the Francis Joseph University was returned to Kolozsvár (q.v.). It functioned there through World War II (q.v.), after which it was transformed into the Hungarian Bólyai University, and then in 1959, it was forcibly merged with its Romanian counterpart. (See University of Kolozsvár.) The University of Szeged continued to function in its host city after 1940, first under the name of Miklós Horthy University *(Horthy Miklós Tudományegyetem)*, and then, after 1945, simply as the University of Szeged. It assumed its current name, József Attila University *(József Attila Tudományegyetem)* in 1961. During the interwar years (q.v.) the University of Szeged had four schools: Law, Philosophy, Medicine, and Natural Sciences. In 1940 it lost its Law School to Kolozsvár, while in 1951 its Medical School became independent. Currently, the University has three schools: Law, Philosophy (Arts), and Natural Sciences. The University of Szeged is one of the important centers for medieval studies in Hungary.

UNIVERSITY OF TECHNICAL SCIENCES [TECHNICAL UNIVERSITY OF BUDAPEST, BUDAPESTI MŰ-EGYETEM]. The roots of the Technical University of Budapest reach back to 1782, when Emperor Joseph II (q.v.) founded the *Institutum Geometricum Hydrotechnicum*. In 1850 this institute merged with the *Joseph Polytechnicum* that had been established in 1846 by Archduke Palatine Joseph (q.v.). In 1872 the school was granted university status and was renamed Royal Palatine Joseph Technical University *(Királyi József Nádor Műegyetem)*. In 1934 it acquired a School of Economic Sciences, which it lost in 1948. The latter became the Budapest University of Economic Sciences (q.v.). In 1949 the university also lost its original name through the purging of its long-dead royal benefactor.

UNIVERSITY OF VESZPRÉM. Established in 1949 as a branch campus of the Technical University of Budapest, in 1951 it became an independent institution under the name Veszprém University of Chemical Engineering *(Veszprémi Vegyipari Egyetem).* In 1990 it was renamed University of Veszprém *[Veszprémi Egyetem],* and was expanded by the addition of a School of Humanities. Currently the University of Veszprém is in the process of further expansion.

UPPER CLERGY see **ECCLESIASTICAL SOCIETY IN HUNGARY.**

UPPER HOUSES [FELSŐ TÁBLA, FŐRENDIHÁZ, FEL-SŐHÁZ]. The upper branch of the Hungarian Diet (q.v.) or Parliament (q.v.) ever since the division of the diet into two branches in 1608. Between 1608 and 1848 the name of the Upper House was *felső tábla,* and its membership consisted of the titled nobility and the country's top secular and ecclesiastical office holders under the presidency of the palatine (q.v.), or in his absence, the lord chief treasurer (q.v.). Following the reorganization of the Upper House in 1885, it was renamed to *főrendház* which it remained until 1918. Its membership was now limited to the top Catholic, Calvinist, Lutheran, and Jewish ecclesiastical office holders; to the top justices of the land; to those members of the titled nobility who met the property qualifications; to the representatives of such institutions as the Hungarian Academy of Sciences (q.v.), Chamber of Commerce, Chamber of Law, and the universities; and to those highly respected personalities who were appointed to life membership by virtue of their unique achievements in the sciences, scholarship, business, or the arts. After going out of existence in 1918, the Upper House was reestablished in 1926, when it was done under the name *felsőház* (1926–45). Its membership was basically identical with that of the *főrendház.* After World War II (q.v.), the Hungarian Parliament (q.v.) remained, and still remains, a unicameral legislative body.

UPPER HUNGARY [FELSŐ-MAGYARORSZÁG]. As used during the Turkish period (q.v.) in the 16th and 17th centuries, this term referred to the eastern half of Northern Hungary (q.v.), that is, to the eastern half of today's Slovakia (q.v.) and all of Carpatho-Ruthenia (q.v.) located to the north of Transylvania (q.v.). The dividing line between Upper and Lower Hungary (q.v.) was the eastern borderline of the counties of Liptó, Zólyom, and Nógrád. Upper Hungary was under the control of the Captain General *(Főkapitány)*, who was headquartered in the city of Kassa (Košice) (q.v.). During the 18th and 19th centuries, the term Upper Hungary gradually lost its currency, and in more recent times it was occasionally used as a synonym of Northern Hungary (q.v.).

UPPER NOBILITY see **ARISTOCRACY, MAGNATES, BARONS.**

URAL-ALTAIC LANGUAGES. Members of a presumed linguistic family with two main branches: Uralic (European) and Altaic (Asiatic). The latter includes various Turkic (q.v.) and Mongol languages in Asia and the Middle East, while the former consists largely of Finno-Ugric languages (q.v.), among them the Finnish, Estonian, and Hungarian or Magyar (q.v.). Both the Uralic and the Altaic languages are agglutinative (q.v.) in character, which means that they rely very heavily on the use of prefixes and suffixes—as explained in conjunction with the Magyar language (q.v.).

URBANISM [URBANISTS]. A counter pole to Populism (q.v.) that drew its inspiration from the urban way of life and expressed its attachment to modernization and Western liberalism both in *belles letters* as well as in sociological works. In Hungary (q.v.) this phenomenon developed especially in turn-of-the-century and interwar Budapest (q.v.), many of its exponents being connected with such sociological and literary periodicals as the *Twentieth-Century (Huszadik Század)* (1900–19), the *West (Nyugat)* (1908–41], and *Our Century (Századunk)* (1926-39).

The Populists and the Urbanists were on two different wave lengths from the start. But the Populist-Urbanist controversy and polarization became especially acute during the 1930s, when it acquired political connotations. Moreover, because the ranks of the

Urbanists included a significant percentage of Hungarians of Jewish origins (q.v.), this controversy also acquired a degree of anti-Semitic versus philo-Semitic coloration. This polarization and controversy was ended by the violence of World War II (q.v.) and the Hungarian Holocaust (q.v.), but it resurfaced once more at the time of the collapse of communism (q.v.). Post-communist Urbanism emerged from the ranks of the dissidents around the samizdat periodical *Speaker (Beszélő)*. In 1988 these dissidents formed themselves into the Federation of Free Democrats [FFD] (q.v.). The Populists, on the other hand, resurfaced at an intellectual gathering in the village of Lakitelek (q.v.) in 1987, where they organized themselves into the Hungarian Democratic Forum [HDF] (q.v.), represented by the weekly *Hungarian Forum (Magyar Forum)*. The first post-communist government (1990–94), headed by József Antall (q.v.) and Péter Boross (q.v.), represented a moderate form of Populism, from which the extremists, under the leadership of István Csurka (q.v.), were expelled in the course of 1992–93. The second post-communist government, currently in power and headed by Gyula Horn (q.v.), on the other hand, is a coalition the Hungarian Socialist Party and the FFD, in which the Urbanists play a significant role.

URBANIZATION IN HUNGARY. The first cities in what later became Historic Hungary (q.v.) were Roman settlements founded in the 1st and 2d century A.D. The most prominent ones included Aquincum (Óbuda) (q.v.), Sabaria (Szombathely), Strigonium (Esztergom) (q.v.), and Apulum (Gyulafehérvár). But they all fell into decay with the collapse of the Roman Empire. Thus, by the time the Hungarians (q.v.) appeared, all they found were ruins. Perhaps the first of these to be reestablished was Esztergom, which became the country's first capital and the birthplace of King St. Stephen (q.v.). Following his accession to the throne, King Stephen's transformation of Hungary into a Christian kingdom was paralleled by his efforts to establish more cities. He invited foreigners, especially Italians, to help him in this undertaking. The great period of city foundation in Hungary, however, began in the mid-12th century, when large groups of Germans ("Saxons") (q.v.)

were invited to establish walled cities and introduce urban skills and artisanship into Hungary. These so called "guests" *(hospes)* (q.v.) settled in Upper Hungary (q.v.), Transylvania (q.v.), as well as in a few select places close to the Danube (q.v.).

Following the Mongol invasion (q.v.) in 1241, King Béla IV (q.v.) redoubled these urbanizing efforts by establishing more cities and by dotting Hungary with scores of new stone fortresses. During the 14th and 15th centuries, the Anjou dynasty (q.v.) and Emperor Sigismund (q.v.) also made great efforts to increase the number and size of the cities in Hungary. Because of the absence of a well-developed feudal system—such as those in Germany (q.v.) and France—most of these cities were placed directly under the king, without any control over them by the local nobility (q.v.). Thus, many of them became "Royal Free Cities" (q.v.), which enjoyed extensive autonomy and self-government. At the time of the division of the Hungarian Diet (q.v.) into two houses in 1608, these Royal Free Cities were given representation in the Lower House (q.v.)—a practice that began informally in the late 14th century.

In addition to the Royal Free Cities, there were also the mining towns (q.v.) and the agricultural towns or *oppidi* (q.v.). The former of these developed out of mining settlements, while the latter grew out of peasant villages. Most of Hungary's medieval cities and mining towns were founded by German-speaking settlers. They functioned under imported German law, which limited access to them by all non-Germans, including Hungarians. The Turkish conquest and occupation (q.v.) of the 16th and 17th centuries destroyed this German preeminence of Hungary's cities, many of which became depopulated. Following the expulsion of the Turks (q.v.), the depopulated cities were settled by migrant foreigners, including Serbians (q.v.) and Vlachs (q.v.) from the Balkans (q.v.), and more Germans from the Holy Roman Empire (q.v.).

This situation began to change during the Hungarian Reform Period (q.v.) and after the Hungarian Revolution of 1848–49 (q.v.), when most cities underwent a rapid process of Magyarization (Hungarianization) (q.v.). This occurred partially through the influx of the rural population into the cities, and partially through a natural process of assimilation of the non-Magyars. Following the Austro-Hungarian Compromise of 1867 (q.v.), the Hungarian government introduced a policy of urban development, which increased the size and urban character of the cities significantly. This policy also made the relatively small cities of Buda (q.v.) and Pest (q.v.) into the modern metropolis of Budapest (q.v.), which became Hungary's main industrial, intellectual, and cultural center.

URBARIUM (1767). A royal decree that dealt with the reorganization of the relationship between the landowning nobility (q.v.) and their serfs (see Serfdom) in order to protect the latter against the increased economic exploitation by the lords. With the spread of seigniorial economy and the enclosure movement, the lords also increased the peasants' feudal work obligations *(robot, corvée)* (q.v.). Desperate and powerless against their lords, the peasants rebelled at several places in Trans-Danubia (q.v.), and then turned to the monarch for help. Maria Theresa (q.v.) responded immediately, partially out of compassion and partially because increased feudal obligations would have undercut the peasants' ability to pay taxes. Collecting these taxes, however, was all the more essential as the Hungarian nobility (q.v.) refused to end their own tax free status.

Although they disliked to have their feudal relations controlled by a royal decree, the frightened nobility went along with the terms of the Urbarium of 1767. This royal document set down the minimum size of a "peasant plot" *(jobbágytelek),* which—depending on the quality of the soil—was to be between thirteen and thirty hectares (thirty-two to seventy-three acres). The smallest subplot that could be held by any peasant was one-eight of a "peasant plot," that is, four to nine acres. The work obligation *(robot, corvée)* was set at 104 days (human labor) or 52 days (labor with draft animals) per year. Decisions made in feudal courts were henceforth to be overseen, not by county courts, but by royal courts. While this was still far from emancipation, the Urbarium of 1767 did eliminate the worst part of feudal arbitrariness and despotism.

- V -

VAJDA see VOIEVOD.

VAJK see STEPHEN I [ST. STEPHEN].

VÁMBÉRY, ÁRMIN [ARMINUS] (1832–1913). A pioneer and widely known Hungarian Orientalist whose books are still being republished and read today. Vámbéry had a unique ability to acquire languages, which he used both in his wide travels throughout the Near East (q.v.) and in Central Asia (q.v.) as well as in his numerous publications. In 1868 he was appointed to the the Chair of Oriental Languages of the University of Budapest (q.v.), a position that he retained until his retirement in 1904. In scholarly circles he is known primarily for the linguistic war he fought with several of his colleagues concerning the origins of the Magyar language (q.v.). While his rivals classified Hungarian (Magyar) as a Finno-Ugric language (q.v.), Vámbéry believed the Hungarians to be of Turkish (q.v.) ethnic-linguistic origin.

Although writing most of his books in Hungarian, many of them appeared also in German and English. His most relevant works include: *About the Eastern Turkic Language (A keleti török nyelvről)* (1869), *Etymological Dictionary of the Turkish and Tatar Languages (A török-tatár nyelvek etymológiai szótára)* (1877), *The Origins of the Hungarians (A magyarok eredete)* (1882), *The Turkish Race (A török faj)* (1885), and *At the Cradle of the Hungarian Nation (A magyarság bölcsőjénél)* (1914). Also interesting are his travelogues, two of which appeared in English: *The Travels of Sidi Ali Reis (alias for Vámbéry)* (1899), and *The Story of My Struggles* (1904). Bram Stoker's *Dracula* (1899), was based on information supplied by Vámbéry about Vlad the Impaler (r.1456-62) or Dracula (q.v.) of Wallachia (q.v.).

VÁMBÉRY, RUSZTEM (1872–1948). A legal scholar and the son of the noted Orientalist Ármin Vámbéry (q.v.) who during World War II (q.v.) was an important spokesman of the left-leaning Hungarian emigration in the United States. After World War II, Vámbéry served as Hungary's (q.v.) second postwar ambassador to the United States (1947–48). Before World War I (q.v.), he had been a practicing attorney and an employee of the Hungarian Ministry of Justice, while during and briefly after the war (1915–20), he served as a professor of law at the University of Budapest (q.v.). During the same period he was also a prominent spokesman of Bourgeois Radicalism (q.v.) in Hungary, represented by Oszkár Jászi (q.v.) and his periodical the *Twentieth Century (Huszadik Század)*.

Following the collapse of Austria-Hungary (q.v.), Vámbéry became a member of the Hungarian National Council headed by Count Michael Károlyi (q.v.), while after the consolidation of the conservative Horthy Regime (q.v.), he returned to the practice of law and to the editing of the radical sociological periodical *Our Century (Századunk)* (1926–39). In light of Hungary's rightward shift, Vámbéry left Hungary in 1939 and emigrated to the United States. In 1941 he founded the American Federation of Democratic Hungarians to oppose the more conservative Movement for Independent Hungary. His federation, however, garnered very little support among Hungarian-Americans.

During the interwar years, Vámbéry was known for defending leftist political opponents of the regime, including a number of the communist peoples' commissars (1920) who had been involved in Béla Kun's (q.v.) Hungarian Soviet Republic (q.v.). Later he also defended Mátyás Rákosi (q.v.), the future "Little Stalin" of Hungary, who, subsequently was instrumental in Vámbéry's appointment as the Hungarian ambassador to Washington. Vámbéry authored several major works on Hungarian criminal law and criminal justice. During and after World War II (q.v.), he likewise published a few political works, including *The Hungarian Problem* (1942), and *Hungary—To Be or Not To Be?* (1946).

VÁRAD   see   NAGYVÁRAD.

VÁRAD, TREATY OF (1538). An agreement between the two rival kings of Hungary—Ferdinand I (q.v.) and John Zápolya (q.v.)— which stipulated that after King John's death the eastern half of Hungary (q.v.) would be reunited with its western half under the control of the Habsburg dynasty (q.v.). The treaty also stated that in case King John would produce some offspring, they would be granted the yet-to-be-established autonomous "Principality of Szepesség," in the center of Upper Hungary (q.v.). Following King John's death in 1540, however, his wife, Isabella (q.v.), and her supporters, refused to abide by the Treaty of Várad. With this act they perpetuated Hungary's fragmentation and made her the battleground of the Holy Roman Emperors (q.v.), the Turkish sultans (q.v.) and the princes of Transylvania (q.v.).

VARNA, BATTLE OF (1444) see VLADISLAV I.

VARNA, CRUSADE OF (1444) see VLADISLAV I.

VASVÁR, PEACE OF (1664). This unfavorable treaty was concluded on August 1, 1664, following the Austro-Turkish War of 1663–64, in which the Turks suffered significant reverses. Fearing French intervention against the Habsburgs (q.v.), Field Marshal Montecuccoli permitted the Ottomans to retain all their holdings in Hungary (q.v.), although both the Ottoman and the Habsburg forces had to withdraw from Transylvania (q.v.). The Treaty of Vasvár produced a widespread consternation and anger throughout Hungary, which was one of the important causes of the Wesselényi Conspiracy (q.v.) as well as of the *kuruc* (q.v.) rebel movement.

VATA (11th c.). The leader of the pagan rebellion in 1046, which came in wake of King St. Stephen's (q.v.) forcible Christianization and centralization of Hungary (q.v.). Vata was a tribal chief who opposed this compulsory Westernization and supported the aspirations of the still pagan Vazul (q.v.), who was probably King St. Stephen's uncle and wished to ascend the Hungarian throne on the basis of the principle of seniority (q.v.).

VAZUL [VÁSZOLY] (11th c.). Hungarian prince of the Árpád dynasty (q.v.), who was probably King St. Stephen's (q.v.) uncle and claimed the throne on the basis of seniority (q.v.). Following the death of Stephen's only son, Emeric (q.v.), Vazul opposed the candidacy of the king's nephew, Péter Orseolo—the future King Péter (q.v.)—and claimed the throne himself (1031). To prevent Vazul's succession, Stephen had him blinded and exiled. According to other sources, it was Stephen's wife, Gisella (q.v.), who was responsible for Vazul's blinding. As a result of his fate, Vazul had subsequently become the hero of those who opposed royal centralization. Still later he also became a hero of many of those, who rejected Westernization in favor of a hazy union of the so-called Turanian peoples of Eurasia (see Turanian Movement).

VENCEL [WENCESLAS] (c.1289–1306). King of Hungary (r.1301–05) and, as Wenceslas III, king of Bohemia (r.1305–06). He was the last member of the Czech Přemyslide dynasty (q.v.). Although crowned king of Hungary with the Holy Crown of Hungary (q.v.), Vencel was unable to outdo his assertive rival, Charles Robert of Anjou (q.v.). Thus, after inheriting the Czech throne in 1305, he returned to Bohemia (q.v.) and transferred his right to the Hungarian throne to Otto Wittelsbach (q.v.) of Bavaria.

VENETIANS see VENICE.

VENICE [VENEZIA, VELENCE]. Venice has been an independent city republic for eleven hundred years (697-1797), during half of which (11th c.-16th c.) it was a naval great power in the Adriatic (q.v.) and the Mediterranean. Medieval Hungary (q.v.) had an ongoing relationship with Venice ever since the late 10th century, when the sister of the future King St. Stephen's (q.v.) married the son of the *doge* of Venice, who soon became the *doge* himself. A few decades later, their son, Peter (q.v.), ascended the Hungarian throne. Following the establishment of these close family ties between the Árpádian dynasty (q.v.) and the Orseolo family of Venice, most of the Hungarian-Venetian relations centered around the control of Dalmatia (q.v.), more specifically, supremacy over such port cities as Zadar (Zara) (q.v.), Spalato (Split) (q.v.), and Ragusa (Dubrovnik) (q.v.). Through most of these centuries, the relationship between Hungary and Venice turned into a three-cornered struggle, with the participation of the Byzantine Empire (q.v.) and, starting with the late 14th century, the Ottoman Empire (q.v.). After the fall of the Kingdom of Hungary following the Battle of Mohács (q.v.) in 1526, Hungary's role vis-à-vis Venice was taken over by the Habsburg Empire (q.v.).

VERECKE PASS [VERCKEI SZOROS]. The mountain pass in the Northeastern Carpathians (q.v.), where the main body of the Hungarian Conquerors entered the Carpathian Basin (q.v.) at the time of the Árpádian Conquest of Hungary (q.v.). The pass is on the northern frontiers of Carpatho-Ruthenia (q.v.), which has been lost to Hungary by the Treaty of Trianon (q.v.) in 1920. During the interwar years (q.v.) Carpatho-Ruthenia and the Verecke Pass was part of Czechoslovakia (q.v.). In 1939 it returned for a few yars to Hungary, only to be lost again after World War II (q.v.), when it was annexed by the Soviet Union (q.v.). Since the collapse of the Soviet Union at the end of 1991, Verecke Pass has been within independent Ukraine (q.v.). In 1996 it was a point of controversy between Hungary and Ukraine, when, in commemoration of the Hungarian millecentennial celebrations, the Hungarians wished to erect a monument there.

VERES, PÉTER (1897–1970). A peasant author and one of the important exponents of Hungarian Populism (q.v.) during the 1930s, and for a while also after World War II (q.v.). Being born into the lowest level of the Hungarian peasantry, possessing only minimal formal education, and having to acquire knowledge through self-education, Veres still became a popular and productive writer. He made his name with his sociographical work entitled *The Peasants of the Great Plain (Az Alföld parasztsága)*in 1936. Thereafter, he wrote scores of essays and many novels dealing with the lives and aspirations of the Hungarian peasantry. In the late 1930s and early

1940s, Veres was involved in most of the movements connected with Hungarian Populism, including the March Front (q.v.) and the Szárszó Conference of 1943 (q.v.). Following World War II (q.v.), he was elected president of the National Peasant Party (q.v.) and became active in party politics. For a while he was even named Hungary's minister of defense (1947–48). But when in 1948 the Peasant Party was suppressed, he too was pushed out of politics. Thereafter, Veres devoted his attention to literary activities, writing significant essays and social novels about the lives of the Hungarian peasants. In contrast to most peasant-based Populist writers, all of whom transformed themselves into intellectuals, Péter Veres never remade himself into an urbanite. He continued to dress and act like a traditional Hungarian peasant to the moment of his death in 1970.

VERHOVAY, GYULA (1849–1906). A popular journalist during the Dualist Period (q.v.) who posed as a Hungarian patriot, but by the 1880s became one of the important exponents of anti-Semitism (q.v.) in Hungary (q.v.). Between 1884 and 1887 Verhovay was a member of the Hungarian Parliament (q.v.), representing the tiny Anti-Semitic Party (q.v.). Being hounded out of politics, in 1892 he withdrew to his wife's country estate in Battonya. In a strange turn of fate, in 1886, when the Hungarian immigrants in the United States founded their first lasting fraternal association, they named it after Gyula Verhovay. It survived under that name up to 1955, when it was renamed the William Penn Fraternal Association. The naming of this association after Verhovay, however, was not the result of his anti-Semitism, but rather of his loudly expressed anti-Habsburg (q.v.) patriotism, which appealed to the simple economic immigrants of those years. (See Emigration from Hungary.)

VESZPRÉM. A city of 70,000 inhabitants in the center of Trans-Danubia (q.v), which during the age of the Árpáds (q.v.) was one of the important royal centers, having been named the "City of the Queens" by King St. Stephen (q.v.). Veszprém was the site of the Orthodox Christian Convent of Veszprémvölgye founded in 1002, as well as of one of the early episcopal sees, the Bishopric of

Veszprém, established in 1009. After attaching Veszprém and its region to his Royal domains, King Stephen also made the city the administrative center of a royal county (q.v.). In 1313, King Charles Robert (q.v.) made the bishop of Veszprém the perpetual *comes (ispán)* (q.v.) of Veszprém County, and the former royal fortress was transformed into an episcopal castle. During the Turkish domination (q.v.) in the 16th and 17th centuries, Veszprém became a frontier fortress and often changed hands. In 1751 the city became the capital of Veszprém County, while in 1949 it acquired its first institution of higher learning, the University of Veszprém (q.v.).

VICE LORD LIEUTENANT [VICE COMES, ALISPÁN]. The elected head of Hungarian county administration between 1870 and 1950. The vice lord lieutenant *(vice comes, alispán)* was nominally under the authority of the lord lieutenant *(comes, főispán]* (q.v.), who was the appointed representative of the royal government. The origins of this office reach back to King St. Stephen (q.v.) in the early 11th century, who transplanted the Carolingian county system (c.v.) to Hungary (q.v.). The word *ispán,* however, is derived from the Slavic word *župan (zhupan)* (q.v.). Second in command after the *ispán* (13th c.), later to the *főispán* (15th c.), the *alispán* played a major role in all aspects of country administration. Between 1723 and 1870 he was elected by the county's nobility (q.v.) from among four persons nominated by the *főispán.* In 1950 these traditional offices were replaced by the Soviet style "council system," and were not revived even after the fall of communism in 1989–90.

VICEROY see VICEROYALTY, VICEROYALTY COUNCIL.

VICEROYALTY [LOCUMTENENTIA, HELYTARTÓSÁG]. The central administrative office of Royal Hungary (q.v.) during the 16th and 17th centuries, when much of the country was under direct or indirect Turkish rule (q.v.). Established soon after Ferdinand's (q.v.) election to the Hungarian throne in 1526, the viceroyalty took its final shape in 1542 under the direction of Pál Várady, the primate-archbishop of Esztergom (r.1526–49). It was based in the city of Pozsony (q.v.), headed by the viceroy *[Locumtenens]* appointed by the king. According to traditions, the palatine (q.v.), was usually appointed to the position of the viceroy. But at times, the Habsburg (q.v.) rulers bypassed the palatine in favor of a more pliable high churchman. Although initially the viceroyalty dealt with all matters concerning Hungary, between the late 16th and late 17th centuries—when Royal Hungary's administration slipped progressively into the hands of the Imperial Government (q.v.)—its authority was limited to judicial matters. In 1723 the viceroyalty was abolished and replaced by the Viceroyalty Council (q.v.).

VICEROYALTY COUNCIL OF HUNGARY [CONSILIUM REGIUM LOCUMTENENTIALE HUNGARICUM, MA-GYAR KIRÁLYI HELYTARTÓTANÁCS]. The chief administrative organ of Hungary (q.v.) under the control of the Imperial Government (q.v.) in the periods between 1723–1848 and 1861–67. The Viceroyalty Council was headed either by the palatine *(nádor)* (q.v.) or by an appointed viceroy. Between 1723 and 1786 it was located in the provisional capital of Pozsony (q.v.), after which it was moved to the old Hungarian capital of Buda (q.v.). The authority of the Viceroyalty Council extended over all matters, with the exception of finances and justice.

VIENNA [WIEN, BÉCS]. A city of two million, the capital of Austria (q.v.), and the former capital of the Holy Roman Empire (q.v.), the Habsburg Empire (q.v.), and Austria-Hungary (q.v.). Built on the site of an ancient Celtic settlement, in the 1st century A.D. it became a Roman outpost under the name of Vindobona. Starting with the 8th century, Bavarian tribes began to move into the area, and by the early 9th century established the province of Ostmark or the Eastern March of the Carolingian Empire.

Medieval written sources first mention Vienna in 881, when invading Hungarians (q.v.) fought a battle in its vicinity against the Franks. During the 10th century Vienna and its vicinity was largely under Hungarian control, but after the defeat of the Hungarians at Augsburg (q.v.) in 955, they were gradually pushed out of that region. In 976 Emperor Otto II the Great (r.973–83) granted Ostmark to Marquis Leopold von Babenberg (q.v.), whose descendants ruled it until 1246. The city's significance increased in 1142, when Marquis Henry II moved his capital from nearby Klosterneuburg to Vienna. In 1156 Ostmark was separated from Bavaria and thereby Vienna became the center of the new principality. In 1237 it rose to the rank of an Imperial City, and in 1282 it became the possession of the new imperial family, the Habsburg dynasty (q.v.). From that year 1282 onward, Vienna remained the center of the dynastic power of the Habsburgs until 1918. In 1485 King Matthias Corvinus (q.v.) conquered Vienna and held it for five years before it reverted to the Habsburgs. The city was besieged by the Ottoman Turks in 1529 and 1683, but without success. In 1814–15 it was the site of the famous Congress of Vienna that reshaped the political map of Europe after Napoleon. At the end of the 17th century, Vienna had a population of 70,000, by 1848 it grew to 400,000, and by the end of the Habsburg Empire [Austria-Hungary] in 1918 to over two million.

VIENNA [HABSBURG IMPERIAL GOVERNMENT]. The name of the capital of the Habsburg Empire (q.v.) was often used as a synonym for the Imperial Government (q.v.), especially by the non-Germanic peoples of the realm.

VIENNA AWARDS (1938–40). Decisions made by Germany (q.v.) and Italy (q.v.) to satisfy part of Hungary's (q.v.) revisionist goals by restoring some of the largely Hungarian-inhabited territories lost with the Treaty of Trianon (q.v.) after World War I (q.v.). Coming soon after the Munich Agreement (September 29, 1938), the First Vienna Award (November 2, 1938) returned about 4,605 square miles of former Hungarian territory from Slovakia (q.v.), with a population of 870,000, of whom 86.5 percent were Hungarians. With the Second Vienna Award two years later (August 30, 1940), Hungary regained from Romania (q.v.) 16,830 square miles of territory, with a population of 2,185,000, the majority of whom were Hungarians (52 percent), a minority Romanians (42 percent), and a small minority Germans (6 percent). The territories regained from Slovakia constituted a narrow strip of Hungarian-inhabited land immediately next to the Hungarian borders. Romania, on the other hand, relinquished the northern half of Transylvania, including the important cities of Kolozsvár (q.v.) and Nagyvárad (q.v.).

VIENNA, CONGRESS OF (1814–15). A meeting of the leaders of the victorious great powers (Austria, Britain, Prussia, and Russia), who triumphed over Napoleon. The peacemakers reorganized Europe on the basis of the principle of legitimacy, with certain compensations to the victors. They also established the Quadruple Alliance and the Holy Alliance for the defense of the social and political order they had established. The chief manipulator of the Congress of Vienna was the chancellor of Austria (q.v.), Prince Metternich (q.v.), who managed to impose his conservative political philosophy on much of Europe for the next several decades.

VIENNA, PEACE OF (1606). An agreement between King/Emperor Rudolph (q.v.) and Prince Stephen Bocskai (q.v.) of Transylvania (q.v.), which ended their war and guaranteed freedom of religion for all Hungarian Protestants (q.v.). The Vienna Peace also stated that Hungary (q.v.) would be governed only by its own palatine (q.v.), and that thenceforth only Hungarians would be appointed to Hungary's high administrative and regional offices. Rudolph likewise acknowledged Transylvania's position as an independent Hungarian principality, and promised to bring the lengthy and bloody war with the Turks (q.v.) to a conclusion. The Treaty of Zsitva-Torok (q.v.) between the Ottoman (q.v.) and the Habsburg Empires (q.v.) was duly concluded a few months later.

VIENNA, SIEGE OF (1529, 1683). The First Siege of Vienna occurred between September 22 and October 15, 1529, three years after Hungary's defeat at the Battle of Mohács (q.v.). Sultan Süleyman (q.v.) besieged the city for over three weeks, but failed to dislodge its defenders, who saved Vienna (q.v.) for the Habsburgs (q.v.). The Second Siege of Vienna took place between July 14 and September 12, 1683, as the climax to the major Ottoman Turkish (q.v.) invasion under the command of Grand Vizier Kara Mustafa. This undertaking was defeated by the united armies of Prince Charles of Lorraine (q.v.), King Jan Sobieski of Poland (q.v.), Prince Maximilian of Bavaria (q.v.), and Prince John George of Saxony. The Turkish defeat at Vienna was so thorough that the Christian armies immediately went on the offensive. This initiated the Liberation Wars (q.v.), which ended in the Treaty of Karlowitz (q.v.) and the expulsion of the Turks from most of Hungary.

VIENNESE ILLUMINATED CHRONICLE [CHRONICON PICTUM VINDOBONENSE, BÉCSI KÉPES KRÓNI-KA] (c.1358). The most ornate Hungarian chronicle prepared in the mid-14th century, containing forty-one miniatures and ninety-five illuminated initial letters. It covers Hungarian history up to the year 1330, coming to an abrupt halt in the middle of a sentence. Most scholars believe that its compiler was Márk de Kált (Márk Kálti) (q.v.), the onetime confessor of the wife of King Charles Robert (q.v.), who may have died in the midst of this compilation work. Chapters 1 through 24 reach back to biblical beginnings and cover the history of the Huns (q.v.). Chapters 25 through 209 narrate the history of the Magyars (q.v.) and of the Kingdom of Hungary up to November 1330.

VILÁGOS. The site of the capitulation of the Hungarian *Honvéd* Army (q.v.) under General Görgey (q.v.) before the invading Russian Army on August 13, 1949. Located in Arad County, Világos signifies the end of Hungary's hopes to triumph in the Revolution of 1848–49 (q.v.).

VILAYET [EYALET] see **PASHALIK**.

VISEGRÁD. A fortress atop a hill overlooking the Danube (q.v.) at the place where it turns form an easterly to a southerly direction.

First mentioned in 1009 as being the property of the Bishopric of Veszprém (q.v.), the early modest fort was replaced after the Mongol Invasion of 1241 (q.v.) by a major stone fortress with a wall stretching down to the river and ending in a powerful donjon or keep. Between 1320 and 1526, the fortress of Visegrád became of home for the Holy Crown (q.v.) of Hungary. In 1323, King Charles Robert (q.v.) made Visegrád his royal residence, where he built a magnificent palace, which in 1335 was the site of the Congress of Visegrád (q.v.). In 1401 the Visegrád donjon was King Sigismund's (q.v.) temporary prison, after he had been taken captive by a group of Barons (q.v.). Visegrád reached its climax under King Matthias Corvinus (q.v.), who extended the fortress, built a 350 room Renaissance palace within the fortress, and made it into his summer residence. In 1529 Visegrád was conquered by the Turks (q.v.), who held it for 155 years. When reconquered in 1684, the palace and the fortress were in total ruins. In 1702 even these ruins were blown up at the orders of Emperor Leopold I (q.v.) to prevent Hungarian rebels from using it. On February 14, 1991, the resort village of Visegrád —situated under the ruins of the former royal castle—was the site of the signing of a Treaty of Mutual Cooperation among the three recently liberated and most developed states of East Central Europe (q.v.): Czechoslovakia (q.v.), Hungary (q.v.), and Poland (q.v.).

VISEGRÁD, CONGRESS OF (1335). A meeting of King Charles Robert (q.v.) of Hungary (q.v.), Casimir the Great (r.1333–70) of Poland (q.v.), and John Luxemburg (r.1310–46) of Bohemia (q.v.) to coordinate their economic policies against the staple rights of Vienna (q.v.), which was having an adverse effect on all three of these states. The monarchs agreed to end all impediments to the free flow of international commerce between Hungary and Bohemia, and between Hungary and Poland. They also made decisions concerning the threat represented by the Teutonic Knights (q.v.) to Poland's northern frontiers. Previously, Charles Robert had sent Hungarian army units to help Casimir in his struggle against the knights. In 1336, it was Charles Robert who received Polish and Czech help in dealing with some rebellious lords, who had allied themselves with the Duke of Austria (q.v.).

VISEGRÁD MEETING (1991). The international meeting on February 14, 1991, which resulted in the first post-communist Treaty of Mutual Cooperation among the three most advanced former Soviet satellite states: Hungary (q.v.), Czechoslovakia (q.v.), and Poland (q.v.). Later the "Visegrád Three" was extended to include such other states as Slovenie, Croatia, and Slovakia (after Czechslovakia's dissolution), but ultimately this attempt at regional coopration went to nowhere. It was soon replaced by the individual states' increased effort to join NATO and the European Union. (See also Visegrád.)

VITÉZ, JÁNOS [JOHANNES VITÉZ] (c.1408–72). A successful diplomat and politician, the bishop of Várad (q.v.) and primate-archbishop of Esztergom (q.v.) (r.1465–72), Johannes Vitéz was at the same time one of the most noted humanist scholars and patrons of 15th–century Hungary (q.v.). Being related to the Hunyadi family (q.v.), Vitéz had a close relationship both to János Hunyadi (q.v.) and his son, Matthias Corvinus (q.v.). As an envoy of Hunyadi, he negotiated with many prominent personalities, including Holy Roman Emperor Frederick III (r.1440–93), King George Poděbrady (r.1458–71) of Bohemia (q.v.), and papal envoy Piccolomini, the future Pope Pius II (r.1458–64).

Vitéz served as tutor and later as guardian of János Hunyadi's two sons, Ladislas and Matthias. Following the death of King Ladislas V (q.v.), Vitéz was in charge of gaining Matthias Corvinus's release from his captivity in Prague (q.v.) and his simultaneous betrothal to Poděbrady's daughter, Elizabeth. Although a close friend and supporter of King Matthias, in 1470 Vitéz turned against the king. He did so partially because he felt that the king's attempt to conquer the Czech kingdom (q.v.) diverted him from his obligation to fight the Turks (q.v.), and partially because he resented Matthias's centralizing policies. The conspiracy was uncovered and Matthias had Vitéz imprisoned in the fortress of Visegrád (q.v.). He was released in the spring of 1472, but only to die a few months later in Esztergom (q.v.).

Having corresponded with most of the top contemporary humanist intellectuals, Vitéz, in his surviving letters presents an intellectual portrait of his age. Some of his correspondence with János Hunyadi and other members of the Hungarian magnates (q.v.) were collected and bound into volumes during his own lifetime (1451 and 1455). Vitéz also collected a large personal library, which later served as a model for King Matthias for his own Corvina Library (q.v.). Vitéz likewise dabbled in astronomy and astrology, and served as the de facto founder of the Academia Istropolitana (q.v.), a university that had been established in the city of Pozsony in 1467. One of Vitéz's most faithful Humanist disciples was his own nephew, Janus Pannonius (q.v.), who also became involved in the anti-Matthias conspiracy and died while fleeing to Italy (q.v.).

VITÉZ, ORDER OF [VITÉZI REND] (1920). A knightly order founded by Regent Horthy (q.v.) in September 1920 for the purpose of rewarding those "unblemished patriots" who—during World War I (q.v.) and the postwar revolutions (q.v.)—"performed valiantly in defense of the Hungarian state." Membership in the Order of Vitéz was accompanied by the grant of a parcel of landed property. The goal was to create a reliable, midlevel propertied class whose members would be upholders of the existing social order.

The members of the order were permitted to put the word "vitéz" (brave, valiant) in front of their names as if it were an aristocratic title like a baron (q.v.) or a count (q.v.). The leadership of the order was concentrated in the National Board of the Order of Vitéz chaired by Regent Horthy in his capacity as the grand master *(főkapitány)*. The title *vitéz* and the landholding that accompanied it could be inherited by the oldest son of the knighted person.

By 1940 the membership in the Order was close to 21,000. The size of its membership increased even further during World War II (q.v.), especially after 1941, when candidates could be inducted into the order even without a grant of land. In Hungary, the Order of Vitéz was dissolved in 1945, but abroad it survived to our own days.

Following the death of Regent Horthy in 1957, Field Marshal Archduke Joseph August (q.v.) became the order's new grand master (1957–62). After his death, he was followed by his grandson, Archduke Joseph Árpád (b.1933). In wake of the fall of communism (q.v.) in 1989–90, the Order of Vitéz was reestablished in Hungary, although without the official approval of the new Hungarian government.

VIZIER [VEZIR, VEZÉR]. A military-administrative rank in the Ottoman Empire (q.v.), just below the Grand Vizier (q.v.). Initially there were only three viziers—one for Europe, one for Asia, and one for the Ottoman Fleet. All of them were members of the Imperial Council or *Divan* (q.v.). Later a few more were added, all of whom held high command positions in the empire. The pasha of Buda (q.v.) often held the rank of a *vizier*.

VLACHS [OLÁH, OLÁHOK]. The name by which the Romanians (q.v.) were known until the unification of Wallachia (q.v.) and Moldavia (q.v.) in 1862. The unified state was renamed Romania (q.v.) and its people Romanians. The artificial terms "Romania" and "Romanian" are derived from the Romanians' belief, developed during the national revival period, that they are in fact descendants of the Romans. This belief is embodied in the theory of Daco-Roman-Romanian Continuity (q.v.), which in more recent times, especially under the rule of Nicolae Ceausescu (r.1965-89), became a virtual national creed. The term "Vlach" gave birth to the Hungarian words "Oláh," by which the Romanians were known to the Hungarians until the early 20th century; as well as to the term "Olasz," which is the still current Hungarian name for the Italians.

VLAD THE IMPALER see DRACULA.

VLADISLAV I [ULÁSZLÓ, WLADYSLAW] (1424–44). Vladislav is the commonly used Western name of Władysław III (r.1434–44), king of Poland (q.v.), who under the name Úlászló I (r.1440–44), was the king of Hungary (q.v.). Vladislav was elected

Hungary's king by a group of Hungarian nobles (q.v.) who opposed
the succession of the child king Ladislas V (q.v.). Crowned king in
May 1440, Vladislav spent the first two years of his reign fighting
against the partisans of King Ladislas. In 1443 he signed an
armistice with his rival and then turned his attention to the Turkish
danger in the Balkans (q.v.). After a successful fall campaign, he
concluded a ten-year peace (July 1444) with Sultan Murad II
(r.1421–51). Then, at the urging of the Papal Legate Cesarini, he
broke the peace and led a new offensive into the Balkans. This so-
called "Crusade of Varna" (q.v.) turned into a total defeat at the Battle
of Varna (November 10, 1944), in which the king himself was
killed. This plunged Hungary into a period of chaos, which lasted
until the rise of Matthias Corvinus (q.v.) to the Hungarian throne.
In the meanwhile, János Hunyadi (q.v.) assumed control over the
affairs of Hungary.

VLADISLAV II [ÚLÁSZLÓ]   (1456–1516). King of Hungary
   (r.1490–1516) and Bohemia (r.1471–1516) after the death of the two
   national kings, the Hungarian Matthias Corvinus (q.v.) (1458–90)
   and the Czech George Poděbrady (r.1458–71). Although it was one
   of the conditions for his election to the throne in Bohemia (q.v.),
   Vladislav was unable to dislodge King Matthias from the conquered
   provinces of Moravia (q.v.) and Silesia (q.v.). Following the latter's
   death, however, Vladislav reunited the Lands of the Bohemian
   Crown (q.v.). He ascended the Hungarian throne in opposition to
   Matthias's natural son, Johannes Corvinus (q.v.). But after consolidating his rule, he was unable to continue his predecessor's policy of
   centralization. Vladislav's weak rule pushed Hungary (q.v.) in the
   direction of total disintegration, which ultimately led to the
   catastrophe at Mohács (q.v.). His reign was characterized by the rapid
   decline of royal power, and by an incessant struggle between the
   lower nobility (q.v.) and the magnates (q.v.). The former were under
   the leadership of Palatine István Zápolya (d.1499) and of his son
   John Zápolya (q.v.), and they wished to assert their legal equality
   with the higher nobility (q.v.). The end of Vladislav's rule witnessed
   the Dózsa Peasant Uprising (q.v.) and the enserfment of the

peasantry in 1514. In 1515 he concluded a pact of mutual succession with the Habsburgs (q.v.), which served as the foundation stone for the Habsburg rule to Hungary. Vladislav tried to strengthen Hungary's position through family pacts with his brothers in the Polish-Lithuanian Commonwealth (q.v.), but these pacts produced no visible success.

VOIEVOD [VOYEVOD, VOYVODA, VAJDA]. The title of the governor of Transylvania (q.v.) within the Kingdom of Hungary (q.v.) from the 11th century until the disintegration of medieval Hungary in the 16th century. The last voievod with nominal powers was István Dobó (q.v.), whose three-year tenure ended in 1556. The voievod was the representative of the king who held all military, judicial, and administrative powers. The rulers of the autonomous principalities of Wallachia (q.v.) and Moldavia (q.v.) were also called voievods, as were the provincial administrators in Poland (q.v.).

VOIVODINA [VOJVODINA, VAJDASÁG]. A former southern province of the Kingdom of Hungary, and now part of Serbia (q.v.). It is located to the north of the Sava River (q.v.), between the Danube (q.v.) and the Tisza (q.v.), but portions of it is to the east of the Tisza River. Its three subdistricts include Baćka *(Bácska)* (q.v.), Banat *(Bánság)* (q.v.), and Srem *(Szerémség)* (q.v.). Before 1918, Voivodina had been part of Historic Hungary (q.v.) for a whole millennium. It is an area of about 8,300 square miles, with over two million inhabitants—half of them Serbians (q.v.), one quarter Hungarians (q.v.), and the other quarter divided among Germans (q.v.), Croats (q.v.), and Romanians (q.v.). The Serbian majority, however, had settled there after the expulsion of the Turks (q.v.), who left the region largely depopulated. Voivodina's largest city and administrative center is the city of Novi Sad *(Újvidék),* which is followed in size by Subotica *(Szabadka),* Zrenjanin *(Nagybecskerek),* Pančevo *(Pancsova),* Sombor *(Zombor),* and Kikinda *(Nagykikinda).*

VÖRÖSMARTY, MIHÁLY (1800–55). One of the great poets of 19th-century Hungary (q.v.), whose heroic epic, *The Flight of Zalán*

(Zalán futása) (1825), made him a national hero and one of the catalysts of the Hungarian Reform Period (q.v.). The epic is a heroic portrayal of the Árpádian conquest (q.v.) of Hungary (q.v.), and in those days served to rouse the patriotic feelings of all Hungarians. *The Flight of Zalán* was followed by several other similar works, as well as by much moving lyrical poetry, most of it written in the classical style, but in the rousing spirit of Romanticism. In 1848 Vörösmarty became involved in politics and was an ardent supporter of Kossuth's (q.v.) at the Hungarian Revolution of 1848-49 (q.v.). For this reason, following the defeat of the revolution (q.v.), he was forced to go into hiding. Vörösmarty was given clemency in 1850, but he was so distraught by this defeat that he spent the remaining years of his life in total depression. His influence, however, continued to pervade Hungarian intellectual life for many years.

- W -

WALLACHIA [HAVASALFÖLD, HAVASELVE]. The south-eastern province of today's Romania (q.v.), which used to be an autonomous or near independent province in the Middle Ages. In the 12th and 13th centuries it was known as Transalpina, part of Cumania (q.v.), and it was under the authority of the Hungarian kings. In the early 14th century, under the suzerainty of the Hungarian Anjou kings (q.v.), it became known as Ungro-Vlachia (Hungarian Wallachia) and was organized as Hungary's (q.v.) vassal state. In the middle of that century Voievod Alexander Bassarab (r.1352–64) was able gain Wallachia's independence, after which he also established the first Christian archbishopric (metropolitanate) for his people in 1359. By this time the native Vlachs (q.v.) had adopted Orthodox Christianity (q.v.) in its Slavic form, and Old Church Slavonic (q.v.) became their liturgical language up to the 19th century. During the late 14th and 15th centuries Wallachia moved back and forth between vassalage and independence. At this time Wallachia's most notorious ruler was Vlad III, the Impaler (r.1456–62), a man of diseased mind, who is also known as Dracula (q.v.). His personality was later incorporated by Bram Stoker into the figure "Count Dracula," who, however, was a much milder character. At the end of the 15th century, the princes of Wallachia paid tribute both to Hungary and to the Ottoman Empire (q.v.). Around 1500, Wallachia came under Turkish rule as an autonomous province of the Ottoman Empire (q.v.). Until 1711 it was ruled by its own princes, while between 1711 and 1821, by the Greek Phanariotes (q.v.), who purchased this right from the Ottoman sultan. Wallachia was unable to extricate itself from Ottoman vassalage until the 19th century. In 1859 it united with Moldavia (q.v.) and in 1862 the two provinces assumed the name Romania (q.v.), and its inhabitants, Romanians (q.v.). Romania gained full independence at the Congress of Berlin (q.v.) in 1878.

WAR COUNCIL [KRIEGSRAT, HOFKRIEGSRAT, HADI-TANÁCS]. The main command center of the Habsburg Imperial Army (q.v.) that was established in 1556. The War Council functioned directly under the emperor, and neither the Hungarian Diet (q.v.), nor the Hungarian palatine (q.v.) had any influence upon it, even when dealing with Hungarian affairs. The interests of Royal Hungary (q.v.) were basically disregarded in favor of the Habsburg Empire (q.v.), even if this meant the violation of the Hungarian Constitution (q.v.). The War Council was abolished in 1848, and it was never reestablished in its original form.

WAR OF AUSTRIAN SUCCESSION (1740–48). Following the death of King Charles III (Emperor Charles VI) (q.v), the last male member of the Habsburg dynasty (q.v.), several claimants contested his daughter's, Maria Theresa's (q.v.), right to the Habsburg throne. These included Charles Albert of Bavaria, Philip V of Spain, and August III of Saxony. Others, like Frederick the Great of Prussia (r.1740–86), simply wanted go gain a portion of the Habsburg Empire (q.v.). Attacked by the Prussians in 1740, who were soon joined by the Bavarians and the French, in 1741 Maria Theresa was close to losing her throne. In desperation she went to the Hungarian capital of Pozsony (q.v.) and asked for the support of the Hungarian nobility (q.v.). They responded enthusiastically, offering their "lives and blood" *(vitam et sanguinem)* to their young queen. They also raised an army of 60,000 men, which, in alliance with England, saved the Habsburg throne for Maria Theresa and her descendants. The Treaty of Aix-la-Chapelle (Aachen) (October 18, 1748), which ended the war, retained the basic unity of the Habsburg Empire, although most of Silesia (q.v.) was annexed by Prussia (q.v.). It also recognized the hereditary rights of the Habsburg-Lorraine dynasty (q.v.) to the Habsburg throne. Maria Theresa was grateful to the Hungarian nobility, which explains her repeated efforts to endear them to her family. One of her tools was the newly founded Hungarian Royal Nobles' Guard (q.v.) in Vienna (q.v.), which, in a sense, backfired. It gave birth to the Hungarian National Revival

Movement (q.v.), and thus to the rise of modern Hungarian nationalism.

WAR OF LIBERATION see **RÁKÓCZI WAR OF LIBERATION, HUNGARIAN REVOLUTION OF 1848-49.**

WARSAW PACT (1955–91). A pact of defense and mutual collaboration among the Soviet bloc states, including Albania, Bulgaria (q.v.), Czechoslovakia (q.v.), East Germany, Hungary (q.v.), Poland (q.v), Romania (q.v.), and the Soviet Union (q.v.). The Warsaw Pact was a Soviet-led organization, which was established as a rival to NATO. It came into being on May 11–14, 1955 and was dissolved on July 1, 1991. Hungary had proclaimed her decision to leave the Warsaw Pact on October 2–4, 1990.

WAR TAX [KRIEGSSTEUER, HADIADÓ, SUBSIDIUM]. A special tax collected in Hungary (q.v.) on the occasion of a major war or invasion, when even the otherwise untaxed noble class was willing to levy a special war tax upon itself. It was first levied under King Sigismund (q.v.) in the late 14th century for the struggle against the Turks. (q.v.) A few decades later it was regularized under King Matthias Corvinus (q.v.). During the 16th and 17th centuries the war tax was collected sporadically. But after 1715, when the standing army was established, it became a permanent levy on the non-noble classes right up to 1848. Initially, a portion of the war tax was collected in kind (food and fodder) and was known as the *porció* (portion). A *porció* was usually a one-day supply for a single soldier. The peasants were often obliged to supply this tax-in-kind immediately to the soldiers themselves, who were quartered in their homes. The value of this *porció* was then supposed to be subtracted from the value of their overall war tax obligations.

WEKERLE, SÁNDOR (1848-1921). A liberal politician and highly regarded financial expert of the Dualist Period (q.v.), who was the only man to serve three times as Hungary's (q.v.) prime minister (1892–95, 1906–10, 1917–18). Wekerle was also the first commoner to head a Hungarian government. He is credited with having reorganized and modernized Hungary's financial affairs, with having put the country on the gold standard, and with having produced a balanced budget. He is likewise credited with continuing the policy of separating the affairs of the church from those of the state by pushing through a number of liberal laws limiting the church's role in politics. Wekerle is remembered as an efficient bureaucrat who, during his final prime ministership, tried desperately to prevent the breakup of Austria-Hungary (q.v.).

WERBŐCZY [WERBŐCZI, VERBŐCZY], ISTVÁN (1458–1541). One of the most powerful personalities in early-16th-century Hungary (q.v.) who is known primarily for his authorship of the *Tripartitum* (q.v.) of 1514, which codified the Hungarian legal system and constitutional law from the vantage point of the Hungarian nobility (q.v.). Coming from a family of common nobles (q.v.), Werbőczy studied law and by 1502 reached the position of a prothonotary within the Hungarian Diet (q.v.). He became one of the leaders of the group of common nobles that supported the right of free election and proposed the candidacy of John Zápolya (q.v.).

In 1514 Werbőczy participated on Zápolya's side in putting down the Dózsa Peasant Revolution (q.v.), and in pushing through the so-called "blood law" *(vérestörvény),* which gave a significant portion of the royal income to Zápolya for having put down the peasant uprising. He was likewise one of the motivators of the law that enserfed the Hungarian peasants by binding them to the land. In 1516 he became the "personalis," that is, the chief justice who represented the king at the nation's highest court. In 1525 Werbőczy was elected Hungary's palatine (q.v.) as the representative of the common nobility. In the following year, however, King Louis II (q.v.) and many of the powerful oligarchs accused him of financial irregularities and he was stripped of his office and much of his wealth. After this personal setback, Werbőczy retired to one of his estates and did not participate in the Battle of Mohács (q.v.).

Following King Louis II's death and John Zápolya's election to the throne, Werbőczy became the latter's chancellor (q.v.), who formulated and supported the Zápolya's pro-Turkish policy against rival King Ferdinand (q.v.). Perhaps to repay this debt, following their capture of Buda (q.v.) in 1541, the Turks (q.v.) appointed Werbőczy the mayor of that city, which now became the capital of Turkish Hungary (q.v.).

WESSELÉNYI CONSPIRACY (1670–71). A conspiracy prompted by the unfavorable Treaty of Vasvár (q.v.) with the Turks (q.v.), which left much of Hungary (q.v.) under Ottoman rule (q.v.) and placed the rest of it under even tighter Habsburg (q.v.) control. The conspiracy evolved slowly between 1664 and 1771, culminating in the arrest and execution of all of the main personalities who were still alive at that time. The leader of the conspiracy, Palatine Ferenc Wesselényi (q.v.) and Primate-Archbishop György Lippay (1600–66) had both died before the planned uprising was revealed. Others included Croatian Ban Péter Zrínyi (q.v.), Lord Chief Justice Ferenc Nádasdy (q.v.), the powerful magnate Ferenc Frangepán (q.v.), and Francis Rákóczi I (q.v.), the elected prince of Transylvania (q.v.). They all wanted to restore Hungary's traditional autonomy.

Initially they only had vague ideas how to achieve their goal, although they did count on the support of Louis XIV (r.1643–1715) of France. The Treaty of Pyrenees (1669), however, destroyed much of their hopes. So did the reluctance of the Ottoman Turks to break their treaty with Emperor Leopold I (q.v.). Although totally unprepared, they began their uprising in 1670, which resulted in total and immediate failure. The leaders of the uprising—with the exception of Rákóczi—were all arrested and brought to trial for high treason. They were condemned, stripped of their titles and property, and then beheaded in Wiener-Neustadt. Those lesser conspirators who were unable to escape to Transylvania (q.v.) or to the Partium (q.v.) were also convicted, stripped of their properties, and imprisoned. Rákóczi escaped at the expense of 400,000 golden *forints* (q.v.) and by transferring all his fortresses to Emperor Leopold. The harshness of these sentences only increased the bitterness against the Habsburgs, which in 1678 erupted into the *kuruc* (q.v.) uprising under the leadership of Imre Thököly (q.v.).

WESSELÉNYI, COUNT FERENC (1605–67). The palatine (q.v.) of Hungary (q.v.) and the leader of the anti-Habsburg Wesselényi Conspiracy (q.v.). Through most of his life, Wesselényi had been a supporter of the Habsburg dynasty (q.v.). He had joined the Imperial Army as a young man and served in many of the Hungarian fortresses on the Ottoman-Habsburg frontier. As the commander of Fülek, he fought against Prince George Rákóczi I (q.v.) of Transylvania (q.v.) and with the help of his future wife, Mária Széchy (1610–79)—known in Hungarian lore as the "Venus of Murány"— he conquered the important fortress of Murány. In return for his military achievements, in 1646 he was given the title of count (q.v.) and was appointed the military commandant of Upper Hungary (q.v.). From 1655 to his death in 1667, he was Hungary's palatine.

In 1663–64 Wesselényi served in the Ottoman-Habsburg War, but after the Treaty of Vasvár (q.v.) he too became disenchanted with Emperor Leopold I's (q.v.) absolutism and the rule of foreigners, who failed to take into account Hungary's national interests. Thus, he allied himself with such powerful oligarchs as Count Péter Zrínyi (q.v.), Count Ferenc Frangepán (q.v.), Count Ferenc Nádasdy (q.v.), and Prince Francis Rákóczi (q.v.) in an ill-fated conspiracy (q.v.) to end Habsburg rule in Hungary. Wesselényi died before the conspiracy became known, thus it was his fellow conspirators and his wife who had to suffer the consequences.

WESSELÉNYI, COUNT MIKLÓS (1796–1850). A prominent Transylvanian-Hungarian magnate, politician, political writer, and one of the leaders of the Hungarian Reform Period (q.v.). In 1820 Wesselényi became a close friend of the great reformer, Count István Széchenyi (q.v.), with whom he explored all of Western Europe (1821–22) so as to prepare for the modernization of Hungary (q.v.). They worked together for the next three decades, although during the early 1840s, Wesselényi took a stand against Széchenyi in the latter's debate with Kossuth concerning the desirable course of political action. During the 1830s, Wesselényi participated both in the Transylvanian Diet (q.v.) and in the Hungarian Diet (q.v.), where he pushed the cause of liberal political and social reforms. In 1835 he was sued by the Imperial Government (q.v.) for alleged political treason. His case, however, dragged on until 1839, when he was finally convicted and sentenced to three years of incarceration.

But his heroic deeds during the great Budapest flood of 1838, his universal popularity, and his growing eye disease prevented the government from applying the full force of the law. Wesselényi spent only a brief time at the fortress prison of Buda (q.v.). He was pardoned in 1840, after which he resumed his political activities. In 1844 Wesselényi lost his eyesight, which prevented him from active participation in the Hungarian Revolution of 1848 (q.v.). In September that year, after having lost his faith in the successful outcome of the revolution, he and his family moved to Bohemia (q.v.) and settled in the spa of Gräfenberg. He remained there until the spring of 1850, and then died on his way back back to Hungary.

Wesselényi was a pragmatic politician, a powerful orator, a great sportsman, and also one of the best agriculturalists of his age. His popularity outlived his death by many decades. His chief political works include *Bad Judgments (Balitéletek)* (1833), and *Manifesto Concerning Hungarian and Slavic Nationalism (Szózat a magyar és szláv nemzetiség ügyében)* (1843), the latter of which summarizes his views concerning political reform and the national minority question.

WESTERN CHRISTENDOM, SHIELD OF. Ever since King St. Stephen's (q.v.) decision to make Roman Catholicism the official religion of his people, Hungarians (q.v.) have prided themselves of being part of Western Christian Civilization. During the period of rising Ottoman power (q.v.), there arose a national myth, which asserted that Hungary is the primary defensive shield of Western Christendom against the Turks (q.v.) and the Tatars (q.v.). The expression "Shield of Christendom" ("Antemurale Christianitatis") was actually coined by the Papacy in conjunction with the 13th-century Mongol Conquest (q.v.). But this idea did not pick up pace and currency until the 15th century, when Aeneas Sylvus Piccolomini (1405-64), the future Pope Pius II (r.1458-64), was active in trying to stem the Turkish tide, and in rallying

Western Christendom against the Ottoman onslaught. The myth became a reality in the 16th and 17th centuries, when Hungary did in fact become the battleground between Christianity and Islam in the duel between the Habsburg (q.v.) and the Ottoman Empires (q.v.). Although continuously voiced during the two centuries of Turkish rule, not until the rise of modern romantic nationalism was this view fully formulated and made part of the Hungarian national myth. The myth itself is backed up by the facts of history. At the same time, the Hungarians are obliged to share this belief with several other nationalities of Southeastern and Central Europe (q.v.), as well as with the Habsburg dynasty (q.v.), which, in those days, represented the only truly viable counterforce against the powerful Ottoman state.

WESTERN HUNGARY see BURGENLAND.

WEST SLAVS see SLAVS.

WHITE TERROR (1919–21). During the two-year period following the collapse of Béla Kun's (q.v.) Hungarian Soviet Republic (q.v.), special officers' detachments or commando units went around the country terrorizing supporters of the defunct regime. Because of the large number of Jews (q.v.) in the leadership of the Kun Regime, these activities also assumed certain anti-Semitic overtones. Following an international protest movement and the consolidation of the Horthy Regime (q.v.) under Prime Minister István Bethlen (q.v.), the commando units were disbanded and the White Terror came to an end. The most prominent commando leaders during the White Terror were Pál Prónay (1874–1945), Mihály Francia-Kiss (1887–1957), Iván Héjjas (1890–1950), and Gyula Ostenburg-Moravek (1886–1944).

WIGNER, EUGENE PAUL [JENŐ PÁL] (1902–95). One of the noted Hungarian-American atomic physicist and Nobel Laureate (1963) who during World War II (q.v.) was involved in the development of the American atomic bomb. Having studied at the

Technical Universities of Budapest (q.v.) and Berlin, Wigner began his career at the latter institution. Sensing the unfavorable turn of events in Germany, he transferred to Princeton University in 1930, with which institution he remained associated through most of his active scientific life (1930–36, 1938–71). Between 1942 and 1948 he worked on the Manhattan Project, while during 1952–57 and 1959–64 he was a member of the American Atomic Commission. For his scientific achievements, in 1950 Wigner received the Franklin Prize, in 1958 the Fermi Award, in 1961 the Max Planck Medal, in 1963 the Nobel Prize, and in 1972 the Einstein Prize. Although part of the team that produced the atomic bomb, Wigner was one of those who constantly promoted peace. Virtually all of his numerous books on atomic physics appeared in German, English, and Hungarian.

WINDISCHGRAETZ, PRINCE ALFRED (1781–1862). An Austrian field marshal who during the middle phase of the Hungarian Revolution of 1848–49 (q.v.) was appointed the commander-in-chief of the Habsburg Imperial Forces (q.v.). In that capacity he defeated the Viennese Revolution (October 1848) and tried to quell the Hungarian Revolution (December 1848–April 1949) as well. His misleadingly rosy reports from Hungary (q.v.) led to the issuance of the Olmütz Constitution (q.v.) on March 4, 1849, which only aggravated Hungary's relations with Austria (q.v.). Following his reverses in the so-called "Spring Campaigns," Windischgraetz was recalled and replaced by General Ludwig von Welden (April 12–May 30, 1849), and then by General Julius von Haynau (q.v.) (May 30, 1849–July 6, 1850). After his recall, Windischgraetz withdrew from active military service and retired to his Bohemian estates.

WITTELSBACH DYNASTY. A ruling family that ascended the throne of Bavaria (q.v.) in the person of Marquis Luitpold (d.907) in the late 9th century, and continued to rule for over a millennium until 1918. In the course of their long history, the Wittelsbachs acquired many provinces and many titles. Some of them even became Holy Roman Emperors (q.v.). But their most lasting titles

—the title of prince (907) and king (1806)—were connected with their rule over Bavaria. One of their members, Otto Wittelsbach (q.v.), became king of Hungary for a short period (r.1305-07), although he was unable to consolidate his rule in face of the more capable and assertive Charles Robert of Anjou (q.v.). Another Wittelsbach, Elizabeth (q.v.), became queen of Hungary, both by virtue of her marriage to King/Emperor Francis Joseph (q.v.), as well as through the insistence of the Hungarians (q.v.) who were attached to her and demandedthat she should also be crowned along with her husband.

WORKERS' COUNCILS [MUNKÁSTANÁCS, SOVIET]. Established first during the Russian Revolution of 1905 and then in 1917, the Workers' Councils, or Soviets, were the alleged representatives of the common people in the new social and political system under communism. In point of fact, however, they became instruments of takeover and control by the Bolsheviks, who ultimately gained power. Similar councils were first established in Hungary (q.v.) after Austria-Hungary's (q.v.) collapse in late 1918. During the period of the Hungarian Soviet Republic (q.v.) in 1919, these councils functioned as institutions of state control. Workers' Councils were also established during the Revolution of 1956 (q.v.), but these councils were anti-Soviet and anti-communist. Thus, their leaders were arrested in December 1956, and they were all disbanded in the summer of 1957.

WORKERS' MILITIA [MUNKÁSŐRSÉG] (1957). Following the defeat of the Hungarian Revolution of 1956 (q.v.), the new communist regime under János Kádár (q.v.) established the Workers' Militia for the protection of the existing order. The militia was organized into regiments, divided into battalions, subdivided into platoons, and placed under the control of the "National Command." The members of the Workers' Militia were made up of dedicated communists whose interests were tied to the Kádár Regime (q.v.). It was disbanded and its property nationalized at the time of the transition from communism to capitalism in 1989-90.

WORLD FEDERATION OF HUNGARIAN HISTORIANS
[MAGYAR TÖRTÉNÉSZEK VILÁGSZÖVETSÉGE]
(1990). Organized in May 1990, the World Federation of Hungarian Historians [WFHH] is an association of Hungarian historians from throughout the world. Its central office is at the Institute of History (q.v.) of the Hungarian Academy of Sciences (q.v.), and until its recent reorganization it was under the direction of a president, a vice president, and a secretary. The WFHH holds periodic congresses in Budapest, in cooperation with other related organizations, such as the American Association for the Study of Hungarian History (q.v.) and the Hungarian World Federation (q.v.). Its past congresses were held in 1990 and 1992, and 1996. Under the reorganization plan implemented in August 1996, the WFHH has changed its name to the International Association of Hungarian Historians *(Magyar Történészek Nemzetközi Társulata)*, and the new leadership structure consists of an executive president, two vice presidents, and a secretary. Thee executive president and the secretary are always Hungarians from Hungary, while the two vice presidents represent the Hungarian minorities of the surrounding states, and those of the Western World, respectively.

WORLD WAR I (1914–18). The main combatants in World War I were the members of the Dual Alliance (q.v.) (Germany and Austria-Hungary) against the members of the Triple Entente (q.v.) (Britain, France, and Russia). The former were joined by the Ottoman Empire (q.v.) and Bulgaria (q.v.), while the latter were joined by Italy (q.v), the United States, and scores of lesser states from all over the world. The war was the result of long-standing colonial, economic, military, and nationality rivalries between the two power groups. The immediate cause, however, was the assassination of Archduke Francis Ferdinand (q.v.) by Serbian revolutionaries in the Bosnian capital of Sarajevo (q.v.). The Dual Alliance was defeated, as a result of which Germany (q.v.) lost some territories and all her colonies, while Austria-Hungary (q.v.) and the Ottoman Empire were completely dismembered. In place of Austria-Hungary, the victorious Allies established a small Austria (q.v.) and a small Hungary (q.v.), created the new states of Czechoslovakia (q.v.) and Yugoslavia (q.v.), and doubled Romania's (q.v.) territory. Of all the states, Hungary was the greatest loser. With the Treaty of Trianon (q.v.) she lost over 70 percent of her territory and over 60 percent of her population. On top of this all, one-third of the Hungarian nation was placed under foreign rule, poisoning her relationship with her neighbors for many decades to come. These factors made her a strong exponent of revisionism (q.v.) and landed her in the German-Italian camp during World War II (q.v.).

WORLD WAR II (1939–45). The main combatants of the war were the members of the Axis Powers (Germany, Italy, and Japan) against the Allies (Britain, France, Soviet Russia, and the United States). The war had two main theaters: Europe and the Far East. During the early phase of the war, both Germany (q.v.) and Japan gained some significant victories, but during the later phase, they and their allies were slowly defeated. As a result, Germany was cut down even more than after World War I (q.v.), while Japan lost all her colonies.

Hungary (q.v.) found itself again on the losing side. This was the direct result of the fact that the only powers that were willing to listen to her revisionist complaints (q.v.) were Germany (q.v.) and Italy (q.v.). In the course of 1938–41, these two countries aided Hungary in regaining from Czechoslovakia (q.v.), Romania (q.v.), and Yugoslavia (q.v.) some of the Hungarian-inhabited territories lost after World War I (q.v.). Given this reality, Hungary was compelled to go along with the German-Italian alliance. When realizing its mistake, the Hungarian government initiated efforts to get out of the war, but these efforts all proved to be unsuccessful. Thus, following the war, Hungary was punished once more, losing not only the regained territories, but also additional lands in the vicinity of the Slovak capital of Bratislava (former Hungarian capital of Pozsony) (q.v.). Hungary also had to share the fate of most other small East Central European (q.v.) countries that were placed under communist rule and forced to become members of the Soviet bloc.

- X, Y -

XANTUS, JÁNOS (1825–94). Hungarian ethnographer, cartographer, and naturalist who spent the years between 1851 and 1864 in the United States. After his repatriation, he became the founder of the Budapest Zoo (1864-66) and the director of the Ethnographic Section of the Hungarian National Museum (1873-94). Xántus was a typical member of the 19th-century Hungarian gentry class (q.v.). He had a legal education, participated in the Hungarian Revolution of 1848-49 (q.v.), was forcibly enlisted in the Austrian Imperial Army (q.v.), and took the first chance to flee to America. During the early 1850s, Xántus went through the trials suffered by most Hungarian gentry immigrants in the United States. According to his own letters, he had worked as a "book salesman, grocer's helper, pharmacist, railroad draftsman, newspaper boy, sailor, piano teacher, as well as a professor of the Greek, Spanish, and Latin languages."

In his published works—which include his *Letters from North America (Levelei Éjszakamerikából)* (1858), and *Travels in the Southern Parts of California (Utazás Kalifornia déli részeiben)* (1960)—Xántus claims that between 1854 and 1864 he was the leader of an expedition commissioned by the U. S. Government to explore and map the Trans-Mississippi West and to collect artifacts for the Smithsonian Institution. In reality, Xántus was an enlistee of the U.S. Army, stationed at Fort Riley, Kansas, and Fort Tejon, California. Thus, most of his expeditions were the products of his rich imagination. Nonetheless, within the limits permitted by his military service, Xántus did collect some animals and artifacts for the Smithsonian, as well as for the Hungarian National Museum in Budapest (q.v.). In the early 1860s he held a minor post as the observer of ocean currents at Capo San Lucas on the southern tip of Baja California. After his repatriation, based largely of his American fame, he was placed in charge of creating the Budapest Zoo, and then also gained appointment to the Hungarian National Museum.

YOUNG HUNGARY [FIATAL MAGYARORSZÁG, IFJÚ MAGYARORSZÁG]. A literary group during the late 1830s and 1840s, whose members emulated the ideas and style of Young Germany *(Junges Deutschland).* They were idealists, dedicated to social and political reform, and rejected the idea of *l'art pour l'art* (art for art's sake). Initially, Young Hungary was a purely literary movement that centered around the person and literary activities of Gábor Kazinczy (1818–84). By the late 1840s, however, it had also become a political movement. At the time of the outbreak of the March Revolution of 1848 (q.v.), many members of the Young Hungary movement became active revolutionaries and came to be known as the March Youth (q.v.).

YUGOSLAVIA (1918–41, 1945–91). The South Slavic state created out of Serbia (q.v.) and of territories carved out of Austria-Hungary (q.v.). Established on December 1, 1918, it was first known as the "Kingdom of the Serbs, Croats, and Slovenes," and was renamed Yugoslavia only in October 1929. Dissolved in April 1941 under the impact of German invasion, it was reassembled at the end of World War II (q.v.) under the leadership of Joseph Broz Tito (1892–1980), who ruled it with an iron hand. Following Tito's death, the antagonisms of Yugoslavia's component nationalities resurfaced once more, leading to ethnic conflicts that tore the state apart in 1991. Several of its component nationalities established independent states under the name of Slovenia (q.v.), Croatia (q.v.), Macedonia, and Bosnia (q.v.). The "Little Yugoslavia" (q.v.) that remained after 1991, consists of Serbia (q.v.) and Montenegro, and of the two Serbian-controlled provinces of Kossovo and Voivodina (q.v.).

Ever since its establishment, Yugoslavia has had a large Hungarian minority (q.v.), which made the relationship between the two countries often very difficult. In 1941, Hungary regained some of the territories lost in 1918, but then was forced to give them up again after World War II. The increasingly difficult position of these minorities in Little Yugoslavia, stemming from the ethnic conflicts unleashed in Bosnian, has made the relationship between Hungary (q.v.) and Serbian-ruled Little Yugoslavia strained in the 1990s.

- Z -

ZADRAVECZ, ISTVÁN (1884-1965). A Catholic army bishop and chaplain-general, and a right-wing politician. A member of the Franciscan Order (q.v.) since 1898, Zadraveczstudied in Rome and was ordained a priest in 1907, and became the abbot of his order's monastery in Szeged (q.v.) in 1915. In 1919 Zadravecz joined the White detachments at Szeged and also became a founding member of the Etelköz Federation *(Etelközi Szövetség)*—one of the several nationalist secret societies established in 1919. In 1921 he was involved in the guerrilla military actions against Austria (q.v.) for the retention of Western Hungary (Burgenland) (q.v.), and then served as a military bishop of the Hungarian Army between 1920 and 1928. During the 1930s he withdrew from active politics and served as the editor of the multivolume *Catholic Encyclopedia [Katolikus Lexikon]*. Following World War II (q.v.) and the Russian occupation of Hungary, he was arrested and imprisoned for three years. After the revolution of 1956 (q.v.), Zadravecz founded and headed the illegal Hungarian Christian National Party *(Magyar Keresztény Nemzeti Párt)*, but it was not permitted to function and eventually ceased to exist.

ZAGREB [ZÁGRÁB, AGRAM]. The capital of Croatia (q.v.), which was founded by King St. Ladislas (q.v.) of Hungary (q.v.) somewhere between 1091 and 1094, after he had occupied Croatia. The Mongols (q.v.) destroyed the city in 1242, but it was quickly rebuilt and Béla IV (q.v.) endowed it with the rank of a Free Royal City (q.v.). During the Middle Ages, Zagreb was the center of the Banat of Slavonia (q.v.), while after the Hungaro-Croatian Compromise of 1868 (q.v.), it became the seat of the autonomous Croatian government until the end of the Austro-Hungarian Empire (q.v.) in 1918. Following the establishment of Yugoslavia (q.v.), Zagreb receded to the position of a provincial city. But after

Yugoslavia's dissolution in 1941 (1941–45), and then again in 1991, it became the capital of an independent state.

ZÁKÓ, ANDRÁS (1898–1968). A general of the Hungarian Royal Army who after World War II (q.v.) settled in Germany (q.v.) and became one of the most noted leaders of the Hungarian political emigration (q.v.). In 1948 Zákó founded the still existing Fraternal Association of Hungarian Veterans *(Magyar Harcosok Bajtársi Közössége)*—known simply as the MHBK. He also established and edited the MHBK's official periodical, *On Warpath (Hadak Útján)* until his death in 1968. Under Zákó's leadership the, MHBK became a worldwide organization with branches in twenty-three countries. It was dedicated to a struggle against communism, and its primary goal was the liberation of Hungary (q.v.). In 1955 Zákó transferred the center of his association from the Austrian town of Absam (near Innsbruck) to Munich in Germany, where it remained with him in charge right up to 1968. General Zákó's posthumous war memoirs were published under the title *Fall Campaign 1944 (Őszi harcok 1944)* (1991).

ZÁPOLYA FAMILY [SZAPOLYAI, DE ZAPOLA]. The family's roots reach back to the Age of the Anjous (q.v) in 14th-century Hungary (q.v.). By the late 14th and early 15th centuries, the Zápolyas produced a number of prominent national leaders. The most outstanding among them were: Imre Zápolya (d.1487), ban of Croatia (1464–66), royal viceroy (1475), and palatine of Hungary (1485–87), who was to assure Matthias Corvinus's natural son's, János Corvin's (q.v.), succession to the throne; John I Zápolya (q.v.), the elected king of Hungary (1526–40); and John II Sigismund (q.v.), the latter's son, who became the founder of the Principality of Transylvania (q.v.).

ZÁPOLYA see JOHN ZÁPOLYA, JOHN SIGISMUND.

ZARA [ZADAR]. An important port city on the Adriatic coast in Dalmatia (q.v.), which for much of the 12th through the 14th centuries (1105–1401) was under Hungarian suzerainty and thus served as an important window to the West. In the early 15th century Zara fell under Venetian (q.v.) control, while after 1797 it went under Habsburg suzerainty. Following World War I (q.v.) the city was gained by Italy (q.v.), while after World War II (q.v.) it was acquired by Yugoslavia (q.v.).

ZEĀMET [ZIAMET]. One of the nonhereditary fiefs (landed estates) in the Ottoman Empire (q.v.), with an income of between 20,000 and 100,000 *akches (akçes)* (q.v.) per year. The other two types of fiefs were the smaller *timar* (q.v.), with an annual income potential less than 20,000 *akches (akçes)* per year, and the larger *hās* (q.v.), that usually brought well over 100,000 *akches (akçes)* per year for its temporary "owner." In the course of the 16th and 17th centuries, Turkish Hungary (q.v.) was divided into thousands of *timars* and *zeāmets*. Most of its major cities and towns were on *hās* lands and, as such, under the control the sultan via his top military administrators.

ZHUPAN [ŽUPAN] see **ISPÁN.**

ZIAMET see **ZEĀMET.**

ZICHY FAMILY. One of the most prominent and largest aristocratic families of Hungary (q.v.) whose origins reach back to the mid–13th century. Initially, the members of the family held only provincial offices in Trans-Danubia (q.v.), but starting with the 17th century they acquired aristocratic titles—baron in 1655 and count in 1676—and also served in many national offices. In the 18th and 19th centuries, the Zichy family spilt into several branches and sub-branches, a number of whose members rose to prominence in the last century. Most of these were conservative politicians and royalist administrators, such as Master of the Horse Count Ödön Zichy (1809–48), who was hanged as a traitor by the Hungarian revolutionaries in 1848. Others became prominent artists and intellectuals, such as Mihály (Michael) Zichy (1827–1906), a great romantic painter, who ended his days in St. Petersburg, Russia (q.v.).

ZIONISM. A movement founded in the late 19th century by the Hungarian-born Theodore Herzl (q.v.) (1860–1904), whose goal was the reestablishment of a Jewish state. He joined forces with Chaim Weizmann (1874–1952) to organize the first Zionist Congress in Basel, Switzerland (1897), where they established a Zionist organization to carry out their goals. The movement was given a boost by the Balfour Declaration of 1917, which stated that the British government is in favor of the creation of a Palestinian "national homeland" for the Jews. During the interwar years, Zionist propaganda produced a mass emigration of European Jews to Palestine, which resulted in a conflict with the Palestinian Arabs. The final boost to the Zionist idea was given by the Holocaust (q.v.), which garnered the universal sympathy of the world for the Jews and the cause of a Jewish homeland. The combination of these factors ultimately resulted in the establishment of the State of Israel in 1948. Following World War II (q.v.), many of the Hungarian survivors of the Holocaust emigrated to Palestine, and later to Israel, where they formed themselves into a still flourishing Hungarian-language cultural community.

ZIPSERS [CIPSZEREK, SZEPESI SZÁSZOK]. The name of the Saxons of Northern Hungary (q.v.), who settled there in the 12th and the 13th centuries. Although most of them were Franks, Bavarians (q.v.), and Austrians (q.v.), their urban law code was derived from the Saxon Law *(Sachsenspiegel),* for which reason they came to be known as Saxons. At the same time, because they lived in the region of Zips (Zipserland, Szepesség, Spiš) they also came to be known as Zipsers. This is one of the factors that distinguishes them from their brethren, the Transylvanian Saxons (q.v.) of southeastern Transylvania (q.v.).

ZIPSERLAND [SZEPESSÉG]. An enclosed region in the north-central section of Historic Hungary (q.v.)—situated between the

High Tátra and the Slovak Ore Mountains—which was first settled by the Zipsers (q.v.) or Zipser Saxons *(szepesi szászok)* in the mid-12th century. Zipserland's most important walled cities included Lőcse (Leutschau, Lovača], Késmárk (Käsmarkt, Kežmarok), and Gölnicbánya (Göllnitz, Gelnica). By the late 14th century, however, there were twenty-four such towns. The fortress of Szepes (Zipsenburg, Spišhrad) had became the administrative center of the Royal County of Szepes in the 11th century, at the time of the country's centralization under King St. Stephen (q.v.). From 1271 until 1878—with occasional brief exceptions—Zipserland enjoyed regional autonomy, which meant that it was directly subject to the authority of the king, and not to the local nobility. The city of Lőcse was the region's most important urban and administrative center, responsible for most of the commerce between Hungary (q.v.) and Poland (q.v.). In 1370 the twenty-four Zipser towns promulgated a joint law code based on the German *Saxonspiegel.* In 1412, in need of money, King Sigismund (q.v.), pawned thirteen of these towns to the king of Poland (q.v.), which were not regained by Hungary until the First Polish Partitions of 1772. Following World War I (q.v.), Hungary lost Zipserland, along with all of Northern Hungary (q.v.), to the new state of Czechoslovakia (q.v.).

ZITA OF BOURBON-PARMA (1892–1989). Wife of Charles IV (Emperor Charles I) (q.v.), last queen of Hungary (q.v.), last empress of Austria (q.v.), and the mother of Archduke Otto von Habsburg (q.v.). Zita married Archduke Charles in 1911, who became the heir to the throne of Austria-Hungary (q.v.) in 1914, following the assassination of Archduke Francis Ferdinand (q.v.) at Sarajevo (q.v.). Zita was crowned queen of Hungary in December 1916 at the time when her husband was crowned king. Following the collapse of Austria-Hungary in November 1918, the royal family moved to Switzerland. Zita made her last visit to Hungary in the fall of 1921, at the time of King Charles's second attempt to regain his Hungarian throne (October 21–November 1, 1921). Following this unsuccessful coup, the royal family was taken to the island of Madeira, where Charles IV died in April 1922. After her husbands death, Queen Zita and her eight children settled in Spain, from where the moved to the Netherlands. During World War II (q.v.), she and her smaller children lived in Montreal, Canada, while between 1982 and her death in 1989, she resided in the Convent of Zizers in Switzerland. Queen/Empress Zita was buried in the Habsburg Crypt in Vienna (q.v.). Following the death of her husband, Zita's whole life was dedicatedto the single goal of regaining the throne for her oldest son, Archduke Otto. These hopes proved to be unattainable.

ZOLTÁN [ZALTAS, ZSOLT, SOLT]. The name of Prince Árpád's (q.v.) youngest son, who was probably the father of Prince Taksony (q.v.), and thus the grandfatherof King St. Stephen (q.v.). Some chronicles claim that Zoltán was Árpád's only son and that he had inherited his father's position immediately after the latter's death in 907. Others, however, assert that he was only the fourth son and may not have ruled at all. The name Zoltán was originally the title of a high office among the Conquering Hungarians, which had been derived from an Arab term that also gave birth to the title "sultan."

ZRÍNYI FAMILY. The roots of the Zrínyi family reach back to early 11th-century Dalmatia (q.v.), where they were known under the name of Subić (Subics). Following the union of Croatia-Dalmatia (q.v.) with Hungary (q.v.) at the turn of the 11th to the 12th century, the family produced prominent personalities for both countries, including some bans of Croatia (q.v.). In 1347, in exchange for their properties in Dalmatia, King Louis the Great (q.v.) granted large estates to the family in Slavonia (q.v.), located between the Dráva (q.v.) and the Sava (q.v.) Rivers. This grant also included the fortress of Zerin (Zrin), which became the center of their family possessions and also gave birth to their new family name. György Subics (Juraj Subić) and his descendants began to call themselves Zrínyi (Zrinski). They intermarried with the powerful Frangepán (q.v.) and Karlovics (Karlović) clans, and thus, by the early 16th century, established themselves as the wealthiest family in Croatia-Slavonia. The most significant members of the Zrínyi family included Miklós (Nicolaus) (q.v.), the hero of Szigetvár;

another Miklós (Nicolaus) (q.v.), the great 17th-century poet and military leader; Péter (Petar) (q.v.), who conspired against the Habsburgs (q.v.) and was beheaded; and Ilona (Helena) Zrínyi (q.v.), who became the wife and the mother of two prominent anti-Habsburg rebels, Prince Ferenc Rákóczi I (q.v.) and Prince Ferenc Rákóczy II (q.v.). The Zrínyi family died out in 1703.

ZRÍNYI, COUNTESS ILONA (1643–1703). The wife (1667) of Prince Ferenc Rákóczi I (q.v.), mother of Prince Ferenc Rákóczi II (q.v.), and after her first husband's death, also the wife of Prince Imre Thököly (q.v.). Because of his involvement in the Wesselényi Conspiracy (q.v.), Ilona's father, Count Péter Zrínyi (q.v.), was beheaded in 1671. This filled her with hatred toward the Habsburgs (q.v.) and may also have prompted her to marry the leader of the anti-Habsburg *kuruc* uprising, Imre Thököly (1681). She supported her husband's efforts with all the income she could muster from the huge Rákóczi estates under her control. After Thököly's defeat in 1685, Ilona Zrínyi continued to defend the fortress of Munkács (q.v.) for over two years. Following her surrender (January 17, 1688), she was taken to a convent in Vienna (q.v.), from where she was ransomed by her husband (1691) in exchange for two captured Habsburg Imperial generals. Thereafter, she shared Thököly's fate in Turkish exile and died in Nicomedia (Izmit) in 1703. Her remains were returned to Hungary in 1906, along with those of her son and her husband. They were interred in the Cathedral of Kassa (q.v.), which, however, was lost to Hungary after World War I (q.v.).

ZRÍNYI, COUNT MIKLÓS [NICOLAUS] THE ELDER. (c.1508–1566). Known as The "Hero of Szigetvár," Zrínyi is one of the most revered personalities in Hungarian history. In 1529 he participated in the defense of Vienna (q.v.), and in 1542 he saved the Christian forces from defeat at Buda (q.v.). This resulted in his appointment as the ban of Croatia (q.v.). The following year he married Katalin Frangepán (q.v.), which marriage increased his personal holdings significantly. Then, in 1546 he purchased the region of Muraköz, an area between the Drava (a.v.) and the Mura

Rivers, and made the fortress of Csáktornya the new center of his personal realm. At this time, Zrínyi also altered his coat-of-arms to indicate his primary identification with Hungary and the Hungarians. He devoted all his remaining time, effort, and money to fight against the expanding Ottoman Empire (q.v.). But he was not supported sufficiently by King Ferdinand (q.v.), wherefore he resigned his position as ban of Croatia and in 1561 assumed the post of the commander of the fortress of Szigetvár (q.v.).

Zrínyi died defending Szigetvár against Sultan Süleyman the Magnificent (q.v.), who was on his way to conquer Vienna (q.v.). Zrínyi's heroic deed in defending his fortress sabotaged the sultan's efforts to take the center of the Habsburg realm. In fact Süleyman himself died during the protracted siege, only a few days before Zrínyi himself fell victim to this violent struggle between Islam and Christianity.

ZRÍNYI, COUNT MIKLÓS [NICOLAUS] THE YOUNGER

(1620–64). Grandson of the "Hero of Szigetvár"—Zrínyi was a poet, military leader, and author of books on military strategy. Being the lord of large estates and the possessor of a broad and sophisticated education, Zrínyi was one of the most distinguished personalities of 17th-century Hungary (q.v.). Although promoted to a general in 1646 and appointed ban of Croatia (q.v.) in 1647, he was increasingly displeased with Vienna's (q.v.) unwillingness to defend Hungary against the Turks (q.v.). He was in close contact with Prince George Rákóczi II (q.v.) of Transylvania (q.v.), which made him suspect in the eyes of Vienna and prevented his being elected the palatine of Hungary in 1655.

The fall (1657) and death (1660) of Prince George Rákóczi II ended Zrínyi's plans for a Hungarian national kingship. With the growing aggressiveness of the Turks under the leadership of Grand Vizier Ahmet Köprülü (q.v.) (r.1661-76), Zrínyi prepared Hungary's defenses. He built the fortress New Zerinvár *(Új Zerinvár)*, and in the course of 1663-64 inflicted a number of major defeats upon the Turks. Yet Emperor Leopold (q.v.) still refused to appoint him the commander-in-chief of the Habsburg Imperial Forces. Thus, at the time of the Ottoman invasion in 1664, the command of the Imperial Army was under the ineffective Field Marshal Montecuccoli (q.v.) who signed the humiliating Treaty of Vasvár (q.v.), which was one of the causes for the anti-Habsburg *kuruc* (q.v.) uprising led by Imre Thököly (q.v.). Zrínyi died only three months later (November 18, 1664), having fallen victim to a wild boar. His death left Hungary without an effective political and military leader.

As testified to by his writings, Zrínyi was one of the greatest military strategists of his age. The most significant of these works is his *Medication against the Turkish Opium (Az török Áfium ellen való orvosság)* (1660–61), in which he outlined an effective military strategy and also called for the establishment of a Hungarian National Army. In 1661 Zrínyi became involved in a major debate with Field Marshal Montecuccoli about the latter's ineffective defense of Transylvania (q.v.), but the debate led to no change in Habsburg policy. In addition to his works on military strategy, Zrínyi was also the greatest Hungarian poet of the 17th century. He wrote lyrics, ballads, and epics. A collection of these appeared in 1651 under the title *The Mermaids of the Adriatic Sea (Adriai tengernek Syrenaia)*. His greatest epic, the *Perils of Sziget (Szigeti veszedelem)*, relates the life and heroic death of his grandfather, Miklós Zrínyi the Elder (q.v.), known as the "Hero of Szigetvár."

ZRÍNYI, COUNT PÉTER [PETAR] (1621–1671). The brother of Count Miklós Zrínyi (q.v.) and, after the latter's death, the ban of Croatia (1665–71). Being disgusted with the ineffective policy of the Habsburgs (q.v.) vis-à-vis the Turks (q.v.), in 1666 Péter Zrínyi joined the Wesselényi Conspiracy (q.v.), which tried to enlist Louis XIV (r.1643/61–1715) of France against the Habsburg rule (q.v.) in Hungary (q.v.). Following the death of Palatine Ferenc Wesselényi (q.v.), Zrínyi assumed the leadership of the group of aristocratic conspirators. But the Imperial Government (q.v.) learned about it. Thus, Zrínyi was arrested in 1670 and then executed in 1671— along with several of his coconspirators. Similarly to his more capable and more famous brother, Péter Zrínyi also did some writing. After Miklós's death, he translated his brother's *Perils of*

Sziget (Szigeti veszedelem) to Croatian, but in doing so, he reworked the epic in a way as to give it a Croatian characteristic.

ZSÁMBOKY, JÁNOS [JOHANNES SAMBUCUS] (1531–84). A humanist historian, physician, and polyhistor who, after a professorship at the University of Bologna (1553–64), became King/Emperor Maximilian's (q.v.) and Rudolph's (q.v.) personal physician in Vienna (q.v.) Prague (q.v.). Zsámboky spoke and wrote many languages and kept close contact with most of the major humanist scholars throughout Europe. Several of his major works deal with Hungarian history. As an example, he was responsible for editing, updating, and publishing the works of Janus Pannonius (q.v.) and Antonio Bonfini (q.v.). He also edited the first collection of Hungarian laws, *Corpus Juris Hungarici*, in 1581. Zsámboky likewise prepared some important historical maps of Hungary (q.v.) and Transylvania (q.v.).

ZSITVA-TOROK, TREATY OF (1606). This treaty between the Habsburgs (q.v.) and the Ottoman Turks (q.v.)—concluded with the mediation of Prince Bocskai (q.v.) of Transylvania—ended the Fifteen Years' War (q.v.) and established a period of peace for twenty years. Both empires retained their respective conquests made during the war, but the Ottoman sultan now recognized the Habsburg emperor as his equal. Although the latter paid a one-time gift of 200,000 gold *forints* to the sultan, henceforth he was freed from having to pay a tribute to the Turks for his Hungarian possessions.

ZUKOR, ADOLF (1873–1976). One of the pioneers of the American film industry who started out as a food store clerk in Hungary (q.v.). Zukor emigrated to the United States in 1888, became a physical laborer, and then a furrier in Chicago. He entered the embryonic movie business in 1904 and became a success immediately. In 1912 he founded the Famous Players Film Corporation, which by 1920 developed into Paramount Pictures. Zukor is generally viewed as one of the founders of Hollywood and one of the "fathers" of the whole American film industry.

Selected Bibliography

1. Basic Handbooks, Atlases, Bibliographies, and Periodicals

American Historical Association's Guide to Historical Literature, The. ed. Mary Beth Norton and Pamela Gerardi. 2 vols. New York and Oxford: Oxford University Press, 1995. The section on Hungary was compiled by Steven Béla Várdy, vol. 2, pp. 1043–51.

Bakó, Elemér, ed. *Guide to Hungarian Studies.* 2 vols. Stanford: Hoover Institution Press, Stanford University, 1973. (Hoover Institution Bibliographical Series, 52.)

Bakó, Elemér, and William Sólyom-Fekete, eds. *Hungarians in Rumania and Transylvania: A Bibliographical List of Publications in Hungarian and West European Languages Compiled from the Holdings of the Library of Congress.* Washington, D.C.: U.S. Government Printing Office, 1969.

Bán, Péter, ed. *Magyar történelmi fogalomtár (Dictionary of Hungarian Historical Terms),* 2 vols. Budapest: Gondolat, 1989.

"Bibliographies. A Selection of Recent Hungarian Historical Writings in Western Languages," in Ervin Pamlényi, ed. *A History of Hungary.* Budapest: Corvina Press, 1973, pp. 634–44.

Braham, Randolph L., ed. *The Hungarian Jewish Catastrophe: A Selected and Annotated Bibliography.* 2d rev. ed. New York: Social Sciences Monographs, and the Institute of Holocaust Studies, Columbia University Press, 1984.

Burant, Stephen R., ed. *Hungary. A Country Study.* 2d ed. Washington, D.C.: Federal Research Division, Library of Congress, 1990.

Canadian-American Review of Hungarian Studies, The, ed. Nándor F. Dreisziger, vols. 1–7. Kingston, Ontario, 1974–80. Three of the volumes are devoted to specific topics and are published under the titles *The Hungarian Revolution Twenty Years After* (vol. 3, no. 2, 1976), *Hungarian Poetry in the English-Speaking World* (vol. 4, no. 2, 1977), and *Hungarian-Canadian Perspectives* (vol. 7, no.1, 1980). See under the name of editor N. F. Dreisziger. Starting with 1981, this periodical was renamed *Hungarian Studies Review.*

Etudes Historiques / Nouvelles Etudes Historiques / Etudes Historiques Hongroises. Budapest: Akadémiai Kiadó, 1955–1990. Two volumes each for 1960, 1965, 1970, 1975, 1980, and 1985; 7 volumes for 1990. Each five-year edition contains extensive bibliography.

Halász de Béky, Iván L., ed. *A Bibliography of the Hungarian Revolution, 1956.* Toronto: University of Toronto Press, 1963.

Hamman, Brigitte. *Die Habsburger.* Vienna: Verlag Carl Ueberreuter, 1988. A historical lexicon of the Habsburg dynasty.

Harvard University Library. Hungarian History and Literature. Classified Schedule, Classification Listing by Call Number, Chronological Listing, Author and Title Listing. Cambridge: Harvard University Library, and Harvard University Press, 1974.

Hungarian Studies. Vols. 1–12. Budapest and Bloomington, Ind.: International Association of Hungarian Studies, 1985–1996. This periodical is published jointly by the International Association of Hungarian Studies and the Hungarian Chair at Indiana University.

Hungarian Studies Review, eds. George Bisztray and Nándor F. Dreisziger, vols. 8–23. Toronto, Ontario, 1981–96. This is the continuation of *The Canadian-American Review of Hungarian Studies.* Many of the volumes are published as special issues under separate titles. These include: *Hungarian Cultural Presence in North America* (vol. 8, nos. 1–2, 1981), *Hungary and the Second World War* (vol. 10, nos. 1–2, 1983), *Minorities and Minority Politics in Hungary* (vol. 11, no. 1, 1984), *Hungarian Experience in Ontario* (vol. 12, no. 2, 1985), *The Tree of Life: Essays Honouring a Hungarian-Canadian Centenary* (vol. 13, no. 2, 1986), *The Early Twentieth Century Hungarian Avant-Garde* (vol. 15, no. 1, 1988), *Forgotten Minorities: The Hungarians of East Central Europe* (vol. 16, nos. 1–2, 1989), *Oscar Jászi: Visionary, Reformer, and Political Activist* (vol. 18, nos. 1–2, 1991), and *Hungarian Artists in the Americas* (vol. 21, nos. 1-2, 1994).

Hungary. Essential Fact, Figures and Pictures. Budapest: MTA Media Data Bank, 1994.

Hupchick, Dennis P., and Harold E. Cox. *A Concise Atlas of Eastern Europe*. New York: St. Martin's Press, 1996.

Information Hungary, ed. Ferenc Erdei. Budapest and Oxford: Akadémiai Kiadó, and Pergamon Press, 1968.

Kabdebó, Thomas, ed. *Hungary*. Oxford and Santa Barbara, Cal.: Clio Press, 1980. (World Bibliographical Series, 15.)

Magocsi, Paul Robert. *Historical Atlas of East Central Europe*. Seattle and London: University of Washington Press, 1993. (History of East Central Europe, vol. 1.)

Magyarország története térképeken elbeszélve [A Narrative Historical Atlas of Hungary], editor-in-chief Ferenc Glatz. 4 vols. Budapest: MTA Történettudomány Intézete, and História Könyvtár, 1995–98). This is an ongoing major project on Hungary's historical geography, with one volume being published every year: 1995, 1996, 1997, and 1998.

Mildschütz, Koloman. *Bibliographie der Ungarischen Exilpresse, 1945–1975*, enlarged and edited by Béla Grolshammer. Munich: Dr. Rudolf Trofenik, 1977.

Rónai, András. *Atlas of Central Europe*. Balatonfüred and Budapest: Institute of Political Sciences of the Count Paul Teleki Research Institute, 1945. Reprinted by the Society of St. Stephen, and the Püski Publishing House, Budapest, 1993.

Sztáray, Zoltán. *Bibliography on Hungary*. New York: Kossuth Foundation, 1960.

Teleki, J. *History of Hungary and Hungarians. A Selected Bibliography*. 2 vols. Toronto: Hungarian Historical Studies, 1972–78.

Tezla, Albert, ed. *Hungarian Authors. A Bibliographical Handbook.* Cambridge: Harvard University Press, 1970.

Tezla, Albert, ed. *An Introductory Bibliography to the Study of Hungarian Literature.* Cambridge: Harvard University Press, 1964.

Tolnai, Márton, and Péter Vas-Zoltán, eds., *Guide to Research and Scholarship in Hungary.* 2 vols. Budapest and Bloomington, Ind.: Akadémiai Kiadó, and Indiana University Press, 1988.

Völgyes, Iván. *The Hungarian Soviet Republic, 1919. An Evaluation and Bibliography.* Stanford: Hoover Institution Press, Stanford University, 1970.

2. DEVELOPMENT OF HUNGARIAN HISTORICAL STUDIES

Arató, Endre. "Die ungarische Geschichtsschreibung nach 1945 und ihre Aufgabe," in *Jahrbücher für Geschichte der UdSSR und der volksdemokratischen Ländern Europas* 8 (1964), pp. 375–424.

Baráth, Tibor. "L'histoire en Hongrie," in *Revue Historique* 177 (1936), pp. 84-144, and *idem*, 178 (1936), pp. 25-74.

Borsody, Stephen. "Modern Hungarian Historiography," in *Journal of Modern History* 24 (December 1952), pp. 398–405.

Deák, István. "Historiography of the Countries of Eastern Europe: Hungary," in *The American Historical Review* 97, no. 4 (October 1992), pp. 1041–63.

Dercsényi, Dezső, "The Age of Louis I in Hungarian Art History," in Várdy-Grosschmid-Domonkos, *Louis the Great, op. cit.,* pp. 371–98.

Dreisziger, Nándor F. "Hungarian History in North American Perspective," in *The Historical Journal* 25, no. 3 (1982), pp. 765–73.

Epstein, Irene Raab. *Gyula Szekfű. A Study in the Political Basis of Hungarian Historiography.* New York: Garland Publishing, 1987.

Fischer, Holger. *Politik und Geschichtswissenschaft in Ungarn. Die ungarische Geschichte von 1918 bis zur Gegenwart in der Historiographie seit 1956.* Munich: Südosteuropa Institut, 1982.

Flegler, Alexander. "Beiträge zur Würdigung der ungarischen Geschichtsschreibung," in *Historische Zeitschrift,* vol. 17–19 (1875–77), vol. 17, pp. 319–78, vol. 18, pp. 236–82, vol. 19, pp. 265–346.

Glatz, Ferenc. "Der Zusammenbruch der Habsburgermonarchie und die ungarische Geschichtswissenschaften," in *Etudes Historiques Hongroises 1980,* 2 vols. Budapest: Akadémiai Kiadó, 1980, vol. 2, pp. 575–93.

_____. "Historiography, Cultural Policy, and the Organization of Scholarship in Hungary in the 1920s," in *Acta Historica Academiae Scientiarum Hungariae* 16 (Budapest, 1970), pp. 273-93.

_____. "Ungarische Historiker—Historiker der Habsburgermonarchie," in *Gesellschaft, Politik und Verwaltung in der Habsburgermonarchie, 1830–1918,* ed. Ferenc Glatz and Ralph Melville. Stuttgart: Fischer Verlag, 1987, pp. 1–21.

Lékai, Louis J. "Historiography in Hungary, 1790–1848," in *Journal of Central European Affairs* 14 (1954), pp. 3–18.

Lukinich, Emeric [Imre], ed. *Les editions des sources des l'histoire hongroise 1854–1930.* Budapest: L'Academie des Sciences Hongroise, 1931.

Lukinich, Imre. *Histoire de la Société Historique Hongroise 1876–1917.* Budapest: L'Academie des Sciences Hongroise, 1918.

Macartney, Carlyle A. *The Medieval Hungarian Historians. A Critical and Analytical Guide.* Cambridge: Cambridge University Press, 1953.

_____. *Studies on the Early Hungarian Historical Sources.* Vols. 1–5. Budapest: Archivum Europae Orientalis, 1938–42; vols. 6-7. Oxford: Oxford University Press, 1951.

Mazsu, János. "Shifting Historiography about the Austro-Hungarian Compromise of 1867." Paper delivered at the 29th Annual Duquesne University History Forum, October 12–14, 1995, Pittsburgh, Penn., USA.

Niederhauser, Emil. *A történetírás története Kelet-Európában (The History of Historical Studies in Eastern Europe).* Budapest: História Könyvtár, 1995.

Pach, Zsigmond Pál, and Ervin Pamlényi. *Les sciences historiques en Hongrie.* Budapest: Studia Historica Academiae Scientiarum Hungaricae, 1975.

Pastor, Peter. "Recent Hungarian Publications on Béla Kun," in *Slavic Review* 48, no. 1 (1989), pp. 89-96.

_____. "Recent Publications on the History of the Hungarian Soviet Republic and Béla Kun," in Pastor, *Revolutions and Interventions, op. cit.,* pp. 467–82.

Pók, Attila, ed. *A Selected Bibliography of Modern Historiography.* Westport, Conn.: Greenwood Press, 1992.

_____. "Rankes Einfluß auf Geschitsschreibung und Geschichtsdenken in Ungarn—ein historisierter Historiker," in *Leopold von Ranke und die moderne Geschichtswissenschaft,* ed. Wolfgang J. Mommsen. Cologne: Europa Verlag, 1988, pp. 201-14.

Rottler, Ferenc. "Beiträge zur Kritik der Historiographie der frühen Mittelalters. Über die Geschichtsanschauung László Erdélyis," in

Annales Sectio Historica, ed. Zoltán Oroszlán (Budapest), vol. 3 (1961), pp. 121–52.

_____. "Beiträge zur Versuch der Bildung einer Gruppe von Kirchlichen Geschichtsschreibern in Ungarn in der 1860-e Jahre," in *Acta Historica Academiae Scientiarum Hungaricae* 19 (1973), pp. 1–53.

Sugar, Peter F. "The Evaluation of Leopold II in Hungarian Historiography," in Várdy–Várdy, *Society in Change, op. cit.,* pp. 435–48.

Szendrey, Thomas L. "Hungarian Historiography and European Currents of Thought from the late Baroque to Early Romanticism, 1700–1830," in Várdy-Várdy, *Society in Change, op. cit.,* pp. 391–411.

_____. "The History of Transylvania: Its Impact and Reception," in *Hungarian Studies Review* 16 (Toronto), nos. 1–2 (1989), pp. 137–50.

_____. *The Ideological and Methodological Foundations of Hungarian Historiography, 1750–1970.* Ph.D. Dissertation. St. John's University, Jamaica, N.Y., 1972.

_____. "The Image of Empire: Louis the Great in the Writings of Bálint Hóman," in Várdy-Grosschmid-Domonkos, *Louis the Great, op. cit.,* pp. 417–25.

_____. "The Writings on Hungarian Historiography by S. B. Várdy," in *The Canadian-American Review of Hungarian Studies* 6, no. 2 (Fall 1979), pp. 107–14.

Várdy, Steven Béla. "An Encyclopedia of Medieval Hungarian History: The Achievement of the 'Szeged School' of Medieval Hungarian Historical Studies," in *Hungarian Studies Review* 22 (Fall 1995), pp. 121–25.

_____. "Antal Hodinka. Historian," in *Hungarian Historical Review,* 3 (Buenos Aires), no. 2 (June 1972), pp. 266–74.

_____. "A Traditional Historian's View of Hungarian History," in *The Canadian-AmericanReview of Hungarian Studies* 4 (Kingston), no. 1 (Spring 1977), pp. 59–65.

_____. *Clio's Art in Hungary and in Hungarian America.* New York: East European Monographs, Columbia University Press, 1976.

_____. "English Language Historiography on Hungary in the 1990s," in *Szomszédaink közt Kelet-Európában. Niederhauser Emil emlékkönyv (Amidst Our Neighbors in Eastern Europe. Emil NiederhauserMemorial Volume),* ed. Ferenc Glatz. Budapest: MTA Történettudomány Intézete, 1993, pp. 393–402. Bilingual.

_____. *Hungarian Historiography and the 'Geistesgeschichte' School.* Cleveland: Árpád Academy, 1974.

_____. *Modern Hungarian Historiography.* New York: East European Monographs, Columbia University Press, 1976.

_____. "Saint Stephen in Hungarian Historiography," in *The Canadian-American Review of Hungarian Studies* 4, no. 2 (Fall 1977), pp. 201–04.

_____. "Selected Bibliography on Louis the Great," in Várdy-Grosschmid-Domonkos, *Louis the Great, op. cit.,* pp. 503–25.

_____. "The Birth of the Hungarian 'Kulturgeschichte' School. A Study in the History of Hungarian Historical Studies," in *Tractata Altaica. Denis Sinor Sexagenario Optime de Rebus Altaicis Merito Dedicata,* ed. W. Heissig, J. R. Krueger, F. J. Oinas, and E. Schütz. Wiesbaden: Otto Harrassowitz Verlag, 1976, pp. 675–93.

_____. *The Changing Image of the Turks in Twentieth-Century Hungarian Historiography.* Pittsburgh: Duquesne University History Department, 1980. (Duquesne University Studies in History, no. 8, ed. Steven Béla Várdy.)

————. "The Development of East European Historical Studies in Hungary prior to 1945," in *Balkans Studies* 18 (Thessaloniki), no. 1 (1977), pp. 53–90.

————. "The Foundation of Hungarian Historical Association and its Impact on Hungarian Historical Studies," in *Südost-Forschungen* 34 (Munich, 1977), pp. 63–77.

————. "The Hungarian Economic History School. Its Birth and Development," in *The Journal of European Economic History* 4 (Rome), no. 1 (Spring 1975), pp. 121–36.

————. "The Image of Louis the Great in Hungarian Historiography," in Várdy-Grosschmid-Domonkos,*Louis the Great, op. cit.*, pp. 349–69.

————. "The Ottoman Empire in European Historiography. A Reevaluation by Sándor Takáts," in *Turkish Review* 2 (Pittsburgh), pp. 1–16.

————. "The Sociological and Ideological Make-up of Hungarian Historiography in the Age of Dualism, 1867–1918, in *Jahrbücherfür Geschichte Osteuropas*, Neue Folge, 24 (Munich), no. 2 (1976), pp. 208–17.

————. "Trianon in Interwar Hungarian Historiography," in Király-Pastor-Sanders, *A Case Study of Trianon, op. cit.*, pp. 361–89.

Várdy, Steven Béla, and Ágnes Huszár Várdy. "Professor Béla Király's Scholarly Publications," in *Király Béla Emlékkönyv. Háború és társadalom (Béla Király Memorial Volume. War and Society)*, ed. Paul Jónás, Peter Pastor, and Pál Péter Tóth. Budapest: Századvég Kiadó, 1992, pp. 36–41. Bilingual.

————. "Béla K. Király's Bibliography," in Várdy-Várdy,*Society in Change, op. cit.*, pp. 15–21.

_____. "Professor Ferenc Somogyi, the Man and the Historian," in Várdy-Várdy, *Triumph in Adversity, op. cit.,* pp. 1–13.

_____. "The 'Dean' of Hungarian Historical Studies. Professor Béla Király and his Scholarly Achievements," in Jónás-Pastor-Tóth, *Király Béla Emlékkönyv, op. cit.,* pp. 25-35.

Várkonyi, R. Ágnes. "Buckle and Hungarian Bourgeois Historiography," in *Acta Historica Academiae Scientiarum Hungaricae* 10 (1963), pp. 49–86.

_____. "The Impact of Scientific Thinking on Hungarian Historiography about the Middle of the 19th Century," in *Acta Historica Academiae Scientiarum Hungaricae*, 14 (1968), pp. 1–20.

3. HISTORICAL SYNTHESES AND ESSAY COLLECTIONS

Bogdan, Henry. *From Warsaw to Sofia: A History of Eastern Europe,* tr. Jeanie P. Fleming, ed. István Feherváry. Santa Fe, New Mex.: Pro Libertate Publishing, 1989.

Braham, Randolph L. "Hungarian Jewry: An Historical Retrospect," in *Journal of Central European Affairs* 20 (April 1960), pp. 3–23.

Dreihundert Jahre Zusammenleben. Aus der Geschichte der Ungarndeutschen. Internazionale Historikerkonferenz in Budapest, 5-7 März, 1987, ed. Wendelin Hambuch, 2 vols. Budapest: Tankönyvkiadó, 1988.

Endrey, Anthony. *The Holy Crown of Hungary.* Melbourne, Australia: Hungarian Institute, 1977.

Hanák, Péter, ed. *One Thousand Years. A Concise History of Hungary.* Budapest: Corvina Press, 1988.

History and Society in Central Europe. Vol. 1. *Vienna–Budapest: Studies in Urban History.* Budapest: Hajnal István Kör, 1992.

History and Society in Central Europe. Vol. 2. *Nobilities in Central and Eastern Europe.* Budapest: Hajnal István Alapítvány, 1994.

Hupchick, Dennis P. *Culture and History in Eastern Europe.* New York: St. Martin's Press, 1994.

————. *Conflict and Chaos in Eastern Europe.* New York: St. Martin's Press, 1995.

Johnson, Lonnie R. *Central Europe. Enemies, Neighbors, Friends.* New York and Oxford: Oxford University Press, 1996.

Jónás Pál, Peter Pastor, and Pál Péter Tóth, ed., *Király Béla emlékkönyv. Háború és társadalom [Béla Király Memorial Volume. War and Society].* Budapest: Századvég Kiadó, 1992. Bilingual.

Kann, Robert A., and Zdenek V. David. *The Peoples of the Eastern Habsburg Lands, 1526–918.* Seattle: University of Washington Press, 1984. (History of East Central Europe, vol. 6.)

Kazár, Lajos. *Facts against Fiction: Transylvania-Wallachian/Rumanian Homeland since 70 B.C.?* Sydney, Australia: Forum of History, 1993.

Komjáthy, Anthony Tihamér. *A Thousand Years of the Hungarian Art of War.* Toronto: Rákóczi Foundation, 1982.

Köpeczi, Béla, ed. *History of Transylvania.* Budapest: Akadémiai Kiadó, 1994. Abbreviated version of a three-volume work in Hungarian.

Kós, Károly. *Transylvania: An Outline of its Cultural History.* Introductory essay by István Nemeskürty. Budapest: Szépirodalmi Könyvkiadó, 1989.

Kosáry, Dominic G. *A History of Hungary*. Cleveland and New York: The Benjamin Franklin Bibliophile Society, 1941. Reprinted by Arno Press, New York, 1971.

Macartney, Carlyle A. *Hungary. A Short History*. Chicago: Adine Publishing Company, 1962.

Nemeskürty, István. *Nos, les hongrois*. Budapest: Akadémiai Kiadó, 1994.

Pamlényi, Ervin, ed. *A History of Hungary*. Budapest: Corvina Press, 1973. To be used with caution because of its Marxist bias, especially for the more recent period.

Portal, Roger. *The Slavs: A Cultural and Historical Survey of the Slavonic Peoples*. New York: Harper and Row, 1969.

Ránki, György, and Attila Pók, eds. *Indiana University Studies on Hungary*. 3 vols. Budapest: Akadémiai Kiadó, 1984–89. Published under the titles: *Hungarian History –World History* (1984), *Bartók and Kodály Revisited* (1987), and *Hungary and European Civilization* (1989).

Sinor, Denis. *History of Hungary*. New York: Frederick A. Praeger, 1959. Reprinted by Greenwood Press, Westport, Conn., 1976.

Sisa, Stephen. *The Spirit of Hungary. A Panorama of Hungarian History and Culture*. Toronto: A Wintario Project of the Rákóczi Foundation, 1983. 2d ed. Morristown, N.J.: Vista Books, 1990.

Somogyi, Ferenc, and Lél Somogyi. *Faith and Fate: A Short Cultural History of the Hungarian People through a Millennium*. Cleveland: Kárpát Publishing, 1976.

Sugar, Peter F., *et al.*, eds. *A History of Hungary*. Bloomington: Indiana University Press, 1990.

Tihany, Leslie C. *A History of Middle Europe: From the Earliest Times to the Age of the World Wars.* New Brunswick: Rutgers University Press, 1976.

Várdy, Steven Béla, and Ágnes Huszár Várdy. *The Austro-Hungarian Mind. At Home and Abroad.* New York: East European Monographs, Columbia University Press, 1989.

_____, eds. *Society in Change. Studies in Honor of Béla K. Király.* New York: East European Monographs, Columbia University Press, 1983.

_____, eds. *Triumph in Adversity. Studies in Hungarian Civilization in Honor of Professor Ferenc Somogyi on the Occasion of His Eightieth Birthday.* New York: East European Monographs, Columbia University Press, 1988.

Wagner, Francis S. *Hungarian Contribution to World Civilization.* Center Square, Penna: Alpha Publications, 1977. A virtual lexicon of Hungarian achievements in the natural sciences, physical sciences, biological sciences, social sciences, economics, business, arts, music, politics, and sports.

Wandycz, Piotr S. *The Price of Freedom. A History of East Central Europe from the Middle Ages to the Present.* London and New York: Routledge, 1992.

4. MEDIEVAL AND EARLY MODERN PERIODS

Ascher, Abraham, Tibor Halasi-Kun, and Béla K. Király, eds. *The Mutual Effects of the Islamic and Judeo-Christian Worlds: The East European Pattern.* New York: East European Monographs, Brooklyn College Press, and Columbia University Press, 1979.

Bak, János M. *Königtum und Stände in Ungarn im vierzehnten-sechzehntenJahrhundert.* Wiesbaden: Steiner Verlag, 1973.

_____. *Medieval Narrative Sources: A Chronological Guide, with a List of Major Letter Collections.* New York: Garland, 1987.

Bak, János M., and Béla K. Király, eds. *From Hunyadi to Rákóczi. War and Society in Late Medieval and Early Modern Europe.* New York: Social Science Monographs, Atlantic Research and Publications, and Columbia University Press, 1982.

Baráth, Tibor E. *The Early Hungarians in the Light of Recent Historical Research.* Montreal: T. E. Baráth, 1983. Contains some interesting, but very far-fetched theories.

Bartha, Antal. *Hungarian Society in the 9th and 10th Centuries.* Budapest: Akadémiai Kiadó, 1975.

Bäuml, Franz H, and Marianna D. Birnbaum. *Attila. The Man and his Image.* Budapest: Corvina Press, 1993.

Bayerle, Gustav, ed. *Ottoman Diplomacy in Hungary. Letters from the Pashas of Buda, 1590–1593.* Bloomington: Indiana University Research Center for the Language Sciences, 1972.

_____. *Ottoman Tributes in Hungary. According to Sixteenth-Century 'Tapu' Registers of Novigrad.* The Hague: Mouton, 1973.

Birnbaum, Marianna D. *Humanists in a Shattered World. Croatian and Hungarian Latinity in the Sixteenth Century.* Columbus, Ohio: Slavica Publishers, 1986.

_____. *Janus Pannonius, Poet and Politician.* Zagreb: Jugoslavenska Akademija Znanosti i Umjetnosti, 1981.

Boba, Imre. *Nomads, Northmen, and Slavs: Eastern Europe in the Ninth Century.* Wiesbaden: Harrassowitz, 1967.

_____. *Moravia's History Reconsidered: A Reinterpretation of Medieval Sources.* The Hague: Martinus Nijhoff, 1971. A most controversial and innovative study that relocated "Great Moravia" to the south, from present-day Czechia and Slovakia to Northern Serbia.

Bowlus, Charles R. *Franks, Moravians, and Magyars. The Struggle for the Middle Danube, 788-907.* Philadelphia: University of Pennsylvania Press, 1995.

Csapodi, Csaba, and Klára Csapodi-Gárdonyi, eds. *Bibliotheca Corviniana. The Library of King Matthias Corvinus of Hungary.* Budapest: Corvina Kiadó, and Magyar Helikon, 1981.

Dienes, István. *The Hungarians Cross the Carpathians.* Budapest: Corvina Press. and Hereditas, 1972.

Domonkos, Leslie S. "Ecclesiastical Patrons as a Factor in the Hungarian Renaissance," in *The New Review: A Journal of East European Studies* 14 (Youngstown), nos. 1–4 (December 1974), pp. 100–16.

_____. "János Vitéz, the Father of Hungarian Humanism, 1408–1472," in *The New Hungarian Quarterly* 20 (Budapest), no. 74 (1979), pp. 142–50.

_____. "The History of the Sigismundean Foundation of the University of Óbuda, Hungary," in *Texts and Studies in the History of Mediaeval Education* 11 (University of Notre Dame), pp. 3–33.

_____. The Origins of the University of Pozsony," in *The New Review: A Journal of East European Studies* 9, no. 4 (December 1969), pp. 270–89.

_____. "The State of Education in Hungary on the Eve of the Battle of Mohács, 1526," in *The Canadian-AmericanReview of Hungarian Studies* 2, no. 1 (Spring 1975), pp. 3–20.

Dunlop, D. M. *The History of the Jewish Khazars*. Princeton: Princeton University Press, 1954.

Dvornik, Francis. *The Slavs in European History and Civilization*. New Brunswick: Rutgers University Press, 1962.

_____. *The Slavs: Their History and Early Civilization*. Boston: American Academy of Arts and Sciences, 1956.

Fehér, Géza. *Turkish Miniatures from the Period of Hungary's Turkish Occupation*. Budapest: Corvina Press, and Magyar Helikon, 1978.

Fodor, István. *In Search of a New Homeland. The Prehistory of the Hungarian People and the Conquest*. Budapest: Corvina Press, 1982.

Fügedi, Erik. *Castle and Society in Medieval Hungary, 1000–1437*, tr. János M. Bak. Budapest: Akadémiai Kiadó, 1986.

_____. *Kings, Bishops, Nobles, and Burghers in Medieval Hungary*, ed., János M. Bak. London: Variorum Reprints, 1986.

Gabriel, Astrik L. *The Medieval Universities of Pécs and Pozsony. Commemoration of the 500th and 600th Anniversary of their Foundation, 1367-1467-1967*. Notre Dame, Ind.: Medieval Institute, University of Notre Dame; Frankfurt-am-Main: Josef Knecht, 1969.

Gerevich, Lajos, ed. *Towns in Medieval Hungary*. New York: Social Science Monographs, Atlantic Research and Publications, and Columbia University Press, 1991.

Gonda, Imre, and Emil Niederhauser. *The Habsburgs*. Budapest: Akadémiai Kiadó, 1977.

Győrffy, György. *King Saint Stephen of Hungary*. New York: Social Science Monographs, Atlantic Research and Publications, and Columbia University Press, 1994.

Handler, Andrew. *An Early Blueprint for Zionism. Győző Istóczy's Political Anti-Semitism*. New York: East European Monographs, Columbia University Press, 1989.

Held, Joseph L. *Hunyadi. Legend and Reality*. New York: East European Monographs, Columbia University Press, 1985.

Hegyi, Klára. *The Ottoman Empire in Europe*. Budapest: Corvina Press, 1989.

Howarth, Patrick. *Attila. King of the Huns*. New York: Barnes and Noble, 1995.

Kelleher, Patrick J. *The Holy Crown of Hungary*. Rome: American Academy in Rome, 1951.

Király, Béla K. *Hungary in the Late Eighteenth Century. The Decline of Enlightened Despotism*. New York: Columbia University Press, 1969.

_____. "The Sublime Port, Vienna, Transylvania, and the Dissemination of Reformation in Royal Hungary, in Király, *Tolerance Movements, op. cit.,* pp. 199–222.

_____, ed. *Tolerance Movements and Religious Dissent in Eastern Europe*. New York: East European Monographs, Columbia University Press, 1975.

Komlós, John. *Nutrition and Economic Development in the Eighteenth-Century Habsburg Monarchy: An Anthropometric History*. Princeton: Princeton University Press, 1989.

Kosáry, Domokos. *Culture and Society in Eighteenth-Century Hungary.* Budapest: Corvina Press, 1987.

Kosztolnyik, Zoltán J. *Five Eleventh-Century Hungarian Kings. Their Policies and their Relations with Rome.* New York: East European Monographs, Columbia University Press, 1981.

_____. *From Coloman the Learned to Béla III, 1095–1196. Hungarian Domestic Policies and Their Impact upon Foreign Affairs.* New York: East European Monographs, Columbia University Press, 1987.

_____. *Hungary in the Thirteenth Century.* New York: East European Monographs, Columbia University Press, 1996.

Kristó, Gyula. *Hungarian History in the Ninth Century.* Szeged, Hungary: Szegedi Középkorász Műhely, 1996.

Laws of the Medieval Kingdom of Hungary. Vol. 1, ed. János M. Bak, György Bónis, and James Ross Sweeney. Historical introduction by Andor Csizmadia. Bakersfield, Calif.: Charles Schlacks, Jr., 1989. (Laws of Hungary, Series 1, vol. 1.)

Laws of the Medieval Kingdom of Hungary. Vol. 2, ed. János M. Bak, Pál Engel, and James Ross Sweeney. Salt Lake City: Charles Schlacks, Jr., Publisher, 1992. (Laws of Hungary, Series 1, vol. 2.)

Laws of the Medieval Kingdom of Hungary. Vol. 3. ed. János M. Bak, Leslie S. Domonkos, and Paul B. Harvey, Jr. Los Angeles: Charles Schlacks, Jr., 1996. (Laws of Hungary, Series 1, vol. 3.)

Macartney, Carlyle A. *The Magyars in the Ninth Century.* Cambridge: Cambridge University Press, 1930.

Makk, Ferenc. *The Árpáds and the Comneni. Political Relations between Hungary and Byzantium in the 12th Century.* Budapest: Akadémiai Kiadó, 1989.

Mályusz, Elemér. *Kaiser Sigismund in Ungarn, 1487–1437.* Budapest: Akadémiai Kiadó, 1990.

Marczali, Henry. *Hungary in the Eighteenth Century.* Introduction by Harold W. V. Temperley. Cambridge: Cambridge University Press, 1910. Reprinted by Arno Press, New York, 1971.

Maenchen-Helfen, Otto J. *The World of the Huns. Studies in Their History and Culture,* ed. Max Knight. Berkeley: University of California Press, 1973.

Moravcsik, Gyula. *Byzantium and the Magyars.* Budapest: Akadémiai Kiadó, 1970.

Obolensky, Dimitri. *The Byzantine Commonwealth: Eastern Europe, 500-1453.* Crestwood, N.Y.: St. Vladimir's Seminary Press, 1982.

Pastor, Peter. "Hungarian-Russian Relations during the Rákóczi War of Independence," in Bak-Király, *From Hunyadi to Rákóczi, op. cit.,* pp. 467–92.

_____. "The Sublime Porte and Ferenc II Rákóczi's Hungary: An Episode in Islamic-Christian Relations," in Ascher-Halasi-Kun-Király, *The Mutual Effect, op. cit.,* pp. 129–48.

Perjés, Géza. *The Fall of the Medieval Kingdom of Hungary: Mohács 1526 – Buda 1541.* New York: Social Science Monographs, Atlantic Research and Publications, and Columbia University Press, 1989.

Püspöki-Nagy, Péter. *On the Location of Great Moravia: A Reassessment.* Pittsburgh: Duquesne University, Department of

History, 1982. (Duquesne University Studies in History, vol. 13, ed. Steven Béla Várdy.)

Rady, Martyn C. *Medieval Buda. A Study in Municipal Government and Jurisdiction in the Kingdom of Hungary.* New York: East European Monographs, Columbia University Press, 1985.

Sugar, Peter F. *Southeastern Europe under Ottoman Rule, 1354–1804.* Seattle: University of Washington Press, 1977.

Szendrey, Thomas. "Inter Arma. Reflections on Seventeenth-Century Educational and Cultural Life in Hungary and Transylvania," in Bak-Király, *From Hunyadi to Rákóczi, op. cit.,* pp. 315–34.

————. *St. Thomas More and East Central Europe: The Impact of his Christian Humanism.* Pittsburgh: Duquesne University Department of History, 1985. (Duquesne University Studies in History, vol. 9, ed. Steven Béla Várdy.)

Szűcs, Jenő, *Nation und Geschichte: Studien.* Cologne: Böhlau Verlag, 1981.

Tardy, Lajos. *Beyond the Ottoman Empire. 14th-16th-Century Hungarian Diplomacy in the East.* Szeged, Hungary: Studio Uralo-Altaica, University of Szeged, 1978.

The Cambridge History of Early Inner Asia, ed. Denis Sinor. Cambridge: Cambridge University Press, 1990.

Thuróczy, János. *Chronicle of the Hungarians.* Introduced by Pál Engel. Bloomington: Indiana University Press, Research Institute for Inner Asian Studies, 1991.

Unghváry, Alexander Sándor. *The Hungarian Protestant Reformation in the Sixteenth Century under the Ottoman Impact. Essays and Profiles.* Lewiston, N.Y.: E. Mellen Press, 1989.

Vajay, Szabolcs de. *Ungarischen Stämmebundes in die europäische Geschichte, 862–933.* Mainz: Hase und Koehler Verlag, 1968.

Várdy, Steven Béla, *Attila.* Introductory essay by Arthur M. Schlesinger, Jr. New York: Chelsea House Publishers, 1990.

_____. "Castle Building and its Social Significance in Medieval Hungary," in *The Canadian-American Review of Hungarian Studies* 6, no. 2 (Fall 1979), pp. 91–97.

Várdy, Steven Béla, Géza Grosschmid, and Leslie S. Domonkos, eds. *Louis the Great, King of Hungary and Poland.* New York: East European Monographs, Columbia University Press, 1986.

Varga, Domokos. *Hungary in Greatness and Decline. The 14th and the 15th Centuries.* Atlanta: Hungarian Cultural Foundation, 1982.

Závodszky, Géza. *American Effects on Hungarian Imagination and Political Thought, 1559–1848.* New York: East European Monographs, Atlantic Research and Publications, and Columbia University Press, 1994.

5. HUNGARY IN THE NINETEENTH CENTURY (TO 1914)

Alföldi, László M. *The Armies of Austria-Hungary and Germany, 1740–1914.* Carlisle Barracks, Penna.: U.S. Army Military History Research Collection, 1975.

Apponyi, Count Albert. *The Memoirs of Count Apponyi.* New York: Macmillan, 1935.

Bárány, George. *Stephen Széchenyi and the Awakening of Hungarian Nationalism, 1791–1841.* Princeton: Princeton University Press, 1968.

Bíró, Sándor. *The Nationalities Problems in Transylvania, 1867-1940.* New York: East European Monographs, Atlantic Research and Publications, and Columbia University Press, 1992.

Bődy, Paul, ed. *Hungarian Statesmen of Destiny, 1867–1956.* New York: Social Science Monographs, Atlantic Research and Publications, and Columbia University Press, 1989.

————. *Joseph Eötvös and the Modernization of Hungary, 1840–1870.* 2d ed. New York: East European Monographs, Columbia University Press, 1985.

Borsi-Kálmán, Béla. *Hungarian Exiles and the Romanian National Movement, 1849–1867.* New York: East European Monographs, Atlantic Research and Publications, and Columbia University Press, 1919.

Deák, George. *The Economy and Polity in Early Twentieth-Century Hungary: The Role of the National Association of Industrialists.* New York: East European Monographs, Columbia University Press, 1990.

Deák, István. *Beyond Nationalism: A Social and Political History of the Habsburg Officer Corps, 1848–1918.* Oxford and New York: Oxford University Press, 1990.

————. *The Lawful Revolution. Louis Kossuth and the Hungarians, 1848-1849.* New York: Columbia University Press, 1979.

Decsy, János. *Prime Minister Gyula Andrássy's Influence on Habsburg Foreign Policy during the Franco-GermanWar of 1870–1871.* New York: East European Monographs, Columbia University Press, 1979.

Deme, László. *The Radical Left in the HungarianRevolution of 1848.* New York: East European Monographs, Columbia University Press, 1976.

Hanák, Péter. *Die Nationale Frage in der Österreichisch-Ungarischen Monarchie, 1900–1918.* Budapest: Akadémiai Kiadó, 1966.

————. *Ungarn in der Donau-Monarchie. Probleme der bürgerlichen Umgestaltung eines Vielvölkerstaates.* Vienna, Munich and Budapest: Verlag für Geschichte und Politik Wien, R. Oldenburg Verlag München, Akadémiai Kiadó Budapest, 1984. A collection of previously published studies by one of Hungary's top historians.

Held, Joseph L., ed. *The Modernization of Agriculture: Rural Transformation in Hungary, 1848–1975.* New York: East European Monographs, Columbia University Press, 1980.

Hoensch, Jörg K. *A History of Modern Hungary, 1867–1986.* London: Longman, 1988.

Ignotus, Paul. *Hungary.* New York and Washington: Praeger Publishers, 1972.

Illyés, Elemér. *Ethnic Continuity in the Carpatho-DanubianArea.* New York: East European Monographs, Columbia University Press, 1988.

János, Andrew C. *The Politics of Backwardness in Hungary, 1825-1945.* Princeton: Princeton University Press, 1982.

János, Andrew C., and William B. Slottman, eds. *Revolution in Perspective. Essays on the Hungarian Soviet Republic of 1919.* Berkeley: University of California Press, 1971.

Jászi, Oscar. *The Dissolution of the Habsburg Monarchy.* Chicago: University of Chicago Press, 1929. Reprinted 1961.

Kann, Robert. *A History of the Habsburg Empire, 1825-1918.* Berkeley: University of California Press, 1980.

_____. *A Study in Austrian Intellectual History from the Late Baroque to Romanticism.* New York: Octagon Books, 1973.

_____. *The Multinational Empire.: Nationalism and National Reform in the Habsburg Monarchy.* 2 vols. New Brunswick: Rutgers University Press, 1950.

Király, Béla K. *Ferenc Deák.* Boston: Twayne Publishers, 1975.

_____. "Ferenc Deák, the Social Reformer in the Revolution of 1848–1849," in *East European Quarterly* 14 (Boulder), no. 4 (Winter 1980), pp. 411–21.

_____. "Galicia: The Hungarians and the Poles between the Partitions and the November Insurrection," in *The Polish Review* 15 (New York), no. 3 (Summer 1970), pp. 19–31.

_____. "Maria Theresa's Hungarian Serf Reforms," in *Topic* 34 (Washington and Jefferson College, 1980), pp. 43–55.

_____. "Neo-Serfdom in Hungary," in *Slavic Review* 34, no. 2 (June 1975), pp. 269–78.

_____. "Peasant Movements in Hungary in 1790," in *Südost-Forschungen* 24 (1967), pp. 140–56.

_____. "The Emancipation of the Serfs in East Central Europe," in *Antemurale* 15 (Rome, 1971), pp. 63–85.

_____. "The November Insurrection and the Hungarians," in *Antemurale* 14 (1970), pp. 229–52.

_____. "The Young Ferenc Deák and the Problem of the Serfs, 1824–36," in *Südost-Forschungen* 29 (1970), pp. 91–127.

Király, K. Béla, and Albert Nofi, eds. *East Central European War Leaders: Civilian and Military.* New York: Social Science Monographs, Atlantic Research and Publications, and Columbia University Press, 1988.

Király, K. Béla, and Walter Scott Dillard, eds. *The East Central European Officer Corps, 1740–1920s: Selection, Social Organization, Education and Training.* New York: Social Science Monographs, Atlantic Research and Publications, and Columbia University Press, 1988.

Komlós, John, ed. *Economic Development in the Habsburg Monarchy in the Nineteenth Century. Essays.* New York: East European Monographs, Columbia University Press, 1983.

————, ed. *Economic Development in the Habsburg Monarchy and its Successor States.* New York: East European Monographs, Columbia University Press, 1990.

————. *The Habsburg Monarchy as a Customs Union. Economic Development in Austria-Hungary in the Nineteenth Century.* Princeton: Princeton University Press, 1983.

Kosáry, Domokos. *The Press during the Hungarian Revolution of 1848–1849.* New York: Social Science Monographs, Atlantic Research and Publications, and Columbia University Press, 1986.

Lukács, John. *Budapest 1900. A Historical Portrait of a City and its People.* New York: Grove Weidenfeld, 1988.

Lukács, Lajos. *The Vatican and Hungary, 1846–1878. Reports and Correspondences on Hungary of the Apostolic Nuncios in Vienna.* Budapest: Akadémiai Kiadó, 1981.

Macartney, Carlyle A. *The Habsburg Empire, 1790–1918.* London: Weidenfeld and Nicolson, 1968; New York: Macmillan, 1969.

McCagg, Jr., William O. *A History of the Habsburg Jews, 1670-1918.* Bloomington: Indiana University Press, 1989.

_____. *Jewish Nobles and Geniuses in Modern Hungary.* New York: East European Monographs, Columbia University Press, 1972. Reprinted 1986.

_____. "Hungary's Feudalized Bourgeoisie," in *Journal of Modern History* 44 (1972), pp. 65–78.

Mályusz, Edith Császár. *The Theater and National Awakening: East Central Europe,* tr. with an introductory essay by Thomas Szendrey. Atlanta: Hungarian Cultural Foundation, 1980.

May, Arthur J. *The Hapsburg Monarchy, 1867–1914.* Cambridge: Harvard University Press, 1965.

Morton, Frederic. *A Nervous Splendor.Vienna 1888-1889.* London: Weidenfeld and Nicolson, 1980.

Niederhauser, Emil. *The Rise of Nationality in Eastern Europe.* Budapest: Corvina Kiadó, 1981.

Pulzer, Peter G. J. *The Rise of Political Anti-Semitism in Germany and Austria.* New York: John Wiley and Sons, 1964.

Rothenberg, Gunther Erich. *The Army of Francis Joseph.* West Lafayette, Ind.: Purdue University Press, 1976.

Schorske, Carl. *Fin-de-Siècle Vienna. Politics and Culture.* New York: Vintage Books, 1981.

Spira, György. *A Hungarian Count in the Revolution of 1848.* Budapest: Akadémiai Kiadó, 1974.

Stroup, Edsel Walter. *Hungary in Early 1848: The Constitutional Struggle against Absolutism in Contemporary Eyes.* Introductory essay by Steven Béla Várdy. Atlanta: Hungarian Cultural Foundation, 1977.

Szabad, György. *Hungarian Political Trends between the Revolution and the Compromise, 1849–1867.* Budapest: Akadémiai Kiadó, 1977.

Seton-Watson, Robert W. *Racial Problems in Hungary.* London: Archibald Constable, 1908. Reprinted by H. Fertig, New York, 1972. Conditions described by Seton-Watson pale beside the events of the past three-quarter century since the collapse of Historic Hungary.

————. *The Southern Slav Question and the Habsburg Monarchy.* London: Archibald Constable, 1911. Reprinted by H. Fertig, New York, 1969. The above comments also hold true for this book.

Sokol, Anthony E. *The Imperial and Royal Austro-Hungarian Navy.* Annapolis, Md.: U.S. Naval Institute, 1968.

Szendrey, Thomas. "Mihály Vörösmarty and the Development of Romanticism in Hungary," in Várdy-Várdy, *Triumph in Adversity, op. cit.,* pp. 155–76.

Taylor, A. J. P. *The Habsburg Monarchy.* London: Hamish Hamilton, 1955.

Tunstall, Jr., Graydon A. *Planning for War against Russia and Serbia. Austro-Hungarian and German Military Strategies, 1871–1914.* New York: East European Monographs, Atlantic Research and Publications, and Columbia University Press, 1994.

Várdy, Steven Béla. *Baron Joseph Eötvös. A Literary Biography.* New York: Social Science Monographs, Columbia University Press, 1987.

_____. "Baron Joseph Eötvös on Liberalism and Nationalism," in *Studies for a New Central Europe* (New York), ser. 2, no. 1 (1967-1968), pp. 65–73.

_____. "Baron Joseph Eötvös's Political Essays in the Cause of Reform during the 1840s," in Várdy-Várdy, *Triumph in Adversity, op. cit.,* pp. 179–93.

_____. "Baron Joseph Eötvös: Statesman, Thinker, Reformer," in *Duquesne Review* 13 (Pittsburgh), no. 2 (Fall 1968), pp. 107–19.

_____. *Baron Joseph Eötvös. The Political Profile of a Liberal Hungarian Thinker and Statesman.* Ph.D. Dissertation. Indiana University, Bloomington, Indiana, 1966; Ann Arbor, Mich.: University Microfilms, 1967.

_____. "National Oppression or Social Oppression? The Nature of Hungarian-Romanian Relations in Historical Transylvania," in Cadzow-Ludányi-Elteto,*Transylvania. Roots of Ethnic Conflict, op. cit.,* pp. 148-54.

_____. "The Age of Romanticism: The Historical Setting to Nikolaus Lenau's Life and Works," in Agnes Huszár Várdy, *A Study in Austrian Romanticism, op. cit.,* pp. 11–26, 122–23.

_____. "The Origins of Jewish Emancipation in Hungary: The Role of Baron Joseph Eötvös," in *Ungarn-Jahrbuch* 7 (Munich, 1976), pp. 137–66.

_____. "The World of Hungarian Populism," in *The Canadian-American Review of HungarianStudies* 5, no. 1 (Spring 1978), pp. 41–50.

Vermes, Gábor. *István Tisza. The Liberal Vision and Conservative Statecraft of a Magyar Nationalist.* New York: East European Monographs, Columbia University Press, 1985.

6. HUNGARY IN THE TWENTIETH CENTURY (SINCE 1914)

Aczél, Tamás, ed. *Ten Years After. A Commemoration of the Tenth Anniversary of the Hungarian Revolution.* New York: Holt, Rinehart, Winston, 1966.

Aczél, Tamás, and Tibor Méray. *The Revolt of the Mind.* New York: Frederick Praeger, 1959.

Banac, Ivo, ed. *The Effects of World War I: Class War after the Great War: The Rise of Communist Parties in East Central Europe, 1918-1921.* New York: East European Monographs, Atlantic Research and Publications, and Columbia University Press, 1983.

Batkay, William M. *Authoritarian Politics in a Transitional State: István Bethlen and the Unified Party in Hungary, 1919–1926.* New York: East European Monographs, Columbia University Press, 1982.

Berend, Iván T. *Central and Eastern Europe 1944–1993. Detour from Periphery to Periphery.* Cambridge: Cambridge University Press, 1996.

————. *The Hungarian Economic Reforms, 1953-1988.* Cambridge: Cambridge University Press, 1990.

Berend, Iván T., and György Ránki. *Economic Development in East-Central Europe in the 19th and 20th Centuries.* New York: Columbia University Press, 1974.

————. *East Central Europe in the 19th and 20th Centuries.* Budapest: Akadémiai Kiadó, 1977.

————. *Hungary: A Century of Economic Development.* New York: Barnes and Noble, 1974.

Bernát, Tivadar, ed. *An Economic Geography of Hungary.* 2d ed. Budapest: Akadémiai Kiadó, 1989.

Bibó, István. *Democracy, Revolution, Self-Determination: Selected Writings,* ed. Károly Nagy, tr. András Boros-Kazai. New York: East European Monographs, Atlantic Research and Publications, and Columbia University Press, 1991.

Borsányi, György, and János Kende. *The History of the Working Class Movement in Hungary.* Budapest: Corvina Press, 1988.

Borsody, Stephen, ed. *The Hungarians: A Divided Nation.* New Haven: Yale Center for International and Area Studies, 1988.

_____. *The Tragedy of Central Europe. The Nazi and Soviet Conquest of Central Europe.* New York: Collier Books, 1962. First published as *The Tragedy of Central Europe* in 1960.

Braham, Randolph L. *The Hungarian Labor Service System, 1939–1945.* New York: East European Monographs, Columbia University Press, 1977.

_____. *The Politics of Genocide: The Holocaust in Hungary,* 2 vols. New York: Columbia University Press, 1981.

Braham, Randolph L., and Béla Vágó, eds. *The Holocaust in Hungary: Forty Years Later.* New York: Social Science Monographs, Columbia University Press, 1985.

Brook, Stephen. *Vanished Empire. Vienna, Budapest, Prague. The Three Capital Cities of the Habsburg Empire as Seen Today.* New York: William Morrow, 1988.

Cadzow, John F., Andrew Ludányi, and Louis J. Elteto, eds. *Transylvania: Roots of Ethnic Conflict.* Kent, Ohio: Kent State University Press, 1983.

Chászár, Edward. *Decision at Vienna. The Czechoslovak-Hungarian Border Dispute of 1938.* Astor, Fla.: Danubian Press, 1978.

_____. *Hungarians in Czechoslovakia Yesterday and Today.* Astor, Fla.: Danubian Press, 1988.

_____. *The International Problem of National Minorities.* Indiana, Penna.: Minority Rights Research Program, Indiana University of Pennsylvania, 1988. 2d ed., 1991.

Daruvár, Yves de. *The Tragic Fate of Hungary: A Country Carved-up Alive at Trianon.* Munich: Nemzetőr, 1974.

Deák, István. "Hungary," in *The European Right: A Historical Profile,* ed. Hans Rogger and Eugene Weber. Berkeley: University of California Press, 1965, pp. 364–407.

Dreisziger, Nándor F. "Between Nationalism and Internationalism: Oscar Jászi's Path to Danubian Federalism, 1905–1918," in *Canadian Review of Studies in Nationalism* 19, nos. 1–2 (1993), pp. 103–16.

_____. "Central European Federalism in the Thought of Oszkár Jászi," in Várdy-Várdy, *Society in Change, op. cit.,* pp. 539–56.

_____. "Civil-Military Relations in Nazi Germany's Shadow: The Case of Hungary, 1939–1941," in *Swords and Covenants: Essays in Honour of the Centennial of the Royal Military College of Canada,* ed. Adrian Preston and Peter Dennis. London: Croom Helm, 1976, pp. 216–47.

_____. "Contradictory Evidence Concerning Hungary's Declaration of War on the USSR in June 1942," in *Canadian Slavonic Papers* 19, no. 4 (December 1977), pp. 480–88.

_____. "Count István Bethlen's Secret Plan for the Restoration of the Empire of Transylvania," in *East European Quarterly* 8, no. 4 (Winter 1974), pp. 413–23.

_____, ed. *Ethnic Armies: Polytechnic Armed Forces from the Time of the Habsburgs to the Age of the Superpowers.* Waterloo, Ontario: Wilfrid Laurier University Press, 1990.

_____. *Hungary's Way to World War II.* Toronto: Helicon, 1968. Paperback edition: Astor Park, Fla.: Danubian Press, 1968.

_____. "New Twist to an Old Riddle: The Bombing of Kassa [Košice], June 26, 1941," in *The Journal of Modern History* 44, no. 2 (June 1972), pp. 232–42.

_____. "Oscar Jászi and the Hungarian Problem: Activities and Writings during World War II," in *Hungarian Studies Review* 18, nos. 1–2 (Spring-Fall 1991), pp. 59–79.

_____. "The Diplomatic Fiasco of the Modern World's First Woman Ambassador: Róza Bédy-Schwimmer," in *East European Quarterly* 7 (1974), pp. 275–82.

_____. "The Evolution of Oscar Jászi's Political Ideas during the First World War," in Jónás-Pastor-Tóth, *Király Béla emlékkönyv, op. cit.,* pp. 159–67.

_____. "The Home Front in Hungary, 1914–1918," in Király-Dreisziger-Nofi, *East Central European Society in World War I, op. cit.,* pp. 124–34.

_____. "The Hungarian General Staff and Diplomacy, 1939–1941," in *Proceedings of the First Banff Conference on Central and East European Studies,* ed. T. M. S. Priestly. Edmonton, Canada, 1977, pp. 247–67.

_____."The Kassa Bombing: The Riddle of Ádám Krúdy," in Dreisziger, *Hungary and the Second World War, op. cit.,* pp. 79–98.

Fejtő, François. *Behind the Rape of Hungary.* Introductory essay by Jean-Paul Sartre. New York: D. MacKay Co., 1957.

Felkay, Andrew. *Hungary and the U.S.S.R., 1956-1988: Kádár's Political Leadership.* Westport, Conn.: Greenwood Press, 1989.

Fenyo, Mario D. *Hitler, Horthy, and Hungary: German-Hungarian Relations, 1941-1944.* New Haven: Yale University Press, 1972.

Gati, Charles. *Hungary and the Soviet Bloc.* Durham, N.C.: Duke University Press, 1986.

Held, Joseph, ed. *The Modernization of Agriculture: Rural Transformation in Hungary.* New York: East European Monographs, Columbia University Press, 1980.

Helmreich, Ernst C., ed. *Hungary.* New York: Frederick A. Praeger, 1957. Reprinted by Greenwood Press, Westport, Conn., 1973.

Hollós, Marida, and Béla C. Maday, eds. *New Hungarian Peasants. An East Central European Experience with Collectivization.* New York: Social Science Monographs, Brooklyn College Press, and Columbia University Press, 1983.

Horthy, Miklós de Nagybánya. *Confidential Papers,* ed. Miklós Szinai and László Szűcs. Budapest: Corvina Kiadó, 1965.

_____. *Memoirs.* Introductory essay by Nicholas Roosevelt. New York: R. Speller, 1957.

Hungarians in Czechoslovakia. New York: Research Institute for Minority Studies on Hungarians Attached to Czechoslovakia and Carpatho-Ruthenia, 1959.

Illyés, Elemér. *National Minorities in Romania. Change in Transylvania.* New York: East European Monographs, Columbia University Press, 1982.

Janics, Kálmán. *Czechoslovak Policy and the Hungarian Minority, 1945–1948.* New York: Social Science Monographs, Atlantic Research and Publications, and Columbia University Press, 1982.

Jászi, Oscar. *Revolution and Counter-Revolution in Hungary.* Introductory essay by R. W. Seton-Watson. Westminster: P. S. King and Son, 1924. Reprinted by H. Fertig, New York, 1969.

Joó, Rudolf, and Andrew Ludányi, eds. *The Hungarian Minority's Situation in Ceausescu's Romania.* New York: East European Monographs, Atlantic Research and Publications, and Columbia University Press, 1994.

Juhász, Gyula. *Hungarian Foreign Policy, 1919–1945.* Budapest: Akadémiai Kiadó, 1979.

Kállay, Miklós. *Hungarian Premier. A Personal Account of a Nation's Struggle in the Second World War.* Westport, Conn.: Greenwood Press, 1970.

Károlyi, Michael. *Memoirs of Michael Károlyi: Faith without Illusions,* ed. Catherine Károlyi. New York: Dutton, 1957.

Katzburg, Nathaniel. *Hungary and the Jews. Policy and Legislation, 1920–1943.* Ramat-Gan, Israel: Bar-Ilan University Press, 1981.

Kertész, Stephen D. *Between Russia and the West: Hungary and the Illusions of Peacemaking, 1945–1947.* Notre Dame, Ind.: University of Notre Dame Press, 1984.

_____. *Diplomacy in a Whirlpool. Hungary between Nazi Germany and Soviet Russia.* Notre Dame, Ind.: University of Notre Dame Press, 1953.

Kessler, Joseph A. *Turanism and Pan-Turanism in Hungary, 1890–1945.* Ph.D. Dissertation. University of California, 1967.

Király, Béla K. "Hungary's Army under the Soviets," in *East Europe* 7, no. 3 (March 1959), pp. 3–14.

_____. "Hungary's Army: Its Part in the Revolt," in *East Europe* 7, no. 6 (June 1959), pp. 24–36.

_____. "Paul Teleki, the Theoretician of Hungarian Revisionism," in Count Paul Teleki, *The Evolution of Hungary and its Place in European History.* Gulf Breeze, Fla.: Academic International Press, 1975, pp. xix–xliv.

_____. "The Danubian Problem in Oscar Jászi's Political Thought," in *The Hungarian Quarterly 5* (New York), nos. 1–2 (April–June 1965), pp. 120–34.

_____. "The First War between Socialist States: Military Aspects of the Hungarian Revolution," in *The Canadian-American Review of Hungarian Studies* 3, no. 2 (Fall 1976), pp. 115–23.

_____. "The Organization and National Defense during the Hungarian Revolution," in *The Central European Federalist* 14, no. 1 (July 1966), pp. 12–22.

_____. "Two Misconceptions about the Hungarian Revolution," in *Scope: A Journal of Social Sciences* 3, no. 1 (1966), pp. 18–31.

Király, Béla K., and Barbara Lotze, and Nándor F. Dreisziger, eds. *The First War between Socialist States. The Hungarian Revolution of 1956 and its Impact.* New York: Social Science Monographs, Brooklyn College Press, and Columbia University Press, 1984.

Király, Béla K., Nándor F. Dreisziger, and Albert A. Nofi, eds. *East Central European Society in World War I.* New York: East European

Monographs, Atlantic Research and Publications, and Columbia University Press, 1985.

Király, Béla K., and Paul Jónás, eds. *The Hungarian Revolution of 1956 in Retrospect.* Introductory essay by Hugh Seton-Watson. New York: East European Monographs, Columbia University Press, 1978.

Király, Béla K., Peter Pastor, and Ivan Sanders, eds. *Essays on World War. Total War and Peacemaking. A Case Study of Trianon.* New York: Social Science Monographs, Brooklyn College Press, and Columbia University Press, 1982.

Kis, János. *Politics in Hungary: For a Democratic Alternative.* New York: Social Science Monographs, Atlantic Research and Publications, and Columbia University Press, 1989.

Kopácsi, Sándor. *In the Name of the Working Class. The Inside Story of the Hungarian Revolution.* New York: Grove Weidenfeld, 1987.

Kostya, Sándor A. *Northern Hungary. A Historical Study of the Czechoslovak Republic,* tr. Zoltán Leskowsky. Toronto: Associated Hungarian Teachers, 1992.

Kovács, Imre, ed. *Facts about Hungary: The Fight for Freedom,* 2d ed. New York: Hungarian Committee, 1966.

Kovács, Mária M. *Liberal Professions and Illiberal Politics. Hungary from the Habsburgs to the Holocaust.* Washington and New York: Woodrow Wilson Center Press, and Oxford University Press, 1994.

Kovrig, Bennett. *Communism in Hungary. From Kun to Kádár.* Stanford: Hoover Institution Press, Stanford University, 1979.

_____. *The Hungarian People's Republic.* Baltimore: Johns Hopkins University Press, 1970.

Lackó, Miklós. *Arrow-Cross Men, National Socialists.* Budapest: Akadémiai Kiadó, 1969.

Lengyel, György, ed. *Hungarian Economy and Society during World War II.* New York: East European Monographs, Atlantic Research and Publications, and Columbia University Press, 1993.

Lévai, Jenő, ed. *Eichmann in Hungary: Documents.* New York: H. Fertig, 1987.

Lomax, William, ed. *Eye-witness in Hungary. The Soviet Invasion of 1956.* Nottingham, UK: Spokesman, 1980.

_____, ed. *Hungarian Workers' Councils in 1956.* New York: Social Science Monographs, Atlantic Research and Publications, and Columbia University Press, 1991.

_____, *Hungary 1956.* New York: St. Martin's Press, 1976.

Lőte, Louis L., ed. *Transylvania and the Theory of Daco-Roman-Rumanian Continuity.* Rochester, N.Y.: Committee of Transylvania, 1980.

Macartney, Carlyle A. *Hungary and Her Successors. The Treaty of Trianon and its Consequences, 1919–1937.* New York: Oxford University Press, 1968.

_____. *October Fifteenth: A History of Modern Hungary, 1929–1945,* 2 vols., 2d ed. Edinburgh, Scotland: Edinburgh University Press, 1961.

Marton, Kati. *Wallenberg.* New York: Random House, 1982.

Max, Stanley M. *The United States, Great Britain, and the Sovietization of Hungary, 1945–1948.* New York: East European Monographs, Columbia University Press, 1985.

Mindszenty, Cardinal József. *Memoirs.* New York: Macmillan, 1974.

Mócsy, István I. *The Effects of World War I. The Uprooted: Hungarian Refugees and their Impact on Hungarian Domestic Politics, 1918–1921.* New York: Social Science Monographs, Brooklyn College Press, and Columbia University Press, 1983.

Molnár, Miklós. *Budapest 1956. A History of the Hungarian Revolution.* London: Allen and Unwin, 1971.

_____. *From Béla Kun to János Kádár. Seventy Years of Hungarian Communism.* New York: Berg; distr. by St. Martin's Press, 1990.

Montgomery, John Flournoy. *Hungary the Unwilling Satellite.* New York: The Devin-Adair Company, 1947. Reprinted by Vista Books, Morristown, N. J., 1993.

Nagy, Ferenc. *Struggle behind the Iron Curtain.* New York: Macmillan, 1948.

Nagy, Zsuzsa L. *The Liberal Opposition in Hungary, 1919–1945.* Budapest: Akadémiai Kiadó, 1983.

Nagy-Talavera, Nicholas M. *The Green Shirts and Others. A History of Fascism in Hungary and Rumania.* Stanford: Hoover Institution Press, Stanford University, 1970.

Orbán, József Gyula. *Friedensbewegung Katholischer Priester in Ungarn.* Budapest: Magyar Egyháztörténeti Enciklopédia Munkaközössége, 1996.

Ormos, Mária. *From Padua to Trianon, 1918–1920.* New York: Social Science Monographs, Atlantic Research and Publications, and Columbia University Press, 1991.

Pacepa, Ion Mihai. *Red Horizons. The True Story of Nicolae and Elena Ceausescus' Crimes, Lifestyle, and Corruption.* Washington, D.C.:

Regnery Gateway, 1987; 2d ed., 1990. Much information about Ceausescus' hatred and treatment of the Hungarians in Romania.

Pastor, Peter. "Franco-Rumanian Intervention in Russia and the Vix Ultimatum: Background to Hungary's Loss of Transylvania," *The Canadian-American Review of Hungarian Studies* 1, nos.1–2 (Spring-Fall 1974), pp. 12–27.

_____. "Hungarian Emigrés in Wartime Britain," in *Eastern Europe and the West*, ed. John Morison. New York: St. Martin's Press, 1992, pp. 81–92.

_____. "Hungarian Prisoners of War in Russia during the War and Revolutions," in Williamson-Pastor, *Essays on World War I, op. cit.*, pp. 149–62.

_____. "Hungarian Territorial Losses during the Liberal-Democratic Revolution of 1918–1919," in Király-Pastor-Sanders, *Essays on World War I: A Case Study on Trianon, op. cit.*, pp. 255-74.

_____. *Hungary between Wilson and Lenin. The Hungarian Revolution of 1918–1919 and the Big Three.* New York: East European Monographs, Columbia University Press, 1976.

_____. "Hungary's Road from Wilsonianism to Leninism," in *East Central Europe* 3, no. 2 (1976), pp. 210-19.

_____. "Mihály Károlyi and Revolutionary Defense, 1918–1919," in Király-Nofi, *East Central European War Leaders, op. cit.*, pp. 85–94.

_____. "Official Nationalism in Hungary since 1964," in *Nationalism in the Era of Brezhnev and Kosygin*, ed. George W. Simmonds. Detroit: Detroit University Press, 1977, pp. 410–19. Reprinted in: *The National Idea in Eastern European Politics: The Politics of Ethnic and Civic Community*, ed. Gerasimos Augustinos. Lexington, Mass.: D. C. Heath, 1996.

_____. "One Step Forward, Two Steps Back: The Rise and Fall of the First Hungarian Communist Party, 1918–1922," in Banac, *The Effects of World War I, op. cit.,* pp. 85-126.

_____, ed. *Revolutions and Interventions in Hungary and its Neighbor States, 1918–1919.* New York: Social Science Monographs, Atlantic Research and Publications, and Columbia University Press, 1988.

_____. "The French Military Mission in Hungary, 1918-1919, in Pastor, *Revolutions and Interventions*, pp. 251–75.

_____. "The French War Aims against Austria-Hungary and the Treaty of Trianon," in Romsics, *20th Century Hungary, op. cit.,* pp. 39–53.

_____. "The Hungarian Critique of Wilsonianism," in *Wilsonian East Central Europe. Current Perspectives,* ed. John S. Micgiel. New York: The Pilsudski Institute, 1995, pp. 1–6.

_____. "The Nationality Policy of the Hungarian Revolutionary Government, 1918-1919," in *Nationalism: Essays in Honor of Louis L. Snyder,* ed. Michael Palumbo and William O. Shanahan. Westport, Conn.: Greenwood Press, 1981, pp. 168–77.

_____. "The Transylvanian Question in War and Revolutions," in Cadzow-Ludányi-Elteto, *Transylvania, op. cit.,* pp. 161–79

_____. "The Vix Mission in Hungary, 1918–1919: A Re-examination," in *Slavic Review* 29 (1970), pp. 481–98

Petri, György. *Effects of World War I: War Communism in Hungary.* New York: Social Science Monographs, Brooklyn College Press, and Columbia University Press, 1984.

Pölöskei, Ferenc. *Hungary after Two Revolutions, 1919–1922,* ed Mária Kovács, tr. E. Csicseri-Rónai. Budapest: Akadémiai Kiadó, 1980.

Prepuk, Anikó. "The Settlement of Jewish Population in the Habsburg Empire in the 18th and 19th Centuries." Paper delivered at the Twenty-Ninth Annual Duquesne University History Forum, October 12–14, 1995, Pittsburgh, Penna., USA.

Radványi, János. *Hungary and the Superpowers. The 1956 Revolution and 'Realpolitik.'* Stanford, Cal.: Hoover Institution Press, Stanford University, 1972.

Romsics, Ignác, ed. *20th Century Hungary and the Great Powers.* New York: East European Monographs, Atlantic Research and Publications, and Columbia University Press, 1995.

————. *Wartime American Plans for a New Hungary. Documents from the U.S. Department of State, 1942–1944.* New York: East European Monographs, Atlantic Research and Publications, and Columbia University Press, 1992.

Rosenfeld, Harvey. *Raoul Wallenberg, Angle of Rescue: Heroism and Torment in the Gulag.* Buffalo, N.Y.: Prometheus Books, 1982.
Sakmyster, Thomas L. *Hungary, the Great Powers, and the Danubian Crisis, 1936–1939.* Athens: University of Georgia Press, 1980.

Sas, Meir.*Vanished Communities in Hungary. The History of the Tragic Fate of the Jews in Újhely and Zemplén County.* Willowdale, Ontario: Memorial Book Committee, 1986.

Seton-Watson, Hugh. *The East European Revolution.* New York: Frederick A. Praeger, 1962.

Shawcross, William. *Crime and Compromise. János Kádár and the Politics of Hungary since the Revolution.* New York: E. P. Dutton, 1974.

Siklós, Pierre L. *War Finance, Reconstruction, Hyperinflation, and Stabilization in Hungary, 1938–1948.* New York: St. Martin's Press, 1991.

Simontsits, Attila L., ed. *The Last Battle for St. Stephen's Crown.* Cleveland: Attila L. Simontsits, 1983.

Sinor, Denis, ed. *Modern Hungary. Readings for the 'New Hungarian Quarterly.'* Bloomington: Indiana University Press, 1977.

Spira, Thomas. *German-Hungarian Relations and the Swabian Problem. From Károlyi to Gömbös, 1919–1936.* New York: East European Monographs, Columbia University Press, 1977.

_____. *The German-Hungarian-SwabianTriangle, 1936-1939. The Road to Discord.* New York: East European Monographs, Columbia University Press, 1990.

Sugar, Peter F., and Ivo J. Lederer, eds. *Nationalism in Eastern Europe.* Seattle: University of Washington Press, 1969.

Szendrey, Thomas. "Philosophy in Hungary before and after 1956: From Staunch Orthodoxy to Limited Revisionism," in Király-Lotze-Dreisziger, *The Hungarian Revolution of 1956, op. cit.* pp. 221–40.

_____. "Remembering 1956: Some Reflections on the Historical Consciousness of a New Generation," in *Hungarian Studies Review* 14 (1987), 27–37.

_____. "The Catholic Intellectual Revival in Hungary in the 1930s: The Journal 'Vigília'," in *Miscellanea Historiae Ecclesiasticae.* Brussels: Editions Neuwalaerts, 1985, pp. 334–45.

_____. "The Origin and Development of Christian Democracy in Hungary: The Role of Alexander Giesswein, Writer, Social Reformer and Scholar, 1856–1923," in *Régi és új peregrináció: Magyarok külföldön, külföldiek Magyarországon [Old and New Wanderings: Hungarians Abroad and Foreigners in Hungary]*, 3 vols. Budapest-Szeged, Hungary: Nemzetközi Magyar Filológiai Társaság, and Scriptum, 1993, vol. 1, pp. 387–95. Bilingual.

Szent-Miklósy, István.*With the Hungarian Independence Movement, 1943–1947.* New York: Praeger Publishers, 1987.

Szilassy, Sándor. *Revolutionary Hungary, 1918–1921.* Astor Park, Fla.: Danubian Press, 1971.

Szinai, Miklós, and László Szűcs, eds. *The Confidential Papers of Admiral Horthy.* Budapest: Corvina Press, 1965.

Teleki, Count Paul. *The Evolution of Hungary and its Place in European History.* New York: Macmillan, 1923. Reprinted by Academic International Press, Gulf Breeze, Fla., 1975.

Tilkovszky, Loránt. *Pál Teleki, 1879–1941. A Biographical Sketch.* Budapest: Akadémiai Kiadó, 1974.

Tőkés, Rudolf L. *Béla Kun and the Hungarian Soviet Republic. The Origins and Role of the Communist Party of Hungary in the Revolutions of 1918–1919.* Stanford and New York: Hoover Institution Press and Praeger Publishers, 1967.

_____. *Hungary's Negotiated Revolution: Economic Reform, Social Change, and Political Succession.* Cambridge: Cambridge University Press, 1996.

Vágó, Béla, and George L. Mosse, eds. *Jews and Non-Jews in Eastern Europe, 1918-1945.* New York and Toronto: John Wiley and Sons, 1974; Jerusalem: Israel Universities Press, 1974.

Vágó, Raphael. *The Grandchildren of Trianon: Hungary and the Hungarian Minority in the Communist States.* New York: East European Monographs, Columbia University Press, 1989.

Váli, Ferenc A. *A Scholar's Odyssey,* ed. Karl W. Ryavec. Ames, Iowa: Iowa State University Press, 1990.

_____. *Rift and Revolt in Hungary. Nationalism versus Communism.* Cambridge: Harvard University Press, 1961.

Várdy, Steven Béla. "Hungarian National Consciousness and the Question of Dual and Multiple Identity," in *Hungarian Studies Review* 20, nos. 1–2 (1993), pp. 53–70.

_____. "Soviet Nationality Policy in Carpatho-Ukraine since World War II: The Hungarians of Sub-Carpathia," in *Hungarian Studies Review* 16, nos. 1–2 (1989), pp. 67–91.

_____. "The Hungarians of Carpatho-Ukraine: From Czechoslovak to Soviet Rule," in Borsody, *The Hungarians. A Divided Nation, op. cit.,* pp. 209–27.

_____. "The Impact of Trianon upon the Hungarian Mind. The Nature of Interwar Hungarian Irredentism," in *Hungarian Studies Review* 10, nos. 1–2 (1983), pp. 21–42.

Vecsey, Joseph, and Phyllis Schlafly. *Mindszenty the Man.* St. Louis, Mo.: Cardinal Mindszenty Foundation, 1972.

Vermes, Gábor. *István Tisza: The Liberal Vision and Conservative Statecraft of a Magyar Nationalist.* New York: East European Monographs, Columbia University Press, 1985.

Völgyes, Iván. *Hungary. A Nation of Contradictions.* Boulder, Colo.: Westview Press, 1982.

_____, ed. *Hungary in Revolution, 1918–19. Nine Essays.* Lincoln: University of Nebraska Press, 1971.

Völgyes, Iván, and Nancy Völgyes. *The Liberated Female. Life, Work, and Sex in Socialist Hungary.* Boulder, Colo.: Westview Press, 1977.

Wagner, Francis S., ed. *The Hungarian Revolution in Perspective.* Washington, D.C.: F. F. Memorial Foundation, 1967.

Williamson, Samuel R., and Peter Pastor, eds. *Essays on World War I: Origins and Prisoners of War.* New York: East European Monographs, Columbia University Press, 1983.

Witnesses to Cultural Genocide: First-Hand Reports on Rumania's Minority Policies Today. New York: American Transylvanian Federation, and Committee for Human Rights in Rumania, 1979.

Wojatsek, Charles. *From Trianon to the First Vienna Arbitral Award: The Hungarian Minority in the First Czechoslovak Republic, 1918–1938.* Montreal: Institut des Civilizations Comparées— Institute of Comparative Civilizations, 1980.

Zinner, Paul. *Revolution in Hungary.* New York: Columbia University Press, 1962.

7. Culture, Education, Folklore, Literature

Balassa, Iván, and Gyula Ortutay. *Hungarian Ethnography and Folklore.* Budapest: Corvina Press, 1974. This is a major compendium of Hungarian folk culture.

Bartók, Béla. *Hungarian Folk Music.* New York: AMS Press, 1981.

Benedek, András, ed. *Development of Education in the Hungarian People's Republic, 1984–1986.* Budapest: Hungarian National Commission for UNESCO, 1986.

Bodolai, Zoltán. *The Timeless Nation. The History, Literature, Music, Art, and Folklore of the Hungarian Nation.* Sidney, Australia: Hungaria Publishing, 1978.

Braham, Randolph L. *Education in the Hungarian People's Republic.* Washington, D.C.: U.S. Department of Health, Education, and Welfare, 1970. Braham fails to differentiate between the university doctorates and the higher level Academy of Sciences doctorates.

Czigány, Loránt. *The Oxford History of Hungarian Literature. From the Earliest Times to the Present.* Oxford: Oxford University Press, 1984.

Dömötör, Tekla. *Hungarian Folk Beliefs.* Bloomington: Indiana University Press, 1982.

Dreisziger, Nándor F. "Emigré Artists and Wartime Politics: The Hungarian-American Council for Democracy, 1943-45," in *Hungarian Studies Review* 21, nos. 1–2 (Spring-Fall 1994), pp. 43–75.

_____. "Watson Kirkconnell and the Cultural Credibility Gap between Immigrants and the Native-Born in Canada," in Kovács, *Ethnic Canadians, op. cit.,* pp. 87–96.

_____. "Watson Kirkconnell: Translator of Hungarian Poetry and Friend of Hungarian Canadians," in *Hungarian Poetry and the English-Speaking World: A Tribute to Watson Kirkconnell.* Ottawa, Canada: Hungarian Readers' Service, 1977, pp. 117–43.

Hungarian Higher Education 1992. Budapest: Hungarian Rector's Conference, Coordinating Office of Higher Education, and Hungarian Equivalence and Information Centre, 1992.

Kampis, Anal. *The History of Art in Hungary.* Budapest: Corvina Press, 1966.

Klaniczay, Gábor. *The Uses of Supernatural Power: The Transformation of Popular Religion in Medieval and Early Modern Europe.* Princeton: Princeton University Press, 1990.

Klement, Tamás. *Three Decades in the History of Hungarian Higher Education.* Budapest: National Pedagogical Library, 1977.

Nemeskürty, István. *Word and Image: History of the Hungarian Cinema.* Budapest: Corvina Press, 1974.

Paládi-Kovács, Attila. *Ethnic Traditions. Classes and Communities in Hungary.* Budapest: Institute of Ethnology, 1996.

Sanders, Ivan. "Hungarians and Germans: A Literary Hassliebe," in *International Journal of Politics, Culture and Society* 9, no.1 (1995), pp. 123–32.

————. "Oriental Flower in Pest," in *Budapest Review of Books* (1995), pp. 19–24.

————. "Post-Trianon Searching: The Early Career of László Németh," in Király-Pastor-Sanders, *Essays on World War I: A Case Study of Trianon, op. cit.,* pp. 347–59.

Sozán, Michael. *The History of Hungarian Ethnography.* Washington, D.C.: University Press of America, 1977.

Szabolcsi, Bence, and György Króo. *A Concise History of Hungarian Music.* Budapest: Corvina Press, 1974.

Várdy, Ágnes Huszár. *A Study in Austrian Romanticism: Hungarian Influences in Lenau's Poetry.* Buffalo, N.Y.: State University of New York College at Buffalo, and Hungarian Cultural Foundation, 1974.

_____. "Literature and Politics in the Age of Reform, 1830-1848: Karl Beck's Role in the *Junges Deutschland* Movement," in *The Canadian-American Review of Hungarian Studies* 6, no. 2 (Fall 1979), pp. 79–89.

_____. "Nikolaus Lenau and Germanic Literary Interests in Hungary during the First Half of the Nineteenth Century," in *The Canadian-American Review of Hungarian Studies* 1, nos. 1–2 (Fall 1974), pp. 28–35.

_____. "The Coffee Houses of Vienna," in *The World And I* 2 (Washington, D.C.), no. 10 (October 1987), pp. 493–505.

_____. *The Image of the Turks in Jókai's Historical Novels and Short Stories*. Pittsburgh: Duquesne University Department of History, 1979. (Duquesne University Studies in History, vol. 7, ed. Steven Béla Várdy.)

_____. "The Turks and Ottoman Civilization in Jókai's Historical Novels and Short Stories," in Várdy-Várdy, *Society in Change, op. cit.,* pp. 449–69.

_____. "Trianon and Transylvanian Hungarian Literature: Sándor Reményik's 'Végvári' Poems," in Király-Pastor-Sanders, *Essays on World War I: A Case Study on Trianon, op. cit.,* pp. 407–22.

Ágnes Huszár Várdy, and Kollar, Walter W., eds. *The Folk Arts of Hungary*. Pittsburgh: Duquesne University Tamburitzans Institute of Folk Arts, 1981.

Várdy, Agnes Huszár, and Steven Béla Várdy. "Peasant Wit in Magyar Folktales," in *The World and I* 2 (Washington, D.C.), no. 6 (June 1987), pp. 520–31.

_____. "Robin Hoods of the Puszta. Part I. Hungarian Betyárs: Rebels against Social Oppression," in *The World and I* 6 (Washington, D.C.), no. 9 (September 1991), pp. 558–69.

_____. "Robin Hoods of the Puszta. Part II. Hungarian Betyárs: Rebels against Habsburg Absolutism," in *The World and I* 6 (Washington, D.C.), no. 10 (October 1991), pp. 640–51.

Várdy, Steven Béla, and Ágnes Huszár Várdy. "A Nation's Sacred Destiny: Part I. Heroic Legends of the Huns and the Magyars," in *The World and I* 3 (Washington, D.C.), no. 7 (July 1988), pp. 492–502.

_____. "A Nation's Sacred Destiny: Part II. Legends of Magyar Heroes after the Conquest of the Lands that Became Hungary," in *The World and I* 3 (Washington, D.C.), no. 8 (August 1988), pp. 524–33.

8. HUNGARIANS IN NORTH AMERICA

Balogh, J. E. *An Analysis of Cultural Organizations of Hungarian Americans in Pittsburgh and Allegheny County.* Ph.D. Dissertation. University of Pittsburgh, 1945.

Barany, George. "The Magyars," in *The Immigrants' Influence on Wilson's Peace Policies,* ed. Joseph P. O'Grady. Lexington: University of Kentucky Press, 1967, pp. 140–72.

Benkart, Paula K. "Hungarians," in *HarvardEncyclopedia of American Ethnic Groups,* ed. Stephan Thernstrom *et al.* Cambridge: Harvard University Press, 1980, pp. 462–71.

_____. *Religion, Family and Community among Hungarians Migrating to American Cities, 1880-1930.* Ph.D. Dissertation. Johns Hopkins University. Baltimore, Md., 1975.

Beynon, Erdman Doana. "Occupational Success of Hungarians in Detroit," in *American Journal of Sociology* 39, no. 5 (1934), pp. 600–10.

_____. "Social Mobility and Social Distance among Hungarian Immigrants in Detroit," *American Journal of Sociology* 41, no. 4 (1936), pp. 423–34.

Birnbaum, Marianna D. "The Hungarians of Hollywood. Image and Image-Making." The unpublished manuscript of a lecture delivered at Indiana University, Bloomington, Indiana, in the mid-1980s.

Bognár, Desi K., ed. *Hungarians in America.* Philadelphia: Alpha Publications, 1971.

Bölöni-Farkas, Alexander [Sándor]. *Journey in North America (Kolozsvár, 1834),* tr.and ed. Theodore Schoenman and Helen Benedek Schoenman. Philadelphia: The American Philosophical Society, 1977.

Bölöni-Farkas, Sándor [Alexander]. *Journey in North America, 1831,* tr. and ed. Árpád Kadarkay. Santa Barbara, Calif: ABC-Clio, 1978.

Boros-Kazai, Mary. "The Emigration Problem and Hungarian Lawmakers, 1880–1910," in *Hungarian Studies Review* 8, no. 1 (Spring 1981), pp. 25–44.

Dreisziger, Nándor F. "'Bridges to the West': The Horthy Regime's Reinsurance Policies in 1941," in *War an Society* 7, no. 1 (May 1989), pp. 1–23.

_____. "Hungarian Revolution of 1956: The Legacy of the Refugees," in *Nationalities Papers* 13, no. 2 (Fall 1985), pp. 198–202.

_____. "Hungarians in the Canadian West: A Research Report," in *Prairie Forum* 10, no. 2 (Fall 1985), pp. 435–53.

_____. "Immigrant Lives and Lifestyles in Canada, 1924-1939," in *Hungarian Studies Review* 8, no. 1 (Spring 1981), pp. 61–83.

_____. "Immigration and Re-Migration: The Changing Urban-Rural Distribution of Hungarian Canadians, 1886–1986," in *Hungarian Studies Review* 13, no. 2 (Fall 1986), pp. 20–41.

_____. "Impact of the Revolutions on Hungarians Abroad," in Király-Lotze-Dreisziger, *The First War between Socialist States, op. cit.*, pp. 411-25.

_____. "In Search of a Hungarian-Canadian Lobby, 1927–1951," in *Canadian Ethnic Studies* 12, no. 3 (1980), pp. 81–96.

_____. "Mission Impossible: Secret Plans for a Hungarian Government-in-Exile in Canada during World War II," in *Canadian Slavonic Papers* 30, no. 2 (June 1988), pp. 245–62.

_____. "National Hungarian-Canadian Organizations," in *Hungarians in Ontario,* ed. Susan Papp. Toronto: Multicultural History Society of Ontario, 1980, pp. 50–54.

_____. "Sub-Ethnic Identities: Religion, Class, Ideology, etc. as Centrifugal Forces in Hungarian-American Society," in *Hungarian Studies: Journal of the International Association of Hungarian Studies* 7 (Budapest and Bloomington), nos. 1–2 (1991–92), pp. 123–38.

_____. "The Critical Visitor: Alexander Bölöni Farkas's Tour of Canada in 1831," in *The Quarterly of Canadian Studies* 5, nos. 3–4 (1982), pp. 147–52.

_____. "The 'Justice for Hungary' Ocean Flight: The Trianon Syndrome in Immigrant Hungarian Society," in Várdy-Várdy, *Triumph in Adversity, op. cit.*, pp. 573–89.

_____. "The 1956 Hungarian Student Movement in Exile," in *Hungarian Studies Review* 20, nos. 1-2 (1993), pp. 103–86.

_____. "The Refugee Experience in Canada and the Evolution of the Hungarian-Canadian Community," in *Breaking Ground: The 1956 Hungarian Refugee Movement to Canada,* ed. R. H. Keyserlingk. North York, Ontario: York Lane Press, and York University Press, 1993, pp. 65–86.

_____, *et al. Struggle and Hope: The Hungarian-Canadian Experience.* Toronto: McClelland and Stewart, 1982. This is a major synthesis of the history of the Hungarian community in Canada.

Fermi, Laura. *Illustrious Immigrants: The Intellectual Migration from Europe, 1930–41.* Chicago: University of Chicago Press, 1969.

Fishman, Joshua A. *Hungarian Language Maintenance in the United States.* Bloomington: Indiana University Publications, Uralic and Altaic Series, 1966.

Gellén, József. "Colonel Prágay's Unknown Letter to American Statesmen," in *Hungarian Studies in English* 11 (University of Debrecen, Hungary), nos. 1-2 (1977), pp. 149–53.

_____. "Emigration in a Systems Framework: The Case of Hungary, 1899-1913," in *Hungarian Studies in English* 17, nos. 1-2 (1984), pp. 85–112.

_____. "Immigrant Experience in Hungarian-American Poetry before 1945," in *Acta Litteraria Academiae Scientiarum Hungariae* 20 (Budapest), no. 1–2 (1978), pp. 81–97.

Gleitman, Henry and Joseph J. Greenbaum. "Attitudes and Personality Patterns of Hungarian Refugees," in *Public Opinion Quarterly* 25, no. 3 (1961), pp. 351–65.

_____. "Hungarian Socio-Political Attitudes and Revolutionary Action," in *Public Opinion Quarterly* 24, no. 1 (1960), 62–76.

Gunda, Béla. "American in Hungarian Folk Tradition," in *Journal of American Folklore* 83, no. 330 (1970), pp. 406–16.

_____. "The Role of Remigrants from America in Hungarian Folklife," in *Sociologus* 36 (Berlin), no. 1 (1986), pp. 79–90.

Hauk-Abonyi, Malvina and James A. Anderson. *Hungarians of Detroit.* Detroit: Center for Urban Studies, Wayne State University, 1977.

Hungarian Ethnic Heritage Study of Pittsburgh, Pennsylvania. Paul Bődy, Director. Pittsburgh: Hungarian Ethnic Heritage Studies, 1981.

Hungarians in America. A Biographical Directory of Professionals of Hungarian Origin in the Americas, ed. Tibor Szy. New York: Hungarian University Association, 1963; 2d ed. New York: The Kossuth Foundation, 1966.

Hungarians in America. A Biographical Directory of Professionals of Hungarian Origin in the Americas, ed. Desi K. Bognár and Katalin Szentpályi. Mt. Vernon, N.Y.: AH Publications, 1971.

Hungarian Studies Review 8, nos. 1–2 (Spring-Fall 1981). Special volume: *Hungarian Cultural Presence in North America.* Parts I and II.

Kalassay, Louis A. *The Educational and Religious History of the Hungarian Reformed Church in the United States.* Ph.D. Dissertation. University of Pittsburgh, 1939.

Katona, Anna. "Hungarian Travelogues on Pre–Civil War U.S.," in *Hungarian Studies in English* 5, nos. 1–2 (1971), pp. 51–94.

_____. "Nineteenth-Century Hungarian Travelogues on the Post-Civil War U.S. Admiration Mixed with Disillusionment. *Hungarian Studies in English* 7, nos. 1–2 (1973), pp. 35–52.

Kerek, Andrew. "Hungarian Language Research in North America: Themes and Directions," in *The Canadian-American Review of Hungarian Studies* 5, no. 2 (Fall 1978), pp. 63–72.

Király, Béla K., and George Bárány, eds. *East Central European Perception of Early America.* Lisse, Netherlands: Peter de Ridder Press, 1977.

Klay, Andor. *Daring Diplomacy. The Case of the First American Ultimatum.* Minneapolis: The University of Minnesota Press, 1957.

Komjáthy, Aladár. *History of the Hungarian Reformed Church in Roebling, New Jersey, 1913–1963.* Trenton, N.J.: Hungarian Reformed Congregation, 1963.

_____. *Hungarian United Church of Montreal, 1926–1976.* Montreal: Hungarian United Church, 1977.

_____. *Seventy Years of Hungarian Reformed Church of Passaic, New Jersey.* Passaic, N.J.: Hungarian Reformed Congregation, 1965.

_____. *The Hungarian Reformed Church in America. An Effort to Preserve a Denominational Heritage.* Ph.D. Dissertation. Princeton Theological Seminary, Princeton, N.J., 1962.

_____. *The Hungarian Reformed Experiment in North America.* New Brunswick, N.J.: Hungarian Reformed Ministerial Association, 1977.

Komlós, John H. *Louis Kossuth in America, 1851–1852.* Buffalo, N.Y.: East European Institute, 1973

Konnyu, Leslie. *Acacias: Hungarians in the Mississippi Valley.* Ligonier, Penna.: Bethlen Press, 1976.

_____. *A History of Hungarian American Literature.* St. Louis: Cooperative of American Hungarian Writers, 1962.

_____. *Hungarians in the U.S.A.: An Immigration Study.* St.Louis: American Hungarian Review, 1967.

_____. *John Xántus. Hungarian Geographer in America, 1851–1864.* Cologne, Germany: American Hungarian Publisher, 1965.

Kósa, John. "A Century of Hungarian Emigration, 1850–1950," in *The American Slavic and East European Review* 16, no. 4 (December 1957), pp. 501–14.

_____. *Land of Choice: The Hungarians of Canada.* Toronto: The University of Toronto Press, 1957.

Kovács, Martin L., ed. *Esterházy and Early Hungarian Immigration to Canada.* Regina, Saskatchewan: Canadian Plains Studies, 1994.

_____, ed. *Ethnic Canadians: Culture and Education.* Regina, Saskatchewan: Canadian Plains Studies, 1978.

_____. *Peace and Strife: Some Facets of the History of an Early Prairie Community.* Kipling, Saskatchewan: Kipling District Historical Society, 1980.

Kramár, Zoltán. *From the Danube to the Hudson. U.S. Consular and Ministerial Dispatches on Immigration from the Habsburg Monarchy, 1850–1900.* Introductory essay by Steven Béla Várdy. Atlanta: Hungarian Cultural Foundation, 1978.

Kretzoi, Miklósné. "The American Civil War as Reflected in the Contemporary Hungarian Press," in *Hungarian Studies in English* 2, nos. 1–2 (1965), pp. 61–92.

Kuné, Julian. *Reminiscences of an Octogenarian Hungarian Exile.* Chicago: Published by the Author, 1911.

Lengyel, Emil. *Americans from Hungary.* Philadelphia: J. B. Lippincott, 1948. Reprinted by Greenwood Press, Westport, Conn., 1974.

Madden, Henry Miller. *Xántus: Hungarian Naturalist in the Pioneer West.* Palo Alto, Calif.: Books of the West, 1949.

Major, Mark Imre. *American Hungarian Relations, 1918–1944.* Astor, Fla.: Danubian Press, 1974.

Makár, János. *The Story of an Immigrant Group in Franklin, New Jersey,* tr. August J. Molnár. Franklin, N.J.: Published by the Author, 1969.

Marchbin, Andrew A. "Hungarian Activities in Western Pennsylvania," in *Western Pennsylvania Historical Magazine* 23, no. 3 (September 1940), pp. 163–74.

McGuire, James Patrick. *The Hungarian Texans.* San Antonio: The University of Texas Institute of Texan Cultures, 1993.

Nadányi, Paul. *The "Free Hungary" Movement.* New York: Amerikai Magyar Népszava, 1942.

Olmsted, Frederick Law. *A Journey through Texas or a Saddle-Trip on the Southwestern Frontier.* New York: Burt Franklin, 1969. Reprint. This famed landscape architect makes references to Hungarian settlers.

Papp, Charles S. *Follow the Sunset. A Dramatic Story of Survival.* Sacramento, Calif.: Entomography Publications, 1988. The personal account of a Hungarian scientist, who left his homeland after World War II in 1945 and emigrated to the United States in 1950.

Papp, Susan M. *Hungarian Americans and Their Communities of Cleveland.* Cleveland: Cleveland Ethnic Heritage Studies, Cleveland State University, 1981.

Park, Robert E. *The Immigrant Press and its Control.* New York: Harper, 1922.

Perlman, Robert. *Bridging Three Worlds. Hungarian Jewish Americans, 1848–1914.* Amherst: University of Massachusetts Press, 1991.

Pivány, Eugene. *Hungarian-American Historical Connections: From Pre-Columbian Times to the End of the American Civil War.* Budapest: Royal Hungarian University Press, 1927.

Prominent Hungarians. Home and Abroad, ed. Márton Fekete. London: Fehér Holló Press, 1973; 3rd ed. London: Szepsi Csombor Literary Circle, 1979; 5th ed. Budapest: HVG Publishing House, 1991.

Puskás, Julianna. *Emigration from Hungary to the United States before 1914.* Budapest: Akadémiai Kiadó, 1975.

_____. *From Hungary to the United States, 1880–1914.* Budapest: Akadémiai Kiadó, 1982.

_____. "Some Recent Results of Historic Research on International Migration," in *Acta Historica Academiae Scientiarum Hungaricae* 23 (1977), pp. 151–169.

_____. "The Process of Overseas Migration from East-Central Europe: Its Periods, Cycles, and Characteristics. A Comparative Study," in *Zeszyty Naukowe Uniwersytetu Jagiellonskiego* (Cracow, Poland, 1983), pp. 33–51.

Rácz, István. "Attempts to Curb Hungarian Emigration to the United States before 1914," in *Hungarian Studies in English* 7, nos. 1–2 (1973), pp. 5–33.

_____. "Emigration from Hungary to the U.S.A.," in *Magyar Történeti Tanulmányok* 10 (University of Debrecen, Hungary), nos. 1–2 (1977), pp. 117–54.

Reményi, Joseph. *Hungarian Writers and Literature*, ed. and introduced by August J. Molnár. New Brunswick: Rutgers University Press, 1964.

Schoenman, Theodore, ed. *The Father of California Wine: Ágoston Haraszthy*. Santa Barbara: Capara Press, 1979.

Sisa, Stephen. *America's Amazing Hungarians*. Huddleston, Va.: Published by the Author, 1987.

Soskis, Philip. "The Adjustment of Hungarian Refugees in New York," in *International Migration Review* 2, no. 1 (Fall 1967), pp. 40–46.

Souders, D. A. *The Magyars in America*. New York: George H. Doran, 1922. Reprinted in by Arno Press, New York, 1969.

Spencer, Donald S. *Louis Kossuth and Young America: A Study in Sectionalism and Foreign Policy, 1848–1852*. Columbia, Mo.: University of Missouri Press, 1977.

Szendrey, Thomas. "Hungarian-American Theater," in *The Ethnic Theater in the United States,* ed. Maxine S. Seller. Westport, Conn.: Greenwood Press, 1983, pp. 191–220.

Széplaki, Joseph, ed. *Hungarians in the United States and Canada. A Bibliography*. Introductory essay by Steven Béla Várdy. Minneapolis: Immigration History Research Center, University of Minnesota, 1977.

_____. *Louis Kossuth, "The Nation's Guest." A Bibliography on His Trip in the United States, December 4, 1851 – July 14, 1852*. Ligonier, Penna.: Bethlen Press, 1976.

_____. *The Hungarians in America, 1583–1974: A Chronology and Fact Book*. Dobbs Ferry, N.Y.: Oceana Publications, 1975.

Táborsky, Otto Árpád. *The Hungarian Press in America*. MSLS Thesis. The Catholic University of America, Washington, D.C., 1955.

Tezla, Albert, ed. *The Hazardous Quest. Hungarian Immigrants in the United States, 1895–1920*. Budapest: Corvina Press, 1993.

Thirring, Gustav. "Hungarian Migration in Modern Times," in *International Migrations*, ed. Imre Ferenczi and Walter F. Wilcox, 2 vols. New York: National Bureau of Economic Research, 1929–31. Vol. 2: *Interpretations*, pp. 411–39.

Várdy, Ágnes Huszár. "Character and Role of Hungarian Literary Journals in North America in the 1970s and 1980s," in Várdy-Várdy,*Triumph in Adversity, op. cit.*, pp. 591–606.

Várdy, Ágnes Huszár, and Steven Béla Várdy. "Research in Hungarian-American History and Culture: Achievements and Prospects," in Várdy-Kollar, *The Folk Arts of Hungary, op. cit.*, pp. 61–116.

Várdy, Steven Béla. "Hungarians in America's Ethnic Politics," in *America's Ethnic Politics*, eds. Joseph R. Roucek and Bernard Eisenberg. Westport, Conn.: Greenwood Press, 1982, pp. 171–96.

_____. "Hungarian Studies at American and Canadian Universities," in *The Canadian-American Review of Hungarian Studies* 2, no. 2 (Fall 1975), pp. 91–121.

_____. "Magyars in America. Early Immigrants and the Great Economic Migration from Rural Hungary," in *The World and I* 2 (Washington, D.C.), no. 3 (March 1987), pp. 462–77.

_____. "Mystery of the Hungarian Talent. Hungarian Intellectual and Political Immigration to America," in *The World and I* 2, no. 4 (April 1987), pp. 488–513.

_____. "The Great Economic Immigration from Hungary, 1880–1920," in Várdy-Várdy, *Society in Change, op cit.*, pp. 189–216.

_____. *The Hungarian-Americans.* Boston: Twayne Publishers, 1985).

_____. *The Hungarian Americans: The Hungarians of North America.* Introductory essay by Daniel Patrick Moynihan. New York: Chelsea House Publishers, 1989.

_____. "The Hungarian Community of Cleveland," in *Hungarian Studies Review* 8, no. 1 (Spring 1981), pp. 137–43.

_____. "The Hungarians [Magyars] in the United States," in *Ethnic Forum: Journal of Ethnic Studies and Ethnic Bibliography* 10 (Kent State University), nos. 1–2 (1990), pp. 63–82. Corrections inserted in *ibid.*, vol. 13, no. 9 (1993).

Várdy, Steven Béla, and Thomas Szendrey. "Hungarian Americans," in *Gale Encyclopedia of Multicultural America,* ed. Rudolph J. Vecoli, *et al.*, 2 vols. Detroit: Gale Research Inc.,1995, vol. 1, pp. 1043–51.

Várdy, Steven Béla, and Ágnes Huszár Várdy. "Historical, Literary, Linguistic, and Ethnographic Research on Hungarian-Americans. A Historiographical Assessment," in *Hungarian Studies: Journal of the International Association of Hungarian Studies*, vol. 1 (1985), pp. 79–124.

_____. "Treaty of Trianon and the Hungarian-Americans," in *Eurasian Studies Yearbook,* 69 (1997), pp. 127-45.

Vassady, Jr., Béla. "Hungarian-American Mutual Aid Associations and Their 'Official' Newspapers: A Symbiotic Relationship," in *Hungarian Studies Review* 19, nos. 1–2 (1992), pp. 7–27.

_____. "Kossuth and Újházi on Establishing a Colony of Hungarian 48-ers in America, 1849–1852," in *The Canadian-American Review of Hungarian Studies* 6, no. 1 (Spring 1979), pp. 21–46.

_____. "The 'Homeland Cause' as Stimulant to Ethnic Unity: The Hungarian-American Response to Károlyi's 1914 American Tour," in *Journal of American Ethnic History* 2, no. 1 (Fall 1982), pp. 39–64.

Vasváry, Edmund. *Lincoln's Hungarian Heroes. The Participation of Hungarians in the Civil War.* Washington, D.C.: The Hungarian Reformed Federation of America, 1939.

_____. *Magyar Amerika [Hungarian America],* ed. György Gyuris and Béla Tóth; introductory essay by András Csillag. Szeged, Hungary: Somogyi-Könyvtár, 1988. An important selection of historical essays by one of the "old-time" Hungarian American historians, who had assembled the largest personal archival collection about the Hungarian immigrants to the United States. His collection is located in the Somogyi Library of Szeged, Hungary, with copies in the archives of the American Hungarian Foundation in New Brunswick, New Jersey.

Vázsonyi, Andrew. "The Cicisbeo and the Magnificent Cuckold: Boarding House Life and Lore in Immigrant Communities," in *Journal of American Folklore* 91, no. 360 (1978), pp. 641–56.

Wagner, Francis S. "The Start of Cultural Exchanges between the Hungarian Academy of Sciences and the American Philosophical Society," in *Hungarian Quarterly* 5, nos. 1–2 (April-June 1965), pp. 90–97.

Weinstock, S. Alexander. *Acculturation and Occupation: A Study of the 1965 Hungarian Refugees in the United States.* The Hague: Martinus Nijhoff, 1969.

Xántus, John. *Letters from North America,* tr. and ed. Theodore Schoenman and Helen Benedek Schoenman. Detroit: Wayne State University Press, 1975. Xántus was a flamboyant 19th-century Hungarian scientist and soldier of fortune.

————. *Travels in Southern California.* tr. and ed. Theodore Schoenman and Helen Benedek Schoenman. Detroit: Wayne State University Press, 1976.

ABOUT THE AUTHOR

STEVEN BÉLA VÁRDY, Ph.D., is professor of European History at Duquesne University, former chairman of the Department of History, director of the Duquesne University History Forum, president of the American Association for the Study of Hungarian History, and board member of the International Association of Hungarian Historians as well as of the International Association for the Study of Hungarian Language and Culture. He is the author or coauthor of well over a dozen books and about three-hundred-fifty articles, chapters, essays, and reviews, some of which are listed in the bibliography of this work. Five of his books deal with two of his favorite topics: Hungarian historiography and Hungarians in America. His newest book on the latter topic, *Hungarians in the New World,* is in the process of publication. He has also resumed research on the development post-World War II Hungarian historical studies under the aegis of Marxism. He is likewise writing on the topic of "dual and multiple identity in historical perspective," especially as it relates to the United States, Hungary, and East Central Europe.

A winner of numerous major grants and fellowships, in 1984 Professor Várdy was the recipient of Duquesne University's Presidential Award for Excellence in Scholarship, and in 1992 the was the cowinner (with Dr. Ágnes Huszár Várdy) of Hungary's "Berzsenyi Prize" — a literary award similar to the Pulitzer Prize in the United States. He is a member of the International P.E.N. Club, and has recently been awarded membership in the Hungarian Writers' Union in Budapest.